Early Childhood Curriculum
A Creative-Play Model
Second Edition

Carol E. Catron
University of Tennessee, Knoxville

Jan Allen
University of Tennessee, Knoxville

Merrill,
an imprint of Prentice-Hall
Upper Saddle River, New Jersey   Columbus, Ohio

Library of Congress Cataloging-in-Publication Data

Early childhood curriculum : a creative play model / Carol E. Catron,
   Jan Allen, editors. — 2nd ed.
       p.   cm.
   Includes bibliographical references and indexes.
   ISBN 0-13-080406-1
   1. Early childhood education—United States—Curricula.
2. Creative activities and seat work.   3. Child development—United
States.   I. Catron, Carol Elaine.   II. Allen, Jan.
LB1139.4.E16   1999
372.19—dc21   98-6057
                                                                   CIP

Cover photo: © Lawrence Migdale
Editor: Ann Castel Davis
Production Editor: Sheryl Glicker Langner
Production Coordination: Tally Morgan, WordCrafters Editorial Services, Inc.
Photo Coordinator: Sandy Lenahan
Design Coordinator: Diane C. Lorenzo
Cover Designer: Susan Unger
Production Manager: Laura Messerly
Electronic Text Management: Karen L. Bretz
Director of Marketing: Kevin Flanagan
Marketing Manager: Suzanne Stanton
Marketing Coordinator: Krista Groshong

This book was set in Century Schoolbook by BookMasters and was printed and bound by Banta Company. The cover was
printed by Phoenix Color Corp.

© 1999 by Prentice-Hall, Inc.
Simon & Schuster/A Viacom Company
Upper Saddle River, New Jersey 07458

Earlier editions, entitled Early Childhood Curriculum, © 1993 by Merrill/Prentice Hall.

Photo credits
Michele Jarnigan, pp. 1, 75, 84, 121, 147 (top), 155; *Jan Allen,* pp. 3, 6, 12, 19, 22, 55, 57, 62, 64, 82, 97, 101, 111, 149,
157, 165, 167, 177, 180, 181, 197, 203, 215, 233, 239, 240, 257, 269, 287, 293, 305, 314; *Anthony Magnacca/Merrill/
Prentice Hall,* p. 26; *Dan Floss/Merrill/Prentice Hall,* p. 35; *Todd Yarrington/Merrill/Prentice Hall,* pp. 44, 69, 292;
Tom Watson/ Merrill/Prentice Hall, p. 45; *Anne Vega/Merrill/Prentice Hall,* pp. 107, 220, 221, 222, 251, 275, 276;
Barbara Schwartz/ Merrill/Prentice Hall, pp. 117, 147 (bottom), 183, 202, 307, 318; *Merrill/Prentice Hall,* p. 135;
Lloyd Lemmerman/Merrill/Prentice Hall, p. 258.

Printed in the United States of America

10 9 8 7 6 5 4 3 2 1

ISBN: 0-13-080406-1

Prentice-Hall International (UK) Limited, *London*
Prentice-Hall of Australia Pty. Limited, *Sydney*
Prentice-Hall of Canada Inc., *Toronto*
Prentice-Hall Hispanoamericana, S.A., *Mexico*
Prentice-Hall of India Private Limited, *New Delhi*
Prentice-Hall of Japan, Inc., *Tokyo*
Simon & Schuster Asia Pte. Ltd., *Singapore*
Editora Prentice-Hall do Brasil, Ltda., *Rio de Janeiro*

*This book is dedicated to
our mothers, Helen Donaldson Catron and Mary Allen Wallace,
who showed us with the example of their lives
how to be teachers, nurturers, and friends to children*

*and to the memory of our fathers,
Bert Gillis Catron and Don William Allen*

Preface

We began writing the first edition of this book in 1985 when we decided that a comprehensive, play-based, developmental curriculum for children was not available for teachers who wanted to match educational philosophy with program focus, to link individual developmental assessment and curriculum planning, and to integrate all aspects of the program for young children, including those with special needs.

Our major purpose in writing this book is to help teachers provide the highest-quality programs possible for children, parents, and teachers. Our focus is on creative-play curriculum as a means of optimizing children's total development in the areas of personal awareness, emotional well-being, socialization, communication, cognition, and perceptual motor skills. Creativity is not simply an additional developmental domain; the potential for creative development is inherent in all domains and is an integral part of a developmentally appropriate curriculum. Creative

processes are essential for children to fully realize skills in problem solving and the generation of innovative ideas; play is the method through which creative potential is fostered and developed.

We have drawn from several sources to develop the creative-play curriculum model. Our educational backgrounds in the disciplines of child development, early childhood education, and teacher education made it possible to use the theoretical and empirical knowledge from these fields to draw conclusions and suggest implications for curriculum development and implementation. From our teaching and administrative experiences in public and private kindergarten, preschool programs, Head Start, child-care cooperatives, and university laboratories, we learned what was effective classroom practice when research and theory failed to provide the answers. This has allowed us to combine research and theory with practical guidelines for using and evaluating curricula.

CONTENT

This text covers basic principles and current research in early childhood curricula; however, it also is a comprehensive guide to planning programs with a play-based, developmental curriculum for children from birth to age 5. This creative-play model presents an integrated, individualized curricular approach that helps teachers to be sensitive to and plan for young children with a variety of developmental and cultural backgrounds.

Several special features contribute to the usefulness and comprehensiveness of the book.

■ A major feature is the emphasis on creative play to support children's learning and development. In addition to presenting an overview of other curriculum models, this text describes using creative play to implement the various components of this curriculum model. This book allows the reader to understand the specific steps in imple-

menting a play-based philosophy of young children's learning in a program setting.

■ Another feature is the comprehensive nature of the curriculum, which demonstrates the complex and interrelated components of the visible and invisible curriculum. This benefits students and practitioners by outlining all the components necessary to plan and implement an effective early childhood curriculum and the relationship of each component to the overall program.

■ A third feature is the integration of developmental assessment and curriculum planning. A developmental checklist is included that is designed to correlate with curriculum objectives. In the text, assessment information is presented to support the belief that curriculum planning and child assessment are integrated and complementary processes rather than separate or parallel functions. Students and practitioners can understand the importance of using information about children's development in both activity planning and child assessment.

- A fourth feature is the integration throughout all curricular components of information for programming for young children with disabilities. Adaptations for use of the curriculum and activ-

ities for children with disabilities are included throughout the book to help early childhood teachers plan for meeting the needs of all young children, including those with special needs, throughout the program.

- An additional feature is the inclusion of sample forms and charts that can be reproduced and used in early childhood programs.

ORGANIZATION _____

The book is organized into four major sections. Part One, *Early Childhood Curriculum,* explains the purpose of curriculum in early childhood programs and influences on curriculum development. It presents several curricula and describes various components of a curriculum. A specific curriculum model, creative play, is described in detail and is the organizing framework of the remainder of the book. The creative-play curriculum model is a flexible, open-ended model that is easily adapted by teachers for a range of age groups from infancy through preschool and for a variety of populations of children. A new chapter, "Children in Contemporary Society," has been added to this new edition. The increasing concern about contemporary stressors and the developmental risks to young children have major implications for teachers as they implement curriculum to promote healthy development and emotional well-being.

Part Two, *Invisible Curriculum,* presents information about early childhood program aspects that significantly affect the teaching and learning environment, yet are not always visible to the observer and, unfortunately, not always carefully planned. These program aspects must be thoughtfully considered and designed before the program is ready for

children and families. In this section, there are separate chapters on the role of the teacher, partnerships with parents, classroom management and guidance, classroom design and organization, and the outdoor play environment. These chapters include both theoretical and practical application information for teachers.

Part Three, *Visible Curriculum,* focuses on the more obvious dimensions of early childhood programs: curriculum activities and child observation and assessment. This section includes a chapter on each developmental domain with a section of classroom activities for each age group.

Part Four, *Professional Issues in Early Childhood Curricula and Programs,* highlights issues for teachers striving to implement quality programs for children. These issues include working environments, staff interactions and relationships, development of a professional identity, and moving beyond mandates and minimal standards to creating excellence in early childhood programs.

The appendices of the textbook contain development assessment instruments, including a developmental checklist and guidelines for writing child observations, which are easily reproducible for use by students and practitioners.

PEDAGOGICAL FEATURES _____

Each chapter begins with a vignette that describes various practical situations and dilemmas with children and families. These "real world" examples encourage readers to critically analyze the situation and consider ways to address the problem. A list of questions following each vignette identifies issues that should be examined before choosing a course of action. Each chapter ends with a sug-

gested solution to the problem. The vignettes are examples derived from our own experiences in early childhood programs and are designed to help readers make the linkage between information and implementation. Each chapter also ends with a chapter summary and a suggested list of discussion questions to facilitate understanding of the material presented.

Each area of children's development is presented in a separate chapter and linked with practical information to help teachers support and facilitate this developmental domain. Curriculum activities for each domain are described at the end of Chapters 11 through 16. Examples for practical application are included throughout the text with lists of guidelines that suggest program evaluation criteria and implementation ideas.

TERMINOLOGY _____

We use the terms *child care, preschool programs,* and *early childhood education* interchangeably to refer to programs that serve children from birth to age 8. The book's emphasis is on programs for children from birth to age 5. We define these groups, for curriculum planning and environmental design purposes, as: infants, 6 weeks to 15 months; toddlers, 15 months to 3 years; and preschoolers, 3 to 5 years. Most programs provide a variety of multiage groupings; teachers should choose and adapt activities and teaching techniques that are appropriate for a specific classroom.

PROFESSIONAL ISSUES _____

This textbook reflects our lifelong professional commitment to creating the best learning environment for young children and our own struggles with securing adequate funding for early childhood programs, designing growth-promoting environments for teachers as well as children, searching for solutions to teacher burnout and turnover, working effectively and compassionately with children and families under stress, and educating administrators and politicians about the needs of children and families. The heart and soul of our writing is a concern for providing excellent programs for children, parents, and teachers. Our hope is that this concern for the quality of young children's lives will have an impact on curricula in early childhood education programs.

ACKNOWLEDGMENTS _____

Many individuals have contributed to the development and publication of the second edition of *Early Childhood Curriculum.* We wish to acknowledge the supportive learning environments provided to us in the course of our own education at Transylvania University and George Peabody College for Teachers at Vanderbilt University and at Louisiana Tech University, Oklahoma Baptist University, the University of Oklahoma, and Purdue University. Special guidance and mentoring from Earline Kendall, Jean Grant Walter, James Broadus, Paul Fuller, Benjamin Burns, Jane Teleki, and Gail Melson have shaped our personal and professional lives and inspired us to reach for the dream of excellence in programs for young children.

Our special thanks go to the staff, students, parents, and children at the University of Tennessee, Knoxville, Child Development Laboratories, for whom and with whom the creative-play curriculum was developed, implemented, and field-tested. The process of developing the creative-play curriculum began in 1985 and was facilitated by staff members and graduate students. We are especially appreciative of longtime laboratory staff members Anne Miller Stott, Diane Bolinger, and Kathy Kidd for their constant commitment and caring.

We are grateful for the insightful comments and suggestions offered by reviewers Corinna D. Calica, Solano Community College (CA); Phyllis Cuevas, McNeese State University (LA); Sister Imelda D'Agostino, formerly of Mount St. Mary's College, Los Angeles; Sima Lesser, Miami-Dade Community College; Karen L. Peterson, Washington State University–Vancouver; and Linda L. Reiten, University of Mary (ND). Their input strengthened the content of the curriculum. For this opportunity to share the curriculum with college students, professors, teachers, and directors, we thank the staff at Prentice Hall, especially Ann Davis, administrative editor.

We are appreciative of the patience, encouragement, and support of our families, friends, colleagues, and students who were gracious enough to "bear with us" during the writing and production of the book. And finally, we are grateful to Mary Alexandra, Carson, Spring, Baylor, Emily, Sam, and Reese, who continue to remind us that the early childhood years are filled with wonderment.

C.E.C.
J.A.

Author Profiles

Carol E. Catron is director of the Early Childhood Education Teacher Licensure Program and a faculty member in the Department of Child and Family Studies at the University of Tennessee, Knoxville. She is former director of the UTK Child Development Laboratories. She was born and raised in Oak Ridge, Tennessee, where she developed a special love and understanding for young children through her relationships with seven nieces and nephews: Karen, Suzan, Gib, Sharon, Jimmy, Kermit, and Christy. She graduated from Transylvania University in Lexington, Kentucky, with a bachelor's degree in elementary education. Her master's and doctoral degrees are in early childhood education from George Peabody College of Vanderbilt University. Prior to her teaching and directing in university settings, she taught kindergarten in public and private schools, taught preschool in parent cooperative and university laboratory settings, and organized and directed the first preschool program in the Nashville, Tennessee, metropolitan school system. She has taught numerous workshops on storytelling with young children and, with her sister, Barbara Catron Parks, has published three storytelling books: *Super Storytelling, Cooking Up a Story,* and *Celebrate with a Story.*

She has been a faculty member at UTK since 1985. She teaches undergraduate and graduate classes in early childhood education and supervises early childhood teaching interns. Her research and writing interests are in the areas of play therapy, curriculum development, staff development and evaluation, and storytelling with young children. She also is involved in child advocacy efforts through professional organizations and agencies, and serves as a mentor and validator for NAEYC's Academy of Early Childhood Programs.

Jan Allen is an associate professor in the Department of Child and Family Studies at the University of Tennessee, Knoxville. She was born and raised in Oakdale, Louisiana, graduated from Oakdale High School, and attended Louisiana Tech University. She graduated from Oklahoma Baptist University, Shawnee, Oklahoma, with a bachelor's degree in home economics education. One of the best things that ever happened to her was that she could not find a job teaching high school home economics and worked in Head Start from 1975 to 1977. She then returned to school for a master's degree (at the University of Oklahoma) and then a doctorate (at Purdue University) in child development to try to figure out what her 3- and 4-year-old Head Start children were trying to teach her.

She has been a faculty member at UTK since 1982. She teaches undergraduate and graduate classes in child development, early childhood education, and children and stress. She conducts research on early childhood work environments and job satisfaction, licensing and policy issues in child care, children's moral development, and young children's political socialization. She is currently writing a book about the children she taught in Head Start and their lives 20 years later. Her interests in public policy and parent education have focused on child care and families, children and stress, and child advocacy. In 1997 Jan was appointed assistant dean of the UTK Graduate School; in 1993 she was chosen as one of the first two Chancellor's Teacher-Scholars at UTK. With her colleague Sky Huck, she developed and coordinates the university's GTA Mentoring Program, an initiative of research, training, and support and recognition for GTAs in their instructional role at a research university. She also directs the UTK's College of Human Ecology's Child Care Resource and Referral Office, a clearinghouse for research, policy development, parent education, and teacher training for sixteen counties in eastern Tennessee.

CONTRIBUTING AUTHORS _____

Bobbie Beckmann is a preschool special-education teacher at the Ft. Craig School of Dynamic Learning in the Maryville (Tennessee) Pubic Schools and a former special education coordinator in the University of Tennessee Child Development Laboratories. She has a master of arts degree in speech pathology from the University of Tennessee and holds a certificate of clinical competence in speech-language pathology.

Kathy Carlson is a former coordinator of the preschool program in the Child Development Laboratories, Department of Child and Family Studies, University of Tennessee, Knoxville. She has a master of science degree in home economics from Purdue University and a master of science degree in child and family studies from the University of Tennessee.

Amy R. Kerlin is a parent advisor with Tennessee Infant Parent Services and a former coordinator of the toddler program in the Child Development Laboratories, Department of Child and Family Studies, University of Tennessee, Knoxville. She has a master of science degree in child development from the University of Tennessee.

Anne Miller Stott is director of the Child Development Laboratories, Department of Child and Family Studies, University of Tennessee, Knoxville; she previously was infant coordinator and toddler coordinator. Her master of science degree is in child and family studies from the University of Tennessee.

Brief Contents

Detailed Contents

EARLY CHILDHOOD CURRICULUM

1.

Role of Curriculum in Early Childhood Programs

■ ■ ■ ■ ■ ■ ■ ■ ■ ■

You are being interviewed for your first job as a teacher of young children. Although you are slightly nervous, you feel you are well trained as an early childhood professional through your course work in child development and early childhood education and your many and varied practical experiences with children. You also feel well prepared for the interview process because the faculty supervisor of your student teaching experience conducted mock interviews with all of the students. As the director of the program begins to ask these questions, you draw on your knowledge and experience to answer them:

- In what type of program environment do you believe young children learn best?
- Can you briefly state your philosophy of early childhood education?
- How will you choose the curriculum used in your classroom? What components will it include?
- Are you able to cite theory or research to support your choice of curriculum?
- How will you evaluate the effectiveness of your curriculum?

■ ■ ■ ■ ■ ■ ■ ■ ■

Suggestions for responding to this vignette will be shared at the end of the chapter.

When reading this chapter, focus on the important role curriculum plays in early childhood programs, the need to develop an educational philosophy as a basis for your curricular choices, and the critical role of theory and research in understanding how young children learn and develop. Also, become aware of the various curricular components as well as various strategies for assessing curricular outcomes.

The word *curriculum* suggests different concepts to the different audiences of teachers, administrators, and parents. A curriculum may be considered to be a set of specific activities that meets prescribed goals and objectives, a framework for making decisions about the choice of materials and activities, or a comprehensive approach to fostering the development of the whole child. Given this ambiguity, it is not surprising that there are many curricular approaches to early childhood education and much debate about which approaches are most effective. Approaches based on various theories of child development and behavior, such as psychoanalytic, behavioral, maturational, and cognitive theories, offer competing explanations of children's development and thus suggest different approaches to the education and care of young children.

PURPOSE OF CURRICULUM

Regardless of the approach or model used in a program, the curriculum is the foundation. The curriculum provides the basis for answering questions about what to teach and how to teach by providing a master plan based on a philosophy of how children develop and learn. It also helps the teacher make decisions about how to organize the classroom and how to guide and respond to children's behavior. In a joint position statement by the National Association for the Education of Young Children and the National Association of Early Childhood Specialists in State Departments of Education (1991), *curriculum* is defined as "an organized framework that delineates the content children are to learn, the processes through which children achieve the identified curricular goals, what teachers do to help children achieve these goals, and the context in which teaching and learning occur" (p. 21).

A curriculum should be specific enough to provide direction and guidance to teachers faced with decisions about teaching and interacting with children: How do I arrange my classroom? What are appropriate materials for the children in my class? What are the most effective strategies for teaching? How do I guide children's behavior? How can I work effectively with parents?

A curriculum should also be flexible enough to allow its adaptation to the special needs—developmental, cultural, financial, and social—of the children and families served by the program and to allow continuing incorporation of new ideas from current research in child development and early childhood education.

Curricula should clarify, explain, and guide, and they should not be rigid or inflexible; teachers must view a curriculum as a process of planning the best possible program for children, parents, and teachers. Planning a program is the process of curriculum and suggests its dynamic nature. Teachers should choose or develop a curriculum—a written document incorporating guidelines, activities, policies, and philosophy—as a basis for the classroom program. The absence of a curricular focus may result in ineffective programming: "[T]he lack of unified, carefully thought-out and considered sources for planning children's experiences promotes slipshod teaching and virtually no accountability or responsibility. Developing a curriculum forces the people involved to think seriously about their purpose and question established practice" (Langenbach, 1976, p. 22).

Regardless of the specific focus of a curriculum, most early childhood educators would agree on the following set of assumptions about curricula (Bredekamp & Copple, 1997; Seefeldt, 1987; Williams, 1987):

1. Curriculum is related to overall program quality. "It defines and clarifies so many other issues, including teacher behavior and questioning style, classroom organization, relationships with families, directive teaching versus child centered learning and so on. The big dividing line between effective and ineffective programs is that the staff of the latter have not made a decision about the curriculum" (Weikart, 1986, p. 8).

2. Curriculum must focus on "the whole child" and programmatically integrate areas of development. "In real life all aspects of the person must be treated together and educated together. Only when this is recognized and provided for in the curriculum can true learning and competence develop" (Hendrick, 1998, p. 3).

3. Play serves many functions for young children; among the most important is that it is the primary mode for learning in early childhood. "The trend toward early academics, for example, is antithetical to what we know about how young children learn. . . . In fact, a growing body of research has emerged recently affirming that children learn most effectively through a concrete, play-oriented approach to early childhood education" (Bredekamp, 1987, p. 1).

Play is the primary mode of learning for young children in early childhood programs.

4. Teachers must agree with the philosophy and practices of the curriculum and understand its content. "The teacher's philosophy of life, of human development, of family dynamics, and of education will be reflected in the program that is developed for children and in the interaction that takes place between and among individuals" (Hildebrand, 1994, p. 367).

5. Teachers also must understand children's development and theories of learning. "The main activity of the teacher is to understand the child. A teacher who understands children's thinking understands how to provide structure and routines, when and how to ask questions, and how to help children formulate and then verbalize their ideas and thoughts" (Seefeldt, 1987, p. 275).

6. Children are active learners. "Early childhood is really the only level of education that has taken developmental principles seriously and developed criteria and procedures for active learning" (Jones, 1986, p. 123).

7. Curriculum should be developmentally appropriate. "Although the quality of an early childhood program may be affected by many factors, a major determinant of program quality is the extent to which knowledge of child development is applied in program practices—the degree to which the program is developmentally appropriate" (Bredekamp, 1987, pp. 2–3).

8. Curriculum should reflect the role of social and cultural context in children's development and learning. "Early childhood teachers need to understand the influence of sociocultural contexts on learning, recognize children's developing competence, and accept a variety of ways for children to express their developmental achievements" (Bredekamp & Copple, 1997, p. 12).

INFLUENCES ON CURRICULUM

In the broader context, curriculum and program development are influenced by social, economic, and political forces. For example, program objectives for the government-sponsored child care centers created by the Lanham Act in 1941 included increasing the labor force participation of women during World War II. Head Start, begun in 1965 as part of President Johnson's War on Poverty, was designed to combat poverty, foster civil rights, and prepare disadvantaged young children for success in school. Passage of P.L. 94-142, the Education for all Handicapped Children Act, enacted in 1975 to mandate individualized education programs in public schools for all school-age children with disabilities, and P.L. 99-457, enacted in 1986 to mandate public educational services to children ages 3 to 5 with disabilities and to support state services for the birth to 2-years special population, underscored the legal right of all children to educational equity (Ballard, Weintraub, & Zantal-Wiener, 1987). The passage of P.L. 101-336, the Americans with Disabilities Act, in 1990 included rights to equal access to enrollment in early childhood programs for young children with disabilities. In addition, the passage in the same year of P.L. 101-576 reauthorized the Education for all Handicapped Children Act, renamed it the Individuals with Disabilities Education Act (IDEA), and included new categories of disabilities (Surr, 1992; Wolery & Wilbers, 1994).

The recent increase in support for public-school kindergarten and preschool programs underscores society's belief in the value of early education. An increase in the demand for child care has been fueled by the rise in single-parent families and the large number of women in the workforce. There were 13 million preschool-age children enrolled in child-care and early childhood education in 1995 (Hofferth, 1996). These statistics reveal a startling increase since the mid-1970s: Four times as many children were enrolled in child care centers in early 1990 (Willer et al, 1991, p. 43). From the early to mid-1990s there has been an almost 50 percent increase in the number of children enrolled in child care. The increasing interest in corporate support for child care reflects economic concerns about productivity of the workforce as well as the need for more high-quality early childhood programs. More direct influences on curricula than these social, economic, and political forces include developmental and learning theories and research.

Theories of Development and Learning

The foundation for all curricula is developmental theory, or beliefs about how children develop and learn. These beliefs guide our view of teaching and supporting children as learners. The developmental theory from which a curriculum originates may be explicit or implicit. The curriculum author may describe the linkage between curriculum practices and theory—showing the relationship between what teachers do and why they do it. A curriculum may not identify the developmental theory on which it is based, but it probably does reflect one of the many theories that explain children's development and learning. Teachers should critically consider and evaluate which of the theoretical approaches as an organizing framework best represents their experience with and understanding of children.

Maturational Theory. A *maturational* orientation to children's development has spawned several similar theories associated with the work of G. Stanley Hall, Robert Havighurst, and Arnold Gesell. Hall (1844–1924) began a tradition of testing and observing large numbers of children and then describing averages or typical behavior for children at each age level. These descriptive age norms were used to determine "typical" child behavior at various ages. Havighurst extensively described tasks in ten behavior categories during five stages of development through the life span. Havighurst believed developmental tasks were "those things a person must learn if he is to be judged and to judge himself to be a reasonably happy and successful person" (Havighurst, 1953, p. 2). For example, in the second stage, Early Childhood (ages 2–3 to 5–7), for the behavior category of developing a conscience, the preschool child's tasks are first, to develop the ability to take directions and to be obedient in the presence of an authority figure, and second, to develop the ability to be obedient in the absence of an authority figure.

Gesell (1880–1961) and his colleagues at the Gesell Institute of Child Development in New Haven, Connecticut, developed an extensive array of measurements and tests to assess and describe children in ten major areas of development: motor, personal hygiene, emotional expression, fears and dreams, self and sex, interpersonal relations, play and pastimes, school life, ethical sense, and philosophic outlook. Each category included several areas. For example, philosophic outlook included time, space, language and thought, war, death, and deity. The data from tests in these areas were used to develop "gradients of growth" that described the norm, or typical child behavior, at each age. Gesell believed that the child's genetic endowment determined development and behavior and that internal maturational factors guided children's growth and development (Gesell & Ilg, 1949). For example, differences in children's abilities to perform physical tasks such as skipping or tying shoes are attributed to differences in their heredity rather than their environment. Children develop, mature, and learn according to their own internal maturational schedule.

Psychodynamic Theory. Sigmund Freud (1856–1939) first described children's development and behavior from a *psychodynamic* or psychoanalytical perspective. Freud, trained as a medical doctor, noted that among his patients were women whose health problems, he believed, could be traced to traumatic emotional experiences in childhood. His emphasis on the emotional and psychological aspects of children led Freud to develop a stage-based theory of development. As children move through the stages (oral, anal, phallic, latency, and genital), their development and behavior is explained by the action of subconscious forces, referred to as the *id,* the *ego,* and the *superego,* that compete to influence behavior. The id consists of the inborn drives present at birth. The ego develops during the second stage (ages 1 to 3) and is the part of personality that controls emotion, thought, and behavior. The superego develops during the phallic stage (ages 3 to 5) and represents ethical values and conscience. Throughout life a struggle exists between the id, representing instinctual drives, and the superego, the moral center. The ego mediates this struggle between pleasure and morality to create behavior that is realistic and acceptable (Freud, 1938).

Erik Erikson (1902–1994), a German-born psychoanalyst, refined Freud's theory of personality development and focused particularly on children's development. His eight psychosocial stages of development parallel Freud's psychosexual stages; they specify an identity crisis or task that each person must resolve at each stage. For example, for children younger than 6, the tasks at each of the first three stages are labeled *trust versus mistrust* (birth to 1 year), *autonomy versus shame and doubt* (ages 2 to 3), and *initiative versus guilt* (ages 3 to 6). The successful resolution of each task during the specified stage results in the ability to perceive the world and the self correctly, development of a healthy personality, active mastery of the environment, and appropriate socialization into the culture (Erikson, 1963, 1968).

Behavioral Theory. Behavioral theories focus on objective, observable principles that influence human behavior. John B. Watson (1878–1959) founded the movement called *behaviorism,* and there are two major frameworks that apply behaviorism to child development. The first, *operant conditioning,* was described by B. F. Skinner (1904–1990), perhaps the most well-known American psychologist. Skinner used the classical conditioning model of Russian psychologist Ivan Pavlov (1849–1936). Pavlov's stimulus-response theory, in which an unconditioned stimulus and unconditioned response are used to elicit a conditioned response to a conditioned stimulus, failed to account for behavior that is emitted but not elicited from any observable stimulus. Skinner's theory of operant conditioning is an explanation of behavior that allows for many actions and behaviors being performed spontaneously, not always in response to something else. In this theory, it is not the prior stimulus, but the consequence of the behavior, that is important. Skinner described these consequences as rewards, or reinforcers, and punishment. Learning is viewed as a process whereby a child is "conditioned" to display expected behavior and knowledge through the use of consequences, or reinforcement and punishment. Skinner described an ideal child-rearing environment and asserted that both human and physical factors in the environment should be "engineered" to produce certain, predictable results (Skinner, 1971, 1974).

Albert Bandura (born in 1925) modified Watson's and Skinner's stimulus-response (S-R) approach into a second behaviorist approach, the theory of social learning. *Social learning theory* includes an attempt to describe the cognition of the individual, or what the child is thinking as he or she acts. Social learning theory also recognizes the roles that observation, imitation, modeling, and incidental learning play in children's behavior and learning (Bandura, 1977).

Cognitive Development Theory. This theory is synonymous with the name of Jean Piaget (1896–1980), whose influence in theory development and education has extended across the human life span. Piaget, originally trained as a biologist, was employed early in his career at the Binet Institute in Paris and was assigned to score children's achievement tests. Piaget became interested in the wrong answers that children of various ages systematically gave to questions on the tests. He discovered that children of similar ages gave the same wrong answers. His discovery led to the development of his theory on intellectual development. He proposed four stages in human cognitive development: the *sensori-motor* stage (birth to 18–24 months), the *preoperational* stage (18–24 months to 6–7 years), the *concrete operations* stage (6–7 years to 12–13 years), and the *formal operations* stage (12–13 years through adulthood) (Piaget, 1926). Regardless of a child's age or stage of development, there are several processes that describe development and learning. Learning occurs as children construct knowledge through active exploration and discovery in their physical and social environments. Two reciprocal processes, *assimilation* and *accommodation,* permit adaptation to the environment. Children assimilate when they match concepts, skills, and information gained from their experiences with the environment to their previously developed sense of pattern or scheme of understanding. Accommodation occurs when mental schemes must be changed to fit the new concept, skill, or information. In the former, information is assimilated or fit into preexisting mental structures. In the latter, the mental structures accommodate or change to fit the new knowledge. In the cognitive development framework, the child actively seeks and processes information and constructs knowledge (Piaget, 1926).

In the 1990s, other theories about cognitive development have gained attention. An information-processing perspective with a mind-as-a-computer model was proposed to explain how information is received, interpreted, stored, and retrieved, yet it did not account fully or accurately for the structure and function of short- and long-term memory, the role of emotions in cognition, or how an individual's goals relate to the perception of stimuli, for example (Thomas, 1996). Bjorklund (1997) suggests that a new theory of cognition is needed and that it must include an understanding of brain development, evolutionary theory, and individual variation.

Multiple Intelligences Theory. Howard Gardner, a professor at Harvard Graduate School of Education, has proposed a framework to describe seven different kinds of intelligence. Although most cognitive theorists and educators have emphasized linguistic and logical-mathematical intelligence, Gardner believes that there are at least five others: musical, bodily-kinesthetic, spatial, interpersonal, and intrapersonal. Children learn about the world through language, logical-mathematical thought, spatial representation, musical thought, using the body to solve problems or create things, understanding others, and understanding self. Children differ in "the strength of these intelligences . . . and in the ways in which such intelligences are invoked and combined to carry out

different tasks, solve diverse problems, and progress in various domains" (Gardner, 1991, p. 12). Children's family, culture, and community influence the development of intelligences, the value placed on various intelligences, and the way the intelligences are expressed. A recognition of cultural influences on the development and valuing of intelligences is critical for teachers in planning curriculum and designing appropriate assessment of young children. Curriculum must offer children a diverse array of opportunities to foster development in all areas of intelligences, and assessment must go beyond the areas typically associated with achievement. This theoretical approach helps teachers to identify children's strengths not always valued in a traditional school setting and enhances children's self-esteem as they play and learn in an enabling environment (Gardner, 1993).

Sociocultural Theory. Lev Vygotsky (1896–1934) was a Russian-born developmental psychologist who emphasized the influence of society and culture on children's development, the role of language in developing higher-order thinking skills, and the importance of play in enhancing children's socially cooperative behavior. His concept of the *zone of proximal development,* "the distance between the actual developmental level as determined by independent problem solving and the level of potential development as determined through problem solving under adult guidance or in collaboration with more capable peers" (Vygotsky, 1933/1978, p. 102), is used by early childhood educators to individualize play experiences. "Play creates a zone of proximal development in the child. In play, the child always behaves beyond his average age, above his daily behavior; in play it is as though he were a head taller than himself. . . . Play contains all developmental tendencies in a condensed form and is itself a major source of development" (Vygotsky, 1933/1978, p. 86). Wood, Bruner, and Ross (1976) introduced the term *scaffolding* to describe the sensitive guidance required of adults involved in children's play and learning. Adults engage children in "interesting and culturally meaningful" activities that include collaboration and problem solving. As children collaborate, a process known as *intersubjectivity* (Newson & Newson, 1975) occurs: Children must share their knowledge with others who may be thinking at a different level. As they work to solve the problem, they arrive at a shared understanding and solution. In this way, children's knowledge is both personally and socially constructed as they discuss, negotiate, and compromise in their problem-solving efforts.

Vygotsky viewed the impact of imaginative play as being complex: It enhances cognitive development, especially strengthening memory and reasoning abilities; it increases social competence; and it enriches language development (Berk & Winsler, 1995). "Vygotsky's theory offers yet another justification for play's prominent place in preschool and primary-grade learning environments. For . . . teachers whose concern with academic progress has led them to neglect or eliminate play from the young child's school life, Vygotsky's analysis offers a convincing argument for change—a powerful account of why make-believe is the ultimate activity for nurturing capacities that are crucial for academic as well as later-life success" (Berk & Winsler, 1995, p. 79).

Comparisons between Vygotsky and Piaget are inevitable because they both focused on the role of language and social experience in the development of children's cognition. Vygotsky's emphasis—on language, particularly inner speech, prompting cognitive development—cotrasts with Piaget's view of cognitive development—sensorimotor exploration in infants, for example—prompting the emergence of language. Vygotsky viewed play as social; Piaget viewed play as initially solitary. As children mature cognitively and become less egocentric, their play becomes more social.

Research

Early childhood curricula must be based on research or empirical knowledge as well as on theory. In the past three decades there has been a dramatic increase in the number of research studies seeking to answer questions about what educational experiences best support young children's learning and development. Much of the developmental research has supported the idea that the preschool years are significant in children's learning. The research on teaching and teacher effects has, in the past, focused more on elementary education, but that body of research, along with more recent studies on early child-

hood programs, allows the application of research findings to the development of curricula in early childhood (Goffin, 1989; Spodek, 1982).

Teachers should be familiar with several areas of development and educational research in an effort to improve their program. These include research on children's cognitive, social, emotional, physical, and creative development; teacher characteristics and behavior; teaching methods and strategies; organizational features of the classroom; management and discipline strategies; children's motivation; and family and peer influences on children. Research from each of these areas can inform teachers' decision making about effective, appropriate curricula.

Since 1985, at least three new journals devoted to the reporting of research in early childhood education have begun publication (*Early Childhood Research Quarterly, Journal of Research in Early Childhood Education,* and *Early Education and Development*). Teachers also have several sources (*Young Children, Childhood Education,* and *Early Childhood Education Journal*) for information that applies the research in early childhood education to classroom practice.

In curriculum development, as well as other areas of early childhood education research, it would be helpful if teachers and researchers discussed these questions: On what topics and issues is more research needed? What are the specific questions whose answers would help classroom teachers? How can the results best be applied in classrooms? What should be the relationship between teachers and researchers in early childhood education, and how can this relationship be encouraged and facilitated? Many producers and consumers of early childhood education research would agree that a dialogue about research and its application would enhance and strengthen our knowledge base in early childhood education (Allen & Catron, 1990). Early childhood educators must use the research available to them as well as think of themselves as classroom researchers (Seefeldt, 1987).

OVERVIEW OF CURRICULUM MODELS _____

Although theories about early childhood development have existed for several centuries, curriculum models in early childhood education have a much more recent beginning. The Russian launching of Sputnik in 1957 created a renewed emphasis on American education

in general. In addition, the federal government's involvement in early childhood education and intervention with the advent of Head Start in 1965 focused attention on educational curricula for preschool children. Beginning in the 1960s, research on education and curricula for young children also expanded rapidly, both in scope and number of studies.

Researchers began to study the effects of early childhood education on program participants, particularly assessing child outcomes of IQ scores, school readiness, language development, and social development and skills. Results of research suggested that specific factors that could help explain the outcomes would need to be examined. Thus, research in early childhood education in the past two decades has increasingly focused on the complex interrelationships and interaction among child variables, teacher variables, family variables, and program or curriculum variables in determining which programs are successful.

Several organizational frameworks for curricula have been derived from developmental theories. These will be described in this section, followed by brief descriptions of several curricula that have been widely implemented and researched. Teachers who are choosing a curriculum should consult the references listed for more complete information about each curriculum.

Several curriculum models that have cognitive development theory as their foundation are referred to broadly as *interactional, transactional,* or *constructivist* models. Although Piaget did not specify educational practice in his theory, many early childhood program designers have done so based on Piaget's theory. In the 1960s, during the debate over the role of heredity versus environment in the development of children's intelligence, many educators began to support and use Piaget's ideas about the child as an active creator and constructor of knowledge. In this model, teachers assess children's levels of development and provide developmentally appropriate materials and experiences. Children are given opportunities to discover answers to questions about the physical environment posed by children themselves, rather than questions whose answers teachers believe children should know.

Psychodynamic models, based on the theories of Freud and Erikson, are concerned with the emotional environment as a supportive climate for children's development and learning. Socioemotional enhancement, such as increasing children's self-esteem and motivation for learning, is the primary focus for these programs. *Maturationist* models are based on understanding typical child maturation and development. Activities are planned that support the attainment of developmental milestones. Teachers provide educational activities and encourage children's social learning but may take a less active role in teaching. *Behavioral* models based on behavioral and social-learning theories usually have a very structured learning environment in which activities are teacher-initiated and objectives include academic and pre-academic skills. The use of rewards, such as tokens or food, and punishment are used to guide children to appropriate behavior. These models provide detailed descriptions of guidance techniques, particularly for children with special needs, that are widely used to modify and guide children's behavior.

High/Scope Cognitively Oriented Curriculum

This curriculum is based on Piaget's theory and was developed beginning in 1964 by David Weikart and colleagues at the High/Scope Educational Research Foundation in Ypsilanti, Michigan. In the curriculum, children are both active learners and active planners in the classroom. The teachers' role is to arrange the classroom and materials and schedule a daily routine that permits children to plan, experience, and review activities and experiments. Research on the effects of the High/Scope curriculum has been ongoing since the 1960s, and follow-up studies, reported on children in the program from their preschool years through age 19, have found positive intellectual, scholastic, and social outcomes (Berrueta-Clement, Schweinhart, Barnett, Epstein, & Weikart, 1984; Hohmann, Banet, & Weikart, 1978).

Bank Street Approach

This model was initiated by Lucy Mitchell and extensively developed and described by Barbara Biber. It was first implemented at the City and Country School in New York City, and its effects have been researched by the Bank Street College of Education. Its theoretical foundation is rooted in the psychodynamic theory of Freud and the progressive-education movement and writing of John Dewey (1859–1952). The approach provides age-appropriate materials but includes the same goals for all children regardless of age. These goals include promoting autonomy, exploration, self-concept, communication, and competence. Materials are often teacher-made and arranged in learning centers in the classroom. Teachers structure the environment and serve as models for skill development and learning in children (Biber, 1984; Biber & Franklin, 1967). The Bank Street approach also includes tenets of the interactional or constructivist model in its curriculum framework.

Montessori Education

This method was developed from the educational principles of Maria Montessori (1870–1952). An Italian physician, Montessori first used her methods in the early 1900s with mentally retarded children and was so successful that she extended her model to preschool children. Dr. Montessori lectured in the United States in 1913 and 1915 and her methods gained popularity when articles about her work were published and the *Association Montessori Internationale* was established in 1929. The Montessori method seeks to support children's personality development and cognitive competence. Children are encouraged to be self-disciplined, self-directed, and independent. The environment and materials are prepared to be self-correcting; that is, the result of children's use of the materials will indicate to the child whether the materials have been used correctly. Most activities occur individually, with the child interacting with materials but not with other children. The teacher's role is to prepare a classroom that is responsive to children's needs as they educate themselves through appropriate use of materials (Montessori, 1949; Perryman, 1966).

Progressive Education

John Dewey (1859–1952) was a philosopher and educator who viewed educational settings as the training ground for democracy. Classrooms were to be centered on working in groups, cooperative effort, and shared responsibility and goals. Children's contributions to the work and life of the group gave them a voice, and being part of the group fostered intellectual and social self-realization. Education was meant to foster "creative individuality." Children learned by actively "doing" both physical and intellectual activities. These activities were to be offered based on children's interests, needs, purposes, and abilities. "Learning is active. It involves reaching out of the mind. It involves organic assimilation from within. Literally, we must take our stand with the child and our departure from him" (Dewey, 1902, p. 9).

Dewey also saw democracy in education as all adults in the community wanting appropriate education for all children. "What the best and wisest parent wants for his own child, that must the community want for all its children. Any other ideal for our schools is narrow and unlovely" (Dewey, 1900, pp. 3–4). Dewey viewed this ideal for our schools as essential to support a democratic society and to teach children to live in a democracy. Dewey's philosophy of progressive education had a most far-reaching impact on public education in the United States than any other theory proposed in the 20th century.

Behavioristic Instructional Technology

Perhaps the most widely discussed example of behavioral theory applied to early childhood education is the Bereiter-Engelmann model. It was designed and widely used, beginning in the 1960s, to provide compensatory education, particularly the development of language skills, to economically disadvantaged children. Teachers use direct instruction to teach math, reading, and language. Lessons and activities are teacher-initiated and -directed and require structured, repetitive teaching. Rewards, including food and praise, are used to motivate and encourage children. Experiences are primarily closed-ended, with the attainment and display of correct answers the expected outcome (Bereiter & Engelmann, 1966).

Reggio Emilia

The Reggio Emilia approach, based on the principle that "things about children and for children are only learned from children," is viewed as a model early childhood education system (Edwards, Gandini, & Forman, 1993, pp. 43–44). Loris Malaguzzi (1920–1994) was the founder and first director of the Reggio Emilia Municipal Early Childhood system in the Emilia Romagna region of Italy. The city of Reggio Emilia funds and operates infant-toddler centers for children from birth to 3 years and preprimary schools for children ages 3 to 6. These are full-day child-care programs open to all children. Education in Reggio Emilia is a sharing of culture and is based on a high degree of parental and community involvement. This cohesive approach, evolved over the past 30 years, emphasizes aesthetic aspects of the curriculum and the classroom environment; high regard for children's ideas and everyday experiences as the basis for an extensive project approach to curriculum; continuity of relationships between children and teachers, which may continue for a period of up to three years; and encouragement for children to express themselves through all their natural "languages," or modes of creative expression (Edwards et al., 1993). Indeed, according to Malaguzzi, the program was designed to be an environment "where children's different languages could be explored by them and studied by us in a favorable and peaceful atmosphere" (p. 68).

Creative Play Approach

The creative-play curriculum, described in detail in the following chapters, was developed and implemented in 1985 at the University of Tennessee, Knoxville. It is based on the Piagetian theory of development, a constructivist model of learning, and developmentally appropiate practices in early childhood education. It is a play-based curriculum that recognizes the importance of the development of creative individuals and the interrelatedness of developmental areas. The curriculum focuses on encouraging and supporting children's play to promote development in six domains: personal awareness, emotional well-being, cognition, communication, socialization, and perceptual motor skills.

Some programs adopt an eclectic approach to curricula and select and modify elements of several curricula in order to better meet the needs of children, to adapt to specific cultural or community expectations, or to work within financial constraints. As a result, the actual curriculum in a program may be composed of the most innovative, economical, or satisfying aspects of several curricula.

DEVELOPING A CURRICULUM FOR YOUR PROGRAM _____

The curriculum designed for a specific program should be characterized by a good match or relationship among children's needs and interests, parental values and expectations, and teacher characteristics and abilities. Many curricula are based on general goals and objectives with which most parents and teachers would agree. Objectives such as fostering independence, responsibility, and self-esteem are common to many models. But the specific content and methods used to accomplish these goals differ from curriculum to curriculum. The debate over which to choose is a healthy one when teachers and parents are involved in discussing their values, expectations, and goals for children's education and care.

In addition to meeting the needs of children, the curriculum "must be culturally salient and locally relevant and meaningful in the context of a specific community" (NAEYC & NAECS/SDE, 1991, p. 23). To reflect and respect the diverse culture, language, values, needs, and interests of families and communities, curriculum practices may differ from program to program and from community to community. Teachers must choose a curriculum that can be adapted to protect this diversity, not homogenize programs and families (Seefeldt, 1987). The curriculum should reflect the needs of children, parents, and teachers, because the conditions of the environment and program for all three groups determine overall program quality and effectiveness. A program that provides poor working conditions for teachers or inadequate sensitivity to the difficult role of parenting is not offering the best program for children.

A position statement by the National Association for the Education of Young Children and the National Association of Early Childhood Specialists in State Departments of Education (1991) offers guidelines for evaluating curriculum content. Its authors suggest that a group of teachers review any proposed curriculum using these questions, which should be answered in the affirmative. Parents also could be included in the review process or given a copy of the questions and informed that the curriculum choice will meet the following guidelines.

1. Does it promote interactive learning and encourage the child's construction of knowledge?
2. Does it help achieve social, emotional, physical, and cognitive goals?
3. Does it encourage development of positive feelings and dispositions toward learning while leading to acquisition of knowledge and skills?
4. Is it meaningful for these children? Is it relevant to the children's lives? Can it be made more relevant by relating it to a personal experience children have had or can they easily gain direct experience with it?
5. Are the expectations realistic and attainable at this time or could the children more easily and efficiently acquire the knowledge or skills later on?
6. Is it of interest to the children and to the teacher?
7. Is it sensitive to and respectful of cultural and linguistic diversity? Does it expect, allow, and

Developmentally appropriate early childhood curriculum promotes active learning that is fun for children.

appreciate individual differences? Does it promote positive relationships with families?

8. Does it build on and elaborate children's current knowledge and abilities?

9. Does it lead to conceptual understanding by helping children construct their own understanding in meaningful contexts?

10. Does it facilitate integration of content across traditional subject-matter areas?

11. Is the information presented accurate and credible according to the recognized standards of the relevant discipline?

12. Is the content worth knowing? Can it be learned by these children efficiently and effectively now?

13. Does it encourage active learning and allow children to make meaningful choices?

14. Does it foster children's exploration and inquiry, rather than focusing on "right" answers or "right" ways to complete a task?

15. Does it promote the development of higher-order abilities such as thinking, reasoning, problem solving, and decision making?

16. Does it promote and encourage social interaction among children and adults?

17. Does it respect children's physiological needs for activity, sensory stimulation, fresh air, rest, and nourishment/elimination?

18. Does it promote feelings of psychological safety, security, and belonging?

19. Does it provide experiences that promote feelings of success, competence, and enjoyment of learning?

20. Does it permit flexibility for children and teachers? (NAEYC & NAECS/SDE, 1991, pp. 31–32; reprinted by permission of NAEYC)

Involving Teachers in Curriculum Design

Teachers are the most important factor in determining program quality, and teachers' roles in decision making about curriculum is essential to a good match between the curriculum and teachers' values, characteristics, and abilities. Teachers should be involved in:

■ Decisions about choosing and designing the curriculum

■ Preservice and in-service training in the use of the curriculum

■ Discussions with parents, in conferences and parent meetings, about the curriculum and the children's daily experiences

■ Ongoing discussions about implementing the curriculum

■ Adapting the curriculum to the special needs of children and families in the program

To determine which curriculum model—or which components of various models—is most appropriate for use in a specific program, certain additional criteria must be considered. These criteria reflect the importance of considering teachers' needs in evaluating a curriculum. A good learning environment for children is also a good environment for teachers. Criteria for evaluating the curriculum based on teachers' needs, experiences, and training are presented in the following series of questions:

■ Does the curriculum allow for the use of a variety of teaching strategies?

■ What teacher qualifications are necessary to effectively implement the curriculum?

■ How much time is required to train teachers in the use of the curriculum? How much preservice and in-service training is needed for teachers?

■ What teacher characteristics and skills are necessary to effectively implement the curriculum?

■ How comprehensive is the curriculum? Does it include all developmental domains, or will the teacher need to supplement the curriculum from other sources?

■ How easily and accurately can the children's development be assessed by teachers?

■ Is the assessment information useful in setting classroom goals and planning activities?

■ Are teachers able to adapt, modify, and change the curriculum based on assessment outcomes, child needs, and family input?

Because early childhood teachers typically have more autonomy than teachers in elementary-school, middle-school, or secondary-school programs, who must adhere to state curriculum guidelines, it is critical that teachers of young children be aware of developmental theory, current research, and curriculum models in order to make decisions about developmentally appropriate curriculum practices for their classrooms.

COMPONENTS OF CURRICULUM

The four major components that compose a comprehensive curriculum are philosophy, goals and objectives, classroom activities, and child assessment. The philosophy component includes the rationale for the development of the remainder of the curricular components. It reflects a set of assumptions about children as learners and about the teacher's and the environment's role in supporting and encouraging children's learning. It should reflect one of the many developmental theories and approaches to early childhood education, or it can be a combination of theories and approaches.

A curriculum includes overall program goals as well as learning objectives in various areas of children's development, referred to as *developmental domains,* such as cognitive, social, emotional, and physical. Although a curriculum may appear to address children's development in each area as a discrete or separate domain, development involves competence across domains. Development is a complex, interrelated process, and the curriculum should recognize and support this integrated development.

The concept of developmentally appropriate practice emphasizes the importance of the early childhood classroom teacher as the primary decision maker about the appropriateness of the curriculum. These decisions are based on teachers' knowledge about the ways in which children develop and learn, knowledge about individual children in the classroom, and knowledge about children's diverse family, social, and cultural backgrounds. As child developmentalists, teachers must continue to learn from research and teaching practices in order to make informed decisions about what is best for young children (Bredekamp & Copple, 1997).

Planning and implementing classroom activities is the component of choosing children's daily experiences. Activities reflect goals for the children and represent all areas of children's development. The implementation of activities also involves preparing a growth-promoting classroom environment and making decisions about the effective use of teaching strategies. If philosophy is the *why* of the curriculum and the goals and objectives are the *what,* then implementation is the *how.* It is carrying out the plans and instructions of the curriculum, the linking of the written document and the actual classroom practices. Implementation of the same curriculum may be different from teacher to teacher or program to program because individuals interpret written instructions in different ways or because adaptations are made to meet the needs of the specific population of children. Implementation of a curriculum will also differ from program to program because the curriculum itself should encourage teacher choice in decisions about how the curriculum is implemented. Teachers continually develop and revise this component of the curriculum to ensure a variety of developmentally appropriate experiences for children.

Child assessment includes the process, methods, and instruments with which children's development and learning is measured. It also is important in producing information that can be shared with parents about their children and as one way to evaluate the overall curriculum and program.

Making decisions about planning and teaching as well as selecting assessment methodology should be based on the philosophical approach to the curriculum. The choices made in these areas also should reflect a responsiveness to the individuals involved in the program; this will determine the overall effectiveness of the curriculum.

ASSESSING CURRICULUM OUTCOMES

Evaluation of curricular effectiveness is a multifaceted process that requires carefully recording children's progress in the various developmental domains, observing children's involvement with activities and use of the classroom environment, and involving parents and colleagues.

Children's development can appropriately be assessed using a variety of observation and record-keeping procedures. The assessment process should be based on an understanding of developmental milestones and should include an emphasis on the uniqueness of each child. Developmental assessment should include the following:

1. Acquiring information from parents
2. Recording observations of children at play and in daily routines and interactions
3. Developing a comprehensive assessment of each child
4. Applying ongoing observations and assessments in curriculum planning, implementation, and evaluation (Leavitt & Eheart, 1991, p. 5)

When assessment is considered to be a comprehensive and ongoing process, it becomes an integral part of the curriculum and can be utilized not only to record the developmental progress of each child, but also to derive information about the effectiveness of the total curriculum. Assessment should be used not to compare children to each other, but to pinpoint any gaps in development that can be addressed through changes in the curriculum.

Children's use of equipment and spaces within the classroom environment, as well as their level of involvement with activities, is an important determinant of curricular effectiveness. Teachers should observe the classroom on a regular basis to analyze the numbers of children using the different areas of the classroom. Teachers can complete an observation in each area of the classroom and determine whether children are using all areas of the environment in a meaningful way.

Teachers also should include an evaluation section on the lesson planning form to encourage evaluation of the success of activities on a daily basis. For example, monitor teaching daily by asking these questions: Did the children ask more questions today? Did they gen-

erate their own answers and good ideas? Did they use materials in a variety of ways? Did they seem confident? Did they appear to be joyfully engaged? By analyzing the results of observations and activity evaluations, teachers can determine necessary changes in the classroom environment or activity planning.

Involving colleagues and parents in assessing the curriculum expands the information base and adds differing perspectives to the evaluation process. Involve parents in a regular written program evaluation and request more informal, verbal feedback during daily interactions and parent conferences. Enlist colleagues to observe the classroom and provide objective information about children's involvement in activities and the effectiveness of teaching strategies.

In addition, the results of published research studies on different teaching strategies or on different curricula can be applied and used to make changes to improve your program. Teachers who develop a philosophy of early childhood education and have a knowledge of curriculum models are best able to make effective choices about implementing curricula that are congruent with a philosophical framework and responsive to the needs of children and families.

■ ■ ■ ■ ■ ■ ■ ■ ■

As you begin to answer the questions posed to you during the interview, you realize the importance of organizing your thoughts and synthesizing your knowledge and skills into a well-articulated philosophical framework. You utilize your background in child development and early childhood education to formulate responses as follows:

- Utilizing information from developmental theories and research, you discuss how young children learn and support your choice of a child-centered educational philosophy and curriculum.

- You discuss your view of the purpose of the curriculum as a comprehensive framework for designing the classroom,

interacting with children and families, and choosing developmentally appropriate activities.

- You describe the various components of the curriculum, including guidelines for establishing program goals and objectives, implementation of activities in all developmental domains, and methods of assessing children's growth and development.

- You describe how you will assess the effectiveness of your curriculum by tracking children's developmental progress, evaluating the use of materials and the environment through classroom observation, and involving parents and colleagues in an assessment process.

■ ■ ■ ■ ■ ■ ■ ■ ■

CHAPTER SUMMARY _____

Chapter 1 focuses on the role of curriculum, including definitions and purposes, in early childhood programs. Teachers have assumptions about curriculum that relate the issues of quality, integrated development, the role of play, teachers' philosophy and

practice, children's development, children as learners, and developmentally appropriate practice to curriculum. Many social, economic, and political factors influence curriculum. Developmental theories—specifically maturational theory, psychodynamic theory, behavioral theory, cognitive developmental theory, multiple intelligences theory, and sociocultural theory, and research—are other major determinants of curriculum in early childhood education. Several curricular models, including the High/Scope cognitively oriented curriculum, the Bank Street curriculum, Montessori, progressive education, behavioristic instructional technology, Reggio Emilia, and the creative-play approach are used in programs.

Choosing and evaluating a curriculum for an early childhood program are important teacher tasks. Four components of curriculum—philosophy, goals and objectives, classroom activities, and child assessment—and the linkages among them are necessary parts of a comprehensive curriculum. Assessing curricular outcomes is described as a multifaceted process with children, parents, and teachers as sources of assessment information.

DISCUSSION QUESTIONS

1. Discuss the vignette at the beginning of the chapter. What other questions or concerns might you have? Discuss the vignette at the end of the chapter. Are there other responses you might have to this situation?

2. Develop a definition of curriculum. Distinguish among the perspectives on curriculum that teachers, parents, and children each might have.

3. Choose one or more of the assumptions about curriculum and describe how it would be put into operation. For example, for the second assumption, describe how curriculum can integrate different areas of development such as cognition and perceptual motor skills.

4. List five to ten statements that describe your beliefs about how children learn and develop. Compare your list to the descriptions of theories of development and learning. Which theory or theories does your list most closely reflect?

5. Describe the curriculum models included in this chapter in a way that illustrates their differences and then their similarities.

6. Choose one or more of the guidelines listed in the position statement of the National Association for the Education of Young Children and the National Association of Early Childhood Specialists in State Departments of Education. Describe an example of what you might observe in a program in order to give an affirmative answer to the guideline question. For example, for the thirteenth guideline—"Does it encourage active learning and allow children to make meaningful choices?"—describe an example of what you would observe in a classroom to be able to answer that the guideline is reflected in the curriculum of a program.

7. Describe the contributions to assessing curricular outcomes made by each of the following: teachers, children, parents, and research.

REFERENCES

Allen, J., & Catron, C. (1990). Researchers at the early childhood center: Guidelines for cooperation. *Young Children, 45*(4), 60–65.

Ballard, B J., Weintraub, F. J., & Zantal-Wiener, K. (1987). *Script for P.L. 99-457: The next step forward for handicapped children*. Reston, VA: Council for Exceptional Children.

Bandura, A. (1977). *Social learning theory*. Englewood Cliffs, NJ: Prentice-Hall.

Bereiter, C., & Engelmann, S. (1966). *Teaching disadvantaged children in the preschool*. Englewood Cliffs, NJ: Prentice-Hall.

Berk, L., & Winsler, A. (1995). *Scaffolding children's learning: Vygotsky and early childhood education*. Washington, DC: National Association for the Education of Young Children.

Berrueta-Clement, J. R., Schweinhart, L. J., Barnett, W. S., Epstein, A. S., & Weikart, D. P. (1984). *Changed lives: The effects of the Perry Preschool program on youths through age 19*. Monographs of the High/Scope Educational Research Foundation. Ypsilanti, MI: High/Scope Press.

Biber, B. (1984). *Early education and psychological development*. New Haven, CT: Yale University Press.

Biber, B., & Franklin, M. (1967). The relevance of developmental and psychodynamic concepts to the education of the preschool child. *Journal of the American Academy of Child Psychiatry, 6*(1), 5–24.

Bjorklund, D. (1997). In search of a metatheory for cognitive development (or, Piaget is dead and I don't feel so good myself). *Child Development, 68*(1), 144–148.

Bredekamp, S. (Ed.). (1987). *Developmentally appropriate practice in early childhood programs serving children from birth through age 8*. Washington, DC: National Association for the Education of Young Children.

Bredekamp, S., & Copple, C. (Eds.). (1997). *Developmentally appropriate practice in early childhood programs.* Washington, DC: National Association for the Education of Young Children.

Dewey, J. (1900). *School and society.* Chicago: University of Chicago Press.

Dewey, J. (1902). *The child and the curriculum.* Chicago: University of Chicago Press.

Edwards, C., Gandini, L., & Forman, G. (1993). *The hundred languages of children.* Norwood, NJ: Ablex.

Erikson, E. (1963). *Childhood and society.* New York: Norton.

Erikson, E. (1968). *Identity: Youth and crisis.* New York: Dutton.

Freud, S. (1938). *An outline of psychoanalysis.* London: Hogarth.

Gardner, H. (1991). *The unschooled mind.* New York: HarperCollins.

Gardner, H. (1993). *Multiple intelligences.* New York: Basic Books.

Gesell, A., & Ilg, F. (1949). *Child development: An introduction to the study of human growth.* New York: Harper & Row.

Goffin, S. (1989). Developing a research agenda for early childhood education: What can be learned from the research on teaching? *Early Childhood Research Quarterly, 4*(2), 187–204.

Havighurst, R. (1953). *Human development and education.* New York: Longman.

Hendrick, J. (1998). *Total learning: Developmental curriculum for the young child* (5th ed.). Columbus, OH: Merrill/Prentice-Hall.

Hildebrand, V. (1994). *Guiding young children* (5th ed.). Columbus, OH: Merrill/Prentice-Hall.

Hofferth, S. (1996). Child care in the United States today. *The Future of Children: Financing Child Care, 6*(2), 41– 61.

Hohmann, M., Banet, B., & Weikart, D. (1978). *Young children in action: A manual for preschool educators.* Ypsilanti, MI: High/Scope Press.

Jones, E. (1986). Perspectives on teacher education: Some relations between theory and practice. In L. Katz (Ed.), *Current topics in early childhood education* (Vol. 6, pp. 123–141). Norwood, NJ: Ablex.

Langenbach, M. (1976). *Day care: Curriculum considerations.* Columbus, OH: Merrill.

Leavitt, R., & Eheart, B. (1991). Assessment in early childhood programs. *Young Children, 46*(5), 4–9.

Montessori, M. (1949). *Childhood education.* Chicago: Henry Regency.

National Association for the Education of Young Children and National Association of Early Childhood Specialists in State Departments of Education (NAEYC & NAECS/SDE). (1991). Guidelines for appropriate curriculum content and assessment in programs serving children ages 3 through 8. *Young Children, 46*(3), 21–38.

Newson, J., & Newson, E. (1975). Intersubjectivity and the transmission of culture: On the social origins of symbolic functioning. *Bulletin of the British Psychological Society, 28,* 437–446.

Perryman, L. (Ed.). (1966). *Montessori in perspective.* Washington, DC: National Association for the Education of Young Children.

Piaget, J. (1926). *The language and thought of the child.* New York: Harcourt Brace Jovanovich.

Seefeldt, C. (1987). *The early childhood curriculum: A review of current research.* New York: Teachers College Press.

Skinner, B. F. (1971). *Beyond freedom and dignity.* New York: Knopf.

Skinner, B. F. (1974). *About behaviorism.* New York: Knopf.

Spodek, B. (Ed.). (1982). *Handbook of research in early education.* New York: Free Press.

Surr, J. (1992). Early childhood programs and the Americans with Disabilities Act (ADA). *Young Children, 47*(5), 18–21.

Thomas, R. M. (1996). *Comparing theories of child development* (4th ed.). Belmont, CA: Brooks/Cole.

Vygotsky, L. (1933/1978). *Mind in society* (M. Cole, V. John-Steiner, S. Scriber, & E. Souberman, Eds., pp. 92–104). Cambridge, MA: Harvard University Press.

Weikart, D. (1986, Winter). *What do we know?* High Scope/ReSource, 6–9.

Willer, B., Hofferth, S. L., Kisker, E. E., Divine-Hawkins, P., Farquhar, E., & Glantz, F. B. (1991). *The demand and supply of child care in 1990: Joint findings from the National Child Care Survey of 1990 and a profile of child care settings.* Washington, DC: National Association for the Education of Young Children.

Williams, L. (1987). Determining the curriculum. In C. Seefeldt (Ed.), *The early childhood curriculum: A review of current research* (pp. 1–12). New York: Teachers College Press.

Wolery, M., & Wilbers, J. (Eds.). (1994). *Including children with special needs in early childhood programs.* Washington, DC: National Association for the Education of Young Children.

Wood, D., Bruner, J., & Ross, G. (1976). The role of tutoring in problem solving. *Journal of Child Psychology and Psychiatry, 17,* 89–100.

ADDITIONAL RESOURCES

Ayers, W. (1989). *The good preschool teacher.* New York: Teachers College Press.

Bagnato, S., & Neisworth, J. (1981). *Linking developmental assessment and curricula.* Rockville, MD: Aspen Systems Corporation.

Berk, L. (1994). Vygotsky's theory: The importance of make-believe play. *Young Children, 50*(1), 30–39.

Bodrova, E., & Leona, D. (1996). *Tools of the mind: The Vygotskian approach to early childhood education.* Columbus, OH: Merrill/Prentice-Hall.

Bredekamp, S. (1993). Reflections on Reggio Emilia. *Young Children, 49*(1), 13–17.

Cuffaro, H. (1995). *Experimenting with the world: John Dewey and the early childhood classroom.* New York: Teachers College Press.

Epstein, A., Schweinhart, L., & McAdoo, L. (1996). *Models of early childhood education.* Ypsilanti, MI: High/Scope Press.

Evans, E. (1982). Curriculum models and early childhood education. In B. Spodek (Ed.), *Handbook of research in early childhood education* (pp. 107–135). New York: Free Press.

Firlik, R. (1996). Can we adapt the philosophies and practices of Reggio Emilia, Italy, for use in American schools? *Early Childhood Education Journal, 23*(4), 217–220.

Gallagher, P. (1997). Teachers and inclusion: Perspectives on changing roles. *Topics in Early Childhood Special Education, 17*(3), 363–386.

Gandini, L. (1993). Fundamentals of the Reggio Emilia approach to early childhood education. *Young Children, 49*(1), 4–8.

Hendrick, J. (1992). Where does it all begin: Teaching principles of democracy in the early years. *Young Children, 47*(3), 51–53.

Hymes, J. L. (1991). *Twenty years in review: A look at 1971–1990.* Washington, DC: National Association for the Education of Young Children.

Janko, S., Schwartz, I., Sandall, S., Anderson, K., & Cottam, C. (1997). Beyond microsystems: Unanticipated lessons about the meaning of inclusion. *Topics in Early Childhood Special Education, 17*(3), 286–306.

Kennedy, D. (1996). After Reggio Emilia: May the conversation begin! *Young Children, 51*(5), 24–27.

Malaguzzi, L. (1993). For an education based on relationships. *Young Children, 49*(1), 9– 12.

Piaget, J., & Inhelder, B. (1969). *The psychology of the child.* New York: Basic Books.

Roopnarine, J., & Johnson, J. (Eds.). (1993). *Approaches to early childhood education* (2nd ed.). Columbus, OH: Merrill/Macmillan.

Seefeldt, C. (Ed.). (1990). *Continuing issues in early childhood education.* Columbus, OH: Merrill/Macmillan.

Stallings, J., & Stipek, D. (1986). Research on early childhood and elementary school teaching programs. In M. Wittrock (Ed.), *Handbook of research on teaching* (pp. 727–753). New York: Macmillan.

Weber, E. (1984). *Ideas influencing early childhood education: A theoretical analysis.* New York: Teachers College Press.

2.

Creative-Play Curriculum Model

■ ■ ■ ■ ■ ■ ■ ■ ■

During a pre-enrollment conference for Jerome, a 3-year-old entering your preschool classroom, his parents express concern about what their child will actually learn in your program. Jerome's parents are very positive about most aspects of your program. They are excited about the well-trained staff and low adult-child ratios, and they are impressed by the cheerful and creative classroom environment. However, they have questions about the creative-play curriculum used in your program.

Jerome's parents question the emphasis on play in your classroom and want assurances that Jerome will learn his alphabet and numbers and other concepts they believe are critical to ensure his success in kindergarten and the primary grades.

To develop a successful relationship with Jerome's parents and to ensure the best possible learning environment for Jerome, you must clarify your program philosophy and curriculum and reach an understanding with the parents.

• How can you justify the importance of play in young children's development?

• What examples can you give to demonstrate the effectiveness of a creative-play curriculum?

• Will you be able to describe what areas of development are critical during the preschool years?

• How can you assure Jerome's parents that your program will prepare him for successful learning experiences in kindergarten and the primary grades?

• What steps will you take to involve Jerome's parents in the program and increase their understanding of how to support learning through play at home?

■ ■ ■ ■ ■ ■ ■ ■ ■

Suggestions for responding to this classroom vignette will be shared at the end of the chapter.

When reading this chapter, focus on the philosophy of the creative-play curriculum and on the many ways that play supports the development of the whole child. Also, understand the components of the invisible curriculum—the role of the teacher, classroom management and guidance, family involvement, classroom design and organization, and the outdoor play environment—and the components of the visible curriculum—activity planning, observation and assessment, and goal setting.

It is a complex process to develop a curriculum design that is responsive to the needs of children, teachers, and parents in a rapidly changing world and that integrates a philosophical framework with research on how children develop and learn. Chapter 1 included an overview of a variety of curriculum models and a discussion of the important role of the early childhood educator in developing curriculum. This chapter outlines a curriculum model that focuses on the optimal development of the whole child in an environment that fosters active exploration through play, nurturing relationships with teachers, and a partnership between the program and parents. This creative-play curriculum model is a flexible, open-ended model that is easily adapted by teachers for a range of age groups from infancy through preschool and for a variety of populations of children.

The creative-play curriculum model has as its central purpose the fostering of optimal development in the young child through an integrated, interactive, creative-play approach to the early childhood learning environment. This approach goes beyond the development of competence to foster optimization or self-actualization, and it goes beyond the idea of a supportive environment to encompass the dynamics of a creative, enabling environment. Fein and Clarke-Stewart (1973) stated that "a broad, educational-developmental approach" leads us to the future aim of early childhood programs as "going beyond promoting competence to fostering 'optimization' or 'self-actualization' for all people" (p. 295). Specifically, optimal development includes:

- A feeling of self-worth and self-confidence
- The capacity to trust, respect, and invest emotionally in people
- Effective interpersonal and social interaction skills
- The ability to act and think independently and to develop self-control
- Skill in communicating ideas and feelings
- Understanding and organizing information about the physical and social environment
- Acquisition and use of problem-solving skills
- Curiosity about the world and pleasure in learning and exploring (Child Development Laboratories Policy Committee, 1985)

In order to face the demands of an increasingly complex society and develop the critical-thinking, problem-solving, and coping skills necessary to adapt and flourish in the 21st century, children's optimal development must be nurtured in an environment that supports creativity.

> Attention to the creative potential of young children lays the foundation for future critical thinking. Children will face situations where the divergent-thinking skills learned now will strengthen the critical-thinking skills to be developed later and empower today's children to solve tomorrow's problems (Tegano, Moran, & Sawyers, 1991, p. 115; used by permission of NEA).

Teachers of young children have a major influence on children's development through the provision of a developmentally appropriate, creative, and stimulating curriculum and classroom environment. In the process of designing and writing this curriculum, certain assumptions have been made about effective teachers of young children:

- Effective teachers want to provide the highest-quality care possible to children in their programs. Standards for safety, supervision, and activities go far beyond the minimal or mandated.
- Effective teachers have both training and experience. This curriculum can be a component of that training and can be used in conjunction with videotapes, teacher supervision and feedback, modeling of effective teaching by master teachers, and other methods of preservice and inservice training and education.
- Effective teachers are resourceful. They will choose to use the resources listed at the end of each chapter or select and use other materials to extend and enrich their learning about the topics and issues presented here.
- Effective teachers respect individual differences. They are sensitive to developmental and cultural diversity and flexible in adapting the curriculum to enhance the creative potential in all young children.
- Effective teachers are autonomous. They will make decisions about the use of this curriculum, and any other materials and resources, in a way that reflects their professionalism, their concern for children, and their commitment to providing the highest-quality care and education for young children.

Curriculum is not viewed as a packaged product but as a dynamic and evolving process that is shaped by the individuals involved in learning together every day. Teachers are expected and encouraged to adapt, revise, and change curriculum to meet the needs of the children, parents, and staff.

THE ROLE OF CREATIVE PLAY IN CURRICULUM _____

Play is the vehicle that enables the optimal development of the young child. Because play is a powerful, growth-promoting, and essential experience in the world of young children, it constitutes the basis of this curriculum model. Play directly influences all areas of development by offering children opportunities for learning about self, others, and the environment. Play gives children the freedom to imagine, to explore, and to create. Children are intrinsically motivated to play; they play to enjoy the activity, to feel competent, and "to match the new with the known" (Rogers, C. S., & Sawyers, 1988,

p. 2). Children are able to gain a sense of mastery over the world and feelings of self-esteem from dynamic, vitalizing, positive play experiences (Caplan & Caplan, 1974). Play is necessary to the lives of children:

> To the young child, play is life itself. Play fills mind and body, mentality, emotionality, and physical being. A child engrossed in play is inventive, free, and happy. Through the variety and depth of play, the child learns and grows. It is serious business; it is his world. (Evans, 1974, p. 267)

Spontaneity, self-expression, and flexibility characterize children's play and allow them to be inventive, imaginative, and creative. Children's curiosity, creative-thinking, and problem-solving abilities are developed in an atmosphere that encourages active exploration, welcomes unconventional ideas, and fosters multiple avenues for self-expression (Vandenberg, 1980). Play provides the opportunity to generate many ideas and thereby maximize the possibility for original ideas; these ideas may be tested in a non-evaluative atmosphere to develop the problem-solving skills of young children (Sawyers, Moran, & Tegano, 1986).

Creativity is enhanced through imaginative-play experiences that allow children to become immersed in pretend play and to produce fresh, innovative ideas in the process of role play (Curry & Arnaud, 1984). Preschool children who engage in imaginative play are shown to produce more original responses to creativity tasks (Moran, Sawyers, Fu, & Milgram, 1984). A play environment does not include rigid expectations for children's behavior and educational outcomes; instead, it fosters risk taking, possibility thinking, nonconformity, and generation of many different ideas, which are important components of children's developing creativity (Starkweather, 1971). A classroom that (1) includes many open-ended play materials such as blocks, Play-Doh with ambiguous props, and water play, and (2) is staffed with teachers who encourage children to experiment with materials, who ask open-ended questions during activities, and who value the process of exploration rather than the aesthetics of a final product, enhances the development of creativity in children. Creative activities are not limited to expressive arts; rather, classroom activities in all developmental areas have the potential to foster creativity if the teacher and the materials encourage exploration, new ideas, and problem solving. Thus, the development of creativity in children is an extension of their learning through play and is supported by the provision of divergent play materials and a flexible, experiential learning environment (Pepler, 1986; Tegano et al., 1991).

The curriculum provides the mechanism for deciding what to teach, and the teacher supplies the methodology for determining how to create a supportive learning environment. Thus, the devel-

Early problem-solving skills can be seen in this child's attempt to wear a dress-up shoe and discover that he must first remove his own shoes.

opment of creative potential in children is enhanced in an exploratory play environment with a teacher whose philosophical and curricular approaches support divergent thinking and problem solving.

Curriculum development and teaching attitudes and behaviors are complementary and integrated processes that set the stage for the development of creativity (Tegano et al., 1991).

FOSTERING THE DEVELOPMENT OF THE WHOLE CHILD

Play is vital to the development of all facets of the young child's emerging self. "A vast amount of research indicates that imaginative play (symbolic play) is a significant causal force in the development of a multitude of abilities, including creativity, sequential memory, group cooperation, receptive vocabulary, conceptions of kinship relationships, impulse control, spatial perspective-taking skill, affective perspective-taking skill, and cognitive perspective-taking skill" (Gowen, 1995, p. 78). All six aspects of children's development in the creative-play curriculum—personal awareness, emotional well-being, socialization, communication, cognition, and perceptual motor skills—are important and must be considered as interactive rather than parallel functions. Creativity is not viewed as an additional developmental domain; rather, the development of creativity is an integral component of a spontaneous play environment, and the potential for creative development is inherent in all developmental areas. Therefore, this curriculum does not single out one area as its primary focus; it supports and encourages children's development in all areas. A creative-play environment is the philosophical basis of the curriculum model; the growth of the whole child in these six developmental domains forms the central focus of the curriculum model.

Creative Play Enables the Development of Personal Awareness

Play supports children as they develop independence and achieve mastery and control over their environment. Through play, children invent, explore, imitate, and practice the routines of everyday living as a step in the development of self-help skills. The successful acquisition of these skills promotes children's feelings of competence. Their emerging independence fosters the ability to make choices about everyday decisions, such as which book to read or whether to paint, play with dolls, or build with blocks.

Children who are given opportunities to explore and experiment with nonstereotypical roles and behaviors are more likely to perceive a diverse range of personal and professional roles as possible options. When children enact a variety of roles through pretend play, they are more likely to see many possibilities for themselves and to make more informed decisions about choices available to them.

Play also supports teaching about personal safety issues to children in appropriate, sensitive, and nonthreatening ways. Teachers can increase children's awareness of appropriate safety practices while also providing them with the security of knowing that caring adults are responsible for their safety and well-being. Teachers who are aware of the importance of child abuse protection and drug abuse prevention measures and who are sensitive to the cognitive limitations and the emotional vulnerability of young children can use play to support developmentally appropriate discussions of health and safety issues with children. Through play, teachers can help children establish the framework that will enable them to make informed personal choices and avoid risks while establishing trust in themselves and adults. Thus, responsible and responsive teachers create a play environment that supports the development of children's positive self-image and increasing independence in day-to-day living. Play promotes the development of personal awareness in the following areas:

- Self-help skills (increases skill to feed and dress self and regulate toileting and sleeping)
- Independence (exhibits control of self and mastery of environment)
- Personal health (develops knowledge of body parts, nutrition, hygiene, drug abuse prevention, wellness)
- Personal safety (learns child abuse protection and passenger and pedestrian safety practices; develops an awareness of hazards within the child's environment)

Creative Play Enables the Development of Emotional Well-Being

Play promotes children's inner growth and self-realization, supports mastery of developmental conflicts, and lessens emotional pain and trauma. Play fosters emotional health by "offering healing for hurts and sadness" (Cass, 1973, p. 12). Through play, young children learn to accept, express, and cope with feelings in a constructive, positive manner.

Play gives children the opportunity to be themselves, to get to know themselves, and to shape a more satisfactory design for living. Children begin to understand themselves in relationship to the world as their play experiences enable them to find out answers to such unspoken questions as: "Is there such a thing as a me? How can I feel sure about my existence? What is the intention of the world toward me?" (Bettelheim, 1981, p. 105). Play also is a valuable therapeutic tool in the lives of young children (Catron, 1981). Children "play out" their feelings and insecurities and arrive at a more satisfactory solution within an accepting, supportive environment.

Play facilitates personality integration and has important implications for human relationships. Seeman (1963) suggests that the principles of psychological integration—the process by which a person comes to know and understand the self—are relevant to the developmental process in children. Children learn about themselves as separate, autonomous, and unique individuals who possess a multitude of thoughts and feelings realized through imaginative play experiences. Encouraging children to understand and accept their emotional selves leads to fuller self-development, enhances relationships, and increases their capacity to cope successfully with stress and change (Seeman, 1963).

Specifically, play promotes the development of these facets of emotional well-being:

- Awareness, acceptance, and expression of emotions (identifies a variety of feelings and expresses feelings to others)
- Coping skills (shows adaptive and healthy responses to stressors, conflict, or change; uses relaxation techniques; resolves emotional conflict and issues)
- Personality integration (exhibits general adjustment, autonomy, positive self-concept)
- Building values (develops empathy, trust, reverence, respect)

Creative Play Enables the Development of Socialization

Play provides an avenue for social development. "When shared with other children, play is a major vehicle for constructive socialization, widening empathy with others, and lessening egocentrism" (Arnaud, 1971, p. 5). Play fosters socialization and enhances children's sense of belonging. Through play experiences, young children learn prosocial behaviors such as taking turns, cooperating, sharing, and helping each other. Dramatic-play situations help children put themselves in another's place and foster the development of empathy and consideration for others. For example, children who engage in pretend play in an imaginary hospital setting may develop a deeper understanding of a peer who has a chronic illness and must be hospitalized frequently.

Play and social interaction with peers promotes the shift from heteronomous moral reasoning, guided by egocentrism, to autonomous moral reasoning, characterized by autonomy, reciprocity, and cooperation (Piaget, 1932). Teachers foster appropriate opportunities for such interactions by providing ways for children to take the role of other people, by allowing children to participate in decisions about classroom policies and rules, by using "other-oriented induction" strategies for behavior management (Hoffman, 1970), and by facilitating social interaction that provides challenges and opportunities to resolve conflict and dissonance (Allen, J., 1988). Teachers can use a play situation, such as a conflict over the use of a toy, to help children learn to express themselves verbally, listen to another child's point of view, and decide on a plan of action that will solve the problem.

Play fosters the growth of peaceful interactions among children. Children learn to be peacemakers through play experiences that help them develop the ability to negotiate, to encourage reconciliation, to resolve conflicts, and to solve problems in a just, constructive atmosphere (Carlsson-Paige & Levin, 1985; Peachey, 1981). When play experiences take place in a classroom environment characterized by positive human relationships and appreciation of the diversity in people, children learn to respect and care for each other and to make peaceful and caring choices about interactions with others (Rogers, V. R., 1973).

Play promotes the development of socialization in the following areas:

- Social interactions (interacts with peers and adults; resolves conflicts)
- Cooperation (helps, shares, takes turns)

- Conservation of resources (uses and cares for materials and the environment appropriately)
- Respect for others (understands and accepts individual differences; understands multicultural issues)

Creative Play Enables the Development of Communication

Play is an especially powerful tool for teaching language skills to children. Children expand their vocabulary and improve their receptive and expressive language skills by interacting with other children and adults in spontaneous play situations.

Pretend play facilitates the development of many language skills by providing a natural setting that is conducive to sharing thoughts, emotions, and novel ideas. Children use language in a creative, colorful way during sociodramatic play to act out roles and communicate needs, ideas, and wishes.

Sociodramatic play involves verbal communication and nonverbal interactions and fosters the development of congruent communication that allows children to send and receive clear, consistent messages. Children's needs to communicate effectively, to understand each other, and to follow directions from peers in play situations encourage proficiency in language development.

Specifically, play promotes the development of these facets of communication:

- Receptive language (follows directions; understands basic concepts)
- Expressive language (expresses needs, wants, feelings; uses words, phrases, sentences; speaks clearly and distinctly)
- Nonverbal communication (uses congruent communication, facial expressions, body gestures, hand gestures)
- Auditory memory/discrimination (understands spoken language; discriminates different sounds)

Creative Play Enables the Development of Cognition

Play is a meaningful and enjoyable activity for children and "acts as an energizer and organizer of cognitive learning" (Arnaud, 1971, p. 5). During play, children encounter new experiences, manipulate materials and equipment, interact with others, and begin to make sense of their world. Play provides the framework for young children to develop an understanding about themselves, other people, and the environment. "Play is the basis of all later cognitive functioning and is, therefore, indispensable in the life of the child" (Athey, 1974, p. 34).

Play serves a critical function in children's development of intellect and the two related processes of assimilation and accommodation. Assimilation involves abstracting information from the outside world and fitting that information into existing knowledge systems. In accommodation, children modify the knowledge systems representing what they already know (Piaget, 1926).

Play allows young children to actively engage the environment, to work through internal and interpersonal conflicts, and to attend to intellectual and cognitive tasks. A play-based curriculum that provides opportunities for choices and self-directed activities encourages children to learn at their own pace and enables children to "gain a sense of autonomy and effectiveness; become motivated to mastery; develop such attributes as self-direction, trust in themselves, self-assurance, and a feeling of self-worth" (Anker, Foster, McLane, Sobel, & Weissboard, 1981, p. 107).

Play supports the development of memory, thinking, and problem-solving skills in young children through learning activities based on observation, investigation, and exploration. Play also provides experiences, information, and skills that form the foundation for future learning (Hendrick, 1996).

Play promotes the development of the following aspects of cognition:

- Problem solving/reasoning (uses divergent thinking; suggests solutions to peer problems, "what if" situations; answers questions; extends sentence or story logically)
- Concept formation (understands spatial relations; identifies colors, numbers, shapes)
- Imitation/memory (imitates; recalls past events; sequences events)
- Association/classification (matches; sorts; groups; classifies; establishes relationships between objects)

Creative Play Enables the Development of Perceptual Motor Skills

Play supports children's needs for active interactions and involvement with the physical environment. As infants, children begin learning about the world through sensorimotor actions upon objects in their environment. Actions become more refined as children develop increasing control and body management skills.

Open and motorically challenging play environments facilitate the development of locomotor skills, involving body movement through space, and nonlocomotor skills, involving more static involvement with the physical environment. Increasingly complex manipulative-play activities support the development of fine motor skills involved in eye-hand/eye-foot coordination.

Extensive opportunities for movement, hands-on learning experiences, and sensorimotor activities that involve the use of large and small muscles enable children to fully develop their emerging motor abilities.

Play promotes the development of perceptual motor skills in the following areas:

- Eye-hand/eye-foot coordination (draws, writes, manipulates objects, tracks visually, throws, catches, kicks)
- Locomotor skills (moves body through space: walks, jumps, marches, skips, runs, hops, gallops, rolls, crawls, creeps)
- Nonlocomotor skills (static: bends, reaches, turns, twists, stretches, sways, squats, sits, stands)
- Body management and control (exhibits body awareness, space awareness, rhythm, balance; ability to start, stop, change directions)

CREATIVE POTENTIAL _____

Creative potential is inherent in all the developmental domains included in the creative-play curriculum model. All young children have creative potential; however, the development of creativity is a highly individualized process influenced by a variety of biological and environmental factors, as is growth in other developmental areas. Tegano et al. (1991) have identified cognitive traits and personality factors that may indicate creativity in young children. Cognitive characteristics that indicate creativity include the following:

- Fantasy—engaging in sociodramatic and imaginative play
- Divergent thinking—developing a variety of responses and ideas
- Curiosity—questioning, exploring, examining
- Metaphoric thinking—being able to produce or comprehend metaphors (Tegano et al., 1991, pp. 23–35; reprinted by permission of NEA)

Personality traits that indicate creativity include:

- Temperament—adaptability, persistence, high levels of involvement in activities and low levels of distractability
- Nonconformity—originality and flexibility
- Risk-taking—willingness to accept a challenge or risk making a mistake
- Motivation—an internal locus of control (Tegano et al., 1991, pp. 35–40; reprinted by permission of NEA)

Teachers of young children who are aware of characteristics that indicate creative potential can recognize individual differences in children and nurture

Creative potential is reflected in a child's curiosity about the world.

the development of creativity throughout the day in all developmental areas.

INVISIBLE CURRICULUM _____

Children's development in the six domains is supported by the following program components: the role of the teacher, partnerships with parents, classroom management and guidance classroom design and organization, and the outdoor play environment. These program components compose the invisible curriculum; they are the foundations of the classroom learning environment that may not be visible or apparent to observers, and they are an integral part of the development of a creative-play curriculum. The teacher's role is to structure the environment to meet the children's needs and capitalize on their interests. Teachers provide a learning environment that challenges without being frustrating, and they act as facilitators for learning by observing, questioning, modeling, and supporting children and by providing information the children would not be able to discover for themselves. Teachers also provide appropriate classroom guidance by setting developmentally appropriate limits on behaviors, supporting the development of positive social interactions, and encouraging children to use problem-solving skills to resolve conflicts.

Forming partnerships with parents is recognized as an important aspect of each child's development and is essential for successful program operation. Efforts should be made to support parents in their child-rearing roles. Their participation should be encouraged through frequent sharing of information about children, solicitation of their ideas concerning program operation and development, and inclusion whenever possible in daily routines and activities at the centers.

Safe, developmentally appropriate, and carefully planned classroom design and outdoor play environments enhance children's total development and set the stage for a variety of learning opportunities. Indoor and outdoor learning environments should be planned by taking into account the importance of schedules, the monitoring of children, and the amount, type, and placement of materials and equipment. The learning environment provided for young children can support them as active organizers of experience and allow children to direct their own play.

VISIBLE CURRICULUM _____

The creative-play curriculum design includes activities planned for infants, toddlers, and preschoolers and includes suggestions for adaptations to meet the needs of young children with special needs participating in an inclusive program. Although the activities included in the creative-play curriculum are appropriate for a range of developmental levels, some adaptations may be necessary to accommodate a child's disabilities, and to help the child enjoy the total learning experience. Activities also reflect the program emphasis on development of the whole child and an integrated, balanced day: indoor/outdoor activities, quiet/active activities, adult-initiated/child-initiated activities, and individual/small-group activities. Process-oriented experiences, rather than product-oriented ones, are emphasized. When the focus is on process, the teacher provides props and materials and acts in a supportive role, but it is the child who explores and directs the play. Open-ended (process) activities provide success for each child at any developmental level. Successful experiences promote self-confidence and enable chil-

dren to continue to actively explore, act on, and interact with their environment.

In addition to the curricular activities, the program includes an emphasis on developmental assessment and child observations that are fully integrated into the curriculum model to provide developmental information on individual children. The assessment approach is the basis for writing individual objectives for each child and setting goals that influence curriculum planning. This flexibility in programming encourages the inclusion of children with special needs stemming from disabilities, unusual family circumstances, and/or developmental delays. The developmental checklist, teacher observations, and children's portfolios emphasize the six developmental domains included in the curriculum and complete the cycle of evaluation, goal setting, and activity planning. This cycle of planning, teaching, and evaluating forms the basis of the visible curriculum—that is, the teaching strategies and activities that are visible and apparent to the classroom observer—and encompasses the fundamental tasks of effective teaching and program planning.

INCLUSION _____

The creative-play curriculum model is an individualized, developmental approach to learning that supports the integration of young children with disabilities into the early childhood classroom. Inclusion is an educational practice advocated by parents, early childhood educators, and early childhood special educators. A working definition of inclusion has four significant components:

1. Young children with and without developmental delays actively participate in the same community program.
2. Professionals from different disciplines plan and collaborate to provide services.
3. Individualized goals—established for children with developmental delays by a multidisciplinary planning team consisting of parents, professionals, and paraprofessionals—are promoted by program services.
4. Children's progress toward their individualized goals is evaluated (Brown, 1997, p. 4).

"A Position on Inclusion," developed by the Division for Early Childhood of the Council for Exceptional Children and adopted by the National Association for the Education of Young Children (1994) supports inclusive practices by recommending:

■ Continued development, evaluation, and dissemination of full-inclusion support services and systems so that the options for inclusion are of high quality.
■ Development of preservice and in-service training programs that prepare families, administrators, and service providers to develop and work within inclusive settings.
■ Collaboration among all key stakeholders to implement flexible, fiscal, and administrative procedures in support of inclusion.
■ Research that contributes to our knowledge of state-of-the-art services.
■ Restructuring and unification of social, education, health, and intervention supports and services to make them more responsive to the needs of all children (p. 78).

To plan and implement an effective inclusion program, invisible curriculum issues must be considered:

Teachers must have an understanding of development and disabilities.

Family needs for support and guidance must be considered when developing the parent partnership program.

Classroom guidance strategies must be flexible enough to accommodate children's different developmental levels and special needs.

Outdoor play areas must be accessible for children with disabilities.

Classroom environments must be designed and arranged to encourage young children with disabilities to explore, interact, and solve problems.

In addition, the visible-curriculum components of assessing children's development, determining individual objectives, setting program goals, and planning and implementing activities based on these goals and objectives provide a flexible and highly individualized program environment that facilitates the inclusion of children with disabilities. Integrating an early childhood classroom involves a great deal more than just including young children with special needs in the program. Inclusion involves treating all young children as children first; obtaining the additional resources to support the educational and developmental needs of young children with special needs; supporting social success and emotional well-being as well as educational opportunities for children with special needs; and encouraging interactive, participatory, and active learning experiences for all children in the classroom (Allen, K. E., 1996; Kaiser, 1991). An individualized, integrated early childhood program enables all young children to learn from each other, from caring adults, and from the environment in order to grow in all areas of development.

CURRICULUM MODEL _____

The curriculum model has creative play as its underlying philosophical basis, the development of the whole child as its center, and the various components of the invisible and visible curriculum as its framework (see Figure 2-1). The broken lines on the curriculum model reflect the inclusion component of the

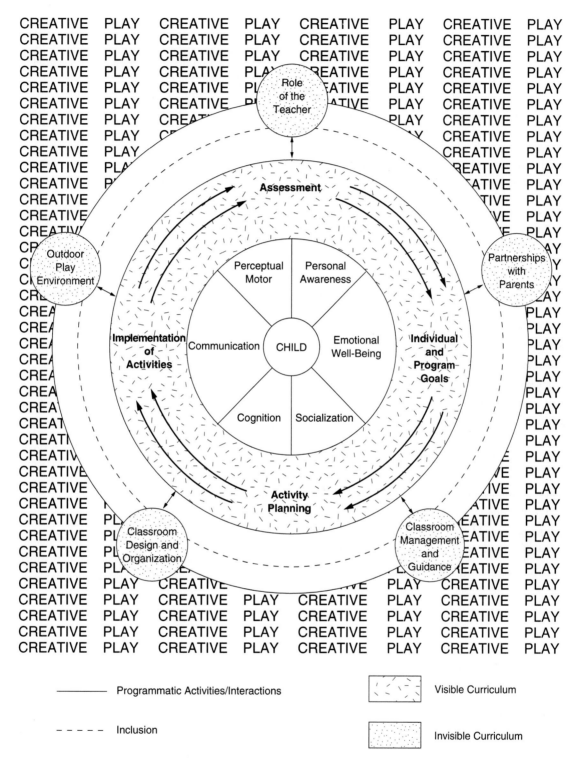

CREATIVE PLAY CREATIVE PLAY CREATIVE PLAY CREATIVE PLAY
CREATIVE PLAY CREATIVE PLAY CREATIVE PLAY CREATIVE PLAY
CREATIVE PLAY CREATIVE PLAY CREATIVE PLAY CREATIVE PLAY

Role of the Teacher

Assessment

Outdoor Play Environment

Partnerships with Parents

Perceptual Motor | Personal Awareness

Implementation of Activities | Communication | CHILD | Emotional Well-Being | Individual and Program Goals

Cognition | Socialization

Activity Planning

Classroom Design and Organization

Classroom Management and Guidance

——————— Programmatic Activities/Interactions

Visible Curriculum

– – – – – Inclusion

Invisible Curriculum

Figure 2-1 Creative-play curriculum model.

program and show the integrative nature of all aspects of the curriculum.

The remaining chapters describe the interrelated components of the creative-play curriculum model and the role they have in guiding children's development. Learning and growing through creative play is an integrated process supported by teachers and parents whose attitudes and behaviors welcome original thinking, by a classroom environment designed to encourage play and exploration, by activities planned to enhance self-direction and problem solving, and by an assessment process designed to recognize the creative potential inherent in all children. Teachers of young children can facilitate all aspects of the creative-play curriculum:

Creativity is fostered in classrooms where learning is valued over performance, where teachers are trained to observe and understand children's play, where ambiguous situations are tolerated by teachers at least for a period of time, where teachers engage children in playful interchange, and in fact, where teachers value their own creativity (Tegano et al., 1991, p. 109; reprinted by permission of NEA).

The creative-play curriculum supports children as they strive toward a unique personhood, explore connections with others and with the environment, and cultivate a sense of wonder and joy in learning and living. Creative play challenges young children toward growth, change, risk, and the realization of their full potential as caring, creative, and thoughtful individuals.

■　　■　　■　　■　　■　　■　　■　　■　　■

It is critical that Jerome's parents become comfortable with your program philosophy and curriculum before enrolling him in your classroom. Parents often need clear explanations about the importance of play in children's development and assurances that time spent playing is not "wasted time" but really is the manner in which young children learn. Use the following suggestions to make Jerome's parents comfortable with your program:

- Discuss the importance of play in supporting children's development in the domains of personal awareness, emotional well-being, socialization, communication, cognition, and perceptual motor skills. Give specific examples.

- Provide a few brief and clear supporting examples from the early childhood literature that define the

importance of play as a child's way of learning about the world.

- Observe the preschool classroom together and point out how the classroom environment and specific activities enhance the learning of certain concepts and skills.

- Show the parents a sample of your developmental assessment and describe how you use the results of the assessment to set individual goals for each child and to aid in planning classroom activities.

- Discuss the importance of your role as the teacher in planning appropriate learning activities and emphasize the necessity of the family's involvement in the program to support Jerome's growth and development.

■　　■　　■　　■　　■　　■　　■　　■　　■

CHAPTER SUMMARY _____

The creative-play curriculum model described in this chapter is designed to foster optimal development through an integrated, interactive, creative-play approach to early childhood education. Curriculum goals include developing self-worth and self-confidence, the capacity to trust and respect others, effective social skills, communication skills, an understanding of the physical and social environment, problem-solving skills, and curiosity about the world and pleasure in learning. Teachers who are effective in curriculum implementation have training and experience, are

autonomous and resourceful, and strive to provide the highest-quality program possible. The creative-play curriculum promotes the development of the whole child in the domains of personal awareness, emotional well-being, socialization, communication, cognition, and perceptual motor skills. Children's creativity is promoted in all domains, interactions, and activities. The invisible curriculum is the foundation of classroom learning and includes the role of the teacher, classroom management and guidance, partnerships with parents, classroom design and organization, and the outdoor play environment. The visible curriculum includes planning and implementing activities for children and developmental assessment. This cycle of planning, teaching, and assessing is the fundamental task of effective teaching. Inclusion of children with disabilities integrates children into all activities and components of the program and environment, and requires that teachers respond to all children based on their individual needs and developmental level.

DISCUSSION QUESTIONS _____

1. Discuss the vignette at the beginning of the chapter. What other questions or concerns might you have? Discuss the vignette at the end of the chapter. Are there other responses you might have to this situation?

2. What objectives or aims for optimal development are included in the creative-play curriculum? Why are each of these important for young children?

3. Describe the characteristics and behaviors of effective teachers that are related to making decisions about selecting and using early childhood curricula.

4. How does play promote children's creativity?

5. What is the role of creative play related to the six developmental domains?

6. What subdomains of development are included in personal awareness? Emotional well-being? Communication? Socialization? Cognition? Perceptual motor skills? How does creative play support development in each of the six domains?

7. Describe the components of the creative-play curriculum. Which are included in the invisible curriculum? Explain the reason for the term *invisible* to describe this part of the curriculum.

8. What is necessary for implementing an effective program for inclusion of young children with disabilities?

REFERENCES _____

Allen, J. (1988). Promoting preschoolers' moral reasoning. *Early Child Development and Care, 33,* 171–180.

Allen, K. E. (1996). *The exceptional child: Inclusion in early childhood education* (3rd ed.). New York: Delmar.

Anker, D., Foster, J., McLane, J., Sobel, J., & Weissboard, B. (1981). Teaching children as they play. In R. D. Strom (Ed.), *Growing through play* (pp. 106–115). Monterey, CA: Brooks/Cole.

Arnaud, S. (1971). Introduction: Polish for play's tarnished reputation. In National Association for the Education of Young Children (Ed.), *Play: The child strives toward self-realization* (pp. 5–12). Washington, DC: Author.

Athey, I. (1974). Piaget, play and problem solving. In D. Sponseller (Ed.), *Play as a learning medium* (pp. 33–51). Washington, DC: National Association for the Education of Young Children.

Bettelheim, B. (1981). What happens when a child plays? In R. D. Strom (Ed.), *Growing through play* (pp. 102–106). Monterey, CA: Brooks/Cole.

Brown, W. (1997). Inclusion: A time to include and support young children. *Dimensions, 25*(3), 3–5.

Caplan, F., & Caplan, T. (1974). *The power of play.* Garden City, NY: Anchor Press/Doubleday.

Carlsson-Paige, N., & Levin, D. (1985). *Helping young children understand peace, war, and the nuclear threat.* Washington, DC: National Association for the Education of Young Children.

Cass, J. E. (1973). *Helping children grow through play.* New York: Schocken Books.

Catron, C. E. (1981). *Play as therapy for young children in a day care setting.* Unpublished doctoral dissertation, George Peabody College for Teachers of Vanderbilt University, Nashville, Tennessee.

Child Development Laboratories Policy Committee. (1985). *The University of Tennessee Child Development Laboratories staff handbook.* Knoxville, TN: Author.

Curry, N. E., & Arnaud, S. H. (1984). Play in developmental settings. In T. D. Yawkey & A. D. Pellegrini (Eds.), *Child's play: Developmental and applied* (pp. 273–290). Hillsdale, NJ: Erlbaum.

Evans, M. W. (1974). Play is life itself. *Theory into Practice, 13,* 267–272.

Fein, G. G., & Clarke-Stewart, A. (1973). *Day care in context.* New York: Wiley.

Gowen, J. (1995). The early development of symbolic play. *Young Children, 50*(3), 75–84.

Hendrick, J. (1996). *The whole child: Developmental education for the early years* (6th ed.). Columbus, OH: Merrill/Prentice-Hall.

Hoffman, M. L. (1970). Moral development. In P. H. Mussen (Ed.), *Carmichael's manual of child psychology* (pp. 261–359). New York: Wiley.

Kaiser, C. (1991). Early intervention and family support for children with special developmental challenges. In D. Elkind (Ed.), *Perspectives on early childhood education: Growing with young children toward the 21st century* (pp. 85–97). Washington, DC: National Education Association.

Moran, J. D. III, Sawyers, J. K., Fu, V. R., & Milgram, R. M. (1984). Predicting imaginative play in preschool children. *Gifted Child Quarterly, 28(2),* 92–94.

National Association for the Education of Young Children (NAEYC). (1994). Position on inclusion. *Young Children, 49*(5), 78.

Peachey, J. L. (1981). *How to teach peace to children.* Scottdale, PA: Herald Press.

Pepler, D. (1986). Play and creativity. In G. Fein & M. Rivkin (Eds.), *The young child at play: Reviews of research* (Vol. 4, pp. 143–153). Washington, DC: National Association for the Education of Young Children.

Piaget, J. (1926). *The language and thought of the child.* New York: Harcourt, Brace, & World.

Piaget, J. (1932). *The moral judgment of the child.* London: Routledge & Kegan Paul.

Rogers, C. S., & Sawyers, J. K. (1988). *Play in the lives of children.* Washington, DC: National Association for the Education of Young Children.

Rogers, V. R. (1973). Helping children with conflict resolution. *Childhood Education, 49*(5), 226–229.

Sawyers, J. K., Moran, J. D., III, & Tegano, D. W. (1986). Model of original thinking. In M. J. Sporakowski & R. P. Densmore (Eds.), *College of Human Resources research conference proceedings, Information Series 87-1* (pp. 59–70). Blacksburg, VA: Virginia Polytechnic Institute and State University.

Seeman, J. (1963). Personality integration as a criterion of therapy outcome. *Psychotherapy: Theory, Research, and Practice, 1,* 14–16.

Starkweather, E. K. (1971). Creativity research instrument designed for use with preschool children. *Journal of Creative Behavior, 5,* 245–255.

Tegano, D. W., Moran, J. D., III, & Sawyers, J. K. (1991). *Creativity in early childhood classrooms.* Washington, DC: National Education Association.

Vandenberg, B. (1980). Play, problem-solving, and creativity. In K. Rubin (Ed.), *New directions for child development: Children's play* (pp. 49–68). San Francisco: Jossey-Bass.

ADDITIONAL RESOURCES _____

Barron, F., & Harrington, D. M. (1981). Creativity, intelligence and personality. *Annual Review of Psychology, 32,* 439–476.

Bomba, A., & Moran, J. D., III. (1989). The relationship of selected temperament characteristics to creative potential in preschool children. *Early Child Development and Care, 41,* 225–230.

Bricker, D. D. (1986). *Early intervention of at-risk and handicapped infants, toddlers, and preschool children.* Glenview, IL: Scott, Foresman.

Bullock, J. (1990). Child-initiated activity: Its importance in early childhood education. *Day Care and Early Education, 18*(2), 14–16.

Christie, J., & Wardle, F. (1992). How much time is needed for play? *Young Children, 47*(3), 28–32.

DeHass-Warner, S. (1994). The role of child care professionals in placement and programming decisions for preschoolers with special needs in community-based settings. *Young Children, 49*(5), 76–78.

Dunlap, L. (1997). *An introduction to early childhood special education.* Boston: Allyn & Bacon.

Frost, J., & Jacobs, P. (1995). Play deprivation: A factor in juvenile violence. *Dimensions, 23*(3), 14–20, 39–40.

Hendrick, J. (1998). *Total learning: Developmental curriculum for the young child* (5th ed.). Columbus, OH: Merrill/Prentice-Hall.

Isenberg, J., & Jalongo, M. (1997). *Creative expression and play in early childhood* (2nd ed.). Upper Saddle River, NJ: Prentice-Hall.

Kugelmass, J. W. (1989). The "shared classroom": A case study of interactions between early childhood and special education staff and children. *Journal of Early Intervention, 13*(1), 36–44.

Millar, S. (1968). *The psychology of play.* Baltimore: Penguin Books.

Monighan-Nourot, P., Scales, B., & Van Hoorn, J. (with Almy, M.). (1987). *Looking at children's play: A bridge between theory and practice.* New York: Teachers College Press.

Moran, J. D. III, Milgram, R., Sawyers, J. K., & Fu, V. R. (1983). Original thinking in preschool children. *Child Development, 54*(4), 921–926.

National Association for the Education of Young Children (NAEYC). (1971). *Play: The child strives toward self-realization.* Washington, DC: Author.

Nourot, P., & Van Hoorn, J. (1991). Symbolic play in preschool and primary settings. *Young Children, 46*(6), 40–50.

Odom, S., Peck, C., Hanson, M., Beckman, P., Kaiser, A., Lieber, J., Brown, W., Horn, E., & Schwartz, I. (1996). Inclusion of young children with disabilities: An ecological analysis. *Social Policy Report of the Society for Research in Child Development, 10,* 18–30.

Odom, S. L., & McEvoy, M. A. (1988). Integration of young children with handicaps and normally developing children. In S. L. Odom & M. B. Karnes (Eds.), *Early intervention for infants and children with handicaps* (pp. 241–267). Baltimore: Brookes.

Paley, V. (1988). *Bad guys don't have birthdays: Fantasy play at four.* Chicago: University of Chicago Press.

Pellegrini, A., & Boyd, B. (1993). The role of play in early childhood development and education: Issues in definition and function. In B. Spodek (Ed.), *Handbook of research on the education of young children* (pp. 105–121). New York: Macmillan.

Piaget, J. (1962). *Play, dreams, and imitation in childhood.* New York: Norton.

Riley, S. S. (1984). *How to generate values in young children.* Washington, DC: National Association for the Education of Young Children.

Sponseller, D. (1974). *Play as a learning medium.* Washington, DC: National Association for the Education of Young Children.

Strom, R. D. (1981). *Growing through play.* Monterey, CA: Brooks/Cole.

Sutton-Smith, B. (1986). The spirit of play. In G. Fein & M. Rivkin (Eds.), *Reviews of research* (Vol. 4, pp. 3–15). Washington, DC: National Association for the Education of Young Children.

Templeman, T. P., Fredericks, H. D., & Udell, T. (1989). Integration of children with moderate and severe handicaps into a day care center. *Journal of Early Education, 13*(4), 315–328.

Torrance, E. P. (1977). *Creativity in the classroom.* Washington, DC: National Education Association.

Torrance, P. (1983). Preschool creativity. In J. Paget & B. Bracken (Eds.), *The psychoeducational assessment of preschool children* (pp. 509–519). New York: Harcourt Brace Jovanovich.

Trawick-Smith, J. (1994). *Interactions in the classroom: Facilitating play in the early years.* New York: Merrill/Macmillan.

Van Hoorn, J., Nourot, P., Scales, B., & Alward, K. (1993). *Play at the center of the curriculum.* New York: Merrill/Macmillan.

Ward, C. (1996). Adult intervention: Appropriate strategies for enriching the quality of children's play. *Young Children, 51*(3), 20–25.

Williams, K. (1997). "What do you wonder?" Involving children in curriculum planning. *Young Children, 52*(6), 78–81.

Wolery, M., & Wilbers, J. (1994). *Including children with special needs in early childhood programs.* Washington, DC: National Association for the Education of Young Children.

CHAPTER

3.

Children in Contemporary Society

As a preschool teacher, you are stunned when a violent crime occurs on the street corner across from your center's playground. An elderly man is shot and robbed while your preschoolers are playing outdoors. Although the emergency medical and police personnel arrive quickly and care for the victim, the children are, of course, extremely upset at witnessing this violent event. Following this terribly stressful event, you notice that many children in the classroom are coping by acting out the scenario in the dramatic-play center by taking on various roles, such as victim, perpetrator, ambulance driver, emergency technician, and police officer, by drawing or painting individual versions of the event, and by talking to teachers and asking questions and eliciting reassurance.

However, one child in the classroom, William, has reacted by becoming more withdrawn and fearful. William is staying close to the teachers and does not want to play outside. He is painting the same picture, one that portrays the victim on the ground after being shot, over and over again. You are very concerned that William's confusion and fears are interfering with his social and cognitive interactions in the classroom and may be threatening his emotional well-being.

- What is the most appropriate way to talk with William about his fears?
- Are there appropriate children's books you can use to facilitate discussion about the event in an open, secure, and nonthreatening manner?
- What type of support can you provide for William to help him cope with his fears?
- What activities or materials can you encourage William to use in his play that will help him "play through" his anxiety and fears?
- How can you provide the reassurance necessary to help William begin to feel safe in the center again, especially in the outdoor play environment?

Suggestions for responding to this classroom vignette will be shared at the end of the chapter.

When reading this chapter, focus on the important role of teacher–child communication and sharing of factual information about stressful life events. Also, become aware of developmentally appropriate strategies, such as facilitating children's play, encouraging expression of ideas and feelings with art experiences, and using children's books about stressors, to help children communicate about, understand, and respond to stressful life events.

Children in contemporary society are confronting stressful life events that threaten their development, their physical and emotional health, and even their survival. Societal, community, and family violence; divorce; illness and hospitalization; death; poverty; homelessness; and many other issues challenge many children every day. Almost all young children have questions about these stressful life events. Garbarino (1995) has described our contemporary society as "socially toxic" for young children: "Violence, drugs, uncaring communities, poverty, abusive families, and custody battles are poisoning their lives. Children's psychological health and overall well-being are endangered as well" (p. 6).

Teachers and parents cannot completely shield children from this reality. We should, however, never try to train or teach children to be responsible for their own safety and protection. We ignore important developmental needs of young children—for trust, safety, security—when we use developmentally, and ethically, inappropriate ways to try to teach children skills for self-protection and survival. It is absolutely the role of teachers to be *with children* to ensure their physical and emotional well-being in a socially toxic world, as well as to work *for children* to decrease the damaging social and physical assaults on their healthy development and ability to thrive.

Research since the 1940s and World War II has helped teachers to identify factors that serve to protect or buffer children from the extreme psychological and developmental harm that can result from significant stress in young children's lives. An early term in the resiliency literature, *invulnerability,* has been rejected because it suggests a fixed or innate characteristic (Rutter, 1987). Instead, the ability to be resilient in the face of risk and challenge is "a capacity that develops over time in the context of person-environment interactions (Egeland, Carlson, & Sroufe, 1993, p. 517). Children are protected from the most damaging effects of stressors when they can develop at least one stable, positive relationship with a parent or other significant adult; have a supportive educational environment; and have social support from others outside their family. Teachers who serve as a social support for children by helping them to develop positive self-esteem, a sense of connection and community, and social skills promote children's resilience and ability to cope with developmental threat from stressors:

> When tragedy strikes, the most valuable contribution teachers can make is to continue to be caring, attentive adults in the lives of children. The very acts of nurturing contradict the fear, anxiety, and chaos that travel with tragedy. It is in our power as educators . . . to stand with children through the hardest times. (Greenberg, 1996, p. 77)

CHILDREN'S UNDERSTANDING OF STRESSFUL LIFE EVENTS

Children's ability to understand, respond and cope with stressful life events varies according to their cognitive development level:

- Three-year-old Molly says to her teacher, "You're dead, you're dead, you're dead today." Her teacher responds, "What does that mean?" Molly replies, "It means that you close your eyes, and when I touch you, you jump up and chase me."

- Four-year-old Taja has awaited the return of the neighbor's cat for several days. The neighbor explains that the cat was very old and left to go find a place to die. Several months later, Taja's parents explain to her that they are divorcing and that her father will be leaving the house to find another place to live. Taja begins to sob and pleads, "I don't want you to leave and die."

- Five-year-old Thad explains to the other children in his class that he will be going to the hospital to have his tonsils taken out. "I have two tonsils, so I have to have two operations."

- Six-year-old Kevin is told by his parents that his cat Scooter is so old that he will have to be put to sleep. Several months later, when Kevin is in the hospital for surgery, his doctor explains that he "will be put to sleep before the operation." Kevin begins to protest loudly: "When you put Scooter to sleep, he never came back."

Children's reactions to stressful life events are determined to a large degree by their level of cognitive development. Knowing children's cognitive abilities and limitations helps teachers to understand children's perceptions and misperceptions of stressors, anticipate children's emotional responses to stressful life events, and adapt explanations of such events to children's ability to understand. Children's responses also vary based on temperament or personality factors (Chess & Hassibi, 1978), the reactions of significant others in the child's life (Slager-Jorne, 1978), and children's previous experience with stressors and resulting coping strategies (Allen & Figley, 1982).

Piaget's cognitive development theory of children's cognition provides a meaningful framework for understanding children's perceptions and responses. Children in the sensorimotor stage respond to changes in their environment involving caregivers and significant adults in the latter half of the first year. Around 8 months of age, infants may exhibit distress in anticipation of repetition of painful experiences. For example, infants older than 7 months will cry when faced with a second injection, particularly if the interval between injections is brief.

In the preoperational period, although children are very verbal and mobile, their thinking is still somewhat limited. Children's egocentrism hinders their understanding and often results in children's misinterpretations of others' actions. Children may consider separation as rejection. Parental divorce may be viewed as a sign of anger toward the child; parental death may be perceived by the child as intentional abandonment. Preoperational children's thinking and belief in immanent justice may lead children to think that they are the cause of changes or stressful life events and believe they are being punished for wrongdoing. For example, if Masako's parents separate or are injured or if she becomes ill, she may assume it's because she isn't "good enough" and this loss or pain is her punishment. Children's authoritarian and magical view of the world may cause them to blame parents, rather than the circumstances, for illness or death. Children may think, "If Daddy really wanted to, he could keep me from having to go to the hospital." Preoperational children also confuse fantasy and reality. Children assume that wishes are powerful and may believe that a sibling's injury was caused by the wish that he or she weren't present anymore. Media, particularly television and movies, can be a source of stress for young children. Children's preoperational thinking, including their inability to distinguish fantasy from reality, often results in fears and confusion about what they see on television. The symbolic representation used in television, for example, may be misinterpreted by children who do not fully understand time, space, distance, sequence, and inference, and who cannot consider multiple pieces of information simultaneously.

Relational and time concepts are difficult for preoperational children to grasp. Statements such as "Mommy will be gone longer this time," or "I'll be back soon," may be more confusing than reassuring to the child. It is better to explain time using a frame of reference with which the child has had experience. Phrases such as "You'll be at the hospital for the same length of time you are at day care each day," or "for about as long as you stayed at Grandma's this summer," may help children understand. It is not as important that children grasp accurate time length as it is that they understand that the experience or separation will end.

This understanding of children's cognitive abilities and limitations can help teachers to anticipate children's questions and fears and to offer developmentally appropriate information as well as reassurance to young children.

Children and Death

Most children ask their first questions about death as preschoolers. "What happened to Grandpa? When is he coming back?" "Why isn't the gerbil moving anymore?" "Mommy, will you die?" "Will I die?" Children's thinking in the preoperational or preschool stage makes understanding the finality, the irreversibility, and the universality of death difficult (Speece & Brent, 1992). Young children do not view death as final. They believe that the dead continue to live, but in another location such as in heaven or under the ground. They may think that adults are being cruel when someone dies and is buried. "He will be cold and lonely; he doesn't have anything to eat down there." Children may think that death is like

going to sleep and then wonder when the person will wake up and come back.

Young children do not understand that death is irreversible; they believe that those who die will come back. They repeatedly ask when they will see their grandma again and may think that her absence is intentional abandonment. The last component of an accurate understanding of the death concept is universality—that everyone will die. Young children believe that some groups are protected from death; Koocher (1973) found that children report that parents, teachers, and children themselves can avoid death. They even knew supposedly successful strategies for preventing illness and death: "Don't eat bugs, don't eat Styrofoam cups, and don't kiss old ladies" (p. 371). Preoperational children's thinking is often egocentric; they may blame themselves when someone is sick, gets hurt, or dies. Children think that wishes are powerful. They believe in magic. They confuse fantasy and reality. So their thinking about death, its causes, and the resulting consequences reflects a less-mature and inaccurate concept of death.

When talking to children about death, avoid confusing and even untruthful explanations. Do not describe death as sleep or a journey. Children may be fearful of going to bed or when a parent leaves on a trip. Do not say, "God loved your daddy so much (or your daddy was so good, or God needed an accountant in heaven) that he took your daddy to live with him." Children then wonder if they perhaps shouldn't be "so good" or decide they don't want God to love them for fear that they too will be taken away. Use simple, concrete explanations of death: "When someone dies, the heart stops beating, and they stop breathing and eating and feeling any hurt. Most people die when they are very, very old. Some people get very, very sick. The doctors and nurses work very hard to take care of people when they are sick. But sometimes there is no medicine that will make them well and they die." It is important to also provide comfort and reassurance to young children when talking about death: "There are many people who love you and take care of you. When you're sick, remember how you take medicine or get a shot to make you better?" For children whose parent or teacher or friend dies, there may be questions about the health and well-being of the surviving parent or friends. Explain to these children: "I try to stay very healthy. I eat food that is good for me, I exercise, and remember how I always wear my seat belt in the car? I do lots of things to take care of myself and be healthy. I plan to live for a very, very long, long time!"

Children and Divorce

Each year, parents of over 1 million children divorce. One-third of all children will experience their parents' divorce by age 18. The process of separation and divorce has powerful and lasting effects on children. Feelings of abandonment, anxiety, confusion, anger, loneliness, sadness, and even self-blame are common among children experiencing parental divorce. Young children experience a pervasive sadness and feelings of loss and abandonment. "Will Daddy leave me, too?" "Who will take care of me?" "Does my mommy still love me?" These questions reflect children's concerns about what will happen to them. Older children may express anger at their parents or fears based on a more realistic understanding of the meaning of divorce: "Will we have to move and leave my school and friends?" Will we have enough money?" Some children may exhibit regressive behaviors; others become disruptive; still others withdraw from their family and friends.

Explain divorce to children by emphasizing that it is their parents' decision; they are not to blame. Reassure children that there will be many people who love them throughout their life. Help children to identify and adjust to the changes that will occur: new home, new neighborhood, new day care and teachers, and changes in routines and schedule. Children who know about these changes and who can identify the skills and strengths that will help them adjust will cope better with their parents' divorce. Children whose parents engage in postdivorce conflict on issues that focus on the children, such as child visitation, child custody, and child support, cope less well with their parents' divorce (Wallerstein & Kelley, 1980).

Children and Violence

Many children in the United States live in virtual war zones. Every three hours an American child dies of gun-related violence. Children growing up in Chicago are fifteen times more likely to be killed than children in Northern Ireland (Garbarino, 1992). In Washington, D.C., 61 percent of children have witnessed violence such as stabbings, muggings, and threats of physical harm (Richters & Martinez, 1993). In New Orleans, 51 percent of young children surveyed had been victims of violence; 90 percent of the children had witnessed moderate to severe violence. Over one-fourth of the children had seen a shooting; almost 40 percent had seen a dead body and almost 50 percent had seen someone wounded by violence (Osoksky, Wewers, Hann, & Fick, 1993). A study of preschoolers in Los Angeles one week after the 1992 riots found that children who had had direct exposure to the violence in the city told stories that reflected aggression and violent characters (Farver & Frosch, 1996).

Almost all children live with another kind of violence—that shown on television. Most children watch three to four hours of television each day, where they may see news coverage and fictionalized depictions of assault, rape, and murder—26,000 killings by the age of 18, by one estimate (Tuchscherer, 1988). "Kidvid," programming designed for children, features 32 acts of violence per hour. Teachers report that they believe the increase in violence among children in their classrooms is a result of television programming and marketing of violence-related toys, videos, and other products (Carlsson-Paige & Levin, 1991).

For many children, the violence is closer to home; in fact, it's in their own home. Between 1985 and 1995, there was a 61 percent increase (to 3.1 million) in the number of children reported abused or neglected. Almost 1 million children each year are victims in confirmed cases of abuse and neglect. Since 1990, the number of children abused and seriously injured has quadrupled. Each day in the United States, three victims of child abuse die (Children's Defense Fund, 1997).

What developmental toll does living with violence and the threat of violence have on young children? Researchers studying children living in violent homes and communities liken the psychological impact that violence has on children to the posttraumatic stress disorders experienced by Vietnam War veterans and children living in war-torn countries such as Iraq, Kuwait, Cambodia, and the Gaza Strip. Children experience sleeping and eating problems, flashbacks, inability to concentrate, and nightmares (Garbarino, Dubrow, Kostelny, & Pardo, 1992). They may identify with the aggressor and imitate models of violence, suffer grief and loss reactions, experience lower levels of moral reasoning and development, feel helpless and hopeless, and believe they will have a much shortened life span (Martinez & Richters, 1993; Osofsky, 1996).

Developmentally, children who live with violence are not able to achieve the important developmental milestones so critical to healthy functioning. Supportive adults and a safe environment that help children to develop trust and autonomy; opportunities to play outdoors and experience social interaction with others; and a chance to see models of, and to develop, conflict resolution skills are not present for most children who live in violent homes and neighborhoods.

In a description of the almost constant violence, fear, and mistrust experienced by young children in inner-city neighborhoods, Kotlowitz (1991) writes of the mother who says, "But you know, there are no children here. They've seen too much to be children" (p. x). And he writes of the children, one of whom reported in response to a question about career aspirations, "If I grow up, I'd like to be a bus driver" (p.8). The children, unsure of even surviving childhood, are just as likely to plan their funerals as to plan their future. Perhaps that is the greatest developmental harm that comes from living with violence—the loss of the experiences of childhood and the time to explore, discover, and construct knowledge of the physical world and of social relationships free from mistrust, harm, and even death.

Wallach (1993) has offered suggestions for teachers who "cannot cure all the hurts experienced by children today, [but who] can make a difference" (p. 7):

■ Our classrooms should provide opportunities for children to develop meaningful relationships with caring and knowledgeable adults. These relationships make "demands on [teachers'] emotions, their energies, and their time. Relationships with children who have inordinate needs and who do not have past experiences in give-and-take partnerships are not 50–50 propositions; adults must meet these children more than halfway" (p. 8).

■ Teachers must organize their time and schedule with children to provide as much consistency as possible. Children need a strong attachment, a consistent relationship, and meaningful interaction with a caregiver. "The best thing to offer children at risk is caring people, people who are available both physically and emotionally—a relationship that touches one's deepest core" (p. 11).

■ Teachers should provide structure and very clear expectations and limits. Children need clear boundaries to help them experience, and then develop, control in their lives.

■ Teachers must help children find appropriate ways to express themselves. Children need to talk about their emotions and to have opportunities to use play, expressive art, and storytelling to gain control over trauma.

Children and Sexual Abuse

Each year, over 150,000 cases of child sexual abuse are reported to authorities. Retrospective studies of adults who are asked to recall childhood experiences

of sexual abuse suggest that at least 20 percent of females and up to 10 percent of males are child sexual abuse victims. Abuse in the preschool population is most likely to go undetected because young children often don't disclose it. Sexual abuse is more likely to occur in environments characterized by parental inadequacy or unavailability. Children whose parents abuse alcohol and drugs, are emotionally unstable, and are punitive or distant are more likely to be abuse victims. Children who have been "emotionally deprived" of a close, warm, responsive relationship with a parent or other adult are more likely to be victimized by an abuser who offers affection, attention, and friendship (Finkelhor, 1994).

Children who are sexually abused exhibit increased levels of fear, anxiety, and problems in concentrating. Child victims suffer from decreased self-esteem, self-efficacy, and sense of trust. Children feel helpless and may blame themselves for the abuse. When violence or threats of harm occur with the sexual abuse, children also may experience heightened fear and emotional distress. Children's distress is diminished when the disclosure of the abuse is believed by significant adults and children are supported, and not punished or blamed for the abuse (Briere & Elliott, 1994).

Children who are sexually abused also have a higher risk of exposure to HIV/AIDS. Special consideration must be given to the physical and emotional needs of children with HIV/AIDS (see, for example, Coleman, 1991; Savage, Mayfield, & Cook, 1993; Wadsworth & Knight, 1996). By far, the most challenging aspect for teachers is working with children whose care, treatment, and shortened life span challenge, overwhelm, and frighten us. It is estimated that over 3,500 preschoolers in the United States have been diagnosed with AIDS (CDC, 1993).

Teachers also need to be aware of children's understanding and misunderstanding of HIV/AIDS. Lindaver, Schvaneveldt, and Young (1989) conducted one of the first studies of young children's thinking about HIV/AIDS. They asked eleven preschoolers, ten first-graders, ten third-graders, and eleven fifth-graders the following questions: "Have you heard the word AIDS?" "What does AIDS mean?" "What causes AIDS?" "What happens to people who get AIDS?" "How can people prevent AIDS?" "How can we help people who have AIDS?" Only 18 percent of the preschoolers had heard of AIDS, compared to 60 percent of the first-graders, and 100 percent of the older children. Older children, but not preschoolers, reported fears that they or their family members would get AIDS and erroneously believed that AIDS was caused by mosquito bites, toilet seats, clothing, and cigarettes. Kistner et al. (1996) asked 608 elementary-school children these questions:

"Have you ever heard of AIDS?" "How do people get AIDS?" "What happens to a person's body when they get AIDS?" "How can people keep from getting AIDS?" Over 80 percent of the children had heard of AIDS. With increasing age, children did not develop more accurate concepts about AIDS, as might be expected, particularly about transmission methods that they generalized from other illnesses or about unhealthy behavior such as smoking cigarettes or drinking alcohol.

Skeen and Hodson (1987) have suggested that teachers avoid giving "scary" information to children about AIDS. Instead, give them "a little information and a lot of reassurance" (p. 69). Tell children who ask about it that AIDS is a serious but rare disease and that a child's chances of getting AIDS are very, very small. If a child asks how a person gets AIDS, say, "It's caused by a virus, a tiny germ" (p. 70). Skeen and Hodson also advise teachers to be prepared to discuss concepts of death and grief when children ask about AIDS.

Children and Developmentally Inappropriate Classrooms

Early childhood education and care programs that do not provide appropriate experiences for children are very stressful for young children. These developmentally inappropriate classrooms include an absence of play opportunities, many large-group activities, and workbooks and worksheets. Children exhibit much higher levels of stress in these classrooms (Burts, Hart, Charlesworth, & Kirk, 1990). Children in preschool programs with an emphasis on teaching academic skills, rather than programs that are more developmentally- and play-focused are no more academically skilled or knowledgeable in kindergarten, but do exhibit more anxiety about school, less creativity, and less-positive attitudes about school (Hirsh-Pasek, Hyson, & Rescorla, 1990). When "academic" activities in preschool are defined narrowly and equated with "technical subskills (e.g., reciting the ABCs or writing out numerical equations) or with rote instruction (e.g., emphasis on worksheets and drill)," then "academics" have no place in early childhood programs (Kostelnik, 1992, p. 21). Children are interested in words and numbers. They enjoy and learn from many activities and experiences that form the foundation for reading and mathematical thinking: looking at books; listening to books being read; repeating words, phrases, and sentences from stories; and counting objects, measuring sizes, and analyzing space problems. Children experience and learn about "academic" concepts daily. The methods for learning and teaching, however, differ in developmentally appropriate and developmentally inappropriate programs. "Programs that focus on isolated skill development and that rely on long periods of whole group instruction or abstract paper-and-pencil activities do not meet the needs of young children. Those that utilize small group instruction, that emphasize concepts and processes, active manipulation of relevant, concrete materials, and interactive learning provide a solid foundation for academics within a context of meaningful activity" (Kostelnik, p. 22). Teachers should use broader literacy and mathematical experiences, recognize the different ways and styles through which children learn and express interest, and let children observe, compare, question, experiment, predict, and derive meaning from their experiences (Kostelnik, 1992). Teachers can plan developmentally appropriate experiences for children that help to prevent and reduce pressure and stress on young children and that increase their enjoyment and learning.

TALKING WITH CHILDREN ABOUT STRESSFUL EXPERIENCES _____

Communication with children about stressful events provides both information and comfort. In fact, providing information that is appropriate to children's age, needs, and cognitive level is the key to helping children understand and cope with stress. Most children want information about the transitions, loss, and separation they experience. They want to talk and will do so if previous attempts to talk to teachers about sensitive subjects have been responded to with reassurance, honesty, and developmentally appropriate information. Use all opportunities to talk with children to convey respect, interest, and a valuing of their ideas and feelings. Figure 3-1 (pp. 42–43) lists guidelines for communicating with young children about stressful events.

Understand that children may be silent or reluctant to share information. Silence may not reflect fear, lack of manners, or low intelligence. Some children may not have established trust in adults yet, or may believe that the teacher's questions are prying or even threatening, or may have been told by others that it is not appropriate to talk about death, divorce, or sexuality. Cultural and family influences may affect children's willingness to talk about stressful

1. For young children, process is as important as the content of your communication. What you do and how you talk to children are as important as what you say.

   "Let's take some time to sit together in the rocking chair and talk about what happened and how you're feeling."

2. Keep in mind children's age and level of understanding. Use language that is developmentally appropriate.

   "The doctor will listen to your heart with a stethoscope. It helps him to hear inside your body better. Here's picture of a stethoscope. How do you think he uses it?"

3. Listen to children's questions and carefully determine what they are really asking. Children can't or don't always ask what they are really thinking about and want to know. Try to discern whether children are asking questions that require factual answers or reassurance (or both).

   "When you ask if you can stay here with me, do you want to know that I will be here with you until your mommy comes to get you? We can play together until then."

4. Begin by finding out what children already know; then you can clarify, correct, and/or extend their knowledge and understanding.

   "What do you think the children in our class know about going to the hospital?"

   "Do you have any ideas about what the word dead means?"

5. Be truthful in answering children's questions and giving explanations. Give honest information about the changes that children will face.

   "Yes, what your daddy told you is right. Peyton is leaving our preschool to move to New Orleans. I think he will miss you, too. We can write letters to him if you what to."

6. Give children information upon which subsequent, more cognitively sophisticated explanations can be based. Do not give information that must be "taken back" or corrected as children mature and require more detailed or cognitively advanced answers.

   "When the dog died, he couldn't eat or bark or move anymore. His heart stopped beating and he died."

7. Use concrete experiences to help children understand information. The best explanations are simple and use children's own experiences and existing information as much as possible.

   "When we go to the doctor today, we'll be there about as long as it took us to walk through the zoo last week. Then we'll be back home in time to watch Mr. Rogers' Neighborhood."

8. Explanations and answers to children's questions shouldn't be lengthy or include everything about the topic. Offer enough information to answer children's questions. Then add more information as children continue to discuss and ask questions.

   "At the doctor's office, the doctor will look in your ears with a flashlight and ask you to open your mouth really big so she can see your throat. What else do you think she will need to do?"

Figure 3–1 Guidelines for talking to children about stress.

9. Avoid explanations that produce fear.

   "No, the doctor doesn't give shots because you are bad; she gives shots to help you stay healthy."

10. Don't avoid children's questions. You can admit that some uncertainty or unknowns exist and that adults don't have all the answers.

    "That's a really good question. I think lots of children who are four years old wonder about that. I don't think all grown-ups really know what heaven looks like. We're not sure either."

11. Emphasize to children that they are not to blame for the stressful event.

    "It's not your fault. No, it wasn't anything you did. Your grandpa didn't want to leave you. When people get that sick, they often die."

12. Try to determine whether children have understood your explanations.

    "Tell the puppet the story I just told you."

    "Will you explain to me what we just talked about what the doctor will do when she uses her stethoscope?"

13. Don't deny children's reactions, feelings, or perceptions. Help children express their feelings without judgment or criticism.

    "I heard you say that you hated that nurse. The shot he gave you must have really hurt."

14. Encourage children to talk about their feelings. It may help children for you to talk about your own feelings and reactions to similar stressors.

    "If you feel sad, you can talk to me about it."

    "I feel bad, too, when that happens to me."

15. Let children know that they can talk to you about anything, and that if you don't have the answer, you'll try to find out.

    "I'm not sure I really know the answer to that question. Let's try to look it up in a book."

16. Don't wait until you feel completely comfortable or totally knowledgeable about a subject before you answer children's questions or offer information.

    "That's hard for me to think about because it makes me sad. Maybe we can ask Miss Diane to help us find a book to read about moving."

17. Assist children in identifying goals and strengths that will help them adjust to change and loss.

    "I know you really miss Sophie and it's hard to think about playing with your new dog. Can you think of all the things you did to take care of and play with Sophie? Your new dog would like those things, too. You really do a good job taking care of animals."

Figure 3-1 *(continued)*

changes within the family. In addition, teachers' own biases, values, and personal childhood and family experiences influence their comfort and the content of communication with children about stressors. Nonverbal communication such as eye contact and facial expressions must be thoughtfully considered by teachers trying to understand children's response to questions and sharing of information. Cultural meanings and family taboos as well as styles of communication are dynamic forces that enhance or diminish our conversations with children (Garbarino, Stott, & Faculty of the Erikson Institute, 1990).

Children's Play and Coping with Stress

"The pressure on children to make social accommodations at the expense of personal assimilations" creates stress in young children; play has an important role as a stress reducer and assimilator for "the hurried child" having to observe, experience, adapt to, and cope with stressful experiences (Elkind, 1988, p. 198). Play—fantasy play, sociodramatic play, and role play—helps children to reduce and cope with stressful experiences in several ways. Play is an important outlet for the fear and anxiety children may feel in response to stress. Play gives children the opportunity to feel what it is like to take the role of another person, to enact frightening experiences in safe surroundings, to express emotions within the safety of a character or role, to rehearse solutions to problems, and to make reality less scary (Allen, 1988; Catron, 1981). Play fosters emotional well-being by "offering healing for hurts and sadness" (Cass, 1973 p. 12). For example, children who are afraid of injections can practice giving shots to a doll and overcome some of the fear and emotions surrounding the real experience. Children who are afraid of doctors, monsters, or separation from parents can confront and control these fears and feelings in play and thus "win in fantasy what they cannot win in reality" (Peller, 1952). Experiences that are frightening or confusing for children can be dealt with repeatedly through play until children can assimilate them into their own understanding and thus are better equipped to develop and use effective strategies to help them cope.

Children's play also helps teachers working with children experiencing stress. Observe children's play for signs of stress and for children's perceptions and misperceptions of the stressor. For example, a child pretending to a doctor who gives an injection to a doll saying, "You're getting this shot because you've been bad," can be reassured by her teacher that shots are not given to punish children but instead to help them get well or to stay healthy by preventing illness. Teachers can prompt children's play about stressful experiences by suggesting themes or roles, providing props, and encouraging dialogue that permits expression of strong emotions, fears, and problem-solving and coping strategies. Ensure that children have an accepting, nonthreatening play environment for exploration, imitation, practice, and mastery (Allen, 1988; Smilansky, 1971).

Children's Books and Coping with Stress

Children's books about stressors are a valuable resource in helping children understand and cope with changes, separation, and loss. Books and stories provide factual information and extend knowledge about stressful events, such as death, divorce, illness and hospitalization. Discussions of stories and pictures help children identify and express their fears, feelings, and ideas. Use children's books, such as those listed in Figure 3-2 (pp. 46–47), to:

- Provide accurate and straightforward information to prepare children for potentially stressful experiences and to help children understand current or past experiences.

- Correct or clarify misinformation children have about stressors.

- Give children the opportunity to hear stories about and see pictures or illustrations of others coping with stressful situations.

Children can learn to cope with frightening experiences through pretend play

Using developmentally appropriate books helps children identify and express their fears and feelings

- Help children feel that they are not alone in experiencing family transitions; stressful circumstances and events happen to other children and families, too.

- Allow children to think and talk about the feelings and thoughts of a story character when children don't yet have the vocabulary or when it is too painful to talk about their own experiences or feelings.

- Let children understand the diversity of values, experiences, rituals, religions, and cultures of other children and families.

- Facilitate children's talking about problems and show children that teachers and other adults can give comfort, information, and other help when fears and other responses to stressors occur.

After children listen to a book, teachers can encourage them to discuss the story or to create their own story based upon their experiences and feelings. Prompt children with questions, such as: "How do you think the child in the story felt?" "What things changed for the little boy?" "What do you think children are afraid of when this happens to them?" "Was the little boy afraid of anything?" "What can children think of when this happens to make them feel better?" "What did his teacher do to help him feel better?" "What did his parent (or grandparent, mom, or dad) do to help him?" "What else do you think his parent (or teacher) could do to help him with this?" "What can children do when this happens to them to make things better?"

Carefully read children's books about stressors before selecting and using them. The most important consideration is to determine whether the book is developmentally appropriate. Some books have pictures that are appealing to young children, but the text is too advanced for preschoolers to understand. Other books may have developmentally appropriate language for young children, but the stories are too long and there is too much information and too many different concepts for young children. In the latter case, teachers may want to use only the portion of the book that addresses an immediate concern or answers a specific question. Consider these additional criteria when choosing books about stressful life events for young children:

- Is the book appropriate for groups of children and can it be used during story time, or is it more appropriate to use one-on-one with a child who has a specific question or stressor with which he or she is dealing?

- Does the book show a diversity of families, perspectives, and ideas? For example, although children's books about adoption have been available for decades, not until 1991 was there a book depicting transracial adoption.

- Does the book show children using a variety of coping strategies that young children can emulate and learn?

- What questions are children likely to ask after hearing the book read and viewing the pictures? Be prepared for children's questions, continuing discussions, and children's play of the themes and issues depicted in the book.

- What feelings are children likely to experience after hearing the book read? Some children will be very sensitive to and saddened by stories of about the death of a pet or grandparent. Some

BEGINNING SCHOOL

Cohen, M. (1967). *Will I have a friend?* New York: Knopf.

Hallinan, P. (1987). *My first day of school.* Nashville, TN: Ideal Children's Books.

Langreuter, J., & Sobat, V. (1997). *Little Bear goes to kindergarten.* Brookfield, CT: Millbrook Press.

Penn, A. (1993). *The kissing hand.* Washington, DC: Child Welfare League of America.

BIRTH/ADOPTION

Cole, J. (1993). *How you were born.* New York: Morrow Junior Books. (birth)

Girard, L. (1983). *You were born on your very first birthday.* Morton Grove, IL: Whitman. (birth)

Koehler, P. (1997). *The day we met you.* New York: Aladdin.

Kroll, V. (1994). *Beginnings: How families come to be.* Morton Grove, IL: Whitman. (birth and adoption)

Livingston, C. (1978). *"Why was I adopted?"* Secaucus, NJ: Lyle Stuart. (adoption)

McCutcheon, J. (1996). *Happy adoption day.* Boston: Little, Brown. (adoption)

Patterson, E., & Prey, B. (1987). *Twice upon-a-time.* Brattleboro, VT: EP Press. (birth and adoption)

Pellegrini, N. (1991). *Families are different.* New York: Holiday. (adoption)

Rogers, F. (1994). *Let's talk about it: Adoption.* New York: Putnam. (adoption)

Sheffield, M. (1991). *Where do babies come from?* New York: Knopf. (birth)

Wabbes, M. (1990). *How I was born.* New York: Tambourine Books. (birth)

Wright, S. (1994). *Real sisters.* Charlottetown, Prince Edward Island: Ragweed Press. (adoption)

CONFLICT RESOLUTION

Burningham, J. (1973). *Mr. Grumpy's motor car.* New York: Puffin Books.

DePaola, T. (1980). *The knight and the dragon.* New York: Putnam.

Emberly, B. (1967). *Drummer Hoff.* Englewood Cliffs, NJ: Prentice-Hall.

Gackenbach, D. (1984). *King Wacky.* New York: Crown.

Leaf, M. (1936). *The story of Ferdinand.* New York: Viking Press.

Minarik, E. (1958). *No fighting! No biting!* New York: Harper & Row.

Scholes, K. (1989). *Peace begins with you.* San Francisco: Sierra Club Books.

Vigna, J. (1986). *Nobody wants a nuclear war.* Niles, IL: Whitman.

Zolotow, C. (1963). *The quarreling book.* New York: Harper & Row.

Zolotow, C. (1969). *The hating book.* New York: Harper & Row.

DEATH

Breebaart, J., & Breebaart, P. (1993). *When I die, will I get better?* New York: Bedrick Books.

Brown, L., & Brown, M. (1996). *When dinosaurs die.* Boston: Little, Brown.

Brown, M. (1965). *The dead bird.* New York: Young Scott Books.

Clifton, L. (1983). *Everett Anderson's goodbye.* New York: Holt.

DePaola, T. (1973). *Nana upstairs and Nana downstairs.* New York: Putnam.

Fassler, J. (1971). *My grandpa died today.* New York: Behavioral Publications.

Greenlee, S. (1992). *When someone dies.* Atlanta, GA: Peachtree.

Mellonie, B., & Ingpen, R. (1983). *Lifetimes: The beautiful way to explain death to children.* Toronto, Ontario: Bantam Books.

Rogers, F. (1988). *When a pet dies.* New York: Putnam.

Sanford, D. (1986). *It must hurt a lot.* Portland, OR: Multnomah Press.

Schlitt, R. (1992). *Robert Nathaniel's tree.* Montgomery, AL: Lightbearers.

Simon, N. (1986). *The saddest time.* Morton Grove, IL: Whitman.

Stein, S. (1974). *About dying: An open family book for parents and children together.* New York: Walker.

Vigna, J. (1991). *Saying goodbye to daddy.* Morton Grove, IL: Whitman.

Viorst, J. (1971). *The tenth good thing about Barney.* New York: Atheneum.

Wilheim, H. (1985). *I'll always love you.* New York: Crown.

Zalben, J. (1997). *Pearl's marigolds for grandpa.* New York: Simon & Schuster.

Zolotow, C. (1972). *The old dog.* New York: HarperCollins.

Figure 3–2 Books to help children deal with stressful situations.

DISABILITIES

Cairo, S. (1985). *Our brother has Down's syndrome.* Toronto, Ontario: Annick Press. (Down's syndrome)

Goldfeeder, C., & Goldfeeder, J. (1973). *The girl who wouldn't talk.* Silver Spring, MD: National Association of the Deaf. (hearing impairment)

Hearn, E. (1984). *Goodmorning, Franny, goodnight, Franny.* Toronto, Ontario: Women's Educational Press. (physical impairment)

Peterson, J. (1977). *I have a sister, my sister is deaf.* New York: Harper & Row. (hearing impairment)

DIVORCE

Brown L., & Brown, M. (1986). *Dinosaurs divorce.* Boston: Little,, Brown.

Clifton, L. (1974). *Everett Anderson's year.* New York: Holt, Rinehart, & Winston.

Girard, L. (1987). *At daddy's on Saturdays.* Morton Grove, IL: Whitman.

Mayle, P. (1988). *Why are we getting a divorce?* New York: Harmony.

Stinson, K. (1984). *Mom and dad don't live together anymore.* Toronto, Ontario: Annick Press.

FAMILIES

Drescher, J. (1986). *My mother's getting married.* New York: Dial Books. (remarriage)

Galloway, P. (1985). *Jennifer has two daddies.* Toronto, Ontario: Women's Educational Press. (remarriage)

Lindsay, J. (1991). *Do I have a daddy? A story about a single-parent child.* Buena Park, CA: Morning Glory Press. (single-parent families)

Stenson, J. (1979). *Now I have a stepparent and it's kind of confusing.* New York: Avon. (remarriage)

Willhoite, M. (1990). *Daddy's roommate.* Los Angeles: Alyson. (gay parents)

FEARS

Mayer, M. (1968). *There's a nightmare in my closet.* New York: Dial Press.

Viorst, J. (1973). *My mama says there aren't any zombies, ghosts, vampires, creatures, demons, monsters, fiends, goblins, or things.* New York: Atheneum.

FEELINGS

Anholt, C., & Anholt, L. (1994). *What makes me happy.* Cambridge, MA. Candlewick Press.

Fernandes, E. (1982). *The little boy who cried himself to sea.* Toronto, Ontario: Kids Can Press.

Modesitt, J. (1992). *Sometimes I feel like a mouse.* New York: Scholastic Books.

Sondheimer, I. (1982). *The boy who could make his mother stop yelling.* Fayetteville, NY: Rainbow Press.

HEALTH CARE/ILLNESS

Brandenberg, F. (1976). *I wish I was sick, too!* New York: Mulberry Books.

Rockwell, H. (1973). *My doctor.* New York: Harper & Row.

Rogers, F. (1986). *Going to the doctor.* New York: Putnam.

Rogers, F. (1988). *Going to the hospital.* New York: Putnam.

HIV/AIDS

Fassler, D., & McQueen, K. (1990). *What's a virus anyway?* Burlington, VT: Waterfront Books.

Hausherr, R. (1989). *Children and the AIDS virus.* New York: Clarion Books.

Merrifield, M. (1990). *Come sit by me.* Toronto, Ontario: Women's Press.

HOMELESSNESS

Kroll, V. (1991). *Shelter folks.* Grand Rapids, MI: Eerdmans.

MOVING

Ballard, R. (1994). *Good-bye, house.* New York: Greenwillow Books.

Hazen, B. (1995). *Goodbye, hello.* New York: Atheneum.

Sharmat, M. (1983). *Gila monsters meet you at the airport.* New York: Puffin Books.

NEW BABY

Corey, D. (1992). *Will there be a lap for me?* Morton Grove, IL: Whitman.

Lansky, V. (1994). *A new baby at KoKo Bear's house.* Minnetonka, MN: Book Peddlers.

Powell, T. (1995). *Hi! I'm the new baby.* Norval, Ontario: Moulin.

Rogers, F. (1985). *The new baby.* New York: Putnam.

Rosenberg, M. (1997). *Mommy's in the hospital having a baby.* New York: Clarion Books.

Vulliam, C. (1996). *Ellen and Penguin and the new baby.* Cambridge, MA: Candlewick Press.

Figure 3-2 *(continued)*

children may be fearful after hearing a story about going to the doctor. Be prepared to talk about feelings and things that we can do to feel better. Be prepared to give children reassurance about their own situation and well-being.

Children's Art and Coping with Stress

Young children often cannot verbalize their thoughts and feelings about stressful events. For these children, art and other forms of creative expression provide a valuable alternative to verbal communication. Children can be encouraged to draw, paint, or construct pictures of themselves, family members, friends, and their house, school, and neighborhood. With pencils, crayons, or markers, children are more likely to express their thoughts and ideas. With finger paint, they ex-

press feelings. After drawing or painting, some children then will tell a story based on their art; these stories provide additional information about their thoughts and feelings. (Figures 3-3, 3-4, and 3-5 are examples of preschoolers' drawings that included shared stories with adults after the children completed their artwork.) Teachers can initiate discussions about stressors and coping, expression of which through their art has made the experience less frightening for children. Children's art experiences can:

■ Help children communicate thoughts and feelings when words are not available.

■ Provide insights to teachers about children's fears, ideas, and emotions, because children's art reflects their cognitive understanding and social relationships.

Figure 3-3 "Person at dentist" (3-year-old's drawing).

Figure 3-4 "Baby is inside lying down because she is sick" (3-year-old's drawing).

■ Allow children to remake and construct experiences through their art; frightening things can be made less scary, and children gain power and control.

■ Remain undisturbed by adult analysis, scrutiny, and discussion. Children should "own" their artwork and should be allowed make the choice to talk or not to talk about their pictures. Art is a therapeutic process for children as they express ideas and deal with emotions that adults do not always know about or understand.

Knowledge about the factors in contemporary environments and lifestyles that threaten children's well-being, coupled with sensitivity to children's feelings and reactions to these stressors, are vital ingredients in the teacher–child relationship. Recognition of children's emotional vulnerabilities, cognitive limitations, and need for support and reassurances in frightening or anxiety-producing situations is the first step in helping young children develop effective coping strategies. Teachers who provide playful environments that encourage expression of feelings and discussion of fears are helping children to name and vanquish their fears and are enabling them to receive support and learn resilience when faced with life's most chaotic and challenging moments.

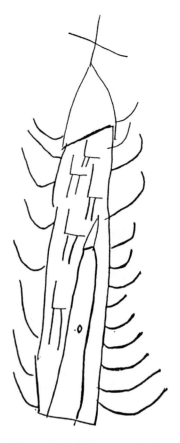

Figure 3-5 "A bug carrying the church away" (4-year-old's drawing).

■   ■   ■   ■   ■   ■   ■   ■   ■

Providing opportunities, activities, and play materials to help children cope with stressors within the safety of the classroom environment is a critical and life-enhancing task for teachers of young children. Helping William find his own way of coping with this violent event involves providing information and resources for play.

• Gently encourage William to express his feelings by asking open-ended questions; listening carefully to his responses and questions; and being honest, simple, and concrete in your explanations.

• Choose developmentally appropriate children's books that deal with the topics of injury, death, and violence to facilitate the discussion and clarify or extend William's understanding of the event.

• Facilitate William's involvement with open-ended play materials that do not force his social involvement with others.

For example, encourage William's use of his painting to help him discover a way to cope with his fear. Acknowledge to William that indeed his picture reflects a scary event. Ask William if he can think of things to put in the picture to make it less scary.

• Talk to William about the people in his classroom, his family, and his community who can help him be safe such as teachers, parents, and police officers.

• Provide a sense of security for William by finding opportunities to let him know that your job is to protect children from harm. Also, provide consistency in the classroom environment, verbal and nonverbal reassurances, and a plentitude of developmentally appropriate play activities. Surround William with your support and strength and enable him to view himself as a competent and resilient person.

■   ■   ■   ■   ■   ■   ■   ■   ■

CHAPTER SUMMARY ——

Children experience many stressful life events that threaten their healthy development, physical safety, and psychological well-being. Violence, homelessness, sexual abuse, death, divorce, and questions about these stressors are common for young children. Knowing about children's cognitive level of understanding of stressors and their emotional responses to them will help teachers use developmentally appropriate communication and activities that can facilitate sharing of information, reduction of emotional distress, and development of effective coping strategies. Children's books, art, and play support children's emotional expression and stress management and reduction. A psychologically safe and physically safe classroom, and teachers who respond with information and reassurance, can help children develop trust and resiliency to enhance their ability to thrive in contemporary society.

DISCUSSION QUESTIONS ——

1. Discuss the vignette at the beginning of the chapter. What other questions or concerns might you have? Discuss the vignette at the end of the chapter. Are there other responses you might have to this situation?

2. What are the major stressful life events for children today? How do young children's cognitive abilities influence the way they understand and misunderstand stressful life events? Give specific examples.

3. What are common emotional responses of young children to stress? How will a teacher use this knowledge to identify children who are unable to cope effectively with stressful life events?

4. List questions that young children are likely to have about death or violence or divorce. Suggest age-appropriate communication for talking to a 3-year-old about these topics.

5. In what ways might you respond to a child who repeatedly draws monsters in his artwork?

6. What are appropriate roles for teachers in facilitating children's play about stressful life events? When is outside and inside intervention appropriate for teachers to use with children experiencing stress?

REFERENCES ——

Allen, J. (1988). Children's cognition of stressful events. *Day Care and Early Education, 16*(2), 21–25.

Allen, J., & Figley, C. (1982, November). *"The sky is falling! The sky is falling!" Helping children and families in stress.* Paper presented at the annual conference of the National Association for the Education of Young Children, Washington, DC.

Bell, C. (1991). Traumatic stress and children in danger. *Journal of Health Care for the Poor and Underserved, 2*(1), 175–188.

Briere, J., & Elliott, D. (1994). Immediate and long-term impacts of child sexual abuse. *The Future of Children, 4*(2), 54–69.

Burts, D., Hart, C., Charlesworth, R., & Kirk, L. (1990). A comparison of frequency of stress behaviors observed in classrooms with developmentally appropriate versus developmentally inappropriate instructional practices. *Early Childhood Research Quarterly, 5*(3), 407–423.

Carlsson-Paige, N., & Levin, D. (1991). The subversion of healthy development and play. *Day Care and Early Education, 19*(2), 14–20.

Cass, J. (1973). *Helping children grow through play.* New York: Schocken Books.

Catron, C. (1981). *Play as therapy for young children in a day care setting.* Unpublished doctoral dissertation, George Peabody College for Teachers of Vanderbilt University, Nashville, Tennessee.

Center for Disease Control (CDC). (1993). *HIV/AIDS surveillance.* Atlanta, GA: Centers for Disease Control.

Chess, S., & Hassibi, M. (1978). *Principles and practice of child psychiatry.* New York: Plenum Press.

Children's Defense Fund. (1997). The state of America's children. Washington, DC: Children's Defense Fund.

Coleman, M. (1991). Caring for preschoolers with the HIV virus. *Dimensions, 20*(1), 14–16, 38.

Egeland B., Carlson, E., & Groufé (1993). Resilience as a process. *Development and Psychopathology, 5*(4), 517–528.

Elkind, D. (1988). *The hurried child: Growing up too fast too soon.* Menlo Park, CA: Addison-Wesley.

Farver, J., & Frosch, D. (1996). L.A. stories: Aggression in preschoolers' spontaneous narratives after the riots of 1992. *Child Development, 67,* 19–32.

Finkelhor, D. (1994). Current information on the scope and nature of child sexual abuse. *The Future of Children: Sexual Abuse of Children, 4*(2), 31–53.

Garbarino, J. (1995). *Raising children in a socially toxic environment.* San Francisco: Jossey-Bass.

Garbarino, J., Dubrow, N., Kostelny, K., & Pardo, C. (1992). *Children in danger: Coping with the consequences of community violence.* San Francisco: Jossey-Bass.

Garbarino, J., Stott, F., & Faculty of the Erikson Institute. (1990). *What children can tell us.* San Francisco: Jossey-Bass.

Greenberg, J. (1996). Seeing children through tragedy: My mother died today—when is she coming back? *Young Children, 51*(6), 76–77.

Hatfield, L., Allen, J., & Bowditch, B. (1981). *Helping young children cope under conditions of stress.* Chicago: Worldbook-Childcraft.

Hirsh-Pasek, K., Hyson, M., & Rescorla, L. (1990). Academic environments in preschool: Do they pressure or challenge young children. *Early Education and Development, 1*(6), 401–423.

Kistner, J., Eberstein, I., Balthazor, M., Castro, R., Foster, K., Osborne, M., Sly, D., & Quadagno, D. (1996). Assessing children's conceptions of AIDS. *Journal of Pediatric Psychology, 21*(2), 269–281.

Koocher, G. (1973). Childhood, death, and cognitive development. *Developmental Psychology, 9,* 369–375.

Kostelnik, M. (1992). Myths associated with developmentally appropriate programs. *Young Children, 47*(4), 17–23.

Kotlowitz, A. (1991). *There are no children here.* New York: Doubleday.

Lindaver, S., Schvaneveldt, J., & Young, M. (April 1989). *Children's understanding of AIDS.* Paper presented at the biennial meeting of the Society for Research in Child Development, Kansas City, MO.

Martinez, P., & Richters, J. (1993). The NIMH Community Violence Project: II. Children's distress symptoms associated with violence exposure. *Psychiatry, 56,* 22–35.

Osofsky, J. (1996). Introduction: Caring for infants and toddlers in violent environments: hurt, healing and hope. *Zero to Six, 3*–6, Vol. 16, No. 6.

Osofsky, J., Wewers, S., Hann, D., & Fick, A. J. (1993). Chronic community violence: What is happening to our children? *Psychiatry, 56,* 36–45.

Peller, L. (1952). Models of children's play. *Mental Hygiene, 36,* 66–83.

Pynoos, R., & Eth, S. (1985). Children traumatized by witnessing personal violence: Homicide, rape, or suicide. In S. Eth & R. Pynoos (Eds.), *Posttraumatic stress disorder in children* (pp. 19–43). Washington, DC: American Psychiatric Press.

Richters, J., & Martinez, P. (1993). The NIMH Community Violence Project: I. Children as victims of and witnesses to violence. *Psychiatry, 56,* 7–21.

Rutter, M. (1987). Psychosocial resilience and protective mechanisms. *American Journal of Orthopsychiatry, 57*(3), 316–331.

Savage, S., Mayfield, P., & Cook, M. (1993). Questions about serving children with HIV/AIDS. *Day Care and Early Education, 22*(1), 10–12.

Skeen, P., & Hodson, D. (1987). AIDS: What adults should know about AIDS (and shouldn't discuss with very young children). *Young Children, 42*(4), 65–71.

Slager-Jorne, P. (1978). Counseling sexually abused children. *Personnel and Guidance Journal, 8*(5), 103–105.

Smilansky, S. (1971). Can adults facilitate play in children? In G. Engstrom (Ed.), *Play: The child strives toward self-realization* (pp. 39–50). Washington, DC: National Association for the Education of Young Children.

Speece, M., & Brent, S. (1992). The acquisition of a mature understanding of three components of the concept of death. *Death Studies, 16,* 211–229.

Tuchschere, P. (1988). *TV interactive toys: The new high tech threat to children.* Bend, OR: Pinnaroo.

Wadsworth, D., & Knight, D. (1996). Meeting the challenge of HIV and AIDS in the classroom. *Early Childhood Education Journal, 23*(3), 143–147.

Wallach, L. (1993). Helping children cope with violence. *Young Children, 48*(4), 4–11.

Wallerstein, J., & Kelley, J. (1980). *Surviving the breakup: how children and parents cope with divorce.* New York: Basic Books.

Zinmeister, K. (1990, June). Growing up scared. *Atlantic Monthly,* 49–66.

ADDITIONAL RESOURCES _____

Amato, P. (1993). Children's adjustment to divorce: Theories, hypotheses, and empirical support. *Journal of Marriage and the Family, 55,* 23–39.

Armstrong, J. (1994). Mad, sad, or glad: Children speak out about child care. *Young Children, 49*(2), 22–23.

Bailey, B. (1992). "Mommy, don't leave me!" Helping toddlers and parents deal with separation. *Dimensions, 20*(3), 25–27, 39.

Berends, M., & Caron, S. (1994). Children's understanding and knowledge of conception and birth: A developmental approach. *Journal of Sex Education and Therapy, 20*(1), 18–29.

Boyatzis, C. (1997). Of Power Rangers and V-chips. *Young Children, 52*(7), 74–79.

Cain, B., & Bohrer, C. (1997). Battling Jurassic Park: From a fascination with violence toward constructive knowledge. *Young Children, 52*(7), 71–73.

Carlsson-Paige, N., & Levin, D. (1985). *Helping young children understand peace, war, and the nuclear threat.* Washington, DC: National Association for the Education of Young Children.

Carlsson-Paige, N., & Levin, D. (1987). *The war play dilemma: Balancing need and values in the early childhood classroom.* New York: Teachers College Press.

Carlsson-Paige, N., & Levin, D. (1992). Making peace in violent times: A constructivist approach to conflict resolution. *Young Children, 48*(1), 4–13.

Chafel, J. (1995). Children's conceptions of poverty. In S. Reifel (Ed.), *Advances in early education and day care* (Vol. 7, pp. 27–57). Greenwich, CT: JAI Press.

Clark, R. (1995). Violence, young children, and the healing power of play. *Dimensions, 23*(3), 28–30, 39.

Craig, S. (1992). The educational needs of children living with violence. *Phi Delta Kappan, 74*(1), 67–71.

Curry, N., & Arnaud, S. (1995). Personality difficulties in preschool children as revealed through play themes and styles. *Young Children, 50*(4), 4–9.

Demaree, M. (1995). Creating safe environments for children with Post-Traumatic Stress Disorder. *Dimensions, 23*(3), 31–33, 40.

Duis, S., Summers, M., & Summers, C. (1997). Parent versus child stress in diverse family types: An ecological approach. *Topics in Early Childhood Special Education, 17*(1), 53–73.

Elkind, D. (1995). The young child in the postmodern world. *Dimensions, 23*(3), 6–9, 39.

Ellerton, M., Caty, S., & Ritchie, J. (1985). Helping young children master intrusive procedures through play. *Children's Health Care, 13*(4), 167–173.

Essa, E., & Murray, C. (1994). Young children's understanding and experience with death. *Young Children, 49*(4), 74–81.

Fortin, A., & Chamberland, C. (1995). Preventing the psychological maltreatment of children. *Journal of Interpersonal Violence, 10*(3), 275–295.

Frieman, B. (1993). Separation and divorce: Children want their teachers to know—meeting the emotional needs of preschool and primary school children. *Young Children, 48*(6), 58–63.

Frieman, B. (1993). What early childhood teachers need to know about troubled children in therapy. *Dimensions, 21*(3), 21–24.

Furman, R. (1995). Helping children cope with stress and deal with feelings. *Young Children, 50*(2), 33–41.

Goldman, L. (1996). We can help children grieve: A child-oriented model for memorializing. *Young Children, 51*(6), 69–73.

Greenberg, P. (1992). Why not academic preschool? Part 2: Autocracy or democracy in the classroom. *Young Children, 47*(3), 54–64.

Groves, B. (1997). Growing up in a violent world: The impact of family and community violence on young children and their families. *Topics in Early Childhood Special Education, 17*(1), 74–102.

Honig, A. (1986). Stress and coping in children (part 1). *Young Children, 41*(4), 50–63.

Honig, A. (1986). Stress and coping in children (part 2). *Young Children, 41*(5), 47–59.

Jackson, B. (1997). Creating a climate for healing in a violent society. *Young Children, 52*(7), 68–70.

Johnson, M. (1996). Television violence and its effect on children. *Journal of Pediatric Nursing, 11*(2), 94–99.

Jordan, N. (1993). Sexual abuse prevention programs in early childhood education: A caveat. *Young Children, 48*(6), 76–79.

Kamii, C., Clark, F., & Dommick, A. (1995). Are violence-prevention curricula the answer? *Dimensions, 23*(3), 10–13.

Kelley, S., Brant, R., & Waterman, J. (1993). Sexual abuse of children in day care centers. *Child Abuse and Neglect, 17,* 71–89.

Knitzer, J., & Aber, L. (1995). Young children in poverty: Facing the facts. *American Journal of Orthopsychiatry, 65*(2), 174–176.

Koplow, L. (1992). *The way home: A child therapist looks at the inner lives of city children.* New York: Mentor.

Kozol, J. (1995). *Amazing grace: The lives of children and the conscience of a nation.* New York: Crown.

Levin, D. (1997). *Remote control childhood: Combatting the hazards of media culture.* Washington, DC: National Association for the Education of Young Children.

Levin, D., & Carlsson-Paige, N. (1994). Developmentally appropriate television: Putting children first. *Young Children, 49*(5), 38–44.

Manning, D., Rubin, S., Perdigao, G., Gonzalez, R., & Schindler, P. (1996). A "worry doctor" for preschool directors and teachers: A collaborative model. *Young Children, 51*(5), 68–73.

Marshall, C. (1995). From Friday to Monday: Preparing inservice teachers to help young children following community violence. *Dimensions, 23*(3), 34–35.

McCormick, L., & Holden, R. (1992). Homeless children: A special challenge. *Young Children, 47*(6), 61–67.

McCracken, J. (Ed.). (1986). *Reducing stress in young children's lives.* Washington, DC: National Association for the Education of Young Children.

McMath, J. (1997). Young children, national tragedy, and picture books. *Young Children, 52*(3), 82–84.

Milling, L., & Martin, B. (1992). Depression and suicidal behavior in preadolescent children. In C. Walker & M. Roberts (Eds.), *Handbook of clinical child psychology* (pp. 319–339). New York: Wiley.

NAEYC position statement on violence in the lives of children. (1993). *Young Children, 48*(6), 80–85.

National Television Violence Study: Key findings and recommendations. (1996). *Young Children, 51*(3), 54–55.

Parry, A. (1993). Children surviving in a violent world—"Choosing non-violence." *Young Children, 48*(6), 13–15.

Peterson, L. (1989). Coping by children undergoing stressful medical procedures: Some conceptual, methodological, and therapeutic issues. *Journal of Consulting and Clinical Psychology, 57*(3), 380–387.

Pynoos, R., & Nader, K. (1988). Psychological first aid and treatment approach to children exposed to community violence: Research implications. *Journal of Traumatic Stress, 1*(4), 445–473.

Rae, W. (1991). Analyzing drawings of children who are physically ill and hospitalized, using the ipsative method. *Children's Health Care, 20*(4), 198–207.

Siegal, M. (1991). *Knowing children: Experiments in conversation and cognition.* Hillsdale, NJ: Erlbaum.

Slaby, R., Roedell, W., Arezzo, D., & Hendrix, K. (1995). *Early violence prevention: Tools for teachers of young children.* Washington, DC: National Association for the Education of Young Children.

Sterling, C., & Friedman, A. (1996). Empathic responding in children with a chronic illness. *Children's Health Care, 25*(1), 53–69.

Stokes, S., Saylor, C., Swenson, C., & Daugherty, T. (1995). A comparison of children's behaviors following three types of stressors. *Child Psychiatry and Human Development, 26*(2), 113–129.

Swenson, C., Saylor, C., Powell, M., Stokes, S., Foster, K., & Belter, R. (1996). Impact of a natural disaster on preschool children: Adjustment 14 months after a hurricane. *American Journal of Orthopsychiatry, 66*(1), 122–130.

Tarnowski, K., & Rohrbeck, C. (1993). Disadvantaged children and families. In T. Ollendick & R. Prinz (Eds.), *Advances in clinical child psychology* (Vol. 15, pp. 41–79). New York: Plenum Press.

Wallinga, C., & Skeen, P. (1996). Siblings of hospitalized and ill children: The teacher's role in helping these forgotten family members. *Young Children, 51*(6), 78–83.

Weinrab, M., (1997). Be a resiliency mentor: You may be a lifesaver for a high-risk child. *Young Children, 52*(2), 14– 20.

Yamamoto, K., Davis, O., Dylak, S., Whittaker, J., Marsh, C., & Westhuizen, P. (1996). Across six nations: Stressful events in the lives of children. *Child Psychiatry and Human Development, 26*(3), 139–151.

INVISIBLE CURRICULUM

4.

Role of the Teacher

■   ■   ■   ■   ■   ■   ■   ■   ■

As you scan your preschool classroom you notice a conflict beginning to escalate in the book corner. When you approach you observe that a small group of children are hovering over Janelle, a 4-year-old who is usually very social and articulate. Janelle is curled up on a beanbag chair, her hands covering her face, whimpering for the other children to go away and leave her alone.

After a little reassurance and gentle prompting from you, Janelle is able to tell you what is wrong. She blurts out, "I don't want children to play with me now. Everybody wants me to do something right now. And it makes me move too fast. In the morning we have to get up and eat breakfast and it's too fast. And the children want me to always play fast. And the teachers say it's time to clean up and go outside fast and then we have to go home and eat dinner and go to bed fast. Everything we do is too fast!"

Janelle has sent you a very clear and strong distress signal.

- How do you feel about Janelle's outburst?
- How do you define the nature and extent of the problem?
- How do you decide what words and behaviors to use in response to Janelle? What will help? What might hurt? Does this situation need both an immediate and a long-term response, or should you assume this is an isolated incident?
- Do you involve the other children who were attempting to play with Janelle? Do you involve the total classroom in resolving this problem?
- Do you involve Janelle's parents in a discussion of this problem? If so, how and when?
- Which of your many skills and roles as a teacher will you need to use to help Janelle cope effectively?

■   ■   ■   ■   ■   ■   ■   ■   ■

Suggestions for responding to this classroom vignette will be shared at the end of the chapter.

When reading this chapter, focus on understanding the important attitudes and skills that caring and competent teachers of young children must possess, and become aware of the variety of roles effective teachers must fulfill. Who you are—your attitudes, feelings, knowledge, and skills—has a tremendous impact on the daily lives of children and constitutes the most important component of the invisible curriculum.

The role of the classroom teacher is perhaps the most important component of the invisible curriculum, as it is critical in determining the effectiveness and quality of care and education for young children. The teacher may be the most important factor in a child's early education and child-care experiences (Feeney & Chun, 1985). Society's expectations of positive outcomes for children in early childhood programs have increased. Teachers are expected to prepare children for academic success in school, socialize them into a culturally diverse society, over-

come environmental disadvantages, and develop children's emotional capacity to cope with the stressors of a rapidly changing world. Early childhood educators must balance these societal and parental expectations with their knowledge of what is most appropriate and growth-promoting for young children. To provide an optimal, creative learning environment for children, teachers must develop and strengthen attitudes, attributes, and abilities that characterize effective teachers and learn to balance the variety of roles they need to assume.

ATTITUDES, ATTRIBUTES, AND ABILITIES OF EFFECTIVE TEACHERS _____

According to Carl Rogers (1983), effective, authentic teachers possess three primary qualities and attitudes. *Realness* or *genuineness* in the teacher facilitates children's development as total human beings.

Prizing the learner, accepting the child's feelings and individuality, and believing that others are fundamentally trustworthy create a supportive climate for learning. Developing *empathic understanding* permits the sensitive teacher to understand children's perceptions of the world.

Other attitude and behavioral traits of authentic teachers include the capacity for risk taking, for establishing loving bridges between people, for modeling joy and spontaneity, for being open to all opportunities to be both a teacher and a learner, and for sharing the magic of their own uniqueness and humanness (Buscaglia, 1984). Authentic teachers have the capacity to enter a child's world, to retain a sense of mystery and awe, and to share in a child's sense of wonder. Children almost always know how to open the doorway to joy if we listen, pay attention, and are open to what young children have to teach us. Indeed, "curriculum making may supply a framework for learning, but it takes adventurous teaching to make any of it come alive" (Frazier, 1980, p. 263).

Good teachers of young children possess many attributes and characteristics. A review of research by Feeney and Chun (1985) found that the best teachers of young children exhibited the following characteristics:

Warmth
Sensitivity
Flexibility
Honesty
Integrity
Naturalness
A sense of humor
Acceptance of individual differences
The ability to support growth without being overprotective
Physical strength
Vitality
Compassion
Self-acceptance
Emotional stability
Self-confidence
The ability to sustain effort
The ability to learn from experience (Hymes, 1968; Read & Patterson, 1980; Yardley, 1971)

In her review of research, Phyfe-Perkins (1981) concluded that effective teachers of young children are positive, encouraging, warm, attentive, child-centered, and involved with children in individual and small-group settings rather than in direct teaching of large groups.

Teachers who effectively encourage the development of creative potential in young children are flex-

ible and open. These teachers were found to have high scores on measures of ambiguity tolerance and playfulness and to have perceiving and intuitive personality traits (Tegano & Catron, 1990). Teachers who facilitate the development of creativity in young children possess the following characteristics:

- They are likely to read between the lines for the possibilities that come to mind.
- They have the capacity to see future possibilities, often creative ones.
- They are open to new evidence and new developments, and are more curious than decisive.
- They show an interest in the new and untried, as well as a preference for learning new materials through an intuitive grasp of meaning and complexities.
- They are more focused on working with theory and imagination than on dealing with tangibles and practical details.
- They adjust easily to the accidental and the unexpected.
- They exhibit flexibility, adaptability, and tolerance (Tegano, Moran, & Sawyers, 1991, p. 102; reprinted by permission of NEA).

Developing the abilities to effectively teach young children requires that early childhood professionals be carefully and thoughtfully trained. They need information about children's development, program planning, and interacting and communicating with children and their parents. They also need supervised experiences that support the development of skills and acquisition of knowledge. Research by Seefeldt (1973) and a review of research by Meissner, Swinton, Shipman, Webb, and Simosko (1973) examined the relationship among teachers' years of formal education, their years of teaching experience, and their effectiveness as teachers. Both reported that children's achievement gains are positively associated with the education and experience of teachers. Snider and Fu (1990) found that the educational level of teachers, the number of courses in child development/early childhood education, and the integration of course work with supervised practical experience were the factors having the most significant effect on teachers' knowledge of and ability to apply developmentally appropriate practice in the classroom environment. Early childhood professionals need training, experience, and opportunities for ongoing professional development to support their commitment to fulfilling diverse roles and responsibilities.

In addition, teachers in integrated classrooms that include children with special needs should have knowledge and skills related to the special population of young children. The teaching competencies necessary for working with all young children are basically the same, but the following are some specific skills needed to work effectively with children with special needs:

1. Knowledge of normal and atypical processes and stages in children's development.
2. Ability to recognize symptoms of specific disabilities.
3. Skill in observing and recording behavior of individual children.
4. Ability to employ informal procedures in diagnosing developmental problems.
5. Ability to prepare long-term goals and short-term objectives that are developmentally appropriate and consistent with each child's style of learning and observed strengths and weaknesses.
6. Ability to structure the environment to adapt to specific needs.
7. Understanding of and belief in the philosophy that underlies the curriculum model in use.
8. Ability to develop a trusting relationship with children through effective communication.
9. Skill in techniques to enhance positive interactions among children of varying levels of ability as well as cultural and ethnic backgrounds.
10. Familiarity with and ability to work effectively as a team member with a wide variety of professionals.
11. Skill in recruiting, training, and working cooperatively with paraprofessionals.
12. Ability to listen reflectively to parents and to develop a viable program of family involvement that demonstrates an understanding of family systems theory.
13. Skill in facilitating children's learning of the social skills necessary for optimal integration.
14. Ability to initiate a formal referral process when indicated.
15. Ability to recognize one's own limitations and to seek assistance when appropriate (Cook, Tessier, & Klein, 1992, p. 7; Safford, 1989, pp. 273–274).

Early childhood educators who understand development as an individualized process and who view children as unique people with individual strengths and challenges possess both the attitudes and knowledge necessary for effective teaching of all young children. Effective teachers of young children have the capability to plan the program and design the environment in order to meet the individual needs of all the children in the group.

ROLE OF THE TEACHER

With a clearer understanding of the attitudes, attributes, and abilities of effective teachers, the different facets of their complex and interrelated roles can be explored. Teachers must learn to understand these varied roles, develop evaluation and judgment skills, and make effective decisions about their role in classroom situations. Figure 4-1 helps to clarify the different aspects of the teacher's role in the classroom: interacting, nurturing, managing stress, facilitating, planning, enriching, problem solving, advocating, and learning.

The Teacher's Role in Interacting

Teachers of young children should interact frequently with children in their care. Interactions can be both verbal and nonverbal and should clearly display respect and affection for children (*Accreditation Criteria and Procedures,* 1991). Teachers should initiate a variety of verbal interactions, such as volunteering information to children, asking them open-ended questions, giving instructions, and simply conversing with them.

Modeling a variety of nonverbal interactions at appropriate times also is critical for teachers of young children. Smiling, touching, hugging, holding, using eye contact, and kneeling or sitting on the child's level are all examples of nonverbal interactions that convey warmth and respect (*Accreditation Criteria and Procedures,* 1991).

Responsive teachers establish positive, trusting, caring relationships with children by carefully listening and answering questions in a patient, sensitive manner. Responsive teachers comfort and reassure children who are hurt, distressed, or anxious. Meeting a child's needs for time, attention, and involvement with a nurturing adult requires that a teacher be flexible and compassionate; it also promotes children's trust and confidence in the teacher. To facilitate enriching and enabling interactions with children, Day (1983) suggests that teachers engage in

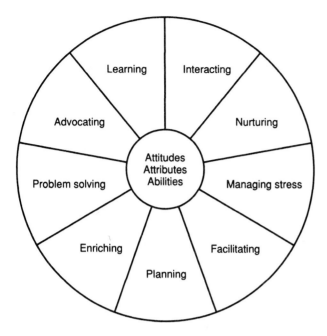

Figure 4-1 A conceptual model of teachers' roles.

activities closely related to what children are doing and involve children in conversations related to the activity. Children's attentiveness to an activity is higher when teachers also are meaningfully involved.

To enhance communication with young children, obtain their attention verbally or nonverbally before beginning conversation, instructions, or requests. Kneel or sit at the child's eye level and make eye contact or say the child's name when you initiate communication. Consider children's developmental, intellectual, and communicative abilities and use language that children can understand (Cherry, 1983). Clear communication reduces the likelihood of failure or misbehavior. For example, saying "Get ready to go outside" may not result in satisfactory responses or preparation from the children. Instead, say "Get your coat and meet me at the door." Children respond better when messages are specific and clear. Supportive interactions characterized by the use of sincere praise, encouragement, and welcoming words can strengthen the relationship between teachers and children, motivate children to learn, and nurture them in their personal growth (Hymes, 1968; Smith, 1982).

Teachers should also establish positive, warm, and responsive relationships with adults. Children need to view teachers engaging in respectful and sensitive interactions with colleagues, volunteers, and parents. Teachers demonstrate respect for both children and adults when they discuss children's behavior or classroom concerns with adults in private and involve children and adults in joint conversations about daily activities, special experiences, and prob-

lem solving when children can appropriately participate in the discussion. Treating information about children and families in a confidential manner is an important component of professionalism and shows sensitivity to others as well as a high regard for the teaching role. Demonstrating appropriate adult interactions enhances children's feelings of security and trust in adults and provides a consistent model of clear and courteous communication.

The Teacher's Role in Nurturing

Early childhood educators are encouraged to nurture children with touch and physical affection (Allen, 1986). Nurturing interactions such as hugging, rocking, cuddling, and holding are necessary for children's physical and psychological development. Physical contact through play, caregiving, and teaching is important in promoting physical growth, emotional health, and attachment to teachers.

Nurturing interactions help children develop positive body images and self-concepts as they experience respectful and responsive physical contact with teachers. Affectionate caregiving and touching enhance both emotional and cognitive development. Children who develop an emotional attachment to their teachers are more competent learners. Children's responses to materials and activities in child care are influenced by the emotional relationship they have with their teachers (Fogel, 1980).

Teachers who use touch and physical affection with children are modeling safe touch. Children can watch teachers exchanging hugs, handshakes, and affectionate touch and can receive respectful and appropriate touch from teachers. This gives children an opportunity to learn and use appropriate touching and helps them distinguish it from less appropriate models of unsafe touch.

Children also are nurtured by verbal support and teacher attitudes that convey the message, "Everyone is someone" (Weiser, 1970, p. 235). Children feel nurtured when teachers are attentive and respectful when listening to and talking with them. Nurturing teachers recognize that real learning is based on valuing children as people with feelings, hopes, and dreams. Actively communicating care and concern to children builds self-esteem:

> It makes individuals visible, for when one is invisible, he is nothing. It means that at the end of each school day each child feels better about himself than he did the day before. It means that he is psychologically secure with his teachers; that he is not

constantly forced to prove himself more capable than someone else, that his efforts are accepted and deemed valuable (Weiser, 1970, p. 237).

Teachers who effectively nurture children help them develop the capacity for reaching out and establishing affectionate, loving relationships. They help children "learn that people matter most of all" (Hymes, 1968, p. 64).

The Teacher's Role in Managing Stress

Children today experience stressful events in a complex developmental-ecological context. Many interdependent elements, including child variables (age, sex, temperament, and developmental stage), family variables (marital status, interactions, child-rearing practices, and socioeconomic status), and variables related to the child's extended social and physical environments (neighborhood, child care, and peers), affect the ways in which children perceive, respond

Nurturing teachers take time to offer comfort and support to hurt or distressed children.

to, and cope with stressors (Benswanger, 1982; Honig, 1986).

Teachers helping children learn to manage stress should create play and learning environments in which stress-management and coping skills can be fostered. Teachers should also give children accurate and developmentally appropriate explanations about stressful events, share children's concerns, acknowledge their feelings, give physical reassurances, and encourage children to ask questions, express feelings, and discuss their own perceptions (Allen, 1988). Play—sociodramatic play, fantasy play, and role play—helps children to reduce and manage stress in several ways. For example, a child who is coping with the stress of a new sibling may choose to role-play taking care of the baby or being the baby to help adjust to this new event. Teachers can use play to help children solve problems, take another person's perspective, make reality more acceptable, and enact frightening experiences in safe surroundings.

Teachers should be prepared to help children understand and cope with stressful events. The teacher's role is a critical one. For many children facing abuse, illness, death, divorce, or other changes in their family and home, the teacher and early childhood education program may be the most stable influence in their young lives (Hatfield, Allen, & Bowditch, 1981).

The Teacher's Role in Facilitating

Young children need opportunities for imaginative play, self-expression, problem finding, exploration of alternatives, and invention to enhance the development of creativity (Curry & Arnaud, 1984; Milgram, Moran, Sawyers, & Fu, 1983; Vandenberg, 1980). Teachers facilitate the development of creativity primarily through an open, nonjudgmental, accepting attitude and a relaxed, flexible learning environment that is rich in resources and abundant with activities.

Teachers who offer young children a variety of opportunities for individual exploration and interpretation of activities encourage self-expression. Many opportunities for imaginative play, with adequate time for children to become immersed in pretend play, fantasy, storytelling, and role-playing activities also foster self-expression and can be "a source of creative imagination" (Piaget, 1962). Children's problem-finding and problem-solving skills are enhanced in an environment that supports curiosity, risk taking, possibility thinking, and nonconformity. Teachers who encourage children to self-select activities, to explore a wide range of alternatives, and to invent new objects or ideas facilitate the development of divergent-thinking skills and original problem solving (Sawyers, Moran, & Tegano, 1986; Starkweather, 1971). Allowing young children blocks of time to play and explore without interruption encourages them to persist with an activity or situation, to fully explore options, and to solve problems creatively.

Spontaneous teachers with a playful attitude and a propensity for fun and enjoyable activities in the classroom facilitate playfulness and spontaneity in young children. A teacher who joyfully engages in bubble play with a group of preschoolers is creating an environment where children are free to experience and are likely to generate questions such as "How do you make a bubble? How many shapes and sizes of bubbles can you make?" Open-minded teachers who value unique, unusual responses to such questions also facilitate creative thought in young children. Teachers best facilitate creative thought in a flexible but well-planned, well-organized environment where children's ideas are valued and where curriculum ideas are generated by children as well as teachers.

Sylvia Ashton-Warner (1963) describes a teacher who believes in balancing discipline and freedom, security and spontaneity, and group needs and individual needs. This type of teacher enjoys "unpredictability and gaiety and interesting people, however small, and funny things happening and wild things happening and sweet, and everything that life is, uncovered" (p. 93). This is the essence of a teacher who facilitates creativity, not chaos, in a classroom for young children.

The Teacher's Role in Planning

Teachers plan for children's security needs by providing a physically and psychologically safe environment. The teacher needs to check for and remove any unsafe or broken toys, materials, and equipment from the classroom and playground areas.

Safety is also an issue in planning activities in the curriculum. Experiences that involve cooking, water play, woodworking, and climbing require thoughtful and thorough consideration and supervision by teachers. Teaching children about safety is a concern for many early childhood professionals. Educators must remember that the safety and security of children in the program is a teacher responsibility. Children should be taught developmentally appropriate concepts about self-awareness, relationships, and problem solving, but they should be assured that adults are responsible for their supervision and protection.

Teachers plan for children's needs for activity, attention, stimulation, and success by providing a balanced and integrated day in the classroom and by implementing curricular activities designed to meet those needs. Teachers also plan for daily routines and transitions. When teachers do not plan routines and transitions, these may become chaotic and frustrating times for children and adults; children who are waiting often become bored and engage in inappropriate behavior, causing teachers to respond to misbehavior and hurry children through transitions. Instead, the many routines and transition times that children go through each day should be learning opportunities for children. When children participate in routines and transitions, the teacher should guide them so that they wait for a minimal amount of time. Children should move efficiently from one area to another in a safe, unhurried manner, in small groups or individually, as they are ready. When children must wait for a short period of time, the teacher should initiate activities such as songs, finger plays, and stories that involve and interest children. Teachers can prepare activities and arrange the environment in ways that stimulate children and help them choose appropriate activities or toys. Teachers can also be flexible and able to quickly reevaluate and use alternative activities depending on weather changes, different interests of children, and extraordinary situations.

The Teacher's Role in Enriching

Another aspect of the teacher's role is to enrich children's learning environment. Teachers should provide children with learning opportunities that are developmentally appropriate. "How young children learn should determine how teachers of young children teach" (NAEYC, 1986, p. 21). The National Association for the Education of Young Children suggests the following guidelines to ensure the use of developmentally appropriate teaching strategies:

- Teachers prepare the environment for children to learn through active exploration and interaction with adults, other children, and materials.

- Children select many of their own activities from among a variety of learning areas the teacher prepares, including dramatic play, blocks, science, math, games and puzzles, books, recordings, art, and music.

- Children are expected to be physically and mentally active. Children choose from among activities that the teacher has set up or that the children spontaneously initiate.

- Children work individually or in small, informal groups most of the time.

- Children are provided concrete learning activities with materials and people relevant to their own life experiences.

- Teachers move among groups and individuals to facilitate children's involvement with materials and activities by asking questions, offering suggestions, or adding more complex materials or ideas to a situation.

- Teachers accept that there is often more than one right answer. Teachers recognize that children learn from self-directed problem solving and experimentation (NAEYC, 1986, pp. 23–24).

These teaching strategies are implemented through the use of both "talking teaching" and "silent teaching" (Hymes, 1968, pp. 98, 103). *Talking teaching* involves sharing information, using opportunities for incidental teaching, and creating new experiences in the classroom. *Silent teaching* involves modeling attitudes and behaviors for children and the process of identification that occurs when the values, points of view, and approach of a teacher become a part of the child. Because silent teaching is more subtle and indirect than talking teaching, the learnings may be unnoticed or unappreciated, but silent teaching can convey important attitudes, values, and behaviors that young children can sense, imitate, and learn. Both modes of teaching contribute to effective, enriching, and developmentally appropriate learning environments.

Young children with disabilities may require more involvement and direction from the teacher in order to achieve mastery of certain skills or behaviors. Although early childhood educators prefer a more child-centered, nondirective approach to teaching,

more structured, directed activities may occasionally be both appropriate and necessary when helping a child with disabilities develop competence and confidence. Teachers may use incidental teaching to present information or pose questions to children as opportunities arise. For children with disabilities, teachers may need to plan or set up situations for using incidental teaching strategies, such as using lunchtime to encourage the development of children's language and social skills (Cavallaro, 1983). Teachers can stage learning experiences, carefully sequence the introduction of specific skills, and offer additional assistance to children while adhering to the tenets of developmentally appropriate practice and activity-based, participatory teaching techniques (Bricker, 1986). Developing skills, achieving control over certain behaviors, and forming satisfying relationships all lead to an increased sense of self-esteem and an eagerness to learn in the child with disabilities.

The Teacher's Role in Problem Solving

The teacher as problem solver uses a process that includes acquiring information, considering alternatives, evaluating outcomes, and applying this feedback to ongoing programs. For example, a problem with a child who frequently hits or shoves other children requires that a teacher identify the reasons for misbehavior; consider the techniques that could be used to prevent, reduce, or respond to the child's behavior; assess the effectiveness of these techniques as well as their compatibility with program philosophy and children's needs; and finally, apply this new

Effective teachers enrich children's learning by providing meaningful experiences and attending to children's questions and comments.

information to maintain or change strategies for classroom management and guidance.

In order to develop problem-solving skills, teachers must develop judgment—the ability to effectively assess and respond to a variety of classroom situations. Judgment is developed through classroom experience, through observing master teachers, through acquiring additional knowledge and insight, and through knowing each child in the classroom as an individual. Teachers need to use judgment to achieve a balance between providing support for children and helping children reach for autonomy, between providing activities children can master and stretching children with new challenges, and between helping children handle problems with peers and encouraging children to resolve their own conflicts. Teachers who know individual children's needs, interests, fears, and frustrations and who have developed good judgment about classroom events can assess problem situations effectively. The most effective problem solvers anticipate and identify questions, issues, and concerns of children and parents and utilize resources to make good decisions about critical classroom issues.

The Teacher's Role in Advocating

Becoming an advocate for children and for the early childhood profession is an important and often overlooked role for the teacher of young children. Teachers have a responsibility to provide the best possible environment and resources for each child enrolled in the program. Teachers must advocate for the highest-quality care and education possible in their classrooms. Each day 13 million children spend all or part of their day with a child-care provider. When this child care and education is of high quality, it promotes healthy development and learning. High-quality child care is particularly advantageous for children from low-income families, with both developmental and socially significant outcomes (Phillips, 1995; Schweinhart & Weikart, 1997; Schweinhart, Weikart, & Larner, 1986). However, for many children, their experiences in child care do not contribute to optimal development; instead it jeopardizes their health and development (Cost, Quality, and Outcomes Study, 1995). Perhaps fewer than 15 percent of the child-care programs in the United States can be termed good or excellent; most are mediocre to poor. In programs with the highest teacher-to-child ratios permitted, child care and developmentally appropriate practice were inadequate or barely adequate for 88 percent of the infants, 78 percent of the toddlers, and

88 percent of the preschoolers (Howes, Phillips, & Whitebook, 1992). The quality of child care and early education in this country—and the resulting problems for parents who search for affordable care, teachers who are underpaid and inadequately trained, and children who experience this care every day—constitutes a crisis for all of us. Children need "choices, meaningful curriculum, connections, teachers who understand active learning. . . . The activities need to promote self-esteem, provide interaction, and be irresistible" (Witmer, 1996). We must advocate for these high-quality programs for all young children.

Teachers must advocate for children in their classrooms who witness and are victimized by violence. Homicide is the third leading cause of death among young children. In some neighborhoods, up to 90 percent of children report witnessing murders and other violent crimes. It is estimated that 3.3 million children in this country witness violence among family members in their home (Kochanek & Hudson, 1995). In these families, children are fifteen times more likely to be physically abused or neglected. "Children need to be safe and secure at home to develop a positive sense of self necessary to their growing into healthy, productive, caring adults; children need to be safe in their communities to be able to explore and develop relationships with other people; and children need to be safe at school in order to successfully learn" (NAEYC, 1993). Children living with violence or the threat of violence need classrooms that provide physical and emotional safety; they need teachers who offer gentle guidance, growth-promoting limits, and stability, and who model and teach alternatives to violence. As teachers we have an educational and moral imperative to advocate for these children who are victimized by violence.

Teachers must advocate for the children in their classrooms with disabilities. Over 10 percent of young children have a disability requiring special services or adaptations (Terman, Larner, Stevenson, & Behrman, 1996). The teacher is the key in determining the success of the child, in determining the quality of inclusion, in creating an attitude of acceptance, and in facilitating skills development. Teachers must prepare children through appropriate, reassuring discussions of the disabling condition and help children have a positive learning experience. Teachers must be aware of the effects of labeling children. Children with the same disability are not alike, and labels emphasize the inabilities, rather than the abilities, of children. Labeling also focuses on deficits in the child instead of, perhaps more appropriately, deficits in the learning environment or in teaching strategies (Cook, Mayfield, & Finn, 1992). Teachers must advocate for children in their classrooms who have disabilities.

Teachers must advocate for the children in their classrooms who are hungry. An estimated 12 million children in the United States, and 195 million worldwide, are undernourished. Reduced energy for play and learning, impaired cognitive functioning, stunted growth, reduced resistance to disease and illness, and even death result from malnourishment (Brown & Pollitt, 1996). Teachers have an educational and ethical obligation to advocate for these children.

Teachers must advocate for the children in their classrooms who have inadequate health care. In most states in this country, fewer than 60 percent of 2-year-olds are immunized against common childhood diseases; in some states the immunization rate is only 30 percent. In the United States the mortality rate for infants is higher than in nineteen other industrialized nations; African-American babies are twice as likely to die in the first year of life as are White infants. For children whose poor health begins early with low birth weight, the resulting total (lifetime) medical costs average $400,000 (Carnegie Corporation, 1994). Teachers must advocate for these children in their classrooms.

Teachers must advocate for children in their classrooms who are homeless. Each day in America, there are 100,000 children who are homeless. In some cities in this country, 1 of every 10 preschool children live in a shelter (Children's Defense Fund, 1997). The homeless and near-homeless—families who live in transitory and temporary situations with friends and family—are also more likely to experience unemployment, violence, and other stressful family circumstances. These children in our class have greater needs—for safety, space, caring relationships, coping skills, and basic necessities (Klein, Bittel, & Molnar, 1993; McCormick & Holden, 1992; Swick, 1997). Teachers must advocate for these children in their classrooms.

In addition, the teacher's role as advocate reaches beyond advocacy for meeting the needs of children in their own classroom into the realm of public policy and commitment to excellence in the field of early childhood education. Teachers should adhere to the highest personal and professional ethics; the National Association for the Education of Young Children's Code of Ethical Conduct (Feeney & Kipnis, 1996) (Appendix A) is a thoughtful and widely accepted standard in the early childhood field. Teachers also need to give voice to children's issues at the community and national level. Being knowledgeable

about program and funding needs, being aware of legislative activities, and writing or calling government officials are avenues for advocacy. Involvement in professional organizations (Figure 4-2) offers opportunities for work in public policy and enables early childhood professionals to combine efforts to bring children's needs to the attention of the public and to advocate for the national, state, and local resources needed to fully support high-quality programs for all young children (Goffin & Lombardi, 1988). Figure 4-3 lists the Internet addresses for some other professional organizations and resources for early childhood educators.

The Teacher's Role in Learning

Finally, the best teachers of young children are committed to continuous learning and developing as effective early childhood professionals. Beginning teachers must realize that initial educational experiences provide the foundation for becoming competent and caring teachers; however, teachers continue to progress through developmental stages and need opportunities for support, networking, professional involvement, and additional training in order to increase teaching skills, avoid burnout, and mature as professionals (Katz, 1977). Katz has identified four stages of professional growth and development in teachers: survival, consolidation, renewal, and maturity. The first developmental stage, *survival,* is marked by teachers' awareness of the realities of teaching, and Katz identifies teachers at this stage as needing support, guidance, and training to develop a baseline of knowledge and skills. In the second stage, *consolidation,* teachers synthesize and consolidate their knowledge and their skills and begin to develop the ability to more effectively focus on individual needs, exceptionalities, and so on. Training for teachers in this stage should focus on using a broader knowledge base and a greater variety of resources. Teachers in the third stage, *renewal,* find that some of their initial enthusiasm, creativity, and commitment has waned, so training should focus on renewal; this should include new experiences such as meeting with other professionals, visiting other programs, reading a wider variety of professional materials, and attending conferences. Figure 4-4 provides a list of professional journals and publications. In the last developmental stage, *maturity,* teachers have integrated their knowledge and skills into a personal philosophy with deeper "insight, perspective, and realism" (p. 11). Training at this stage should include opportunities for teachers to share with others their own insights through workshop presentations, writ-

```
Administration for Children, Youth and Families
Office of Human Development Services
Department of Health and Human Services
200 Independence Ave. SW
Washington, DC 20201

American Academy of Pediatrics
141 Northwest Point Rd.
P.O. Box 927
Elk Grove Village, IL 60007

American Association of Elementary, Kinder-Nursery
  Educators
1201 16th St. NW
Washington, DC 20036

Association for Childhood Education International (ACEI)
11141 Georgia Ave.
Suite 200
Wheaton, MD 20902

Bureau of Education for the Handicapped
U.S. Office of Education
Department of Health and Human Services
7th and D Streets SW
Washington, DC 20036

Children's Defense Fund
122 C Street NW
Washington, DC 20001

Child Welfare League of America, Inc.
67 Irving Pl.
New York, NY 10003

The Division of Early Childhood of the Council for
  Exceptional Children (CEC)
1920 Association Dr.
Reston, VA 22091

Head Start Bureau
Department of Health and Human Services
P.O. Box 1882
Washington, DC 20013

National Association for the Education of Young
  Children (NAEYC)
1834 Connecticut Ave. NW
Washington, DC 20009

National Black Child Development Institute
1463 Rhode Island Ave. NW
Washington, DC 20005

Organisation Mondiale pour l'Education Préscolaire
  (OMEP)
World Organization for Early Childhood Education
1718 Connecticut Ave. NW
Suite 500
Washington, DC 20009

Southern Early Childhood Association (SECA)
Box 5403
Brady Station
Little Rock, AR 72215
```

Figure 4-2 List of early childhood organizations.

ing and publication of articles, and consultation with other teachers and programs to develop ideas and solve problems.

Teachers at any stage of professional development can benefit from personal reflection about their teaching identity, philosophy, and abilities. Reflection can take several forms. It can involve the use of "inner conversations" within the minds and hearts of individual teachers. It can involve the use of journaling to record feelings and reactions to classroom situations, individual children, and their family circumstances. It can involve collegial discussions that promote self-reflection and individual professional growth. A more formal, but also dynamic, process of reflection involves the development of a teaching portfolio. The teaching portfolio is a reflective activity that includes an ever-changing collection of examples of teaching experiences and classroom activities coupled with reflections on the teaching role. The teaching portfolio may be used by preservice teachers and by experienced teachers; it is a creative activity that encourages teachers to paint individual self-portraits that change and evolve as teachers develop skills, wisdom, and insight.

Teachers who are reflective practitioners view teaching as a journey—a journey that increases self-understanding while also developing greater sensitivity to young children and greater knowledge of how to facilitate learning. "Teachers must understand that even as they teach, they will also be taught; even as they help others develop, they will themselves change and grow. . . . This, of course, involves a certain amount of plunging into the unknown, listening and hearing; a certain willingness to take risks" (Ayers, 1993, p. 80). Reflective teaching is a challenging, risk-taking, ethical, personal, and professional activity. It is what keeps teachers honest, renewed, and focused on the important and meaningful rather than the urgent and the trivial. It is a perspective-making and life-altering exercise. The process of reflection

Administration for Children and Families
http://www.acf.dhhs.gov

Child Trends
http://www.childtrends.org

Children's Defense Fund
http://www.childrensdefense.org/index.html

Children Now
http://www.dnai.com/~children

Children Now—Link to Other Resource on Children's Issues
http://www.dnai.com/~children/links.html

Early Childhood Educators' and Family Web Corner
http://www.nauticom.net/www/cokids/

Early Childhood Education On Line (ECEOL)
http://www.ume.maine.edu/~cofed/eceol/welcome.shtml

ERIC Clearinghouse on Assessment and Evaluation
http://ericae.net/

ERIC Clearinghouse on Elementary and Early Childhood Education
http://ericps.ed.uiuc.edu/ericeece.html

Kids Campaigns
http://KidsCampaign.org

National Association for the Education of Young Children (NAEYC)
http://www.naeyc.org/haeyc

National Association of Child Care Resource and Referral Agencies
http://www.childcarerr.org/

National Child Care Information Center (NCCIC)
http://ericps.ed.uiuc.edu/nccic/nccichome.html

National Resource Center for Health and Safety in Child Care
http://nrc.uchsc.edu

National Institute on Out-of-School Time
http://www.wellesley.edu/WCW/CRW/SAC

Stand for Children
http://www.stand.org

THOMAS—Legislative Information on the Internet (U.S. Congress)
http://thomas.loc.gov

U.S. Department of Education
http://www.ed.gov

Figure 4-3 Internet addresses for resources in early childhood education. (*Source:* Adapted from Melissa Grove's *Useful Web Sites in Early Childhood Education,* The University of Tennessee)

Teachers who share children's excitement about learning have a commitment to professional growth.

is a step beyond the process of evaluation. It does not involve judgment of others—it is looking inward and determining what individual teachers can do to take responsibility for changing within themselves.

Teachers who (1) have an awareness of their own attitudes, attributes, and abilities; (2) effectively make decisions about interacting, nurturing, managing stress, facilitating, planning, enriching, problem solving, advocating, and learning; and (3) have a commitment to professional and personal excellence make a true difference in the lives of young children. For authentic, responsive early childhood educators, teaching is indeed "a passionate profession that can challenge both our hearts and minds" (Smith, 1982).

Child Care Quarterly
Human Sciences Press
72 Fifth Ave.
New York, NY 10011

Child Development
University of Chicago Press
5801 Ellis Ave.
Chicago, IL 60637

Childhood Education
Association for Childhood Education International (ACEI)
11141 Georgia Ave.
Suite 200
Wheaton, MD 20902

Dimensions
Southern Early Childhood Association (SECA)
Box 5403
Brady Station
Little Rock, AR 72215

Early Childhood Research Quarterly
National Association for the Education of Young Children (NAEYC)
1834 Connecticut Ave. NW
Washington, DC 20009

Early Childhood Education Journal
Human Sciences Press
72 Fifth Ave.
New York, NY 10011

Early Education and Development
Psychology Press, Inc.
39 Pearl St.
Brandon, VT 05733-1007

Journal of Early Intervention
Council for Exceptional Children (CEC)
1920 Association Dr.
Reston, VA 22091

High Scope/ReSource
High/Scope Educational Research Foundation
600 North River St.
Ypsilanti, MI 48197

International Journal of Early Childhood Education
World Organization for Early Childhood Education (OMEP)
1718 Connecticut Ave. NW
Suite 500
Washington, DC 20009

Topics in Early Childhood Special Education
PRO-ED
8700 Shoal Creek Blvd.
Austin, TX 78758-6897

Young Children
National Association for the Education of Young Children (NAEYC)
1834 Connecticut Ave. NW
Washington, DC 20009

Figure 4-4 List of professional journals and publications.

■   ■   ■   ■   ■   ■   ■   ■   ■   ■

Responding to children's needs requires that teachers quickly assess the situation and respond appropriately based on their experience and personal attributes. Further evaluation of a child or situation may be necessary later and will require use of additional knowledge and skills. In Janelle's case, the teacher must make a decision to move through a variety of overlapping roles—nurturer, interactor, stress manager, problem solver, planner, and facilitator—as we will describe here.

Examine your own feelings about Janelle's outburst. Were you irritated at the disruption? Were you concerned for Janelle's distress and somewhat confused about how to respond to her? All of these feelings are natural responses. Being aware of your own feelings and then reaching past them to understand the level of the child's pain and distress is the first step.

Next, evaluate the seriousness of this incident and determine how to respond. An appropriate immediate response is a nurturing one. This is an unusual behavior for Janelle; she is clearly upset and needs an affectionate, understanding response. Janelle may need assistance in choosing a quiet, individual activity such as reading a book, working a puzzle, or becoming involved in an art activity. Let Janelle set the pace and tone of further interactions during the day. Otherwise, explain to the small group of children who were attempting to play with her that Janelle is feeling stressed and needs some play time alone right now. Acknowledge Janelle's feelings and convey an attitude of respect for Janelle's need to be alone. Help the other children make a choice for a different play activity until Janelle feels like joining them in play. If Janelle is able to express her feelings to the other children, encourage her to do so.

When Janelle's parents pick her up, find a private place to tell them about her day. Reassure the parents that children experience the same stressors of daily life that adults do, and tell them that you will appreciate their helping to observe Janelle for any signs that this is an area of continual concern for her. The parents may have additional insight into this behavior, or it may be the first time they have seen it also.

At the end of the day, you will need to reevaluate Janelle's behavior and determine whether there is a need for long-term strategies to help Janelle cope with stressors. The first step in making this decision is to observe and keep anecdotal records of Janelle's play and interactions for the next several weeks. If you determine that stress is a significant issue for Janelle, you will want to take the following steps to help solve the problem:

1. Plan a parent conference to explore in depth the reasons Janelle might be having difficulty dealing with stress. Enlist the parents' support and assistance in determining strategies for helping Janelle manage stress at school and at home and ensuring that Janelle has adequate time for play and rest.

2. Evaluate the total classroom schedule and structure to make sure that the expectations for the children are developmentally appropriate and that there are ample opportunities for quiet time and solitary play. Plan more opportunities for imaginative and creative play activities that allow children to pace themselves and facilitate problem finding and problem solving.

3. Make use of opportunities in the classroom to identify and label stressful events and enrich the classroom environment, with opportunities for role play and conflict resolution that help children learn to manage stress.

■   ■   ■   ■   ■   ■   ■   ■   ■

CHAPTER SUMMARY _____

The teacher has the most important role in determining program quality for young children. Attitudes, attributes, and abilities are all important. Teachers must be authentic, genuine, and empathic; they must create a supportive environment for learning. Attributes include flexibility, openness, and playfulness. Abilities include skills in program planning, interacting, and communicating, and applying knowledge of children's development. Child development, early childhood education, and special-education courses, as well as supervision and feedback from experienced teachers, are important in the training of skilled professionals. Teachers must understand and effectively implement their roles in interacting, nurturing, managing stress, facilitating, planning, enriching, problem solving, advocating, and learning.

DISCUSSION QUESTIONS _____

1. Discuss the vignette at the beginning of the chapter. What other questions or concerns might you have? Discuss the vignette at the end of the chapter. Are there other responses you might have to this situation?

2. Ask your fellow students to recall their favorite teachers. What were the traits and characteristics of these teachers? Discuss the attitudes, attributes, and abilities of effective early childhood educators.

3. What teacher characteristics are associated with the development of creativity in young children?

4. What skills are necessary to work effectively with young children with disabilities?

5. Consider the different teacher roles of interacting, nurturing, managing stress, facilitating, planning, enriching, problem solving, advocating, and learning for young children. Describe ways you can prepare for each of these roles.

6. Identify statements that teachers make that are unclear or confusing to children, such as "Be nice" or "Get ready to go." Discuss examples of clear communication that will convey teachers' actual intent.

7. Distinguish between "talking teaching" and "silent teaching."

8. Discuss some of the current issues for which strong advocates are needed: children in poverty, homeless children, children who lack medical care and are uninsured, children with HIV/AIDS, and "crack" babies, for example. Discuss ways to effectively advocate in local, state, and national arenas for these children.

9. Discuss opportunities locally, in your state or region, and nationally to be professionally active, such as in the local and state NAEYC affiliates.

REFERENCES _____

Accreditation criteria and procedures of the National Academy of Early Childhood Programs. (1991). Washington, DC: National Association for the Education of Young Children.

Allen, J. (1986). Safe touch: Reassurances for child care workers. *Day Care and Early Education, 14*(3), 14–16.

Allen, J. (1988). Children's cognition of stressful events. *Day Care and Early Education, 16*(2), 12–16.

Ashton-Warner, S. (1963). *Teacher.* New York: Simon & Schuster.

Ayers, W. (1993). *To teach: The journey of a teacher.* New York: Teachers College Press.

Benswanger, E. (1982). Stressful events in early childhood: An ecological approach. *Child Care Quarterly, 11*(4), 267–279.

Bown, J., & Pollitt, E. (1996, February). Malnutrition, poverty, and intellectual development. *Scientific American,* 38–43.

Bricker, D. D. (1986). *Early education of at-risk and handicapped infants, toddlers, and preschool children.* Glenview, IL: Scott, Foresman.

Buscaglia, L. (1984). Landmarks in discovering the human dimension. *Childhood Education, 60*(3), 154–165.

Carnegie Corporation. (1994). *Starting points: Meeting the needs of our youngest children.* New York: Author.

Cavallaro, C. C. (1983). Language interventions in natural settings. *Teaching Exceptional Children, 16*(1), 65–70.

Cherry, C. (1983). *Please don't sit on the kids: Alternatives to punitive discipline.* Belmont, CA: Pitman Learning.

Children's Defense Fund. (1977). *The State of America's Children.* Washington, DC: National Association for the Education of Young Children.

Cook, M., Mayfield, P., & Finn, D. (1992). To refer or not to refer: Evaluation for special education. *Day Care and Early Education, 19*(4), 45–47.

Cook, R. E., Tessier, A., & Klein, M. D. (1992). *Adapting early childhood curricula for children with special needs* (3rd ed.). Columbus, OH: Merrill/Macmillan.

Cost, Quality, and Outcomes Study. (1995). *Cost, quality, and child outcomes in child care centers.* Denver: Department of Economics, University of Colorado at Denver.

Curry, N. E., & Arnaud, S. H. (1984). Play in developmental settings. In T. Yawkey & A. Pellegrini (Eds.), *Child's play: Developmental and applied* (pp. 273–290). Hillsdale, NJ: Erlbaum.

Day, D. (1983). *Early childhood education: A human ecological approach.* Glenview, IL: Scott, Foresman.

Feeney, S., & Chun, R. (1985). Effective teachers of young children. *Young Children, 41*(4), 47–52.

Feeney, S., & Kipnis, L. (1996). *Code of ethical conduct.* Washington, DC: National Association for the Education of Young Children.

Fogel, A. (1980). The role of emotion in early childhood education. In L. Katz (Ed.), *Current topics in early childhood education* (Vol. 3, pp. 1–14). Norwood, NJ: Ablex.

Frazier, A. (1980). Making a curriculum for children. *Childhood Education, 56*(5), 258–263.

Hatfield, L., Allen, J., & Bowditch, B. (1981). *Helping young children cope under conditions of stress.* Chicago, IL: Childcraft Resource Reports.

Heekin, S., & Mengel, P. (Eds.). (1984). *New friends mainstreaming activities to help young children understand and accept individual differences.* Chapel Hill, NC: Chapel Hill Training Outreach Project.

Honig, A. S. (1986). Stress and coping in children. In J. B. McCracken (Ed.), *Reducing stress in young children's lives* (pp. 142–167). Washington, DC: National Association for the Education of Young Children.

Howes, C., Phillips, D., & Whitebook, M. (1992). Thresholds of quality: Implications for the social development of children in center-based child care. *Child Development, 63,* 449–460.

Hymes, J. L. (1968). *Teaching the child under six* (3rd ed.). Columbus, OH: Merrill.

Katz, L. G. (1977). *Talks with teachers.* Washington, DC: National Association for the Education of Young Children.

Klein, T., Bittel, C., & Molnar, J. (1993). No place to call home: Supporting the needs of homeless children in the early childhood classroom. *Young Children, 48*(6), 22–31.

Kochanek, K., & Hudson, B. (1995). Advance report of final mortality statistics, 1992. *Monthly vital statistics report, 43,* 6.

McCormick, L., & Holden, R. (1992). Homeless children: A special challenge. *Young Children, 47*(6), 61–67.

Meissner, J. A., Swinton, S., Shipman, V., Webb, P., & Simosko, S. (1973). *Disadvantaged children and their first school experiences. ETS—Head Start longitudinal study: Preschool teachers of disadvantaged children: Characteristics and attitudes* (Report No. H-8256). Washington, DC: Project Head Start. (ERIC Document Reproduction Service No. ED 109 136)

Milgram, R. M., Moran, J. D., III, Sawyers, J. K., & Fu, V. R. (1983). *Predicting original problem-solving in children: A multidimensional theoretical model.* Unpublished document: Tel-Aviv University.

National Association for the Education of Young Children (NAEYC). (1986). Position statement on developmentally appropriate practice in programs for four- and five-year-olds. *Young Children, 41*(6), 20–29.

National Association for the Education of Young Children. (1993). Positive statement on violence in the lives of children. *Young Children, 48*(6), 80–84.

Phillips, D. (Ed.). (1995). *Child care for low-income families: Summary of two workshops.* Washington, DC: National Academy Press.

Phyfe-Perkins, E. (1981). *Effects of teacher behavior on preschool children: A review of research.* Washington, DC: National Institute of Education. (ERIC Document Reproduction Service No. ED 211 176.)

Piaget, J. (1962). *Play, dreams, and imitation in childhood.* New York: Norton.

Read, K., & Patterson, J. (1980). *The nursery school and kindergarten* (7th ed.). New York: Holt, Rinehart & Winston.

Rogers, C. (1983). *Freedom to learn for the 80's.* Columbus, OH: Merrill/Macmillan.

Safford, P. L. (1989). *Integrated teaching in early childhood.* White Plains, NY: Longman.

Sawyers, J. K., Moran, J. D., III, & Tegano, D. W. (1986). Model of original thinking. In M. J. Sporakowski & R. P. Densmore (Eds.), *College of Human Resources conference proceedings, Information Series 87–1* (pp. 59–70). Blacksburg, VA: Virginia Polytechnic Institute and State University.

Schweinhart, L., & Weikart, D. (1997). The High/Scope Preschool Curriculum comparison study through ages 23. *Early Childhood Research Quarterly, 12,* 117–143.

Schweinhart, L., Weikart, D., & Larner, M. (1986). Consequences of three preschool curriculum models through age 15. *Early Childhood Research Quarterly, 1,* 15–45.

Seefeldt, C. (1973). Who should teach children? *Journal of Teacher Education, 24*(4), 308–311.

Smith, C. A. (1982). *Promoting the social development of young children: Strategies and activities.* Palo Alto, CA: Mayfield.

Snider, M. H., & Fu, V. R. (1990). The effects of specialized education and job experience on early childhood teachers' knowledge of developmentally appropriate practice. *Early Childhood Research Quarterly, 5*(1), 69–78.

Starkweather, E. K. (1971). Creativity research instrument designed for use with preschool children. *Journal of Creative Behavior, 5,* 245–255.

Swick, K. (1997). Strengthening homeless families and their young children. *Dimensions, 25*(3), 29–34.

Tegano, D., & Catron, C. (1990). *Early childhood educators: Encouraging the creative potential of young children.* Unpublished manuscript.

Tegano, D. W., Moran, J. D. III, & Sawyers, J. K. (1991). *Creativity in early childhood classrooms.* Washington, DC: National Education Association.

Terman, D., Larner, M., Stevenson, C., & Behrman, R. (1996). Special education for students with disabilities. *The Future of Children, 6*(1), 4–24.

Vandenberg, B. (1980). Play, problem-solving, and creativity. In K. Rubin (Ed.), *New Directions for child development: Children's play* (pp. 49–68). San Francisco, CA: Jossey-Bass.

Weiser, M. G. (1970). Teaching and the new morality. *Childhood Education, 46*(5), 234–238.

Witmer, J. (1996). From our readers. *Young Children, 51*(3), 3.

Yardley, A. (1971). *The teacher of young children.* London: Evans Brothers

ADDITIONAL RESOURCES _____

Arnaud, S. (1971). Introduction: Polish for play's tarnished reputation. In National Association for the Education of Young Children (Ed.), *Play: The child strives toward self-realization* (pp. 5–12). Washington, DC: Author.

Baker, K. (1950). *The nursery school: A human relations laboratory.* Philadelphia: W. B. Saunders.

Baker, K. (1992). The nursery school: A human relations laboratory. *Young Children, 47*(3), 4–5.

Brooks, G. (1994). My personal journey toward professionalism. *Young Children, 49*(6), 69–71.

Carson, R. (1956). *The sense of wonder.* New York: Harper & Row.

DeVries, R., & Zan, B. (1995). Creating a constructivist classroom atmosphere. *Young Children, 51*(1), 4–13.

Dill, D. D. (Ed.). (1990). *What teachers need to know: The knowledge, skills, and values essential to good teaching.* San Francisco: Jossey-Bass.

Duff, R., Brown, M., & Van Scoy, I. (1995). Reflection and self-evaluation: Keys to professional development. *Young Children, 50*(4), 81–88.

Edgerton, R., Huthings, P., & Quinlan, P. (1991). *The teaching portfolio: Capturing the scholarship of teaching.* Washington, DC: American Association of Higher Education.

Goffin, S. G. (1989). Developing a research agenda for early childhood education: What can be learned from the research on teaching? *Early Childhood Research Quarterly, 4*(2), 187–204.

Goffin, S. G., & Lombardi. J. L. (1988). *Speaking out: Early childhood advocacy.* Washington, DC: National Association for the Education of Young Children.

Goodlad, J. I., Soder, R., & Sirotnik, K. A. (Eds.). (1990). *The moral dimensions of teaching.* San Francisco: Jossey-Bass.

Gratz, R., & Boulton, P. (1996). Erikson and early childhood educators: Looking at ourselves and our profession developmentally. *Young Children, 51*(5), 74–78.

Kontos, S., & Wilcox-Herzog, A. (1997). Teachers' interactions with children: Why are they so important? *Young Children, 52*(2), 4–12.

Kurth-Schai, R. (1991). The peril and promise of childhood: Ethical implications for tomorrow's teachers. *Journal of Teacher Education, 42*(3), 196–204.

Lieber, J., Beckman, P., Hanson, M., Janko, S., Marquart, J., Horn, E., & Odom, S. (1997). The impact of changing roles on relationships between professionals in inclusive programs for young children. *Early Education and Development, 8*(1), 67–82.

Lombardi, J. (1992). Early Childhood 2001—advocating for comprehensive services. *Young Children, 47*(4), 24–25.

McCracken, J. B. (Ed.). (1986). *Reducing stress in young children's lives.* Washington, DC: National Association for the Education of Young Children.

Moustakas, C. (1971). *The authentic teacher.* Cambridge, MA: Doyle

Osofsky, J. (1995). Children who witness domestic violence: The invisible victims. *SRCD social policy report, 9*(3), 1–16.

O'Connell, J. C. (1986). Managing small group instruction in an intregrated preschool setting. *Teaching Exceptional Children, 18*(3), 166–171.

Pratt, C. (1948). *I learn from children.* New York: Simon & Schuster.

Rogers, D., & Webb, J. (1991). The ethic of caring in teacher education. *Journal of Teacher Education, 42*(3), 173–181.

Ryan, J., & Kuhs, T. (1993). Assessment of preservice teachers and the use of portfolios. *Theory into Practice, 32*(2), 75–81.

Seldin, P. (1991). *The teaching portfolio.* Bolton, ME: Anker.

Swanson, L. (1994). Changes. *Young Children, 49*(4), 69–73.

Tegano, D. W., Sawyers, J. K., & Moran, J. D., III. (1989). Problem-finding and solving in play: The teacher's role. *Childhood Education, 66*(2), 92–97.

Warren, R. M. (1977). *Caring: Supporting children's growth.* Washington, DC: National Association for the Education of Young Children.

Wishon, P. (1994). On our watch: Connecting across generations of early childhood advocates. *Young Children, 49*(2), 42–43.

Zanolli, K., Saudargas, R., Twardosz, S. ((1997). The development of toddlers' responses to affectionate teacher behavior. *Early Childhood Research Quarterly, 12,* 99–116.

5.

Partnerships with Parents

■   ■   ■   ■   ■   ■   ■   ■   ■

As a teacher in an infant classroom you have become concerned that one of your children's parents seems to be increasingly agitated about leaving her child each morning. The infant, 8-month-old Gustavo, has been enrolled in your program for about three months and has recently begun to have a difficult time separating from his mother in the morning.

Gustavo now typically cries and clings to his mother as she attempts to leave each morning. His mother has responded by becoming more and more upset, verging on tears herself. Several mornings she has left the classroom only to return minutes later because of her concern about Gustavo's being upset. Of course, the return of his mother to the classroom increases the severity of Gustavo's crying.

Although this parent has not verbalized her concern to you, it is clear from her actions and her body language that she is very upset about leaving Gustavo and worried about his well-being. In order to help both Gustavo and his mother cope with separation you must take steps to discuss this problem and help the mother learn how to deal with this situation.

- How can you approach Gustavo's mother about the problem?
- When is the appropriate time to discuss the issue of separation?
- Will you be able to help Gustavo's mother decide on a way to cope with these difficult morning good-bye times?
- How can you provide assurance and support for Gustavo's mother as well as meet his needs for comfort and security?
- What strategies will you utilize to communicate with Gustavo's parents about this issue on both an immediate and ongoing basis?

■   ■   ■   ■   ■   ■   ■   ■   ■

Suggestions for responding to this classroom vignette will be shared at the end of the chapter.

When reading this chapter, focus on the important role teachers play in supporting families, providing positive interactions with parents, and inviting families' participation in the program. Also become aware of the strategies needed to communicate effectively with families, such as providing daily information in both verbal and written form, scheduling regular parent conferences and parent meetings, and encouraging parents to volunteer and participate in the program.

Forming partnerships with parents is an ecological approach to involving, teaching, and supporting families; to enhancing the total experience of children through increased interactions and continuity between the home and the center; and to enriching the program through parents' participation and contributions. Forming partnerships with parents is a process of sharing information and establishing relationships; it is one of the foundations of the invisible curriculum and provides the bridge of consistency between children's worlds.

Parents' involvement in the early childhood program helps to meet the needs of children, families, and the program. Children have the opportunity to interact with an expanded group of adults with diverse occupational interests, cultural backgrounds,

Amy R. Kerlin also contributed to writing this chapter.

and ideas. Children feel supported and secure in the classroom environment when parents are involved in a variety of the program's activities. Working parents can increase the amount of time in interaction with their children when opportunities and encouragement for their involvement are provided. Working parents' participation in the program can relieve the stress and guilt that often accompany the use of nonparental child care. Parents also can feel supported by teachers who listen to them, share information about their child, offer help with child-rearing problems, and encourage them in their role as parents. Opportunities for communication and interaction with other families in the program also can provide support and encouragement for parents.

When parent participation is high, teachers gain additional information and insight about children in the broader context of their home and family environment. The total child perspective enables teachers to be more sensitive to individual needs, stressors, concerns, and changes associated with the children's home environments and to more effectively meet the needs of children and families through more responsive, comprehensive, child-centered planning. Parents have special knowledge and skills that can be very helpful to teachers. It is important to respect and value the contributions parents can make. A programmatic emphasis on sharing, open communication, and involvement between the home and the center allows both parents and teachers an opportunity to mesh their dreams, hopes, and aspirations for children's development. Children should perceive consistency in expectations for their behavior, in setting the stage for successful learning experiences, and in values and goals for their development and education between home and program environments.

Often present in the parent–teacher relationship, however, are problems and tension created by a number of factors. Job stress (both parents' and teachers'), parents' guilt about the use of nonparental care, jealousy over the relationship and attachment between teacher and child, and confusion over roles and boundaries of responsibility can create tension and conflict that make positive parent–teacher relationships a challenge to even the best teachers (Galinsky, 1988; Powell, 1989a).

Historically, a precedent for parent education and involvement can be traced from early parenting books in the fifteenth century, essays on parenting published during the Reformation and the Colonial era, parents' magazines begun in the 1800s in the United States, the government's child-rearing publications, White House Conferences on the Family, and the focus on families as a component of Head Start and other early-intervention experiences (Berger, 1991). Even more recently, two primary factors have emerged to reemphasize the importance of educating parents and involving them in early

childhood programs. First, the number of preschool children and the workforce participation of their mothers has steadily increased since 1980. In 1995, of the 22.5 million children younger than 6, almost two-thirds of the total population of preschool children, or 13 million, had mothers in the labor force (Hofferth, 1996); the use of nonfamilial child care, in centers or family day-care homes, will continue to increase. Second, research of the past three decades has demonstrated both the value of parents' participation in children's education and the critical role of both family and child care as child-rearing environments in young children's development. As a result of the first factor, cooperation and continuity between home and early childhood education programs must be strengthened; a consequence of the second factor is renewed interest in educating and supporting parents (Powell, 1989a).

The complexity of modern life, the pressures of balancing work and family commitments, and the demands on parents' time are factors that contribute to an expanded view of parent participation. This view emphasizes the strengths of individual families and enables the formation of equal partnerships between the family and the center. These partnerships are based on the beliefs that both parents and teachers contribute something valuable and meaningful to the relationship, share a common concern for the well-being of the child, and feel a shared responsibility for meeting common goals. This view of the parent–teacher partnership also recognizes that families have limited time to engage in typical parent involvement activities. A wide range of parent participation opportunities allows parents to choose those that are meaningful and possible in their lives. Teachers also realize that the most important type of involvement occurs within the home, where parents are involved with their own children. Teachers support parents' caring involvement with their children as well as their involvement with the early childhood program (Workman & Gage, 1997).

INCREASING INTERACTION AND CONTINUITY BETWEEN THE HOME AND THE CENTER _____

Children, parents, and teachers benefit from strong connections between home and center. Staff members set the stage for a continuous relationship with parents during the initial contacts. Parents interested in enrolling a child in the program should be encouraged to visit the center and discuss program policies and philosophy to ensure compatibility of

goals and values. Parents should also be encouraged to bring the child for a visit to assess the child's comfort level with the program environment.

Once the decision to enroll the child has been made, the pre-enrollment conference is held. The director meets with parents to discuss program policies and procedures and to plan for the child's first day in the program. (Figure 5-1 is a sample pre-enrollment conference checklist form.) Parents complete the pre-enrollment parent questionnaire (Figure 5-2) to communicate to teachers their goals and concerns about their child's participation in the program. A shortened version of the pre-enrollment conference is held when the child is older and ready to make a transition to another classroom. The current teacher and the receiving teacher meet with parents to discuss the similarities and differences in classroom procedures and to restate center policies. The child, accompanied by a current teacher, visits the new classroom to gain familiarity with the new teachers, children, and the environment prior to the move.

Parents who make frequent visits to the center to eat lunch with their child, to observe their child at play, and to participate in special activities send a message to the child that the early childhood program experience is important and enjoyable. Parents also become more familiar with the program's curricular activities and management and guidance policies and can provide consistency between home and center. Teachers who plan home visits demonstrate a high level of concern for the child as a whole person and strengthen relationships with the family. Home visits can be social visits, information-gathering and -sharing visits, or parent training visits. Teachers and parents can share activities that complement the curriculum.

ENRICHING THE PROGRAM THROUGH PARENT PARTICIPATION AND CONTRIBUTIONS _____

In addition to encouraging parents to visit and observe the early childhood program, teachers should encourage parents to participate as volunteers. By participating, parents can gain a broader understanding of children's development, instructional strategies, and enabling caregiving. Parents can use the knowledge and skills to enrich children's experiences at home and at the center.

For parents to visit and participate, they must feel welcomed, comfortable, and useful. Some parents, as well as other volunteers, may benefit from a list of guidelines similar to those in Figure 5-3 to give them a basic orientation to interacting with a group of children.

Most parents will respond to opportunities to volunteer. They can make significant contributions and have meaningful involvement with children and staff. There are several ways to involve parents in volunteering, either directly in the classroom or indirectly. Parents can be chaperones or sponsors for special field trips and events. Parents can share their knowledge by leading a special activity for the children based on their culture, occupation, or hobby. Parents can be active participants in fund-raising projects. With some prior organization, parents can participate in Saturday work days where they can

help build blocks, plant a garden, or construct large climbing equipment. Overall, the experience of volunteering should benefit parents as well as contribute to the early childhood facility.

Parents also contribute to the program as policymakers and child advocates. Parents can be active in decisions involving the policies and procedures of the program. Parents on the advisory council or board of directors of your early childhood program have an active voice in the decisions that affect their child's experiences at school. Parents also can be children's advocates. They can promote the rights of children in local, state, and regional child-care issues. Improving quality of care, increasing the status of early childhood professionals, raising salaries, decreasing staff turnover, and raising consciousness about child care as a responsibility of society, government, and businesses are all goals that both parents and teachers as child advocates can cooperatively address in seeking to improve the quality of all programs. The role of advocate is empowering for parents of children with special needs. As they work to ensure the existence of programs and services for children, this effort fosters acceptance and adjustment and helps parents to acknowledge their strength and commitment to their child.

INVOLVING, TEACHING, AND SUPPORTING FAMILIES _____

Parents' needs for information, encouragement, and stress reduction can be met through family involvement in the program. Several ways to accomplish

this are listed and described here. It is important that these methods include two-way communication, with teachers being open and responsive to parents

PRE-ENROLLMENT CONFERENCE CHECKLIST

Child's Name_____ Child's Birthdate_____

_____ Program Descriptions
          _____ Summary of Licensing Requirements
          _____ NAEYC Accreditation Pamphlet
_____ Purpose
          _____ Parent Handbook
          _____ Consent Form (field trips, photographs, research)
_____ Educational Philosophy and Curriculum
_____ Inclusion
_____ Staffing (ratio, staffing patterns, students, and volunteers)
_____ Calendar

PROGRAM POLICIES

_____ Enrollment Fees
_____ Payment of Tuition
_____ Attendance (call center if absent or late)
          _____ Release Form and Card
          _____ Late Fee Policy
_____ Staff Interaction/Communication (confidentiality)
_____ Personal Data Sheet
_____ Child's Health Record
_____ Dispensing of Medication Form
_____ Physician's Release Form
_____ Illness/Informal Health Check
          _____ Centers for Disease Control Handbook
_____ Accidents and Emergencies
          _____ Emergency Notification Form and Card
_____ Field Trip Permission Form
_____ Exit Procedure Form/Leave of Absence and Vacation Policy

PROGRAM ROUTINES

_____ Children's Folders (confidentiality)
_____ Daily Schedule
_____ Field Trip Guidelines
_____ Diapering/Toileting/Lunch and Snack Routines
_____ Extra Clothing
_____ Dressing for Outdoor Play

Figure 5-1 A sample pre-enrollment conference checklist form.

WAYS PARENTS ARE INVOLVED AND KEPT INFORMED

_____   Enrollment Procedure
_____   Parent Handbook
_____   Parent Visitation
_____   Parent Meetings
_____   Parent Conferences
_____   Assessment Process
_____   Newsletters
_____   Bulletin Boards
_____   Daily Contacts
_____   Child-Care Advisory Committee

PARENT QUESTIONS AND PLAN FOR CHILD'S FIRST DAY

Child's Start Date_____

I verify that all of the items on the Pre-Enrollment Conference Checklist have been discussed with me prior to enrolling my child. I have received a copy of the Parent Handbook, licensing standards, Centers for Disease Control Parent Handbook, and all necessary forms. I understand that it is my responsibility to be aware of and follow all policies and procedures.

_____   _____
Parent's Signature   Date

_____   _____
Parent's Signature   Date

Conference Conducted by:

_____   _____
Staff Member's Signature   Date

Figure 5-1 (*continued*)

and their concerns, questions, and input. Early childhood educators must also work to enable and empower parents to participate in the education of their children.

Daily Interactions

In most programs, the daily interaction between parents and teachers that occurs at arrival and depar-

ture times is the means by which most information is shared (Powell, 1989b). Teachers must recognize the importance of initiating communication; being receptive to information shared by parents concerning the child's health, mood, or experiences; and offering information to parents about significant occurrences in the child's day.

Teachers must create a setting for this interaction and communication. Staff schedules must be

---

PRE-ENROLLMENT PARENT QUESTIONNAIRE

1. What do you view as the *most important* areas of development for your child?

2. What are the most important concerns you have about your child being in child care?

3. Please list any areas or issues regarding child development about which you would like information.

4. Are there any individuals or family needs/concerns with which you feel the child-care program should/could assist you or your family?

5. Parent participation in a child-care program is a very important factor in the parents' satisfaction with the program and in the child's growth and development while enrolled in the program. Please mark any of the following ways you will be involved with your child's program:

    _____   Attending parent meetings

    _____   Attending parent conferences

    _____   Collecting items for art and/or other activities

    _____   Driving/chaperoning field trips

    _____   Helping with minor repairs around the center

    _____   Donating children's outgrown clothes and/or toys

    _____   Demonstrating activity for children (for example, a talent, hobby, or special interest you have)

    _____   Arranging a visit or tour of your workplace for children

    _____   Reading stories for children

    _____   Collecting items for the imaginary play center (for example, clothing, used food containers, purses, "pretend" items)

    _____   Sewing items such as doll clothes, sheets, extra clothes, cloth toys

    _____   Building equipment such as furniture, wooden toys, play structures

    _____   Gardening and nature activities

Figure 5-2 Sample pre-enrollment parent questionnaire.

arranged so that a teacher is available to greet and talk with parents, and other staff are available to greet and interact with children. Discussions about a child should not occur in the child's presence, unless the child is to be included in the conversation. Both parents and teachers may be hurried and stressed during arrival and departure times, but teachers must convey to parents the importance of this brief time for sharing and interacting.

Ineffective communication is the major barrier to establishing positive parent–teacher relationships. Teachers who learn effective communication techniques

Parents who visit the program and participate in special activities help provide consistency for children between the home and the center.

develop self-knowledge, demonstrate sensitivity to parents' ideas and feelings, and create a climate of mutual support and respect. Effective communication techniques include establishing eye contact, listening attentively, acknowledging feelings, sharing information, asking open-ended questions, helping parents feel comfortable, respecting differences, treating parents as individuals, maintaining a friendly and nonjudgmental disposition, and using problem-solving skills when needed.

When conflicts between parents and teachers arise, teachers must examine their own feelings and biases and also understand that parents filter their perceptions through their own experiences, stereotypes, and ideas about educational settings. Communication difficulties may stem from stress, hurriedness, guilt, differing values, and personality conflicts. Most teachers prefer to avoid conflicts and hope they will be resolved

without confrontation or intervention; however, conflicts often escalate and the resulting tension can be harmful to children as well as to parents and teachers. It is important for teachers to acknowledge and deal with conflicts, tensions, and hurt feelings. When parents are antagonistic, hostile, negative, or unresponsive, teachers should remain patient and professional. Specifically, teachers can avoid becoming defensive, attacking the parent personally, or arguing with the parent. When a situation becomes uncomfortable, teachers should maintain control of their emotions, seek assistance from a colleague, and end the exchange until tempers cool and a calmer climate prevails. Teachers should demonstrate respectful and courteous behavior and expect the same behavior from parents (Boutte, Keepler, Tyler, & Terry, 1992; Brand, 1996).

Galinsky (1988) has identified four major areas of job stress for parents: number of work hours, lack of job autonomy, job demands, and relationship with supervisor. Teachers experience job stress, too, with some areas in particular creating tension, conflict, and jealousy among parents and teachers: income disparity (with other working parents' income), lack of training to work with parents, job status, blaming parents, and possessive feelings toward children. To address these tensions, she suggests that teachers:

- Understand their own expectations
- Understand parents' point of view
- Understand parent development
- Consider their own attitude
- Accept diversity
- Get support
- Set appropriate limits on their role
- Think about the words they use with parents

There are some roles that teachers cannot assume with parents. Many teachers think they are expected to be a counselor or therapist with parents of the children in their program. Most teachers are not trained for the counseling role, and time spent talking to parents who would better be helped by talking with a trained therapist could be spent in the classroom with children or working with parents in more appropriate ways. When teachers find themselves being pushed into the role of counselor, there are several steps "that clarify without abandoning or ignoring the distress or confusion that parents may feel" (Hauser-Cram, 1986, p. 19). Acknowledge what the parents have been feeling and sharing. Determine whether the problem is a classroom issue, a parenting issue, a family issue, or another type of issue. If the problem is a classroom issue, decide on a plan to begin resolving the issue. For other problems,

GUIDELINES FOR VOLUNTEERS

1. On your first few visits to the classroom, tell children your name. Explain "I will be coming to your classroom on Monday mornings." Such an explanation lessens confusion for children in classrooms that have many volunteers.

2. Quickly learn and use children's names. Say their names often when talking to them, asking questions, or singing songs and reciting rhymes into which children's names are inserted.

3. Position yourself in the classroom so that your back is to the wall and not to the children. Maintain visual observation of as many children as possible.

4. Make plans to ensure children's success. Give children manageable, developmentally appropriate tasks. Say to children, "Can you think of a way to do this?" Suggest strategies for children who seem to become frustrated.

   Say: "Try turning all the colored sides of the puzzle up before you start. Now, does that help you decide where the pieces fit?"

5. Get a child's attention before beginning to talk, ask questions, or give instructions. Position yourself—in a small chair, on your knees, or sitting on the floor— at the child's eye level. Use a gentle touch on the child's shoulder or arm to gain the child's attention.

6. Communicate with children in a positive way. Children who are told what not to do may not understand what they should do.

   Say: "We walk inside."
   "Our feet stay on the floor."
   "Touch him gently."

   Not: "Don't run."
   "Don't put your feet on the chair."
   "Don't be so rough."

7. Children often misbehave and ignore instructions, rules, or requests when the messages are unclear or not specific.

   Say: "It's time to clean up."
   "Put on your mittens before you go outside."
   "Tell him, 'I want the trike next.'"

   Not: "It's too messy in here."
   "It's cold outside today."
   "Be nice to him."

8. Children should be reinforced, praised, and encouraged for their effort rather than for their products or possessions.

   Say: "You worked hard on that picture."
   Not: "I like the pretty dress you are wearing today."

9. When appropriate, use encouragement that emphasizes effort rather than praise that only focuses on completed products.

   Say: "This puzzle has a lot of pieces, but I think you will be able to work it."
   "This puzzle is hard, but I think you can learn to do hard things."

   Not: "You finished that so quickly."
   "What a nice job you did."

10. When you do praise, make it sound sincere, not phony or superficial.

    Say: "What big arm strokes you are using to put the paint on the paper."

    Not: "Your painting is the most beautiful I have ever seen."

11. Use physical touch with children in appropriate ways for routine caregiving (such as diapering and changing clothes), for providing comfort to a child in distress, for providing physical guidance (such as redirecting a child), and for promoting self-esteem and positive social interactions among children and adults. Touch and affection are important and necessary for healthy child development and quality caregiving. Children have their individual temperaments, emotional styles, and needs for physical attention and touch. Be sensitive to children's varying needs for physical contact. If you have questions about giving or receiving physical affection from children, please ask.

12. Consult the parent and staff bulletin boards when you come to the center for posted information about daily schedules, menus, and special events.

13. Some of the children have special needs. Before you begin your participation in the program, we will inform you of special routines, meals, or equipment, such as wheelchairs or prosthetic devices, that we use.

14. If you have questions about anything you observe, or if you are unsure about any of our policies and procedures, please ask. If you have concerns or questions about the children, do not discuss them in the children's presence. Wait for a more appropriate time, such as during naptime or after children leave, and discuss them in a professional manner with a teacher or the director.

15. Confidentiality is very important. Information about children and their families should not be shared with anyone unrelated to the program. We welcome you sharing information with others about the center and its program and philosophy; however, when you do, the identities of the children and families we serve must remain anonymous.

Your participation in the program is very helpful to us. We appreciate you sharing your time and talents with us!

Figure 5-3 A suggested list of guidelines for volunteers. (*Source:* Allen, J., & Carlson, K. (1989). Volunteers in the classroom: Guidelines for orientation. *Day Care and Early Education, 16*(1), 4–6. Reprinted by permission of Human Sciences Press.)

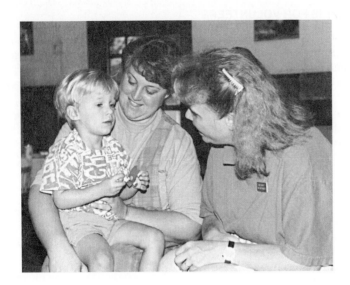

Parent–teacher communication at arrival time that makes children transition into the morning's activities.

teachers should be prepared to suggest resources, such as parent support groups, pediatricians, psychologists, therapists, or other agencies or programs. Finally, teachers can agree to offer help appropriate to their role as a classroom teacher. "Teachers are trained to notice and respond to the needs of other human beings. [They] should think more about where they can be most helpful and where being helpful lies in pointing the way to more appropriate resources" (p. 20). Teachers who are able to relate to parents honestly and openly while also establishing appropriate boundaries in parent relationships will be more effective partners with parents.

Teachers and parents who are able to relate to each other as real people with strengths and vulnerabilities are able to validate each other, share responsibilities, and focus on the common goal of providing the best growing ground for the child. In this way, teachers and parents develop authentic relationships as partners, collaborators, co-educators, and co-decisionmakers in the life of the child (Coleman, 1997).

Parent Conferences

Parent conferences are an excellent way to give and receive information about a child and should be conducted at least three times a year. As information is shared, the teacher and parent can collaborate on providing mutually beneficial and reinforcing experiences at child care and at home. Bjorklund and Burger (1987, pp. 26–28) suggest the following guidelines for the parent conference:

1. *Advance preparation.* Communication with parents is an ongoing process. Establishing relationships through daily contacts with parents is vital to the conference preparation. As you know the family better, you can anticipate what the parents may want to discuss in a formal conference. Knowing the parents well will assist you in anticipating the parents' approach to the conference. Advance preparation for the parents also is important. In addition to the general information about the conference, you may want to provide the parents with concrete information about the goals for the conference and things for them to consider before you meet. Suggest that they bring a list of questions or information about the child's experience at home. Set a convenient date and time for the conference. Prepare, organize, and review all written materials necessary to conduct the conference efficiently and productively. Include current copies of the developmental checklist, child observations, portfolios, and other assessment data.

2. *Setting the stage.* Create a comfortable, nonthreatening climate for the meeting. Ensure privacy. At the beginning of the conference, introduce those attending (director, teacher, student assistant, and so on) and explain the roles of each in the conference. A brief review of the conference agenda should be provided.

3. *Talking to parents.* During the conference you should try to:

    ■ Help parents feel relaxed, comfortable, and welcome.

    ■ Communicate with parents on their level. Try to avoid educational jargon.

    ■ Emphasize the positive attributes of the child.

    ■ Provide specific ways the curriculum will address individual needs and activities for their child and suggest activities the parents can do at home.

■ Ask open-ended questions to elicit parents' opinions and ideas.

■ Be an active listener. to encourage information sharing. *Active listening* requires you to pay attention to the stated and implied feelings of the parent and respond in a reflective manner that promotes further communication.

4. *Content.* During the conference, be sure to cover all that is listed on the parent conference checklist (see Figure 5-4), the developmental assessment information, and any parental concerns or ideas.

■ *Child's daily experience.* Teachers should share information about the child's daily experiences, including discussions of the child's general adjustment, the child's favorite activities, and anecdotal information about the child's experiences at the early childhood program. Parents should be encouraged to share information and questions regarding their child's development and participation in the program. Ask parents to describe children's daily experiences at home.

■ *Developmental assessment information.* Parent conferences are an excellent time to share assessment information based on the

---

PARENT CONFERENCE CHECKLIST

Child's Name_____

Date_____

_____ **I. WELCOME AND INTRODUCTIONS**

_____ **II. ANNOUNCEMENTS**

The purpose of the announcement section is to share current information about the program with parents. This can be a "reminder" time. The information shared at this time should be relevant for the time of the year that the conference is held. Please use you best judgment when deciding which announcements to share with parents. You may use some of the examples that are listed, add additional ones, or not share any at all if they are not relevant. (For example, do not share the inclement weather policy with parents in June.)

—holidays or in-service closings
—upcoming parent meetings
—recent or projected field trips
—others

III. ASSESSMENTS

_____ **A.** Developmental Checklist/Observations/Portfolios

_____ **B.** Objectives

The purpose of this section is to discuss each child's development. This information should include a summary of the developmental checklist/observations/portfolios that have been completed since the last conference. This summary should focus on how skills have developed during the past several months and should document how unique and individual each child's development is. Encourage parents to share observations and insights about their child's development and ask parents for suggestions about setting objectives.

_____ **IV. PARENT QUESTIONS OR CONCERNS**

This is an appropriate time to discuss a new child's adjustment to the program (first conference only). This also is a time to answer any questions a parent might have, discuss a child's behavior changes, or discuss any concerns a parent might have.

_____ **V. SUMMARY AND CLOSING**

Figure 5-4 Sample of a parent conference checklist.

child's growth and development. The information is obtained through daily observations of the child, the use of a developmental checklist, and the compilation of work samples in the child's portfolio. Parents can contribute to this by reporting on the child's development in the home setting, helping to set individual goals, and discussing activities appropriate for the child's development.

5. *Ending the conference.* Summarize major points and goals; agree on a plan of action, and a follow-up plan, if needed. Always ask whether there are questions or concerns and thank the parents for coming.

6. *After the parents leave.* The follow-up to a parent conference is as critical as the conference itself. Immediately after the conference, fill out the conference summary form (see Figure 5-5). Include in it suggestions that were made and questions that were raised. If a response from you is expected, be sure to follow up as soon as possible.

Written Communication

Parent Newsletters. Parent newsletters containing anecdotal information about children, descriptions of special events, and parent education information can be compiled periodically throughout the year by the staff members. Parents can contribute to this process by sharing information about their child (summer vacations, special trips, favorite bedtime stories, and so on).

Parent Bulletin Board. Bulletin boards are centers for disseminating information, making announcements, sharing articles, displaying photographs, exhibiting children's artwork and other creations, and posting daily lesson plans and menus. Bulletin boards can be two-way communication resources; a section can be designated for parents to post messages to teachers. Other options for sharing written communication include individual parent mailboxes and wipe-off boards with felt markers. Bulletin boards should be in a prominent place with colorful and creative displays to ensure their effectiveness as information centers.

Hug Notes. These short, anecdotal messages to parents describe something especially positive, humorous, or significant that occurred during a child's day and should be shared routinely with parents (see Figure 5-6). Variations on hug notes include any type of short, preprinted form that can be individualized to share daily information.

Parent Meetings

Parent group meetings should provide information, create awareness, or teach parents about children's development, parenting issues, and the early childhood program. Meetings also allow parents and teachers to socialize in a relaxed atmosphere. Before planning a parent meeting, assess the current interests and needs of the parents. Create a needs assessment or questionnaire and ask parents to respond. The needs assessment form allows parents to choose or suggest certain topics of interest. For an effective parent meeting, advance arrangements are nec-essary. Select a room with appropriate size, seating, ventilation, lighting, and audiovisual equipment. Make special efforts to greet and welcome parents. Name tags, displays of children's photographs or artwork, refreshments, and an ice-breaking activity should be arranged in advance. Use these and other methods to create a warm climate in which parents and teachers will begin to socialize and share information.

Welcome parents more formally as a group, outline the meeting's agenda and purpose(s), and make necessary announcements. Large-group parent meetings may include a potluck dinner, picnic supper, or pizza party. These are usually more formal, with a planned program, special topic, and guest speaker. Small-group parent meetings allow parents to choose among several meeting times and topics throughout the year and offer parents greater flexibility. A series of brown-bag lunch seminars on a variety of parenting issues offers parents an opportunity for ongoing education in parenting skills and time to interact informally with staff members.

Some topics for parent meetings are suggested here. Other topics relevant to parents' needs and interests can be added.

1. *Building self-concept.* Objective: To give parents information on the importance of children's self-concept and to give examples of ways to foster positive self-concept.

2. *Sibling rivalry.* Objective: To offer practical guidelines and real-life examples for fostering cooperative sibling relationships.

3. *Health issues.* Objective: To have relevant group-care health issues discussed by a medical professional. These could include upper-respiratory infections, ear infections, hepatitis A virus, HIV, thrush, chicken pox, and so on.

4. *Creativity.* Objective: To explain the development of creativity and to suggest activities that could enhance self-expression, imagination, invention, and exploration.

5. *Discipline.* Objective: To explain methods of discipline and guidance and to discuss methods of preventing inappropriate behavior and using praise, logical consequences, and conflict resolution.

6. *Communication.* Objective: To teach effective listening, explain the importance of determining

PARENT CONFERENCE SUMMARY FORM

Child _Audrelle Williams_

Parent(s) Attending _John & Delores Williams_

Teacher(s) Attending _Melissa Rogers_

Date _5/14_   Program _Preschool_

Points Covered (list briefly):

1) Shared developmental assessment information.
2) Discussed issues of safety awareness.
3) Talked about Audrelle's expression of emotion at school.
4) Related examples of Audrelle initiating more play with other children.

Parental Reactions/Staff Response:

1) Parents were pleased with Audrelle's developmental progress.
2) Delores asked if Audrelle seems preoccupied with safety issues. She mentioned that Audrelle expresses concern over safety situations at home (e.g. a person drowning). I responded that while Audrelle shows an awareness of safety, such as asking teachers to watch her at the climber, she does not seem preoccupied with the subject.
3) John asked if Audrelle cries or shows anger at the preschool. I replied that she does infrequently & seems to recover quickly.
4) I related examples of Audrelle initiating more play with other children.

Concluding Remarks (summarize tone of conference, goals set, and any other pertinent information):

The conference was very pleasant. The Williams expressed pleasure at Audrelle's growth and development over the past months, especially her appropriate expression of emotions and her willingness to take initiative to play with peers. The Williams are pleased with the program and the teachers.

Monitoring Teacher _Melissa Rogers_

Figure 5-5 Sample of a parent conference summary form.

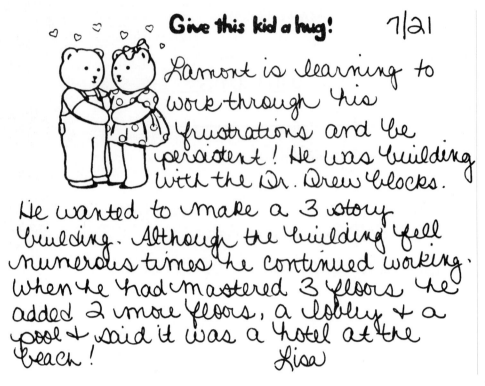

Give this kid a hug! 7/21

Lamont is learning to work through his frustrations and be persistent! He was building with the Dr. Drew blocks. He wanted to make a 3 story building. Although the building fell numerous times he continued working. When he had mastered 3 floors he added 2 more floors, a lobby + a pool + said it was a hotel at the beach!

Lisa

Figure 5-6 A completed sample hug note.

the child's feelings and meanings, and to respond to the child by giving open-ended responses (Berger, 1991).

7. *Nutrition for children.* Objective: To provide helpful hints about nutrition for children with a nutritionist or dietitian as guest speaker. Recipes for nutritious foods that children enjoy in the center can be shared with the parents.

8. *Storytelling and finger plays.* Objective: To give suggestions to parents on effective ways to use storytelling and finger plays. Provide several handouts on how to make finger puppets and how to lead a finger-play activity (Croft, 1979).

9. *Transition to school.* Objective: To help parents consider relevant issues and develop strategies for assisting children in the transition from child care to kindergarten.

These topics should be discussed and meetings should be planned using a variety of formats and methods. Roundtable discussions, buzz sessions, workshops, classroom observations and field trips, role playing

and dramatizations, and panels are formats that can be used to vary the method of providing information to parents (Berger, 1991). Be prepared to evaluate your parent meetings by one or more methods. Elicit verbal feedback or written comments, and use this information to plan subsequent meetings.

Parent Resource Center

This may simply be a shelf above the children's lockers or a room that doubles as a staff workroom or a parent-teacher conference room. It holds a variety of resource materials, including books, magazines, videos, and brochures on child development and behavior, parenting, and family relationships. These materials can be used at the center or loaned to the parents to take home. Teachers may extend the availability of resources to include a parent lending library for children's literature and child-created books for parents and children to read together at home.

SUPPORTING FAMILIES IN CRISIS

A special challenge in working with parents is presented to teachers when families face crisis. Families may experience changes in structure, with the addi-

tion or loss of family members through birth, death, divorce, or separation. They may be faced with changes in family functioning as roles and responsibilities are altered through changes in employment status or illness and hospitalization. Teachers may be asked to provide information, suggest coping strategies, and make referrals for family assistance and counseling. Some special cases of family stress are discussed in this section.

Families with Children with Disabilities

Parent participation is especially important for the family of a child with disabilities. Parents experience additional financial, medical, marital, and emotional stressors. Teachers are challenged to provide information, encouragement, and stress reduction.

Parents respond to the birth of a child with disabilities or the later occurrence of a disabling condition by moving through various stages of adjustment and acceptance. Although these stages occur in similar sequence for most families, the stages often overlap, and the length of time parents take to move through the stages varies from family to family. Parents of infants, toddlers, and preschoolers with disabilities may still be confronting the psychological, marital, and familial adjustments that must be made. Denial, projection of blame, fear, guilt, mourning or grief, withdrawal, rejection, and acceptance are stages through which parents may go before they are psychologically and emotionally able to accept the disabling condition and accompanying changes (Chinn, Winn, & Walters, 1978). Teachers should understand this struggle to adjust and provide support and encouragement. This understanding is crucial to helping parents accept the child and the disabling condition (Moses & Dreidler, 1981). As parents of children with disabilities become partners with the center, they should be helped to avoid comparing their child with the other children in the program. Teachers can model this by focusing on children's strengths, skills, and progress.

Families with Children with Chronic Illness

Many children with birth defects, organ transplants, or formerly fatal conditions are now being successfully treated with the help of current medical science and new technologies. These children often are part of regular early childhood programs, and some special considerations must be made in working with their families. Parent–teacher communication about medical conditions and care, more detailed health and medical forms, identification of community ser-

vices, and collaboration with health-care consultants are all special issues for teachers working with parents of children with chronic health conditions (Fauvre, 1988; Association for the Care of Children's Health, 1990).

Families and Divorce

Current divorce statistics indicate that 50 percent of all marriages today end in divorce. In 1996, over 27 percent of children lived in single-parent households (Children's Defense Fund, 1997). About half of the decline in the number of two-parent families in the past two decades was due to the increase in the number of never-married parents (Corcoran & Chaudry, 1997). Parenting, a difficult job without family stressors, is significantly affected by marital conflict, separation, and divorce. Parents experience lowered self-esteem, loneliness, depression, and ambivalence about their new role as a single parent. These feelings alter the parent–child relationship; changes in discipline, nurturance, attachment, and amount of time for parenting may hurt the quality of the relationship (Skeen & McKenry, 1986). Teachers may be expected to provide additional support and encouragement, suggest information about single parenting and helping children cope with divorce, and show sensitivity to special concerns of single parents. Scheduling a parent conference for each parent, sharing copies of children's records with each parent, and encouraging parents to communicate regularly about the child's early childhood program are to be considered when working with single parents. It is important that teachers remain impartial and supportive of the entire family.

Families and Child Abuse

Over 1,000 children in the United States die each year as a result of maltreatment. In 1995, almost 3.1 million children were reported abused or neglected, a 61 percent increase from a decade earlier. The number of children who were seriously injured by abuse nearly quadrupled in the past decade (Children's Defense Fund, 1997). The number of child sexual abuse victims is more difficult to identify because most cases of child sexual abuse are never reported. It is estimated, however, that there are between 200,000 and 300,000 new child sexual abuse victims each year. Since 1980, the number of child sexual abuse reports has increased at a significantly higher rate than other child abuse reports (Finkelhor, 1994).

Parents whose children are abused by nonfamily members may feel angry, guilty, and helpless. They will need assistance in dealing with these feelings in constructive, adaptive ways. Some parents try to repress their feelings and even deny that the abusive experience occurred. These parents need help to face the reality of the abuse, openly discuss their emotions, and help their child receive communication, reassurance, and support. Some parents become overprotective of their children. With these parents, discuss appropriate protection measures but encourage them to return to more adaptive parenting that lets children feel safe and secure and able to proceed with healthy development (Schetky, 1988).

Parents who abuse their own children also need support from teachers. Teachers first must deal with their own emotions, particularly negative feelings, about the parent who is abusive. The blame for child abuse most accurately lies in a complex set of variables—economic, social, and environmental—that are all factors leading to abuse. Teachers who learn as much as possible about abuse and neglect can deal effectively and empathically with parents without condoning the abuse (Fontana & Schneider, 1978).

Support for abusive parents includes first, of course, reporting the abuse to the appropriate local child protection agency. Many states mandate this reporting for teachers. Next, identify community resources for counseling, parent education, and other assistance to address specific causative factors such as unemployment/employment stress and financial problems. Convey to parents that you want to help them to develop more adaptive coping skills as well as to restore a positive, loving relationship with their child.

WORKING WITH DIVERSE GROUPS OF PARENTS

The changing demographics in the United States suggest an increasingly diverse culture. These ethnolinguistically diverse groups, previously referred to as minority or underrepresented groups, are now majority groups in many areas of the country. It has been estimated that, compared to 1995, in the year 2005 there will be 3 million more Hispanic children, 1 million more African–American children, 1 million more Asian–American children, almost 40,000 more Native American children, and 1.5 million fewer White children, thus increasing the proportion of ethnolinguistically diverse children in the United States from one-fourth to almost one-third of the childhood population (*Kids Count Data Book,* 1997). Clearly, the cultural, linguistic, and ethnic diversity of the United States population is increasing, and early childhood professionals must be prepared to work with more families whose values, language and communication style, child-rearing practices, and family relationships may be different from their own. For example, small bruises on Indo-Chinese children may not be indicators of abuse; instead, they may indicate the use of *coining,* or applying pressure with coins to reduce illness or pain (Berger, 1991). Some Pacific American families view a child's disability as punishment for a wrongdoing, or the result of foods the mother ate during pregnancy, or evil spirits in the child with special needs (Chan, 1986). A "thumbs up" sign is seen as an obscene gesture in some South American cultures, and patting a child on the head is inappropriate in Asian and Muslim families (Han-son, Lynch, & Wayman, 1990). Children in Black families often exhibit a relational, rather than analytical, cognitive style that is more affective, people-oriented, and characterized by significant nonverbal communication (Hale-Benson, 1981). Children who speak a dialect of English, rather than Standard English, actually may be effective and powerful communicators in their own neighborhoods. Teachers who are not sensitive to the needs, customs, and values of families from diverse cultures and who are not able to communicate, through both parental and curricular avenues, an appreciation and valuing of this cultural diversity miss opportunities for growth and learning for children, parents, and teachers.

Another demographic change in the United States has resulted in a larger number of families with young children living in poverty. About 24 percent of all children—46 percent of Black children, 40 percent of Hispanic children, 19 percent of Asian–American children, 41 percent of Native American children, and 16 percent of White children—live in poverty (Children's Defense Fund, 1997; Corcoran & Chaudry, 1997). Among all children, 35 percent of Black children, 25 percent of Hispanic children, 20 percent of Asian–American children, 24 percent of Native American children, and 21 percent of White children live in families where no parent is employed (Children's Defense Fund, 1997). For these families, additional services are essential, such as book- and toy-lending libraries, health and medical care, affordable housing, job training, and other social services. Although early childhood educators will not be providing all of these services, they must advocate for the availability of economic and social-service supports as well as provide information and make referrals to help address the complex needs of families in poverty. Some programs may employ a family services director, or give the responsibility to another staff member, who identifies needs and makes referrals to appropriate agencies.

Other demographic changes have resulted in an increased number of children living in single-parent families. Divorce and births to unmarried women, particularly teenage mothers, have resulted in 27 percent of the preschool population living with one parent (Children's Defense Fund, 1997). Another recent social change is the increased number of children who live with a single father as well as gay and lesbian couples who either adopt or who have custody of children from an earlier marriage. Increasing numbers of children also live with grandparents—1.4 million, an increase of 66 percent in only six years—and with foster parents—almost a half million children, a 16 percent increase in just four years (Children's Defense Fund, 1997). These living arrangements create the need for teachers to understand and learn to work with many different individuals—including single parents, dual-career parents, stepparents, foster parents, grandparents, and same-gender parents—who are filling a parenting role.

Escobedo (1983) has suggested some special cultural, educational, and economic considerations to remember when working with a culturally diverse parent group and with families of various structures:

1. With what cultural background do parents identify, and what terminology do they prefer (for example, Chicano or Mexican–American)?
2. What language is primarily spoken in the child's home? Do the parents feel comfortable speaking English?
3. What is the reading level of the parents? In what language should letters to parents be written?
4. Does the child live with one or both parents? Are there other adults living in the household who function in a parent role?
5. Do all parents living with the child work outside the home? When would it be most convenient to

schedule a parent conference? Can they take time off from work? Is transportation a problem? (p. 117)

These demographic and cultural changes point to the critical need to include parents as partners in promoting positive values about diversity. A rationale for including families in multicultural learning is based on the following concepts:

1. The early childhood years are the most influential period for influencing children's development of cultural understanding, attitudes, and perspectives.
2. Parents are the most powerful models, guides, and designers of children's social and cultural experiences.
3. Teachers' use of parent and family involvement strategies is highly influential in promoting multicultural learning (Swick, Boutte, & Van Scoy, 1994, p. 17).

Parents are cultural role models for children and influence their cultural perspectives by nurturing positive attitudes about racial, ethnic, cultural, and developmental diversity. Teachers who focus on parents' strengths help families and children explore their own culture and develop the confidence to share aspects of their culture with others in the program. Reciprocal communication between teachers and parents is a critical factor in creating an anti-bias, culturally diverse curriculum. Teachers and parents can support each other's efforts to broaden their cultural knowledge and can share decision making about promoting children's multicultural learning. Together, parents and teachers can support children as they become sensitive, aware, and positive members of a diverse community (Swick et al., 1994).

Parent participation is essential for optimal development of children because it integrates the experiences of home with the experiences in early childhood programs. It is the responsibility of the program to develop or strengthen a positive working relationship with parents so that children's optimal development can occur. Parent participation promotes and supports children's learning and development and enables the growth and development of parents and teachers in a mutually beneficial and reinforcing environment.

■   ■   ■   ■   ■   ■   ■   ■   ■

Gustavo and his mother clearly need your assistance to help resolve the conflict surrounding their morning separation. It appears that Gustavo's mother is not comfortable dis-

cussing this issue with you, so it is your responsibility to approach her and communicate in a manner that will help alleviate her anxiety and lead to a solution of the problem. Clear communication and positive relationships with parents are a critical component of the invisible curriculum.

Approach Gustavo's mother during one of your daily interactions in the afternoon to express your concern about the difficulty Gustavo is having with separation. Make sure this brief discussion takes place in a private place and is confidential. Avoid approaching Gustavo's mother in the morning when she is upset over leaving her child. If you have difficulty arranging a time to discuss this issue during the afternoon hours, make a telephone call during the day to arrange a time to talk informally.

Be calm and reassuring as you discuss this issue with Gustavo's mother. Because this is clearly a difficult problem for the mother, you probably will want to schedule a special parent conference right away.

During the parent conference, be prepared to listen empathically to Gustavo's mother and assure her that separation anxiety is a common developmental issue for children of this age. Also reassure Gustavo's mother by giving examples of how quickly he recovers from his crying after she leaves and how he continues to enjoy playing during the day. Together,

decide on strategies to help Gustavo's mother remain in control of the separation time by being calm and reassuring to Gustavo and leaving the classroom promptly.

Determine procedures for communicating with Gustavo's mother that will help her cope with this stage in Gustavo's development. You may encourage her to telephone you after she reaches work in the morning so you can report on Gustavo's well-being after she leaves. You will want to communicate both verbally and with written notes each day about Gustavo's progress. It will also be helpful to regularly send home hug notes, reassuring Gustavo's mother that he has many enjoyable experiences during the day. Finally, schedule a follow-up parent conference to discuss progress.

Because the issue of separation anxiety is a common one for parents of infants, you may want to plan a parent meeting to discuss it with the entire group of parents. This meeting can offer important information to parents, as well as provide a forum for discussion and reassurances for your families.

■   ■   ■   ■   ■   ■   ■   ■

CHAPTER SUMMARY _____

Parent participation in the early childhood program benefits children, parents, and teachers. Establishing and encouraging this partnership with parents is important because of the large numbers of children in nonparental care and the value of cooperation and continuity between the home and the early childhood education program for children's learning. Pre-enrollment conferences, daily interactions, parent visits, parent conferences, newsletters, bulletin boards, "hug" notes, parent meetings and resource centers all help to support, educate, and share information with parents. A special challenge occurs when families experience crisis, such as divorce, violence, or having children with chronic illness or disabilities. The diversity of parent groups requires teachers to understand and be sensitive to special cultural, educational, and economic concerns of parents.

DISCUSSION QUESTIONS _____

1. Discuss the vignette at the beginning of the chapter. What other questions or concerns might you have? Discuss the vignette at the end of the chapter. Are there other responses you might have to this situation?

2. Discuss the value to parents, to children, and to programs and staff of parents' interest and participation in their child's early childhood program.

3. What factors have contributed to renewed or increased emphasis on parental involvement in early childhood programs?

4. Describe the information that is shared and discussed in a pre-enrollment conference. What other information might be included for special programs or populations?

5. What behaviors or activities other than those listed in the chapter support parents working as volunteers in a center?

6. Why are daily interactions among teachers and parents so important in early childhood programs?

7. Describe strategies for an effective parent conference.

8. How can teachers support families experiencing various kinds of family stress?

REFERENCES _____

Association for the Care of Children's Health. (1990). *Family-centered care for children with HIV infection: A checklist for early childhood programs.* Bethesda, MD: Author.

Berger, E. H. (1991). *Parents as partners in education: The school and home working together* (3rd ed.). Columbus, OH: Merrill/Macmillan.

Bjorklund, G., & Burger, C. (1987). Making conferences work for parents, teachers, and children. *Young Children, 42*(2), 26–31.

Boutte, G., Keepler, D., Tyler, V., & Terry, B. (1992). Effective techniques for involving "difficult" parents. *Young Children, 47*(3), 19–22.

Brand, S. (1996). Making parent involvement a reality: Helping teachers develop partnerships with parents. *Young Children, 51*(2), 76–81.

Chan, S. (1986). Parents of exceptional Asian children. In M. K. Kitano & P. C. Chinn (Eds.), *Exceptional Asian children and youth* (pp. 36–53). Reston, VA: Council for Exceptional Children.

Children's Defense Fund. (1997). *The state of America's children.* Washington, DC: Author.

Chinn, P., Winn, J., & Walters, R. (1978). *Two-way talking with parents of special children: A process of positive communication.* St. Louis, MO: Mosby.

Coleman, M. (1997). Families and schools: In search of common ground. *Young Children, 52*(5), 14–21.

Corcoran, M., & Chaudry, A. (1997). The dynamics of childhood poverty. *The Future of Children: Children and Poverty, 7*(2), 40–53.

Croft, D. J. (1979). *Parents and teachers: A resource book for home, school and community relations.* Belmont, CA: Wadsworth.

Escobedo, T. (1983). Parent and community involvement: A blueprint for a successful program. In O. Saracho & B. Spodek (Eds.), *Understanding the multicultural experience in early childhood education* (pp. 107–122). Washington, DC: National Association for the Education of Young Children.

Fauvre, M. (1988). Including young children with "new" chronic illness in an early childhood education setting. *Young Children, 43*(6), 71–77.

Finkelhor, D. (1994). Current information on the scope and nature of child sexual abuse. *The Future of Children: Sexual Abuse of Children, 4*(2), 31–53.

Fontana, V., & Schneider, C. (1978). Help for abusing parents. In L. E. Arnold (Ed.), *Helping parents help their children* (pp. 259–269). New York: Brunner/Mazel.

Galinsky, E. (1988). Parents and teacher-caregivers: Sources of tension, sources of support. *Young Children, 43*(3), 4–12.

Hale-Benson, J. (1981). Black children: Their roots, culture, and learning styles. *Young Children, 36*(2), 37–50.

Hanson, M., Lynch, E., & Wayman, L. (1990). Honoring the cultural diversity of families when gathering data. *Topics in Early Childhood Special Education, 10*(1), 112–131.

Hauser-Cram, P. (1986). Backing away helpfully: Some roles that teachers shouldn't fill. *Beginnings, 3*(1), 18–20.

Hofferth, S. (1996). Child care in the United States today. *The Future of Children: Financing Child Care, 6*(2), 41–61.

Kids Count data book. (1997). Baltimore: The Annie E. Casey Foundation.

Moses, K., & Dreidler, K. (1981). Bridging the gaps training manual. Chicago: Association for Retarded Citizens.

Powell, D. (1989a). *Families and early childhood programs.* Washington, DC: National Association for the Education of Young Children.

Powell, D. (1989b). Toward a socioecological perspective of relations between parents and child care programs. In S. Kilmer (Ed.), *Advances in early education and daycare* (Vol. 1, pp. 203–226). New York: JAI Press.

Schetky, D. (1988). Treatment of the sexually abused child. In D. Schetky & A. Green (Eds.), *Child sexual abuse: A handbook for health care professionals* (pp. 193–208). New York: Brunner/Mazel.

Skeen, P., & McKenry, P. (1986). The teacher's role in facilitating a child's adjustment to divorce. In J. McCracken (Ed.), *Reducing stress in young children's lives* (pp. 64–69). Washington, DC: National Association for the Education of Young Children.

Swick, K., Boutte, G., & Van Scoy, I. (1994). Multicultural learning through family involvement. *Dimensions, 22*(4), 17–21.

Workman, S., & Gage, J. (1997). Family-school partnerships: A family strengths approach. *Young Children, 52*(4), 10–14.

ADDITIONAL RESOURCES _____

Bailey, D., Simeonsson, R., Winton, P., Huntington, G., Comfort, M., Isbell, P., O'Donnell, K., & Helm, J. (1986). Family-focused intervention: A functional model for planning, implementing, and evaluating individualized family services in early intervention. *Journal of the Division for Early Childhood, 10*(2), 156–171.

Barber, P., Turnbull, A., Behr, S., & Kerns, G. (1988). A family systems perspective on early childhood special education. In S. Odom & M. Karnes (Eds.), *Early intervention for infants and children with handicaps* (pp. 179–198). Baltimore: Brookes.

Brazelton, T. B. (1983). *Working and caring.* Reading, MA: Addison-Wesley.

Briggs, N., Jalongo, M., & Brown, L. (1997). Working with families of young children: Our history and our future goals. In J. Isenberg & M. Jalongo (Eds.), *Major trends and issues in early childhood education* (pp. 56–70). New York: Teachers College Press.

Brock, D., & Dodd, E. (1994). A family lending library: Promoting early literacy development. *Young Children, 49*(3), 16–21.

Bundy, B. (1991). Fostering communication between parents and preschools. *Young Children, 46*(2), 12–17.

Cataldo, C. (1987). *Parent education for early childhood.* New York: Teachers College Press.

Caulfield, R. (1996). Partnership with families. *Early Childhood Education Journal, 24*(2), 125–128.

Coleman, M. (1991). Planning for the changing nature of family life in schools for young children. *Young Children, 46*(4), 15–20.

Cryer, D., & Burchinal, M. (1997). Parents as child care consumers. *Early Childhood Research Quarterly, 12,* 35–38.

Cunningham, B. (1994). Portraying fathers and other men in the curriculum. *Young Children, 49*(6), 4–13.

Davies, D. (1997). Crossing boundaries: How to create successful partnerships with families and communities. *Early Childhood Education Journal, 25*(1), 73–78.

Delpit, L. (1988). The silenced dialogue: Power and pedagogy in educating other people's children. *Harvard Educational Review, 58*(8), 280–298.

Delpit, L. (1995). *Other people's children: Cultural conflict in the classroom.* New York: New Press.

Derezotes, D., & Snowden, L. (1990). Cultural factors in the intervention of child maltreatment. *Child and Adolescent Social Work, 7*(2), 161–175.

Diffily, D., & Morrison, K. (Eds.). (1996). *Family-friendly communication for early childhood programs.* Washington, DC: National Association for the Education of Young Children.

Fitzgerald, L., & Goncu, A. (1993). Parent involvement in urban early childhood education: A Vygotskian approach. In S. Reifel (Ed.), *Advances in early education and day care: Perspectives on developmentally appropriate practice* (Vol. 5, pp. 197–212). Greenwich, CT: JAI Press.

Foster, S. (1994). Successful parent meetings. *Young Children, 50*(1), 78–80.

Frost, J. (1986). Children in a changing society. *Childhood Education, 62*(4), 242–249.

Gage, J., & Workman, S. (1994). Creating family support systems: In Head Start and beyond. *Young Children, 50*(1), 74–77.

Gonzalez-Mena, J. (1992). Taking a culturally sensitive approach to infant-toddler programs. *Young Children, 47*(2), 4–9.

Gorham, P., & Nason, P. (1997). Why make teachers' work more visible to parents? *Young Children, 52*(5), 22–26.

Greenberg, P. (1989). Parents as partners in young children's development and education: A new American fad? Why does it matter? *Young Children, 44*(4), 61–75.

Greenspan, S., & Greenspan, N. (1989). *The essential partnership.* New York: Penguin.

Halpern, R. (1987). Major social and demographic trends affecting young families: Implications for early childhood care and education. *Young Children, 42*(6), 34–40.

Harding, N. (1996). Family journals: The bridge from school to home and back again. *Young Children, 51*(2), 27–30.

Hasson, J. (1996). Grandparents' day: What to do for children who don't have a grandparent. *Young Children, 51*(3), 28–31.

Honig, A. S. (1979). *Parent involvement in early childhood education.* Washington, DC: National Association of the Education of Young Children.

Jacobs, N. (1992). Unhappy endings. *Young Children, 47*(3), 23–27.

Joffe, C. (1977). *Friendly intruders: Childcare professionals and family life.* Berkeley, CA: University of California Press.

Jones, I., White, C., Aeby, V., & Benson, B. (1997). Attitudes of early childhood teachers toward family and community involvement. *Early Education and Development, 8*(2), 153–168.

Knitzer, J., & Page, S. (1996). Young children and families: The view from the States. *Young Children, 51*(4), 51–55.

Lewis, E. (1996). What mother? What father? *Young Children, 51*(3), 27.

Lightfoot, S. (1978). *Worlds apart: Relationships between families and schools.* New York: Basic Books.

Manning, D., & Schindler, P. (1997). Communicating with parents when their children have difficulties. *Young Children, 52*(5), 27–33.

McBride, B. (1989). Interaction, accessibility, and responsibility: A view of father involvement and how to encourage it. *Young Children, 44*(5), 13–19.

McBride, B., & Raine, T. (1997). Father/male involvement in early childhood programs: Issues and challenges. *Early Childhood Education Journal, 25*(1), 11–16.

Montanari, E. (1993). Keeping families happy: Communication is the key. *Child Care Information Exchange, 90*(3), 21–23.

Morgan, E. (1989). Talking with parents when concerns come up. *Young Children, 44*(2), 52–56.

Neugebauer, R. (1982, September/October). Tips on publishing a center newsletter. *Child Care Information Exchange,* pp. 26–31.

National Center for Children in Poverty. (1990). *Five million children: A statistical profile of our poorest young citizens.* New York: Author.

Phillips, C. (1988). Nurturing diversity for today's children and tomorrow's leaders. *Young Children, 43*(2), 42–47.

Powell, D., Batsche, C., Ferro, J., Fox, L., & Dunlap, G. (1997). A strength-based approach in support of multi-risk families: Principles and issues. *Topics in Early Childhood Special Education, 17*(1), 1–26.

Printz, P. (1996). Enhancing collaboration for all our children and families. *Journal of Early Intervention, 20*(1), 14–15.

Rosenberg, S., & Robinson, C. (1988). Interactions of parents with their young handicapped children. In S. L. Odom & M. B. Karnes (Eds.), *Early intervention for infants and children with handicaps* (pp. 159–177). Baltimore: Brookes.

Stipek, D., Rosenblatt, L., & DiRocco, L. (1994). Making parents your allies. *Young Children, 49*(3), 4–9.

Stone, J. (1987). *Teacher-parent relationships.* Washington, DC: National Association for the Education of Young Children.

Stroud, J., Stroud, J., & Staley, L. (1997). Understanding and supporting adoptive families. *Early Childhood Education Journal, 24*(4), 229–234.

Sturm, C. (1997). Creating parent-teacher dialogue: Intercultural communication in child care. *Young Children, 52*(5), 34–38.

Swick, K., & McKnight, S. (1989). Characteristics of kindergarten teachers who promote parent involvement. *Early Childhood Research Quarterly, 4*(1), 19–29.

Turnbull, A., & Turnbull, H. R. (1985). *Parents speak out: Then and now* (2nd ed.). Columbus, OH: Merrill/Macmillan.

6.

Classroom Management and Guidance

After a period of several weeks you notice that Lin, a 3-year-old, has become increasingly aggressive in her interactions with other children in the preschool classroom. Lin's behavior has been characterized recently by a refusal to share materials and by hitting and pinching when other children attempt to enter her play space. This is a dramatic change in Lin's behavior, and it is having a negative impact on the classroom environment.

After discussing the change in Lin's behavior with her parents, you realize there have been no significant changes in her home environment that would account for this dramatic change in behavior. At this point, it is imperative that you analyze your relationship with Lin and the appropriateness of the classroom management and guidance procedures you have been using.

- What is the first step in analyzing and addressing this problem in behavior management?
- What is the most effective way to work with children engaged in this type of inappropriate behavior?
- What skills can you teach children to help them manage their difficulties in peer interaction and to guide their own behavior?
- Are there ways you could have prevented the inappropriate behavior?
- Will you need to involve the parents further in analyzing and responding to this change in behavior?

Suggestions for responding to this classroom vignette will be shared at the end of the chapter.

When reading this chapter, focus on understanding the importance of a supportive classroom environment that includes specific goals for guidance that are clearly communicated to children. Also, become aware of the specific techniques for fostering positive interactions among children and managing behavior, such as ignoring minor annoyances, praising effort and accomplishment, redirecting children from misbehavior, using natural and logical consequences, teaching conflict resolution skills, and implementing a sit-and-watch procedure. Designing growth-promoting guidance strategies is an important component of the creative-play curriculum.

Decisions about classroom management are among the most important that a teacher makes. Policies and practices related to guidance can (1) prevent or reduce behavior and management problems, (2) allow humane and growth-promoting responses to children's misbehavior when it occurs, (3) support the classroom instructional and learning climate, and (4) enhance children's self-esteem, develop their ability to take responsibility and make decisions, help them develop self-control and self-discipline, and provide a model of appropriate conflict resolution.

Effective policies and practices for classroom management and guidance arise from the teacher's philosophy of early childhood education, much in the same way that decisions about teaching strategies and activities do. Decisions about policies for guidance must be carefully considered and developed prior to interacting with children. Growth-promoting guidance, a component of the invisible curriculum, is necessary to teach and interact in a positive, humane manner. Based on the philosophical tenets of the creative-play curriculum, the following guidelines will help teachers develop responsive, effective, and developmentally appropriate guidance strategies.

DEVELOPING GOALS FOR GUIDANCE

An initial step in developing a plan for guidance is for teachers to determine in advance the goals they want to achieve through classroom management. Simply reducing occurrences of misbehavior is only one goal of good guidance. Other important objectives are to (1) help children learn strategies for self-control and self-discipline; (2) meet children's needs for support, nurturing, and protection balanced with the teacher's needs for structure, control, and flexibility; (3) enhance or support children's self-esteem; (4) help children develop their own skills for resolving conflicts and making peace; and (5) support the curriculum by providing a positive and productive learning environment. These goals are met when teachers choose strategies for guidance rather than punishment. "Children who are punished feel humiliated, hide their mistakes, have a poor self-concept, and fail to develop inner controls to handle future problems. Children who are disciplined learn to balance their needs with those of other people, feel good about themselves, and become increasingly independent" (Miller, 1984, p. 15). These comprehensive goals for classroom guidance reflect the interrelated nature of children's development as well as the positive, integrated focus of the creative-play curriculum.

A guidance approach to children's behavior requires that teachers reconsider the meaning of the term *misbehavior.* Gartrell (1995) has offered a new perspective— that teachers should consider children's inappropriate behavior as "mistaken behavior" instead of misbehavior. His reconsideration is based on the work of Rudolf Dreikurs (1968) and Steven Harlow (1975). Dreikurs proposed that children behave in ways that gain them social acceptance. Children misbehave to get attention, to seek power, to seek revenge, and to display inadequacy— all inappropriate ways to gain social acceptance. Harlow's work contributed the idea that children often make mistakes in the ways they seek social approval and acceptance. Instead of traditional guidance, which "punishes children for having problems they cannot solve, . . . guidance teaches children to solve their problems in socially acceptable ways" (Gartrell, 1995, p. 27). To do this, teachers must view children's behavior as a mistake occurring because of problems in one of three relational patterns: encountering, adjustment, and survival.

Children at the first stage, *encountering,* are experimenting, exploring, and engaging in the discovery and construction of new knowledge. Teachers in Piagetian, constructivist classrooms encourage children's exploration and experimentation. When this behavior results in a "mistake," teachers provide guidance that accepts the child's striving for learning and new knowledge, but also helps the child to avoid repeating the same behavior—that is, making the same mistake. For example, a child who is building a block tower to see how many blocks he can construct and in what pattern he can construct without it collapsing may inadvertently cause blocks to fall into the play space of, or onto, another child. Teacher guidance in the form of pointing out natural consequences of a tower that is too high and reminding the child of the classroom rule that children build towers not higher than they are tall helps the child to avoid repeating the mistake.

The second level of mistaken behavior is *adjustment.* Children's behavior is often socially influenced, and they adjust their behavior based on the responses of others. Parents, teachers, peers, and others who are significant in the child's life are models and influences on the child's behavior. Children learn mistaken behavior by imitating others and having this behavior reinforced by others. The child who builds a block tower so high that it collapses onto others with the goal of gaining attention or approval can be helped to find other, more appropriate ways to interact with other children that will enhance his self-esteem and meet his needs for attention and approval.

The third level of mistaken behavior, *survival,* is related to the child's needs for safety and security in an environment that may threaten the child's physical and emotional well-being and even survival. Children with a survival relational pattern often have very deep pain and suffering that requires more than teacher guidance. "As Harlow suggests, strong-needs mistaken behavior results from psychological and/or physical pain in the child's life that is beyond the child's ability to cope with and understand. Often children show strong-needs mistaken behavior in the classroom because it is a safe haven in their environment. . . . These children are asking for help in the only way they can" (Gartrell, 1995, p. 30). If a teacher determines that the child building the block tower is deliberate in his attempt to hurt other children, the teacher must respond to the child's behavior with logical consequences and to the child's deep-seated pain and hostility with attempts to provide physical safety and emotional support. Often there is much in the child's environment—whatever is causing the pain and psychological harm—that must be addressed and changed.

SETTING REALISTIC EXPECTATIONS

Effective teachers of young children understand the developmental process and acknowledge the differences in individual rates of development. Clearly, developmental level affects behavior, interactions with the environment, and relationships with peers and teachers. It is important for teachers to use children's developmental age to help determine whether their behavior is appropriate. For example, a 4-year-old who is at a 2-year-old developmental level will be less verbal, have fewer problem-solving skills, and be more likely to express frustration, fatigue, or fear in less-mature ways than most 4-year-olds. Teachers should have realistic expectations based on developmental age rather than chronological age and respond with developmentally appropriate and growth-promoting guidance strategies.

PREVENTING MISBEHAVIOR

An important step in developing a plan for guidance is to determine ways to prevent behavior problems. A classroom that is well-designed and well-organized can eliminate or reduce management problems and suggest to children appropriate behaviors and use of the environment. For example, an art center should be located away from the traffic flow and areas with high mobility. It should be organized so that supplies are accessible and should be arranged to suggest sequential steps in the process (for example, put on apron, put paper on table, get paint jars, return supplies, hang up apron). This arrangement can prevent or reduce behavior problems caused by children waiting until an adult is available to supply art materials.

Also, the room arrangement has consequences for children with disabilities. For example, suppose a child who uses a wheelchair is instructed to return the blocks to a shelf before leaving the block area. The shelf is inaccessible to the child, so the child begins to toss the blocks onto the shelf and is reprimanded for breaking the rule about throwing materials. Instead, the teacher should rearrange the block area so the child has access to remove or return blocks, or the teacher should give more appropriate and clear instructions: "Jesse, please put away the blocks; ask Michone to put the blocks on the shelf as you hand them to her."

Similarly, a well-planned and well-implemented curriculum can prevent behavior problems that result from a schedule of activities that is not balanced or that is not developmentally appropriate. For example, a schedule that is not balanced (that is, with quiet and active periods, indoor and outdoor play, small-group and large-group activities) or a schedule with activities that are too simple or too complex may create confusion, frustration, and fatigue in young children and result in misbehavior.

Children's misbehavior may also occur as a result of skill deficit. For example, an art activity that involves paper cutting may be too challenging for a child with motor impairments, so the child may begin to throw the scissors or disrupt other children. Instead, the teacher should ask the child to tear the paper while other children are using scissors. In this case, it is the teacher's expectations and activity planning that require modifying, rather than the child's behavior.

CREATING A CLIMATE OF SUPPORT

Another important prerequisite for designing effective guidance strategies is to create a climate of trust, support, and security for young children. Reducing stress in children's environment, respecting children and their abilities and needs, and sharing warm, reciprocal interactions with young children characterize the authentic, responsive teacher. Building positive adult–child relationships involves demonstrating mutual respect, taking time to share enjoyable activities, providing encouragement, and communicating caring through words and actions (Dinkmeyer & McKay, 1982). Using meaningful praise and avoiding sarcasm, threats, and humiliation reinforce a trusting environment.

This climate can only be created if there are reasonable rules and a system to enforce them. Children need the presence of strong, confident teachers who can set and maintain limits fairly and consistently, provide help and intervention when needed, and provide security and protection so children feel supported as they play and learn. When children trust teachers to empathize, to allow them to fail, to give encouragement when they are ready to try again, and to give recognition when they succeed, then the climate exists for children to risk exploration, adventure, and learning (Cherry, 1983).

COMMUNICATING EFFECTIVELY _____

Communication with children is important both in preventing inappropriate behavior and in discussing with children the consequences of their behavior. The following guidelines for communication can help teachers create a trusting climate and avoid behavior problems arising from unclear verbal and nonverbal messages.

Get children's attention before engaging in conversation or making requests. Place yourself at the child's eye level by kneeling or sitting beside the child. Use touching to get and maintain children's attention (Cherry, 1983). Speak quietly to a child: "Maria, I need you to listen to me now." "Savannah, look at me. I need to talk with you." Be sensitive to individual or cultural differences among children. Some children can attend to your message without making eye contact. Avoid trying to get a child's attention by raising your voice. Instead, speak more firmly. Reciprocally, be responsive to children's attempts to appropriately get your attention.

Use language that is developmentally appropriate and easily understood by children. Be aware of the pitch, pace, and tone of your language and the message that these can convey. Communications must be congruent; the content of your message and the tone in which it is delivered must match. Your words must fit your feelings or children will detect insincerity or confusion. If you ask children to put away toys now, do not sound as if the request can be ignored or that you intend to repeat it many times before you expect their response. Or, as you welcome children into your classroom, let your voice show that you are truly happy to see them.

Address your communication to the situation and the child's behavior rather than to the child's character or personality. Do not say "You are mean (or bad or selfish)," but rather "That is an unkind word to call your friend," or "Your playmates don't like it when you scream."

Sometimes children's misbehavior occurs when limits and rules are not clearly explained to children. Examples of unclear or nonspecific messages include the following: "Behave." "It's time to go outside." "This room is a big mess." "Act your age." Children may hear these statements but not be able to determine the request the teacher is intending. Instead, say: "Use gentle touches." "Put on your coat." "We need to put these toys back on the shelf." "Use your words to tell me what you want."

When you use understandable language to describe rules, children are more likely to follow them. Say to children:

"We talk inside."
"We take care of each other here."
"We take care of our materials."
"We use encouraging words with friends."
"We clean up what we use."
"There are some things we only do outside."

Children are also more likely to remember and follow rules when teachers phrase rules and requests using positive language rather than simply stating the prohibition. Children are more likely to understand what to do when teachers use clear, positive phrases, such as the previous examples. In contrast, children will hear only what not to do if you simply say: "Don't yell." "Don't hit." "Don't tear the book." "Don't use unkind words." "Don't mess up the room."

To help children understand and follow rules, teachers should determine guidelines, very few in number, that children can remember or be reminded of with a simple, "Remember the rule?" Other rules necessary for classroom and child management, such as how many children can safely play on a piece of equipment, become guidelines for teachers to follow. These limits may change with different activities, equipment, or room arrangements. Children should not be expected to know the limits but can be told and reminded of these by teachers. Children are confused and frustrated by being expected to remember too many rules. The primary responsibility for protection and guidance of young children lies with adults in the classroom.

Clear communication with children helps to establish a positive climate, prevent inappropriate behavior, and point out consequences of behavior.

RESPONDING TO CHILDREN'S BEHAVIOR _____

When dealing with children's misbehavior, it is important to first determine the reasons for the child's behavior. Often children will cause problems when they are tired, overstimulated, frustrated, ill, hungry, or bored. Their misbehavior is a signal to teachers to identify problems in the curriculum, daily schedule, staffing patterns, or classroom routines and to make appropriate adjustments.

It is important that the methods teachers use to address misbehavior meet children's needs. Often, a teacher's own anger, fatigue, frustration, or need to be in control results in discipline that meets the teacher's needs and ignores the true cause and intention of the child's behavior. Physical punishment, for example, does nothing to enhance children's self-esteem, teach self-control, or reinforce a positive and nurturing relationship between child and adult. It only meets the adult's need to gain control, exhibit power, or release frustration. There is substantial evidence from the social sciences that physical punishment simply does not work and, in fact, is detrimental to the emotional development of children. A look at the short-term and long-term consequences of physical punishment underscores its ineffectiveness:

1. Physical punishment focuses on behavior that is undesirable rather than illustrating socially acceptable behavior, so it does very little to teach children what is acceptable or expected behavior.

2. Contrary to what many adults who use physical punishment believe, children's negative reactions and emotional responses to punishment are more likely to be associated with the person who is the punisher rather than with the behavior for which the child is punished. Because children learn better from adults with whom they have a positive emotional relationship, these negative reactions and emotional responses may actually hinder teaching (Clarizio & Yelon, 1974; LeFrancois, 1992).

3. There is evidence that physical punishment sometimes produces opposite effects to those intended. For example, children who are physically punished for aggressive behavior tend to be more aggressive; children who are punished for bed wetting continue to wet the bed much longer than children whose parents respond in more positive ways. The use of arbitrary punitive strategies is correlated with the highest rates of antisocial behavior and delinquency in adoles-

cents. In addition, some children crave the attention they receive for misbehavior, and, in these cases, punishment actually reinforces and increases the very behavior teachers seek to extinguish (LeFrancois, 1992; Sears, Maccoby, & Lewin, 1957).

4. Physical punishment appears to be effective in changing children's behavior in the short term—children will stop their misbehavior or exhibit desired behavior in the presence of the punisher. But this apparent effectiveness often reinforces and increases the adult's use of punishment to the degree that it becomes harsh, unjust, or abusive.

5. Physical punishment also has been shown to be associated with lowered self-esteem, lower levels of moral reasoning, and fewer acts of prosocial, positive behavior in children (Hoffman, 1970). Children are less likely to seek advice and counsel from adults whom they perceive as being punitive and coercive.

Negative emotional responses, increased misbehavior, and ineffectiveness characterize physical punishment. In addition, many adults feel that there are obvious ethical and humanitarian reasons for not using physical punishment with children. The use of physical punishment is not compatible with the philosophy of this curriculum. NAEYC's accreditation standards (*Accreditation Criteria and Procedures,* 1991) require that teachers avoid using corporal punishment or other humiliating or frightening discipline techniques. In 40 states, the licensing regulations for centers prohibit corporal punishment for some or all age groups of children from infancy to age 5 (NAEYC Information Service, personal communication, January 2, 1992).

Teachers must learn to appropriately handle the anger that often occurs when children are destructive or aggressive toward other children. Expressed constructively, teachers' anger can communicate ideas and feelings, release tension, focus on the child's behavior without degrading the child, and serve as a model for children who are learning how to handle their own angry feelings. When teachers express anger in irrational and destructive ways, they communicate negativity, attack the child rather than the child's behavior, escalate anger in the child, experience guilt or embarrassment, and provide a poor model for children. Teachers should learn and use an "expanded vocabulary" to express anger, such as: "I'm antagonized, bugged, incensed, irked, mortified"

(Cherry, 1983, p. 19). Distinguish between rational and irrational expressions of anger. For example, "You've ruined my whole day. You've upset the whole class." sends the message that the child is bad and has power and control over the emotions of the teacher and other children. Saying, "Please stop that screaming. It annoys me," is a simple and truthful statement that does not degrade the child or demean the teacher. "I" messages are helpful as rational expressions of anger that avoid an accusing tone. Teachers who express their anger appropriately and constructively help children maintain their self-esteem as they learn how to control both their behavior and their angry feelings (Cherry, 1983).

GROWTH-PROMOTING GUIDANCE _____

Some humane, developmentally appropriate, and growth-promoting strategies that are effective in guiding children's behavior and that support a creative-play classroom environment are discussed in this section.

Ignore Minor Annoyances

Some children misbehave for the attention they receive for acting out. Ignoring inappropriate attention-seeking behavior is often the most effective strategy for guiding these children to behave appropriately and to be reinforced for that. Teachers should clarify for the child what behavior is inappropriate or ineffective. "When you whine as you talk, I can't understand you. I will listen to you when you talk in your own voice." This helps to avoid sending the message that the child is being rejected by the teacher. After a brief clarification or explanation, the teacher should ignore subsequent occurrences of the behavior. Deliberately ignoring minor annoyances and misbehavior (for example, whining, crying, or tantrum throwing) means not giving *any* reinforcement—that is, not doing anything that the child would perceive as rewarding or reinforcing, which would increase, not decrease, the attention-getting behavior. Do not react to the child's behavior by looking at or saying anything to the child or about the child to another person. Others in the room, both other teachers and children, also should not react emotionally or behaviorally to the child. When the child is behaving or responding in appropriate ways, be sure to encourage and praise the child for the more appropriate and acceptable behavior (Cherry, 1983).

Encourage Children

Pay attention when children are behaving appropriately, doing something difficult, or helping another child. Verbal praise should be sincere and succinct. To express nonverbal praise, make eye contact with the child and smile or nod approval. A hug or pat on the back is another nonverbal demonstration of approval (Cherry, 1983). Praise that is insincere or that is overused, however, may undermine a teacher's attempt to enhance children's self-esteem and to manage children's behavior.

Recent reviews of the pertinent research on the effectiveness of praise suggest that encouragement is more effective than praise with many children and in many circumstances (Brophy, 1981; Hitz & Driscoll, 1988; Seefeldt, 1987). Encouragement enhances children's self-concept, fosters independence and autonomy, motivates children, and guides children to appropriate behavior (Hitz & Driscoll, 1988). Encouragement involves "a positive acknowledgment . . . that focuses on [children's] efforts and/or specific attributes of work completed" (p. 10). Hitz and Driscoll offer the following guidelines for the effective use of encouragement.

1. Encouragement is specific: "Your picture has lots of big, bright circles in it," rather than "Good job."
2. Encouragement is teacher-initiated and generally takes place in private: "I saw the way you worked hard to pick up the blocks before you went outside this morning," rather than "Everyone, look at how hard Steven is working."
3. Encouragement focuses on improving a process rather than evaluating a completed product or task: "You are really working hard on your book," rather than "That is a very nice picture you painted."
4. Encouragement involves sincere, direct comments delivered with a natural voice: "Fatima, your choice of orange and white for the flowers in your picture reminds me of the lilies in my yard," rather than "That is the most beautiful painting I've ever seen."
5. Encouragement helps children to succeed: "Anu, you returned Brian's scissors promptly after you used them, and I'm sure he liked that," rather than "You're always so sweet."

6. Encouragement helps children to appreciate their own behavior and achievements. "You must be very proud of your skipping," rather than "I'm very proud of you."

7. Encouragement avoids comparison or competition among children: "Gina, your tower has good balance because you put the bigger blocks at the base," rather than "Your block structure is the best of all the ones built today" (pp. 10–12).

Redirect Children from Misbehavior

When too many children are attempting to play in one area or when children are beginning to dispute over rights to play with a toy, redirecting one or more children to another activity or area is often the most effective guidance and can prevent escalation of inappropriate behavior. A teacher may say to children, "It appears there are too many children in the loft; it doesn't look safe to me," or "Five children at the puzzle table doesn't give everyone enough work space; one of you needs to choose a book or string beads at the other table now." Such comments help children to recognize that a problem or potential problem exists and suggest appropriate choices for them instead. Offering suggestions or choices, rather than using commands or prohibitions, is more effective in getting children to comply (Honig, 1985a, 1985b). Offering legitimate choices to children, such as "There is not a teacher at the loft now, so you may not climb up; but you can paint or play with blocks or listen to a record," helps to redirect children to appropriate behavior, with an opportunity to foster their independence and decision-making skills (Clemens, 1983).

Discuss Consequences

Consequences that help children develop self-discipline are based on recognition of equality, mutual respect, and order in the classroom. Natural consequences are based on the natural flow of events and are those that take place without adult intervention. For example, when a child tips the tricycle over, the teacher says, "When you make a fast turn with this tricycle, it tips over." The teacher can effectively use the naturally occurring consequences of children's inappropriate or undesirable behavior to help children recognize the relationship between their own behavior and the unfortunate consequences. Logical consequences are structured and arranged by the teacher. They must be considered logical by the child. It is important that the adult verbalize and clarify logical consequences of children's behavior. For example, after a child spills another child's glue during an art activity, the teacher says, "You can share your glue with Taja because she doesn't have any now." Consequences involve a learning process for the child and distinguish between the deed and the doer. The child is accepted, but his or her behavior is not. The teacher must remain objective and be firm yet fair. Discussing consequences with a harsh, negative, or accusing tone makes the strategy punitive. Disciplining is teaching, and it should be done in a calm, supportive, and encouraging manner. The use of consequences allows the child to make decisions and helps the teacher to remain an educator and facilitator, rather than become involved in power struggles with the children.

One specific type of logical consequence is the use of sit-and-watch. When a child can't control his or her behavior, a logical response is to have the child leave the activity until he or she can regain emotional and behavioral control. Sit-and-watch or time-out strategies are appropriate when children are aggressive (for example, hitting, kicking, pushing, spitting, biting) or when they are destructive (for example, throwing materials, destroying toys). The teacher must convey the message that the child does not have a choice (for example, "Taneika, please play without throwing the blocks; you may build with them."). If the child does not comply, the teacher should remove her from the activity or interaction and place her in sit-and-watch. First, the teacher must explain to the child why she is in sit-and-watch (for example, "You are in sit-and-watch because you hit Maury. We take care of our friends. I won't let children be hurt here. Children who play without hurting their friends are allowed to play."). The explanation is important, so that children do not perceive the teacher's anger or frustration rather than their own behavior as the reason for being in sit-and-watch.

After the child has watched the other children for a short time (no more than three to five minutes), briefly explain again and discuss with the child the reason sit-and-watch was used before she returns to the activity: "Do you feel calm enough now to play again?" "Do you understand that blocks are for building, not for throwing, and can you use them in a safe way now? If you can do that, you may return to the group." This teaches the child to monitor her own feelings, allows her to help determine the length of sit-and-watch, and facilitates teacher–child discussion of feelings and behavior. Once the child is engaged in the activity, praise and encourage appropriate behavior. In this way the child does not feel threatened or humiliated and is able to learn appropriate behaviors. Sit-and-watch is used after other strategies have proved ineffective (except for instances of aggression or destruction, in which sit-and-watch is used immediately); thus, the sit-and-watch strategy will not be used as often as other methods. In Figure 6-1 a sample sit-and-watch chart records uses of the technique and children's reactions (that is, the effectiveness or lack of effectiveness). The chart is used to gather information about the pattern of a child's behavior over time and about teachers' frequency of use of the sit-and-watch technique. The primary misuse of sit-and-watch is that it is used to respond to behaviors that are best addressed by other methods. Sit-and-watch must appear to the child to be a logical response to the misbehavior, one that helps to teach more appropriate behavior rather than be a punitive strategy to control the child and relieve the teacher's anger. If sit-and-watch is used too often, it suggests that changes in the environment—space arrangement, materials, staffing patterns, teacher expectations, or teacher–child interactions—should be made to reduce conflict and misbehavior. Another misuse is having a specific sit-and-watch location, such as a designated chair. This becomes punitive because it appears to "display" the child. Instead, simply remove the child from the activity or interaction to a nearby location from which the child can observe the continuing, appropriate behaviors of the other children (Clewett, 1988).

In some situations, particularly involving child-to-child aggression or destruction of materials, a teacher may need to help a child calm down. Holding the arms of a child who is hitting or holding the legs of a child who is kicking is sometimes helpful with a child who has lost control. "I will help you get calm. Let me help you stop kicking. We can talk when you are ready." Physical restraint should be done in a supportive, positive way. A teacher who is harsh and punitive will only escalate the child's anger and length of outburst.

Teach Conflict Resolution

When conflict occurs, children and adults need to know how to resolve it peacefully and without displaying negative behaviors. Conflict resolution is an opportunity for children to evaluate what caused the disagreement and to find ways to resolve future problems before they create conflict; discussing the situation helps children learn to talk about their feelings and solve their own problems with the support of each other and an adult (Cherry, 1983). "Teaching children to describe their own emotions and motives, to listen empathetically to what others have to say and [resolve differences] are among the most important skills teachers can impart" (p. 147).

In a conflict situation, teachers should encourage children to talk about their ideas and emotions, listen to the ideas and feelings of the other child, then discuss what each child wants. The final step is agreeing on a mutually satisfying plan. Teachers can model or prompt questions or statements that let children substitute words and discussion for physical conflict (Cherry, 1983). For example, when two children begin to fight over the use of a toy and their argument is not leading to a resolution of the conflict, the teacher can help them find effective words with a series of questions and statements:

"Alex, what is it you want?"

"Ted, what do you want?"

"Alex, what does Ted want?"

"Ted, what is Alex asking for?"

"I see you both want the trike."

"Alex, how do you think Ted feels about wanting the trike and not getting to play with it?"

"Ted, how do you think Alex feels?"

"Can you think of a way you both could feel happy instead of angry? Can you come up with a plan so both of you could use the trike before we go inside?"

Gradually children will carry on discussions and resolve conflicts with less and less help. Learning conflict resolution skills helps children to become effective communicators and creative problem solvers.

In unusual cases in which preventive techniques, consequences, conflict resolution, and sit-and-watch are not effective, parents and teachers should agree on an alternative plan. Behavior management for some children may require using play therapy, behavior modification, or cognitive modification strategies. In many cases, teachers select and adapt strategies depending upon the individual needs and circumstances of a child. A combination of strategies may be used with children who have limited language comprehension, verbal skills, or cognitive abilities. As important as the specific technique is, the process teachers use to arrive at the best decision about appropriate guidance is more critical. Information from multiple sources—parents, teachers, the director—about the child's behavior, development, and special circumstances should be used to develop a strategy or combination of strategies that conveys concern and respect for the child, fosters self-control, and allows for positive, growth-promoting teacher–child interactions.

Sit and Watch Record

Date	Time	Child	Reason for Sit and Watch	Child's Reaction	Teacher's Initials
10/5	10:05	Chris	Hit peer during group time	Screamed & kicked	MR
10/5	11:30	Chris	Tackled peer outside	Complied	MR
10/7	10:45	Chris	Hit another child with toy	Cried & talked about his feelings	CH
10/8	9:30	Chris	Tackled peer	Complied	MR
10/8	10:15	Chris	Threw block at peer	Cried	EK
10/10	11:10	Chris	Pushed peer off of tricycle outside	Ran away from teacher	AB
10/13	9:15	Chris	Pinched a peer	Screamed & threw a chair	CH
10/13	10:00	Chris	Scratched peer on the back during group time	Complied	AB
10/13	11:20	Chris	Tackled peer outside	Complied	EK
10/15	11:05	Chris	Hit teacher	Ran away from teacher	MR
10/16	10:25	Chris	Pushed peer down	Screamed & knocked over a trashcan	CH

Figure 6-1 Sample sit-and-watch chart.

Teachers who encourage conflict resolution help children learn to talk about their feelings and solve their problems.

Children who have special circumstances in their lives, such as physical or emotional abuse, physical or behavioral limitations caused by a disability, or overly stressed families in which children's healthy development is not a primary concern, need authentic, responsive teachers who are aware of the many difficulties confronting the child. Children who hurt inside, who feel broken, unsure, and afraid, are often children who lash out at others and exhibit aggressive or other inappropriate behaviors. It is essential that teachers respond to the hurt and pain of these children as well as to their needs for growth-promoting guidance, a physically and psychologically safe environment that fosters the development of trust, and opportunities to develop self-discipline. Teachers must be sensitive to the whole child and the child's total environment and should individualize guidance strategies to meet the needs of each child.

MAKING EFFECTIVE DECISIONS ABOUT GUIDANCE _____

Decisions about classroom management and guidance help teachers foster a warm and humane learning environment, provide support and security to young children, reduce or manage behavior problems, and meet the goals of a creative-play curriculum. For children, the benefits of growth-promoting guidance are even more valuable and long-lasting. For example, children who understand the consequences of their behavior for others and empathize with the physical or emotional hurt of another person have been found to have higher levels of moral-reasoning skills. Similarly, children who understand the rationale and need for rules in a classroom or society are more likely to internalize a rule system and thus develop true self-discipline (Hoffman, 1970).

In addition, teachers who demonstrate and encourage peaceful, nonaggressive conflict resolution are helping children learn important skills for living in a society in which violence or the threat of violence is an unfortunate but common experience. Like children, teachers often feel helpless and frustrated in response to living in a violent society. Early childhood educators have been encouraged to take action (Day, 1982), and one strategy is to begin by teaching young children peaceful solutions to conflict. Early childhood educators would agree with Gandhi's claim that "If we are to teach real peace in this world and if we are to carry on a real war against war, we shall have to begin with the children" (Allen & Pettit, 1987).

■   ■   ■   ■   ■   ■   ■   ■   ■

Determining a plan for classroom management and guidance that meets the needs of children and teachers is a crucial component of the invisible curriculum and preparing to teach effectively. In this situation, a necessary first step is to discover the reasons for Lin's misbehavior.

Evaluate your own teaching strategies for having realistic expectations, providing a supportive climate, and using clear communication.

Determine whether you are responding appropriately to Lin's misbehavior by using the following techniques consistently:

ignoring minor annoyances, praising efforts, redirecting, discussing consequences, teaching conflict resolution skills, and using sit-and-watch.

As you evaluate your teaching behavior and response to Lin, you realize that the negative behavior has been established. What probably began as Lin having a day or two of unusually negative behavior has become a cycle because of your response. You have responded negatively to Lin's behavior and have not been supportive and encouraging enough to her in the last several weeks.

By keeping a record of your use of sit-and-watch with Lin, you realize that in your frustration you have been using sit-and-watch too frequently and this also has escalated the negative behavior pattern. Also, you have neglected to teach conflict resolution skills to help Lin learn to express her feelings to her peers rather than to react with aggressive behavior.

Upon further discussion with Lin's parents, you find that they also have reacted to the change in Lin's behavior by being more negative and punitive than usual. Although you still cannot determine what caused the behavior change initially, you and the parents are able to decide together to be more positive and encouraging with Lin and help her to break this negative cycle.

By teaching conflict resolution skills to Lin, you can help her to solve her own problems with less adult intervention. This allows her the opportunity to learn and to practice a strategy that is so important to successful social relationships. The use of these positive methods promotes more constructive, appropriate behavior and does not result in negative behavior patterns. Children are helped to make decisions, observe the consequences of their actions, and take responsibility for their own behavior, and they are treated with respect by teachers.

■   ■   ■   ■   ■   ■   ■   ■   ■

CHAPTER SUMMARY _____

Guidance helps prevent and reduce children's misbehavior and mistaken behavior, supports growth-promoting teacher–child interactions, promotes a positive environment for learning, and increases children's self-esteem as they learn self-control. Effective guidance strategies include having realistic expectations for children's behavior, preventing misbehavior through appropriate curriculum and classroom organization, and giving clear instructions and communica-

tion. Physical punishment is neither growth-promoting nor appropriate. It models undesirable behavior, creates negative emotions, often produces opposite results to those intended, can become overly punitive and abusive, and can decrease children's self-esteem and positive behavior. Positive, effective, growth-promoting guidance includes ignoring minor annoyances, praising and encouraging, redirecting, discussing consequences, and teaching conflict resolution.

DISCUSSION QUESTIONS _____

1. Discuss the vignette at the beginning of the chapter. What other questions or concerns might you have? Discuss the vignette at the end of the chapter. Are there other responses you might have to this situation?

2. How do guidance practices support teaching effectiveness?

3. List goals that positive guidance can help to accomplish.

4. Discuss ways in which inappropriate behavior might be prevented.

5. Explain mistaken behavior and appropriate teacher responses to aggression or name-calling at each of the three levels of mistaken behavior.

6. Discuss examples of rules and examples of limits.

7. List or describe teacher behaviors that would not be permitted by licensing requirements in your state.

8. Explain why physical punishment is ineffective.

9. Contrast the use of encouragement with the use of praise.

10. Discuss the appropriate use and possible misuses of ignoring, redirecting, discussing consequences, teaching conflict resolution, and sit-and-watch.

REFERENCES _____

Accreditation criteria and procedures of the National Academy of Early Childhood Programs. (1991). Washington, DC: National Association for the Education of Young Children.

Allen, J., & Pettit, R. (1987). Mighty Mouse and MX missiles: Children in a violent society. *Day Care and Early Education, 15*(1), 5–7.

Brophy, J. (1981). Teacher praise: A functional analysis. *Review of Educational Research, 41*(1), 5–33.

Cherry, C. (1983). *Please don't sit on the kids: Alternatives to punitive discipline.* Belmont, CA: Fearon Pitman.

Clarizio, H., & Yelon, S. (1974). Learning theory approaches to classroom management: Rationale and intervention techniques. In A. R. Brown & C. Avery (Eds.), *Modifying children's behavior: A book of readings* (pp. 44–56). Springfield, IL: Thomas.

Clemens, S. (1983). *The sun's not broken, a cloud's just in the way: On child-centered teaching.* Mt. Rainier, MD: Gryphon House.

Clewett, A. (1988). Guidance and discipline: Teaching young children appropriate behavior. *Young Children, 43*(4), 26–31.

Day, D. (1982). Our response to nuclear madness. *Young Children, 37*(6), 10–12.

Dinkmeyer, D., & McKay, G. (1982). *The parent's handbook: Systematic training for effective parenting (STEP).* Circle Pines, MN: American Guidance Service.

Dreikurs, R. (1968). *Psychology in the classroom* (2nd ed.). New York: Harper & Row.

Gartrell, D. (1994). *A guidance approach to discipline.* Albany: Delmar.

Gartrell, D. (1995). Misbehavior or mistaken behavior. *Young Children, 50*(5), 27–34.

Harlow, S. (1975). *Special education: The meeting of differences.* Grand Forks, ND: University of North Dakota.

Hitz, R., & Driscoll, A. (1988). Praise or encouragement? New insights into praise: Implications for early childhood teachers. *Young Children, 43*(5), 6–13.

Hoffman, M. (1970). Moral development. In P. Mussen (Ed.), *Carmichael's manual of child psychology* (3rd ed., pp. 261–359). New York: Wiley.

Honig, A. (1985a). Compliance, control, and discipline. *Young Children, 40*(2), 50–58.

Honig, A. (1985b). Compliance, control, and discipline. *Young Children, 40*(3), 47–52.

LeFrancois, G. (1992). *Of children.* Belmont, CA: Wadsworth.

Miller, C. (1984). Building self-control: Discipline for young children. *Young Children, 40*(1), 15–19.

Sears, R., Maccoby, E., & Lewin, H. (1957). *Patterns of child rearing.* Evanston, IL: Row, Peterson.

Seefeldt, C. (1987). Praise—good or bad? *Dimensions, 15*(4), 18–20.

ADDITIONAL RESOURCES _____

Bauer, K., Sheerer, M., & Dettore, E. (1997). Creative strategies in Ernie's early childhood classroom. *Young Children, 52*(6), 47–52.

Betz, C. (1994). Beyond time-out: tips from a teacher. *Young Children, 49*(3), 10–14.

Crosser, S. (1992). Managing the early childhood classroom. *Young Children, 47*(2), 23–29.

Eaton, M. (1997). Positive discipline: Fostering the self-esteem of young children. *Young Children, 52*(6), 43–46.

Fields, M., & Boesser, C. (1994). *Constructive guidance and discipline: Preschool and primary education.* Columbus, OH: Merrill/Prentice Hall.

Gartrell, D. (1997). Beyond discipline to guidance. *Young Children, 52*(6), 34–42.

Greenberg, P. (1988). Avoiding "me against you" discipline. *Young Children, 44*(1), 24–29.

Heath, H. (1990). Dealing with difficult behaviors. *Young Children, 49*(5), 20–24.

Honig, A. (1991). The tasks of early childhood: The development of self-control. *Day Care and Early Education, 18*(4), 21–26.

Kelman, A. (1990). Choices for children. *Young Children, 45*(3), 42–45.

Kostelnik, M. (1992, September). Building spaces, finding words—creating the context for positive discipline. *Child Care Information Exchange,* pp. 34–37.

Marion, M. (1995). *Guidance of young children* (4th ed.). Columbus, OH: Merrill/Prentice-Hall.

Morrison, J. (1991). The art of redirection. *Day Care and Early Education, 18*(4), 4–7.

Stephens, K. (1992, September). What so positive about positive discipline? . . . and other mysteries of child guidance. *Child Care Information Exchange,* 30–33.

Stone, J. G. (1969). *A guide to discipline.* Washington, DC: National Association for the Education of Young Children.

7.

Classroom Design and Organization

Midway through the week, you realize that the group of toddlers in your classroom seems to be much more active and aggressive than usual. Children are playing in larger groups than is typical and seem constantly to be getting in each other's way, resulting in an increase in shoving and hitting and a higher level of noise and activity in the classroom.

Several children have responded by becoming increasingly more dependent, clinging, and crying easily. Other children are more demanding and impatient. Everyone seems to be frustrated.

You begin to evaluate the situation by thinking through possible changes that may be affecting the children's behavior. Have there been changes in the weather, routine, staffing patterns, or the composition of the group of children? Are there any significant events involving changes in the children's families or home environments? None of these variables would seem to cause such a profound change in the children's behavior, but you know something is definitely creating upheaval in the classroom.

- How do you proceed in your analysis of the cause of the disruption to the classroom?
- Do you make changes in the classroom structure or activities?
- Do you decide to rearrange the centers or materials in the room?
- How do you involve the children in solving this problem?
- How can you involve colleagues in assessing the nature of this situation?
- Which principles of classroom design and organization will you need to apply to evaluate and solve this problem effectively?

Suggestions for responding to this classroom vignette will be shared at the end of the chapter.

When reading this chapter, focus on understanding the various components of effective room arrangements for infant, toddler, and preschool classrooms and on learning about the importance of staffing assignments and daily activities and routines. A safe, secure, and stimulating classroom environment is the foundation of the invisible curriculum and enhances children's sense of well-being, encourages positive socialization, and extends the possibilities of learning through play.

The environment has a strong influence on how people feel and how they act. Therefore, the goal of a well-planned environment for young children is that both the children and their teachers can say, "I like it here. I can be successful here. This is a good place for me to be!" For these feelings to occur, many details in addition to the design of the physical space must be considered. The architectural features, the type and placement of materials in a classroom, the schedule of daily activities, and the staff assignments all influence children's behavior and learning

This chapter was written by Kathy Carlson; Carol E. Catron and Bobbie Beckmann also contributed to writing this chapter.

and support the implementation of the creative-play curriculum (Twardosz, 1984).

Researchers have identified ways in which the classroom environment can affect children's play and learning: Children are happier, more socially and cognitively competent, work longer, use more language skills, and engage in more cooperative play in environments that are appropriately designed (Trawick-Smith, 1992). These effective classrooms must allow for individual differences for stimulation and rest, for noise and quiet, and for interactions and privacy. Teachers can ensure that early childhood classrooms reduce the crowding and hurrying of children that is so pervasive today by appropriate design and scheduling.

CHARACTERISTICS
OF A WELL-PLANNED ENVIRONMENT _____

A well-planned environment will be safe and healthful, will meet the needs of both children and adults, will facilitate classroom management, will enhance the process of learning through play, and will support the implementation of program goals and objectives. A priority in designing a center for young children is to ensure their safety and well-being. Teachers should be aware of and follow state licensing requirements, which typically provide minimum standards to ensure the health and safety of young children. Another resource to consult is the *Accreditation Criteria and Procedures of the National Academy of Early Childhood Programs* (1991); this resource gives guidelines for maintaining the health and safety of children, with an emphasis on the development of centers that are of the highest quality. Figure 7-1 contains safety guidelines for early childhood classrooms. Figure 7-2 includes guidelines for a healthful classroom environment. With the increased concern about the spread of infectious diseases in early childhood settings, universal health precautions are recommended by the Centers for Disease Control and the Food and Drug Administration (1988). Universal precautions are based on using barrier techniques to prevent the spread of disease. Wear gloves when touching body fluids (blood, stool, urine, and vomit). Disinfect with bleach (a solution of sodium hypochlorite diluted 1:10 to 1:100) to clean up body fluid spills. Wash toys also with this bleach solution. Dispose of bloody materials and cleaning materials in a tightly-closed, child-proof container. The most effective practice in limiting disease spread is frequent hand washing before and after diapering children (Crocker, Cohen, & Kastner, 1992; Edelstein, 1995).

Once physical safety and health have been ensured, the staff can direct their attention to children's emotional safety. One way to ensure emotional safety is to see that both children and adults have their needs met. Children's need for nurturing will be enhanced by a safe and secure environment that includes opportunities for rest and relaxation and that offers opportunity for exploration and enjoyment. Children's need for privacy in a group-care setting will be enhanced by an environment that includes space for storage of personal items and space for private play within the classroom. Children's need for variety and complexity will be enhanced by an environment that provides chances to explore, offers opportunities to make choices, and includes materials and activities that encompass a wide range of children's abilities and interest levels. Children's need for recognition of individual differences will be enhanced by an environment that provides for differences in energy levels, thinking styles, social interaction styles, and cultural diversity (Appelbaum, Day, & Olds, 1984; Caples, 1996; Caruso, 1984; Greenman, 1984; Prescott, 1984). Children's need for self-expression will be enhanced by an environment that encourages imaginative play, fantasy, original thought, and creative problem solving (Rogers & Sawyers, 1988).

Children's needs will not be met unless adults' needs are met as well. An adult's need for nurturing can be met by having other adults in a classroom who will share responsibilities, by providing adequate information about the staff's daily responsibilities, by allowing staff to give and receive feedback about their job performance, and by providing occasions for continued learning through staff meetings, in-service opportunities, and staff development workshops. An adult's need for privacy can be met by making sure the schedule allows for time away from children. Staff need time for rest and relaxation as well as for planning and paperwork. Adults also need space for storage of personal belongings (Catron & Kendall, 1984).

An adult's need for variety and complexity will be met by a system of staff assignments that allows staff to rotate various responsibilities. An adult's need for recognition of individual differences can be met by encouraging staff members to learn from each other's strengths by sharing ideas for planning and implementing program goals and objectives. An adult's need for self-expression will be met by an atmosphere that acknowledges and supports staff members as autonomous, creative, playful, and thoughtful individuals.

A well-planned environment facilitates classroom management by reducing the possibility that problems will occur. A first step is to define the behaviors to be encouraged and discouraged, and then to arrange the environment so that desired behaviors can occur and undesired behaviors will be less likely to occur (Hart, 1978). Teachers need to ask themselves, "What do we want children to be able to do here, and how can we make sure they are able to do it?" Teachers also need to consider what teachers want or need to be doing and how to make that possible. A classroom should be open for staff supervision, yet divided into functional areas with low boundaries that encourage appropriate movement

A safety-conscious teacher should always be thinking, "How could a child get hurt here?" and "How can that possibility be prevented?" Very young infants and toddlers have no idea how certain objects can hurt them because they often have no previous experience with the object. It is the teacher's responsibility to ensure that their environment is as safe as possible. Making sure that the environment is safe demands time and thought. Even safety basics should never be assumed.

1. Strangers entering the centers or classroom areas should be greeted and questioned for approval to have access to the classroom.

2. Staff members must be sure that children leave the center with their parent(s) or other persons listed on the release form, unless prior arrangements have been made by the parent(s). Parents should initial the attendance list to sign children in and out at arrival and departure times.

3. Careful adult supervision at all times is critical. Any time a teacher leaves the classroom, he or she must notify another teacher before leaving and upon return.

4. Always position yourself in such a manner that you face as many children as possible. This usually means standing or sitting with your back to a wall, corner, or fence. Scan the environment continually for potentially dangerous situations and intervene as necessary.

5. Always be alert for possible accidents and use necessary preventive measures. If you question the safety aspect of any activity, redirect the children.

6. Protect all electrical outlets with ground-fault circuit interrupters or use tamper-resistant outlets.

7. Keep all knives, sharp objects, and tools out of children's reach.

8. Make certain all plastic wrap and bags, chemicals, and cleaners are kept in locked cabinets that are inaccessible to children.

9. Put safety catches or locks on all doors, cabinets, and drawers that children should not enter.

10. Always supervise infants or toddlers on high surfaces such as the diaper table; they may roll or fall off.

11. Be aware of all sharp corners on tables, desks, and counters, because young children can run into them or fall on them and be injured. Check to be sure that bolts and screws do not protrude from under low surfaces of furniture or equipment because these could injure a young child who tried to stand while underneath. Check up above, too; make sure there is nothing that could fall or be pulled off on an infant or toddler.

12. Check toys and equipment daily for broken or loose parts. Fix them immediately or remove them from the environment. Make sure all rough or splintered edges on wooden materials are sanded. Check for loose nails or screws that stick out of equipment and that might cause an injury to a child.

13. Avoid using staples, thumbtacks, pins, nails, paper clips, and other small office and household items. Balloons can be potential hazards for children; if they pop, children can swallow the broken rubber and suffocate. Never use glass or breakable objects around young children. When glass breaks, it can shatter into slivers that can't be seen, but young crawlers and walkers can find them with bare hands, feet, and knees. Also, some hard plastics can crack or break and be as sharp as glass. Choose unbreakable plastics only. Check any metal toys or objects daily to make sure edges are not sharp, pointed, or rusted.

14. Check infant cribs for safety features. The bars on infant cribs should be no farther apart than $2\frac{3}{8}$ inches. Check any equipment attached to cribs or design work carved into the crib to make sure there are no spaces where an infant's head could get stuck. When infants begin to pull up in their cribs, it is time to remove all crib gyms and mobiles. These often have small pieces on them that infants can swallow. Make sure infant crib mattresses are set low enough so that children cannot fall or climb out of cribs.

(continued)

Figure 7-1 Suggested list of safety guidelines.

15. Carefully supervise play where a toy with a long string is involved. Infants who are just beginning to roll over can get the string caught around their necks and strangle themselves. Also, take care that all long strings, electrical cords, and curtain or blind chains are placed out of children's reach so that they won't get tangled in them or pull a heavy object off onto the floor or themselves.

16. Keep hot objects away from children (such as hot plates, irons, matches, candles, hot pans, or dishes). Some sources of burns are not nearly so obvious; for example, hot food or liquids (especially ones heated in a microwave oven, which often heats unevenly) can burn mouths. Any metal surface such as a bench, swing, or slide that has been facing the sun may burn bare legs and tummies. Water faucets that turn quickly to the hot water or other water sources that start especially hot (water in a hose or pipe lying in the sunshine) may scald children.

17. Make sure that infants chew only on safe objects—objects that cannot be swallowed and will not chip, crack, break, or come apart in an infant's mouth. Also, watch for chipping and peeling paint on toys or objects that are chewed. Make sure paints are lead-free and nontoxic. It is important to investigate supplies used for art projects, such as glue, paints, markers, crayons, play dough, and the like, and determine that they are nontoxic.

18. When infants are beginning to pull up and walk, they look straight ahead rather than down toward the floor. Make sure they have a clear path for practicing this newly acquired skill. Toys and equipment should be moved so that children will not trip. Small throw rugs can slide on slick floors and cause children to fall, or they can become wrinkled and cause a child to trip. Pointed objects in the play environment, such as wooden clothespins, wooden stacking ring poles, spoons, sticks, and wooden pegs, must not be in the hands and mouths of children when they are walking, running, or climbing.

19. Block structures should be built no higher than the child's head.

20. When serving infants and toddlers table foods, remember that they often don't have many teeth and have limited experience with chewing, so they can swallow foods whole and choke easily. Make sure foods are broken into very small pieces. Avoid giving young children foods such as whole peanuts, hot dog slices, some dry cereals, uncooked dry beans, apple peels, chicken skin, grapes, and raw foods. These are just the right size to block a child's windpipe; they are difficult to chew and may cause choking. Also, carefully supervise children while they are eating peanut butter and jelly sandwiches. The consistency can easily cause choking when children eat too much at one time.

21. When preparing a child for a nap, always check for objects around the child's neck or in the child's mouth. Make sure a child has finished chewing after lunch before putting the child down for a nap.

22. If pet animals are kept in the environment, petting times should be carefully supervised by an adult. Be especially careful that infants and toddlers don't scare or overwhelm animals. If angry or frightened, animals may scratch or bite children. To avoid spreading any germs, hand washing needs to be incorporated in the routine each time children touch the animals. Also be aware of any children with allergies to pets before bringing animals into the classroom.

Figure 7-1 *(continued)*

throughout the classroom. Plan a schedule that maximizes children's involvement with the environment and includes few, if any, periods of unnecessary waiting (Twardosz & Risley, 1982).

Teachers must organize the environment and create a classroom climate where there are many opportunities to say "yes" to children and few times it is necessary to say "no"; in such a classroom children have many opportunities for success and few chances for failure. Growth-producing environments are not focused on things that children should not do, but instead send the message that many things are possible.

Only when safety is ensured, needs are met, and problems are prevented or diminished can the staff

1. Require current health examinations and immunization records for all children and staff members. Be aware of allergies or special physical conditions that necessitate modifications in the environment.

2. Develop and communicate to parents clear health policies concerning care of mildly ill children, guidelines for exclusion of ill children, procedures for managing communicable illnesses, preparedness for emergency care of sick or injured children, infection control practices, and policies for dispensing medication.

3. Maintain current training and certification in CPR and first aid for staff members. Post emergency care procedures by each telephone.

4. Conduct an informal health check when greeting children as they arrive each morning and discuss possible health problems with parents.

5. Minimize the spread of disease by establishing regular hand-washing routines for adults and children. Both should wash hands with soap and running water before handling food, after diapering or toileting, and after nose wiping. Help children develop these self-help skills; for children too young to do so, adults should wash their hands for them.

6. Follow careful diapering procedures, including keeping supplies conveniently stored so they are within easy reach; disposing of diapers, wipes and plastic gloves in plastic-lined and covered containers; washing the child's hands after dressing; disinfecting the diapering area; and washing hands thoroughly.

7. Give medication only with signed parental consent, written directions, and physician's prescription. Designate a place in the classroom to keep detailed medication and health- or injury-related records for parents.

8. Store all medications in locked cabinets or locked containers in the refrigerator, so that they are inaccessible to children.

9. Check for environmental pollutants and hazards in building materials. Improve air quality by prohibiting cigarette smoking, opening windows daily, and cleaning air filters regularly.

10. Separate food areas and diapering areas as much as possible, and adhere to health department guidelines for food preparation and food handling.

11. Maintain adequate cleaning of the environment including disposing of garbage; disinfecting of toileting, diapering, and food areas; laundering sheets and blankets; and sanitizing toys and materials mouthed by children.

12. Develop relationships with health and environmental consultants who will provide consultation, review program policies, and monitor the classroom environment on a regular basis.

Figure 7-2 Guidelines for a healthful environment. (*Sources:* Deitch, 1987; Kendrick, Kaufmann, & Messenger, 1995.)

turn their full attention to implementing the program goals and objectives for enhancing children's growth and development. In a well-planned environment routine tasks run smoothly, and teachers can turn their attention to implementing special activities or one-to-one involvement with children.

ROOM ARRANGEMENTS _____

A well-planned environment contains a variety of defined areas where children and adults find materials that suggest a particular type of activity. The provision of specific activities and materials within those areas depends on the age of the children in the classroom, the number of children in the classroom, and the goals of the program. In an infant classroom, for example, the major activity areas are eating, sleeping, diapering, and play. A toddler classroom needs all these areas plus access to a toileting area. In ad-

The environment should be planned to meet children's needs, including the need for privacy and quiet interaction with peers.

dition, in a toddler classroom the play area can be subdivided into more specific play areas such as blocks, small-motor activities, imaginary play, art, books, and large-motor activities. A preschool classroom needs space for eating, napping, toileting, and specific play areas. However, a preschool classroom may have more kinds of specific play areas and/or the materials within the areas will be more complex. Although a preschool classroom does not usually need a diapering table, provisions for diapering children who are not yet toilet-trained or who have disabilities that require diapering and/or catheterization must be considered.

There are several general features to consider when organizing the physical space. These include the distribution of activities, the amount of space required per activity, the number and variety of activities, the flow of traffic between activities, the convenience (in terms of visibility, cleanup, and storage), the responsiveness of the environment to children, and the wall displays and decorations (Caples, 1996; Hildebrand, 1987).

The distribution of activities in a room should be considered according to their compatibility with one another. It is preferable to have active centers such as imaginary play and blocks separated from quiet centers such as books and manipulatives. It also is desirable to have messy activities such as art and water play separate from areas that need protection from paint and water, such as books and imaginary play.

The amount of space required for an activity is an extremely important consideration. Some activities require plenty of space in which to move around and work (block building, motor activities). Other activities require much less space. A book area, quiet corner, or reading loft can be relatively small but still be quite cozy and functional. Several areas in the rooms could be multi-use space. For example, tables can be used for art, snack, and lunch. At lunchtime, highchairs can be brought into the area infants use for play and then returned for storage when lunch is finished. Large-group activities could be conducted in the block area or the large-motor area because all of these require plenty of space. At nap time for toddlers and preschoolers, cots can be brought into the room and then returned to storage after nap.

The number and variety of activities depend on the number of children in the room. Consider the number of things to do per child. If the classroom contains only enough activities and materials for just one activity or item per child, the result will be boredom, misbehavior, or problems with sharing. A guideline of 50 percent more play items and activities than the total number of children will set the stage for active, positive involvement with materials and peers. For example, in a classroom of twelve children, there should be at least eighteen play items and materials available at all times. The number of play items and activities can be increased by the inclusion of many complex units in a classroom. Prescott (1984) has defined simple, complex, and super units. For example, a sand pile with no equipment is a simple unit. Add digging equipment and it is a complex unit. If you add water as a third element, it becomes a super unit. Play dough by itself is a simple unit; with toothpicks, it is a complex unit; with toothpicks and cookie cutters, it is a super unit (Prescott, 1984).

Complex and super units hold children's interest longer and "geometrically increase the number of things that can be done" (Prescott, 1984). Variety is provided not only by considering the complexity of activities but also by considering the type of activities. Children need to have choices that include active play, quiet play, and play that is in between. Children also need choices that involve socialization and choices that involve playing alone or with a friend.

The flow of traffic within a classroom can prevent or cause problems. Clear pathways are needed to the bathroom area, to the outside areas, and between activity areas. Protection is needed for areas where play requires freedom from intrusion, such as the block area. If the pathway to the bathroom leads right through the block center, block structures are likely to be knocked down by children on their way to the bathroom. Moving the block center to an area that is not used as a pathway diminishes that possibility. The book area and manipulatives area also need protection from intrusion. Areas can be protected by providing low boundaries that adults can see over but that children will notice and recognize. Boundaries can be made with classroom furniture, room dividers, with large carpeted wooden blocks, or by changes in the floor surface (different colors or different textures). Small carpet pieces can be used on the floor (on top of the regular carpet) to designate specific areas for puzzles, games, or other activities. Children will learn to walk around the carpet pieces rather than through the activity on the carpet. Lines on the floor created with masking tape also may be used to designate a boundary for an area.

Another important consideration concerning the flow of traffic is the accessibility of the outdoor play environment. All children's classrooms should provide direct access to a protected outdoor play area. This direct linkage of the indoor and outdoor play areas allows greater in-and-out movement of children throughout the day and maximizes use of outdoor space as an extension of the learning environment.

The convenience of activity areas should be planned in terms of visibility, cleanup, and storage. Two kinds of storage are needed. Low storage shelves should be within each area for storage of materials to which children have access. High, closed cabinets or closets should be in or near each activity area for storage of materials to which teachers need access and for storage of children's materials that are not in use. Messy activities such as art and eating need to be near a sink. If the flooring in messy areas is tile, cleanup is easier, and teachers will not need to continually caution children to be careful (Hildebrand, 1987). Eating areas need to be near the kitchen, if possible. If not, rolling carts may be used to provide children and adults with items needed for food service. Coats and other personal belongings should be stored conveniently. The location of electrical outlets often determines how a classroom is arranged. Record players, tape recorders, and appliances used for cooking activities must be used near an outlet. Therefore, the location of outlets determines where certain activities may take place.

Environments should be responsive to children and their actions. Materials that respond to children include soft places to sit such as rugs, pillows, couches, beanbag chairs, laps, and grass. Responsive materials also include sand, water, play dough, finger paint, scarves, plants, toys that move or make a sound when a child touches them, and other materials that do what the children want them to do. These kinds of responsive materials help lessen fatigue for children and adults, enhance variety, and encourage

further exploration (Caruso, 1984; Greenman, 1984; Prescott, 1984).

Wall displays and decorations are an important part of the environment. Pictures and other displays for children should be at the child's eye level. For toddlers and preschoolers, the displays should be concentrated on the lower half of the wall. For babies, find ways to make ceilings and the undersides of furniture interesting and functional. Mobiles above changing tables, ceiling displays, textures along the baseboards, and pictures attached to the underside of tabletops should be incorporated.

Another consideration for wall displays is that the majority of materials should be the children's creations. Children will be delighted by the fact that their own work is being used to decorate the room. Also, commercial displays are expensive, and teacher-made displays are time-consuming. When teachers occasionally do select items for wall displays, they should use the opportunity to enrich children's knowledge by using pictures of people from a variety of cultures; families and museums may be a source of culturally diverse paintings and art objects. It also is important to avoid clutter in wall displays. Too many or too-complicated displays result in visual pollution or "visual noise" (Greenman, 1984, p. 25). There is always a lot of detail and movement in a classroom because of the numbers of people moving around. There should be adequate "blank" space, or space where the eyes see nothing but the wall.

Classroom lighting influences children's learning and play as well as their sense of comfort and security. The fluorescent lights found in most classrooms flash 120 times a second: imperceptible to the eye but having an effect on mood, physical health, and learning (Olds, 1988; Hathaway, Hargreaves, Thompson, & Novitsky, 1992). When possible, use a variety of lighting options: skylights and windows for natural, outdoor light; incandescent light for the "home-like" atmosphere it provides; and full-spectrum light, which includes wavelengths at all points on the spectrum and has positive effects on children's health, activity level, and academic performance (Schreiber, 1996).

These guidelines will help determine not only what should be in the classroom but also where items generally should be located. The next step is to make a floor plan. Hart (1978) suggests trying out various ideas by sketching alternatives and evaluating them according to the established guidelines and priorities. Once the "best" plan has been decided, the next step is to move furniture and materials into place. View the room from the perspective of the teacher as well as from the perspective of the child. Get down on your knees (or hands and knees) and view the room as children would. Check on supervision possibilities from several locations within the room. Once you are satisfied with the initial arrangement, children's behavior in the room will provide an evaluation of the success of the arrangement. If misbehavior or misuse of materials occurs, the first thing to do is to reevaluate the arrangement to see whether the environment is causing problems. Even when a satisfactory arrangement is discovered, teachers and children enjoy changing the room occasionally. There is seldom just one successful arrangement. Materials in the play areas should be rotated daily, weekly, or biweekly according to the specific area and children's involvement with it. In general, the art area may need daily changes. Book, small-motor, large-motor, imaginary-play, and block areas may need to be changed weekly or biweekly. Teacher judgment is important. Teachers can evaluate the need to change a center by watching children's level of involvement with the materials. Children's participation in selecting and changing materials will result in higher levels of engagement and exploration.

The Infant Classroom

Young children learn about the world of people and objects through their senses and motor activities, so a physical environment that supports exploration, play, and learning is critical. The four basic activity areas for infants are playing, eating, diapering, and sleeping. The majority of the space should be devoted to playing. Although some authors recommend a separate room for sleeping, researchers have found that sleep patterns are not adversely affected by having a sleeping area in the same room as a play area (Twardosz, Cataldo, & Risley, 1974). Having all the activity areas in the same room maximizes supervision possibilities. An example of an infant classroom arrangement is shown in Figure 7-3.

Exploratory play is important for the cognitive development of infants because as infants interact with their environment, they receive feedback. For infants to be able to explore, materials must be visible and readily accessible. An infant play area needs structures that can be used for grasping, reaching, or pulling up. Carpet-covered blocks of various heights made from sturdy plywood make excellent low room dividers and safe climbing areas for infants. Pillows, foam mattresses, slightly raised platforms, and changes in the textures of surfaces make a play area with space for infants to sit, crawl, or walk short distances (Greenman, 1984).

It is neither necessary nor preferable for the entire play area to be carpeted. The area where infants will be involved in messy activities (art, water play) should have an easily cleanable surface such as tile or linoleum. This area also can serve as the eating area. "Even floor surfaces help [infants] learn about the world. For example, a ball goes a long way with a little push on a tile floor, but not on the rug. On the other hand, crawling is easier on the less slippery rug" (Willis & Ricciuti, 1980, p. 138).

Infants' exploratory play will be enhanced by the variety and complexity of materials in the play area. When evaluating the appropriateness of a toy or piece of equipment it is helpful to ask, "What can an infant learn from this toy?" Avoid equipment designed to keep children constrained and passive, such as walkers and motorized swings. Instead, infants need to be down on the floor with toys to look at, listen to, feel, chew on, push, pull, stack, roll, turn, squeeze, shake, and drop (Shaw & Chatt, 1985).

Variety and complexity also are important because of infants' rapid growth and development. Even if several infants are the same age, their interests and abilities will be highly individual. The same play area must work for infants who are lying, sitting, crawling, and/or walking. There will be some who are focused on large-motor activities, some who are focused on small-motor activities, and others who are interested in books and pictures.

Careful consideration also should be given to meeting the emotional and social needs of infants by providing a warm and home-like environment in the classroom. A classroom that contains small, cozy spaces as well as open spaces for active exploration provides the balance needed by young children through the day. All young children, especially infants, need spaces that invite nurturing adult–child interactions and provide continuity between the home environment and the early childhood program environment.

The remainder of the space in an infant room is for eating, sleeping, and diapering. The eating area needs to be close to the kitchen and near a sink where teachers and infants wash hands before and after eating. There are two important considerations for the diapering area. The first is that it be located so that the teacher can take a position that permits diapering a child while still seeing the remainder of the room. The second is that all needed materials for diapering be within the reach of the teacher, including a sink to wash hands. The teacher must not leave an infant unattended on the diaper table to search for diapers, washcloths, or other needed items. Important considerations for the cribs is that they all be in the same room and opposite from the play area. Another important consideration for the cribs is that children are in them only for sleeping. Cribs should not be used inappropriately for "caretaking" purposes when children are awake and need to be active.

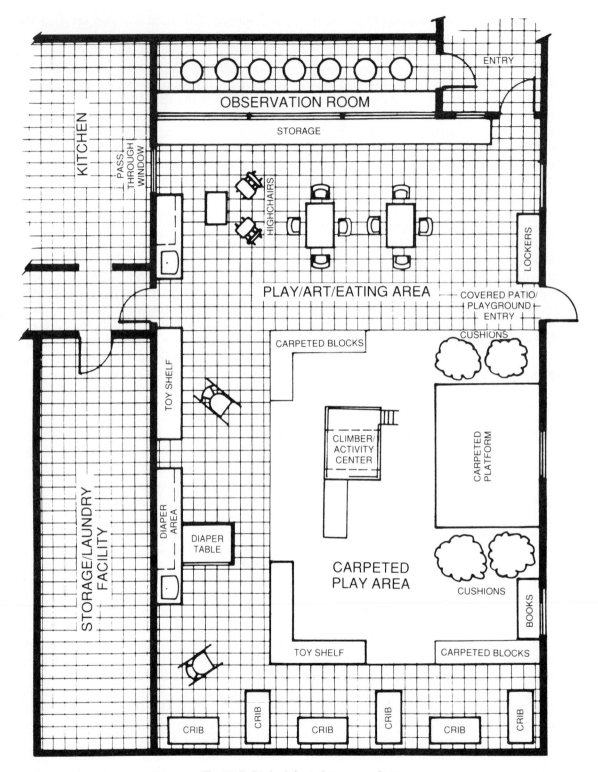

Figure 7–3 An infant classroom plan.

The Toddler Classroom

The activity areas for toddlers include spaces for eating, napping, diapering, toileting, and playing. As was the case for infants, the play area is the largest area in the room. However, the play area for toddlers can be subdivided into more specific play areas such as imaginary play, art, small-motor activities, large-motor activities, block building, and a quiet corner for looking at books.

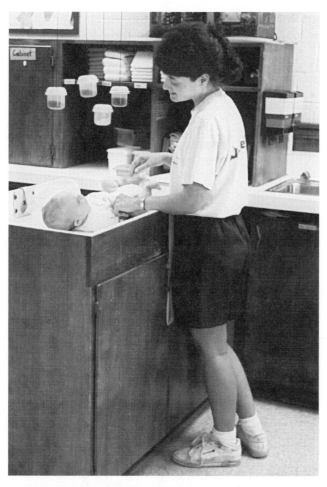

The diapering area should be designed to give teachers easy access to the sink and diapering supplies.

Although a toddler room may look more like a preschool room because play areas are more defined, it is important to realize that toddlers are not miniature preschoolers. Such thoughts will lead to inappropriate and unrealistic expectations (Gonzalez-Mena, 1986). "Toddlers need space to explore, experiment, discover and move. This age child is constantly on the go and needs to have many opportunities to practice newly emerging skills" (Vartuli, 1987, p. 29). The toddler classroom must reflect these understandings about toddlers. A sample room arrangement is shown in Figure 7-4.

The large-motor area should contain space and equipment for climbing, jumping, and moving in, over, or around obstacles. Small slides and climbers, steps, tunnels, snap wall structures, rocking boats, and boxes to crawl in and around are some examples of appropriate equipment. If a record/cassette player is located nearby, the large-motor area can be used for large-group music and movement activities as well.

The small-motor area should contain a variety of materials toddlers can explore with their hands. Simple three- or four-piece puzzles, large beads to string, nesting toys, stacking toys, shape sorters, and large interlocking construction toys are examples of appropriate equipment. Each toy or set of materials should have its own storage space or container. Toddlers like to dump, sort, and collect. Provide toddlers with a specific place to dump, sort, and collect; give them buckets labeled with pictures of the specific items to collect (Duplos, beads, toy cars) and make a game of these activities. It is important to make sure that all these materials are too large to be swallowed.

The art area needs to contain materials for a specific art project as well as aprons or smocks to protect children's clothing from messy activities. It is helpful to have a sink immediately adjacent to the art area. If this is not possible, a bucket of soapy water and paper or cloth towels provide easy cleanup. Use smocks with Velcro closures that toddlers can try to put on and fasten themselves. The art materials for the day's project should be completely ready before children begin the project. Behavior problems are likely to occur if children have to wait while the teacher looks for paper or brushes. In addition to materials for a specific project, the art center should contain crayons and paper to which children have access.

The block-building area contains large cardboard blocks and/or basic wooden unit blocks. The area needs clear boundaries so that block building will be protected from intrusion. Carpeting in the block area reduces noise, but the carpeting must be of the low, dense pile type so that structures will stay balanced. Storage shelves in the block area can be labeled with pictures or outlines of block shapes so toddlers can put blocks away according to size and shape. Accessories for block building include transportation toys and wooden or plastic people and animals. Masking tape may be used to make roads or pathways, ponds, or shapes that children can build in, on, or around.

The basic materials in the imaginary-play area include housekeeping items such as a stove/sink combination, cabinets for dishes, pots and pans, table and chairs, dolls and a doll bed, telephones, dress-up clothes and hats, and a Plexiglas mirror. Other types of imaginary play can be suggested by additional props such as grocery store supplies or doctor's office equipment. It is not always necessary to change the entire area; adding the additional props to one corner of the area may be enough to encourage and extend a different kind of imaginary play.

The book corner needs to be in a protected, quiet area. Books that contain mostly pictures and few words should be selected. The books should be sturdy enough for the kind of exploration toddlers enjoy and need. Soft pillows, couches, beanbags, and a plush rug will make the book corner cozy and inviting. Puppets and

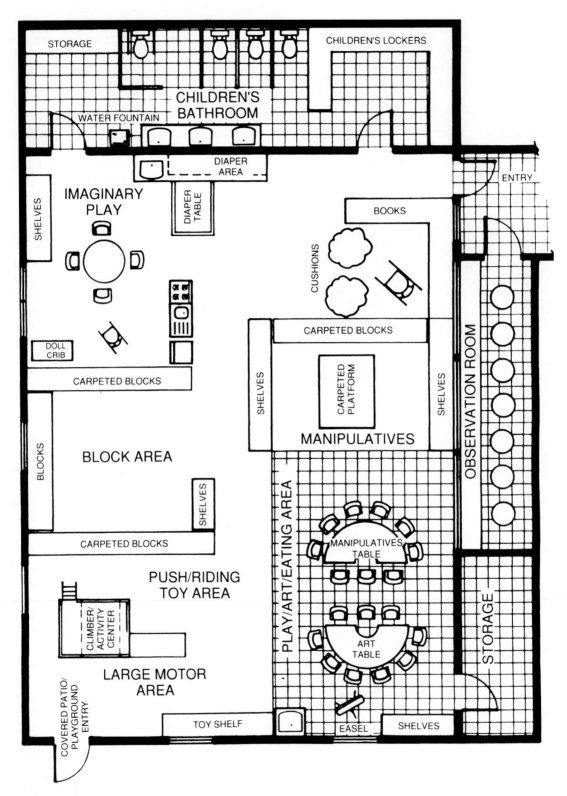

Figure 7-4 A toddler classroom plan.

flannel-board activities may be added to this area to extend language activities and promote imaginative play.

A classroom pet is an important addition to a toddler classroom. Toddlers will enjoy watching and playing with the pet, as well as helping take care of the pet. Because pets require consistent, nurturing care, and since some children may have allergies to or fears about certain animals, make choices regarding a classroom pet accordingly.

Toddlers eat snack and lunch at the low tables and chairs used for other kinds of table activities throughout the day. It is helpful if these tables are near the kitchen. It also is helpful if the eating area is near the bathroom area so that hand washing and toileting before and after eating can be more easily supervised.

For nap time, cots may be brought in from the storage area and placed in all the available locations throughout the room. Nap time usually occurs right after lunch, and teachers can encourage a restful atmosphere by gradually turning out the lights as children finish lunch and begin the transition to nap. Soft, relaxing music also helps encourage a restful atmosphere.

The diapering area in a toddler room is the same as the diapering area in an infant room. However, toddlers who are beginning to use the toilet need child-sized toilets and sinks in a room adjacent to the play area. If the children's lockers also are in this room, teachers have easier access to children's extra clothing when it is needed.

The Preschool Classroom

The preschool classroom is similar to the toddler classroom except that it does not include a diapering area. The play area is subdivided into specific centers. Materials are more complex and varied to match the preschooler's developmental abilities and interests. There are more kinds of play areas in a preschool classroom as well. Sample preschool classrooms are outlined in Figures 7-5 and 7-6. Figure 7-5 demonstrates a design for two preschool classrooms that are shared by two groups of preschoolers who spend a large block of play time in each classroom during the day. Materials and equipment are different in each of the shared preschool classrooms. Figure 7-6 shows a self-contained preschool classroom plan where one group of children spends the entire day, and a wide variety of materials and equipment is included in a single room.

The guidelines for the play areas in the preschool room are the same as those for the toddler room. In addition to the large-motor materials mentioned for toddlers, large-motor materials for preschoolers can include items requiring more complex movement such as balance beams, beanbag targets, and hopscotch grids. If space is available, materials may be used in combinations to make an obstacle course. Materials also may be included for simple games such as a bowling game involving blocks and a beach ball.

The small-motor area (also called the puzzles and games or manipulatives area) contains puzzles with more and smaller pieces, smaller beads to string,

pegs and peg boards, lotto or other matching games, and a wider variety of construction materials such as Duplos, Legos, Bristle Blocks, Towerifics, Rig-a-Jigs, and so on. Preschoolers will get involved with these materials on a wide range of levels. For some, dumping the Legos will be enjoyable and challenging. Others will become absorbed in using the Legos to make very intricate structures.

In the art area preschoolers should have access to a greater variety of materials. Crayons and markers; paper of various shapes, sizes, and colors; scissors; magazines; and glue bottles permit preschoolers to become involved in a wide variety of self-initiated art projects. Materials for writing can be included in the art center; writing materials also can be included in a separate writing center to facilitate the whole-language approach to developing emergent literacy skills. Plastic or cardboard letters and numerals, cards with children's names on them, and both large- and regular-diameter pencils will encourage children to experiment and play with the writing process and develop graphomotor skills (Carlson & Cunningham, 1990).

The block-building area includes more complex materials because the preschoolers are able to build more complex structures. In addition to the accessories listed for toddlers, preschoolers want materials to decorate their structures (cardboard tubes, wooden or plastic thread spools, for example) or materials to make signs for their structures.

Imaginary play also is more complex because of preschoolers' abilities. The center can be changed to become a doctor's office, a veterinarian's office, a hair salon, a grocery store, a beach/picnic area, a fishing lake, a skating pond, a travel center, and so on. Extending the availability of books and writing materials to imaginary-play settings such as an office or a library also may increase children's play-related literary activity and increase development in emergent literacy skills.

The book corner contains books with more words; however, the major portion of each page should still be pictures. Books created by the children about particular concepts (Red Things, Square Things, Things We Like to Eat) or about a field trip can be included. Books also may be selected to extend learning about particular play themes or special activities.

An additional area for the preschool classroom is the discovery center. This center contains science-related materials such as magnets, prisms, balance scales, materials for measuring and pouring (for example, sand, water, birdseed, dirt, dry beans), and color-mixing materials. Too often a discovery/science area contains a few rocks, plants, or other items just to view. Although it is fine to have these items, the main focus of the discovery area is on materials

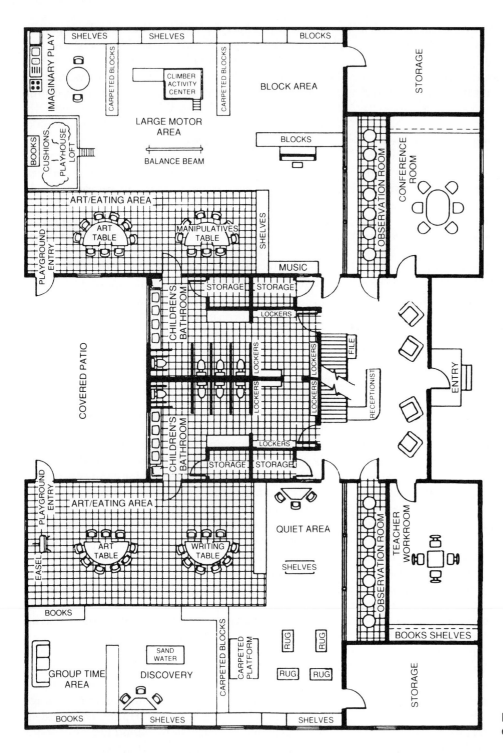

Figure 7-5 A shared preschool classroom plan.

preschoolers can become involved with and act upon. Classroom pets such as hamsters, guinea pigs, or fish can be located in the discovery area as well.

Another activity preschoolers enjoy is woodworking. This center requires careful and continuous supervision. Preschoolers can hammer nails into wood, tree stumps, Styrofoam blocks, and/or cardboard boxes. Sawing also is a popular activity. Although a hacksaw is not usually used for cutting wood, it is a sturdy saw that preschoolers can learn to manipulate. A clamp can be used to attach the wood to the workbench so preschoolers can use both hands to saw.

If the preschool room contains a piano or keyboard, preschoolers will enjoy playing it by themselves or with a friend. Some preschoolers will enjoy playing simple songs by matching colors or numbers on the

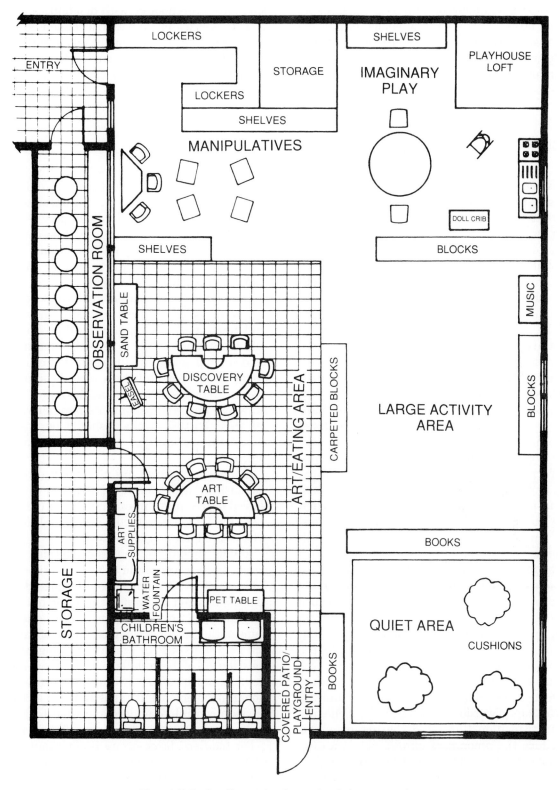

Figure 7-6 A self-contained preschool classroom plan.

piano keys to colored notes or numerals. Music experiences can be extended by the provision of musical instruments, records, tapes, and props for movement and relaxation activities.

The guidelines for eating, sleeping, and toileting areas are the same for preschoolers as for toddlers. If there are preschoolers with disabilities who need to be catheterized or diapered, a cot can be designated for this use only and brought out into the bathroom area. The bathroom area can be closed off temporarily to provide for privacy.

SCHEDULES

Schedules can be a blessing if they are used to help children and teachers know what comes next and to contribute to the feeling of security such knowledge produces. Or they can be a burden if they are allowed to dominate the day in a rigid, minute-by-minute fashion that ignores children's needs and prevents teachers from exercising good judgment. A well-designed schedule not only provides for orderly planning, but also allows for flexibility so that time periods can be extended or contracted depending on whether the children are deeply occupied or particularly restless (Hendrick, 1998, p. 44).

In planning schedules, consider and incorporate a balance of activities on the following dimensions: (a) indoor/outdoor; (b) quiet/active; (c) individual/small-group/large-group; (d) large-muscle/small-muscle; (e) child-initiated/staff-initiated (*Accreditation Criteria and Procedures,* 1991, p. 22). The schedule also must incorporate time for routine care (eating, sleeping, and diapering or toileting) and the transitions from one type of activity to the next. When planning schedules, also consider hours of operation, the kind of facility, the number of staff available, the fixed events, and the time of year.

The schedule should provide for a reasonable pace during the day. Children need time to become "truly engrossed in what they are doing. Plans that cause children to be constantly shifted back and forth from one thing to another reduce their chances for concentration and deep involvement, to say nothing of the general feeling of harassment" (Hendrick, 1998, p. 39).

Minimize or omit periods of unnecessary waiting. Waiting leads to boredom, restlessness, and unpleasant interactions (Twardosz & Risley, 1982). Schedule purposeful transition times and concurrent activities to reduce the amount of unnecessary waiting. For example, during a transition from outdoor play to lunch, one teacher can read a story as children come in from the playground while another teacher finishes getting lunch materials ready. Children can be dismissed slowly from story time to wash hands and come to the table.

Plan the daily schedule by blocking out the routine and fixed events, adding large uninterrupted blocks of time for free play and guided play with children making choices from a variety of creative learning activities, and providing for transitions. Figures 7-7, 7-8, and 7-9 contain sample schedules for infant, toddler, and preschool classrooms.

Younger infants are on individual schedules for eating and sleeping. Older infants may eat snacks and lunch on a more regular schedule. Some take one nap after lunch, some take both a morning and afternoon nap, and a few take only a morning nap. The young children usually have a bottle or are breastfed every three or four hours and have juice or water in between. The younger infants nap before and/or after their bottles. A chart should be posted in the classroom explaining each child's current daily schedule.

Whenever children are not involved in a caregiving task or a planned activity, they should be involved in free play. Infants need time outdoors every day. The change to outdoors is enjoyable for an infant who is tired, cranky, or fussy.

Infants should not be rushed through the routine care activities. These can be a special time for talking individually with infants about facial and body parts, about warm and cold water, and so forth. Toddlers also need plenty of time for routine care, especially because some of the "major accomplishments of this stage are self-help skills such as dressing, feeding, washing, and toileting. All of these skills involve a great deal of practice . . . [and include physical, intellectual, and emotional involvement]. It takes time for a child to gain physical control, to understand what to do, and to be willing to do it" (Gonzalez-Mena, 1986, p. 48).

For toddlers, large-group times should be limited to a very few activities, such as eating and a short story or music time. Provide other activities for young toddlers to do when they lose interest. Older toddlers will soon enjoy and want to be involved in group activities for a longer period of time (Gonzalez-Mena, 1986).

7:30–9:00	Children arrive and engage in free play
9:00–9:30	Diapering[a] and free play
9:30–10:00	Snack[b] and gradual transition to activity time
10:00–10:30	Guided-play/creative-activity time
10:30–11:15	Outdoor time, walks, some morning naps (individual schedules)
11:15–11:45	Diapering and free play; then hand washing and preparation for lunch
11:45–12:30	Lunch
12:30–1:00	Free play and individual nap preparation
1:00–2:30	Nap time
2:30–3:00	Diapering and free play
3:00–3:30	Snack and gradual transition to outdoor play
3:30–4:15	Outdoor play
4:15–4:45	Diapering and free play
4:45–5:30	Guided-play/creative-activity time or free play

[a] Diapering throughout the day as needed.
[b] Young infants on individual eating and sleeping schedules.

Figure 7-7 Sample schedule for infant program daily routines.

7:30–9:00	Children arrive and engage in free play; then toileting or diaper changing[a], hand washing, and transition to snack
9:00–9:30	Snack and gradual transition to outdoor play
9:30–10:30	Outdoor play
10:30–11:30	Guided-play/creative-activity time; then toileting or diaper changing, hand washing, and preparation for lunch
11:30–12:30	Lunch; then toileting or diaper changing, hand washing, and preparation for nap
12:30–2:15	Nap time and gradual transition to outdoor play
2:15–3:00	Outdoor play; then toileting or diaper changing, hand washing, and transition to snack
3:00–3:30	Snack and gradual transition to free play
3:30–4:00	Free play inside
4:00–5:00	Inside or outside free play
5:00–5:30	Guided-play/creative-activity time or free play

[a] Toileting and diaper changing as needed throughout the day and on individual schedules for children who are involved in toilet learning.

Figure 7-8 Sample schedule for toddler program daily routines.

Preschoolers are ready for larger group activities. The large-group times could be 10 to 15 minutes long at the beginning of the year or for younger preschoolers, and could extend to 15 or 20 minutes long later in the year or for older preschoolers. The main group time should be in the morning, before children become tired from the morning's activities. Group time for preschoolers includes songs, finger plays, movement activities, discussions, and storytelling or reading. If there is a group activity before lunch as part of a transition, it should be limited to a few calming songs or a story.

It is helpful to plan for rainy days. Otherwise, these days can be hectic. Rainy-day activities can be written on file cards for easy reference. Remember that the children still need large-motor activity even if they cannot be outside. Take advantage of any covered outdoor space where a few children at a time can play. Especially in colder climates, it is helpful to have an indoor large-motor room or area. Children may become too active at times as well. Be ready to conduct an impromptu "calm down" activity such as relaxation exercises whenever a change of pace is needed.

7:30–8:30	Children arrive and engage in free play
8:30–9:10	Indoor and outdoor play (if weather permits); then toileting[a], hand washing, and transition to snack
9:10–9:30	Snack and gradual transition to group time
9:30–9:45	Group time
9:45–11:00	Guided-learning/creative-activity time and gradual transition to outdoor play
11:00–11:50	Outdoor play
11:50–12:00	Transition to lunch (toileting, hand washing)
12:00–1:00	Lunch
1:00–1:10	Transition to nap time (toileting, hand washing, select book)
1:10–2:30	Nap time
2:30–3:00	Free play
3:00–3:30	Snack and gradual transition to outdoor play
3:30–4:30	Outdoor play
4:30–5:30	Guided-learning/creative-activity time or free play

[a] Toileting throughout day as needed.

Figure 7-9 Sample schedule for preschool program daily routines.

STAFF ASSIGNMENTS

Staff assignments need to be specific enough for people to know when, where, and what they are to do. Therefore, the assignments include not only the working hours, but also who will be responsible for monitoring children, lesson planning, and implementation of activities and routines.

Work Schedules

The staff work schedule must include adequate staff to carry out the goals of the program. Licensing standards usually indicate the minimum number of staff members that must be present. However, a much lower staff-child ratio is recommended (Table 7.1) by the National Academy of Early Childhood Programs, a division of the National Association for the Education of Young Children. These lower staff-child ratios increase the quality of care for children and reduce the stress levels of the adults.

Another way to reduce stress levels for staff is to have at least two adults in each classroom. Being alone all day with children is not safe and leads to quick burnout. Combine classrooms during the early-morning and late-afternoon hours if the number of children present is fewer at those times. It also is helpful to have additional staff available during the busy times of the day, such as lunch. It is preferable that staff rotate working hours occasionally. The late-afternoon hours are always the hardest. Sample work schedules for infant, toddler, and preschool staff are presented in Table 7.2.

Monitoring of Children

For children to form secure relationships with adults, the children should be assigned to a set of teachers who stay with them throughout the day and who will be consistent throughout the week. Within the group, children can be assigned to a specific staff person for purposes of monitoring and assessment. The number of children assigned to each teacher depends on the number of staff in each group who are qualified to provide reliable information to parents regarding the day's activities and on the child's individual goals and objectives derived from a variety of assessment procedures. Monitoring teachers are responsible for the following: (1) keeping children's folders up-to-date; (2) making sure parents receive daily information (both written and verbal) about their child's experiences in the program; (3) observing and recording children's development; (4) setting individual objectives and planning program activities appropriate for each child; (5) conducting parent conferences and writing parent conference summaries; (6) bringing any problems or concerns regarding the child's development to the attention of the supervisor and family.

Planning

Planning assignments depend on the number of staff available and the amount of planning that

TABLE 7.1 Recommended Staff-Child Ratios Within Group Size[a]

Age of Children	GROUP SIZE										
	6	8	10	12	14	16	18	20	22	24	28
Infants (birth–12 mos.)	1:3	1:4									
Toddlers (12–24 mos.)	1:3	1:4	1:5	1:4							
2-year-olds (24–30 mos.)		1:4	1:5	1:6							
2½-year-olds (30–36 mos.)			1:5	1:6	1:7						
3-year-olds					1:7	1:8	1:9	1:10			
4-year-olds						1:8	1:9	1:10			
5-year-olds						1:8	1:9	1:10			
6- to 8-year-olds								1:10	1:11	1:12	
9- to 12-year-olds										1:12	1:14

[a] Smaller group sizes and lower staff–child ratios have been found to be strong predictors of compliance with indicators of quality, such as positive interactions among staff and children and developmentally appropriate curriculum. Variations in group sizes and ratios are acceptable in cases where the program demonstrates a very high level of compliance with criteria for interactions, curriculum, staff qualifications, health and safety, and physical environment.

Source: Accreditation Criteria and Procedures of the National Academy of Early Childhood Programs, p. 41 (1991). Washington, DC: National Association for the Education of Young Children. Reprinted by permission of NAEYC.

can be shared. In some programs, the lead teacher in each classroom does all the planning. In other programs, planning responsibilities are shared equally by all the caregivers. Shared responsibility not only lessens fatigue but builds staff esteem, professional relationships, and sense of involvement. Sharing can be done by taking turns planning everything for a period of time or by continually dividing up the responsibilities within a period of time.

Implementing Daily Activities and Routines

When there is more than one teacher in each classroom, teachers can divide and share responsibilities for daily routines and specific activities. LeLaurin and Risley (1972) recommend a *zone staffing* procedure. In the zone method, staff are assigned to an area or an activity and children circulate through the zone. For example, in a classroom with two teachers,

TABLE 7.2 Staff Schedule for Work/Planning/Breaks
Infants: 6 children, 1 to 3 ratio
Toddlers: 10 children, 1 to 5 ratio
Preschoolers: 15 children, 1 to 8 ratio

7:30	8:30	9:30	10:30	11:30	12:30	1:30	2:30	3:30	4:30	5:30

A
└──────────── *10:00–10:30 ──────────── *1:00–1:30 ──────────┘
(Full-time teacher)

        C
        └─────────────────────── 1:30–2:30 ─────────────────┘
            (Full-time teacher)

B   D
└──────────── **9:30–10:00 ──────────┘   └─── **2:30–3:00 ──────────────┘
(Part-time teacher)   (Part-time teacher)

Each room:
 * Two full-time teachers—40 hrs/week; 1 hour paid break/plan time
 ** Two part-time teachers—25 hrs/week; ½ hour paid break/plan time
 Staffing is arranged to provide time for breaks/planning and to provide additional help during lunch setup/cleanup/nap transition and during nap time (two teachers to provide adequate supervision and necessary help in case of emergency).

each teacher can be assigned to supervise the centers in one half of the room. If there is an activity that requires very close guidance (for example, cooking), one teacher can supervise the specific activity while the other teacher circulates and manages the remaining centers. In an infant room, one teacher can do all the diapering while the other teachers supervise play or eating. Staff members may wish to decide on a day-to-day basis who will take which responsibilities for the day. Other staffs may be more comfortable with having a specific weekly assignment. The decision should be made, in part, according to the staff members' experience and the effectiveness of their classroom management. Begin with specific assignments until all staff members are comfortable with managing each zone or activity.

CLASSROOM ADAPTATIONS _____

The design and organization of the classroom have a strong impact upon the successful inclusion of children with disabilities in early childhood programs. The classroom's design and organization can enhance socialization skills, promote appropriate use of materials, facilitate development of targeted skills, and manage behavior.

Play for children with disabilities may not emerge as naturally and informally as it does with their peers. Social integration of children is unlikely to occur unless situations are structured to ensure this interaction. The design of center areas and play areas and the types of activities chosen must encourage social interaction. The teacher can facilitate socialization by "staging" interactions in various centers or during daily routines. For example, mealtime can be an excellent time to foster peer interactions naturally and easily. Careful attention to seating arrangements can greatly enhance the socialization process. By seating the child with disabilities near the teacher, social interactions can be verbally prompted: "Jennifer, tell Joey about the tower we built." The child with disabilities is seated between two other children so that interaction is increased. This positioning also enhances the opportunities for utilizing the language skills of peers as a model.

Having peers assist the child with disabilities in activity transitions can promote opportunities for socialization. Other routines also can be utilized to enhance socialization. For example, during the premeal hand-washing routine, encourage another child to assist by modeling the skill and helping to remember the steps involved.

As children model appropriate use of materials, the child with disabilities can learn from and with them. The materials chosen should provide a wide range of challenges so that the children can choose items that they can successfully use. For example, choices in the puzzle area should include a range of puzzles that encompass the skill levels of all children. With this range, the child with disabilities can be encouraged to play with harder puzzles and peers can be encouraged to provide assistance and/or modeling.

When integrating children, specific areas of individual need should be addressed and considered in program planning. Intervention occurs naturally by supplying the materials to enhance the development of specific skills, structuring the activity, and then providing assistance if needed. Most materials that are appropriate for early childhood classrooms are appropriate for use by children with disabilities. However, to maximize the benefits of classroom materials, the following guidelines can be used:

- If necessary, assist children in learning to play with toys and materials.
- Select toys and materials based on children's preferences and interests.
- Provide toys and materials that encourage engagement, play, interaction, and learning.
- Adapt toys and materials to promote attention, engagement, and play (Wolery, 1994, pp.108–110).

Many children with disabilities require additional time in certain activities to fully explore and benefit from the material. The daily schedule should provide adequate time for the child to participate in centers.

The integration of a child with disabilities into the classroom need not necessitate additional staff. Rather, the staff assignments for monitoring, supervising, and providing individual instruction can adequately and appropriately facilitate inclusion. With the recommended teacher–child ratios, the teacher is available to provide physical assistance if it is needed, while providing verbal instructions for the other children in the group. Behavior becomes more manageable with a low teacher–child ratio, close proximity of the teacher, and availability of the teacher for direction of individual activities.

The following adaptations to the environment are suggested to make the space more easily accessible for children with disabilities and to help prevent accidents:

1. Classroom spaces should be accessible to children who use wheelchairs, braces, crutches, or other forms of mobility assistance; this includes learning centers, bookshelves, computers, doorways, and space to move within the classroom (Smith, Polloway, Patton, & Dowdy, 1995, p. 358).

2. Children with wheelchairs, walkers, and braces will climb ramps and steps more easily with handrails on ramps and steps that are wide and shallow (Garwood, 1979, p. 114).

3. Tables should be high enough for a child in a wheelchair to sit comfortably at the table. Mirrors, sinks, toilets, and drinking fountains should be low enough for children to use easily (Garwood, 1979, p. 114).

4. Floors should have a nonslip surface. Deep-pile, shag, or sculptured rugs limit mobility; carpet should be tightly looped, commercial-grade carpet, which is smooth enough to allow wheelchairs to move easily and durable enough for heavy use (Salend, 1990, p. 301).

5. Special seating may be needed for some children. A chair with arms and with sides high enough to prevent a child from falling to either side, or a high-backed chair to support a child's trunk and head, might be needed (Spodek, Saracho, & Lee, 1984, p. 69).

6. Design and arrange the bathroom so a child using crutches, a walker, or a wheelchair can easily use it. Placement of bars and width of door stalls must be considered (Safford, 1978, p. 255).

Evaluating the daily flow of activity in the classroom involves observing how children interact, how they engage materials, and how they move from one activity to another. In this situation the teacher must determine, as described in the closing vignette, whether children's needs are being met by the classroom environment, staffing, and scheduling:

■   ■   ■   ■   ■   ■   ■   ■   ■

Once you have determined that no significant changes have occurred in staff assignments or in the daily schedule, the next step is to evaluate the current room arrangement. Because this room arrangement is new this week, there may be factors in the distribution of activities; amount of space for activities; the number, variety, and convenience of activities; the flow of traffic; or the responsiveness of this room arrangement that are causing changes in the children's behavior.

Observing the classroom is the critical first step in this evaluation process. It may be helpful to enlist the assistance of a co-worker to help get a clear idea of how the children are involved in use of the classroom. Requesting the director's assistance in scheduling time for observation will enable the observer to give you objective and thorough feedback.

As you observe, you realize that one large corner of the classroom is almost totally avoided by the children. A new activity center filled with carpet squares and manipulatives on the shelves is virtually unused. The result is that too many children are using the remaining space and activities, causing overcrowding and a shortage of materials, especially in the popular imaginary-play center. These remaining activities do not have adequate space for the numbers of children, and traffic flow is concentrated at one end of the classroom. Children's needs for privacy and variety are not being met. As a consequence, children who feel crowded and fatigued are exhibiting increased behavioral problems.

In order to solve this classroom design problem you need to do the following:

1. Make a change in the distribution and variety of activities, and alter the space allocated to different centers. By creating a smaller space for the manipulatives and making a larger space for the imaginary-play center, which is being used regularly, you decrease the overcrowding problem. Also, by adding a small canopy covering to the manipulatives center you create a cozy space that will attract children and meet the needs for privacy. By taking several sets of manipulatives off the shelves and opening the boxes of materials onto the floor you invite the children to play with the variety of materials available to them and help distribute the numbers of children more equally throughout the room. The traffic flow problem is greatly relieved.

2. Continue to observe and monitor children's play patterns and behavior throughout the week. Encourage children's involvement in a variety of activities and alter materials as needed. By making a few simple changes in the classroom design you have created an environment where children can be both positive and productive.

■   ■   ■   ■   ■   ■   ■   ■   ■

CHAPTER SUMMARY

Characteristics of a well-planned environment include consideration of and planning for physical safety and health. The environment also should be planned to meet both children's needs and adults' needs for nurturing, privacy, variety and complexity, recognition for individual differences, and self-expression. Room arrangements must include consideration of distribution of activities, amount of space, number and variety of activities, flow of traffic, and convenience. Environments must be responsive to children by the inclusion of soft materials. Special consideration and planning is required for the special developmental needs of infants, toddlers, preschoolers, and children with disabilities. Scheduling within the planned space should include a balance of indoor/outdoor, quiet/active, individual/small-group/large-group, large-muscle/small-muscle, and child-initiated/staff-initiated activities. Staff assignments should allow time for monitoring, assessment, and planning, as well as for supervising, interacting, and teaching.

DISCUSSION QUESTIONS

1. Discuss the vignette at the beginning of the chapter. What other questions or concerns might you have? Discuss the vignette at the end of the chapter. Are there other responses you might have to this situation?

2. Describe how children's needs and teachers' needs can be met by a well-planned environment.

3. What should a teacher consider when designing a classroom?

4. Describe ways to plan a classroom environment that supports the creative play of infants, toddlers, and preschoolers.

5. In what ways should a toddler classroom differ from an infant classroom? A toddler classroom from a preschool classroom?

6. What objects can be placed in the art area for preschoolers?

7. What should be considered, and avoided, when planning a classroom schedule?

8. Describe different types of staff assignments for classroom responsibilities.

REFERENCES

Accreditation criteria and procedures of the National Academy of Early Childhood Programs (1991). Washington, DC: National Association for the Education of Young Children.

Applebaum, M., Day, D., & Olds, A. (1984, Summer). Fine details: Organizing and displaying materials. *Beginnings*, pp. 13–16.

Caples, S. (1996). Some guidelines for preschool design. *Young Children, 51*(4), 14–21.

Carlson, K., & Cunningham, J. (1990). Effect of pencil diameter on the graphomotor skill of preschoolers. *Early Childhood Research Quarterly, 5*(2), 279–293.

Caruso, D. (1984). Infants' exploratory play. *Young Children, 40*(1), 27–30.

Catron, C. E., & Kendall, E. D. (1984). Staff evaluation that promotes growth and problem solving. *Young Children, 39*(6), 61–66.

Centers for Disease Control. (1988). Update: Universal precautions for prevention of transmission of human immunodeficiency virus, hepatitis B virus, and other bloodborne pathogens in health care settings. *Morbidity and Mortality Weekly Report, 37,* 377–387.

Crocker, A., Cohen, H., & Kastner, T. (1992). *HIV infection and developmental disabilities.* Baltimore: Brookes.

Deitch, S. R. (Ed.). (1987). *Health in day care: A manual for health professionals.* Elk Grove Village, IL: American Academy of Pediatrics.

Edelstein, S. (1995). *The healthy young child.* Minneapolis, MN: West.

Garwood, S. G. (1979). *Educating young handicapped children.* Germantown, MD: Aspen.

Gonzalez-Mena, J. (1986). Toddlers: What to expect. *Young Children, 42*(1), 47–51.

Greenman, J. (1984, Summer). Worlds for infants and toddlers: New ideas. *Beginnings,* pp. 21–25.

Hart, B. (1978). Organizing program implementation. In K. E. Allen, V. A. Holm, & R. L. Schiefelbusch (Eds.), *Early intervention: A team approach* (pp. 309–330). Baltimore: University Park Press.

Hathaway, W., Hargreaves, J., Thompson, G. & Novitsky, D. (1992). A study into the effects of light on children of elementary school age—a case of daylight robbery. Edmonton, Canada: Alberta Department of Education.

Hendrick, J. (1998). *Total learning: Developmental curriculum for the young child* (5th ed.). Columbus, OH: Merrill/Prentice Hall.

Hildebrand, V. (1987). Organizing: A key aspect of classroom management. *Dimensions, 15*(4), 6–8.

Kendrick, A. S., Kaufmann, R., & Messenger, K. P. (1995). *Healthy Young Children: A Manual for Programs.* Washington, DC: National Association for the Education of Young Children.

LeLaurin, K., & Risley, T. (1972). The organization of day care environments: "zone" versus "man-to-man" staff assignments. *Journal of Applied Behavior Analysis, 5*(3), 225–232.

Prescott, E. (1984, Summer). When you think about spaces. *Beginnings,* pp. 3–5.

Rogers, C. S., & Sawyers, J. K. (1988). *Play in the lives of children.* Washington, DC: National Association for the Education of Young Children.

Safford, P. (1978). *Teaching young children with special needs.* St. Louis, MO: Mosby.

Salend, S. (1990). *Effective mainstreaming.* New York: Macmillan.

Schreiber, M. (1996). Lighting alternatives: Considerations for child care centers. *Young Children, 51*(4), 11–13.

Shaw, J., & Chatt, M. (1985). Ideas: Toy selection for day care centers. *Dimensions, 13*(2), 15–18.

Smith, T., Polloway, E., Patton, J., & Dowdy, C. (1995). *Teaching students with special needs in inclusive settings.* Boston: Allyn & Bacon.

Spodek, B., Saracho, O., & Lee, R. (1984). *Mainstreaming young children.* Belmont, CA: Wadsworth.

Trawick-Smith, J. (1992). The classroom environment affects children's play and development. *Dimensions, 20*(2), 27–30, 40.

Twardosz, S. (1984). Environmental organization: The physical, social, and programmatic context of behavior. In M. Hersen, R. M. Eisler, & P. M. Miller (Eds.), *Progress in behavior modification* (Vol. 18, pp. 123–161). New York: Academic Press.

Twardosz, S., Cataldo, M., & Risley, T. (1974). Open environment design for infant and toddler day care. *Journal of Applied Behavior Analysis, 7*(4), 529–546.

Twardosz, S., & Risley, T. (1982). Behavioral-ecological consultation to daycare centers. In A. M. Jeger & R. S. Slotnick (Eds.), *Community mental health and behavioral ecology: A handbook of theory, research, and practice* (pp. 147–159). New York: Plenum Press.

Vartuli, S. (1987). Ideas: Teacher decisions that maximize learning and minimize disruptions in early childhood settings. *Dimensions, 15*(4), 28–31.

Willis, A., & Ricciuti, H. (1980). *A good beginning for babies: Guidelines for group care.* Washington, DC: National Association for the Education of Young Children.

Wolery, M. (1994). Designing inclusive environments for young children with special needs. In M. Wolery & J. Wilbers (Eds.), *Including children with special needs in early childhood programs* (pp. 97–118). Washington, DC: National Association for the Education of Young Children

ADDITIONAL RESOURCES _____

Donowitz, L. (Ed.). (1991). *Infection control in the child care center and preschool.* Baltimore: Williams & Wilkins.

Golbeck, S. (1995). The social context and young children's spatial representations: Recreating the world with blocks, drawings, and models. In S. Reifel (Ed.), *Advances in early education and day care: Social contexts of early development and education* (Vol. 7, pp. 213–252). Greenwich, CT: JAI Press.

Greenman, J. (1988). *Caring spaces, learning places: Children's environments that work.* Redmond, WA: Exchange Press.

Hirsch, E. (Ed.). (1984). *The block book.* Washington, DC: National Association for the Education of Young Children.

Kendall, E., & Moukaddem, V. (1992). Who's vulnerable in infant child care centers? *Young Children, 47*(5), 72–78.

Kennedy, D. (1991). The young child's experience of space and child care center design: A meditation. *Children's Environments Quarterly, 81*(1), 37–48.

Lanser, S., & McDonnell, L. (1991). Creating quality curriculum yet not buying out the store. *Young Children, 47*(1), 4–9.

Maldonado, N. (1996). Puzzles: A pathetically neglected, commonly available resource. *Young Children, 51*(4), 4–10.

Morris, S. (1995). Supporting the breastfeeding relationship during child care: Why is it important? *Young Children, 50*(2), 59–62.

Morrow, L. M. (1990). Preparing the classroom environment to promote literacy during play. *Early Childhood Research Quarterly, 5*(4), 537–554.

Petrakos, H., & Howe, N. (1996). The influence of the physical design of the dramatic play center on children's play. *Early Childhood Research Quarterly, 11*(1), 63–77.

Piaget, J. (1976). *The grasp of consciousness: Action and concept in the young child.* Cambridge, MA: Harvard University Press.

Presler, B., & Routt, M. (1997). Inclusion of children with special health care needs in early childhood programs. *Dimensions, 25*(3), 26–31.

Readdick, C. (1993). Solitary pursuits: Supporting children's privacy needs in early childhood settings. *Young Children, 49*(1), 60–64.

Schickedanz, J. (1986). *More than the ABC's: The early stages of reading and writing.* Washington, DC: National Association for the Education of Young Children.

Surr, J. (1992). Early childhood programs and the Americans with Disabilities Act (ADA). *Young Children, 47*(5), 18–21.

Taylor, S., Morris, V., & Rogers, C. (1997). Toy safety and selection. *Early Childhood Education Journal, 24*(4), 235–238.

Tegano, D., Moran, J., Delong, A., Brickey, J., & Ramassini, K. (1996). Designing classroom spaces: Making the most of time. *Early Childhood Education Journal, 23*(3), 135–142.

Warrick, J., & Helling, M. (1997). Meeting basic needs: Health and safety practices in feeding and diapering infants. *Early Childhood Education Journal, 24*(3), 195–200.

Weinstein, C., & David, T. (Eds.). (1987). *Spaces for children: The built environment and child development.* New York: Plenum Press.

Zeavin, C. (1997). Toddlers at play: Environments at work. *Young Children, 52*(3), 72–77.

8.

Outdoor Play Environment

Your director has recently informed you that a new child will soon be entering your classroom of fifteen 4-year-olds. After meeting Marta and her parents you are excited about completing the enrollment procedures. Marta is a delightful child, open and friendly and very articulate. Her parents are interested, warm, and supportive.

During the preenrollment conference and visit to the classroom, Marta is full of energy and quickly maneuvers her way around the classroom to explore the variety of materials and learning centers. Her wheelchair is not at all an impediment to her access to centers within the classroom. However, as you open the classroom door to show her the playground, you realize that you are faced with a difficult problem. Marta cannot maneuver her wheelchair over the ledge of the door, and it also is quickly apparent that much of the playground is inaccessible to her.

It is evident you must take steps to evaluate the playground's accessibility and make appropriate modifications so Marta can have full advantage of her learning environment.

- How do you approach Marta's parents about the problem of accessibility facing their daughter?
- What role will your director play in making necessary changes to the outdoor play area?
- Will you need to enlist the help of a consultant to help evaluate the playground and make recommendations for modifications?
- What types of play areas and equipment will you need to evaluate?
- Will the renovations to the playground require special funds?

Suggestions for responding to this classroom vignette will be shared at the end of the chapter.

When reading this chapter, focus on the important role that the outdoor play environment has in supporting children's development and in extending the curriculum. Also, focus on gaining an understanding of the issues of playground safety, playground design, and the accessibility of outdoor play areas for children with disabilities.

A safe, carefully planned outdoor play environment can enhance the development of personal awareness, emotional well-being, socialization, communication, cognition, and perceptual motor skills in young children. Stone (1970) views outdoor play as an integral part of the educational experience rather than simply a time to engage in recreational activities to let off excess energy. Range (1979) called attention to the mistaken belief that outdoor play is of little developmental value for children. She argued that, when challenged appropriately, young children can benefit greatly from their outdoor play experiences. The outdoor curriculum is an important component of the invisible curriculum

Anne Miller Stott and Bobbie Beckmann also contributed to writing this chapter.

and can be utilized to enhance the growth and development of the young child in a creative-play environment.

Providing outdoor places for children with disabilities to benefit from play experiences presents a great challenge. Many times, the nature of the disability limits the child's experiences and interactions with the environment. However, many of the identified educational goals for children with disabilities can be met through the naturalistic setting of play. Young children with disabilities require outdoor play experiences to promote the development of personal awareness, emotional well-being, socialization, communication, cognition, and perceptual motor skills and to assist them in generalizing these skills to the mainstream of life.

OUTDOOR CURRICULUM _____

Planning a balanced and varied outdoor curriculum involves understanding children's perceptual motor development, integrating the flow of activities between the indoor and outdoor play areas, regularly altering the outdoor environment to enhance opportunities for skill development, and fostering young children's exploration of the natural world. A carefully planned outdoor curriculum will enhance children's sense of well-being, extend the level of body awareness, facilitate social interactions, promote problem-solving skills, enrich movement vocabulary, develop perceptual motor skills, heighten respect for nature, and support creative expression.

When we think of the outdoor play environment, we usually envision young children in motion. Children are physical beings, and body movement is perhaps the most important way that children express themselves. "To the young child, movement means life" (Whitehurst, 1971, p. 52). Learning to move and learning through movement are equally important and interrelated processes:

> Learning to move . . . involves continuous development in ability to use the body effectively and joyfully, with increasing evidence of control and quality in movement. It involves the development of the ability to move in a variety of ways, in unexpected and expected situations, and in increasingly complex tasks. . . . Learning through movement . . . is a means through which a child may learn more about himself, about his environment and about his world. (Halverson, 1971, p. 18)

Movement allows children to engage in self-discovery and self-expression, explore the physical and social environment, establish contact and communication, and experience enjoyment and sensory pleasure (Whitehurst, 1971, p. 55). Movement is the vehicle through which young children experience the outdoor environment and curriculum.

To meet the needs of the whole child, the outdoor curriculum also must engage children's minds and sense of wonder. Children's inherent curiosity and sensitivity to the natural world around them is readily enhanced in the outdoor play environment. Adults who share children's wonder and excitement and who join children in exploration of nature have the opportunity to model respect and care for the environment and teach the interconnectedness of all life. Cornell (1979) has suggested five guidelines for nature education with young children:

Teach less and share more.

Be receptive.

Focus the child's attention.

Look and experience first, talk later.

A sense of joy should permeate the experience of being outdoors.

Nature offers children and adults the perfect classroom for discovery, adventure, challenge, and learning about the mystery and majesty of the world. "Climbing big rocks, mucking in puddles, whacking sticks on trees, collecting acorns and pinecones, looking for life under logs, and wallowing in the snow are all perfect, and frequent, opportunities for learning" (Fenton, 1996, p. 10).

The outdoor curriculum can be fully integrated into the overall curriculum by planning activities and experiences that meet goals for the development of the whole child. To meet the needs of all children in the program, teachers must appreciate differences in development, consider individual needs and objectives in the planning process, adapt and modify the environment and activities as needed, and add challenges gradually to develop children's competence as well as confidence in their abilities. Teachers should be knowledgeable about playground types, playground safety, and playground design features in order to plan an appropriate and adaptable playground environment.

PLAYGROUND TYPES _____

Various types of playgrounds have been advocated at different times in the United States and Europe. The traditional playground, with nonmovable, steel play equipment, has been criticized as being one-dimensional and anchored, with no natural landscaping (Datner, 1969; Frost & Klein, 1979). Traditional playgrounds tend to impede child experimentation and do not provide enough experiences to support basic play needs. The contemporary playground is usually designed by a professional architect. Designer playgrounds often use expensive materials and have a high level of aesthetic appeal (Frost, 1986).

The adventure playground concept originated in 1943 with a Danish landscape artist, C. Th. Sorensen, who noticed that children did not play on the elaborate, static traditional playground sites. He began to design playgrounds that reflected the actual play patterns of young children (Frost, 1992a). Yerkes (1982) describes these playgrounds as having novel forms and textures and different heights that are aesthetically arranged. Adventure playgrounds usually are very informal play areas that utilize scrap building materials (Frost, 1986). The adventure playground combines the concepts of exploration and creative pursuits, and permits children to develop their own ideas of play (Yerkes, 1982).

Frost (1986) defines the creative playground as one that is a compromise between formal, traditional playground design and the highly informal adventure playground. The creative playground features a semiformal environment and uses a variety of manufactured and handmade equipment. Henninger (1994) describes major characteristics of a creative playground: "First, children must have opportunities for healthy risk taking. Secondly, playgrounds must provide graduated challenges for young children. A third characteristic of good outdoor play spaces is the ability to promote a variety of play types. Finally, creative playgrounds should allow children to manipulate the materials and equipment found there" (p.10).

Creative playgrounds provide a flexible environment that can be adapted to meet the needs of children and support the curricular goals. When viewed as an extension of the classroom, the outdoor curriculum becomes an important setting to enhance the natural mode of children's learning and exploration (Yerkes, 1982).

PLAYGROUND SAFETY

To enhance children's mobility and creativity in playground areas, careful consideration must be given to creating and maintaining safe outdoor play environments. Frost describes the major problems associated with playgrounds for young children: "They are developmentally sterile" (Frost, 1992b, p. 6). "They are inappropriate to the developmental needs of children and they are hazardous" (Frost, 1986, p. 200). The majority of playground injuries are the result of children falling onto hard surfaces; a high number of injuries and deaths also are the result of inappropriate equipment that is poorly installed and maintained. Snow, Teleki, Cline, and Dunne (1992) reviewed reports on childhood injuries and found that playground injuries that require a visit to the doctor or emergency room occur at a rate of up to 7 per 100 children annually. Minor injuries not requiring medical assistance occur at the rate of up to 284 injuries per 100 children each year. It is interesting that up to 48 percent fewer serious injuries occur to children in child care than in other locations, including their homes. Unlike reports of injuries at home, where boys have higher injury rates, there are no gender differences in playground injury rates in child care, perhaps because both boys and girls are equally supervised in child-care programs. Children are most likely to be injured on climbing structures, followed by slides and swings, falls on the pavement, and occasionally wheel-toy accidents. About 30 percent of the injuries occur when children poke, hit, pinch, or collide with another child (Snow et al., 1992).

Ensuring outdoor play safety for young children includes selecting developmentally appropriate equipment that is durable, nontoxic, and securely fastened or installed; providing a resilient surface of at least 8 to 10 inches of pea gravel, wood chips, rubber matting, or other cushioning material under all climbing structures. To prevent entrapment of children, spacing between slats and railings on equipment should be less than $3\frac{1}{2}$ inches or more than 9 inches apart. Surround the playground areas with a well-constructed fence to protect children from hazards or intrusion (Frost, 1986, 1997; Wallach, 1997). Figure 8-1 includes a checklist for rating a playground for safety and appropriateness.

Equipment for the playground should be chosen using carefully established criteria. Consider the usefulness of a piece of equipment. Does the equipment meet the developmental needs of the children in the program, and can it be used in multiple ways by the children? In order to be safe and effective, equipment needs to be suitable for the ages and sizes of the children, durable and economical, and easily maintained (Sciarra & Dorsey, 1995). There are no *mandatory* national safety standards for play equipment and design; however, a national playground safety movement has been responsible for the development of voluntary standards designed to reduce playground injuries. The United States Consumer Product Safety Commission has established voluntary federal guidelines for playground safety (1994). The American Society for Testing and

Instructions:

Rate each item on a scale from 0–5. High score possible on Section 1 is 100 points, Section II is 50 points, and Section III is 50 points, for a possible grand total of 200 points. Divide the grand total score by 2 to obtain a final rating.

SECTION I. WHAT DOES THE PLAYGROUND CONTAIN?

Rate each item for degree of existence and function on a scale of 0–5 (0 = not existent; 1 = some elements exist but not functional; 2 = poor; 3 = average; 4 = good; 5 = all elements exist, excellent function).

_____ **1** A hard-surfaced area with space for games and a network of paths for wheeled toys.

_____ **2.** Sand and sand play equipment.

_____ **3.** Dramatic play structures (playhouse, car or boat with complementary equipment, such as adjacent sand and water and housekeeping equipment).

_____ **4.** A superstructure with room for many children at a time and with a variety of challenges and exercise options (entries, exits and levels).

_____ **5.** Mound(s) of earth for climbing and digging.

_____ **6.** Trees and natural areas for shade, nature study and play.

_____ **7.** Zoning to provide continuous challenge; linkage of areas, functional physical boundaries, vertical and horizontal treatment (hills and valleys).

_____ **8.** Water play areas, with fountains, pools and sprinklers.

_____ **9.** Construction area with junk materials such as tires, crates, planks, boards, bricks and nails; tools should be provided and demolition and construction allowed.

_____ **10.** An old (or built) vehicle, airplane, boat, car that has been made safe, but not stripped of its play value (should be changed or relocated after a period of time to renew interest).

_____ **11.** Equipment for active play: a slide with a large platform at the top (slide may be built into side of a hill); swings that can be used safely in a variety of ways (soft material for seats); climbing trees (mature dead trees that are horizontally positioned); climbing nets.

_____ **12.** A large soft area (grass, bark mulch, etc.) for organized games.

_____ **13.** Small semi-private spaces at the child's own scale: tunnels, niches, playhouses, hiding places.

_____ **14.** Fences, gates, walls and windows that provide security for young children and are adaptable for learning/play.

_____ **15.** A garden and flowers located so that they are protected from play, but with easy access for children to tend them. Gardening tools are available.

_____ **16.** Provisions for the housing of pets. Pets and supplies available.

_____ **17.** A transitional space from outdoors to indoors. This could be a covered play area immediately adjoining the playroom which will protect the children from the sun and rain and extend indoor activities to the outside.

_____ **18.** Adequate protected storage for outdoor play equipment, tools for construction and garden areas, and maintenance tools. Storage can be separate: wheeled toys stored near the wheeled vehicle track; sand equipment near the sand enclosure; tools near the construction area. Storage can be in separate structures next to the building or fence. Storage should aid in children's picking-up and putting equipment away at the end of each play period.

(continued)

Figure 8-1 Sample playground rating system. *Source: Play and Playscapes* by J. L. Frost, 1992, pp. 107–109. New York: Delmar Publishers, Inc. Copyright 1992 by Joe L. Frost. Reprinted with permission of Joe L. Frost.)

_____ **19.** Easy access from outdoor play areas to coats, toilets, and drinking fountains. Shaded areas and benches for adults and children to sit within the outdoor play area.

_____ **20.** Tables and support materials for group activities (art, reading, etc.).

SECTION II. IS THE PLAYGROUND IN GOOD REPAIR AND RELATIVELY SAFE?

Rate each item for condition and safety on a scale of 0–5 (0 = not existent; 1 = exists but extremely hazardous; 2 = poor; 3 = fair; 4 = good; 5 = excellent condition and relatively safe yet presents challenge).

_____ **1.** A protective fence (with lockable gates) next to hazardous areas (streets, deep ditches, water, etc.).

_____ **2.** Eight to ten inches of noncompacted sand, wood mulch (or equivalent) under all climbing and moving equipment, extending through fall zones and secured by retaining wall.

_____ **3.** Size of equipment appropriate to age group served. Climbing heights limited to 6–7 feet.

_____ **4.** Area free of litter (e.g., broken, glass, rocks), electrical hazards, high voltage power lines, sanitary hazards.

_____ **5.** Moving parts free of defects (e.g., no pinch and crush points, bearings not excessively worn).

_____ **6.** Equipment free of sharp edges, protruding elements, broken parts, toxic substances, bare metal exposed to sun.

_____ **7.** Swing seats constructed of soft or lightweight material (e.g., rubber, canvas).

_____ **8.** All safety equipment in good repair (e.g., guard rails, signs, padded areas, protective covers).

_____ **9.** No openings that can entrap a child's head (approximately $3\frac{1}{2}$–9 inches). Adequate space between equipment.

_____ **10.** Equipment structurally sound. No bending, warping, breaking, sinking, etc. Heavy fixed and moving equipment secured in ground and concrete footings recessed in ground. Check for underground rotting, rusting, termites in support timbers.

SECTION III. WHAT SHOULD THE PLAYGROUND DO?

Rate each item for degree and quality on a scale of 0–5 (0 = not existent; 1 = some evidence but virtually nonexistent; 2 = poor; 3 = fair; 4 = good; 5 = excellent). Use the space provided for comments.

_____ **1.** Encourages play:

Inviting, easy access

Open, flowing, and relaxed space

Clear movement from indoors to outdoors

Appropriate equipment for the age group(s)

_____ **2.** Stimulates the child's senses:

Change and contrasts in scale, light, texture, and color

Flexible equipment

Diverse experiences

(continued)

Figure 8-1 (continued)

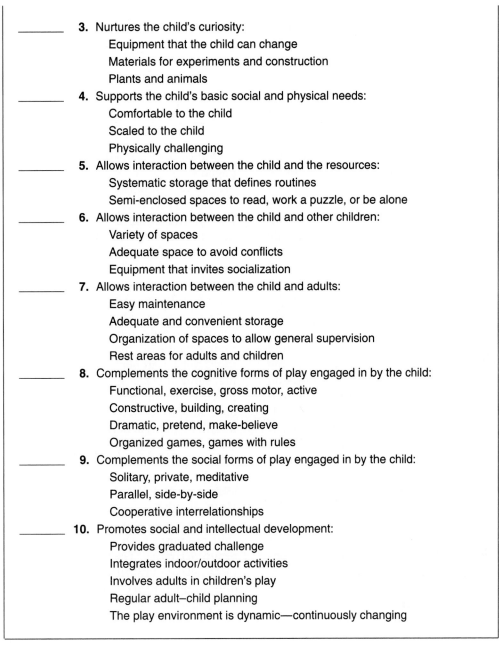

        3. Nurtures the child's curiosity:

                Equipment that the child can change

                Materials for experiments and construction

                Plants and animals

        4. Supports the child's basic social and physical needs:

                Comfortable to the child

                Scaled to the child

                Physically challenging

        5. Allows interaction between the child and the resources:

                Systematic storage that defines routines

                Semi-enclosed spaces to read, work a puzzle, or be alone

        6. Allows interaction between the child and other children:

                Variety of spaces

                Adequate space to avoid conflicts

                Equipment that invites socialization

        7. Allows interaction between the child and adults:

                Easy maintenance

                Adequate and convenient storage

                Organization of spaces to allow general supervision

                Rest areas for adults and children

        8. Complements the cognitive forms of play engaged in by the child:

                Functional, exercise, gross motor, active

                Constructive, building, creating

                Dramatic, pretend, make-believe

                Organized games, games with rules

        9. Complements the social forms of play engaged in by the child:

                Solitary, private, meditative

                Parallel, side-by-side

                Cooperative interrelationships

      10. Promotes social and intellectual development:

                Provides graduated challenge

                Integrates indoor/outdoor activities

                Involves adults in children's play

                Regular adult–child planning

                The play environment is dynamic—continuously changing

Figure 8-1 (*continued*)

Materials has developed national voluntary standards for playground equipment safety (1995). Teachers will always be the most important decision makers in the selection of playground equipment and the supervision of children for safety. Teachers must be aware of suggested safety guidelines and monitor the use and condition of playground equipment (Frost, 1986).

PLAYGROUND DESIGN _____

A creative playground design that is safe, secure, and stimulating encourages young children to learn about themselves, their peers, and the environment through play and exploration. A growth-promoting playground design will recognize variations in developmental stages and abilities of children and include equipment and activities appropriate for each age group. A well-designed outdoor play area consists of separate play areas for the different age groups of children: infants, toddlers, and preschoolers. Although children of each age group need appropriate playground equipment and play space, they also need opportunities to learn from one another. Playground placement adjacent to each classroom and scheduling of time to play outdoors should allow for interaction of different ages of children in the outdoor environment. Scale drawings (see Figures 8-2, 8-3, and 8-4) are included to illustrate a sample design of each of these play areas. Ample outdoor play space is essential to support children's perceptual motor development and to meet curricular objectives by providing a variety of creative play activities. The National Academy of Early Childhood Programs (*Accreditation Criteria and Procedures,* 1991) recommends a minimum of 75 square feet of outdoor play space per child; many early childhood playground environments include up to 150–200 square feet per child. Playgrounds should be carefully designed to incorporate the different developmental needs of these age groups of children and to encourage children to explore their outdoor environment actively.

Children's active exploration involves an element of risk taking. It is important that the children have control over decision making about their capabilities to meet motoric challenges. Giving opportunities for these challenges enhances children's feelings of accomplishment and self-worth and promotes the use of imagination and problem-solving skills. There is a distinction, however, between risks and hazards in the outdoor play environment. It is the responsibility of the teacher to eliminate playground hazards and to allow children to experience adventure, challenge, and risk. "The enjoyment and accomplishment of risk on the equipment should remain as an element of positive play and growth" (Wallach, 1997, p. 97).

Children with disabilities also should be fully engaged in outdoor exploration and should be considered in the preparation of playground designs. Table 8.1 lists specific adaptations to provide accessible playground equipment and structures for the infant, toddler, or preschool child with disabilities. The outdoor surface of the ground must be considered for accessibility as well. Manuvering a wheelchair on an outdoor surface should require no more force than it takes to propel the wheelchair up a ramp with a 14-degree slope. The surface must not catch a crutch tip, walker, or caster wheel. Resilent or cushioning material placed under swings or climbers must not be an obstacle for wheelchairs. For example, sand and pea gravel require up to six times as much effort for wheelchair movement as most indoor surfaces. Wood fibers as cushioning, after a month or more of settling and compacting, may provide less challenge, particularly with adequate draining and regular maintenance. Rubber matting, a more expensive option, may be the most accessible material for outdoor spaces (Henderson, 1997; Wallach, 1997).

Playgrounds should be designed with equipment that promotes both quiet and active, individual and group activities. Traditional playgrounds often promote active play with their large, open spaces. They often limit solitary play with their lack of quiet, private spaces. Both the playground design and the choice of equipment should create a balance between opportunities for individual and group experiences. Additional program goals, which may include staff training and research, may be supported by incorporating a research area and observation areas into the playground design.

Playground equipment can be classified into three broad categories according to the curricular objectives they support: sensory and tactile experiences; creative-play and dramatic-play opportunities; and large motor challenges. Each of the three playground areas, although planned for different age groups of children, should provide a wide variety of play equipment and play opportunities that encourage exploration and development in each of these categories and extends the classroom program outdoors.

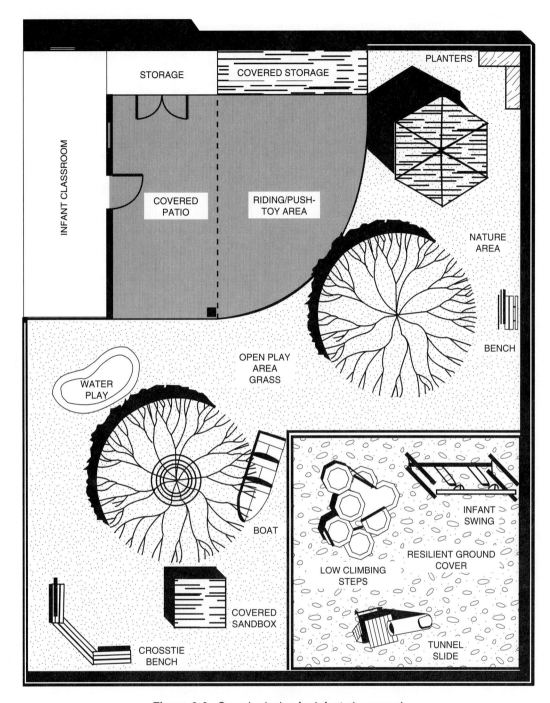

Figure 8-2   Sample design for infant playground.

Sensory and Tactile Equipment and Experiences

Providing a variety of sensory and tactile experiences on the playground supports cognitive development and encourages children to learn many basic concepts as they are exposed to various sights, sounds, textures, smells, and tastes outdoors. Children learn by manipulating, constructing, and experimenting with diverse materials available to them in the outdoor play area. Four specific categories of sensory/tactile experiences are water play, sand play, gardening, and nature activities.

Water Play. Numerous choices for water play involvement should be available on the playgrounds. Each playground design that includes a water play area should have wading areas, water tables, and water-fall/sprinkler systems that are appropriate for the specific age range of children. The wading areas and water tables on each playground may be connected

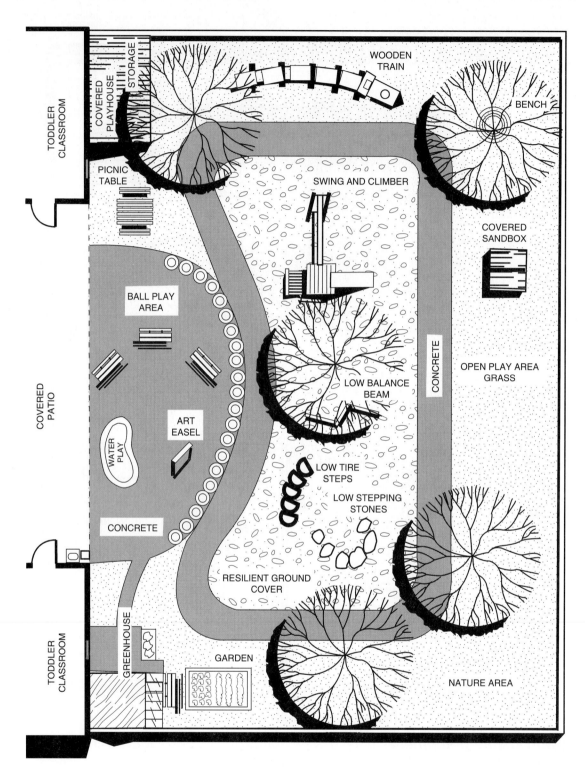

Figure 8-3 Sample design for toddler playground.

by a series of mini-canyons, gullies, and waterfalls so children can observe the natural flow of water and attempt to control the flow by building dams to check the water flow or by adding water to increase the flow.

Water play areas must be planned to offer a safe, healthy, developmentally appropriate medium for learning such concepts as wet-dry, sink-float, hot-cold, dip-pour, heavy-light, full-empty, and clean-dirty. Another goal of providing water play for young children is to offer a progression of exposure to water so that children can learn to respect water and not fear it.

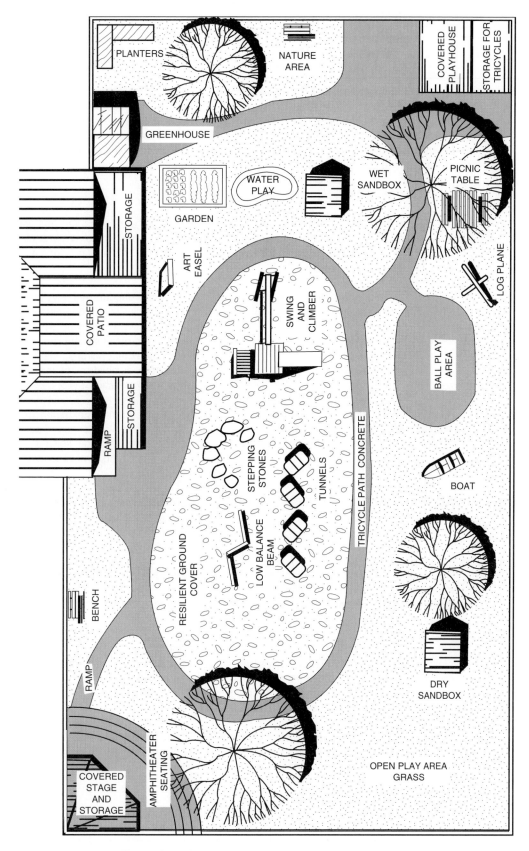

Figure 8-4 Sample design for preschool playground.

TABLE 8.1 Playground Adaptations for Inclusion

Structure	Adaptations of Design for Children with Disabilities	Expected Benefits
Climber	A platform at the ground level of this structure provides wheelchair accessibility to the child who cannot climb. The sizes of the rails are designed to accommodate various prosthetic devices used by amputees. The close spacing of the climbing section provides a safe and easy structure to promote climbing for children who have motor difficulties.	This structure promotes socialization, motor skills, motor coordination, balance, challenge, imagination, and problem solving. This also provides the *novel* experience of being "elevated" to the child with physical impairments.
Playhouse	A ramp provides access for children who use wheelchairs and other motorically impaired children. The door inside the playhouse is wide enough for a wheelchair.	This play area enhances imagination, dramatic play, motor skills, socialization, and creativity. This also provides a space for a quiet corner.
Tricycle Path	This path accommodates a tricycle and a wheelchair, side by side.	This area encourages development of motor skills, socialization, coordination, balance, imagination, and playing games with rules. Language development is enhanced by actually experiencing spatial-relationship concepts, as children move through, over, and under structures along the path.
Greenhouse/Garden	A table structure at the appropriate height is accessible to a child in a wheelchair.	This area promotes experiences in manipulative play, language development, creative play, problem solving, use of tools, nurturing, caring, and sensory/tactile stimulation.
Water Table and Pool	A child in a wheelchair can readily use a waist-high water table.	This area encourages socialization skills, creativity, manipulative skills, problem solving, concept development, and sensory/tactile stimulation.
Swing Structure	The various slats and platforms on this structure are designed to permit safe experiences for children with motor impairments.	This structure provides vestibular stimulation, sensory integration, movement stimulation, and balance activities.
Sandboxes	The low side structures allow access for a motorically impaired child. These sides are designed to give support, in a sitting position, for children who cannot sit unaided. Adapted tools will be provided for fine motor limitations.	These areas promote tactile stimulation, socialization, creative play, problem solving, and imagination.
Amphitheater	A ramp to the stage provides accessibility for children who use wheelchairs and other children who are motorically impaired. The design of the terrain on the preschool playground provides accessibility from the upper level of the playground to the lower level and amphitheater area.	This area enhances creativity, dramatic play, novelty, storytelling, variety of play, and socialization.

Children's cognitive development is supported by providing a variety of sensory and tactile experiences in the outdoor play environment.

In colder climates, it may not be practical or cost-effective to design a wide variety of water play areas when children's use of these areas is restricted to a few months during the year. Instead, the outdoor play area may be planned to include an open area for snow play. Examples of snow play activities include building snow sculptures and structures and carefully supervised sledding and sliding. Play is facilitated by providing plastic shovels, pails, scoops, and other open-ended materials. Children also are exposed to concepts such as wet-dry, hot-cold, and solid-liquid when experimenting with snow as a learning medium.

Sand Play. Sand play is another important means of sensory/tactile stimulation for young children. The texture, weight, and consistency of sand make it a versatile material for manipulation, through which children can practice gripping a shovel, scooping, sifting, shoveling, digging, filling containers, sculpting, and molding forms. Practicing these fine-motor techniques provides children with a basic understanding of the properties of sand such as heaviness, particle sizes, and textures; beginning measurement opportunities; and chances for creative expression. Children should be exposed to sand play along with a variety of tools and utensils for exploration. Sandboxes should be located close to the water play areas so children can combine the two ingredients for additional learning if they so desire. Sandboxes should be designed with folding doors or snap-on canvas tops to cover them when they are not in use to ensure the cleanliness of the sand.

Gardening. In keeping with the creative playground philosophy, teachers may include a third sensory/tactile experience in the playground design, a gardening area. With exposure to seeds, plants, soil, water, fertilizer, and the plant growth process, children can begin to understand firsthand the basics of the plant life cycle, manipulate a variety of materials, and learn basic properties of substances. Children also will have tasks such as feeding, watering, and repotting plants and can begin to share small amounts of responsibility. Children will learn basic cause-and-effect relationships with situations such as too little water, too much sunlight, too little soil, and too much water. Flowers and vegetables grown by the children can be picked, washed, arranged, smelled, and tasted, providing children with numerous sensory experiences.

Within the gardening areas, greenhouses may be included to provide additional space for outdoor planting. Greenhouses positioned between the playground areas will be accessible to several groups of children. The greenhouses should be designed with solar panels, a water source, actual space for potting and growing plants, and storage areas for gardening supplies.

Nature Activities. In addition to planned gardening areas, a more natural area that includes trees and plants can provide an outdoor habitat for wildlife such as birds and butterflies. Children can observe and delight in these wonders of nature and learn to protect their natural environment. "People seem to have a fundamental need to care for things outside themselves. This need can be met—and human life enriched—by caring for the natural world. A genuine concern for wild creatures and their habitats can promote great fulfillment in one's individual life and a sense of caring for other people" (Wilson, 1995, p. 7). In this environment, in addition to enhancing children's cognitive and sensory/tactile development, children's sense of emotional well-being is allowed to flourish.

This natural area can fulfill children's needs for privacy and time alone. Here children can experience solitude and the quieting effects of nature. These are

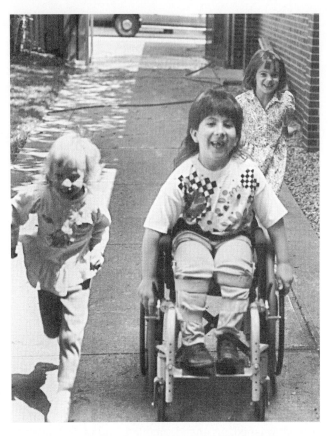

An effective playground design includes adaptations such as wider concrete paths to accommodate children with disabilities.

places to "watch, wonder, and retreat" (Readdick, 1993). This environment meets children's needs for privacy and supports children as they construct a sense of self, address autonomy issues, regulate social interaction, and understand person–environment relations (Readdick, 1993).

Rivkin (1995) suggests that this peaceful, quieting environment is a condition of human exisistence. We need peace as much as we need food and sleep. "Peace is a need, not a byproduct of exhaustion or overpowering violence" (p. 58). When we have time for peace and solitude, we are better able to deal with conflict, another condition of human existence. The playground and outdoor environment can be used to teach peace, provide solitude, and help children learn to engage in and value peaceful social interactions. "A belief in the possible—imagine a playground without fights (a world without wars!)—can lead to action" (p. 66).

Creative-Play and Dramatic-Play Equipment and Experiences

Opportunities for creative and dramatic play on the playground enhance early socialization, expression of emotions, acting out different roles, development of language,

and children's imagination. Pretend play presents children with the option of stopping and starting play scenarios at will (Yamamoto, 1979) and gives children a positive sense of control over their environment. Creative art activities allow children to express themselves in their own unique way. These activities combine to support the development of a positive self-concept in the young child. Playground equipment that supports creative- and dramatic-play opportunities can be divided into four major categories: stage/amphitheater areas, pretend transportation equipment, playhouses, and creative art.

Stage/Amphitheater Areas. Creative, dramatic play activities present children of all ages and developmental levels with circumstances in which they must work together toward a common goal. The stage/amphitheater areas provide opportunities for group work in acting out a story together, pretending to be characters in a nursery rhyme, and creating and performing skits together. While working together on these projects, children will have opportunities both to initiate interactions with other children and adults and to respond to interactions initiated by other children and adults. They can practice being a leader, giving instructions, being a follower, carrying out instructions, and helping a friend. Children can begin to discriminate between their own appropriate and inappropriate interactions by the responses of others.

To provide a catalyst for dramatic-play activities for toddlers and preschoolers, include a stage/amphitheater area composed of a raised stage area with a cover, rows of multilevel seats on one side of the stage for viewing a production, and a storage area under the stage for props and other stage equipment.

Because the amphitheater area is inappropriate for the developmental levels of infants and young toddlers, their dramatic-play needs can be met by providing pretend transportation equipment on the infant and toddler playgrounds. Suggestions for transportation pieces include a boat, an airplane, and train with an engine, cars, and caboose. Each vehicle should have a steering wheel, knobs, levers, bells, horns, flags, and window shutters, which the older infants can manipulate while they pretend to drive the vehicle.

Playhouses. Playhouses can serve dual purposes; they can promote social interaction and solitary play. One of the main goals of the outdoor curriculum is to provide children with many experiences that encourage them to interact with each other and practice social skills. Exposure to the spectrum of personalities within a group can offer continual learning experiences for young children, and the outdoor "classroom" is designed to facilitate interactions. Child-size houses with space for numerous materials will foster interaction among children. Within this area the youngest children can begin imitating actions they observe and then progress to acting out different feelings, emotions, and roles with a mixture of playmates.

Another goal of the outdoor curriculum is to provide children with areas that encourage individual pursuits. Playhouses, treehouses, and other niches can provide children "glassy-eyed moments of daydreaming or 'cocooning'" and allow children to "remove themselves from the hustle and bustle around them" (Readdick, 1993, p. 60). Teachers can help children understand that time to be alone is valuable and important in learning to live with others.

Playhouses may have front doors that open wide to allow for constant supervision, windows for authenticity, a division wall to simulate rooms, shelves for storage, and space to arrange various materials such as housekeeping supplies, hospital props, grocery store merchandise, and so on. Another playhouse feature may be a "garage" for the storage of tricycles and other wheel toys.

Creative Art. Children need to have creative-art materials constantly available to them, and one way of providing them on the playground is by using art easels designed for outdoor use. Playground areas may have easels attached to the outside fence, close to a water source. These art easels should be designed to store all needed supplies for painting and other easel activities within the easel. In colder climates it is more practical to take indoor easels outside when weather permits, rather than investing in specially designed outdoor easels. Children should be free to use this area at all times; however, younger children will need supervision during the activity. The availability of art materials and spaces should foster children's individual exploration and creation of unique masterpieces. These creative pursuits can be either solitary or social and allow children to choose their mode of creative expression and level of interaction with others.

Large-Motor Equipment and Experiences

Large-motor challenges are essential for young children who are just learning to control their physical movements. Young children need constant access to areas and equipment that will allow them to practice climbing and being on different height levels, balancing both statically and dynamically, coordinating movements such as pedaling and steering a wheel toy, and standing, walking, and running on a variety of surfaces. Some additional perceptual motor skills to be encouraged through the use of the equipment are motor planning ability, flexibility, agility, strength, endurance, timing, sequencing, and rhythm (Beckwith, 1979). Providing a variety of motor challenges for young children ages 6 weeks to 5 years

Creative art experiences encourage self expression as well as the development of fine motor skills.

means creating play opportunities for infants who are just beginning to hold their heads up; for toddlers who are beginning to creep, walk, and climb; and for preschoolers who are running, jumping, and climbing to greater heights. The four categories of equipment designed to foster physical/motor development are wooden climbing structures, swings, concrete areas for wheel toys, and balancing apparatus.

Wooden Climbing Structures. Large wooden climbing structures that have been designed to provide appropriate motor challenges for specific age groups of children are essential elements in promoting large-motor development. The climbing structures should be composed of a series of wooden platforms arranged on different levels to offer children various perspectives when observing their outdoor environment. The wooden climbers may be accessible through a variety of routes such as steps, ramps, ladders, slides, rope ladders, bridges, and poles. Navigating through these structures affords children chances to increase upper arm strength, coordinate hand grips with leg movements while climbing, and increase their stamina.

Swings. Swings provide an opportunity for children of all ages to practice cooperation and problem skills. Deciding how to get in and out of a swing, how to control a swing by pushing it, how to make the swing move while sitting in it, and how to maneuver a swing using more than one person are all learning experiences for young children.

A tire swing provides an outlet for social interactions, because two or three children can easily ride in it at one time. Another type of swing, the hammock swing, offers less support because of its flexible form; it requires greater effort from the children for balance while sitting in the swing, for gripping the ropes to hold onto the swing, and for aid while climbing into the swing. Still another type of swing is a flat platform swing used primarily with infants, toddlers, and children with disabilities. Young infants can lie on the swing and be challenged to lift their heads to view their environment. This swing also is accessible to creepers and toddlers and is useful in challenging children with disabilities.

Concrete Areas for Wheel Toys. Concrete areas for wheel toys afford challenges for all aspects of motor development. Children need opportunities to practice coordinating their arms and feet through steering, pedaling, and navigating a variety of terrains. Sharing, cooperating, and taking turns can be emphasized through the use of tricycles, wagons, and scooters. Children's observation skills and reaction times also can be enhanced through continued avoidance of collisions. Infant playground areas may include concrete areas where older infants can begin crawling and pushing wheel toys, walking and pushing wheel toys for support, and climbing on the wheel toys to maneuver them.

Toddler and preschool playground areas may have streetlike tricycle paths that wind around the playground area. These tricycle paths should be wide enough to allow a wheelchair and a wheel toy to pass at the same time and may follow the contour of the playground with hills of varying degrees of steepness. A covered bridge adds a greater element of challenge and fascination to the tricycle path.

Maneuvering a wheel toy on these terrains is a challenge for young children who are just beginning to gain control over their own physical movements. Mastering control over a wheel toy and successfully maneuvering it around the playground is an important confidence booster for young children.

Balancing Apparatus. Another aspect of perceptual motor development that should be addressed in the playground design is balance. Children need situations that enhance their ability to balance, not only while they are moving but also while they are stationary. Equipment designed to facilitate the practice of balance includes multilevel tree-stump "stepping stones," balance beams, or logs; climber ladders; and geometric stepping stones between functional areas.

Practical Considerations

Unfortunately, funds are often not available to purchase the wide variety of playground equipment needed to enhance all aspects of children's development. Creative teachers can improvise by moving indoor equipment outdoors temporarily and by enlisting the help of parents or community groups to construct simple, inexpensive equipment. For example, sensory/tactile experiences can be provided by moving a portable water table outdoors, using inexpensive equipment such as sprinklers, and constructing a sand play area inside a large donated tire. A gardening area for the playground can be prepared by parent volunteers. A natural area can be enhanced by child-constructed bird feeders made from milk cartons, wood scraps, or pinecones. Creative- and dramatic-play opportunities can be included by moving imaginary-play props and clothes outdoors and covering plastic snap walls and tables with sheets and blankets to make playhouses or stage areas. Large appliance boxes are one of the most enjoyed and open-ended materials teachers can use to promote creative play. Books and a blanket under a tree provide the impetus for storytelling and dramatization. Creative-art activities also can be provided by moving easels, tables, and art supplies outdoors and by taping large sheets of paper to fences and sidewalks. Children may be involved for lengthy periods of time in an activity as simple as painting the side of the brick building with water. This creative activity requires only buckets, paint brushes, and water. Perceptual motor challenges can be created by taking balance beams, balls, parachutes, jump ropes, and hoops outdoors. Inexpensive climbing areas and swings can be carefully constructed using donated materials. Teachers also can supplement the motor challenges available outdoors by planning field trips to area parks and community playgrounds.

The development of a high-quality, creative playground is a complex endeavor that requires consideration of safety and design features, knowledge of children's development and curriculum goals, and the ability to use resources and materials effectively and imaginatively. A creative playground supports curriculum goals and objectives by offering opportunities for the development of personal awareness, emotional well-being, socialization, communication, cognition, and perceptual motor skills for young children. In addition, an innovative playground design provides a solution to the challenge of creating a play facility for the child with disabilities.

■   ■   ■   ■   ■   ■   ■   ■   ■   ■

Creating a learning environment that is accessible to all young children requires that a teacher possess knowledge about children with disabilities, an attitude of acceptance, and the commitment to make environmental changes when needed. To meet Marta's needs for accessibility to the outdoor play environment the following steps are necessary:

Discuss your concerns with both your director and Marta's parents. Ask for assistance in evaluating the playground area, and take suggestions from both your supervisor and the parents.

Enlist the aid of someone with more expertise, such as a special educator familiar with adapting environments or a playground planner with experience planning outdoor play areas for inclusive programs.

Together, the teacher, director, and special educator should evaluate the playground area for accessibility. Upon evaluation you find that the concrete tricycle path is already wide enough for a tricycle and a wheelchair to pass each other; this is a positive aspect of the environment. You also realize that the sandbox has a wide ledge that will support Marta's ability to sit and play with other children in the sand

area. Water play is available with a movable water table that is the right height to accommodate Marta's wheelchair. Also, the door to the playhouse has no ledge, so Marta will have no difficulty maneuvering her wheelchair into that space. The need for change also is apparent. The most immediate need is for a ramp from the classroom door to the playground area. Another need is to purchase a swing with a back and sides; Marta will have too much difficulty with the tire swing currently being utilized. The addition of an S hook will make it possible for alternate use of both types of swings.

Request funds from your director for the immediate renovations needed. Be a strong advocate for Marta's needs. Marta's parents also may be able to offer suggestions for support, as may area organizations for children with disabilities.

Once the plans for renovation are made, involve Marta and the other children in discussing the need for the changes and watching the renovations when appropriate. This can be a wonderful learning experience for your preschoolers!

With the help of your consultant, make a long-range plan to add accessible climbing equipment and a gardening area.

■   ■   ■   ■   ■   ■   ■   ■   ■   ■

CHAPTER SUMMARY _____

This chapter describes ways that outdoor play and activities support children's development and learning. Different playground types include traditional, designer, adventure, and creative. Playground safety information and a checklist for rating playgrounds help to ensure children's safety in the outdoor play environment. Playground design, including scale drawings and adaptations

for children with disabilities, is discussed. Outdoor equipment to support sensory/tactile experiences, creative and dramatic play, and perceptual motor development should be included in playground design. Activities and equipment for water play, sand play, gardening, nature exploration, playhouses, outdoor art, transportation play, and climbing promote children's creative play.

DISCUSSION QUESTIONS _____

1. Discuss the vignette at the beginning of the chapter. What other questions or concerns might you have? Discuss the vignette at the end of the chapter. Are there other responses you might have to this situation?
2. Identify and distinguish among the four playground types.
3. Identify the three major categories of playground equipment and examples of specific objects in each category.

4. Describe considerations that help adapt playground designs and equipment to accommodate children with disabilities.
5. What playground areas and equipment can teachers create with limited resources?

REFERENCES _____

Accreditation criteria and procedures of the National Academy of Early Childhood Programs (1991). Washington, DC: National Association for the Education of Young Children.

American Society for Testing and Materials. (1995). *Safety performance specifications for playground equipment for public use.* Washington, DC: Author.

Beckwith, J. (1979). *Playground planning and fundraising.* Tacoma, WA: Schoolyard Big Toys.

Cornell, J. (1979). *Sharing nature with children.* Nevada City, CA: Ananda.

Datner, R. (1969). *Design for play.* Cambridge, MA: MIT Press.

Fenton, G. (1996). Back to our roots in nature's classroom. *Young Children, 51*(3), 8–11.

Frost, J. (1986). Children's playgrounds: Research and practice. In G. Fein & M. Rivkin (Eds.), *The young child at play: Reviews of research* (Vol. 4, pp. 195–211). Washington, DC: National Association for the Education of Young Children.

Frost, J. (1992a). *Play and playscapes.* Albany, NY: Delmar.

Frost, J. (1992b). Reflections on research and practice in outdoor play environments. *Dimensions, 20*(4), 6–10, 40.

Frost, J. (1997). Child development and playgrounds. *Parks and Recreation, 32*(4), 54–60.

Frost, J., & Klein, B. (1979). *Children's play and playgrounds.* Boston: Allyn & Bacon.

Halverson, L. (1971). The significance of motor development. In G. Engstrom (Ed.), *The significance of the young child's motor development* (pp. 17–33). Washington, DC: National Association for the Education of Young Children.

Henderson, W. (1997). Catching kids when they fall: Guidelines to choosing a playground surface. *Parks and Recreation, 32*(4), 84–92.

Henninger, M. (1994). Planning for outdoor play. *Young Children, 49*(4), 10–15.

Prescott, E., & Jones, E. (1972). *Day care as a child-rearing environment* (Vol. 1). Washington, DC: National Association for the Education of Young Children.

Range, D. (1979, September). Outdoor play, a year 'round adventure. *Texas Child Care Quarterly,* 17–19.

Readdick, C. (1993). Solitary pursuits: Supporting children's privacy needs in early childhood settings. *Young Children, 49*(1), 60–64.

Rivkin, M. (1995). *The great outdoors: Restoring children's right to play outside.* Washington, DC: National Association for the Education of Young Children.

Sciarra, J., & Dorsey, A. (1995). *Developing and administering a child care center* (3rd ed.). Albany, NY: Delmar.

Snow, C., Teleki, J., Cline, D., & Dunn, K. (1992). Is day care safe? A review of research on accidental injuries. *Day Care and Early Education, 19*(3), 28–31.

Stone, J. (1970). *Play and playgrounds.* Washington, DC: National Association for the Education of Young Children.

U.S. Consumer Product Safety Commission (CPSC). (1994). *Handbook for public playground safety.* Washington, DC: Author.

Wallach, F. (1997). Playground safety update. *Parks and Recreation, 32*(4), 95–99.

Whitehurst, K. (1971). The young child: What movement means to him. In G. Engstrom (Ed.), *The significance of the young child's motor development* (pp. 51–55). Washington, DC: National Association for the Education of Young Children.

Wilson, R. (1995). Nature and young children: A natural connection. *Young Children, 50*(6), 4–11.

Yamamoto, K. (1979). Trails of many, and of one: The wholesome child, the troubled child. In K. Yamamoto (Ed.), *Children in time and space* (pp. 59–75). New York: Teachers College Press.

Yerkes, R. (1982). *A playground that extends the classrooms.* DeKalb, IL: Northern Illinois University. (ERIC Document Reproduction Service No. ED 239 802)

ADDITIONAL RESOURCES _____

Adams, L., Hayslip, W., & Norman-Murch, T. (1997). Interest areas support individual learning. *Child Care Information Exchange, 114,* 61–64.

Betz, C. (1992). The happy medium. *Young Children, 47*(3), 34–35.

Burnett, R., & Davis, N. (1997). Getting to the heart of the matter. *Child Care Information Exchange, 114,* 42–44.

Castle, K., & Wilson, E. (1992). Creativity is alive in outdoor play! *Dimensions, 20*(4), 11–14, 39.

Clemens, J. (1996). Gardening with children. *Young Children, 51*(4), 22–27.

Dighe, J. (1993). Children and the earth. *Young Children, 48*(3), 58–63.

Dinwiddie, S. (1993). Playing in the gutters: Enhancing children's cognitive and social play. *Young Children, 48*(6), 70–73.

Ebensen, S.B. (1987). *The early childhood playground: An outdoor classroom.* Ypsilanti, MI: High/Scope Press.

Frost, J., & Wortham, S. (1988). The evolution of American playgrounds. *Young Children, 43*(5), 19–28.

Gallahue, D. (1993). Motor development and movement skill acquisition in early childhood education. In B. Spodek (Ed.), *Handbook of research on the education of young children* (pp. 24–41). New York: Macmillan.

Galvin, E. (1994). The joy of seasons: With the children, discover the joys of nature. *Young Children, 49*(4), 4–9.

Gonzalez, S. (1974). Adventure playgrounds. *Parks and Recreation, 9,* 22–23.

Griffin, S. (1992). Wondering about trees: Playground discoveries can lead to new learning. *Dimensions, 20*(4), 31–34.

Guddemi, M., & Eriksen, A. (1992). Designing outdoor learning environments for and with children. *Dimensions, 20*(4), 15–18, 23–24, 40.

Haugen, K. (1997). Using your senses to adapt environments. *Child Care Information Exchange, 114,* 50, 55–56.

Jaelitza. (1996). Insect love: A field journal. *Young Children, 51*(4), 31–32.

Jensen, M. (1990). Playground safety: Is it child's play? *Parks and Recreation, 25*(8), 36–38.

Meyer, A. (1997). More than a playground: Accessible outdoor learning centers. *Child Care Information Exchange, 114,* 57–60.

Odoy, H., & Foster, S. (1997). Creating play crates for the outdoor classroom. *Young Children, 52*(6), 12–16.

Passantino, E.D. (1975). Adventure playgrounds for learning and socialization. *Phi Delta Kappan, 56,* 329–332.

Piaget, J. (1962). *Play, dreams, and imitation in childhood.* New York: Norton.

Sher, A. (1976). *The importance of play.* Rutland, VT: College of St. Joseph the Provider. (ERIC Document Reproduction Service No. ED 248 964)

Smilansky, S. (1968). *The effects of sociodramatic play on disadvantaged preschool children.* New York: Wiley.

Taylor, S., & Morris, V. (1996). Outdoor play in early childhood education settings: Is it safe and healthy for children? *Early Childhood Education Journal, 23*(3), 153–158.

Thompson, S. (1994). What's a clothesline doing on the playground? *Young Children, 50*(1), 70–71.

Tomich, K. (1996). Hundreds of ladybugs, thousands of ladybugs, millions and billions and trillions of ladybugs—and a couple of roaches. *Young Children, 51*(4), 28–30.

Vaughn, E. (1990). Everything under the sun: Outside learning center activities. *Dimensions, 16*(4), 20–22.

Wallach, F. (1990). Playground safety update. *Parks and Recreation, 25*(8), 46–50.

Wallach, F. (1992). Playing safe: Eliminating hazards on children's playgrounds. *Dimensions, 20*(4), 28–30.

Wardle, F. (1990). Are we taking play out of playgrounds? *Day Care and Early Education, 18*(1), 30–34

Wardle, F. (1994). Viewpoint: Playgrounds. *Day Care and Early Education, 22*(2), 39–40.

Wardle, F. (1997). Playgrounds: Questions to consider when selecting equipment. *Dimensions, 25*(1), 9–15.

Wilson, R. (1996). The development of the ecological self. *Early Childhood Education Journal, 24*(2), 121–124.

Wilson, R. (1997). A sense of place. *Early Childhood Education Journal, 24*(3), 191–194.

Wortham, S., & Wortham, M. (1992). Nurturing infant and toddler play outside. *Dimensions, 20*(4), 25–27.

Yinger, J., & Blaszka, S. (1995). A year of journaling—a year of building with young children. *Young Children, 51*(1), 15–20.

Youcha, V., & Wood, K. (1997). Enhancing the environment for ALL children. *Child Care Information Exchange, 114,* 45–49.

THREE. . . . .

VISIBLE CURRICULUM

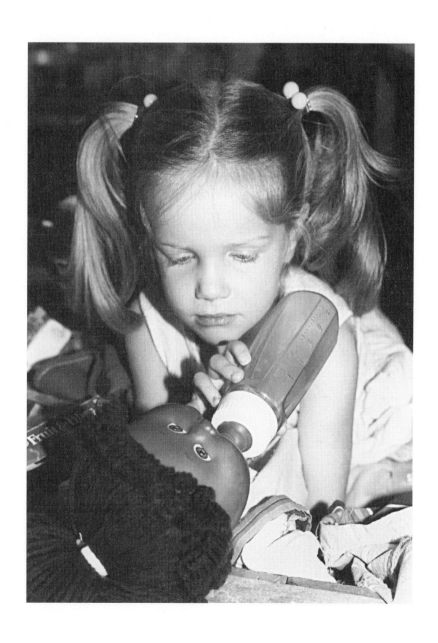

9.

Child Observation and Assessment

Compiling assessment information such as developmental checklists, child observations, and portfolios is an ongoing process in your program. The developmental information is shared with parents in parent conferences. As you are sharing information from the developmental checklist with 4-year-old Tanika's parents in a parent conference, they begin to ask a variety of questions about Tanika's development:

- How does Tanika's social development compare with that of the other children in her classroom?

- Why doesn't your program use a standardized assessment that yields an IQ score?

- Tanika's best friend, Jamie, seems to have a much larger vocabulary than Tanika. Is Tanika delayed in her language development?

- Tanika cannot yet count beyond 5; does this mean she will have difficulty in school next year?

- Tanika's older sister seemed to be much more sensitive to others' feelings when she was 4 years old. Why is Tanika different? Does this mean she is insensitive or difficult to get along with?

These are important issues to Tanika's parents. How will you explain your approach to developmental assessment, answer the parents' questions, and help reassure Tanika's parents about her growth and development?

Suggestions for responding to this classroom vignette will be shared at the end of the chapter.

When reading this chapter, focus on the important role that developmental assessment plays in early childhood programs and the importance of a linkage between assessment and curricula. Learn the criteria for evaluating developmentally appropriate assessment procedures and how to choose assessment instruments for your classroom. Also, become aware of the components of authentic assessment—such as developmental checklists, child observations, portfolios, and specialized assessment instruments—and the role that teachers and parents have in the assessment process.

Assessment procedures provide a systematic method of verifying and clarifying what teachers intuitively know about the development of individual children. When implemented as an integral part of the curriculum development process, assessment helps teachers to broaden and deepen their understanding of children; form stronger, more meaningful relationships with children; and individualize instructional strategies effectively to meet the needs of children. When families are involved in the assessment procedure, teachers gain an understanding of children in the context of their total environment and form partnerships with parents to support children's growth.

One of the basic precepts in assessment of young children is that development is a highly individualized process. "Normal" development at any one age level includes a broad spectrum of skills and behavior. The

Bobbie Beckmann also contributed to writing this chapter.

highly individualized nature of development is readily apparent when observing a group of children of the same age; physical characteristics, social behavior, and cognitive and language skills may vary tremendously and still fall within a normal range. Use of any assessment process requires a basic understanding of child development, a knowledge of observation and assessment techniques, and a consideration of the role of the teacher and parents in the assessment process.

Assessment is an important component in the development and implementation of a comprehensive creative-play curriculum. What is lacking in many assessment processes is the linkage between assessment and curriculum; this linkage, however, provides the integration of children's developmental needs with program goals and activities and completes the cycle of the visible curriculum, which includes assessing development, setting individual and program goals, and planning and implementing curricular activities.

GOALS FOR DEVELOPMENTAL ASSESSMENT _____

There are a variety of reasons for assessing young children. Most early childhood educators agree that a comprehensive assessment process should be designed to obtain specific developmental information about children, to aid teachers in setting goals and planning programs, and to provide a profile of each child's growth and development to share with parents. In addition, some programs use assessment for the diagnosis of disabilities or developmental delays. Assessment of children with disabilities also is appropriately used to determine individual education plans (IEPs) that include goals and objectives for adapting the classroom environment and activities for preschool children's needs and abilities, or to develop individual family service plans (IFSPs) that include goals and objectives for family support and developmental activities for infants and toddlers with disabilities. Other programs inappropriately use assessments as a criterion to determine readiness for a program or classroom placement and to label, group, or track children according to skill level (Meisels & Atkins-Burnett, 1993; NAEYC & NAECS/SDE, 1991; Schweinhart, 1993).

In a joint position paper on appropriate curriculum and assessment in programs serving children ages 3 through 8, the National Association for the Education of Young Children and the National Association of Early Childhood Specialists in State Departments of Education state:

> Assessment is the process of observing, recording and otherwise documenting the work children do

and how they do it, as a basis for a variety of educational decisions that affect the child. Assessment is integral to curriculum and instruction. In early childhood programs, assessment serves several different purposes: (1) to plan instruction for individuals and groups and for communicating with parents, (2) to identify children who may be in need of specialized services or intervention, and (3) to evaluate how well the program is meeting its goals. (NAEYC & NAECS/SDE, 1991, p. 32)

Developmental assessment is a systematic, continuous method of observing individual children and their unique development. The process includes the following:

- A collection of milestones that can be charted using observational techniques
- A method for direct, objective observation of specific skills and behaviors in each developmental domain
- A documentation of the unique and individual development of each child through the use of comments, anecdotes, and work sampling
- A system for communicating with parents, for sharing a child's strengths and identifying areas of concern, and for discussing the next levels of development
- A useful mechanism for assessing program effectiveness and for enhancing program planning

CHOOSING DEVELOPMENTALLY APPROPRIATE ASSESSMENTS _____

Developmentally appropriate assessment techniques will provide a variety of ongoing procedures for assessing the development of the whole child over time. Assessing the development of the whole child, not just cognitive development, is critical if teachers are to understand what is important in children's lives and what the needs of children are, because in the words of Winnie-the-Pooh, "There are days when spelling Tuesday simply doesn't count" (Milne, 1957,

p. 221).[1] Teachers should use the assessment information to support children's growth and make daily decisions about programming, not to compare children's development or to evaluate the achievement of narrow academic goals.

NAEYC and NAECS/SDE (1991, pp. 34–35) guidelines include a series of questions to ask to evaluate a program's assessment procedures. Teachers should be able to answer all of these questions in the affirmative.

---

[1]Excerpts from Winnie-the-Pooh titles that appear throughout this book are used by permission of Dutton Children's Books, a division of Penguin Books USA Inc., and Metheun Children's Books. *The House at Pooh Corner* by A. A. Milne. Copyright 1928 by E. P.

Dutton, renewed ©1956 by A. A. Milne; *Winnie-the-Pooh* by A. A. Milne. Copyright 1926 by E. P. Dutton, renewed ©1954 by A. A. Milne; *The World of Pooh: The Complete Winnie-the-Pooh and the House at Pooh Corner* by A. A. Milne. Copyright 1957.

1. Is the assessment procedure based on the goals and objectives of the specific curriculum used in the program?

2. Are the results of assessment used to benefit children, that is, to plan for individual children, improve instruction, identify children's interests and needs, and individualize instruction, rather than label, track, or fail children?

3. Does the assessment procedure address all domains of learning and development—social, emotional, physical, and cognitive—as well as children's feelings and dispositions toward learning?

4. Does assessment provide useful information to teachers to help them to do a better job?

5. Does the assessment procedure rely on teachers' regular and periodic observations and record-keeping of children's everyday activities and performance so that results reflect children's behavior over time?

6. Does the assessment procedure occur as part of the ongoing life of the classroom rather than in an artificial, contrived context?

7. Is the assessment procedure performance based, rather than only testing skills in isolation?

8. Does the assessment rely on multiple sources of information about children, such as collections of their work, results of teacher interviews, and dialogues, as well as observations?

9. Does the assessment procedure reflect individual, cultural, and linguistic diversity? Is it free of cultural, language, and gender biases?

10. Do children appear comfortable and relaxed during assessment rather than tense or anxious?

11. Does the assessment procedure support parents' confidence in their children and their ability as parents rather than threaten or undermine parents' confidence?

12. Does the assessment examine children's strengths and capabilities rather than just their weaknesses or what they do not know?

13. Is the teacher the primary assessor and are teachers adequately trained for this role?

14. Does the assessment procedure involve collaboration among teachers, children, administrators, and parents? Is information from parents used in planning instruction and evaluating children's learning? Are parents informed about assessment information?

15. Do children have an opportunity to reflect on and evaluate their own learning?

16. Are children assessed in supportive contexts to determine what they are capable of doing with assistance as well as what they can do independently?

17. Is there a systematic procedure for collecting assessment data that facilitates its use in planning instruction and communicating with parents?

18. Is there a regular procedure for communicating the results of assessment to parents in meaningful language, rather than letter or number grades, that reports children's individual progress?[2]

In addition, in a position statement on developmentally appropriate assessment, the Southern Early Childhood Association (SECA, 1990) lists the following cautions on the use of assessment:

- Assessment information is not to be used as tests for grading, labeling, grouping, or retaining children.
- Children have different styles, rates, and motivations for learning.
- Diversity among children should be expected, and all children should be treated with respect and dignity.
- All forms of assessment and evaluation can be misused and influenced by biases about race, gender, income level, and culture; and professionals must guard against personal bias.

Early childhood educators who understand the importance of developmentally appropriate assessment will choose components of the assessment process that support children's growth and facilitate program planning.

TEACHER AS EVALUATOR

Teachers can be very effective observers of children's development when they follow appropriate guidelines. They must use knowledge of children's development, be objective when evaluating children, and be able to make informed decisions about support for children's development. To be effective as evaluators and obtain an accurate total picture of each child, early childhood educators must become committed and understanding observers of young children. "Observing children purposefully and carefully is a way

[2]Reprinted by permission of NAEYC.

to get to know them, a way to look more deeply. We need as full and realistic a picture as possible of the child in motion—interacting, choosing, constructing, learning, responding, functioning. Observing individual children helps us to keep in mind that each child is different, and each is his or her own universe" (Ayers, 1993, p. 34).

Using observation to determine the extent of a learning or development problem can be a challenging task for teachers of young children. Teachers observe and interact with young children in naturalistic play settings over long periods of time and often are well qualified to determine when a developmental problem exists. However, because the rate of children's development is so individual, teachers often are unsure about how to react to differences in children's behavior or skill level.

Teachers should not overreact to changes in children's behavior or skills but should observe over a period of time, discuss the observations with parents to determine whether changes in the family situation may be affecting the child, and alter the environment or teaching strategies to help the child succeed. In general, "a learning difficulty is a problem only if it continues over a significant length of time, resists casual efforts to help, or impedes the child in her daily functioning" (Pitcher, Feinburg, & Alexander, 1989, p. 290). However, if the problem does exist over time, and efforts to help the child succeed in the classroom environment are not productive, the teacher needs to pursue developmental screening or a diagnostic referral in order to obtain needed assistance for the child and family.

Teachers also must realize the importance of the issue of confidentiality and ensure that the developmental information obtained for each child is treated in a professional, confidential manner. Parents should, of course, always have access to their child's developmental information, but teachers must develop specific procedures that require parental permission to release developmental information to other agencies or professionals.

Most important, however, effective teachers of young children must be more than good observers, accurate record keepers, and trained evaluators. Teachers must know each individual child, be aware of each child's dreams and fears and feelings, and be alert to problems or changes that may require special assistance or additional support. What is most significant in a child's life is not always observable and is rarely quantifiable, for "what is essential is invisible to the eye" (Saint-Exupéry, 1943, p. 70). How do you measure a child's capacity for joy, a child's curiosity, or a child's sense of humor? These all are important characteristics of healthy, well-adjusted children that are not measurable but are certainly knowable. How do you measure the depth of a child's pain, the extent of a child's inner turmoil, or the intensity of a child's fears? For children in emotional distress, these are significant factors that are not likely to be determined through testing, but may be revealed through interactions with caring, supportive teachers. The best teachers of young children are sensitive to what is essential in the child's world and are able to use a variety of assessment techniques to create a comprehensive assessment process that will enlarge their understanding of each individual child.

PARENT PARTNERSHIPS IN ASSESSMENT

Teachers can gain an understanding of the whole child in the context of the child's total environment by involving families in the assessment process. Developing a picture of the whole child involves viewing the child as an individual, a group member, and a family member. Benner (1992) discusses the importance of ecologically valid assessments that include an analysis of the child's family, culture, and community and that consider the child as part of a home and community environment, not as an isolated individual.

All parents should have input into the developmental assessment process, but this is especially critical for families with children who are at risk or have disabilities. Public Law 99-457 requires family involvement in the development of an individual family service plan (IFSP). The family, together with appropriate professionals, evaluates the family's strengths and needs and determines goals and services for the child and the family. Family-focused assessment considers the child as part of a family system, respects the uniqueness of each family, and recognizes the influence of the family on the development of the young child (Bailey & Simeonsson, 1988).

Information concerning a family's strengths and needs can be obtained through a variety of methods, including interviews, observations, tests, or a combination of these. Data-collection methods should be individualized as appropriate for the family and the situation, but any methods used should reflect the philosophical framework of the ecological perspective:

- Effective intervention techniques address family systems issues and, therefore, must be accompanied by data gathering related to family strengths and needs.
- The ongoing consistent influence in a child's life is his or her family.
- Families are the decision makers and, therefore, are partners with professionals in the early-intervention process.

- Comprehensive services that meet broad-ranging needs of all family members are more beneficial than segmented delivery systems (Benner, 1992, p. 116).

Besides implementing these family-focused assessment processes with families who have young children with disabilities, early childhood educators can utilize some of these family assessment techniques when a situation with any individual child or family may necessitate a higher level of family involvement.

COMPONENTS OF THE ASSESSMENT PROCESS _____

An authentic, comprehensive assessment process should include several components: a developmental checklist, child observations, portfolios, and the use of specialized screening instruments as needed. These components differ by data-collection method and by the type of results or information they yield. Using multiple sources of information results in greater validity and, most important, is an interactive process that helps teachers see children in a total environmental context. The *developmental checklist* charts children's development through sequenced stages and uses a combination of teacher observations and limited staged testing of children. *Child observations* yield anecdotal information from teachers' observations of individual children and focus on what is unique about each child in development, behavior, and interaction. *Portfolios* are a type of performance-based assessment that provide teachers with a tool for compiling work samples to complete the developmental picture of each child. *Screening instruments* use staged testing and interviewing of children to yield standardized, developmental information, to confirm the validity of teachers' observations of children's development, and to suggest the need for diagnostic assessment of specific developmental delays. Comprehensive assessment must be viewed as a continuing process that occurs and reoccurs at regular intervals.

A comprehensive assessment process involves parents by eliciting parental reports of children's developmental progress in the home setting and by requesting parents' input into the formulation of individual objectives for the child. This sharing of developmental assessment information is best accomplished in regularly scheduled parent conferences.

Developmental Checklist

A checklist of developmental milestones in the same domains that are included in the curriculum will provide insight into children's individual development and will foster the linkage between assessment and curriculum planning. The developmental domains included in the checklist directly correspond to the areas of development in the curriculum. The developmental checklist (Appendix B) for the creative-play curriculum provides teachers with a systematic method of observing the individual child's development in six areas: personal awareness, emotional well-being, socialization, communication, cognition, and perceptual motor skills. The checklist includes a wide range of behaviors and skills in sequential developmental order to facilitate observations and ratings by the teacher/evaluator. The primary purpose of the checklist is not to obtain a developmental age of the child or to predict future development, but to assist in describing the child's unique development and areas of strength.

Although skills or behaviors in many developmental areas or domains overlap, the purpose of the developmental checklist is to assign specific milestones to each area to ensure a comprehensive observation and assessment process. This sequential design reduces duplication and minimizes assessment time.

Areas of the Developmental Checklist. Milestones observed in the *personal awareness* domain are in the four subdomains:

1. Self-help skills (SH): Increases skill to feed and dress self and regulate toileting and sleeping.
2. Independence (I): Exhibits control of self and mastery of environment.
3. Personal health (PH): Develops knowledge of body parts, nutrition, hygiene, drug abuse prevention, wellness.
4. Personal safety (PS): Learns child abuse protection and passenger and pedestrian safety practices; develops an awareness of hazards within the child's environment.

The domain of *emotional well-being* directs teachers/evaluators to observe the following subdomains:

1. Awareness, acceptance, and expression of emotions (AAEE): identifies a variety of feelings and expresses feelings to others.
2. Coping skills (CS): Shows adaptive and healthy responses to stressors, conflict, or change; uses relaxation techniques; resolves emotional conflict and issues.
3. Personality integration (PI): Exhibits general adjustment, autonomy, positive self-concept.
4. Building values (BV): Develops empathy, trust, reverence, respect.

Socialization provides the teacher/evaluator with a sampling of skills from the following subdomains:

1. Social interactions (SI): Interacts with peers and adults; resolves conflict.
2. Cooperation (C): Helps, shares, takes turns.
3. Conservation of resources (CR): Uses and cares for materials and the environment appropriately.
4. Respect for others (RO): Understands and accepts individual differences; understands multicultural issues.

Communication skills are observed in the four subdomains that constitute language development:

1. Receptive language (RL): Follows directions; understands basic concepts.
2. Expressive language (EL): Expresses needs, wants, feelings; uses words, phrases, sentences; speaks clearly and distinctly.
3. Nonverbal communication (NV): Uses congruent communication, facial expressions, body gestures, hand gestures.
4. Auditory memory/discrimination (A): Understands spoken language; discriminates different sounds.

In the *cognition* area, development is observed in the following four subdomains:

1. Problem solving/reasoning (PS/R): Uses divergent thinking; suggests solutions to peer problems, "what if" situations; answers questions; extends sentence or story logically.
2. Concept formation (CF): Understands spatial relations; identifies colors, numbers, shapes.
3. Imitation/memory (I/M): Imitates; recalls past events; sequences events.
4. Association/classification (A/C): Matches; sorts; groups; classifies; establishes relationships between objects.

Observation of *perceptual motor skills* include the following subdomains:

1. Eye-hand/eye-foot coordination (EHC or EFC): draws, writes, manipulates objects, tracks visually, throws, catches, kicks.
2. Locomotor skills (LS): moves body through space: walks, jumps, marches, skips, runs, hops, gallops, rolls, crawls, creeps.
3. Nonlocomotor skills (NLS): static: bends, reaches, turns, twists, stretches, sways, squats, sits, stands.
4. Body management and control (BMC): exhibits body awareness, space awareness, rhythm, balance, and ability to start, stop, and change directions.

Figure 9-1 includes a sample portion of the developmental checklist (see Appendix B) to illustrate the linkage between the developmental milestones that form the focus of the curriculum model and the developmental checklist.

An emphasis of the creative-play curriculum is the development of creativity in young children. All young children have creative potential, but creative development is highly individualized and varies from child to child. Although research on young children's creative development is relatively new and this assessment is not designed to identify creative young children, the teacher/evaluator should comment on indicators of creativity in the Observations section of the developmental checklist. Recognizing individual children's creative traits will help teachers of young children to plan the curriculum and prepare the program environment to support the development of creativity. Although no reliable indicators of creativity have been determined in children under age 3, some indicators of creativity in preschool-age children are these:

- Child is willing to take risks, do things differently, try new things; willing to try the difficult.
- Child has an extraordinary sense of humor in everyday situations.
- Child is opinionated, outspoken, willing to talk openly and freely.
- Child is a nonconformist, does things his or her own way.
- Child expresses imagination verbally; for example, makes up funny words, fantastic stories.
- Child is interested in many things, is curious, questioning.
- Child is self-directed, self-motivated.
- Child is imaginative, enjoys fantasy.
- Child engages in deliberate, systematic exploration, develops a plan of action.
- Child likes to use his or her imagination in play, prefers pretend play.
- Child is innovative, inventive, resourceful.

DEVELOPMENTAL CHECKLIST
EMOTIONAL WELL-BEING

24 to 30 months
1. Smiles in recognition of own image in mirror. (PI)
2. Voluntarily slows down for nap or rest. (CS)
3. Begins to use words or complex gestures to express needs or feelings. (AAEE)
4. Begins to exhibit ability to set limits for self. (CS)
5. Begins to instigate activities based on own needs and desires rather than by imitation alone. (PI)

30 to 36 months
1. Expresses emotions through pretend play. (AAEE)
2. Relates warmly and positively to adults but is not overly dependent. (BV)
3. Begins to enjoy small-group activities and interactions. (PI)
4. Can describe a memory of an emotional situation or interaction. (CS)

36 to 42 months
1. Verbalizes emotions he/she is feeling. (BV)
2. Is able to recover from anger or temper tantrum and be cooperative and organized. (CS)
3. Expresses displeasure through verbalization rather than physical aggression. (BV)
4. Separates from parent without reluctance. (PI)

42 to 48 months
1. Recognizes emotions in others. (BV)
2. Verbalizes consequences of behaviors. (CS)
3. Maintains an appropriate, stable temperament most of the time. (PI)
4. Begins to differentiate between fact and fantasy. (PI)

Emotional Well-Being Subdomains:

AAEE   Awareness, acceptance, and expression of emotions
CS   Coping skills
PI   Personality integration
BV   Building values

Figure 9-1 Sample portion of the developmental checklist.

- Child explores, experiments with objects; for example, pulls things apart purposefully.
- Child is flexible.
- Child is good at designing things (Tegano, Bennett, & Pike, 1990, pp. 35–36; Tegano, Moran, & Sawyers, 1991, p. 120; reprinted by permission of NEA).

Before administering the developmental checklist, the teacher/evaluator should become very familiar with the milestones and the criteria. Administration of the checklist should begin at one developmental age level below the child's chronological age level, continue through the child's age level, and end at one age level above the chronological age. (For example, if a child is 22 months old, then the three developmental levels to be assessed would be 12 to 18 months, 18 to 24 months, and 24 to 30 months.) The checklist is scored with a (+) symbol to denote that the child can perform the task consistently and with confidence and ease and a (−) to denote that the child can perform the task not at all, rarely, or only with help.

When assessing an item on the developmental checklist, it is most appropriate to set up the necessary materials or activity in one area of the classroom. For example, to determine whether a 55-month-old child can count four objects, you may need to set up small blocks on a table and invite the child to play. While playing, put four blocks in front of the child and ask the child to count them for you, one at a time. Then the child can continue in block play. The checklist is designed to be used in the naturalistic classroom environment.

The Observations section follows each set of questions in the checklist. It is extremely important to use this space to list the skills the teacher/evaluator observed in unstructured observational assessment, to record any questions or comments concerning the child's ability in a specific area, and to include observations related to the child's developing creativity.

Child Observations

The record of child observations is designed to complement and complete the assessment information obtained through the use of the developmental checklist. The observations of behavior in each domain provide important information that is descriptive of the uniqueness and individuality of each child. Recording of child observations may include the use of anecdotal records that are brief narrative statements about a significant occurrence, daily logs of a child's activities that are written at the end of the day, or play observation diaries that use play behaviors as the basis for observation (Mindes, Ireton, & Mardell-Czudnowski, 1996). The record of child observations should contain specific, objective information that allows teachers and parents to extend the developmental "picture" of the child and that highlights the subtle differences in development in each domain. Results of the child observations may be recorded in the Observations section of the checklist, or a more extensive narrative report may be attached to the checklist if more in-depth information is needed. Use of formal, report-writing style is recommended, because this information will become a part of the child's

Observing children in a natural play environment completes the total picture of the individual child's development.

permanent file. Guidelines for preparing accurate, professional, and well-written observation comments or reports are offered here:

1. Preparation

    a. An important first step is to read over previous observation comments written about the children. To update and expand the development information concerning a particular skill, describe changes that have occurred, or use a completely different type of observation to describe development. For example, if a child's block-building structures have been discussed before, find another creative activity to discuss.

    b. In order to complete accurate and meaningful observation comments, it is critical to reach an understanding of the developmental domains. It is helpful to start by reading about the developmental milestones in each developmental domain and to become familiar with the checklist items. The subdomains are useful explanations of the skill areas under each domain. Also, to prepare for observing and writing, refer to the Guidelines for Child Observations (Appendix C).

    c. The most important aspect of the assessment process is to know the children about whom you are writing. Observe each child on a regular basis and take time to get to know each child.

2. Purpose

    The primary purpose of the observation comments is to provide unique information about each child's total development. Observe how the child is developing in his or her own way. Someone who is familiar with the child and reads the report should be able to identify the child by the specific descriptions of the child's behaviors, without seeing the child's name.

3. Process

    a. Begin the assessment process by making notes about the children on a regular basis. When something significant occurs, write it down and describe it in detail. Later you can decide where to place the information in the Observations section.

    b. Develop a system for remembering what you have observed. Use note cards in your pocket or an observation clipboard in the classroom—whatever works best for you.

Daily charts or logs, journals, or diaries also may be useful for obtaining details for the report.

   c. The comments will be more comprehensive if observations are made over time. To make the task more manageable and the comments more accurate and complete, spread the observation period out over several weeks. The process of observing and recording children's development should be an ongoing one.

4. Product

   a. The Observations section is the product of classroom observations. It should be written in the form of summary paragraphs in each of the developmental domains.

   b. The tone of the observation comments should be formal. Avoid the use of "I," "me," "mine," other people's names, and value judgments (well, wonderful, good, improved.)

   c. As in any professional report, it is necessary to write, spell, and punctuate correctly. If needed, use a grammar handbook and dictionaries as references.

   d. Positive descriptions of what the child is doing rather than what he or she is not doing are most appropriate. If a concern needs to be expressed, do so in a positive manner. This can be difficult, but it is essential. Also, describe effective methods that are being used to cope with the problem in the classroom.

   e. Comments concerning children's development should be written objectively. Give specific anecdotal examples that are dated, and avoid making subjective assumptions about feelings or intentions and using feeling words. When it is important to describe a subjective interpretation such as "child enjoys music activities," back that up with specific examples of the child taking part in these types of activities and his or her evidence of enjoyment (smiles; expresses excitement, enthusiasm, or eagerness).

   f. It is important to write clearly and concisely and to use definite, specific, concrete language. Another person who reads your comments should have a clear picture (like a videotape) of the child's behavior and development.

   g. To strengthen the observation comments consider the following points:
      1) Contrast the observed skill/behavior indoors and outdoors.
      2) Contrast the observed skill/behavior with various materials, situations, or people.
      3) Describe the frequency and duration of the behavior.
      4) Describe whether the child engages in the behavior spontaneously or with encouragement.
      5) Describe whether the behavior was initiated by the child or was in response to someone else.

5. Professionalism

   a. The developmental checklist with comments usually becomes a part of the child's permanent record; and parents, staff members, and other professionals who work with the child in the future may have access to it. It is essential that the information be accurate and the comments written in a professional manner.

   b. Developmental assessment information always is considered confidential. Keep observation notes and drafts of the comments with you or in a locked file cabinet. In the notes and drafts it is helpful to assign each child an assessment number rather than using the child's name or initials to ensure confidentiality.

6. Proofread

   To ensure that the comments are accurate and complete, always go over the report thoroughly before sharing it with parents or colleagues and make any needed corrections or changes.

PORTFOLIOS _____

Portfolios are a type of child-centered authentic assessment that are based in the context of the child's real world and show the child's accomplishments over time. Teachers make decisions about the organization of young children's portfolios—what to include and how frequently to collect work samples. Creating a portfolio is a dynamic process that can involve the child, teacher, and parents. As children get older they will want to participate more fully and make choices about the work samples to include in their portfolios. Portfolios may be organized in a variety of ways: by content area, by themes, or by developmental domains. The method of organization most effective for integrating the portfolio with the developmental checklist and child observation is to use the developmental domains—personal awareness, emotional well-being, socialization, communication, cognition, and perceptual motor skills—as the organizing structure. Portfolios organized in this manner consist of a collection of each child's work in each developmental area. Work samples may include children's artwork, child-created stories, books read, and photographs of special projects. The portfolio also may include technologically assisted sampling of children's play and performance as documented in videotapes or audiotapes.

Teachers may choose to keep observational records, developmental checklists, and parent conference reports in the portfolio, or may choose to keep these in a separate file to be used in conjunction with portfolio information. Portfolios may be kept in notebooks, file folders, file boxes, or other appropriate containers. They provide important insight into developing a picture of the child's total development (Wortham, 1995).

GOAL-SETTING PROCEDURES _____

The results of the developmental assessments are a valuable tool in curriculum planning. Through the identification of the child's developmental milestones, goals can be set to enhance the next stage of development. Developing educational objectives for young children is the step that provides the linkage between assessment and curriculum. Translating the results of the developmental assessment into a specific educational objective for the child involves analyzing the results of the assessment, determining the most important developmental goals for the child, breaking down the goals into specific, observable skills or behaviors, and writing the objective you want the child to achieve in clear, concrete language. Using children's objectives when writing activity plans and selecting materials and equipment for the classroom links the objectives to the curriculum and creates a meaningful basis for individualized teaching.

Teachers and parents can set goals and plan appropriate activities that help achieve the child's individual goals (see Figure 9-2 for a sample form for individual objectives and activities). Using assessment informa-

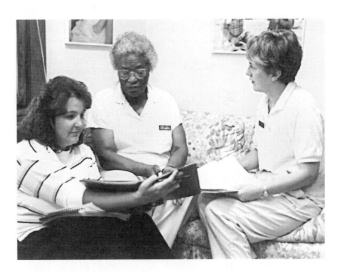

Teachers can use assessment information to set individual children's objectives and enhance curriculum planning.

tion from every child to set individual and program goals and plan activities is the task that completes the cycle of the visible curriculum and solidifies the linkage between assessment and curriculum.

PARENT CONFERENCES _____

The parent conference is a time to share assessment information. Not only should the teacher/evaluator report developmental information, but also the parents should supply information. Parental comments concerning the child's development may be added to the observation comments. This information sharing helps to complete the total picture of the child, inform the parents of the uniqueness of their child's devel-

opment, and enlist parental participation in supporting their child's growth. General guidelines for parent conferences and sample forms are in Chapter 5. Specific suggestions for sharing assessment information in parent conferences are offered here:

1. Prepare in advance for the conference by organizing and reviewing current copies of the

Individual Objectives and Activities

Date: _July 1, 1991_   Domain: _Emotional Well-being_

Sarah _____ will _begin to return_
(child)   (behavior)

to equilibrium after experiencing stress
(behavior continued)

as evidenced by _Calming down more quickly
after stressful events._

Some activities to encourage this behavior are:

1. _During group, read the book I'm So Mad & discuss using words & staying calm._

2. _In art give crayons & paper, say "color as if you are is very angry, mad, sad, calm, happy, silly, etc." As children (esp. Sarah) color talk about how the emotions feel._

Figure 9-2 Sample of an individual objective and activity form.

developmental checklist, observation comments, portfolios, and any additional assessment data. Bring these materials to the conference and be ready to share the information with parents in an understandable and meaningful way.

2. Communicate to parents:

   a. the uniqueness of their child's development

   b. the importance of not using this assessment information to compare their child to other children

   c. how assessment information is used to set goals, plan program curriculum, and implement individual activities

   d. ways to use this information to facilitate their child's development at an appropriate level and pace at home

3. Ask parents to share:

   a. information about their observations of the child's behavior in the home setting

   b. anecdotes describing the uniqueness of their child's development

   c. suggestions for individual objectives

   d. ways they facilitate the child's development at home

4. Together, agree on the individual objectives to be set for the child and brainstorm ideas for activities that can be implemented at home and in the classroom to foster development in these areas.

5. Before finishing the conference, ask parents if they have other questions or issues to discuss about their child's development. Be sensitive to parents' concerns about assessment information. Ensure that parents leave the conference with a positive view of their child's development and with appropriate strategies or resources for addressing concerns.

DEVELOPMENTAL SCREENING _____

Occasionally the results of the developmental checklist, child observations, and portfolio assessments may indicate a concern about a child's development in a particular area. Teachers may choose to conduct an additional developmental screening to determine whether the child may have a problem that indicates a need for further testing. Although a screening instrument cannot be used to identify a specific developmental problem or to develop intervention techniques, its results can extend the information obtained from the developmental checklist and child observations and may indicate the need to make a referral for diagnostic assessment.

Developmental screening instruments typically encompass a variety of developmental domains including cognition, communication, perceptual motor skills, and socialization. The basis for selecting a screening instrument should include considerations of the length of the screening process, the difficulty in learning to administer the screening instrument, the inclusion of a parent questionnaire in the screening process, the adaptability of the instrument for use with children from a variety of cultures, and the reliability (how often identical results are obtained) and validity (how accurate the instrument is) of the instrument (Meisels & Atkins-Burnett, 1993). Standardized tests are classified as either criterion-referenced or norm-referenced assessment instruments. *Criterion-referenced* tests compare a child's performance or skill level to a specified standard of skill mastery. *Norm-referenced* tests compare a child's performance or skill level to a larger population in the same age range. This type of standardized screening instrument should be individually administered by a person who has good rapport with children, is sensitive to cultural diversity, and has specialized training in testing procedures.

REFERRAL _____

Communicating concerns about a possible developmental delay to parents can be very difficult. Many times, the child's teacher is the first person to identify these concerns, especially if the problems are very subtle. Keep in mind that the developmental checklist and screening assessment process can only identify the need for further testing. They are not diagnostic tools. Teachers of young children have a responsibility to identify children who may need more thorough assessment and to support families through the early identification and intervention processes.

During the parent conference, follow the guidelines and accentuate the positive aspects of the child's development first. Have written information about the delays or problems you have observed and be very specific. Present only information related to what you have observed and avoid making personal judgments. Listen attentively to parents' opinions and ideas about the problem and discuss options and make decisions using a problem-solving approach.

If through the assessment and developmental screening process a child exhibits problems or delays, further professional evaluation may be needed. Diagnostic assessment typically will "identify a child's specific areas of strength and weakness; determine the nature of a child's problems; suggest the cause of the problem or deficiency, if possible; and make general recommendations about suitable remediation strategies" (Meisels & Atkins-Burnett, 1993, pp. 5–6). The types of professionals who are qualified to provide various types of diagnostic testing are listed in Figure 9-3. Departments of public health, school systems, Head Start programs, and pediatricians can be a source of information on how to gain access to the necessary evaluation instruments and qualified evaluators. Have a list of the names and phone numbers of professionals who can further assess the child or provide the parent with more information. Comprehensive diagnostic assessments of young children are best obtained by using a multidisciplinary team of professionals. By using a team approach to deal with the delay or problem, you provide much-needed support to parents in obtaining services that the child needs.

Developmental delays or problems rarely occur in total isolation. Because developmental domains are interrelated and a problem in one area often affects other areas, it is critical that diagnostic assessments yield information about the development of the whole child. This whole-child assessment approach also supports the choice of individual goals, intervention strategies, and program placement to address the developmental needs of the child. These decisions should be determined through an M-team

The following professionals are trained to provide comprehensive evaluations and/or therapy. If you suspect a medical or developmental problem, a referral to one of the following professionals is recommended.

Audiologist   Screens for and diagnoses hearing problems, recommends hearing aids if needed and suggests resources for people with hearing impairments. The audiologist can provide information about the nature of a child's hearing loss, the sound frequencies and decibel levels the child can and cannot hear, the usefulness of a hearing aid, the care of a hearing aid, and the availability of special programs for children with hearing impairments.

Neurologist   A medical doctor who diagnoses and treats brain and nervous system disorders. A neurologist performs a physical examination to determine how the body gains information from the sense organs and how it uses the muscular system to perform motor acts. He or she may do special tests such as lumbar punctures or electroencephalograms (EEGs). The EEG is used to determine abnormal patterns of activity in the brain. This test can help the neurologist decide whether the child's abnormal behavior is related to some underlying central nervous system condition.

Nutritionist   Evaluates a person's food habits and nutritional status. This specialist can provide advice about normal and therapeutic nutrition.

Occupational Therapist   Evaluates and treats children who may have difficulty performing self-help, play, or school-related activities. The aim is to promote self-sufficiency and independence in these areas. The therapist chooses exercises and activities designed to improve the child's motor skills in feeding, dressing, toileting, washing, sitting, walking, and handling objects. The occupational therapist will work with the child and suggest activities that the child's family and teachers can do to promote independence.

Opthalmologist   A medical doctor who diagnoses and treats diseases, injuries, or birth defects that affect vision. He or she may also conduct or supervise vision screening. The opthalmologist examines a child's eyes using lights, simple pictures, toys, and a variety of instruments to determine how well the child sees. Opthalmologists use different procedures in treating children, depending on the eye condition. They may prescribe glasses or medication or perform surgery. They may also be able to suggest special modifications for teaching the child (such as in materials and seating arrangements).

Orthopedist   A medical doctor who deals with the development, function, and disorders of the skeletal system (muscles, joints, and bones). An orthopedist sets broken bones, prescribes prosthetic devices and braces, and makes recommendations to physical therapists in cases where exercises are advised.

Otolaryngologist   A medical doctor who diagnoses and treats disorders of the ear, nose, and throat. He or she also can perform ear, nose, and throat surgery. This specialist may also be known as an E.N.T. (ear, nose, and throat doctor). An *otologist* is an otolaryngologist who works exclusively in the area of ear disorders. The otolaryngologist may undertake a comprehensive examination of the external ear, the ear canal, the eardrum, and the middle ear (the space behind the eardrum). He or she may also administer a gross test of hearing acuity to get an idea of where the problem lies and to determine what further tests should be given. Surgery may be advised when there is a problem with the bone structure of the ear or when fluid is present in the ear.

(*continued*)

Figure 9-3   List of professionals in child assessment. *Source:* Frakes, P., & Porter, M. (1986). Glossary of diagnosticians and treatment specialists. *Guide to conditions which place children at developmental risk* (pp. 78–80). Nashville, TN: The Tennessee Children's Services Commission.)

Pediatrician   A medical doctor who specializes in the health care of children. A pediatrician can examine general health and nutritional conditions. If there are specific health problems, the pediatrician may prescribe medication, or may suggest another specialist: a *pediatric allergist* specializes in allergies of the skin and respiratory system; a *pediatric cardiologist* specializes in heart conditions, diseases and defects; a *pediatric endocrinologist* specializes in metabolic disorders; a *pediatric hematologist* specializes in children's blood disorders; a *pediatric pulmonary specialist* diagnoses and treats lung diseases in children.

Physical Therapist   A licensed professional who evaluates and plans physical therapy programs for young children. He or she directs activities for promoting self-sufficiency primarily related to posture and gross motor skills such as walking, sitting, and shifting position. The pediatric physical therapist also helps select special equipment used for moving, such as wheelchairs, braces, and crutches. The therapist may help a child practice walking, crawling, hopping, skipping, and going up and down stairs. The physical therapist can suggest activities that the child's family and teachers can do to promote motor development.

Psychiatrist   A medical doctor who diagnoses and treats psychological, emotional, behavioral, and developmental or organic problems. Psychiatrists can prescribe medication. They generally do not administer tests. There are different kinds of psychiatrists. A *child psychiatrist* is a medical doctor who specializes in psychological, behavioral and developmental problems of childhood. A psychiatrist spends time talking to or playing with a child. He or she may interview the child's parents. While observing how the child relates to others, communicates, and plays, the psychiatrist is also alert for signs of some physical problem that might indicate a nervous system disorder.

Psychologist   A nonmedical licensed professional who diagnoses and treats social, emotional, psychological, behavioral, or developmental problems. There are many different kinds of psychologists. Psychologists may ask children questions, observe them at play, ask the parents questions, and observe the children interacting with the parents. They may choose to administer standardized tests to assess intellectual abilities and adaptave behavior (ability to use language, play with others, and do things independently). Psychologists sometimes use play activities to understand and treat children. At times they may want to talk with the whole family to help with problems they might have concerning a particular child. Some psychologists also can help to decide what kinds of educational programs and activities would be best to improve children's intellectual abilities and adaptive behavior.

Speech/Language Pathologist   A licensed professional who screens, diagnoses, and treats communication disorders. This person also may be called a speech clinician or speech therapist. Depending upon the results of testing, observation, and parent and teacher interviews, the speech/language pathologist may design and carry out a therapy program for the child. When the speech/language pathologist feels that there may be other problems contributing to the language disorder, he or she may recommend that the child see an audiologist, psychologist, otolaryngologist, or other professional for further examination and recommendations. The speech/language pathologist can provide the child's family and teachers with specific instructional activities to help stimulate language development or to help correct speech problems.

Figure 9-3   (*continued*)

(multidisciplinary team) process. Participants include parents, teachers, diagnosticians, and additional qualified personnel who will determine educational and support services for the child with disabilities.

Early childhood educators concerned with fostering the optimum development of each child, planning a growth-promoting curriculum and program environment, and providing intervention strategies for individual children as needed must

rely on developmentally appropriate assessment practices in order to be effective. Child observation, assessment procedures, and supplementary screening procedures can provide the framework for gathering information about specific areas of a child's development. The authentic assessment process increases teaching effectiveness, supports program goals, and strengthens the partnership between teachers and parents.

■   ■   ■   ■   ■   ■   ■   ■   ■

Most parents are extremely concerned about their children's development and often are anxious about any differences they may see in their child's developmental progress. Parents frequently want to compare their children to other children in the program or to a larger population of children in order to be reassured that their child's development is occurring within a normal range. Parents also may feel threatened by differences in development that might suggest a concern or a developmental delay.

Teachers must have the ability to describe the purposes of developmental assessment in early childhood programs and to inform parents about the possible misuses of developmental information. Teachers also must be very knowledgeable about child development and be able to explain to parents the individual growth patterns and rates of development in young children. Helping parents to understand that each child's development is unique and that the value of assessment is not in comparing children but in evaluating each individual child's development in all areas is a critical task for the teacher/evaluator. For example:

- Help Tanika's parents understand that her behavior in all areas is within the normal range and that the value of the assessment process is not in comparing Tanika's development with other children's but in determining how to help Tanika grow to her fullest capabilities.
- Explain that there is minimal value in assessing IQ at this

age, that young children do not test well, and that the most appropriate assessment procedures involve teacher and parent observation.

- Reassure Tanika's parents that each child develops at an individual rate and that certainly they can expect to see differences between Tanika and other children, including her sister. The results of the developmental assessment confirm that Tanika's social and cognitive development are quite typical for a 4-year-old and there is no need to be concerned about Tanika's relationship with others or her ability to master cognitive tasks that she will encounter in school.
- Finally, give Tanika's parents many examples of her developmental strengths to help them appreciate her for the unique, delightful child she is and to gain their assistance in fostering Tanika's development at home.

Using the information obtained in the developmental checklist, child observations, and portfolio as a basis, teachers also must include parents in setting individual developmental goals for their child and describe how these goals are utilized to aid in curricular planning. Being well prepared for the parent conference, knowledgeable about the child's development, and sensitive to parents' concerns will help the teacher/evaluator use the developmental assessment information effectively and appropriately.

■   ■   ■   ■   ■   ■   ■   ■   ■

CHAPTER SUMMARY _____

Assessment is an integral part of early childhood programs that helps teachers better understand children and better plan instruction that is individualized and developmentally appropriate. Good assessment practices assume an understanding of child development and a knowledge of observation and assessment techniques. NAEYC and NAECS/SDE have issued guide-

lines for selecting and implementing assessment procedures in early childhood programs. The guidelines focus on purposes, scope, use of results, teachers' role, children's response, and parents' involvement. Teachers' observation and interactions with children are important in assessment; confidentiality of information is critical. Parents' input in assessment is important, especially for children with disabilities. P.L. 99-457 mandates family involvement in determining goals and services for children. Comprehensive assessment can include several components: checklist, child observation reports, portfolios, and screening instruments. The developmental checklist assesses a wide range of behavior and skills in six domains: personal awareness, emotional well-being, socialization, communication, cognition, and perceptual motor skills. Child observation reports include anecdotal reports or event sampling. It is important that this information be accurate, professional, and well written. Portfolios include a collection of children's work over time that reflects the child's development in all domains. Information from the assessment process is used to develop goals and objectives upon which selection of classroom activities, equipment, and materials is based. Assessment information is also shared in parent conferences. Developmental screening may be used when the results of the developmental checklist and child observation reports indicate concern about a child's development. Referral of the child and family to other professionals to further assess the child or to provide information and services may occur.

DISCUSSION QUESTIONS _____

1. Discuss the vignette at the beginning of the chapter. What other questions or concerns might you have? Discuss the vignette at the end of the chapter. Are there other responses you might have to this situation?

2. Discuss the concept of "normal" development.

3. What are the various reasons for assessing young children?

4. Describe the ways and settings in which teachers assess children.

5. Discuss parents' role in assessment.

6. Describe the different components of a comprehensive assessment procedure.

7. Discuss reliable indicators of creativity in preschool children. Describe examples of behaviors you would expect to observe related to each indicator.

8. Explain why administration of the checklist for a child should include three developmental levels.

9. Discuss decisions about, and making, referrals.

REFERENCES _____

Ayers, W. (1993). *To teach: The journey of the teacher.* New York: Teachers College Press.

Bailey, D. B., Jr., & Simeonsson, R. J. (1988). *Family assessment in early intervention.* Columbus, OH: Merrill/Macmillan.

Benner, S. M. (1992). *Assessing young children with special needs.* White Plains, NY: Longman.

Frakes, P., & Porter, M. (1986). *Guide to conditions which place children at developmental risk.* Nashville, TN: The Tennessee Children's Services Commission.

Meisels, S. J., & Atkins-Burnett, S. (1993). *Developmental screening in early childhood: A guide.* Washington, DC: National Association for the Education of Young Children.

Milne, A. A. (1957). *The world of Pooh: The complete Winnie-the-Pooh and the house at Pooh corner.* New York: Dutton.

Mindes, G., Ireton, H., & Mardell-Czudnowski, C. (1996). *Assessing young children.* Albany, NY: Delmar.

National Association for the Education of Young Children and National Association of Early Childhood Specialists in State Departments of Education (NAEYC & NAECS/SDE). (1991). Guidelines for appropriate curriculum content and assessment in programs serving children ages 3 through 8. *Young Children, 46*(3), 21–38.

Pitcher, E. G., Feinburg, S. G., & Alexander, D. A. (1989). *Helping young children learn* (5th ed.). Columbus, OH: Merrill/Macmillan.

Saint-Exupéry, A. de. (1943). *The little prince.* New York: Harcourt, Brace, & World.

Schweinhart, L. (1993). Observing young children in action: The key to early childhood assessment. *Young Children, 48*(5), 29–33.

Southern Early Childhood Association, (SECA). (1990). *Developmentally appropriate assessment: A position statement.* Little Rock, AR: Author.

Tegano, D., Bennett, E., & Pike, G. (1990). *Constructing a measure of preschool children's creativity through social validation.* Manuscript submitted for publication.

Tegano, D. W., Moran, J. D., III, & Sawyers, J. K. (1991). *Creativity in early childhood classrooms.* Washington, DC: National Education Association.

Wortham, S. (1995). *Measurement and evaluation in early childhood education* (2nd ed.). Englewood Cliffs, NJ: Prentice-Hall.

ADDITIONAL RESOURCES _____

Abbott, C. F., & Gold, S. (1991). Conferring with parents when you're concerned that their child needs special services. *Young Children, 46*(4), 10–14.

Allen, K. E., & Marotz, L. (1994). *Developmental profiles: Pre-birth through eight.* Albany, NY: Delmar.

Bagnato, S. J., Neisworth, J. T., & Munson, S. M. (1989). *Linking developmental assessment and curricula: Curriculum-based prescriptions.* Rockville, MD: Aspen.

Bailey, D. B., Jr., & Wolery, M. (1989). *Assessing infants and preschoolers with handicaps.* Columbus, OH: Merrill/Macmillan.

Bentzen, W. R. (1997). *Seeing young children: A guide to observing and recording behavior* (3rd ed.). Albany, NY: Delmar.

Boehm, A. E., & Weinberg, R. A. (1987). *The classroom observer: Developing observation skills in early childhood settings.* New York: Teachers College Press.

Bredekamp, S., & Rosegrant, T. (Eds.). (1992). *Reaching potentials: Appropriate curriculum and assessment for young children* (Vol 1). Washington, DC: National Association for the Education of Young Children.

Bredekamp, S., & Rosegrant, T. (Eds.). (1995). *Reaching potentials: Transforming early childhood curriculum and assessment* (Vol. 2). Washington, DC: National Association for the Education of Young Children.

Bredekamp, S., & Shepard, L. (1989). How best to protect children from inappropriate school expectations, practices, and policies. *Young Children, 44*(3), 14–24.

Curry, N. E., & Arnaud, S. H. (1984). Play in developmental settings. In T. D. Yawkey & A. D. Pellegrini (Eds.), *Child's play: Developmental and applied* (pp. 273–290). Hillsdale, NJ: Erlbaum.

Frost, J. L., & Sunderlin, S. (Eds.). (1985). *When children play.* Wheaton, MD: Association for Childhood Education International.

Fuchs, L. S., & Fuchs, D. (1986). Linking assessment to instructional intervention: An overview. *School Psychology Review, 15*(3), 318–323.

Goodwin, W., & Goodwin, L. (1993). Young children and measurement: Standardized and nonstandardized instruments in early childhood education. In B. Spodek (Ed.), *Handbook of research on the education of young children* (pp. 441–463). New York: Macmillan.

Guidry, J., van den Pol, R., Keeley, E., & Neilsen, S. (1996). Augmenting traditional assessment and information: The videoshare model. *Topics in Early Childhood Special Education, 16*(1), 51–65.

Gullo, D. (1994). *Understanding assessment and evaluation in early childhood education.* New York: Teachers College Press.

Guralnick, M. J., & Weinhouse, E. (1983). Child–child social interactions: An analysis of assessment instruments for young children. *Exceptional Children, 50*(3), 268–271.

Haney, M., & Cavallaro, C. (1996). Using ecological assessment in daily program planning for children with disabilities in typical preschool settings. *Topics in Early Childhood Special Education, 16*(1), 66–81.

Hills, T. (1993). Assessment in context—Teachers and children at work. *Young Children, 48*(5), 20–28.

Hrncir, E. J., & Eisenhart, C. E. (1991). Use with caution: The "at risk" label. *Young Children, 46*(2), 23–27.

Kamii, C. (Ed.). (1990). *Achievement testing in the early grades: The games grown-ups play.* Washington, DC: National Association for the Education of Young Children.

Leavitt, R. L., & Eheart, B. K. (1991). Assessment in early childhood programs. *Young Children, 46*(5), 4–9.

Lidz, C. S. (1983). Issues in assessing preschool children. In J. Paget & B. Bracken (Eds.), *The psychoeducational assessment of preschool children* (pp. 17–27). New York: Harcourt Brace Jovanovich.

McAfee, O., & Leong, D. (1994). *Assessing and guiding young children's development and learning.* Needham Heights, MA: Allyn & Bacon.

Meisels, S. (1993). Remaking classroom assessment with the work sampling system. *Young Children, 48*(5), 34–40.

Meisels, S. (1994). Designing meaningful measurements for early childhood education. In B. Mallory & R. New (Eds.), *Diversity and developmentally appropriate practices* (pp. 202–222). New York: Teachers College Press.

Meisels, S. J. (1987). Uses and abuses of developmental screening and school readiness testing. *Young Children, 42*(2), 4–9, 68–73.

Milgram, R. M., Moran, J. D., III, Sawyers, J. K., & Fu, V. R. (1983). *Predicting original problem-solving in children: A multidimensional theoretical model.* Unpublished document, Tel-Aviv University.

National Association for the Education of Young Children. (1988). NAEYC position statement on standardized testing of young children 3 through 8 years of age. *Young Children, 43*(3), 42–47.

Paget, J., & Bracken, B. (1983). *The psychoeducational assessment of preschool children.* New York: Harcourt Brace Jovanovich.

Pepler, D. (1986). Play and creativity. In G. Fein & M. Rivkin (Eds.), *The young child at play: Reviews of research* (Vol. 4, pp. 143–153). Washington, DC: National Association for the Education of Young Children.

Puckett, M., & Black, J. (1994). *Authentic assessment of the young child: Celebrating development and learning.* New York: Merrill/Macmillan.

Runco, M. A. (1984). Teachers' judgments of creativity and social validation of divergent thinking tests. *Perceptual and Motor Skills, 59,* 711–717.

Salvia, J., & Ysseldyke, J. E. (1995). *Assessment* (6th ed.). Boston: Houghton Mifflin.

Seefeldt, C. (1998). Assessing young children. In C. Seefeldt & A. Galper (Eds.), *Continuing issues in early childhood education* (2nd ed., pp. 311–330). Columbus, OH: Merrill/Prentice-Hall.

Spodek, B., & Saracho, O. (Eds.). (1997). *Issues in early childhood educational assessment and evaluation.* New York: Teachers College Press.

Torrance, P. (1983). Preschool creativity. In J. Paget & B. Bracken (Eds.), *The psychoeducational assessment of preschool children* (pp. 509–519). New York: Harcourt Brace Jovanovich.

Vandenberg, B. (1980). Play, problem-solving, and creativity. In K. Rubin (Ed.), *New directions for child development: Children's play* (pp. 49–68). San Francisco: Jossey-Bass.

Wortham, S. (1997). Assessing and reporting young children's progress: A review of the issues. In J. Isenberg & M. Jalongo (Eds.), *Major trends and issues in early childhood education* (pp. 104–122). New York: Teachers College Press

10

Activity Planning

As a teacher of 3- and 4-year-olds in an early childhood program, you are asked to participate in joint planning sessions with several other preschool teachers in order to ensure consistency in curriculum goals and activity-planning procedures. You discover that each teacher has a different idea about what is essential in the activity-planning process. One teacher is a very vocal advocate of the theme-based planning approach to curriculum development. Another teacher is concerned about early academic achievement and is convinced that a skills-based planning approach is superior. Still another teacher is concerned about how to plan effectively for the young children with special needs enrolled in his classroom.

To facilitate the joint planning process, adhere to the program philosophy, and arrive at a consistent activity-planning format, you realize that you must address the following issues:

- What curriculum goals and practices are consistent with the program's philosophy?
- Is there an effective method of combining the theme-based and skills-based approaches to activity planning?
- What type of activity-planning format will be useful to all the preschool teachers and provide consistency within the program?
- How will you ensure that the individual developmental objectives for each child are incorporated into the activity-planning process?
- What additional planning strategies are necessary to meet the developmental and educational needs of young children with special needs enrolled in the preschool program?

Suggestions for responding to this classroom vignette will be shared at the end of the chapter.

When reading this chapter, focus on these topics: the importance of planning developmentally appropriate classroom activities, the use of guidelines for activity planning and for developing a comprehensive curriculum, and ways to select activities and learning centers for the early childhood classroom. Also, gain an understanding of how to individualize learning experiences; plan for diverse cultural, social and racial groups of children; and incorporate strategies for inclusion of children with disabilities into the classroom environment.

The creative-play curriculum includes activities that respond to young children's individual developmental needs and that enhance the development of the whole child. It is important that the general goals adopted as the curricular framework be compatible with the program philosophy, and that the objectives for specific activities reflect the developmental needs of individual children. Planning appropriate activities for the classroom setting is one step in the continuous cycle of child assessment, individual and program goal setting, activity planning, and implementation of activities that constitute the visible curriculum.

Activity plans as well as instructional procedures must be appropriate for the developmental level of the young child. Young children learn through an active

Bobbie Beckmann also contributed to writing this chapter.

process of seeing, hearing, touching, feeling, asking, exploring, and creating, not through a passive process of sitting, listening, and receiving information. A flexible, open, learning environment coupled with a responsive, creative teacher sends an invitation to young children to interact with the environment and others, and to choose activities that reflect their needs and interests.

When early childhood programs fail to base curricular activities on an understanding of how young children learn and develop and instead emphasize formal instruction and academic skills at an early age, the result can be children who feel overly regimented and pressured to succeed rather than children who develop a sense of excitement and enthusiasm for learning. "When we ignore what the child has to learn and instead impose what we want to teach, we put infants and young children at risk for no purpose" (Elkind, 1987, p. 23). This type of miseducation of young children is far too prevalent in today's schools and centers, and it denies young children access to a developmentally appropriate environment that encourages involvement in play as the primary mode of learning (Elkind, 1987).

In contrast, an essential ingredient in planning an integrated, experiential, creative curriculum is a conceptual and attitudinal framework that supports children's learning through play. Children are viewed as people with feelings who need opportunities for success, for making choices and decisions, for laughter and movement and activity, and for supportive, loving interactions with others. Learning is seen as a joyful, meaningful process that fosters the development of a positive self-concept, invites curiosity about the world, promotes independent thought and problem-solving skills, and challenges children toward continuous growth and development.

Providing young children with many opportunities to explore the indoor and outdoor classroom environment as well as to experience close relationships with peers and adults leads to meaningful learning about themselves, others, and the world:

I sincerely believe that for the child . . . it is not half so important to know as to feel. If facts are the seeds that later produce knowledge and wisdom, then the emotions and the impressions of the senses are the fertile soil in which the seeds must grow. Once the emotions have been aroused—a sense of the beautiful, the excitement of the new and the unknown, a feeling of sympathy, pity, admiration, or love—then we wish for knowledge abut the object of our emotional response. Once found, it has lasting meaning. It is more important to pave the way for the child to want to know than to put him on a diet of facts he is not ready to assimilate. (Carson, 1956, p. 45)[1]

GUIDELINES FOR ACTIVITY PLANNING

An important goal for curricular planning is to choose activities that enhance children's growth in a variety of developmental areas, including personal awareness, emotional well-being, socialization, communication, cognition, and perceptual motor skills. For example, providing blocks of assorted shapes and sizes with which a group of children can create structures and build together may have as its primary objective the development of social skills, but also may enhance the development of perceptual motor skills, communication skills, and problem-solving skills. Creative and flexible teachers can adapt activities to use with children of different age groups and varying levels of development. Many activities also are adaptable for both the indoor and outdoor play environments. General considerations and guidelines for activity planning by the teacher are described by Moyer, Egertson, and Isenberg (1987), who say that the effective teacher:

- Recognizes and affirms individual differences in children's growth and development
- Sets curriculum goals and individual goals appropriate for children's developmental levels
- Accepts play as the fundamental, essential framework for children's daily activities
- Adopts a wholistic approach by responding to children as total, integrated human beings
- Provides multiple opportunities for learning through a variety of activities

- Fosters active experience, discovery, participation, and child choice through open-ended, creative activities
- Utilizes integrated programming with a balance in quiet/active, indoor/outdoor, teacher-initiated/child-initiated, and individual/small group/large group activities
- Values the process of exploration and learning rather than the final product
- Includes opportunities for experiences with multicultural, nonsexist materials and activities

To enhance children's creativity in all developmental areas, it is essential to plan process-oriented activities that encourage self-expression, imaginative ideas, divergent thinking, and problem-solving skills. General guidelines and techniques to foster problem-solving and creative thought are described by Sawyers and Tegano (1986):

- Be aware of the many facets of problem solving, particularly divergent problem solving (creativity). Creative problem solving is not limited to the arts. It is possible in all curricular areas.
- Encourage children to take part in the decision-making process. Allow them to have a part in the control of their learning experiences.

[1]Excerpt from *The sense of wonder* by Rachel Carson. Copyright ©1956 by Rachel L. Carson; copyright renewed ©1984 by Roger Christie. Reprinted by permission of HarperCollins Publishers Inc.

Process-oriented activities that encourage self-expression enhance the development of creativity in young children.

- Incorporate and adapt to children's interests and ideas.
- Create a warm, supportive atmosphere and a climate of mutual respect and acceptance. This environment provides the freedom and security necessary for individual or group exploration and divergent problem solving.

- Allow time for children to think about and develop their ideas. Very few problems are solved immediately or spontaneously.
- Accept unusual ideas and responses of children. Avoid unnecessary rewards/reinforcement.
- Suspend judgment or evaluation of children's attempts at divergent problem solving.
- Foster divergent problem solving by providing resources, participating, and guiding exploration and play through the use of questions (for example, descriptive exploration questions: "What do you think it is? What else could it be?" followed by similarity/difference exploration questions: "Are they shaped differently? Are they both smooth?").

In a creative-play classroom environment, children are encouraged to learn through imaginative-play experiences instead of being expected to work quietly with dittos, flash cards, and other paper-and-pencil tasks. Open-ended play activities support children's learning through interactions with peers, adults, and the environment and release children's creative potential (Tegano, Moran, & Sawyers, 1991).

SELECTING ACTIVITIES AND LEARNING CENTERS _____

When selecting activities and materials for learning centers, make sure that what is chosen fits with the program philosophy and program goals. It is important to remember that the activities selected reflect our understanding of children's development and our values as teachers. According to Thurman (1981), if we value

- children's time, we select worthwhile activities;
- content, we select what is honest, correct, and worth knowing;
- creativity, we select activities that allow children to make choices and use their own ideas;
- thinking, we select activities that allow a wide variety of correct answers;
- independence, we select activities that allow children to do as much for themselves as they are developmentally able;
- other people, we select activities that present people as human beings, not stereotypes;

- ourselves, we select activities based on our own professional judgment, experience, and knowledge of children.

The following questions from Thurman (1981) may help teachers select the best from all the good activities that exist for young children:

1. Is the activity safe?
2. Is the activity appropriate for the age group?
3. Does the activity allow for several levels of ability?
4. Does the activity allow children to make choices? Think? Create?
5. Is the activity designed so that directions can be presented clearly and briefly?
6. Does the activity allow children to be successful?
7. Is the expense of the activity justified by its value?
8. Is the activity the child's work?

9. Does the activity meet children's needs by providing for growth in several developmental areas (perceptual motor, social, emotional, cognition)?

10. Has the activity been tried by the teacher ahead of time?

NAEYC offers the following guidelines for teachers in selecting and designing curriculum that is developmentally appropriate (Bredekamp & Copple, 1997):

■ Developmentally appropriate curriculum meets children's needs in all areas of development.

■ Curriculum integrates content across subject areas and is meaningful and engaging for children.

■ Curriculum uses what children already know to help them learn and assimilate new concepts and skills.

■ Curriculum fosters the development and use of critical-thinking skills.

■ Curriculum reflects children's native culture and language and promotes children sharing information about, learning about, and respecting others' family and culture.

■ Curriculum goals are appropriate and obtainable for the developmental and skill level of children in the classroom.

■ When used, technology should be integrated into the philosophy, curriculum, and teaching strategies of the early childhood program.

Teachers should choose from the wide variety of activities available on the basis of a knowledge of children's needs, their compatibility with curricular goals, and the potential for fostering creativity in young children. Activity guides may assist the teacher of young children in the search for fresh ideas and spark the imagination in order to create innovative activities for the classroom.

THEME, SKILL-BASED, AND PROJECT PLANNING _____

Activities can be implemented in the classroom through the use of three alternative but complementary approaches to planning and organization. In one approach, activities are planned by developmental domain and can be implemented by using a sequenced planning scheme based on a hierarchy of skill development. Use of this approach emphasizes children's developmental readiness for specific tasks and incorporates activities into the classroom to meet individual goals for children's development.

Another approach to planning and implementation of activities is to organize classroom activities around a unit topic or theme that can be changed weekly or biweekly throughout the year. Thematic planning provides a helpful organizational and conceptual framework for teachers as they plan program activities. Activities can be selected and adapted to correspond with the current theme. Some suggestions for theme topics include the following:

Self
People Are Special
Everybody Has Feelings
Things We Want
  to Learn
Things We See/Hear
Things We Taste/
  Smell/Touch

Families/Holidays
New Year Celebrations
  (Chinese New Year,
  New Year's Day)
Family Celebrations
  (birthdays, adoption
  days)
Cultural Celebrations

(Kwanzaa, American
  Indian Day)
Harvest Festivals
  (Thanksgiving, corn
  festivals, Oktoberfest)
Winter Holidays
  (Hanukkah,
  Christmas)
Vacations
Families
Babies (human and
  animal)
Community
Transportation—Land
Transportation—Air
  and Water
People Who Help Us
What We Do in School
Safety/Health
Driver/Passenger Safety
Personal Safety
Staying Healthy
Safety at Home
  and School
Things We Eat
Plants We Eat

Friends, Helping,
  Sharing
Sharing with
Friends
Helping at Home and
  School
Ways We Communicate
Making Friends
Animals
Animal Habitats
Forest Animals
Farm Animals
Backyard Animals
Zoo Animals
Animal Families
Caring for Pets
Our World/Science
Air
Tools and Machines
Seasons
Day and Night
Things That Grow
Taking Care of Our
  World
Nature/Camping
Life at the Seashore

Activities can be planned around a unit topic, such as the family, and also can be individualized for each child's level of development.

Themes can be developed by teachers and children together. Examples of themes that can encompass a variety of specific activities, challenge children's and teachers' thinking and values, and promote meaningful explorations into diverse ideas and cultures suggested by children and teachers include the following:

1. We respect ourselves and our world.

   a. Every living thing has needs.
   b. I am somebody important.
   c. We all have a cultural heritage.
   d. We need to live in peace.

2. We send messages when we communicate.

   a. Communication is two way.
   b. We communicate in many languages and in many ways.
   c. Stereotypes are contained in cartoons, books, magazines, and TV.
   d. TV can be dangerous to our health.

3. We can make a difference on planet earth.

   a. We have been shaped by the past, we shape the future.
   b. African American people have contributed greatly to our nation.
   c. We celebrate the contributions of women.
   d. People of all nationalities have worked for justice and equality.
   e. We need to overcome prejudice and racism.

4. We share stories of the world.

   a. My family's story is important.
   b. We learn about other people through their stories.
   c. We can all be storytellers and actors (Ayers, 1993, p. 98–99).

Developing a list of themes is a useful framework for activity planning. However, it is important to remain flexible, to be responsive to the current needs, interests, and diverse backgrounds of children, and to change themes and plans to meet individual and group needs. It also is important to adapt topic ideas and specific activities to the varying developmental levels within the group.

The *project approach* is an in-depth study of a topic or concept that has personal meaning to children. Projects often are suggested by children, who actively participate in planning for the activity, which may extend for several days or weeks. Project work is neither direct instruction nor spontaneous play, but emerges from children's interest in real-life concepts or experiences. Both the planning and carrying out of the project foster children's thinking, problem-solving, and social-negotiation skills (Katz & Chard, 1989).

A comprehensive approach to activity planning includes a combination of the skill development, thematic, and project approaches. Activities are selected to (1) correspond to a topic, theme, or project; (2) support the goals set for individual children based on developmental assessment information; and (3) foster the development of the total child by supporting the program's curricular goals. Daily activities that are chosen to enhance skill development and correspond to the unit topic should be planned for each center in the classroom as well as for group-time activities, transition activities, and outdoor play activities.

The process of curriculum webbing provides an excellent framework for creating comprehensive curriculum plans and linking themes or projects with skill development. *Webs* are dynamic plans that link different areas of the curriculum and increase the possibilities for integrating the curriculum. Webbing extends the planning process and becomes a mechanism for organizing activities and skills around a project or theme. For example, the topic of "Friends" is written in the middle of the page with lines drawn outward to the different areas, including language/communication activities, perceptual motor activities, cognitive activities, and others; specific activities and ideas are listed under each area, creating a plan for the teacher to follow. Both teachers and children generate ideas for activities to be included in the web, resulting in a flexible, responsive, and creative curriculum-planning process (Katz & Chard, 1989; Workman & Anziano, 1993).

Planning includes determining the objectives for the activity, outlining the materials needed and the methods for implementing the activity, describing the teacher's role, and suggesting criteria for evaluating the success of the activity. Figure 10-1 includes a master planning sheet for brainstorming activities to include in a weekly unit or theme plan. Figure 10-2 is a sample of an activity plan that is designed as one component of a daily schedule of classroom activities.

DIVERSITY IN THE CLASSROOM

Children's learning, both how they learn and what they learn, is influenced by their culture. Cultural differences between children and their teachers can profoundly affect teaching and learning. It can "lead teachers to misunderstand children, to misassess their developmental competence, and to plan incorrectly for their educational achievement" (Bowman & Stott, 1991, p. 121). Developmentally appropriate curriculum must include an emphasis on the social and cultural contexts in which both children and teachers live. Providing developmentally appropriate experiences with diversity for young children requires that teachers have a respect for individual differences and a sensitivity to the diverse cultural and ethnic populations represented in our society.

An effective program includes

- Teacher sensitivity to and knowledge of cultural diversity
- Meaningful curriculum activities and experiences
- Carefully selected instructional materials
- Appropriate instructional resources (Saracho & Spodek, 1983, p. 77)

Teacher attitudes that reflect positive feelings about diverse family groups and that value the uniqueness of all children help to foster the growth of self-esteem in young children and help children develop empathy and respect for the differences in people. Goals for an effective program that celebrates diversity might include the following:

1. To help children learn that people of all cultures have worth.
2. To help children recognize and accept differences in people.
3. To help children increase their self-esteem through appreciation of their own heritage.
4. To help children understand that they are part of a larger world.
5. To contribute to peace and harmony in the world through helping children recognize the common bond of humanity in people of all cultures. (Phenice & Hildebrand, 1988, p. 15)

The National Association for the Education of Young Children recently adopted a position statement titled *Responding to Linguistic and Cultural Diversity—Recommendations for Effective Early Childhood Education* (1996a). Its purpose is to help teachers construct programs that are sensitive to children's language, culture, and race and responsive to the families and communities

Interactions among children from diverse cultural backgrounds develop empathy and respect for the differences in people.

Theme: _Many Ways to Travel (Land)_   Date: _August 5-9_

Puzzles & Games	Drawing/Writing
Wooden train Flexi blocks School bus puzzle Vehicle puzzle Horse puzzle Parquetry blocks - use to make vehicles	Maps - encourage children to make their own maps

Discovery
Sand table - add plastic
  cars, trucks, bulldozers.
Encourage children to
  make roads + mountains
Globe with magnifying
  glass
	Books
	And to Think I Saw It on
	  Mulberry Street
	The Train
	The Horse in Harry's Room
	A Walk in the City
	Freight Train
	Big Joe's Trailer Truck
	Big Wheels

Blocks
Make "roads" with
  masking tape
Add cars, trucks, gas
  pumps
	Imaginary Play
	Travel Office - travel brochures,
	  telephone, phone book,
	  maps, "tickets," calendar
	Suitcase
	"Vehicle" (van, bus, train) -
	  put large snap walls
	  together, attach cloth strips
	  to chairs for safety belts

Art
Paint with plastic cars
Collage on truck shape - cut
  out furniture + glue
  inside truck
Footprint mural
Paint to fast + slow music
Imagination paper - cut out
  pictures of vehicles, paste on
  paper. Children finish w/ crayons
	Outdoor
	Set up gas pump
	Special event - Tricycle Wash
	  (brushes + buckets of
	  water w/ small amount
	  of soap)
	Hopscotch game
	Obstacle course
	Wooden wagon

Figure 10-1 Sample master planning sheet.

Activity/Plan

Theme Many Ways to Travel (Land)   Teacher Carleon

Center Puzzles, Games, & Manipulatives   Week of August 5-9

Materials

Wooden train and tracks
Flexiblocks
Puzzles - horse, school bus, vehicles, truck
Parquetry blocks
Stringing Beads

Child's Role/Procedure (include concepts, skills, objectives)

Personal Awareness - keep small objects out of mouth
Perceptual Motor - string beads, connect flexiblocks
Cognition - Put puzzles back together; problem solve how to create
    structures with flexiblocks; identify colors, shapes of
    parquetry blocks; use parquetry blocks to make vehicles;
    count beads on string; make up stories about vehicles
    being built or about puzzles.
Socialization - Return materials to containers when finished; cooperate
    with peers to build and play with train and tracks;
    share materials; respect others' creations
Communication - ask for turns; use words to resolve conflict; ask for help
Emotional well-being - experience satisfaction; make independent choices

Teacher's Role/Questions (include safety considerations)

Encourage identification of colors, shapes
Facilitate counting, sorting
Ask open-ended questions; what can you add to this structure?
    where can we go on a trip? Where should I put this block?
Facilitate conflict resolution
Redirect inappropriate use of materials

Adaptations/Comments

Make sure (DB) spends a few minutes working puzzles. Encourage
    him to stay on track.
Assist (DZ) with stringing beads. Hold the string so she can use
    right hand to put beads on.

Figure 10-2 Sample activity planning form.

in which these children live. There is often dissonance between the culture of the family and community and the culture of school; this disruption and its potential consequences challenge teachers to "accept . . . respect . . . value . . . promote and encourage the active involvement and support of all families, including extended and nontraditional family units" (NAEYC, 1996a). Specifically, teachers should:

- Recognize that all children are cognitively, linguistically, and emotionally connected to the language and culture of their home.

- Acknowledge that children can demonstrate their knowledge and capabilities in many ways.

- Understand that without comprehensible input, second-language learning can be difficult.

- Actively involve parents and families in the early learning program and setting.

- Encourage and assist all parents in becoming knowledgeable about the cognitive value for children of knowing more than one language, and provide them with strategies to support, maintain, and preserve home-language learning.

- Recognize that parents and families must rely on caregivers and educators to honor and support their children in the cultural values and norms of the home (NAEYC, 1996a, pp. 7–9).

Many early childhood educators also use the anti-bias curriculum approach. Anti-bias curriculum in the early childhood classroom goes beyond teaching about cultural diversity and places the emphasis on helping young children "to understand and comfortably interact with differences, to appreciate all people's similarities through the different ways they are human, and to recognize and confront ideas and be-

haviors that are biased" (Derman-Sparks & A.B.C. Task Force, 1989, p. 7).

An anti-bias curriculum broadens children's perspectives and challenges stereotypical views of people based on gender, age, special needs, and racial, ethnic, cultural, or social backgrounds. In some instances, an anti-bias curriculum may need to counter prevailing societal attitudes toward specific groups or populations and actively teach children to view all individuals in a positive and unbiased manner.

Putting an anti-bias curriculum into practice involves acquiring knowledge about the needs and practices of a variety of populations and demonstrating a commitment to a rich, diverse, and nonstereotypical classroom environment. To implement an anti-bias curriculum teachers must do the following:

- Model behaviors and interactions that demonstrate an appreciation of differences in individuals and that reflect the absence of bias or prejudice.

- Practice enrollment procedures that follow affirmative-action guidelines and actively pursue diversity in the population of children and families, including young children with disabilities.

- Select a variety of materials for the classroom that are free of stereotypes and show varying populations of people in positive, productive situations.

- Plan classroom activities that involve nonstereotypical and diverse views of people, that provide children of differing developmental levels and from a variety of backgrounds with opportunities for success and mastery, and that promote respect for individual differences.

- Involve parents and members of the community in providing diverse resources, sharing experiences, and planning activities that facilitate children's learning about a variety of cultures and populations.

TECHNOLOGY IN THE CLASSROOM _____

In the last decade researchers have examined the use and outcomes of computers in the early childhood education classroom. The ensuing debate has centered on the appropriate use of computers with young children—they are not a replacement for nor simply an addition to a developmentally appropriate curriculum. Computers can be an important part of an integrated curriculum when their use is planned into the total curriculum, when children are using them actively and not passively, and when appropri-

ate software is chosen. A multifaceted view of children and their intelligences can be strengthened by computer use: teachers can "provide various kinds of experiences that are often overlooked but that could offer children with diverse intelligences an opportunity to learn and express themselves in different ways" (Wright, 1994, p. 9).

Initially children's computer use was studied for its value in promoting cognitive and language skills. But it also can promote the development of a broad spectrum of intelligences. "Computer experience should tap children's potential for imaginative, creative, and emotive as well as logical and empirical thinking" (Bowman & Beyer, 1994, p. 20). For example, children may use computers as artists and storytellers, designers, authors, mechanics, and logical thinkers (Wright, 1994).

In response to concern about the use of computer and related technology, such as telecommunications and multimedia that can be integrated with computer technology, in early childhood classrooms, NAEYC has developed a position statement titled *Technology and Young Children—Ages Three through Eight* (1996b). Its seven major recommendations are listed here:

- In evaluating the appropriate use of technology, NAEYC applies principles of developmentally appropriate practice and appropriate curriculum and assessment. In short, NAEYC believes that, in any given situation, a professional judgment by the teacher is required to determine whether a specific use of technology is age-appropriate, individually appropriate, and culturally appropriate.

- Used appropriately, technology can enhance children's cognitive and social abilities.

- Appropriate technology is integrated into the regular learning environment and used as one of many options to support children's learning.

- Early childhood educators should promote equitable access to technology for all children and their families. Children with special needs should have increased access when this is helpful.

- The power of technology to influence children's learning and development requires that attention be paid to eliminating stereotyping of any group and eliminating exposure to violence, especially as a problem-solving strategy.

- Teachers, in collaboration with parents, should advocate for more appropriate technology applications for all children.

- The appropriate use of technology has many implications for early childhood professional development (NAEYC, 1996b, pp. 11–15).

The role of the teacher in creating the classroom environment, choosing software, and establishing an overall climate for computer use by young children is critical. Teachers who view computer use as another opportunity for play and exploration, for developing social relationships, and for increasing children's communication skills are promoting the developmentally appropriate use of technology in the classroom. Teachers who integrate computer usage into the total curriculum choose software to support the theme or unit plan, use computers as center choice, and introduce interactive storybook or new software at group time. Teachers often are less comfortable with computer technology than are children. What teachers view as a deficit—their need for resources, support, and training in the use of computer technology—can also allow a positive view of themselves as co-learners with children. Teachers who enhance children's critical-thinking and problem-solving skills use open-ended questioning techniques when using developmentally appropriate software. "The goal of such questioning is to help children become aware of 'thinking about thinking.' Three basic questions to use in the facilitation process include: (1) What do you think you should do? (2) Why do you think that is the thing you should do? and (3) How did you decide that? (Snider & Badgett, 1995, p. 103).

Establishing a classroom environment that provides easy accessibility to computers and a variety of software is the first step in supporting children's computer usage. Early childhood classrooms should be equipped with powerful and updated computer hardware that supports children's multisensory exploration through the use of graphics, sound, recording, animation, and touch (Bredekamp & Rosegrant, 1994). In addition to hardware that gives children choice and control, software should be chosen to meet the needs of young children. Instead of emphasizing the use of computers for drill-and-practice activities, software should be chosen that encourages discovery and exploration. The teacher's role as decision maker in the selection of developmentally appropriate software involves the evaluation of "child features, teacher features, and technical features" (Shade, 1996, p. 19). Appropriate child features of software can be evaluated with this set of questions:

Does the software foster children's independent use of computers?

Does it encourage active learning?

Does it encourage child-controlled interaction?

Does it encourage experimentation?

Does it encourage discovery learning?

Does it encourage creativity?

Is the software open-ended?

Can it be operated from a picture menu?

Does the software include age-appropriate concepts?

Does it allow children to set their own pace for the activity? (Shade, 1996, p. 17).

Teacher features to be included when choosing software are the following:

What is the software's educational value?

Does it reflect diversity of cultures, ages, family structures, and the like?

Is the software congruent with the curriculum philosophy and goals?

Can the software be customized for individual children's differing abilities?

Questions about the technical features to be considered include the following:

Is the software aesthetically pleasing?

Is it available for both Macintosh and IBM-compatible computers?

Is the software easy and fast to install?

Are there realistic graphics and sound effects?

Is the sound and speech clear and distinct? (Shade, 1996, p. 17)

Consider these questions to select software that is age-appropriate, encourages children to be active participants by initiating and controlling events, has clear spoken directions, allows children to manipulate and explore the software without adult supervision, is process oriented, provides opportunities to try alternative responses, and is of high technical quality (Haugland & Shade, 1988, p. 39). Computer software that allows for playfulness and exploration and provides activities that encourage divergent thinking and creative expression supports children's developing creativity (Tegano, Moran, & Sawyers, 1991). Although computer software for young children is improving, children do not engage in the same high level of playfulness as they do when engaged in play with more open-ended materials such as blocks and art materials (Henninger, 1994).

There are other considerations for the selection of appropriate hardware and software to be used with young children with disabilities. Computers are one aspect of assistive technology that can enhance children's communication and learning opportunities. The Technology-Related Assistance for Individuals with Disabilities Act of 1988 (P.L. 100-407) requires that equipment be modified or customized for appropriate use by individuals with disabilities. Modifications to hardware for young children with disabilities may include alternative keyboards, touch screens, pressure switches, eye-gaze control devices, and voice-activation devices. It is essential that software include animation, auditory prompts and feedback, and digitized voice quality (Behrmann & Lahm, 1994).

Teachers who are excited about the creative possibilities of computer use, who encourage children's exploration, and who interact in nonjudgmental ways are creating a positive and supportive climate for the construction of new knowledge. Interactions with peers, teachers, and the environment are critical components of early childhood curricula. Teachers who keep their focus on the child and the integrative nature of curriculum will find a creative use for computers in young children's play and learning.

INDIVIDUALIZED LEARNING EXPERIENCES _____

Each child is a unique individual growing and developing at an individual rate and in a unique fashion. In order to truly individualize instructional practices, early childhood educators must effectively assess each child's developmental level, set specific objectives for each child, and translate the objectives into developmentally appropriate classroom activities. In addition, individualized instruction is essential for the successful inclusion of young children with disabilities.

Goals for early childhood programs that include children with disabilities are:

- To support families in achieving their own goals.
- To promote children's engagement, independence, and mastery.

- To promote children's development in key domains.
- To build and support children's social competence.
- To promote children's generalized use of skills.
- To provide and prepare children for normalized life experiences.
- To prevent the emergence of future problems or disabilities (Bailey & Wolery, 1992, p. 35).

To facilitate the implementation of individualized learning experiences for children with disabilities, early childhood educators should become familiar with the development of individual education plans (IEPs) and individual family service plans (IFSPs). Developed for children age 3 and older, the IEP is a child-centered plan for educational services. It is developed through a multidisciplinary team process that involves the parents as well as professionals, uses assessment results to describe the child's strengths as well as areas of developmental concern, and produces goals and objectives for the child in all developmental domains. The IEP includes the following components: a description of the child's current level of development and functioning; developmental and educational goals; specific instructional objectives; educational services to be provided; type and amount of support services needed; a determination of the program placement where the child's goals can best be accomplished; and procedures for evaluating the child's progress and the effectiveness of the program placement (Allen, 1996; Bricker, 1986).

The IFSP is a family-centered plan to identify and provide resources to help families reach goals for themselves and their children in the birth-to-age-2 population. The IFSP focuses on the child in the context of the family, recognizes the role of parents as the primary teachers of the young child, and enables families to become more active and better equipped to meet the needs of the young child with special needs. The IFSP is developed through a multidisciplinary team process that involves parents and profession-als, determines the needs of the child and family, and identifies the resources and support services to be provided. The IFSP includes the following components: a description of the child's current developmental level; identification of the family's strengths and needs; annual goals for the child and the family; early-intervention services to be provided; family support services to be provided; a determination of the appropriate placement (home-based, program-based, or a combination of services); and criteria, procedures, and timelines for evaluating the plan (Johnson, McGonigel, & Kaufmann, 1989).

Effective teachers of young children will recognize the need to obtain information about the conditions of young children with disabilities enrolled in their classroom. A variety of specialists and organizations are available to provide information and services that will help teachers meet the developmental and educational needs of children with disabilities. Using the resources available in the community to create a multidisciplinary and collaborative approach to providing appropriate classroom environments for children with disabilities is a basic component of effective inclusion (Cook, Tessier, & Klein, 1992; Wolery & Wilbers, 1994).

ADAPTATIONS FOR CHILDREN WITH DISABILITIES _____

This section includes additional suggestions for adaptations of classroom activities for five general types of disabilities: physically impaired, speech/language impaired, visually impaired, hearing impaired, and behaviorally disordered/emotionally disturbed. Not included are adaptations for mentally retarded children. Instead, these are addressed indirectly through adaptations for children with speech/language impairments. Mental retardation usually manifests itself as a cognitive and speech/language delay in young children, and teachers should choose adaptations that are appropriate for the individual child.

The purpose of the suggested adaptations is to provide the teacher with ways to make activities more appropriate for the child with disabilities. Most of these adaptations require a small amount of teacher time. These adaptations are provided to enhance the experience for the child with disabilities and assist the teacher in allowing the child to participate as independently and successfully as possible. When implementing these activities, some general guidelines should be followed. Agencies and organizations that provide information to assist in program planning are listed in Figure 10-3.

Guidelines for Children with Physical Impairments

Children with physical impairments often have difficulties with locomotor skills and may need the assistance of a wheelchair, walker, or braces to move around the classroom. Some children may be able to navigate in the classroom environment by pushing something, such as a large wooden container, in front of them. The classroom environment should be barrier free and traffic patterns should facilitate ease of movement. Positioning the child is extremely important for enhancing opportunities for learning and preventing muscle deformity. A general rule is to position the child, when seated or standing, with the body symmetrical and head in midline. Carrying the child in a flexed (legs and hips bent) and upright position is easier and is a better vantage point for seeing the environment. When pulling a child with a physical impairment to a sitting position, always rotate the shoulders in toward the body and pull from the body, not the arms.

Alexander Graham Bell Association
  for the Deaf
3417 Volta Place NW
Washington, DC 20007

American Council of the Blind
1155 15th St. NW, Suite 720
Washington, DC 20005

American Foundation for the Blind
15 W. 16th St.
New York, NY 10011

American Speech-Language-Hearing Association
10801 Rockville Pike
Rockville, MD 20852

Association for the Care of Children's Health
3615 Wisconsin Ave. NW
Washington, DC 20016

Children with Attention Deficit Disorders
499 NW 70th Ave., Suite 308
Plantation, FL 33317

Epilepsy Foundation of America
4351 Garden City Dr.
Landover, MD 20785

March of Dimes Birth Defects Foundation
1275 Manaroneck Ave.
White Plains, NY 10605

Muscular Dystrophy Association
810 7th Ave.
New York, NY 10019

National Association for Retarded Citizens
2510 Avenue J
Arlington, TX 76011

National Association of Hearing and
  Speech Agencies
814 Thayer Ave.
Silver Springs, MD 20910

National Consortium for Child Mental
  Health Services
3615 Wisconsin Ave. NW
Washington, DC 20016

National Easter Seal Society for Crippled
  Children and Adults
2023 W. Ogden Ave.
Chicago, IL 60612

National Institutes of Mental Health
5600 Fishers Lane
Rockville, MD 20857

National Society for Children and
  Adults with Autism
1234 Massachusetts Ave. NW
Suite 107
Washington, DC 20005

Office of Special Education and
  Rehabilitation Services
U.S. Department of Education
Room 3132, Switzer Bldg.
Washington, DC 20202-2524

Spina Bifida Association of America
343 S. Dearborn
Suite 317
Chicago, IL 60604

United Cerebral Palsy Associations, Inc.
66 E. 34th St.
New York, NY 10016

Figure 10-3 List of agencies and organizations that provide assistance to families and professionals.

Children with physical impairments, especially children with poor arm and hand control, may need to have materials or activities adapted in order to have successful learning experiences. Providing special adaptive equipment such as a bolster, wedge, or supportive seating will help to position children for participation in classroom activities. Attaching manipulative materials and toys to a board; providing large crayons, paint brushes, and writing tools; taping large pieces of paper to the table; and providing large handles on toys are a few simple but effective adaptations. Children's play and learning also may be augmented by the use of other assistive technology devices such as battery-operated toys, head pointers, Velcro fasteners, and computers (Allen, 1996; Brett, 1997; Dolinar, Boser, & Holm, 1994).

To provide an appropriate program for the child with a physical impairment, teachers should consult with professionals who can help identify appropriate goals for the child and suggest program modifications. A physical therapist provides therapy to restore or improve motor functioning. An occupational therapist provides treatment programs designed to facilitate activities of daily living, such as feeding and dressing skills. Physical therapists and occupational therapists are usually employed by hospitals, rehabilitation centers, or school systems.

To locate the appropriate professionals, contact the child's pediatrician, the local department of public health, area hospitals, rehabilitation centers, local school systems, or home health-care agencies.

Guidelines for Children with Speech/Language Impairments

Inclusion of the child with a speech/language impairment provides a natural setting for enhancing language development. A nurturing and naturalistic language-enriched environment can greatly enhance the development of receptive and expressive language skills. Communication and attempts at communication should be encouraged and praised. Guidelines for teaching language-delayed children include modeling correct language usage and facilitating communication with peers. This modeling is the basis of naturalistic intervention and enhances language development in infants, toddlers, and preschool children. Children who are unable to communicate through speech may need to use alternative communication systems such as sign language, or assistive technology such as communication boards and computers (Hecht, 1997).

Speech pathologists and audiologists can provide assistance with program planning for a child with a speech/language delay. A speech pathologist is qualified to provide evaluation and therapy for disorders such as articulation delay, receptive language delay, expressive language delay, disorders of the voice (nasality, hoarseness, pitch, and so on), and disorders of fluency. An audiologist is qualified to assess the child's hearing acuity, provide auditory training for hearing-impaired children, and provide hearing aids. Both professionals usually work in speech and hearing centers, hospitals, rehabilitation centers, or local school systems.

Guidelines for Children with Visual Impairments

Although many early childhood classroom activities, such as art, may seem to require sight for participation, the child with a visual impairment can enjoy and benefit from being included in all activities. Activities can be adapted to provide alternative sensory inputs and allow children to experience the activity through touching, smelling, and tasting.

During activities, use visual words such as *look, see,* and *show.* The child with a visual impairment generally uses these words to express his or her method of seeing. Provide "tours" for the child with a visual impairment and provide verbal cues pinpointing the location of equipment and toys in the room. Repeat tours any time the room arrangement or toy locations are changed. Always try to explain the location of objects in relation to static items such as a door or sink. Use verbal descriptions frequently to increase the child's awareness of what equipment or toys are available and what activities are occurring in the room. The classroom environment should include good lighting, a variety of magnifiers, large-print books and signs, a beginning system of Braille, and numerous sensory activities. The classroom also should be language rich and include verbal interaction, taped stories, and talking books to facilitate the development of language and social skills (Dolinar, Boser, & Holm, 1994).

When a child with a visual impairment is in the program, teachers should always identify themselves by name and encourage the other children to do this. Eventually the child will be able to identify classmates and teachers by their voices. However, this is a difficult skill, and the stating of names eases the stress of identifying the voice. Also encourage children to identify various sounds in the classroom environment, such as the sound of running water or blocks being stacked together.

Many children with visual impairments exhibit associated mannerisms such as rocking or rubbing their eyes. When these mannerisms are observed, tell the child what you see and encourage the child to stop the behavior. Praise times when the child does not exhibit the mannerism.

Encourage the child to be as independent as possible. More trial-and-error attempts at all activities are to be expected for the child with visual impairments. If the child requires assistance moving around the room or playground, encourage a peer to be the guide, allowing the child who is visually impaired to hold onto the peer's arm at the elbow. The child with a visual impairment should walk one-half step behind the guide. Encourage the leader to explain directions and upcoming obstacles such as stairs and narrow hallways verbally.

Many school systems employ certified vision specialists who can provide information and assistance in program planning for the child with a visual impairment. If the local school system does not employ a vision specialist, a special-education resource teacher would be qualified to assist with providing appropriate activities. Many states provide residential schools for blind children or have established state commissions for the blind. These schools or the commissions can be an excellent resource.

Guidelines for Children with Hearing Impairments

In general, early childhood activities are as appropriate for the child with a hearing impairment as for any other child. Total communication—a combination of talking and signing to the child—is often the recommended method of teaching. Some professionals, however, are advocates for the use of American Sign Language (ASL), which does not include the use of voice communication. Children with hearing impairments often have delayed speech and language development; teachers should choose the appropriate combination of activity adaptations to meet the needs of individual children. Children with severe hearing impairments often are socially isolated and need the support and encouragement of teachers to develop positive relationships with peers.

If the child wears a hearing aid, consult the child's parents for information regarding the length of time it should be worn, placement in the ear, how to check volume and correct functioning, and how to replace the batteries. Each day you will need to check the hearing aid to see that it is working, and the ear mold for wax buildup or improper fit. If you observe an abrupt change in the child's auditory abilities, recheck the hearing aid. An alternative type of assistive technology appropriate for early childhood classroom settings is the wireless frequency modulated (FM) transmission device. The FM device provides sound amplification like a hearing aid, but has several advantages. It amplifies the teacher's voice and minimizes noise from the classroom environment because a transmitter/microphone is worn by the teacher and a receiver is worn by the child. It also allows the teacher freedom of movement in the classroom because sound signals are received from a greater distance (Scalise-Annis, 1997).

Specialists who serve children with hearing impairments can be excellent resources to assist the early childhood teacher with program planning. An audiologist is certified to assess the child's hearing loss, prescribe hearing aids, and provide auditory training therapy. A speech/language therapist has the training to evaluate speech and language delays and determine the need for a prescribed speech/language program. Both professionals may be employed by local school systems, rehabilitation centers, hospitals, or speech and hearing centers.

Guidelines for Children with Behavior Disorders/Emotional Disturbances

Inclusion of the child who has a behavior disorder or who is emotionally disturbed can be successful with minimal adaptations and planning. Activity centers in the classroom provide an excellent environment for the child's participation, especially with clearly defined boundaries and explanations of appropriate uses of materials. Provide low screens or dividers to decrease distractibility when the centers are close to each other.

Consistency is a key in teaching children with behavior disorders or emotional disturbances. Always prepare the child for new activities or events. Be consistent in classroom management techniques, always accentuating the child's positive behaviors. Set well-defined, consistent limits.

Providing a nurturing and supportive classroom environment encourages the development of children's self-esteem and trust in others. Facilitating children's involvement with open-ended play materials encourages self-expression and provides the opportunity for validation of children's feelings. Teaching the use of effective coping skills allows children to deal with fears, frustrations, and hurts in a socially acceptable manner.

Professionals who can assist with program planning for children with behavior disorders or emotional disturbances include psychologists, child psychiatrists, social workers, play therapists, and special educators. These professionals are usually employed by mental health centers, children's hospitals, or local school systems, or are in private practice.

ACHIEVING DEVELOPMENTAL GOALS THROUGH EFFECTIVE PLANNING _____

Teachers who effectively incorporate children's individual objectives into activity plans make the linkage between assessment and curriculum, meet the developmental and educational needs of children, and complete the cycle of the visible curriculum. In addition, a consideration of the range of developmental levels of young children, understanding how young children learn, valuing the diversity of children's cultural and social backgrounds, and knowing strategies for inclusion of children with disabilities will provide the framework for choosing activities and learning materials that foster the development of the whole child and support curricular goals. The early childhood professional who values teacher autonomy, creativity, and judgment, and who is focused on children as individuals, will continually create and adapt new and exciting activities for the particular classroom environment.

■ ■ ■ ■ ■ ■ ■ ■ ■

To provide consistency in your program, it is critical that the group of teachers first discuss the philosophy of how children learn. Using that philosophy as a basis, then you can make decisions about the curriculum goals and types of activities to plan for the classroom. Consider the following:

- Curriculum goals reflect what we believe is important for young children to learn. Discuss the importance of the development of skills and competencies and how these can be fostered by a creative-play curriculum approach.
- Discuss the differences in theme-based planning and skills-based planning. Identify the contributions each can make to your program and determine how to integrate the two approaches into a comprehensive curriculum plan.

- List guidelines for planning appropriate activities for the early childhood classroom. Decide on activity-planning forms that will facilitate planning and that will incorporate children's objectives into the curriculum.
- Discuss the importance of integrating multicultural and anti-bias experiences into the curriculum. Also, decide together about your attitudes toward and the possible uses and benefits of computers in the classroom.
- Emphasize the importance of providing individualized learning experiences that meet the needs of all children in the classroom. Discuss strategies for inclusion of children with disabilities, and determine resources and consultants available to assist with planning appropriate classroom adaptations.

■ ■ ■ ■ ■ ■ ■ ■ ■

CHAPTER SUMMARY _____

Activities must support children's growth in all areas of development. Activities can be planned in each developmental domain based on a hierarchy of skill development, or activities can be planned around a theme or unit topic. Activities should reflect the diversity and variety of children's experiences. Anti-bias curriculum is another approach that helps children learn about and understand differences. Teachers should consider carefully the use of computers. Appropriate use includes programs and software that are high quality, age-appropriate, and interactive. Activities and other classroom learning experiences must be individualized for children with disabilities. Adaptations that allow appropriate and full participation by all children can be made for children with physical impairments, speech/language impairments, visual impairments, hearing impairments, and behavior disorders/emotional disturbances.

DISCUSSION QUESTIONS _____

1. Discuss the vignette at the beginning of the chapter. What other questions or concerns might you have? Discuss the vignette at the end of the chapter. Are there other responses you might have to this situation?
2. Describe developmentally appropriate education versus "miseducation" of young children. Characterize each in terms of their philosophy, goals, and curricular activities.
3. Describe the effective teacher's role as an activity planner.
4. How can teachers foster children's problem solving and creativity through the activities they plan?

5. Describe what *you* value as a teacher, and then explain how what you value is reflected in activities planned for children.

6. Describe the different approaches to planning activities: project, theme-based, and skill-based.

7. Describe the purpose and use of curriculum webs.

8. Describe the appropriate use of computers in early childhood classrooms.

9. Describe the special considerations for teaching young children with various disabilities.

REFERENCES _____

Allen, K. E. (1996). *The exceptional child: Inclusion in early education* (3rd ed.). Albany, NY: Delmar.

Ayers, W. (1993). *To teach: The journey of a teacher.* New York: Teachers College Press.

Bailey, D. B. & Wolery, M. (1992). Teaching infants and preschoolers with disabilities. 2nd ed. Columbus, OH: Merrill.

Behrmann, M., & Lahm, E. (1994). Computer applications in early childhood special education. In J. Wright & D. Shade (Eds.), *Young children: Active learners in a technological age* (pp. 105–120). Washington, DC: National Association for the Education of Young Children.

Bowman, B., & Beyer, E. (1994). Thoughts on technology and early childhood education. In J. Wright & D. Shade (Eds.), *Young children: Active learners in a technological age* (pp. 19–30). Washington, DC: National Association for the Education of Young Children.

Bowman, B., & Stott, F. (1994). Understanding development in a cultural context: The challenge for teachers. In B. Mallory & R. New (Eds.), *Diversity and developmentally appropriate practices: Challenges for early childhood education* (pp. 119–133). New York: Teachers College Press.

Bredekamp, S., & Copple, C. (Eds.). (1997). *Developmentally appropriate practice in early childhood programs* (Rev. ed.). Washington, DC: National Association for the Education of Young Children.

Bredekamp, S. & Rosegrant, T. (1994). Learning and teaching with technology. In J. L. Wright & D. D. Shade (Eds.), *Young children: Active learners in a technological age* (pp. 53–62). Washingtion, DC: National Association for the Education of Young Children.

Brett, A. (1997). Assistive and adaptive technology—Supporting competence and independence in young children with disabilities. *Dimensions, 25*(3), 14, 18–20.

Bricker, D. (1986). *Early education of at-risk and handicapped infants, toddlers, and preschool children.* Glenview, IL: Scott, Foresman.

Carson, R. (1956). *The sense of wonder.* New York: Harper & Row.

Cook, R., Tessier, A., & Klein, M. (1992). *Adapting early childhood curricula for children with special needs* (3rd ed.). Columbus, OH: Merrill/Macmillan.

Derman-Sparks, L., & A.B.C. Task Force. (1989). *Antibias curriculum: Tools for empowering young children.* Washington, DC: National Association for the Education of Young Children.

Dolinar, K., Boser, C., & Holm, E. (1994). *Learning through play: Curriculum and activities for the inclusive classroom.* Albany, NY: Delmar.

Elkind, D. (1987). *Miseducation: Preschoolers at risk.* New York: Knopf.

Haugland, S., & Shade, D. (1988). Developmentally appropriate software for young children. *Young Children, 43*(4), 37–43.

Hecht, S. (1997). Speech and language services. In L. Dunlap (Ed.), *An introduction to early childhood special education* (pp. 156–176). Needham Heights, MA: Allyn & Bacon.

Henninger, M. (1994). Computers and preschool children's play: Are they compatible? *Journal of Computing in Childhood Education, 5*(3/4), 231–239.

Johnson, B., McGonigel, J., & Kaufmann, R. (Eds.). (1989). *Guidelines and recommended practices for the individualized family service plan.* Chapel Hill, NC: National Early Childhood Technical Assistance System.

Katz, L., & Chard, S. (1989). *Engaging children's minds: The project approach.* Norwood, NJ: Ablex.

Moyer, J., Egertson, H., & Isenberg, J. (1987). The child-centered kindergarten. Position paper of the Association for Childhood Education International. *Childhood Education, 63*(4), 235–242.

National Association for the Education of Young Children (NAEYC). (1996a). NAEYC position statement: Responding to linguistic and cultural diversity—recommendations for effective early childhood education. *Young Children, 51*(2), 4–12.

National Association for the Education of Young Children (NAYEC). (1996b). NAEYC position statement: Technology and young children—ages three through eight. *Young Children, 51*(6), 11–16.

Phenice, L., & Hildebrand, V. (1988). Multicultural education: A pathway to global harmony. *Day Care and Early Education, 16*(2), 15–17.

Saracho, O., & Spodek, B. (Eds.). (1983). *Understanding the multicultural experience in early childhood education.* Washington, DC: National Association for the Education of Young Children.

Sawyers, J., & Tegano, D. (1986, November). *General guidelines and techniques for problem solving.* Paper presented at the annual conference of the National Association for the Education of Young Children, Chicago.

Scalise-Annis, M. (1997). Services for children with hearing impairments. In L. Dunlap (Ed.), *An introduction to early childhood special education* (pp. 177–196). Needham Heights, MA: Allyn & Bacon.

Shade, D. (1996). Software evaluation. *Young Children, 51*(6), 17–21.

Snider, S., & Badgett, T. (1995). "I have this computer, what do I do now?" Using technology to enhance every child's learning. *Early Childhood Education Journal, 23*(2), 101–106.

Tegano, D. W., Moran, J. D., III, & Sawyers, J. K. (1991). *Creativity in early childhood classrooms.* Washington, DC: National Education Association.

Thurman, B. (1981). Informal lecture at the University of Tennessee, Knoxville.

Wolery, M., & Wilbers, J. Eds.). (1994). *Including children with special needs in early childhood programs.* Washington, DC: National Association for the Education of Young Children.

Workman, S., & Anziano, M. (1993). Curriculum webs: Weaving connections from children to teachers. *Young Children, 48*(2), 4–9.

Wright, J. (1994). Listen to the children: Observing young children's discoveries with the microcomputer. In J. Wright & D. Shade (Eds.), *Young children:Active learners in a technological age* (pp. 3–17). Washington, DC: National Association for the Education of Young Children.

ADDITIONAL RESOURCES _____

Banks, J. (1993). Multicultural education for young children: Racial and ethnic attitudes and their modification. In B. Spodek (Ed.), *Handbook of research on the education of young children* (pp. 236–250). New York: Macmillan.

Beckman, P., Robinson, C., Jackson, B., & Rosenberg, S. (1986). Translating developmental findings into teaching strategies for young handicapped children. *Journal of the Division for Early Childhood, 10*(1), 99–122.

Benjamin, A. (1994). Observations in early childhood classrooms: Advice from the field. *Young Children, 49*(6), 14–20.

Bergen, D. (1997). Perspectives on inclusion in early childhood education. In J. Isenberg & M. Jalongo (Eds.), *Major trends and issues in early childhood education* (pp. 151–171). New York: Teachers College Press.

Billman, J. (1992). The Native American curriculum: Attempting alternatives to tepees and headbands. *Young Children, 47*(6), 22–25.

Boutte, G., Van Scoy, I., & Hendley, S. (1996). Multicultural and nonsexist prop boxes. *Young Children, 52*(1), 34–39.

Bredekamp, S., & Rosegrant, T. (Eds.). (1992). *Reaching potentials: Appropriate curriculum and assessment for young children* (Vol. 1). Washington, DC: National Association for the Education of Young Children.

Bredekamp, S., & Rosegrant, T. (Eds.). (1995). *Reaching potentials: Transforming early childhood curriculum and assessment* (Vol. 2). Washington, DC: National Association for the Education of Young Children.

Bronson, M. (1995). *The right stuff for children birth to 8: Selecting play materials to support development.* Washington, DC: National Association for the Education of Young Children.

Brown, J. (Ed.). (1982). *Curriculum planning for young children.* Washington, DC: National Association for the Education of Young Children.

Catron, C., & Parks, B. (1996). *Celebrate with a story.* Grand Rapids, MI: Instructional Fair/Dennison.

Chandler, P. (1994). *A place for me: Including children with special needs in early care and education settings.* Washington, DC: National Association for the Education of Young Children.

Chupman, M. (1997). Valuing cultural diversity in the early years: Social imperatives and pedagogical insights. In J. Isenberg & M. Jalongo (Eds.), *Major trends and issues in early childhood education* (pp. 43–55). New York: Teachers College Press.

Clemens, S. (1983). *The sun's not broken, a cloud's just in the way: On child-centered teaching.* Mt. Rainier, MD: Gryphon House.

Clements, D. (1987). Computers and young children: A review of research. *Young Children, 43*(1), 34–44.

Clements, D., & Nastasi, B. (1993). Electronic media and early childhood education. In B. Spodek (Ed.), *Handbook of research on the education of young children* (pp. 251–275). New York: Macmillan.

Diamond, K., Hestenes, L., & O'Connor, C. (1994). Integrating young children with disabilities in preschool: Problems and promise. *Young Children, 49*(2),68–75.

Dodge, D. T. (1988). *The creative curriculum for early childhood.* Washington, DC: Teaching Strategies.

Eliason, C., & Jenkins, L. (1990). *A practical guide to early childhood curriculum* (4th ed.). Columbus, OH: Merrill/Macmillan.

Elkind, D. (1996). Young children and technology: A cautionary note. *Young Children, 51*(6), 22–23.

Escobedo, T. (1993). Curricular issues in early education for culturally and linguistically diverse populations. In S. Reifel (Ed.), *Advances in early education and day care: Perspectives on developmentally appropriate practice* (Vol. 5, pp. 213–246). Greenwich, CT: JAI Press.

Forman, G., & Kuschner, D. (1983). *The child's construction of knowledge: Piaget for teaching children.* Washington, DC: National Association for the Education of Young Children.

Garcia, E. (1993). The education of linguistically and culturally diverse children. In B. Spodek (Ed.), *Handbook of research on the education of young children* (pp. 372–384). New York: Macmillan.

Garcia, E. (1997). The education of Hispanics in early childhood: Of roots and wings. *Young Children, 52*(3), 5–14.

Gonzalez-Mena, J. (1993). *Multicultural issues in child care.* Mountain View, CA: Mayfield.

Green, E. (1997). Guidelines for serving linguistically and culturally diverse young children. *Early Childhood Education Journal, 24*(3), 147–154.

Greenfield, P. (1984). *Mind and media: The effects of television, video games, and computers.* Cambridge, MA: Harvard.

Guddemi, M., & Mills, H. (1991). Supporting literacy growth through word processing. *Dimensions, 19*(2), 18–21.

Hale, J. (1991). The transmission of cultural values to young African American children. *Young Children, 46*(6), 7–15.

Haugland, S. (1997). How teachers use computers in early childhood classrooms. *Journal of Computing in Childhood Education, 8*(1), 3–14.

Haugland, S. (1997). Outstanding developmental software. *Early Childhood Education Journal, 24*(3), 179–184.

Holder-Brown, L., & Parette, H. (1992). Children with disabilites who use assistive technology: Ethical considerations. *Young Children, 47*(6), 73–77.

Jackman, H. (1997). *Early education curriculum: A child's connection to the world.* Albany, NY: Delmar.

Jones, E., & Nimmo, J. (1994). *Emergent curriculum.* Washington, DC: National Association for the Education of Young Children.

Lavatelli, C. S. (1970). *Piaget's theory applied to an early childhood curriculum.* Boston: Center for Media Development.

Levin, D. (1986). Weaving curriculum webs: Planning, guiding, and recording curriculum activities in the day care classroom. *Day Care and Early Education, 13*(4), 16–19.

Mallory, B., & New, R. (Eds.). (1994). *Diversity and developmentally appropriate practices: Challenges for early childhood education.* New York: Teachers College Press.

McCormick, L., & Feeney, S. (1995). Modifying and expanding activities for children with disabilities. *Young Children, 50*(4), 10–17.

Morrison, J., & Rodgers, L. (1996). Being responsive to the needs of children from dual heritage backgrounds. *Young Children, 52*(1), 29–33.

National Association for the Education of Young Children. (NAEYC). (1990). NAEYC position statement on media violence in children's lives. *Young Children, 45*(5), 18–21.

Neugebauer, B. (Ed.). (1992). *Alike and different: Exploring our humanity with young children.* Washington, DC: National Association for the Education of Young Children.

Raines, S. (1997). Developmental appropriateness: Curriculum revisited and challenged. In J. Isenberg & M. Jalongo (Eds.), *Major trends and issues in early childhood education* (pp. 75–89). New York: Teachers College Press.

Shade, D., & Davis, B. (1997). The role of computer technology in early childhood education. In J. Isenberg & M. Jalongo (Eds.), *Major trends and issues in early childhood education* (pp. 90–103). New York: Teachers College Press.

Sheerer, M., Dettore, E., & Cyphers, J. (1996). Off with a theme: Emergent curriculum in action. *Early Childhood Education Journal, 24*(2), 99–102.

Shilling, W. (1997). Young children using computers to make discoveries about written language. *Early Childhood Education Journal, 24*(4), 253–260.

Smith, M. (1996). Fostering creativity in the early childhood classroom. *Early Childhood Education Journal, 24*(2), 77–82.

Soldier, L. (1992). Working with Native American children. *Young Children, 47*(6), 15–21.

Southern Early Childhood Association. (1988). *Appropriate uses of computers in the early childhood curriculum: Position statement.* Little Rock, AR: Southern Association on Children under Six.

Southern Early Childhood Association. (1988). *Multicultural education: A position statement.* Little Rock, AR: Southern Association on Children under Six.

Spiegel-McGill, P., Zippiroli, S. M., & Mistrett, S. G. (1989). Microcomputers as social facilitators in integrated preschools. *Journal of Early Intervention, 13*(3), 249–260.

Trawick-Smith, J. (1997). *Early childhood development: A multicultural perspective.* Columbus, OH: Merrill/Prentice-Hall.

Williams, C. K., & Kamii, C. (1986). How do children learn by handling objects? *Young Children, 42*(1), 23–26.

Wilson, L. C. (1986). *Infants and toddlers: Curriculum and teaching.* Albany, NY: Delmar.

Wright, J., & Shade, D. (Eds.). (1994). *Young children: Active learners in a technological age.* Washington, DC: National Association for the Education of Young Children.

Zeece, P. D., & Graul, S. K. (1990). Learning to play: Playing to learn. *Day Care and Early Education, 18*(1), 11–15.

11.

Curriculum for Developing Personal Awareness

As a teacher in a toddler classroom you have become increasingly concerned about a 2-year-old who is extremely aggressive toward other children. Ahmed's aggressive behavior seems to be escalating and he hits, pushes, and yells at his peers with very little provocation. Ahmed also exhibits new behaviors such as crying and screaming when going near the bathroom, not wanting you to touch him to change his diaper, and attempting to touch his friends' penises. Ahmed's peers are avoiding him, and he is beginning to withdraw. This cycle of aggression and withdrawal coupled with Ahmed's other behavioral and emotional changes causes you extreme concern and prompts you to arrange a conference with Ahmed's mother.

During the conference, as you express your concerns to Ahmed's mother, she begins to cry and reveals that her boyfriend has been sexually abusing Ahmed for the past several months. She is upset and ashamed as well as frightened for her child and herself. You discuss the possible consequences of sexual abuse and emphasize the urgent need to protect Ahmed and help him cope with the physical, emotional, and behavioral consequences of abuse. You also inform Ahmed's mother that you have a professional, ethical,

and legal obligation to report the abuse to the state's human services department so it can investigate and arrange counseling for Ahmed. The mother is very upset and defensive but says, "Maybe they can stop him. I can't stop him. And I don't want my baby to be hurt anymore."

As you consider your role as Ahmed's teacher in helping him to work through his anger, frustration, and mistrust of adults, you realize you must decide:

- How will you help to strengthen Ahmed's positive body image after such traumatic experiences?
- What can you do to help Ahmed identify with positive male role models and become comfortable with his own sexual identity?
- How can you teach Ahmed about safe and unsafe interactions with adults in a developmentally appropriate manner, without further violating his sense of trust in others?
- What can you do to help Ahmed understand his right to privacy and to saying "no" without making him feel responsible for his own safety?
- How can you help Ahmed to feel less a victim and more a person who can exercise some control over his environment?

Suggestions for responding to this classroom vignette will be shared at the end of the chapter.

When reading this chapter, focus on the developmental milestones in personal awareness that are necessary for young children's healthy development. Also, become aware of how to foster growth in personal awareness through teaching strategies and daily transition times, as well as specific activities developed for the creative-play curriculum.

Personal awareness is one of six developmental domains identified in the creative-play curriculum. Although all facets of children's development are integrated and interrelated, these six developmental areas are discussed separately in order to present an in-depth picture of developmental issues and suggestions for curricular activities in each area.

The primary developmental tasks in achieving personal awareness for young children involve developing

Activities were written by Kathy Carlson, Amy R. Kerlin, and Anne Miller Stott; adaptations were written by Bobbie Beckmann.

independence and control, understanding sexuality, and developing a sexual or gender identity. Young children who are comfortable with themselves as sexual beings and as members of a particular gender have positive body images and higher levels of self-esteem, and establish more satisfying relationships with members of both sexes. Young children who begin to achieve independence develop a degree of control over bodily functions and become aware of practices to support their personal health and safety. Children's development in the area of personal awareness involves building a positive body image and sex-role identity, learning about ways to be safe and healthy, and practicing a variety of self-help skills. Growth in personal awareness involves the emergence of independence and is closely related to the development of a positive self-concept, the cognitive ability to understand safety and health issues, the ability to communicate with others, and the motor skills needed to begin to care for one's own physical needs. Understanding the develop-

mental milestones and research results surrounding the personal and sexual development of young children will facilitate the process of curriculum planning and inform teachers' attitudes and reactions to children's sexual play, formation of gender identity, and attempts to control the environment.

DEVELOPMENTAL MILESTONES IN PERSONAL AWARENESS

Infants are completely dependent upon adults for their nurturing and well-being. As children grow physically, cognitively, and emotionally, they begin to discover new abilities to achieve mastery over the environment. The growth of independence involves taking gradual steps away from the security of an adult's presence and protection and fulfilling the drive toward separateness and individuality. The most intense period for developing independence occurs between 18 and 30 months; however, "the mastery of the steps toward independence will take the rest of childhood and most of adulthood" (Brazelton, 1974, p. 223). Becoming a separate, autonomous person is a process that is sometimes turbulent and stressful and involves both advancing into independence and retreating into dependence as the child learns to balance these conflicting developmental needs.

Children's drive toward independence involves developing "a pattern of self-controlling behavior" (Brazelton, 1984, p. 57) that begins in infancy when children learn to quiet themselves and establish routines for eating and sleeping. Learning self-control continues during the toddler years as children develop mastery over fears and bodily functions, and into the preschool years when children cope with aggression and learn prosocial group behaviors.

Another facet of developing independence is children's ability to gain mastery and control over the environment. Children's need for mastery and control is evidenced by the frequent verbalization of "do it myself" during the toddler years. Toddlers struggle to match their desire for independent actions with their physical and cognitive abilities. Developing mastery and control continue to be significant issues during the preschool years, when young children's abilities allow them to create changes in the environment, influence the behavior of others, and engage in increasingly complex play and learning activities.

Another lifelong component of personal awareness is the development of an understanding of sexuality. Infants are sexual from birth. They sense pleasure

and engage in behaviors that would be labeled sexual in older children and adults, but their actions lack the intent and sexual consciousness that appear later. As infants begin to explore their environments, their own bodies are included in this exploration. They determine that some parts of their own bodies are more pleasurable to touch. This exploration is healthy. Infants also are beginning to understand human sexuality through their interaction with other people. Hugging, holding, rocking, cuddling, and other pleasurable interactions between children and adults help children learn that close, physical contact with another person is enjoyable.

Young children continue their exploration of sexuality in the toddler and preschool years as their level of curiosity about male and female body parts increases. Typical behavior includes asking questions about physical differences in males and females and attempting to observe differences during toileting, bathing, or dressing routines. Another aspect of children's curiosity about sexuality, usually emerging during the preschool years, is questioning where babies come from and how they are born. Young children may develop complex but inaccurate theories about conception and birth and need simple, honest explanations from adults that are appropriate for their age and developmental level. Young children need reassurances from adults that this sexual curiosity and exploration is natural and healthy, so that this stage of sexual development is not characterized by shame and guilt and in order to develop positive images of themselves as sexual beings.

A parallel developmental task in the domain of personal awareness is understanding and identifying with either primarily masculine or primarily feminine traits. The development of gender or sexual identity is a learning process that begins at birth and continues throughout life. Developing gender- or sex-role identity is related to the process of physical sexual development, but also involves the emotional development of self-esteem and the socialization process that occurs in the family, the peer group, and society (Lively & Lively, 1991).

Family influences, especially the role models provided by the mother and father, are the most significant factor in helping the child develop a strong identity, which includes "establishing a definition of the human body, and creating an awareness of what males and females are, what they can do, and how they are related to each other" (Lively & Lively, 1991, p. 82). Sex-role behaviors are learned early as children begin to distinguish between male and female and masculine and feminine in the second year of life. By age 3, most children are certain of their own gender, another person's gender, and the clothing and occupations typically associated with males and females. By age 4 or 5, most children can differentiate between physical cues of maleness and femaleness and psychological cues of masculinity and femininity. Children's cognitive categorization by gender as well as gender-segregated socialization may create rigid gender barriers and biases. This stereotyping may lead to disregard for individual differences and problems in communication and interaction with others perceived as being different (Powlishta, 1995).

Creating conditions that favor the development of the whole child involves breaking down rigid definitions of roles for males and females and eliminating the idea of exclusivity in certain occupations and the stereotyping of roles in relationships. The characteristics of masculinity and femininity are not mutually exclusive: rather, the healthy integrated person can be achievement-oriented, assertive, and competent as well as nurturing, expressive, and understanding (Harris & Liebert, 1987; Morrison, 1988). Well-balanced people have psychological advantages over individuals who have developed more rigidly defined sexual identities. Children who possess sex-role behaviors of both genders exhibit more frequent analytical thinking and greater creativity. Indeed, research suggests that integrated people, who have characteristics of both sexes, "may be more flexible and more competent, and may have greater self-esteem" (Harris & Liebert, 1987, p. 296).

RESEARCH ON YOUNG CHILDREN'S SEXUALITY AND SEX-ROLE IDENTITY

Early research on children's sex-role development showed that by age 4, many children have developed restrictive and stereotyped ideas about sex roles. Children of both sexes viewed the male role as more desirable; males and their activities were given higher status and visibility (Brown, 1956, 1957; Shepherd-Look, 1982). Research also showed that children's books, toys, and television programs, all important socializing agents for young children, were predominantly sex-stereotyped in their portrayal of social and occupational roles for males and females (Chambers, 1983; Yawkey & Yawkey, 1976). This distortion and rigidity limit children's images, goals, and aspirations.

More recent research on children's sex-role development and early childhood education has shown that preschool children who spent time in child care are more independent of their mothers when proximity-seeking is measured. A child without child-care experience is more dependent and seeks to be near or interact with his or her mother. A sex difference is noted among this latter group; girls are much more dependent than boys. But among children with child-care experience, there is no gender difference; girls and boys are equally independent. The authors of these studies suggest that child care programs may foster independence in both boys and girls; these children may be less likely to behave in stereotypical ways and more likely to show a balance of both female/feminine and male/masculine traits and behavior (Cornelius & Denny, 1975).

Several useful studies have examined children's knowledge of human sexuality and reproduction. Children's knowledge about "Where do babies come from?" has been categorized into five levels, with the first three describing young children. At the first level, the "geographers" believe that babies always existed, but they are not sure where. At the store, in mommy's stomach, in a cloud, and with God are typical responses at this stage. In level two, the "manufacturers," ages 4 to 8, realize that some action or behavior is necessary to make a baby. Construction analogies, heavenly powers, fathers' magic, or the digestive fallacy, in which swallowing something such as a seed begins the process of human life, are characteristic of children at this stage. At level three, children ranging in age from 5 to 10 and still exhibiting preoperational thinking are in a transitional period. Children's ideas about procreation combine the technology of the previous manufacturing stage and the physiology of a more advanced understanding of the physical action and contributions of both mother and father (Bernstein & Cowan, 1975).

Children in these first three stages are likely to ask questions about labels and vocabulary ("What is that?" "What do you call that?"), about function ("What's that for?" "What do you do with that?"), and perhaps purpose or causality ("Why are they doing that?" "Why do they want to kiss?"); later they begin to ask questions about the emotions, relationships, and values that adults associate with human sexuality.

Another study of children's knowledge of human sexuality and reproduction compared the responses of children in North America with those of children in England, Australia, and Sweden. Children in North America were the slowest to develop an accurate understanding of reproduction and did not catch up to other children until ages 13 to 15. Most preschool children believed babies always existed or

that they were created by some artificial or manufacturing process. There also was evidence of sex stereotypes in the children's answers as they grew older. Mothers had a more passive role and fathers a more active role in human reproduction rather than equivalent or reciprocal roles (Goldman & Goldman, 1982).

Five things children should know by the age of 4 about human sexuality and reproduction are names of the body's sexual parts, socially accepted words for elimination, the basic fact that babies develop in their mother's body, an understanding of observable differences between boys and girls, and, as soon as they ask, the fact that both mothers and fathers create a baby (Bernstein, 1978, p. 73).

FOSTERING PERSONAL AWARENESS THROUGH CREATIVE-PLAY CURRICULUM _____

The development of personal awareness is a process of building independence and control over the self and the environment as well as developing gender identity and a positive image of self as a healthy, sexual person. For a teacher of young children, fostering growth in personal awareness involves creating an open classroom environment where children can participate in natural sexual exploration without negative consequences, where children are encouraged to participate in all activities and enact a wide variety of gender roles, where children become increasingly independent in regulating bodily functions, and where children engage in activities to learn about the importance of personal health and safety. Classrooms for young children offer many opportunities to develop personal awareness skills. Children can use the many transition and routine periods of the day, including toileting, washing hands, setting the table for lunch, putting on coats to go outside, and helping to clean up after snack, to practice emerging skills in independence and master self-help skills with the support of adults. It is especially critical for teachers to structure these routines to encourage young children with special needs to develop self-help skills and independent functioning within the classroom environment.

Independence and Control

As children learn that they have the capabilities to act on and control the environment, they begin to test the

limits of the adults who care for them and provide for their safety and security. Teachers of young children must recognize children's drive toward independence as well as their need for safety and reassurance. A supportive learning environment for young children includes many opportunities to explore and experiment with new activities, challenges, and interactions, but also provides the security of reasonable limits and guidelines for acceptable behaviors.

Developing independence, including the ability to take initiative and responsibility, is a critical developmental task that can be fostered and reinforced by teachers of young children. Giving children responsibility in developmentally appropriate ways at an early age can help children become productive and self reliant. Children receive satisfaction and feelings of accomplishment when given age-appropriate tasks. Helping children to see how their contributions benefit other individuals will promote feelings of self-respect and self-confidence.

Young children develop independence through interactions with the environment and others and test their emerging independence during a variety of play activities. Brian Sutton-Smith (1981) has classified young children's play as being imitative, exploratory, testing, and model-building. During infancy and toddlerhood, children's play is characterized by imitating the actions and behaviors of adults and other children; by exploring their own bodies as well as objects and language; by testing their physical, cognitive, and social/emotional capabilities; and by modeling or planning a variety of play themes.

Children develop independence through interactions with the environment and others during play activities.

The play of children becomes more complex as they grow in ability and self-confidence. A classroom environment that provides a variety of opportunities for active, exploratory, and pretend play enables children to test their abilities, gain mastery over the environment, and build competence and confidence.

Developing Sexuality

Teachers and parents who establish physically affectionate relationships with young children help children to learn about safe, appropriate touches and enable children to develop positive attitudes about their bodies. Attitudes about sexuality also are learned when adults respond to children's sexual exploration. Telling an infant that touching his penis is bad and stopping exploration of his genitals contributes to the child's own negative feelings about his body and behavior. Or in a game of "there are your eyes, this is your nose, here are your ears," refusing to acknowledge or label the genitals robs the child of necessary knowledge and a positive, respectful attitude about the body. These experiences begin infants' learning about human sexuality and sexual relationships.

As children get older, their sex play becomes more intentional and deliberate. They may engage in genital play, referred to as masturbation when the behavior is recognized by the child as bringing pleasure, soothing distress, or calming to induce sleep. Children also may engage in sex play with other children. This usually takes the form of "playing doctor" or "I'll show you mine, you show me yours" and is a natural part of children's curiosity and learning about their social and physical world. Preschoolers also may repeat obscene words, either for their usefulness in shocking others or in an attempt to gain a definition or context for use of the word. Adults should not overreact to the use of obscene language but should ignore or in a matter-of-fact manner state the appropriate and inappropriate usages of this type of language. The response of adults to these words usually provides children with both factual information and an understanding of attitudes and values associated with the public use of such language (Koblinsky, Atkinson, & Davis, 1980).

Teachers also facilitate young children's understanding of sexuality when they respond to children's questions about anatomy and childbirth in a developmentally appropriate manner. Young children do not require detailed answers to their questions about where babies come from or why boys have penises and girls do not; rather, they need explanations that are simple, clear, and honest. Teachers should provide a classroom environment where open communication is fostered and children feel free to question and discuss issues of sexuality.

Children's development of an understanding of human sexuality and relationships has recently been emphasized as teachers and parents have searched for effective and appropriate ways to educate children about and prevent child sexual abuse. A vocabulary and knowledge about human sexuality is one component; teaching children both respect for their bodies and the expectation that others will respect children's bodies is another vital component.

Gender Identity

The child begins to develop gender identity by evolving a self-image as a male or a female and by forming attitudes about what it means to be a member of a particular sex. Teachers and parents communicate to young children a set of attitudes about male and female roles and reinforce behaviors that are considered appropriate for each sex (Lively & Lively, 1991). Young children learn gender identity through imitating same-sex role models. Toddlers begin to pattern their behavior after that of the same-sex parent or teacher and respond to adults who offer praise for appropriate male or female behaviors. Preschoolers extend their concept of gender identity through a socialization process that involves taking on a variety of roles during pretend play with peers and by responding to cues from peers and adults.

Teachers of young children who encourage them to explore a variety of roles and engage in the entire spectrum of classroom activities will facilitate the development of children with a healthy and balanced, not a restricted and stereotypical, view of gender identity. For example, encouraging girls to play with blocks and in the woodworking center and encouraging boys to engage in dramatic play and art activities help to balance children's development and establish the view that people of both genders are capable of having many talents and interests and of being both nurturant and competent. In addition, selecting books and materials for the classroom that are free of stereotypes will facilitate children's learn-ing about the multiple roles available to them and reinforce attitudes of openness and flexibility toward gender identity.

Safety Issues

A comprehensive safety curriculum for young children recognizes their emotional, cognitive, and physical vulnerabilities. Young children are small; they cannot easily get away from harmful or frightening situations. Young children are naïve; they sometimes do not have the capability to evaluate the potential danger of a situation. Young children are trusting; they usually are unable to prevent adults, strangers, or friends from involving them in harmful or abusive activities. A developmentally appropriate safety curriculum is comprehensive in scope and includes activities in a variety of areas, such as environmental safety, fire safety, vehicular safety, and personal safety.

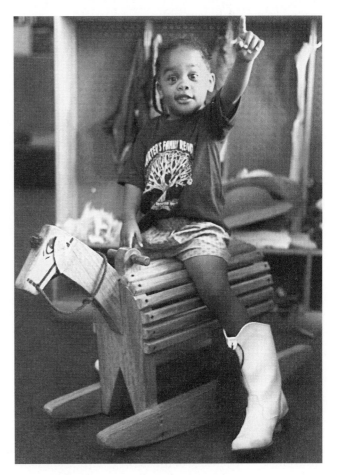

An environment that encourages both boys and girls to enact a variety of roles helps children develop healthy, balanced gender identities.

Concern about an increase in the frequency and number of cases of child abuse has led to a recent emphasis on child sexual abuse prevention and has created an explosion in the number of books for children and curriculum guides for teachers. When choosing books and activities, it is important to consider that a critical developmental task for young children is establishing trust in adults; therefore, the materials should contain realistic information but not be excessively or unnecessarily frightening. An essential factor in the development of trust is children's feelings of security in the knowledge that adults will keep them safe. The safety and protection of young children is the responsibility of adults, and young children should not be taught through prevention curricula that they are responsible for preventing child abuse or keeping themselves safe. It also is important to consider the developmental level of the child; it is not appropriate to use specific child abuse prevention materials with children under the age of 3. Clearly the concepts provided to a 3-year-old should be less specific than the information presented to a 5- or 6-year-old.

Appropriate goals of child sexual abuse prevention curricula include helping children do the following:

- Develop a positive self-concept.
- Establish loving relationships with others.
- Build a healthy respect for their bodies.
- Express emotions and communicate effectively.
- Learn problem-solving and conflict resolution skills.
- Become independent and assertive.
- Distinguish between safe and unsafe situations.
- Understand basic safety rules.
- Know how to respond to an unsafe situation.

A comprehensive child safety curriculum does not overemphasize child sexual abuse prevention; rather, it integrates a variety of issues involving personal safety throughout the creative-play curriculum. Teaching young children about personal safety involves not only planning appropriate activities, but also utilizing classroom routines and free-play situations to emphasize safety procedures.

Personal Health

Developing curricula for personal health requires an awareness of the issues of illness in group care, an understanding of the nutritional needs of infants and young children, insight into the development of physical control over a variety of bodily functions, and

recognition of the choices children face regarding their personal health and well-being. Ensuring the development of healthy young children involves setting appropriate program policies for requiring up-to-date medical and immunization records for children, excluding ill children from the classroom, planning nutritious meals and snacks, establishing appropriate diapering and toilet-learning procedures, and helping children learn to make healthy choices.

Parents and teachers must accept responsibility for children's health by working as partners to implement the program's health policies. Health policies should include a daily health check administered by the teacher at arrival time, criteria for excluding sick children, guidelines for administering medication, and procedures for caring for mildly ill children in the classroom. Written health policies will facilitate mutual understanding and cooperation between teachers and parents. Health practices that best protect young children, their teachers, and their families from the spread of infectious diseases include regular hand washing for adults before and after diapering and for adults and children after toileting, wiping noses, and before eating. Diapering and toileting areas should be separated from eating areas and both should be regularly sanitized with a bleach solution (Kendall, 1988).

Meeting the nutritional needs of children involves providing infants and young children with adequate nutritional intake as well as planning activities to teach children about healthy nutrition habits. Meals and snacks should meet the requirements recommended by the Child Care Food Programs of the U.S. Department of Agriculture. Infants' feeding times and intake of food should be closely monitored and highly individualized. Mealtime also should be a pleasant experience, with small groups of children and teachers eating family style. Mealtime is an excellent time to teach children sound nutritional habits and encourage children to learn to choose healthy foods and regulate their intake of food (*Accreditation Criteria and Procedures,* 1991; Lee, 1988).

Policies and procedures for toilet learning must be based on children's developmental level. Toilet learning should be a highly individualized process that considers both the child's physical and cognitive readiness for control of bodily functions. Children must show signs of interest in using the toilet, verbalize an awareness of wet or soiled diapers, and demonstrate evidence of bladder or bowel control. Teachers who encourage children toward independence in toileting, but do not push or punish children who are not ready, help children develop bodily control and a positive self-concept.

As children grow, they will be faced with making increasingly complex choices about behaviors that will affect their personal health and well-being. Introducing young children to issues such as drug abuse prevention and AIDS prevention can be accomplished by sharing developmentally appropriate health information and emphasizing goals similar to those used in sexual abuse prevention curriculum, such as helping children develop positive self-concepts and respect for their bodies, establishing caring relationships with others, and learning effective communication and problem-solving skills.

Children can be taught developmentally appropriate health practices in the context of a creative-play curriculum when teachers use a variety of opportunities in the daily schedule to facilitate the understanding and control of bodily functions and help children develop increasing confidence, competence, and self-help skills. Planned activities that allow for exploration of healthy practices also support the development of well children with positive attitudes toward personal health.

GOALS AND ACTIVITIES FOR PERSONAL AWARENESS _____

The development of personal awareness is dependent upon growth in four major subdomains: (1) self-help skills; (2) independence; (3) personal health; and (4) personal safety. Both the creative-play curriculum and the assessment process support children's growth in these areas. The following sections include specific developmental goals in each subdomain as well as sample activities for infants, toddlers, and preschoolers, with adaptations for children with disabilities.

Self-Help Skills

The first subdomain in the area of personal awareness encompasses developing a variety of self-help skills. Young children learn self-control by beginning to regulate bodily functions such as sleeping, eating, and toileting. Children's abilities become increasingly complex as their motor skills develop and they are able to care for their physical needs more independently. Specific developmental goals in this subdomain include the following:

1. Increase children's ability to dress and remove their own articles of clothing.
2. Encourage children to regulate their own needs for activity and calm and to provide their own self-cues to quiet for rest/sleep when necessary.
3. Foster independence in serving and eating a variety of foods at mealtime.
4. Help children to learn to regulate toilet patterns.

The development of self-help skills can be fostered through helping children establish and follow routines and allowing children both the time and the opportunity to test their emerging abilities. Here are some suggested sample activities for infants, toddlers, and preschoolers that can be adapted for a variety of developmental levels (an asterisk [*] denotes an activity that is also appropriate for use in the outdoor play environment).

INFANT ACTIVITY
Sock Party (Quiet Game)
_____

In the invitation to the sock party, ask parents to bring in a variety of socks that have lost a mate. Also save all mismatched socks from the child care center. Infants should be barefooted for the sock party. Show the infants a variety of socks and describe each type. Have sport socks, dressy socks, tennis socks, heavy winter socks—all in infant sizes. For very young infants, take their hands and help them to put the socks on their feet. For older infants, model putting on a sock and then encourage them to do the same. Refreshments for the sock party are optional.

Comments:

"These heavy wool socks will keep your feet warm in winter."

"Look at these dressy socks. They would be perfect to wear with a romper."

"You could wear these sport socks with your tennis shoes."

Additional Skills:

Socialization (social interaction); perceptual motor (coordination)

Adaptations for Children with Disabilities:

Physically Impaired: Provide assistance as needed. Observe the child's response to the various textures to avoid any tactile sensitivity or tactile defensiveness that would interfere with the enjoyment of this activity.

Speech/Language Impaired: None needed.

Visually Impaired: Encourage the child to feel the various textures of the socks; verbally explain which ones feel the same.

Hearing Impaired: Use signs and/or gestures to explain the activity and names of socks.

Behavior Disordered/Emotionally Disturbed: None needed.

TODDLER ACTIVITY
Pouring Party (Science/Nature)*

In a water table (or large tub) provide plastic containers (cups, pitchers, bowls, and so on) that children can use for pouring water back and forth. Add food coloring to the water to increase interest. Have children experiment with pouring/filling containers slowly/fast and halfway/to the top; encourage them to think about and discover which techniques would cause fewer spills. Talk about what they can do when something spills. Experiment with different kinds of paper to discover why certain kinds (paper towels) are best to use for cleanup. Talk about what to do at snack and lunch times to prevent spills as well as what to do when spills occur.

Additional Skills:

Perceptual motor (eye-hand coordination); cognition (concept formation)

Adaptations for Children with Disabilities:

Physically Impaired: Upper-extremity involvement: Use pitchers with large handles and cups with wide

mouths for more successful pouring. The child may need slow, gentle physical assistance from the teacher. Lower-extremity involvement: Properly seat the child in a chair so that the water table is at a comfortable level for the child to participate in this activity.

Speech/Language Impaired: Encourage the child to make verbal requests for containers for pouring from the other children. Provide verbal modeling as needed.

Visually Impaired: For the pouring, ask the child to pour with one hand and insert the index finger of the other hand into the glass to feel when to stop pouring.

Hearing Impaired: Label containers and use signs and/or gestures to describe pouring activity.

Behavior Disordered/Emotionally Disturbed: None needed.

PRESCHOOL ACTIVITY
Zip-a-Dee-Doo-Dah (Music)

Provide a zipper for each child and tell them they're going to be in a zipper band. Practice zipping and unzipping the zippers while listening to the sound the zipping makes. Sing "Zip-a-dee-doo-dah" and zip/unzip the zippers as you sing. You may want to zip/unzip only when you (slowly) say the word, "Z-Z-Z-Z-Z-Zip!"

Additional Zipper Songs:

1. (Tune: "If You're Happy") "If you can zip and you know it, show me now (zip, zip)"
2. (Tune: "Mulberry Bush") "This is the way we zip the zippers, early in the morning."
3. (Tune: "Looby Lou")

Here we go zip-ity-zip
Here we go zip-ity-zy,
Here we go zip-ity-zoo
All on a Saturday night.

Note: When zipping real zippers on clothing, the hard part is getting the zipper started, especially on thick jackets. Have children watch you and listen as you stand behind them (so your hand position will be like theirs would) and verbalize the idea of putting the thin metal piece down in the slot on the other side and then listening for it to "click" in place. Then pull the zipper up several inches and have children finish the job. Continue getting them started, doing less for them as they are able to do more.

Additional Skills:

Personal awareness (independence); perceptual motor (eye-hand coordination)

Adaptations for Children with Disabilities:

Physically Impaired: Tie a ribbon through the zipper making a loop (for a bracelet). Help the child move his or her arm slowly to make the zipper move up and down.

Speech/Language Impaired: Because the /z/ sound is a later-developing sound, many speech-impaired children

may not be able to make this sound. However, encourage verbal participation.

Visually Impaired: Allow the child to feel the zipper from top to bottom at the beginning of the activity.

Hearing Impaired: Use signs and/or gestures to explain the activity. Use overly exaggerated body movements to enhance the rhythm of the songs.

Behavior Disordered/Emotionally Disturbed: None needed.

Independence

The second subdomain in the area of personal awareness is growth in independence. An important developmental task for young children is learning independence, including becoming a separate individual, developing responsible behavior, and gaining mastery and control over the environment. Specific developmental goals in this subdomain include the following:

1. Encourage children to accept responsibility for personal possessions, toys, and so on.
2. Help children to learn to separate from their family (Hendrick, 1998).

3. Help children to make choices and decisions about interactions with the environment.
4. Encourage children to exercise control over their environment.

The development of independence can be facilitated by adults who encourage children to make choices and attempt new challenges while providing a safe and secure environment. Here are some suggested sample activities for infants, toddlers, and preschoolers that can be adapted for a variety of developmental levels.

 **INFANT ACTIVITY
All by Yourself (Music)**

To encourage infants' independence, make up a song "All by Yourself." Sing a variety of verses that focus on tasks infants can do by themselves. For example,

> Eating, eating, eating snack,
> Eating, eating, eating snack,
> Eating, eating, eating snack,
> All by yourself!

Other verses can be washing hands, holding a bottle, walking alone, going to sleep, and so on. Use hand motions that fit the verse and encourage infants to imitate the motions.

Additional Skills:

Communication (receptive language); cognition (imitation /memory)

Adaptations for Children with Disabilities:

Physically Impaired: Initially assist the child to perform the activities you are singing about. Then give the child opportunities to participate without assistance.

Speech/Language Impaired: None needed.

Visually Impaired: Initially, physically assist the child to perform the activity you are singing. Then give the child opportunities to participate without assistance.

Hearing Impaired: Use signs and/or gestures for vocabulary. Physically move the child to "feel" the rhythm of the song.

Behavior Disordered/Emotionally Disturbed: None needed.

TODDLER ACTIVITY
Good-Bye Book (Quiet Game)

Prepare a simple picture book of ways to say good-bye to parents. This book can be made by choosing pictures (pictures from magazines or photographs taken at the center), mounting pictures on construction paper or tagboard, laminating, and so forth; punching three holes in the paper; and tying the book together with string or yarn. Some suggestions for pictures are children hugging parents, children kissing parents, children waving good-bye to parents at the door or window, children making silly faces to parents, and a blank page for children to choose their own unique way of saying good-bye. Before parents leave children at the center, the children can choose a way to say good-bye from the book and the teacher can help the children carry out their choices.

Additional Skills:

Communication (nonverbal)

Adaptations for Children with Disabilities:

Physically Impaired: None needed.

Speech/Language Impaired: None needed.

Visually Impaired: Use a heavy black marker to outline the pictures or describe the pictures and make this more of a discussion activity.

Hearing Impaired: Use signs and/or gestures to explain the activity and name the pictures.

Behavior Disordered/Emotionally Disturbed: None needed.

PRESCHOOL ACTIVITY
Let's Use the Tape Recorder (Discussion)

Young children can learn to use a tape recorder for listening to prerecorded stories if they are given clear instructions and if they are given opportunity to practice the skill before being left on their own to use the equipment. Cassette book sets can be purchased or teacher made. If the teacher reads a story to make the cassette recording, a tapping sound can be used as the clue for the child to turn the page. With a small group of children, talk about the tape recorder and what all the parts are. Emphasize the parts of the tape recorder that the children will need to use as well as the parts that they should avoid touching (inside the cover, etc.). Color-code the buttons they need to use (green for "play," red for "stop," blue or yellow for "rewind"). Let each child take turns starting, stopping, and rewinding a tape. Show them how to listen (when the tape is rewinding) for the sound of rewinding as well as the sound of the click when the rewinding is finished. That will be their signal to push the stop button again. Children also will need to learn to listen for the clue that tells them when to turn the page. When children first begin to use the tape recorder on their own, have them demonstrate to you that they remember how to stop, start, and rewind.

Variation: Use the technique to show children how to use other classroom equipment or special equipment you bring in (woodworking tools, typewriters, and so on).

Additional Skills:

Socialization (conservation of resources); communication (receptive language)

Adaptations for Children with Disabilities:

Physically Impaired: If the child has difficulty with fine motor skills, pushing the button may be impossible. Use of cones made of sturdy cardboard or wood can assist the child if he or she can grasp the large end and push the button on the tape recorder with the pointed end.

Speech/Language Impaired: None needed.

Visually Impaired: Use glue dots to provide a Braille simulation of the first letters of the name of the color (for example, *g* for green, *r* for red, *b* for blue). This can go on top of the buttons. Encourage the child to feel the separate keys and explore the Braille letters.

Hearing Impaired: Encourage the child to feel the vibration of the sound coming out of the tape recorder to indicate sound on versus off. Otherwise, the child would probably not choose to participate in this auditory activity.

Behavior Disordered/Emotionally Disturbed: None needed.

Personal Health

The third subdomain in the area of personal awareness is developing personal health. Becoming a whole and healthy individual involves an awareness and acceptance of the physical attributes of sexuality and developing gender identity. Young children also need to learn healthy habits in order to develop increasing levels of responsibility for their physical well-being. Specific developmental goals in this subdomain are as follows:

1. Teach children to identify body parts and strengthen their positive body image (Hendrick, 1998).

2. Help children to understand gender differences and become comfortable with their sex role and sexual identity.

3. Increase children's awareness of the need for cleanliness and healthy personal practices.

4. Encourage children to practice good nutritional habits through eating a variety of healthful foods.

The development of personal health can be fostered through relationships with caring, affectionate adults who create an open classroom atmosphere where children are comfortable exploring a variety of roles. Teachers also need to model appropriate hygienic and nutritional practices and provide educational experiences for children in the area of health and wellness. Here are some suggested sample activities for infants, toddlers, and preschoolers that can be adapted for a variety of developmental levels (an asterisk [*] denotes an activity that is also appropriate for use in the outdoor play environment).

INFANT ACTIVITY
Washing (Science/Nature)*

Place a tub of water on an old shower curtain. Have ready washcloths, soap, towels, sponges, and containers for pouring. Infants, dressed in diapers, can be encouraged to explore with the water, but the focus of the activity should be washing. Help infants to get soap on the washcloth, wash hands and face, and rinse and dry. Emphasize the importance of washing regularly to be sure we are clean. Discuss during the activity how soap and water can be used to make us clean, how soap feels, and how towels can be used to dry off water.

Comments:

"We use soap and water to make us clean. Watch, let's lather up the soap and wash your hands and face."

"Oh, the soap feels slick! Look at the soap bubbles! They pop!"

"Now, let's get a towel. The towel feels rough. It can help dry the water off of you. Look! You are all dry!"

Additional Skills:

Cognition (imitation/memory); socialization (cooperation); personal awareness (self-help skills)

Adaptations for Children with Disabilities:

Physically Impaired: Adult assistance may be required for the child's participation. Have washcloths of various textures available to prevent or lessen tactile sensitivity or defensiveness.

Speech/Language Impaired: Pair vocalizations with various actions during water play. Encourage the infant to imitate the sound you make.

Visually Impaired: Slowly introduce the child to the water and washing materials. Show the child how to wash by verbally describing your actions as you assist the child to wash himself or herself. Once the child appears comfortable with the water and materials, allow for independent exploration, experimentation, and practice.

Hearing Impaired: Use signs and/or gestures to explain the activity.

Behavior Disordered/Emotionally Disturbed: None needed.

TODDLER ACTIVITY
The Washing Hands Song (Music)

Use the "Mulberry Bush" tune to sing about the sequence used in washing hands. Verses may include: "This is the

way we turn on the water; get our hands wet; get the soap; make the bubbles; rinse off the soap; turn off the water; get a paper towel; dry our hands; throw the towel away." Children will enjoy acting out the procedures as they sing. Emphasize the importance of making lather not only on palms of hands, but on the backs of hands and in between fingers. Also emphasize the importance of drying palms and backs of hands, and so on.

Additional Skills:

Cognition (imitation/memory); communication (expressive language)

Adaptations for Children with Disabilities:

Physically Impaired: Praise the child for attempts at acting out the procedure.

Speech/Language Impaired: None needed.

Visually Impaired: Verbally explain how to act out the various procedures. Provide physical assistance when needed.

Hearing Impaired: Use signs and/or gestures to explain the activity and "sing" the song.

Behavior Disordered/Emotionally Disturbed: None needed.

PRESCHOOL ACTIVITY
Friendship Soup/Salad (Science/Nature)

Have children plan with you what ingredients should be in their soup/salad. Children could bring one item from home or go on a field trip to purchase one item. Provide containers of water for children to use to wash the ingredients. Have them use plastic knives to cut up the ingredients. (You may have to do some preliminary preparation after they wash the ingredients but before they cut them. For example, cut apples and potatoes into wedges and have them cut the wedges into smaller pieces.) As children work, talk about where the ingredients grow, how they grow, and why they help children grow. Talk about color, shape, texture, and so on.

Additional Skills:

Socialization (cooperation); perceptual motor (eye-hand coordination); cognition (concept formation)

Adaptations for Children with Disabilities:

Physically Impaired: Physically assist the child with cutting through foods if necessary.

Speech/Language Impaired: Encourage the child to verbalize about what children are doing, using longer phrases and/or sentences. This is an excellent activity for using the other children as good language models.

Visually Impaired: Allow time for the child to carefully explore the dull edge of the plastic knife and the various foods. Give verbal directions on how to cut and assist as needed.

Hearing Impaired: Use signs and/or gestures to explain the activity.

Behavior Disordered/Emotionally Disturbed: None needed.

Personal Safety

The fourth subdomain in the area of personal awareness is learning about personal safety. Helping children to develop an awareness of safety issues and the ability to distinguish between safe and unsafe situations is the primary task in teaching personal safety. Specific developmental goals in this subdomain include the following:

1. Encourage children to be aware of pedestrian safety rules and passenger safety rules for riding in vehicles and on bicycles.
2. Increase children's awareness of safe and unsafe interactions with adults.
3. Teach children to value their right to privacy and ownership of their bodies.

4. Teach children to be aware of environmental hazards in the classroom, on the playground, and at home.

Young children learn personal safety when responsible, caring adults help them develop an awareness of safe and unsafe situations in the classroom environment. Children also learn about personal safety when adults recognize and respect children's right to privacy as well as their right to choose when to engage in physically affectionate behaviors. Here are some suggested sample activities for infants, toddlers, and preschoolers that can be adapted for a variety of developmental levels (an asterisk[*] denotes an activity that is also appropriate for use in the outdoor play environment).

INFANT ACTIVITY
Buckle Up (Imaginary Play)

Use an infant car seat and let infants take turns sitting in it and "buckling up." Talk about the importance of buckling up when riding in a car. Name the parts of the car seat and describe what you are doing as you buckle each child in. Talk about the children swapping and taking turns. Praise them for taking turns. Let the children manipulate the parts of the car seat. Encourage them to help buckle their friends into the car seat so they can ride safely.

Additional Skills:

Socialization (cooperation); perceptual motor (coordination)

Adaptations for Children with Disabilities:

Physically Impaired: Help the child manipulate the various parts of the car seat.

Speech/Language Impaired: None needed.

Visually Impaired: Provide enough time for the child to explore the seat fully before the activity. Give the child verbal descriptions about parts of the car seat and also when it is his or her turn.

Hearing Impaired: Use signs and/or gestures to describe the activity and name the parts of the seat.

Behavior Disordered/Emotionally Disturbed: None needed.

TODDLER ACTIVITY
Painting with Cars (Art)*

Tape a large piece of butcher paper to the floor. Draw or paint roads and stop lights or stop signs. In several pie pans put assorted colors of tempera paint. Dip plastic cars into each pie pan and allow the children to drive the cars on the "roads." Tell them to stop at each red light that they see. Ask the children as they are playing with the cars to identify the colors of the paint and cars and to count the stop lights and stop signs.

Additional Skills:

Perceptual motor (eye-hand coordination); cognition (concept formation)

Adaptations for Children with Disabilities:

Physically Impaired: Use cars large enough for the child to grasp or push with open or fisted hand.

Speech/Language Impaired: Encourage the child to verbalize what children are doing.

Visually Impaired: Use corrugated strips to make the road or use narrow corrugated strips to outline the roads. Cut out red lights from cardboard and attach at the crossroad. Encourage the child to feel for the stop sign or to distinguish a crossroad and stop until a friend comes to help. Add food extracts such as vanilla and peppermint to two paints to enhance the activity through the sense of smell.

Hearing Impaired: Use signs and/or gestures to describe the activity.

Behavior Disordered/Emotionally Disturbed: None needed.

PRESCHOOL ACTIVITY
Three Little Children Climbing on the Climber (Discussion)

Adapt the words and motions to "Five Little Monkeys Jumping on the Bed" to incorporate playground safety rules and consequences:

Three little children climbing on the climber,
One jumped off and hit his head.
Teacher called the doctor and the doctor said,
"No more jumping off the climber!"

Two little children walking by the swings,
One walked too close and got knocked down.
Teacher called the doctor and the doctor said,
"No more walking too close to the swings!"

One little child was sliding down the slide.
She slid head first and banded her chin.
Teacher called the doctor and the doctor said,
"No more sliding head first down the slide!"

After each verse, discuss the safe way to do the activity. Encourage children to think of additional situations that could be dangerous and incorporate those ideas in the finger play.

Additional Skills:

Communication (receptive and expressive language); cognition (problem-solving/reasoning)

Adaptations for Children with Disabilities:

Physically Impaired: Assist the child as needed to perform the movements you are singing.

Speech/Language Impaired: None needed.

Visually Impaired: Initially, physically assist the child to perform the movements in the song. Then give the child opportunities to participate without assistance.

Hearing Impaired: Use signs and/or gestures to describe the activity and words to the song. Use overly exaggerated body movements to enhance the rhythm of the song.

Behavior Disordered/Emotionally Disturbed: None needed.

CHAPTER SUMMARY _____

Children are physical beings. The formation of a positive body image includes developing an awareness of sexuality, increasing control over the environment, regulating elimination and acquiring bladder and bowel control, establishing sound nutritional habits, and making healthy personal choices. Teacher attitudes play a vital role in the development of children's physical and sexual images of themselves.

Teachers who convey positive verbal and nonverbal messages about sexual feelings and bodily functions help children develop a healthy respect for their bodies. Teachers who create a safe, healthy, and secure classroom environment help children learn respect for themselves, others, and the environment and encourage children to engage in healthy and safe practices.

■　　■　　■　　■　　■　　■　　■　　■　　■

In order to grow as complete, healthy, productive human beings, children must develop positive images of themselves as physical, sexual individuals. For a child like Ahmed, whose trust has been violated and whose sexual identity has become associated with shame and discomfort, it is especially critical to convey an attitude of respect for the body and provide classroom activities to foster healthy and safe practices. Specifically, it is important for a teacher to do the following:

- Accept children as physical beings and react positively to their attempts to regulate their bodies.
- Help children explore a variety of sex roles and become comfortable in establishing a gender identity by providing

positive role models and a wide range of nonstereotypical classroom materials and activities.

- Incorporate a comprehensive safety curriculum into the creative-play curriculum and teach personal safety in the context of broader safety issues.
- Teach children about their right to privacy and their right to safe and healthy interactions with others.
- Help children understand that it is adults' responsibility to keep them safe; however, you should also teach them developmentally appropriate techniques for obtaining help from a trusted adult in unsafe situations.
- Institute classroom policies and procedures to ensure a healthy and safe environment for all children.

■　　■　　■　　■　　■　　■　　■　　■　　■

DISCUSSION QUESTIONS _____

1. Discuss the vignette at the beginning of the chapter. What other questions or concerns might you have? Discuss the vignette at the end of the chapter. Are there other responses you might have to this situation?

2. What are the primary tasks in achieving personal awareness for young children?
3. Describe the development of independence in young children.

4. Describe how children develop an understanding of human sexuality.

5. Describe children's levels of knowledge about human reproduction. What misconceptions might children have at each level?

6. How can teachers help young children develop independence and control?

7. Describe appropriate sex abuse prevention activities for young children.

8. Describe classroom policies and practices that promote health in young children.

9. Describe the four subdomains in the area of personal awareness.

REFERENCES

Accreditation criteria and procedures of the National Academy of Early Childhood Programs. (1991). Washington, DC: National Association for the Education of Young Children.

Bernstein, A. (1978). *The flight of the stork.* New York: Delacorte.

Bernstein, A., & Cowan, P. (1975). Children's concepts of how people get babies. *Child Development, 46,* 77–91.

Brazelton, T. B. (1974). *Toddlers and parents.* New York: Dell.

Brazelton, T. B. (1984). *To listen to a child: Understanding the normal problems of growing up.* Reading, MA: Addison-Wesley.

Brown, D. (1956). Sex role preference in young children. *Psychological Monographs, 70* (Whole No. 421).

Brown, D. (1957). Masculinity-femininity development in children. *Journal of Consulting Psychology, 21,* 197–202.

Chambers, B. (1983). Counteracting racism and sexism in children's books. In O. Saracho & B. Spodek (Eds.), *Understanding the multicultural experience in early childhood education* (pp. 91–105). Washington, DC: National Association for the Education of Young Children.

Cornelius, S., & Denny, N. (1975). Dependency in day-care children. *Developmental Psychology, 11,* 575–582.

Goldman, R., & Goldman, J. (1982). How children perceive the origin of babies and the roles of mothers and fathers in procreation: A cross-national study. *Child Development, 53,* 491–504.

Harris, J. R., & Liebert, R. M. (1987). *The child.* Englewood Cliffs, NJ: Prentice-Hall.

Hendrick, J. (1998). *Total learning: Developmental curriculum for the young child* (5th ed.). Columbus, OH: Merrill/Prentice-Hall.

Kendall, E. (1988). Disease spread in day care: Cautions for infant programs. *Tennessee's Children, 30*(1), 5–9.

Koblinsky, S., Atkinson, J., & Davis, S. (1980). Sex education with young children. *Young Children, 35*(1), 21–31.

Lee, K. C. (1988). Good nutrition for infants. *Tennessee's Children, 30*(1), 2–4.

Lively, V., & Lively, E. (1991). *Sexual development of young children.* New York: Delmar.

Morrison, G. (1988). *Education and development of infants, toddlers, and preschoolers.* Glenview, IL: Scott, Foresman.

Powlishta, K. (1995). Gender segregation among children: Understanding the "cootie phenomenon." *Young Children, 50*(4). 61–69.

Shepherd-Look, D. (1982). Sex differentiation and the development of sex roles. In B. B. Wolman (Ed.), *Handbook of developmental psychology* (pp. 452–470). Englewood Cliffs, NJ: Prentice-Hall.

Sutton-Smith, B. (1981). Children at play. In R. Strom (Ed.), *Growing through play* (pp. 26–34). Monterey, CA: Brooks/Cole.

Yawkey, T., & Yawkey, M. (1976). Analysis of picture books. *Language Arts, 53,* 545–548.

ADDITIONAL RESOURCES

Allen, J. (1986). Safe touch: Reassurances for child care workers. *Day Care and Early Education, 14*(3), 14–16.

Allen, J. (1988). Sexual abuse and child care: Turning stumbling blocks into stepping stones. *Dimensions, 16*(4), 12–14.

Aronson, S. (1983). Injuries in child care. *Young Children, 38*(6), 19–20.

Birch, L., Johnson, S., & Fisher, J. (1995). Children's eating: The development of food-acceptance patterns. *Young Children, 50*(2), 71–78.

Brazelton, T. B. (1987, June). Are we frightening our children? *Family Circle,* pp. 98, 100, 124–125.

Calderone, M., & Raney, J. (1982). *Talking with your child about sex.* New York: Random House.

Caughery, C. (1991). Becoming the child's ally: Observations in a classroom for children who have been abused. *Young Children, 46*(4), 22–28.

Comer, D. (1987). *Developing safety skills with the young child.* New York: Delmar.

Corbett, S. (1991). Children and sexuality. *Young Children, 46*(2), 71–77.

Cosgrove, M. (1991). Cooking in the classroom: The doorway to nutrition. *Young Children, 46*(3), 43–46.

Deitch. S. (Ed.). (1987). *Health in day care: A manual for health professionals.* Elk Grove Village, IL: American Academy of Pediatrics.

Donowitz, L. (Ed.). (1991). *Infection control in the child care center and preschool.* Baltimore: Williams & Williams.

Finkelhor, D. (1984). *Child sexual abuse: New theory and research.* New York: Free Press.

Good, L. (1996). When a child has been sexually abused: Several resources for parents and early childhood professionals. *Young Children, 51*(5), 84–85.

Jurs, J., & Mangili, L. (1989). Having fun with health: Providing activities for young children. *Day Care and Early Education, 16*(4), 18–20.

Kendrick, A., Kaufmann, R., & Messenger, K. (Eds.). (1995). *Healthy young children.* Washington, DC: National Association for the Education of Young Children.

Koblinsky, S., & Behana, N. (1984). Child sexual abuse: The educator's role in prevention, detection, and intervention. *Young Children, 39*(6), 3–15.

Maukaddem, V. (1990). Preventing infectious diseases in your child care setting. *Young Children, 45*(2), 28–29.

Mobley, C. (1996). Assessment of health knowledge in preschoolers. *Children's Health Care, 25*(1), 11–18.

Mogharreban, C., & Nakhikian-Nelms, M. (1996). Autonomy at mealtime: Building healthy food preferences and eating behaviors in young children. *Early Childhood Journal, 24*(1), 29–35.

Perlmutter, J. C. (1990). Fostering children's fantasy play. *Dimensions, 18*(3), 23–24, 32.

Richey, D. (1985). Understanding child abuse. *Dimensions, 13*(4), 12–14.

Rothbaum, F., Grauer, A., & Rubin, D. (1997). Becoming sexual: Differences between child and adult sexuality. *Young Children, 52*(6), 22–28.

Rothlein, L. (1989). Nutrition tips revisited: On a daily basis, do we implement what we know? *Young Children, 44*(6), 30–36.

Satter, E. (1984). Developmental guidelines for feeding infants and young children. *Food and Nutrition News, 56*(4), 21–24.

Sheldon, A. (1990). "Kings are royaler than queens": Language and socialization. *Young Children, 45*(2), 4–9.

Stephens, K. (1988). The first national study of sexual abuse in child care: Findings and recommendations. *Child Care Information Exchange, 60,* 9–12.

Taylor, J., & Taylor, W. (1989). *Communicable disease and young children in group settings.* Boston: Little, Brown.

Wanamaker, N., Kearn, K., & Richarz, S. (1979). *More than graham crackers: Nutrition education and food preparation with young children.* Washington, DC: National Association for the Education of Young Children.

Wellhousen, K. (1996). Girls can be bullriders, too! Supporting children's understanding of gender roles through children's literature. *Young Children, 51*(5), 79–83.

What to do to stop disease in child care centers: A handbook for caregivers (1984). Washington, DC: U.S. Department of Health and Human Services, the Public Health Service, and the Centers for Disease Control.

Zeitlin, S. (1997). Finding fascinating projects that can promote boy/girl partnerships. *Young Children, 52*(6), 29–30.

12.

Curriculum for Developing Emotional Well-Being

Most of the children in your preschool classroom are actively engaged in exploring materials and interacting with peers. However, 3-year-old Megan is extremely hesitant to attempt new activities or to initiate play with other children. When encouraged to participate in a new art activity or explore a new climber she moves away and says, "I can't do that." When encouraged to join in play with other children she lowers her head and says, "They don't like me." Clearly, Megan's feelings of insecurity and inferiority are limiting her ability to enjoy interacting with peers and participating in activities in the classroom and are interfering with the development of a positive self-concept.

In a discussion with Megan's father you discover that her older sibling, who seldom lets Megan join in play or special activities, is the dominant figure in the home. The sibling expresses many negative emotions to Megan, calling her "stupid," "silly," "dumb," and "brainless," and makes her feel even more powerless, small, and unimportant.

Although initially resistant to the idea that a problem exists, Megan's father eventually realizes that the situation is out of control, and he too becomes concerned that Megan's emotional development is at risk. Together you determine several issues to consider in order to help Megan:

- What types of activities and interactions can you plan for Megan so she can experience success? What types will enhance her feelings of self-esteem?
- How can you help Megan develop the ability to express her emotions, including her anger and frustration with her older sibling?
- What types of creative-play experiences and materials can you make available to Megan so she can use pretend play to help resolve her emotional conflicts and problems?
- How can you organize the classroom environment and choose activities to help foster the development of Megan's decision-making and problem-solving skills?
- What teaching skills can you use to help Megan learn to cope with change and stress?

Suggestions for responding to this classroom vignette will be shared at the end of the chapter.

When reading this chapter, focus on understanding the major developmental milestones for young children in the domain of emotional well-being. Also, consider the variety of ways the development of emotional competence can be facilitated through creative-play activities, peer and adult interactions, and growth-promoting teaching techniques.

Young children who develop emotional competence usually recognize emotions and express them appropriately; develop self-esteem; establish warm, empathic relationships with others; cope effectively with life's stressful events; become unique, positive, autonomous individuals; and understand the value of life. Children who thrive emotionally have high levels of self-esteem and feel good about themselves, their relationships with others, and their abilities. Young children with high self-esteem are self-accepting, are individualistic, allow themselves to feel, are able to express feelings, are self-motivated, do not fear failure, generally like and trust people, respect fair and loving authority from adults, have low levels of guilt, have a high level of empathy for others, and are generally nonviolent (Quinn, 1986, pp. 127–129). Thus, the development of emotional competence is clearly integrated with the development of independence, social skills, and competence in the cognitive, communication, and perceptual motor realms. Knowledge of the important milestones in children's development and consideration of the many ways a creative-play classroom supports positive emotional growth enables teachers to nurture young children's emotional development and plan a curriculum to foster the development of emotional well-being.

Activities were written by Kathy Carlson, Amy R. Kerlin, and Anne Miller Stott; adaptations were written by Bobbie Beckmann.

DEVELOPMENTAL MILESTONES IN EMOTIONAL WELL-BEING

Erik Erikson (1963), a psychologist, described development as occurring through eight stages. Each stage is characterized by a crisis in development that must be resolved in order for children to grow and develop positively. During the first year of life, the developmental crisis is between basic trust and mistrust. During this stage, the young infant learns to rely on others to provide basic needs. Children also learn to trust their own bodies to deal with a variety of urges. Children successfully resolve the crisis in this stage and develop "trust born of care" (Erikson, 1963, p. 250) if the adults in the child's world are sensitive and responsive to individual needs. When children are involved in positive, nurturing, consistent relationships with adults, they leave this stage believing that both self and others are trustworthy.

During the second year of life, the developmental crisis involves autonomy versus shame and doubt. Children at this stage of development are struggling to gain control over their own impulses and bodily functions. Success in these areas leads children to feel secure and independent; lack of success on a regular basis results in children who feel insecure about themselves and their abilities, who have a tremendous "sense of being small" (Erikson, 1963, p. 254) and powerless. The developmental crisis involving initiative versus guilt begins about the third year of life. Children at this age have energy and curiosity and become more fully aware of their emerging selves. Three-year-olds are constantly in motion, exploring, planning, and attacking "a task for the sake of being active and on the move" (Erikson, 1963, p. 255). Children who frequently experience failure or blame during this stage will become hesitant to initiate activities or relationships. On the other hand, children who experience a reasonable number of successful, positive experiences will be able to reach out and attempt new challenges consistently.

The fourth stage of the eight is the last to occur during the early childhood years. This stage begins between the ages of 4 and 5. The developmental crisis during this stage is between industry and inferiority. Children at this stage are exploring more complex tasks and relationships and are testing their newly developed capabilities. Children who consistently feel unsuccessful when confronted with new activities or tasks may feel inadequate and unworthy, in contrast with children who gain mastery over new events and feel proud and successful.

Another perspective comes from T. Berry Brazelton, a pediatrician who views development in the first years of life as being centered on the issues of attachment and detachment. Strength of attachment to others is the primary developmental issue in the infant's first year of life. During the first few weeks of life, infants begin to distinguish between humans and objects, and by 3 months are usually able to distinguish the mother from other people. When the child begins to miss the mother as she leaves, between about 6 and 9 months, the attachment to another person is complete, and reciprocal adult–child relationships have been established.

During the child's second year of life, detachment begins and becomes the primary developmental task. Detachment is the beginning of the development of independence. At times the process of separation is extremely difficult and reflects "the strength of the ties which are being loosened" (Brazelton, 1974, p. 223). Children may be afraid to let go, yet at the same time feel the excitement of having increased control over people and events. The push for independence needs to be balanced with adult support and with the setting of reasonable, firm limits. These give children a sense of security while they test their emerging independence (Brazelton, 1974; 1992).

During the toddler and preschool years, children establish a unique identity by exploring through play, expressing newly acquired complex language, and by learning new behaviors through imitating and modeling. This is a period of testing, trying, ups and downs, and turbulent struggles. "The adult learns that he must allow the child to settle his own struggles; the child learns that he can!" (Brazelton, 1974, p. 220). The child's awareness of self and the child's positive view of self increase by attempting new challenges, interacting with others, and resolving conflicts in a supportive environment.

Stanley Greenspan, M.D., has completed a detailed study of children's emotional development from birth to age 4. According to Greenspan, six emotional milestones occur during the first four years of life. During the birth-to-3-months stage, the major emotional milestone involves self-regulation and interest in the world. The infant needs to develop the capacity for regulation, to become calm when in a state of excitement. The baby also begins to use all his or her senses to become interested in the world. The baby's interest in the adult's face or voice, or response to rocking or cuddling, often helps to relax the baby when he or she is upset. Thus, the two tasks of self-regulation and of developing interest in the world are complementary and interrelated processes (Greenspan & Greenspan, 1985).

Between 2 and 7 months the emotional milestone involves falling in love. Children at this stage become more socially alert and more deeply attached to significant adults. Children begin to look around, smile in response to parents, and establish deep emotional bonds. Parents and their children become involved in a "mutual love affair" during this period (Greenspan & Greenspan, 1985, p. 49).

During the 3-to-10-months period, the major emotional milestone is developing intentional communication. It is critical to the child that parents and teachers learn to understand and respond to the infant's efforts at communication at this stage. Young children begin to realize that they can cause certain actions and events to take place, and they begin to be involved in two-way communication with adults. Infants learn to develop trust when they discover that their actions result in reciprocal actions from adults. "For example, when your baby is gleeful and happy and you vigorously return these emotions, the baby begins to realize that his joy can cause your joy" (Greenspan & Greenspan, 1985, p. 76).[1] Emergence of an organized sense of self is the emotional milestone during the period of 9 to 18 months. During this beginning stage of toddlerhood, children become involved in more complex communications and become more organized in both their behaviors and emotions. Toddlers are developing independence, taking more initiative when expressing needs and interests, and establishing relationships with other children. During this stage, children need adults who express admiration, set reasonable limits, and help them expand the complexity of their play (Greenspan & Greenspan, 1985).

Between 18 and 36 months, the emotional milestone involves creating emotional ideas. Children at this stage have more complex communication skills and are able to express ideas, emotions, and needs or desires. Children learn about labeling feelings and learn to express a wider range of emotions, particularly in situations such as pretend play. Developing the ability to regulate self and to express feelings to help resolve conflicts are both important for a child who is developing independence and learning to respect individual differences in others. During the period from 30 to 48 months, the major emotional milestone is emotional thinking: the basis for fantasy, reality, and self-esteem. Children at this stage begin to be capable of separating themselves from others and separating reality from make-believe. The child is able to understand complex cause-and-effect interactions, use more complex emotional ideas and understand complex relationships, and understand and express a complex range of emotions (Greenspan & Greenspan, 1985).

In the last few years researchers have focused on "emotional intelligence" as a way to expand our notion of intelligence. Individuals use their "intrapersonal intelligence" to understand their feelings and use them to make choices about their behavior and interactions with others (Gardner, 1993). New research on brain development and behavior suggests that the abilities to "rein in emotional impulse, to read another's innermost feelings, to handle relationships smoothly" are key to healthy, balanced development because of the interplay of physical and emotional well-being. This research suggests the importance of bringing together "mind and heart in the classroom" and recognizing that children's individual gifts and talents also are visible through children's emotional intelligence (Goleman, 1995, pp. xiii–xiv).

Young children develop at varying rates and master developmental milestones at different times. An important consideration for the teacher of young children is how to organize a classroom environment and plan a program curriculum to enhance children's potential to develop emotional competence. Examining the results of research on children's play and emotional development can result in a clearer definition of the role of creative-play in enhancing the development of emotional well-being.

RESEARCH ON PLAY AND EMOTIONAL WELL-BEING _____

A behavior highly valued in our society is the expression of empathy and nurturing toward others. This involves understanding the internal state, emotions, and needs of another and then using that understanding and information to respond and offer help. This has become particularly important as more children interact with many different peers and teachers earlier in life.

Adults usually expect more nurturing behavior from girls than boys, and research has found this to be true in many situations. One area in which there are few differences in children's nurturing behavior is children's interaction with infants. Both boys and girls in the preschool years display attention to, knowledge of, and interaction with babies. Researchers who have studied young children's nurtur-

[1]From *First feelings* by Stanley Greenspan and Nancy Thorndike Greenspan. Copyright ©1985 by Stanley Greenspan and Nancy Thorndike Greenspan. Used by permission of Viking Penguin, a division of Penguin Books, USA Inc.

ing suggest that exposing children to pets, babies, the elderly, or people with special needs and then guiding and encouraging appropriate caregiving and interaction will foster nurturing behaviors. Because children, particularly boys, associate caregiving with females, it is important that children see men engaging in nurturing, caregiving behavior. Male teachers or fathers in the classroom who change diapers, feed babies, or play with children can model nurturing caregiving (Melson & Fogel, 1988).

In his description and discussions of children's cognitive development, Piaget also emphasized the role of emotions in children's cognition. Children's feelings influence which events receive attention and how information is processed. Feelings can foster and facilitate learning or interfere with the learning process (Fogel, 1980; Yarrow, 1979). Children learn better with adults with whom they have a warm, positive relationship (Ainsworth, Blehar, Waters, & Wall, 1978). Teachers who display a caring, warm demeanor with children actually help children approach, rather than avoid, opportunities for learning.

Young children's ability to control or regulate their emotions is a skill useful for play and interactions with others. Infants have very little ability to regulate their emotions; their brain and nervous system are organized to express their feelings—of hunger or pain, for example—immediately (Izard & Kobak, 1991). Infants do, however, develop strategies to self-comfort. Sucking a thumb or using attachment objects are first attempts at emotional self-regulation (Fogel & Thelen, 1987). As toddlers, children begin to control emotions through their play as they pretend to be happy or sad. Preschoolers learn to restrain emotions and even learn the "cultural display rules" for emotional expression through observation of others' appropriate and inappropriate emotional displays (Hyson, 1994). As children play, they observe, practice, and are reinforced for their appropriate expression of emotions.

Children's play, both spontaneous and structured, also fosters children's emotional well-being in times of stress. Play allows children to express emotions and gain a sense of control over their feelings and fears in a safe environment. This environment is one in which children may create characters, assign roles, act out struggles, display behavior, and confront fears—all of their own choosing and at their own pace. This play is a nonthreatening rehearsal for life in the real world. "To play out is the most natural auto-therapeutic measure childhood affords. Whatever other roles play may have in the child's development . . . the child uses it to make up for defeats, sufferings, and frustrations" (Erikson, 1940, p. 561). For example, research on children's medical play, or play that involves acting out doctor and patient roles—practicing medical procedures such as giving and receiving shots, and using play materials such as syringes without needles and blood-pressure cuffs—has shown that the opportunity to engage in pretend and sociodramatic play before hospitalization or medical procedures reduces children's anxiety, increases their knowledge and understanding of the events, and in some cases reduces children's perception of pain and the length of hospitalization (Yap, 1988).

The degree of structure and academic orientation in classroom situations also affects children's stress levels. A study designed to explore the differences in stress behaviors of children in developmentally appropriate and developmentally inappropriate kindergarten classroom environments found that children enrolled in the developmentally inappropriate classroom exhibited significantly higher levels of stress than their counterparts in the developmentally appropriate classroom (Burts, Hart, Charlesworth, & Kirk, 1990). In developmentally appropriate classrooms, children had more self-selected center time and could move freely from one activity to another. Children in the developmentally inappropriate classroom, characterized by more teacher-directed instruction, large-group time, and workbook/worksheet activities, exhibited an increase in stress behaviors during large-group activities and during workbook or worksheet tasks. These findings reinforce the concerns of many early childhood educators that there are negative consequences and increased stress levels of children in classrooms that emphasize inappropriate teaching practices and academically oriented activities. "Since children today experience much stress in their lives, additional stress from an inappropriate curriculum may leave children even more vulnerable and unable to cope effectively" (Burts et al., 1990, p. 417).

FOSTERING EMOTIONAL WELL-BEING THROUGH CREATIVE-PLAY CURRICULUM _____

The growth of emotional well-being is a journey of developing awareness and acceptance of the emerging self. The journey toward selfhood involves discovering the individual self, forming loving attachments to others, becoming a separate and autonomous person, and developing emotional strength and competence. The major emotional tasks faced by children from birth to age 5 can be summarized as follows:

- Distinguishing the self as a separate person
- Forming positive, trusting attachments to objects and adults
- Establishing reciprocal, loving relationships with others
- Developing independence and autonomy as creative individuals
- Taking initiative to explore, play, learn, and grow
- Establishing a unique identity with the ability to express emotions, relate to others, cope with change, and develop self-esteem

Fostering the emotional development of young children involves creating a supportive classroom environment where children are nurtured through loving relationships with adults and encouraged to develop their uniqueness through pretend play as well as a variety of planned classroom activities.

Distinguishing the Self

Infants who become aware of their separate selves and who become attached to their parents may begin to have difficulty separating from parents when they leave the program each morning. One 15-month-old child coped with her parents' leaving the early childhood center each morning by playing a "separation game." Although the child's teacher welcomed her eagerly each morning, entering the classroom continued to be a difficult adjustment until they devised the separation game. Teacher and child would go to the window and wave as the parents walked outside toward the window. With the parents on the other side of the glass, the child and parents would make funny faces at each other, throw kisses to each other, and wave good-bye. At this point the child was able to remain calm and begin to enter into the activity of the classroom. A consistent ritual during a transition time gives a sense of security and comfort to the young child coping with a difficult change. A sensitive, understanding teacher will help the child develop resources to cope and then begin to engage him or her in creative-play activities.

Establishing Trusting Relationships

Forming attachments to people and objects is a critical task in the development of very young children. Teachers foster attachment to adults when they provide consistent, warm, nurturing care to children and help children cope effectively with separation from parents by establishing morning good-bye rituals and being reassuring and comforting. Teachers foster attachment to peers when they set up play areas and activities that promote peer interaction. Teachers foster attachment to objects when they have a posi-

tive attitude toward children bringing an "attachment object," such as a blanket or teddy bear, from home. Some children use attachment objects to help them cope effectively with separation from parents and with changes and transitions during the day.

Children also may use attachment objects to help them express fears or concerns. For example, one 3-year-old who liked to sleep with a stuffed dog, named Yellow Dog, had Yellow Dog speak for him at nap time. The child got off his cot, came close to the teacher, and said, "Yellow Dog's barking and keeping me awake. He's barking at the dark because there's not much light in here." This, of course, was a cue to the teacher to let more light into the classroom to allay the child's fear of sleeping in the dark. Teachers who create flexible and creative environments encourage children to use attachment objects in many wonderful and creative ways. Children who establish positive attachments with others and who use objects or people to help meet emotional needs and develop effective coping strategies are growing a positive sense of self. A growth-promoting classroom environment must support many such opportunities because a child's self-concept is developed through experiences encountered day by day (Kendall & Elder, 1980).

An open and flexible classroom environment that includes an emphasis on nurturing adult–child relationships enables a young child to reach out in trust to others as well as to respond to appropriate expressions of affection and care from adults. One 2-year-old devel-

Children who use an attachment object for reassurance and comfort are developing effective strategies to cope with separation, change, and transition.

oped an especially warm and loving relationship with his teacher. Each morning when the child entered the classroom, he would run to his teacher with arms outstretched and jump into her lap. He then would look up, smile shyly, and say, "Guess how many 'sugars' I have for you today?" The teacher would guess a number, the child would say "no," and they would play the guessing game until the child responded with, "Yes, I have four 'sugars' for you today. One is on my nose." (The teacher would lightly kiss his nose.) "One is on my ear." (The teacher would lightly kiss his ear.) "One is on my cheek." (The teacher would lightly kiss his cheek.) "And the last one is right here by my hair!" (The teacher would kiss him lightly on his forehead.) Because of his nurturing, caring relationships with adults, this young child is able to enter the world each day completely open to love, eager to express affection, and unafraid to reach out and trust others. He is delighted with himself, his teacher, and the world!

Developing Autonomy and Independence

Teachers enable children to trust themselves as well as others and to develop independence and initiative when they provide security as well as challenges for children. For example, a very timid and fearful 3-year-old spent the first several weeks of preschool clinging to the teacher or curled up in a little ball on the beanbag couch. She was insecure and afraid of contacts with others. For the first month of school the teacher gradually drew her out of herself into activities with small groups of children and helped her to achieve success and begin to

Teachers who reassure and comfort children when they are upset or frightened help them to establish trusting relationships with adults.

build self-confidence. When walking side by side down the hall one day, the teacher automatically reached for the child's hand. The little girl, who was skipping along beside the teacher, looked up, smiled, and said, "You don't need to hold my hand anymore." Teachers who support children but also encourage children to try, to risk, and to experiment, and who are available to delight in their successes and reassure them in their failures, provide a classroom environment where children are free to grow and develop at their own pace.

Taking Initiative to Play and Learn

A stimulating, developmentally appropriate classroom that includes a multitude of learning centers, activities, and manipulative toys will invite young children to play, explore, and learn. Children who have success in play will continue to take initiative and will develop a more positive self-concept. "A child-centered curriculum is the responsive conversations shared between adult and child, the atmosphere of delight in learning that is established, . . . the growing mastery of body and mind" (Curry & Johnson, 1990, pp. 121–123).

Some children, however, may have difficulty taking initiative, being involved in play, and achieving mastery. For example, a preschooler who uses a wheelchair may have difficulty becoming involved in classroom activities for fear of being unsuccessful. Teachers must adapt the classroom environment appropriately, and peers should be encouraged to provide assistance as needed. In one instance a preschooler helped a child position her wheelchair so she had access to the water table in the classroom. The preschooler went to get smocks and helped the other child with her smock. The two children played together enthusiastically and energetically for quite some time. Teachers who adapt the classroom environment appropriately and have the attitude that all children are people first, and that the special need or disabling condition is secondary to the person, are also likely to foster positive interactions with peers. In this type of open and play-oriented classroom environment, all children can have successes, take initiative, learn through play, and develop self-esteem.

Expressing Emotions and Developing Self-Esteem

Preschool children are better able to express a range of emotions when interacting with adults and peers. Classroom environments that include many opportunities for play with individuals and in small groups support young children's attempts to communicate, negotiate, and relate successfully to others. For example, three preschoolers playing in the imaginary-play center may negotiate about the use of dress-up clothes and the assignment of roles. In this instance, two of the preschoolers decided to dress up as the mother and the grandmother and designated the third child to pretend to be the baby, a role he was not eager to assume. After a few minutes of play, the "baby" resisted, saying he was unhappy and wanted to be the grandfather instead of the baby. The "baby" also said he wasn't going to play anymore if he couldn't be the grandfather. The other two children, when faced with a playmate able to articulate his frustration and unhappiness, decided it would be great to have a grandfather in the house, and they got a plastic doll to play the part of the baby. Children communicate, negotiate, and redefine themselves through play and interactions with peers.

Play also is an important therapeutic tool. As children develop through the stages of emotional growth, they must resolve a variety of conflicts and cope with emotional turmoil. Teachers who implement a creative-play curriculum have the opportunity to enhance and support children's emotional development through dramatic- and pretend-play activities. Dramatic play gives children opportunities to take on a variety of roles, achieve mastery in relationships, and gain control over frightening situations. Involvement in pretend play can lessen a child's emotional pain, help a child master developmental conflicts, and strengthen a child's sense of self-esteem.

Coping with Change and Stress

Play also supports children as they learn to cope with extremely difficult, stressful life events. Young children experience a variety of stressful events in their lives, from the personal issues of dealing with divorce or death of a parent to making sense out of societal tragedies such as the violence of crime, assassination, or war (Brown, Curry, & Tittnich, 1971). For example, children use play to express their feelings when hospitalized for illness or surgery. Assuming the persona of a hulking monster, a 4-year-old in the hospital greeted his doctor. The child's voice and behavior reflected a massive character who is powerful and brave and strong. The child assumed this character with increasing frequency as the day for surgery approached. Play allowed this child to become an active participant in his hospitalization and to gain a sense of mastery, power, and control in an institution where helplessness and passivity too often characterize the patient role.

Involvement in dramatic play with peers strengthens the development of children's self-esteem.

Play is vitally important for children who do not have adequate language and vocabulary to express their feelings. It is also helpful for children who do not believe they can talk openly and honestly about sensitive subjects such as illness, death, or divorce. Play allows a child experiencing any stressor to examine and reconstruct reality without surrendering the defenses that may help the child cope. Indeed, play in times of stress " is not only the child's response to life; it is his life, if he is to be a vital, growing, creative individual" (Hartley & Goldenson, 1963, p. 1).

Developing autonomy, coping with stressors, expressing emotions, and establishing relationships contribute to building the child's self-concept. A creative-play curriculum includes specific developmental goals and sample activities designed to foster the growth of emotional well-being in the young child.

GOALS AND ACTIVITIES FOR EMOTIONAL WELL-BEING_____

The development of emotional well-being depends on growth in four major subdomains: (1) awareness, acceptance, and expression of emotions; (2) coping skills; (3) personality integration; and (4) building values. Both the creative-play curriculum and the assessment process support children's growth in these areas. The following sections include specific developmental goals in each subdomain as well as sample activities for infants, toddlers, and preschoolers, including adaptations for children with disabilities.

Awareness, Acceptance, and Expression of Emotions

The first subdomain in the area of emotional well-being encompasses developing an awareness, acceptance, and expression of emotions. Young children move through a developmental progression that begins with recognizing and labeling emotions, continues with children learning to accept the wide range of feelings they experience as natural and healthy, and culminates with children learning to express their emotions appropriately in a variety of happy, sad, frustrating, and loving situations. Specific developmental goals in this subdomain include the following:

1. Teach children to recognize and verbalize a wide variety of emotions.
2. Help children to learn to separate their emotions from those of other people.
3. Help children remain in contact with all their feelings while learning to control what they do about them (Hendrick, 1998).
4. Encourage children to express a wide range of emotions in appropriate ways.

The development of the awareness, acceptance, and expression of emotions can best be fostered through children's interactions with teachers who model acceptance of emotions and openly share their feelings. In addition, specific activities can be developed for each age group to facilitate emotional competence in this area. Here are some suggested sample activities for infants, toddlers, and preschoolers that can be adapted for a variety of developmental levels.

INFANT ACTIVITY
Baby Emmy (Storytelling)

Use a large doll (it can be homemade) with a large featureless face. Place Velcro dots on the spaces for the eyes and mouth. Affix a variety of eyes and mouths to the doll's face to reflect different emotions: happy, sad, angry, funny. Talk about the different emotions and make up a short story to go with each. For example: "Look! Emmy is so angry. Look at her face. She is so angry. Let me tell you what happened. She was playing with a bright yellow ball like this one and someone took it away from her. That made Emmy angry. She is so angry." "Now Emmy is happy. Look at her face. She has a big smile on it now. She is so happy. Do you know why she is so happy? She is so happy because I am giving her a great big hug. Hugs make Emmy very happy."

Additional Skills:

Communication (receptive language); cognition (concept formation)

Adaptations for Children with Disabilities:

Physically Impaired: None needed.

Speech/Language Impaired: None needed.

Visually Impaired: Encourage the child to explore Emmy's face by touch, emphasizing how Emmy's face shows her emotions.

Hearing Impaired: Use signs and/or gestures to tell the story and name the emotions.

Behavior Disordered/Emotionally Disturbed: None needed.

TODDLER ACTIVITY
What's My Name and How Do I Feel? (Art)

Provide the children with a large piece of butcher paper, crayons, and markers. As the child lies flat on the paper, draw an outline of the child's body. Then ask children to draw in their features. As the child draws the face, ask the child, "How do you feel? Are you happy or sad or angry?" Give the child plenty of time to express emotions and feelings. Write the child's name on the picture and label the picture with the feelings expressed by the child.

Additional Skills:

Communication (expressive language)

Adaptations for Children with Disabilities:

Physically Impaired: If the child cannot grasp a crayon or marker, ask the child how he or she feels and ask a peer to draw the face.

Speech/Language Impaired: Encourage the child to verbalize feelings. Model the appropriate words or phrases when needed. For example, "Susie, I see a big smile on your face. You look happy. Say, 'I am happy'."

Visually Impaired: Provide glue, yarn, and premade faces depicting emotions. Have the child feel how the happy-face mouth curves upward. Encourage the child to glue the yarn on a "face" in an upward curve. Do the same for the other emotions. Encourage the child to choose the emotion he or she is feeling.

Hearing Impaired: Use signs and/or gestures to explain the activity.

Behavior Disordered/Emotionally Disturbed: Provide additional support and prompts for the child who has difficulty recognizing and accepting his or her own feelings.

PRESCHOOL ACTIVITY
How Would You Feel? What Would You Do? (Discussion)

Using colorful pictures, present situations that evoke specific feelings. Children choose a picture, describe the situation, and are encouraged to discuss answers to the questions, "How would you feel?" and "What would you do?" Encourage all children to join in by suggesting alternatives. These situations may lead to discussions of relationships, appropriate social behaviors, and personal-safety issues. Suggested situations include:

1. You spill your milk at lunch.
2. A classmate knocks down your blocks.
3. You want play dough and no one will share.
4. Someone offers you the first turn at the swings.
5. Someone calls you a dummy.
6. Someone pinches you on a private part of your body.
7. Someone calls you his or her friend.
8. Someone gives you a toy.
9. Someone smiles at you.
10. Some people you don't know ask you to get in a car with them.

Additional Skills:

Communication (expressive language); emotional well-being (coping skills); personal awareness (personal safety)

Adaptations for Children with Disabilities:

Physically Impaired: None needed.

Speech/Language Impaired: Use puppets or flannel-board characters to prompt conversation about the suggested situations.

Visually Impaired: None needed.

Hearing Impaired: Use signs and/or gestures to explain the activity and describe the situations.

Behavior Disordered/Emotionally Disturbed: Provide additional encouragement for the withdrawn or aggressive child who may have difficulty accepting and expressing emotions appropriately.

Coping Skills

The second subdomain in the area of emotional well-being is coping skills. Young children need to develop increasingly complex and competent coping behaviors by using creative-play situations to identify and resolve emotional conflicts. Learning these behaviors will help children adapt to life changes and develop techniques for dealing with stressful events. Specific developmental goals in this subdomain include the following:

1. Encourage children to use play and creative materials to clarify feelings and resolve emotional problems (Hendrick, 1998).
2. Help children develop an internal locus of control (Greenspan & Greenspan, 1985).
3. Increase children's ability to face reality and adjust to change (accept what cannot be changed, accept alternative satisfactions) (Hendrick, 1998).
4. Help children learn healthy techniques for coping with stressful events and crisis situations (relaxation techniques, humor, verbalization, and exercise).

Although the development of coping skills is best facilitated in an environment where adults encourage children to discuss feelings, play out conflict situations, and develop individual techniques to deal with stress, specific activities for implementation in the classroom can emphasize the importance of learning coping skills. Here are some suggested sample activities for infants, toddlers, and preschoolers that can be adapted for a variety of developmental levels (an asterisk [*] denotes an activity that is also appropriate for use in the outdoor play environment).

INFANT ACTIVITY
Tiny Bubbles (Science/Nature)*

When infants seem to need a slow, comforting activity, blow bubbles. If lots of children are involved, the bubble wand can be held up in front of an air conditioner or a fan so that lots of bubbles are produced at one time. If only one or two children are involved, then the teacher can blow the bubbles. Talk about how light the bubbles are, how big or little they are, how they pop when touched, and whether there are lots of bubbles or just a few bubbles. Encourage children to try to blow bubbles or to dip the wand in and out of the bottle.

Comments:

"Look at those bubbles—they are so light, they float up."

"There are lots of little bubbles. Oh, look! Here is a great big bubble!"

"Watch. When I touch the bubble, it goes 'pop.'"

Additional Skills:

Cognition (concept formation); emotional well-being (personality integration)

Adaptations for Children with Disabilities:

Physically Impaired: None needed.

Speech/Language Impaired: As the bubbles appear, vocalize a sound, such as "o-o-o-o" or "a-a-a-h." As the bubbles pop, say, "Pop, pop, pop."

Visually Impaired: Assist the child with dipping the bubble wand and feeling the bubbles.

Hearing Impaired: Use signs and/or gestures while talking about the bubbles.

Behavior Disordered/Emotionally Disturbed: None needed.

TODDLER ACTIVITY
Hammering (Imaginary Play)*

Provide each child with a wooden or plastic "play" hammer. Set up a table of clay and wood. Encourage the children to pound the clay and to bang on the wood. This can be used as a venting activity so that children have an opportunity to express their anger, frustrations, or aggressions in an appropriate way by pounding on the various materials.

Additional Skills:

Perceptual motor (locomotor skills)

Adaptations for Children with Disabilities:

Physically Impaired: If it is needed, provide physical assistance to hammer or pound.

Speech/Language Impaired: None needed.

Visually Impaired: None needed.

Hearing Impaired: Use signs and/or gestures to explain the activity.

Behavior Disordered/Emotionally Disturbed: For the aggressive child, provide additional praise for the appropriate expression of anger or frustration.

PRESCHOOL ACTIVITY
If You're Angry and You Know It (Music)

Help children discover ways to deal with emotional upsets by discussing alternative strategies. Adapt the song, "If You're Happy and You Know It" to include "angry," "sad," "scared," and so forth. Have children suggest what to do. If their suggestions are inappropriate, discuss why. Ask children to think about acceptable things to kick (balls), push (friends at the swings), tear (paper), and pound (play dough, nails). Act out the appropriate activities as you sing: "If You're Angry and You Know It, Pound the Play Dough" (or draw a picture, or tear some paper).

Variation: As you help children review acceptable actions, offer the additional alternative of using words. Have them sing, "If you're sad and you know it, use your words: I'm sad!" Teach them other words to use: "If you're angry and you know it, use your words: I'm aggravated!" (irritated, exasperated, upset, annoyed).

Additional Skills:

Cognition (problem solving/reasoning); communication (expressive language)

Adaptations for Children with Disabilities:

Physically Impaired: None needed.

Speech/Language Impaired: None needed.

Visually Impaired: None needed.

Hearing Impaired: Use signs and/or gestures to explain the activity and while singing the song.

Behavior Disordered/Emotionally Disturbed: Provide additional support for the child who has difficulty coping with upsetting feelings.

Personality Integration

The third subdomain in the area of emotional well-being involves developing personality integration. Children's development of a positive self-concept is related to respecting individual differences in people and growing as an autonomous person. Specific developmental goals in this subdomain are as follows:

1. Enhance children's feelings of self-esteem (Hendrick, 1998).
2. Cultivate positive feelings about the child's gender and ethnic/cultural heritage (Hendrick, 1998).
3. Help children to learn to respect individuality and uniqueness in relationships with others.

4. Encourage children to demonstrate increasing autonomy in decision making and problem solving.

The development of personality integration occurs when children have a variety of opportunities to make decisions and experience success in the classroom. The development of self-esteem and positive feelings about others is primarily the result of establishing positive relationships with children from different backgrounds and learning from teachers who model respect for differences in people. In addition, specific activities can be developed for each age group to foster the development of personality integration. Here are some suggested sample activities for infants, toddlers, and preschoolers that can be adapted for a variety of developmental levels (an asterisk [*] denotes an activity that is also appropriate for use in the outdoor play environment).

INFANT ACTIVITY
Where is _____? (Music)*

The teacher uses a large unbreakable hand mirror and sings (to the tune of "Where Is Thumbkin?"):

> Where is Susie, where is Susie?
> There she is, there she is (show child's face in mirror)
> She is very special, she is very special
> Watch her smile, watch her smile. (show child's face in mirror again)

The teacher should hold the mirror for each child who shows an interest in the activity in order to make each child feel special and loved.

Additional Skills:

Communication (receptive language)

Adaptations for Children with Disabilities:

Physically Impaired: None needed.

Speech/Language Impaired: None needed.

Visually Impaired: Touch the child as a cue when it is his or her turn.

Hearing Impaired: Use signs and/or gestures while singing the song.

Behavior Disordered/Emotionally Disturbed: None needed.

TODDLER ACTIVITY
Pictures of My Friends (Discussion)

Take several photographs of the children playing with one another. Show these pictures to the children and ask them to describe what they are doing with their friends. Talk about how the children feel about playing or sharing toys with the other children: "Does it make you happy to play with your friends?" "What other kinds of games do you play with your friends?"

Compile the pictures and children's descriptions of the activities, which you write on construction paper or cards, into a photo book that can be kept in the book corner in the classroom.

Additional Skills:

Socialization (cooperation and social interaction); communication (expressive language)

Adaptations for Children with Disabilities:

Physically Impaired: None needed.

Speech/Language Impaired: None needed.

Visually Impaired: Ask another child to describe the pictures for the child who is visually impaired.

Hearing Impaired: Use signs and/or gestures to explain the activity.

Behavior Disordered/Emotionally Disturbed: Provide additional encouragement and support for the child who has difficulty interacting with peers.

PRESCHOOL ACTIVITY
Guess-Who Stories (Storytelling)

Work with children individually to tape-record a story about each one. Include descriptions of each child such as hair color, eye color, where the child lives; what makes the child happy, sad, angry; and what is easy or hard for the child to do. Listen to the tape during a group time and ask the children to "guess who" by identifying the child's voice and using the information the child provides. (Leave the tape in the listening center for several days so children can listen over and over if they wish.) Encourage children to recall what makes other children happy, sad, and angry, so all can be kinder to each other at school.

Additional Skills:

Communication (auditory memory/discrimination, receptive and expressive language); socialization (respect for others)

Adaptations for Children with Disabilities:

Physically Impaired: None needed.

Speech/Language Impaired: None needed.

Visually Impaired: None needed.

Hearing Impaired: Have the child cut out magazine pictures of the things that make him or her happy, sad, and angry.

Building Values

The fourth subdomain in the area of emotional well-being is the process of building values. Helping children to become trusting, empathic, caring individuals who exhibit concern for others and value all of life is the major task of building values. Specific developmental goals in this subdomain include the following:

1. Foster basic attitudes of trust, autonomy, and initiative in children (Hendrick, 1998).
2. Help children to begin to build empathy for other people (Hendrick, 1998).
3. Teach children to understand and value life (Hendrick, 1998).

Read the child's responses on the tape for the other children. Use signs to interpret the taped stories for the child.

Behavior Disordered/Emotionally Disturbed: Provide additional support and prompts for the child who has low self-esteem or difficulty relating with peers.

4. Help children to recognize, understand, and exhibit concern for emotions in others.

Although building values that encompass a concern for others and a reverence for life is best accomplished in a classroom where all individuals and all living things in the environment are treated with dignity and respect, specific activities can be developed for each age group to support the development of these values. Here are some suggested sample activities for infants, toddlers, and preschoolers that can be adapted for a variety of developmental levels (an asterisk [*] denotes an activity that is also appropriate for use in the outdoor play environment).

INFANT ACTIVITY
Empathy (Discussion)*

Infants and young toddlers who are just beginning to walk and crawl often take minor tumbles in spite of classroom safety features and close teacher supervision. When they do, the teacher should make use of this "teachable" moment. Encourage another child to go with you to get a frozen sponge and help hold it on the hurt child's bump. Explain that "Yolanda just fell down and got hurt. Let's give a hug to help her feel better," or "Let's give Max a sponge to help his/her bump feel better." The teacher can also talk about how sorry we are that the child fell, how falls hurt people, and how we should try to help the child who has been hurt. Use a quiet, soothing tone of voice to comfort the hurt child and to explain the situation to other children. Model giving comfort to the hurt child by hugs, pats, and saying you're sorry it happened. Use a puppet or stuffed animal to role-play this situation before a child is injured.

Additional Skills:

Socialization (social interaction, cooperation); emotional well-being (awareness, acceptance, and expression of emotions, coping skills)

Adaptations for Children with Disabilities:

Physically Impaired: None needed.

Speech/Language Impaired: None needed.

Visually Impaired: None needed.

Hearing Impaired: Use signs and/or gestures to explain the activity.

Behavior Disordered/Emotionally Disturbed: None needed.

TODDLER ACTIVITY
Helping Others (Discussion)

Use puppets to describe certain situations that might enhance children's ability to understand and help other children. For example, enact a puppet story of a child riding a tricycle and then tell the children to imagine the child falling off the tricycle. Ask the children, "How would you help the child who is hurt?" Another example is to use a puppet whose toy is broken. Ask the children, "What would you do if a friend's toy breaks?" or "What happens if a toy you are playing with breaks?" Make up puppet stories that are relevant to your daily circumstances.

Additional Skills:

Socialization (social interaction, cooperation); emotional well-being (awareness, acceptance, and expression of emotions); communication (expressive language)

Adaptations for Children with Disabilities:

Physically Impaired: None needed.

Speech/Language Impaired: None needed.

Visually Impaired: Describe the picture in detail.

Hearing Impaired: Use signs and/or gestures to explain the activity.

Behavior Disordered/Emotionally Disturbed: Provide prompts for the child who has difficulty relating to peers.

PRESCHOOL ACTIVITY
Familiar Tales a New Way (Storytelling)

Tell a familiar story (The Three Little Pigs, The Three Bears, Little Rabbit Foo Foo, or Three Billy Goats Gruff) but involve children in extending the ending so that the characters become friends at the end. For example: The Three Pigs rescue the wolf from the fireplace and he decides to be their friend; the three bears invite Goldilocks to stay for supper; Little Rabbit Foo Foo decides the field mice would be fun to play with and they give each other hugs; the Three Billy Goats Gruff decide the troll is mean because he is lonely and they bring him a picnic lunch and ask to be his friend. Have children discuss the differences between the traditional ending and the new ending with an emphasis on the way the characters found ways to get along with each other. Continue the discussion by talking about situations at school when classmates get angry with each other, but then find a way to get along by understanding each other better.

Additional Skills:

Communication (receptive and expressive language); socialization (social interaction, conflict resolution)

Adaptations for Children with Disabilities:

Physically Impaired: None needed.

Speech/Language Impaired: None needed.

Visually Impaired: None needed.

Hearing Impaired: Use signs and/or gestures to tell the story.

Behavior Disordered/Emotionally Disturbed: Provide additional encouragement and prompts for the child who has difficulty expressing feelings or difficulty relating to peers.

CHAPTER SUMMARY _____

Teachers who want children to become their best and most fully human selves will be open and expressive with children. "Even when our children are very young, we can and must share the real stuff of living—the hurts, disappointments, fears, joys, successes, and triumphs" (Kendall & Elder, 1980, p. 70). Teachers who want children to cope effectively with changes and stressful events provide many opportunities for pretend play in the classroom. Teachers who want children to develop positive self-esteem and to respect and value others foster a variety of interactions among children in the classroom, where they can play and learn in a supportive, successful environment. Teachers who want children to take increasing initiative in problem solving and decision making plan play activities that promote problem finding, exploration of alternatives, and risk taking. A classroom based on a creative-play curriculum will foster the development of emotional competence, self-esteem, and appreciation of others.

■   ■   ■   ■   ■   ■   ■   ■   ■

The development of a sense of emotional well-being is central to the ability to function productively, creatively, and lovingly in the classroom and in life. All children need support and nurturing to develop as whole, healthy individuals. For children like Megan who are hurt and unhappy and who feel unloved and incapable, it is critical to structure the classroom environment and curriculum to give children opportunities to do the following:

- Develop secure attachments and trusting relationships with adults.
- Become increasingly independent and differentiate the boundaries between self and others.
- Become involved in reciprocal loving relationships with others.

- Develop the ability to express feelings and emotional ideas.
- Regulate one's own behavior and begin to practice self-control.
- Develop a positive view of self.
- Become active, industrious, and autonomous in activities and relationships with others.
- Develop empathy and respect for others and learn to value all life.

Young children thrive in an open, flexible environment where they are cared for and have honest, loving relationships with teachers. In this type of creative-play environment, children can learn to value themselves and others, express feelings clearly and directly, establish positive relationships with peers and adults, and learn to cope constructively with stress and change.

■   ■   ■   ■   ■   ■   ■   ■

DISCUSSION QUESTIONS _____

1. Discuss the vignette at the beginning of the chapter. What other questions or concerns might you have? Discuss the vignette at the end of the chapter. Are there other responses you might have to this situation?
2. Describe the characteristics of a child with high self-esteem.
3. How did Erikson describe the process of development? What are the first four stages of the eight stages of development? What important milestone is emphasized in each stage?
4. What did T. Berry Brazelton describe as the most important issues in the first year of life? How are these successfully developed?

5. Discuss the six emotional milestones in the first four years of life described by Stanley Greenspan. What is the adult's role at each stage?
6. How can adults foster nurturing behaviors in young children?
7. What is the role of emotions in children's learning?
8. Describe the role of play as a stress reducer for young children.
9. Describe stress from an inappropriate classroom and describe a stress-reducing classroom.
10. How can teachers facilitate the development of trusting relationships with children?
11. Describe the subdomains in emotional well-being.

REFERENCES _____

Ainsworth, M., Blehar, M., Waters, E., & Wall, S. (1978). *Patterns of attachment.* Hillsdale, NJ: Erlbaum.

Brazelton, T. B. (1974). *Toddlers and parents.* New York: Dell.

Brazelton, T. B. (1992). *Touchpoints: Your child's emotional and behavioral development.* Reading, MA: Addison-Wesley.

Brown, N., Curry, N., & Tittnich, E. (1971). How groups of children deal with common stress through play. In National Association for the Education of Young Children, *Play: The child strives toward self realization* (pp. 26–38). Washington, DC: Author.

Burts, D., Hart, C., Charlesworth, R., & Kirk, L. (1990). A comparison of frequencies of stress behaviors observed in classrooms with developmentally appropriate versus developmentally inappropriate instructional practices. *Early Childhood Research Quarterly, 5*(3), 407–423.

Curry, N., & Johnson, C. (1990). *Beyond self-esteem: Developing a genuine sense of human value.* Washington, DC: National Association for the Education of Young Children.

Erikson, E. (1940). Studies in the interpretation of play. *Genetic Psychology Monographs, 22,* 561–570.

Erikson, E. (1963). *Childhood and society.* New York: Norton.

Fogel, A. (1980). The role of emotion in early childhood education. In L. Katz (Ed.), *Current topics in early childhood education* (Vol. 3, pp. 1–14). Norwood, NJ: Ablex.

Fogel, A., & Thelan, E. (1987). Development of early expressive and communicative action: Reinterpreting the evidence from a dynamic systems perspective. *Developmental Psychology, 23,* 747–761.

Gardner, R. (1993). *Multiple intelligences.* New York: Basic Books.

Goleman, D. (1995). *Emotional intelligence.* New York: Bantam Books.

Greenspan, S., & Greenspan, N. T. (1985). *First feelings.* New York: Viking Penguin.

Hartley, R., & Goldenson, R. (1963). *The complete book of children's play.* New York: Crowell.

Hendrick, J. (1998). *Total learning: Developmental curriculum for the young child* (5th ed.). Columbus, OH: Merrill/ Prentice-Hall.

Hyson, M. (1994). *The emotional development of young children: Building an emotion-centered curriculum.* New York: Teachers College Press.

Izard, C., & Kobak, R. (1991). Emotions system functioning and emotion regulation. In J. Garber & K. Dodge (Eds.), *The development of emotion regulation and dysregulation* (pp. 303–321). New York: Cambridge University Press.

Kendall, E., & Elder, B. (1980). *Train up your child: A guide for Christian parents.* Nashville, TN: Abingdon.

Melson, G., & Fogel, A. (1988). The development of nurturance in young children. *Young Children, 43*(3), 57–65.

Quinn, P. (1986). *The well-adjusted child: How to nurture the emotional health of your children.* Nashville, TN: Thomas Nelson.

Yap, J. (1988). A critical review of pediatric preoperative preparation procedures: Processes, outcomes, and future directions. *Journal of Applied Developmental Psychology, 9,* 359–389.

Yarrow, L. (1979). Emotional development. *American Psychologist, 34,* 951–957.

ADDITIONAL RESOURCES _____

Axline, V. (1964). *Dibs in search of self.* New York: Ballantine.

Axline, V. (1969). *Play therapy.* New York: Ballantine.

Bettelheim, B. (1950). *Love is not enough: The treatment of emotionally disturbed children.* New York: Macmillan.

Brazelton, T. B. (1969). *Infants and mothers: Differences in development.* New York: Dell.

Brazelton, T. B. (1984). *To listen to a child: Understanding the normal problems of growing up.* Reading, MA: Addison-Wesley.

Briggs, D. (1974). *Your child's self-esteem: The key to his life.* New York: Doubleday.

Bullock, J. (1993). Lonely children. *Young Children, 48*(6), 53–57.

Buzzelli, C., & File, N. (1989). Building trust in friends. *Young Children, 44*(3), 70–75.

Cadiz, S. (1994). Striving for mental health in the early childhood center setting. *Young Children, 49*(3), 84–87.

Caruso, D. (1984). Infant exploratory play: Implications for child care. *Young Children, 40*(1), 27–30.

Charlesworth, R. (1996). *Understanding child development* (4th ed.). New York: Delmar.

Curry, N., & Arnaud, S. (1995). Personality difficulties in preschool children as revealed through play themes and styles. *Young Children, 50*(4), 4–9.

DesRosiers, F., & Busch-Rossnagel, N. (1997). Self-concept in toddlers. *Infants and Young Children, 10*(1), 15–26.

Diantoniis, J., & Yawkey, T. (1984). Child's play as therapy. In T. D. Yawkey & A. D. Pellegrini (Eds.), *Child's play and play therapy* (pp. 79–84). Lancaster, PA: Technomic.

Eisenberg, N., Fabes, R., Shepard, S., Murphy, B., Guthrie, I., Jones, S., Friedman, J., Poulin, R., & Maszk, P. (1997). Contemporaneous and longitudinal prediction of children's social functioning from regulation and emotionality. *Child Development, 68*(4), 642–664.

Feeny, N., Eder, R., & Rescorla, L. (1996). Conversations with preschoolers: The feeling state content of children's narratives. *Early Education and Development, 7*(1), 79–97.

Fraiberg, S. (1959). *The magic years.* New York: Scribner's.

Furman, R. (1995). Helping children to cope with stress and deal with feelings. *Young Children, 50*(2), 33–41.

Honig, A. (1985). High quality infant/toddler care. *Young Children, 41*(1), 40–46.

Honig, A. (1993). Mental health for babies: What do theory and research teach us? *Young Children, 48*(3), 69–76.

Hyson, M. (1996). Preface to the special issue: Emotional development and early education. *Early Education and Development, 7*(1), 5–6.

Jalango, M. (1987). Do security blankets belong in preschool? *Young Children, 42*(3), 3–8.

Katz, L. (1993). Are we confusing self-esteem and narcissism? *Young Children, 49*(1), 2–3.

Kosnik, C. (1996). Everyone is a V.I.P. in this class. *Young Children, 49*(1), 32–37.

Kuebli, J. (1994). Young children's understanding of everyday emotions. *Young Children, 49*(3), 36– 47.

Marshall, H. (1989). The development of self concept. *Young Children, 44*(5), 44–49.

Mills, B., & Spooner, L. (1988). Preschool stress and the three R's: Is play an answer? *Dimensions, 16*(2), 8–10.

Morris, J. (1994). Introverts in young children. *Young Children, 49*(2), 32–33.

Moustakas, C. (1953). *Children in play therapy.* New York: Ballantine.

Moustakas, C. (Ed.). (1966). *The child's discovery of himself.* New York: Ballantine.

Pearce, J. (1977). *Magical child.* New York: Dutton.

Pipp-Siegel, S., & Foltz, C. (1997). Toddlers' acquisition of self/other knowledge: Ecological and interpersonal aspects of self and other. *Child Development, 68*(1), 69–79.

Raikes, H. (1996). A secure base for babies: Applying attachment concepts to the infant care setting. *Young Children, 51*(5), 59–67.

Rogers, C. S., & Sawyers, J. K. (1988). *Play in the lives of children.* Washington, DC: National Association for the Education of Young Children.

Satir, V. (1975). *Self esteem.* Millbrae, CA: Celestial Arts.

Schaefer, C. (Ed.). (1976). *The therapeutic use of child's play.* New York: Aronson.

Smith, D., Allen, J., & White, P. (1990). Helping preschool children cope with typical fears. *Dimensions, 19*(1), 20–21.

Solter, A. (1992). Understanding tears and tantrums. *Young Children, 47*(4), 64–68.

Vaughn, S. (1985). Facilitating the interpersonal development of young handicapped children. *Journal of the Division for Early Childhood, 9*(2), 170–174.

Warren, R. (1977). *Caring: Supporting children's growth.* Washington, DC: National Association for the Education of Young Children.

Wheat, R. (1995). Help children work through emotional difficulties—sand trays are great! *Young Children, 51*(1), 82–83.

White, B. (1975). *The first three years of life.* Englewood Cliffs, NJ: Prentice-Hall.

Wieder, S., & Greenspan, S. (1993). The emotional basis of learning. In B. Spodek (Ed.), *Handbook of research on the education of young children* (pp. 77–90). New York: Macmillan.

Wolf, D. P. (Ed). (1986). *Connecting: Friendship in the lives of young children and their teachers.* Redmond, WA: Exchange Press.

13.

Curriculum for Developing Socialization

As a teacher of 4- and 5-year-olds, you are pleased that your group of children interact frequently and engage in a great deal of cooperative play. The children seem to enjoy playing together in small groups, and there is very little conflict or aggression in the classroom. Because the classroom climate seems very positive and children always seem to be actively and productively involved in play activities, you are quite surprised to have a visit from a parent who is concerned about her child's well-being.

Andrew's mother has asked to talk with you because she is concerned that he is exhausted at the end of each day. She describes an experience that is typical behavior for Andrew. When he arrived home about 3:30 P.M. yesterday, Andrew's younger sister was waiting to play with him. She asked him to help her build a castle as soon as he finished his snack. Andrew turned to her, carefully put down his glass of milk, and said, very seriously, "Just give me a minute, please? I've been covered up with people all day long!"

It is apparent from Andrew's very insightful words and from his lack of energy and enthusiasm for the remainder of the day that his experience in preschool is emotionally, socially, and physically draining for him. You and Andrew's mother discuss ways to help him have a more enjoyable and less fatiguing day at preschool. You need to consider the following:

- Is it possible that the children in your classroom are spending too much time in active, cooperative play?
- Are there times during the day when children can play alone and engage in quiet, relaxing activities?
- Does your classroom environment include private spaces where children can be alone and away from peers?
- Have you given enough consideration to differences in children's personalities and energy levels when planning your curriculum?
- How can you individualize your program more, to enable children like Andrew to pace themselves and choose to engage in solitary play as well as cooperative play?

Suggestions for responding to this classroom vignette will be shared at the end of the chapter.

When reading this chapter, focus on understanding the developmental milestones in the domain of socialization and on becoming aware of the influences on young children's social behaviors. Also, consider the types of play that young children engage in and how a creative-play classroom environment contributes to the development of social skills.

The growth of social beings begins with children who are very egocentric and focused on their own needs and desires and continues as children move through a process of developing understanding and concern for the well-being of others. The development of social skills, or socialization, is also the process of acquiring behaviors, beliefs, and values determined acceptable or valuable by members in a society. Children's socialization begins at birth, primarily through their observations of and interactions with, first, adults and, later, peers. Agents of socialization for young children include families, neighborhoods, churches, communities, early childhood programs, and media.

DEVELOPMENTAL MILESTONES IN SOCIALIZATION _____

It is generally agreed that the most important influence in children's socialization is the family. In his psychoanalytic theory of children's development, Freud

Activities were written by Kathy Carlson, Amy R. Kerlin, and Anne Miller Stott; adaptations were written by Bobbie Beckmann.

(1938) discussed the important role parents have as young children develop attachments to the opposite-sex parent and then resolve this conflict as they identify with and take on the role, traits, and behavior of the same-sex parent. The parent–child relationship, with both the same-sex and the opposite-sex parent, helps children explore and develop roles and relationships that provide the foundation for multifaceted social experiences in adolescence and adulthood. Within the family, the parents' relationship also influences children's notions about social interactions with others. Interactions with siblings, which usually precede social experiences with peers, also contribute to the influence of the family on children's socialization.

As infants and children enter early childhood programs, peers become an important part of a child's social world. Although peers as socialization agents have been emphasized primarily in adolescent development, preschool children do learn about the social world from other children as they actively participate with them. Piaget and Inhelder (1969) described the value of children's social interactions with other children. As children engage in play, they negotiate roles and rules. Children are exposed to others' needs, viewpoints, beliefs, and ways of thinking; from this interaction, their own perspectives and thinking mature. Piaget described parent–child interactions as being characterized by a hierarchy in which parents usually make and enforce the rules. In contrast, child–child interaction is much more reciprocal, democratic, and characterized by the give-and-take of discussion and negotiation of mutually satisfying play themes, roles, and use of play materials. Piaget and Inhelder even found value in the less-than-positive interactions that occur among playmates. When disagreements or conflicts over play or toys arise, children must consider the viewpoint, needs, or wants of another person. With peer relationships reflecting a more egalitarian nature, children must move from egocentric or self-centered thought to more other-centered thinking in order to continue their play.

Piaget also described the role of peers and socialization in young children's moral development. Piaget believed that changes in children's cognitive reasoning, accompanied by changes in social and emotional development, promote moral reasoning. He investigated children's thinking about rules and social justice as he observed them playing marbles and as he interviewed them about the origin, legitimacy, and alterability of rules. In other conversations with children, Piaget told moral dilemmas or stories about children who committed various misbehaviors and asked children to judge the rightness, wrongness, and appropriate punishment for the story character. From his research, Piaget described two stages of children's moral development. In the *heteronomous* stage, children up to the age of 7 or 8 are guided by moral realism and egocentrism. Young children in their social interactions are very much aware of the presence of authorities and the rules they insist should be followed. Young children believe that rules are sacred and unalterable. They acknowledge the

rules, but because rules remain external to their conscience, rules do not always guide their behavior. Piaget noted that even when young children realize that rules can be invented or altered, they still affirm the involvement of a divine or higher authority. Responding to a question about the origin of a new rule he had just made up, a 6-year-old said, "All of a sudden, God told it to me" (Piaget, 1932, p. 59).

Young children believe that behaviors are either totally right or totally wrong and that everyone has similar views of right and wrong. For young children, the importance of an act's consequences outweighs the importance of an actor's intentions. The emphasis is on whether or not the behavior elicits punishment. Young children also believe in immanent justice, the concept that misbehavior and the violation of rules are followed by physical accidents caused by innate objects or misfortune divined by God. For example, in his research Piaget used a story of a child who fell into a river while walking on a bridge of rotten boards. Young children attribute this misfortune to the existence of divine or expiatory punishment. Responses typical of young children included: "God made him [fall] because he had touched the scissors." "It served him right. You shouldn't disobey." "The bridge must have known, since it gave way" (Piaget, 1932, pp. 253–258).

In the second, *autonomous* stage, one of reciprocity and cooperation, children ages 9 and older realize that rules have no divine origin but are established through reciprocal social agreement and changed by mutual consent. Punishment is no longer impersonally assigned but fits the situation, such as in restitution to the victim. Intentions are given more importance than consequences. The child, now less egocentric, is able to take the perspective of others and recognizes the diverse views of right and wrong among individuals and cultures.

Piaget proposed that children's development from heteronomous to autonomous moral reasoning was fostered first by cognitive maturation and second by children's social experiences. Early social interactions with parents are regulated by adult constraint and characterized by the child's unilateral respect for authority and submission to parents. Later interactions with peers are characterized by equality, cooperation, and a more mature and broad perspective supplied by diverse peer interactions. Experiences with peers permit greater opportunities for the child to experience democratic and reciprocal social discourse, diverse perspectives, and challenging social interactions (Allen, 1988).

Harry Sullivan wrote extensively on the role of social experiences with peers, and, like Piaget, believed that children get a different kind of socialization from peers than they do from adults, particularly parents. A child overly dependent on adults learns independence as peers refuse to do everything for the child. A child who is overindulged by parents quickly recognizes that peers do not give up all resources at the child's wish for them. And the child who believes that all rules and decisions emanate from adults realizes that discussion and negotiation can lead to a mutually agreed-upon set of guidelines, which can be suspended and renegotiated in the next play session (Sullivan, 1953).

A system for categorizing children's social participation based on play was developed by Parten (1932). These categories are not simply hierarchial; they overlap—children continue to engage in all of these types of play as they mature and move primarily into more organized play. These categories can be used to demonstrate the role of play in socialization. Children's early play is usually solitary. Children explore their own bodies and the immediate physical surroundings, such as crib, mobiles, and clothing. This early play contributes to a sense of identity, "me-ness," that must be established before the recognition can occur that there are others in the world, the concept of "not me." Infants do interact with parents and other caregivers before this recognition develops; they just believe that others are an extension of themselves and, usually, under their control. But before their first birthday, infants are aware that others exist as individuals, and social play begins to occur. This play facilitates the development of a sense of self in relationships with other people. Toddlers' and preschoolers' solitary play may occur in the presence of others, but children make no attempt to talk or coordinate play. Children's interest focuses on their own activity, toys, or space. In the *onlooker* behavior type, children watch others play. Talking, asking questions, and interjecting suggestions all may occur, but children remain physically uninvolved yet nearby. Children can and do learn a great deal about social relationships and interaction from this type of participation. Particularly for shy children, this behavior is an important step to more participatory play. In *parallel play,* children remain centered on their activities or toys, but are playing near other children who are engaged in a similar activity or playing with the same materials. In *associative play,* children play together. They talk, share materials, and try to direct or influence the play of others. In *cooperative* or *organized play,* children's play interactions are more structured and organized by the children themselves; they work toward a goal or purpose, organize to complete a task more efficiently or make a product, or orchestrate role play or an acting out of an event. A few children may assume leadership positions and direct the group. Children work together, with their interest and efforts centered more on the group than on the individual.

RESEARCH ON CHILDREN'S SOCIALIZATION _____

Interest in children's socialization has increased as children have been exposed at an earlier age to larger numbers of nonparental caregivers and peers. Questions and concern about the effects of nonparental care on children's development, particularly on social development, have created debate focusing on two issues:

What effect does early childhood education have on children's social interactions with adults?

What effect does early childhood education have on children's social interactions with other children?

Children's Social Interaction with Adults

Children's social experiences with adults begin at birth and have important implications for social development as well as cognitive, language, and emotional development. One of the most significant and enduring contributions to understanding the effect of parents on children is research on parenting styles by Diana Baumrind (1967, 1991). She identified four primary patterns that parents use in interactions with their children—authoritative, permissive, authoritarian, and rejecting-neglecting.

The *authoritarian* parents are very firm with children and expect unquestioning and unwavering obedience. Rules are set by parents, and misbehavior is often met with physical punishment or threats. Authoritarian parents also may use love withdrawal, or threats to withdraw affection or their presence, as a response to misbehavior. Children of authoritarian parents are often unhappy, fearful, withdrawn, inhibited, hostile, and aggressive. They have low self-esteem and difficulty with peers. *Permissive* parents appear to be the opposite of authoritarian parents. They are not firm or controlling. They have few expectations or demands. They may be warm and caring, but they appear to be uninvolved and uninterested. Many children in these families believe their parents do not care about them or their behavior. Without limits or expectations set for them, these children are often impulsive and aggressive and lack self-control. As preschoolers, these children show low levels of independence and responsibility. In contrast, *authoritative* parents achieve a happy compromise. They are firm yet loving. They have clear and reasonable expectations and limits for their children. They treat children with respect and warmth and are likely to respond to misbehavior with a type of discipline strategy called induction. This method focuses on helping the child to understand (that is, the method induces understanding) why the misbehavior is not acceptable and what the consequences of the child's actions are on self and others. Children of authoritative parents are socially competent, self-reliant, and have a greater ability to use self-control. They have higher self-esteem and as preschoolers are much more likely to engage in new or mildly stressful situations with interest and curiosity. In Baumrind's fourth and newest category, *rejecting-neglecting* parents are disengaged from their children. They are neither demanding of nor responsive to their children. They provide no structure, supervision, support, or guidance. Children from these homes have been found to be least competent in their overall functioning.

Others also have examined different types of parenting and caregiving for their effects on children's development. In a review of many observational studies of maternal functioning, five caregiving behaviors in adult–infant interactions were found to have significant effects on children's social, emotional, and cognitive development: (1) attentiveness—that is, looking at, holding, speaking to the infant; (2) physical contact, both static (holding) and kinesthetic (rocking, jiggling, and other active movement); (3) verbal stimulation—that is, talking and trying to elicit a response from the child; (4) material stimulation, ranging from simply providing age-appropriate toys to directing the child's attention to the toys, talking about interesting properties of the toys, and playing with the toys with the child; and (5) responsive care—that is, contingently responding to infants' smiles, vocalizations, and behaviors and being sensitive to children's needs. A sixth behavior, restrictiveness or physically and verbally limiting infants' exploration, has a negative influence on development (Belsky, Lerner, & Spanier, 1984).

Adults other than parents also influence children's development. In particular, the quality of social interactions among teachers and children affects children's development. In early childhood programs, when teachers provided high levels of cognitive and social stimulation to 2-year-olds, these children scored higher on social competence measures at age 3 (Golden et al., 1978). Children in programs where there were higher levels of verbal interaction between teachers and children were rated higher on consideration of others and sociability (Phillips, Scarr, & McCartney, 1987). Chil-

dren who were encouraged by teachers and given opportunities to practice and discuss helping, sharing, and cooperating showed an increase in these prosocial behaviors (Honig & Pollack, 1990; Smith, Leinbach, Stewart, & Blackwell, 1983).

Other program effects on children's socialization have been studied. Innocenti et al. (1986) examined preschool environmental factors that influenced peer interaction during free-play, snack/lunch, individual-activity, and group-activity times. Preschool teachers' behaviors that occurred in conjunction with peer interaction were observed. Peer interaction occurred more frequently when children engaged in free play and when teachers directed children the least—that is, when teachers attempted to direct children through questions, prompts, or reprimands, less peer interaction occurred. Teacher behaviors such as prompting and praising peer interaction can facilitate peer interaction and maintain or increase positive social interactions in children who regularly interact with peers, yet teachers seldom encouraged peer interaction or praised ongoing peer interaction. Other teacher behaviors, such as suggesting play themes, offering play props, assigning roles, or encouraging specific dialogue, are helpful in increasing social interaction among children who lack social skills.

Several studies have sought to examine the effect on children's social development of children's experiences in both early childhood programs and their homes. A study of 140 Swedish children, begun while the children were on waiting lists for child-care centers and completed one year later after 53 children entered child care and 33 entered family child care, found that the type and quality of nonparental child care had no significant effect on the outcome of children's peer social skills, sociability with strange adults, and personality. Several factors did have an effect, however: family's socioeconomic status, quality of care at home, child's temperament, and support from grandparents (Lamb et al., 1988).

Children's Social Interaction with Peers

Children's ability to play and socialize with other children has long been a goal of most parents and teachers. Children's social interactions with other children outside the family provide opportunities to engage in same-status or egalitarian interactions, develop meaningful relationships for social comparison and identity formation, find social resources different from those in the family, and develop skills that characterize a socially competent child and, later, adolescent and adult.

Research on children's friendships helps us to understand children's thinking about their social interactions and the development of friendship relationships (Selman, 1976). Preschool children, ages 3 to 5, conceive of friends as momentary physical playmates, the peers one is playing with at any given time. When asked to describe their friends, preschoolers discuss physical attributes and shared activities of friends. "We're friends because we play together." "He's my friend because I like him." "She has lots of toys and we play with them." "We're friends now because we know each other's names" (Damon, 1977).

A second stage of reasoning about friendship occurs by age 11 or 12 as children's friendship selection is based on psychological attributes such as personality traits and shared interests, needs, and values. "Friends listen and understand each other. You have the same problems and want to help." "We believe in the same things." "A friend is someone you can share secrets with at three in the morning" (Damon, 1977). Selman described children's friendships as progressing and maturing as children are able to broaden their perspective-taking ability, view people as psychological rather than only physical entities, and view social relationships as more than temporal interactions but as social systems that endure over time. This progression in thinking about friendships reflects children's changing cognitive development as well, from egocentrism to decentration (considering another's perspective), from concrete to abstract, and from simple to complex.

One issue in children's socialization that concerns teachers, parents, and policymakers is that of aggression and children. Several researchers have studied the question, "Are children in nonparental care more aggressive with peers than children cared for in the preschool years by their parents?" In one study of 55 toddlers, children in programs of higher quality who had had fewer previous child-care arrangements showed lower aggression levels. Family variables also were important, however. Children from more nurturing families were less likely to display aggressive behavior (Howes & Rubenstein, 1981).

A study of 32 kindergarten children found no differences on measures of aggressiveness between a group of children who had had at least 30 hours of preschool child-care experience per week and a group who had had less than 12 hours of preschool child-care experience per week. Children with more preschool child care experience were no more likely to engage in negative or nonsocial behaviors (Hegland & Rix, 1990).

Several researchers, however, have found evidence that children enrolled in child care exhibit more negative, nonsocial, or aggressive behavior than children without nonparental care in the preschool years (Finkelstein, 1982; Haskins, 1985; Schwarz, Strickland, & Krolick, 1974). There are major limitations in this research, however. Several studies examined lower-income children, who tend to exhibit more aggressive behavior regardless of previous child-care experience. In some studies the measure of children's aggression was rated by the children's teachers, who "were not blind to," or were knowledgeable about, the children's previous child-care attendance and who could have been biased by that knowledge in their ratings of the children's aggressiveness. One conclusion that has been drawn from the research on the issue of aggression and child care is that outcomes are program-specific. It is not simply children's participation in an early childhood program that promotes aggression. It is that some programs fail to provide children with the supportive environment that fosters more positive social interaction. These supports include (1) teachers who model positive interactions and avoid using physical punishment or verbal aggression, (2) opportunities to practice positive social interaction, (3) programs with lower teacher-child ratios, and (4) toys and materials that do not suggest or support aggressive themes.

In their social interaction with peers and adults, children notice racial differences beginning in infancy. As preschoolers they develop a concept of race and can classify into categories using racial cues, yet gender is a more salient characteristic than race in preschoolers' friendship preferences (Jarrett & Quay, 1983; Katz, 1976). When preferences have been found, White children are more likely to have same-race friendships than are African American children (Hallinan & Teixeira, 1987) and "are more at risk for developing own-race bias in their friendships" (Ramsey, 1995). Beyond the preschool years, information about the social status of different racial groups influences children's understanding and attitudes. Children view race as more than physical attributes and are influenced by the stereotypes and attitudes of significant adults (Ramsey, 1995). When classrooms are very diverse, cross-race play preferences are more likely to occur, particularly when teachers provide encouragement and structure for interracial friendships (Howes & Wu, 1990).

Preschool children are less cognizant of social-class differences. They can distinguish rich people from poor people by their possessions and are beginning to understand the power and influence related to wealth. Children associate having money with being happy and liked (Ramsey, 1991) and have opinions about the social justice and injustice associated with wealth and poverty (Ramsey, 1991; Allen, Freeman, & Osborne, 1989). It is clear that children's understanding and attitudes about racial and class differences and valuing of diversity are influenced by their cognitive and moral reasoning, experiences with others, their social environment, and prevailing values and attitudes (Ramsey & Myers, 1990).

FOSTERING SOCIALIZATION THROUGH CREATIVE-PLAY CURRICULUM

Play is the socializing experience that allows young children to develop positive, caring attitudes toward others and to build effective skills for interacting with others. Young children learn about themselves in relationship to other people when they establish trusting relationships with adults, make friends within their peer group, learn to cooperate with others and resolve conflicts, and exhibit kindness and respect toward different groups of people. A creative-play classroom environment enables young children to learn about themselves as social beings in relationship to other children through a variety of play settings and activities.

Developing Social Competence and Responsibility

Through a variety of play situations, young children become increasingly aware of the needs of others, respond to verbal and nonverbal social cues, and learn responsibility and control over their own behaviors. Children begin to establish their separateness from others as they learn to distinguish their emotions from the emotions other children are experiencing. As children begin to label their feelings they also begin to recognize feelings of sadness, distress, and joy in adults and peers. A significant step in the process of developing concern and empathy is recognizing and responding to the distress or delight expressed by another person. For example, a young toddler may try to pat or hug a playmate in distress from a fall off a wheel toy. A preschooler may use more complex, sophisticated methods of offering comfort to a peer, such as talking about a conflict over a favorite book and offering both verbal and nonverbal reassurances. Children who develop the capacity to identify and respond to the feelings and social cues of peers during a variety of play situations are better able to establish meaningful friendships.

In order to develop social competence, young children also must learn to cooperate with peers and act in a socially responsible manner. Children develop a cooperative spirit through participating in a variety of dramatic-play and small-group activities. Children who are unable to cooperate and restrain their aggressive or egocentric impulses often have difficulty forming relationships and becoming an accepted member of the group. For example, children who frequently argue and fight or whine and complain typically are not well accepted by peers and may have difficulty joining in play. On the other hand, children who are positive, friendly, and caring easily develop

peer relationships and often are sought out by other children to participate in play. Children's involvement in play fosters their ability to influence peers, understand another's viewpoint, develop helping behaviors, learn cooperation, practice problem solving, become both leaders and followers, and control their impulses. All of these skills characterize children who have successfully entered the world of social relationships (Rogers & Sawyers, 1988; Smith, 1982).

Children's playful interactions with peers in classrooms where the social ambience affirms differences and avoids stereotypes create empathy and respect for others. Children learn to appreciate differences and celebrate uniqueness—in physical traits, abilities, culture, race, and gender—in a play-based environment where equality, worth, and dignity are important values. They learn to be responsible for their treatment of others, to demonstrate courteous and compassionate behaviors, and to avoid hurtful exclusion of other children from play activities from teachers who model justice and fairness. Play provides an opportunity for "building bridges across cultural, racial, and ability lines" and promotes the understanding that "children can learn to care about every other person's feelings, beliefs and welfare" (Teaching Tolerance Project, 1997, p. i; Katz & McClellan, 1997; Wittmer & Honig, 1994).

Meeting Social Needs through Play

During the early childhood years, the frequency of social play increases as children grow and mature.

Young children learn about themselves as social beings through playful interactions with peers.

However, young children continue to have a need to engage in many types of play at different times and in different situations. For example, although solitary play is the primary mode of play for infants and young toddlers, older toddlers and preschool children also have an emotional and social need to have defined spaces in the classroom where they can be and play alone. Teachers should design the classroom environment and schedule to allow for solitary, private play, and alone time so children do not become overwhelmed by constantly being in a group situation.

Parallel and associative play are characteristic of toddlers and young preschoolers. Children need opportunities for play with objects and play themes without the requirement to share with peers. Sharing is a difficult developmental task for young children to master and involves beginning to understand the needs of others and sometimes delaying gratification. Sensitive teachers will recognize children's conflict over sharing playthings and will respect children's right to play alongside others without sharing. At the same time, effective teachers of young children will help children learn simple rules of life in a group situation and teach children that play is "free movement within prescribed limits" (Erikson, 1972, p. 133).

Cooperative play is most frequently seen beginning with the preschool years, but it does occur in younger children and continues to be practiced in more complex ways with larger groups of children in the primary grades. Young children at this stage discover that experiences are more fun and more meaningful when shared with a friend. As Pooh and Piglet noticed, "it was much more Friendly with two" (Milne, 1957, p. 66)! Teachers must achieve a balance between encouraging children to express their newfound individuality and helping children learn socially responsible behaviors. As children grow, they gradually develop a set of inner controls over their behaviors and interactions with others and can resolve conflicts with less teacher intervention.

Children may engage in onlooker or unoccupied play at any age. Teachers should not respond negatively to children who occasionally engage in these types of play. Young children do not need an overly structured day or to be actively occupied every minute of the day. Adults, whose lives are often fast-paced and tightly scheduled, sometimes forget the value of "just watching" or "doing nothing." As Christopher Robin is leaving the Enchanted Forest he tells Pooh, 'I'm not going to do Nothing any more.' 'Never again?' 'Well, not so much. They don't let you'" (Milne, 1957, p. 312). Christopher Robin is describing

Preschoolers discover that activities are more fun and more meaningful when shared with a friend.

the adult perspective that requires children to leave behind their childhood and be productively engaged at all times. Young children need opportunities and support for disengaging from other people and from play experiences from time to time in order to renew and refresh their emotional and social selves.

Some children, however, may engage in onlooker or unoccupied play the majority of the time. For these children, low self-esteem, immaturity, or a developmental problem may prevent them from participating in play with peers. These children need special support from teachers in order to grow as social individuals. Teachers can best offer support by accepting children at their current level of development and including them as important members of the group in whatever role they choose to play. For example, Chenfeld (1989) describes a teacher who always includes children in the classroom activity, expressing appreciation for the child even if he or she is an onlooker, such as " 'Oh, who will be the audience for our circus? Randy, thanks for volunteering!' " (Chenfeld, 1989, p. 26). Teachers who accept and appreciate young children, whatever their level of social development and participation in play, help them to establish a positive identity as a member of a group. Helping children feel socially accepted means teachers must involve all children in the life of the classroom. A teacher who had been successful with a nonparticipatory child described her experience: "Because we never let his circles leave us out and because we always drew circles that took him in," he became a vital part of the group (Chenfeld, 1989, p. 27). Teachers who draw young children into the circle of the classroom enable them to grow at their own pace and in their own way as contributing members of the group.

GOALS AND ACTIVITIES FOR SOCIALIZATION

In the following sections are included specific goals for children's socialization in the subdomains of (1) social interaction, (2) cooperation, (3) conservation of resources, and (4) respect for others. There are also suggested activities for infants, toddlers, and preschoolers.

Social Interaction

The first subdomain in the area of socialization involves the development of social interaction skills. A major developmental task for young children is developing relationships with both adults and peers and learning to interact in a socially acceptable manner. Specific developmental goals in this subdomain include the following:

1. Help children to learn to interact in a positive, affectionate, and trusting way with adults.

2. Increase children's ability to make friends and interact positively with peers (Hendrick, 1998).

3. Teach children to resolve conflicts with others in socially appropriate ways.

4. Help children to acquire the ability to restrain their unsocial impulses and build inner controls (Hendrick, 1998).

The development of social competence in young children can best be fostered in a classroom environment that encourages interaction with others and teaches children to resolve conflicts and problems with peers. Here are some suggested sample activities for infants, toddlers, and preschoolers that can be adapted for a variety of developmental levels (an asterisk [*] denotes an activity that is also appropriate for use in the outdoor play environment).

INFANT ACTIVITY
A-Visiting We Will Go (Music)

To encourage positive interactions among children, take one infant and "visit" other children in the classroom. Sing the song "A-Visiting We Will Go" (to the tune of "A-Hunting We Will Go"):

> A-visiting we will go, a-visiting we will go,
> Hi ho the merry-o, a-visiting we will go.

As you move around the room you should visit each infant. Help the visiting infant give a gentle pat or a hug when "visiting" another child. The visiting infant also can take a toy to each child he or she visits. Praise all positive interactions.

Additional Skills:

Emotional well-being (building values)

Adaptations for Children with Disabilities:

Physically Impaired: None needed.

Speech/Language Impaired: None needed.

Visually Impaired: As the child visits, assist with gently touching the other children's faces, hair, clothes, and so on. Use this sensory input to explain who the other child is.

Hearing Impaired: Use signs and/or gestures while singing the song.

Behavior Disordered/Emotionally Disturbed: Provide additional support for the child who has difficulty relating positively to peers.

TODDLER ACTIVITY
Roll-On Deodorant Bottles (Art)*

Fill empty plastic roll-on deodorant bottles with different colors of tempera paint. Provide children with several pieces of newsprint paper and allow them to use the roller bottles to paint pictures or designs on the paper. As the children experiment with the materials, encourage them to share the bottles with one another. Encourage them to use their words to ask for a different color to use. Also encour-

age the children to make a big design or picture together by allowing them to paint on a big piece of butcher paper.

Additional Skills:

Socialization (cooperation); perceptual motor (eye-hand coordination)

Adaptations for Children with Disabilities:

Physically Impaired: If it is needed, provide physical assistance. Encourage the other children to assist the child by bringing paper, roll-on bottles, or paint. Encourage the child to ask friends for help with difficult activities.

Speech/Language Impaired: If the child has limited expressive language skills, model the necessary words or phrases for the child to imitate. For example, if the child wants the blue paint, model the sentence, "I want the blue paint," or the phrase, "blue paint," depending on the child's skill level.

Visually Impaired: Add food extracts to the colors so the child can identify them by smell. Encourage a partner to tell the child what colors are available. Cue the child by saying, "Joe, you have used red and blue. Joan has the yellow. How can you get the yellow one?" If the child has difficulty asking, prompt child to say, "Joan, pass me the yellow one, please." Encourage the child to repeat the request.

Hearing Impaired: Use signs and/or gestures to explain the activity. Encourage the child and the other children to communicate their requests by using signs or gestures.

Behavior Disordered/Emotionally Disturbed: None needed.

PRESCHOOL ACTIVITY
Gingerbread Hunt (Storytelling)

After telling the story of Gingerbread Man have children help make sugar cookie dough and use cookie cutters to make gingerbread boys and girls. Provide raisins or chocolate chips to decorate the cookies to be sent to the kitchen for baking. Later, have the cook come and tell you that something strange has happened. The cookies have disappeared from the kitchen. Have children help you look around the room and then begin a (prearranged) tour of the center to hunt for the missing gingerbread cookies. At each stop in the tour (director's office, teachers' office, library, laundry room, and so on) children will find a (preplaced) note that says, "Run, run, run, as fast as you can. You won't find me, I'm the gingerbread man!" Use the opportunity to acquaint the children with various areas in the center and the people who provide services to the center. Also, use the opportunity to acquaint children with important field-trip guidelines such as staying with the group and holding hands. End the tour by finding the cookies and having a picnic. You may wish to take pictures of each step of the process and place them in a photo album along with captions that tell the story of the missing cookies and what was done to find them.[1]

Additional Skills:

Communication (receptive language); socialization (cooperation)

Adaptations for Children with Disabilities:

Physically Impaired: When planning the tour, plan for stops that would be accessible to the child using a wheelchair or a walker.

Speech/Language Impaired: None needed.

Visually Impaired: Ask another child to be the "tour guide."

Hearing Impaired: Use signs and/or gestures to tell the story and to read the notes.

Behavior Disordered/Emotionally Disturbed: None needed.

Cooperation

The second subdomain in the area of socialization is learning cooperation. In order to live productively and peacefully in groups, young children must learn about themselves in relationship to others and develop the skills to relate to peers in a positive way. Specific developmental goals in this subdomain include the following:

1. Encourage children to find satisfaction in helping each other and the group (Hendrick, 1998).
2. Teach children socially acceptable ways of getting what they want and need (Hendrick, 1998).
3. Help children learn about their place in the world (Hendrick, 1998).

4. Increase children's ability to function successfully as part of a group (Hendrick, 1998).

The growth and development of cooperative skills can best be facilitated in a classroom where children have many opportunities to test their abilities to relate to peers in a variety of group activities. Here are some suggested sample activities for infants, toddlers, and preschoolers that can be adapted for a variety of developmental levels (an asterisk [*] denotes an activity that is also appropriate for use in the outdoor play environment).

[1]Resource: Catron, C. E., & Parks, B. C. (1986). *Super Storytelling*. Minneapolis, MN: T. S. Denison.

INFANT ACTIVITY
Wagon Rides (Movement)*

Use a small wooden cart or metal wagon. Encourage infants to help push a friend (a young infant) in the wagon. Beginning walkers can help push the wagon. Sturdy walkers can help pull the wagon. Nonwalkers can take turns riding in the wagon. The focus of the activity should be helping our friends ride, sharing the wagon, and taking turns riding.

Additional Skills:

Perceptual motor (locomotor skills); emotional well-being (building values)

Adaptations for Children with Disabilities:

Physically Impaired: None needed.

Speech/Language Impaired: None needed.

Visually Impaired: None needed.

Hearing Impaired: Use signs and/or gestures to explain the activity.

Behavior Disordered/Emotionally Disturbed: None needed.

TODDLER ACTIVITY
Puppet Show (Imaginary Play)*

From a large box cut out a large space to make a puppet stage. Provide the children with several hand puppets: animals, story characters, people, and so forth. Encourage the children to make up their own story using the puppets and acting out the story together. Ask questions that allow the children to explain their story. For instance, "How can you make up a story with the frog puppet, the lion puppet, and the bear puppet?" "Can you pretend all those animals are walking through the forest?" "What will Mr. Frog do? Will he jump or will he crawl?"

Additional Skills:

Socialization (social interaction); communication (expressive language)

Adaptations for Children with Disabilities:

Physically Impaired: If it is needed, provide physical assistance to enable the child to use hand puppets. If the

child cannot use the puppet with a hand inside, attach a Velcro bracelet to the back of the puppet or attach a ribbon to the top of the puppet's head and connect the ribbon to a large ring so the child can move the puppet.

Speech/Language Impaired: Encourage the child to verbalize about the puppet and make up a story. If needed, use prompts (pictures and verbal cues) to encourage participation and verbalization.

Visually Impaired: Provide time for the child to explore the puppets and identify them.

Hearing Impaired: Use signs and/or gestures to explain the activity. Sign the story that the other children are performing. Encourage the child to sign the puppet story either before or after the puppets "perform."

Behavior Disordered/Emotionally Disturbed: None needed.

PRESCHOOL ACTIVITY
Let's Do It Together (Art)*

Plan an art project that encourages group participation. Provide several cardboard boxes (small, medium, and large) and invite children to work together to build one structure. use glue, string, or tape to hold the structure together. Emphasize that the completed structure can be enjoyed and used by everyone. After the structure is completed, provide tempera paint and a variety of brushes. Children will enjoy painting their creation.

Variation: Work together on murals to decorate the room; have children decorate the bulletin boards together.

Additional Skills:

Cognition (problem solving/reasoning)

Adaptations for Children with Disabilities:

Physically Impaired: If it is needed, provide physical assistance or encourage the other children to assist the child. Provide a Velcro bracelet to attach the brush to the child's wrist if the child cannot grasp the brush.

Speech/Language Impaired: None needed.

Visually Impaired: Encourage the children to assist the child by giving specific directions on where to place the block, string, and so on. Add food extract to the tempera paint to add a smell to the coloring.

Hearing Impaired: Use signs and/or gestures to explain the activity. Encourage the other children to use signs and gestures while building together.

Behavior Disordered/Emotionally Disturbed: Provide additional encouragement for the child who has difficulty relating positively to peers.

Conservation of Resources

The third subdomain in the area of socialization involves learning the importance of conservation of resources. Children's understanding of the principles of conservation is related to their awareness of and respect for the environment as well as their ability to begin to accept responsibility. Specific developmental goals in this subdomain include the following:

1. Help children learn to use play materials constructively.
2. Encourage children to take responsibility for the appropriate care of materials and the environment.
3. Help children to learn to respect and care for the natural world.
4. Increase children's awareness of ecological problems and conservation practices.

Learning about the conservation of resources occurs when teachers model an attitude of respect and care for both the indoor and outdoor environment and give children developmentally appropriate opportunities to take responsibility for the care of materials and resources. Here are some suggested sample activities for infants, toddlers, and preschoolers that can be adapted for a variety of developmental levels (an asterisk [*] denotes an activity that is also appropriate for use in the outdoor play environment).

INFANT ACTIVITY
Grass Watering (Science/Nature)*

During dry weather, hook up one or two garden hoses to water sources and help infants undress so they are wearing diapers. Encourage children to hold the hose individually and take turns watering the grass. Two infants also can be encouraged to hold the hose together and water the grass. The teacher can talk about how the grass feels and looks dry and needs water and then discuss the contrast with the watered grass that feels and looks wet. The infants also may drink from the hose or spray each other or feel the water on their bodies.

Additional Skills:

Cognition (concept formation); socialization (social interaction, cooperation); perceptual motor (coordination, nonlocomotor, body management and control)

Adaptations for Children with Disabilities:

Physically Impaired: If needed, provide physical assistance to hold the hose.

Speech/Language Impaired: None needed.

Visually Impaired: None needed.

Hearing Impaired: Use signs and/or gestures to explain the activity.

Behavior Disordered/Emotionally Disturbed: None needed.

TODDLER ACTIVITY
Washing Toys and Equipment (Science/Nature)*

Provide the children with a large tub of soapy water and several sponges. Bring transportable equipment (easels, small tables, and so on) and various plastic toys (dolls, balls, and so on) outdoors. Allow the children to wash the materials in any way they choose. Use the opportunity to ask open-ended questions about the importance of taking care of our toys and equipment.

Additional Skills:

Perceptual motor (eye-hand coordination); socialization (cooperation)

Adaptations for Children with Disabilities:

Physically Impaired: If it is needed, provide physical assistance to enable the child to work or play with the toy.

Speech/Language Impaired: Encourage the child to name the toys presented. If the child has limited expressive language skills, present two toys and ask the child to choose the one you name.

Visually Impaired: If the child cannot identify the object by feel, provide verbal descriptions. If necessary, provide verbal or physical prompts to encourage the child to work or play with the toys.

Hearing Impaired: Use signs and/or gestures to explain the activity and name the toys.

Behavior Disordered/Emotionally Disturbed: None needed.

PRESCHOOL ACTIVITY
The Clean-Up Club (Storytelling)*

Tell a story about some children who wanted to play together at a park, a playground, or a similar place but could not enjoy it because the area was littered by trash (see the example that follows). Include in the story how the children decided to work together to clean up the area and then decided to form a club that would always be on the lookout for trash and garbage. Act out the story in the classroom by using wadded-up newspaper for the trash. Provide bags for the "Clean-Up Club" to use to collect the trash. Extend the activity by going outside on the school playground to look for and pick up trash. Provide membership cards or badges for all those who wish to be members of the club. Encourage children to continue to look for and pick up trash at school or at home.

Clean-Up Club Story:

Close your eyes and try to imagine a beautiful summer day—bright blue sky, soft breeze blowing, flowers blooming, birds singing. Can you picture it in your mind? Well, that's the kind of day it was when some children just like you found that their mothers were taking them to their favorite park to play. They were so excited because this park had swings and slides and climbers, and even a duck pond! When they got to the park, their happy faces changed into sad faces. The park looked awful. There were papers and trash everywhere they looked. The park wasn't at all like they remembered. They were really upset. Then, one of the girls said, "We can make the park look better!" What do you think she wanted to do? That's right! She suggested they

could all work together and clean up the park and that's just what they did. Soon all the trash was in the garbage cans where it belonged. The park looked great again. One of the boys said, "Let's form a club that will always look for paper and trash and put it where it belongs. We can call ourselves the Clean-Up Club!"

Additional Skills:

Socialization (cooperation); communication (receptive and expressive language)

Adaptations for Children with Disabilities:

Physically Impaired: While cleaning up the room or cleaning outside, encourage the child to participate by doing a job that can be done independently, such as holding the trash bag or pushing the trash can.

Speech/Language Impaired: None needed.

Visually Impaired: Ask another child to be the "tour guide" and take the child to the area that needs to have the trash cleaned up. Have the guide tap the trash can. Encourage the child to face the tapping noise and put the trash in the can.

Hearing Impaired: Use signs and/or gestures to explain the activity and tell the story.

Behavior Disordered/Emotionally Disturbed: None needed.

Respect for Others

The fourth subdomain in the area of socialization is developing respect for others. Helping young children to understand and value the differences and similarities in people and to develop empathic, compassionate attitudes and behaviors is a major component of learning respect for others. Specific developmental goals in this subdomain include the following:

1. Help children understand that all people are similar in some ways and different in some ways (Hendrick, 1998).
2. Encourage children to demonstrate respect and understanding of differences in people (race, gender, cultural backgrounds).

3. Help children exhibit kindness, generosity, compassion, and nurturing behaviors toward others (Smith, 1982).
4. Encourage children to recognize and respond to others' needs in an affirmative, supportive way.

Young children are best able to develop respect for others when teachers model respectful, appreciative behaviors toward all children and families and when teachers encourage positive, nurturing interactions among children. Here are some suggested sample activities for infants, toddlers, and preschoolers that can be adapted for a variety of developmental levels.

INFANT ACTIVITY
Baby Faces (Discussion)

Make a collection of pictures of each infant. Parents may bring some from home to help. Post pictures of each infant on a separate piece of poster board and list the child's age in each picture if desired. Use the posters in an activity to discuss individual differences among the children. Show the infants a particular child's poster and talk about blue eyes, brown hair, a big smile, lots of teeth, pierced ears, brown skin, a hearing aid, and so on. Keep all descriptions objective and positive and end each with a comment about how special and unique each child is. Let the infants carefully hold and touch the posters and pictures. Talk about how infants change over time. "When Johnny was a younger baby, he didn't have much hair, but now that he's older, he has more hair."

Additional Skills:

Emotional well-being (personality integration); cognition (association/classification)

Adaptations for Children with Disabilities:

Physically Impaired: None needed.

Speech/Language Impaired: None needed.

Visually Impaired: None needed.

Hearing Impaired: Use signs and/or gestures while describing each child.

Behavior Disordered/Emotionally Disturbed: None needed.

TODDLER ACTIVITY
Different Clothes (Imaginary Play)

Locate clothing from several different cultures or countries. Show the children the difference in what people wear. If clothes, hats, shoes, and so on can be located, allow the children to try the clothes on; then leave them out in the imaginary-play center. You also can construct clothes and costumes for children to wear (for example, a turban can be made by wrapping a thin piece of material around a child's head).

Variation: Invite parents or other community resource people from other countries and cultures to the classroom to show traditional clothes, foods, and the like.

Additional Skills:

Socialization (social interaction); communication (receptive language)

Adaptations for Children with Disabilities:

Physically Impaired: If needed, physically assist the child with trying on the clothes.

Speech/Language Impaired: None needed.

Visually Impaired: Use actual clothing for the child to explore. Explain the tactile differences in the clothing.

Hearing Impaired: None needed.

Behavior Disordered/Emotionally Disturbed: None needed.

PRESCHOOL ACTIVITY
Hard Things/Easy Things (Discussion)

Use the book *Is It Hard, Is It Easy?* as a way to begin a group discussion about things that are hard or easy for children in the classroom to do. Talk about things that are hard for you as an adult to do, to reinforce the idea that it's okay to talk about things that are hard to do. Talk about things that were once hard but are now easy because children have learned how as they have grown bigger. Talk about things that may always be hard for some people and things that will always be easy for some people. Reinforce the idea that each person has different things that are hard and easy and that we don't all have to do the same things in the same way.[2]

Additional Skills:

Communication (receptive and expressive language); emotional well-being (personality integration)

Adaptations for Children with Disabilities:

Physically Impaired: Discuss how movements (and what types) are hard for the child. You also can use this

activity to problem-solve situations that would be difficult for the child and talk about ways we help our friends. Be sure also to point out what activities are easy for the child.

Speech/Language Impaired: None needed.

Visually Impaired: Use this activity to discuss how and why some activities are hard for the child who is visually impaired and suggest ways to solve some of these difficulties.

Hearing Impaired: Use signs and/or gestures to explain the activity. Discuss how and why some activities are hard for the child who is hearing impaired.

Behavior Disordered/Emotionally Disturbed: None needed.

CHAPTER SUMMARY _____

Teachers encourage the development of social competence in young children when they model caring, nurturing interactions with others and establish a classroom climate that promotes cooperation, respectful communication, and mutual problem solving. In addition, providing a classroom environment rich in opportunities for social interactions during creative-play activities allows children to recognize their individual differences and supports their development as social beings.

■ ■ ■ ■ ■ ■ ■ ■ ■

As an effective and sensitive teacher of young children, you realize the need to evaluate your classroom practices based on children's comments and responses. Andrew has sent you a clear message that the activity level and amount of social interaction in the classroom is, at times, simply too much for him. You realize you may have overemphasized the importance of developing social skills and must recognize children's varying needs for periods of quiet and solitary activity during the day. You plan to make the following changes to help Andrew and the other preschoolers make good choices about their time, activity, and social interactions:

- Intersperse periods of quiet, relaxing activity with the active play periods during the day.

- Rearrange the classroom environment to include cozy private spaces where children can relax or rest with books, music, and soft toys.

- Be more sensitive to children's individual needs; if a child is reluctant to join in a group activity, allow the child to make another appropriate choice of activity or to be an onlooker.

- Discuss with children the importance of pacing oneself through the day and encourage children to let you know when they are tired or overstimulated.

- Give attention and encouragement to children engaged in solitary, parallel, or associative play as well as to children actively engaged in cooperative play with a group.

Children, like adults, have differing needs for activity, stimulation, and social interaction. Planning the classroom

[2]Resource: Green, M. M. (1960). *Is It Hard, Is It Easy?* New York: Young Scott Books.

schedule and arranging the classroom environment to encourage children to make choices that will meet their individual needs

is an important component of helping children grow as social beings and understand themselves in relationship to others.

■ ■ ■ ■ ■ ■ ■ ■ ■

DISCUSSION QUESTIONS _____

1. Discuss the vignette at the beginning of the chapter. What other questions or concerns might you have? Discuss the vignette at the end of the chapter. Are there other responses you might have to this situation?

2. What role do both positive and negative peer interaction have in children's socialization, according to Piaget?

3. Describe Parten's categories of children's play. What is the value of each type of play?

4. Describe the different parenting styles described by Baumrind and the outcomes associated with each style.

5. What variables or factors associated with child-care programs promote children's social competence and prosocial behavior?

6. Describe children's stages of reasoning about friendship, according to Selman.

7. Summarize what is known from the research about center-based child care and aggressiveness in children. What are the limitations of this research?

8. How does creative-play support children's socialization in early childhood? How can teachers encourage and support children's social interactions with peers?

9. How can teachers encourage children who have difficulty initiating or maintaining social play and interactions with other children?

10. Describe the four domains of development in socialization.

REFERENCES _____

Allen, J. (1988). Promoting preschoolers' moral reasoning. *Early Child Development and Care, 33,* 171–180.

Allen, J., Freeman, P., & Osborne, S. (1989). Children's political knowledge and attitudes. *Young Children, 44*(2), 57–61.

Baumrind, D. (1967). Child care practices anteceding three patterns of preschool behavior. *Genetic Psychology Monographs, 75,* 43–88.

Baumrind, D. (1991). Parenting styles and adolescent development. In R. Lerner, A. Peterson, & J. Brooks-Gunn (Eds.), *Encyclopedia of Adolescence* (pp. 758–772). New York: Garland.

Belsky, J., Learner, R., & Spanier, G. (1984). *The child in the family.* Reading, MA: Addison-Wesley.

Chenfeld, M. B. (1989). From catatonic to hyperactive: Randy snapped today. *Young Children, 44*(4), 25–27.

Damon, W. (1977). *The social world of the child.* San Francisco: Jossey-Bass.

Erikson, E. H. (1972). Play and actuality. In M. W. Piers (Ed.), *Play and development* (pp. 127–167). New York: Norton.

Finkelstein, N. (1982). Aggression: Is it stimulated by day care? *Young Children, 37*(6), 3–9.

Freud, S. (1938). *An outline of psychoanalysis.* London: Hogarth.

Golden, M., Rosenbluth, L., Grossi, M., Policare, H., Freeman, H., & Brownlee, M. (1978). *The New York infant*

day care study. New York: Medical and Health Research Association of New York City.

Hallinin, M., & Teixeira, R. (1987). Opportunities and constraints: Black-White differences in the formation of interracial friendships. *Child Development, 58,* 1358–1371.

Haskins, R. (1985). Public school aggression among children with varying day-care experience. *Child Development, 56,* 689–703.

Hegland, S., & Rix, M. (1990). Aggression and assertiveness in kindergarten children differing in day care experiences. *Early Childhood Research Quarterly, 5,* 105–116.

Hendrick, J. (1998). *Total learning: Developmental curriculum for the young child* (5th ed.). Columbus, OH: Merrill/Macmillan.

Honig, A., & Pollack, B. (1990). Effects of a brief intervention program to promote prosocial behaviors in young children. *Early Education and Development, 1,* 438–444.

Howes, C., & Rubenstein, J. (1981). Toddler peer behavior in two types of day care. *Infant Behavior and Development, 4,* 387–393.

Howes, C., & Wu, F. (1990). Peer interactions and friendships in an ethnically diverse school setting. *Child Development, 61,* 537–41.

Innocenti, M., Stowitschek, J., Rule, S., Killoran, J., Striefel, S., & Boswell, C. (1986). A naturalistic study of the relation between preschool setting events and peer interaction in four activity contexts. *Early Childhood Research Quarterly, 1,* 141–153.

Jarrett, O., & Quay, L. (1983). *Cross-racial acceptance and best friend choice in racially balanced kindergarten and first-grade classrooms.* Paper presented at the biennial meeting of the Society for Research in Child Develoment, Detroit, MI.

Katz, L., & McClellan, D. (1997). *Fostering children's social competence: The teacher's role.* Washington, DC: National Association for the Education of Young Children.

Katz, P. (1976). The acquisition of racial attitudes in children. In R. Katz (Ed.), *Toward the elimination of racism* (pp. 125–154). New York: Pergamon.

Lamb, M., Hwang, C., Bookstein, F., Broberg, A., Hult, G., & Frodi, M. (1988). Determinants of social competence in Swedish preschoolers. *Developmental Psychology, 24*(1), 58–70.

Milne, A. A. (1957). *The world of Pooh: The complete Winnie-the-Pooh and the House at Pooh Corner.* New York: Dutton.

Parten, M. (1932). Social participation among preschool children. *Journal of Abnormal Social Psychology, 27,* 243–270.

Phillips, D., Scarr, S., & McCartney, K. (1987). Child care quality and children's social development. *Developmental Psychology, 23*(4), 537–543.

Piaget, J. (1932). *The moral judgment of the child.* London: Routledge & Kegan Paul.

Piaget, J., & Inhelder, B. (1969). *The psychology of the child.* New York: Basic Books.

Ramsey, P. (1991). Young children's awareness and understanding of social class differences. *Journal of Genetic Psychology, 152*(1), 71–82.

Ramsey, P. (1995). Growing up with the contradictions of race and class. *Young Children, 50*(6), 18–25.

Ramsey, P., & Myers, L. (1990). Young children's responses to racial differences: Relations among cognitive, affective, and behavioral differences. *Journal of Applied Developmental Psychology, 11,* 49–67.

Rogers, C. S., & Sawyers, J. K. (1988). *Play in the lives of children.* Washington, DC: National Association for the Education of Young Children.

Schwarz, J., Strickland, R., & Krolick, G. (1974). Infant day care: Behavioral effects at a preschool age. *Developmental Psychology, 10,* 502–506.

Selman, R. (1976). Toward a structural analysis of developing interpersonal relations concepts. In A. Pick (Ed.), *Minnesota Symposium on Child Psychology* (Vol. 10, pp. 156–200). Minneapolis, MN: University of Minnesota Press.

Smith, C., Leinbach, M., Stewart, B., & Blackwell, J. (1983). Affective perspective-taking, exhortations, and children's prosocial behavior. In D. Bridgeman (Ed.), *The nature of prosocial development: Interdisciplinary theories and strategies* (pp. 113–134). New York: Academic Press.

Smith, C. A. (1982). *Promoting the social development of young children: Strategies and activities.* Palo Alto, CA: Mayfield.

Sullivan, H. (1953). *The interpersonal theory of psychiatry.* New York: Norton.

Teaching Tolerance Project. (1997). *Starting small: Teaching tolerance in preschool and the early grades.* Montgomery, AL: Southern Poverty Law Center.

Wittmer, D., & Honig, A. (1994). Encouraging positive social development in young children. *Young Children, 49*(5), 4–12.

ADDITIONAL RESOURCES _____

Athey, I. (1984). Contributions of play to development. In T. D. Yawkey & A. D. Pellegrini (Eds.), *Child's play: Developmental and applied* (pp. 9–27). Hillsdale, NJ: Erlbaum.

Brown, M., Althouse, R., & Anfin, C. (1993). Guided dramatization: Fostering social development in children with disabilities. *Young Children, 48*(2), 68–71

Cooney, M., Hutchinson, L., & Costigan, V. (1996). From hitting and tattling to communication and negotiation: The young child's stages of socialization. *Early Childhood Education Journal, 24*(1), 23–29.

DeKlyen, M., & Odom, S. L. (1989). Activity structure and social interactions with peers in developmentally integrated play groups. *Journal of Early Intervention, 13,* 342–352.

Dinwiddie, S. (1994). The saga of Sally, Sammy, and the red pen: Facilitating children's social problem solving. *Young Children, 49*(5), 13–19.

Eddowes, E. A. (1991). Review of research: The benefits of solitary play. *Dimensions, 20*(1), 31–34.

Eifermann, R. R. (1971). Social play in childhood. In R. E. Herron & B. Sutton-Smith (Eds.), *Child's play* (pp. 270–297). New York: Wiley.

Fry-Miller, K., & Myers-Walls, J. (1990). Caring for the environment. *Day Care and Early Education, 18*(2), 17–19, 21.

Goffin, S. G. (1987). Cooperative behaviors: They need our support. *Young Children, 42*(2), 75–81.

Greenberg, P. (1992). How to institute some simple democratic practices pertaining to respect, rights, roots, and responsibilities in any classroom. *Young Children, 47*(5), 10–17.

Griffin, S. (1988). Conservation seeds: Pollution awareness. *Day Care and Early Education, 16*(1), 28–29.

Guralnick, M. (1990). Social competence and early intervention. *Journal of Early Intervention, 14,* 3–14.

Hale, J. (1992). Dignifying black children's lives. *Dimensions, 20*(3), 8–9, 40.

Hatch, J., & Johnson, L. (1991). Guiding the social development of young children. *Day Care and Early Education, 18*(4), 29–33.

Howes, C. (1987). Social competency with peers: Contributions from child care. *Early Childhood Research Quarterly, 2,* 155–167.

Howes, C., Droege, K., & Phillipsen, L. (Eds.). (1992). Contribution of peers to socialization in early childhood. In

M. Gettinger, S. Elliott, & T. Kratochwill (Eds.), *Preschool and early childhood treatment directions* (pp. 113–150). Hillsdale, NJ: Erlbaum.

Kemple, K. (1991). Preschool children's peer acceptance and social interaction. *Young Children, 46*(5), 47–54.

Kemple, K. (1997). Getting along: How teachers can support children's peer relationships. *Early Childhood Education Journal, 24*(3), 139–146.

LeBlanc, L. (1989). Let's play: Teaching social skills. *Day Care and Early Education, 16*(3), 28–31.

McCall, R. (1979). Stages in play development between zero and two years of age. In B. Sutton-Smith (Ed.), *Play and learning* (pp. 35–44). New York: Gardner.

McMath, J. (1989). Promoting prosocial behaviors through literature. *Day Care and Early Education, 17*(1), 25–27.

Mallory, B., & New, R. (Eds.). (1994). *Diversity and developmentally appropriate practices: Challenges for early childhood education.* New York: Teachers College Press.

Paley, V. (1986). *Mollie is three: Growing up in school.* Chicago: University of Chicago Press.

Paley, V. (1992). *You can't say you can't play.* Cambridge, MA: Harvard University Press.

Piers, M. (Ed.). (1972). *Play and development.* New York: Norton.

Roedell, W., Slaby, R., & Robinson, H. (1976). *Social development in young children: A report for teachers.* Washington, DC: National Institute of Education.

Rogers, D. (1987). Fostering social development through block play. *Day Care and Early Education, 14*(3), 26–29.

Rogers, D. L., & Ross, D. D. (1986). Encouraging positive social interactions among young children. *Young Children, 41*(3), 12–17.

Spodek, B., & Saracho, O. (1994). *Dealing with individual differences in the early childhood classroom.* New York: Longman.

Stockdale, D., Hegland, S., & Chiaromonte, T. (1989). Helping behaviors: An observational study of preschool children. *Early Childhood Research Quarterly, 4,* 533–543.

Trawick-Smith, J. (1988). "Let's say you're the baby, OK": Play leadership and following behavior of young children. *Young Children, 43*(5), 51–59.

Wolf, D. (Ed.). (1986). *Connecting: Friendship in the lives of young children and their teachers.* Redmond, WA: Exchange Press.

Zeece, P., & Graul, S. (1990). Learning to play: Playing to learn. *Day Care and Early Education, 18*(1), 11–15.

Zick, R. (1980). *Children's friendships.* Cambridge, MA: Harvard University Press.

14.

Curriculum for Developing Communication

■ ■ ■ ■ ■ ■ ■ ■ ■ ■

As a toddler teacher, you are constantly in awe over the amazing language development that takes place between 18 months and 3 years of age. The children's vocabularies grow rapidly during this period, and soon they are uttering two-word sentences and then multiple-word sentences. You truly enjoy being involved in helping toddlers acquire and practice language skills.

However, you are concerned about one particular toddler who turned 2 years old last month. Trey has virtually no language and has not even attempted a two-word sentence. For some time you have assumed that Trey was just somewhat immature in his language skills and that he would develop in his own time. The parents have expressed concern, but you have reassured them that the lack of language is not serious. Now you are not so sure. You talk with the parents again and together you consider these questions:

- Is it likely that Trey is still just somewhat delayed in his language development and he will begin talking in his own time?

- What are the possible causes for Trey's language delay if it really is a developmental problem?

- What type of physical or developmental assessments should be conducted to determine whether Trey has a significant language problem?

- Is it possible that there is something in the home or center environment that is keeping Trey from talking or wanting to talk?

- How can you and the parents encourage Trey to begin to use language without making him feel pressured and developing negative feelings about himself?

■ ■ ■ ■ ■ ■ ■ ■ ■ ■

Suggestions for responding to this classroom vignette will be shared at the end of the chapter.

When reading this chapter, focus on understanding major developmental milestones for young children in the domain of communication. Also, consider ways that the development of communication skills can be fostered through creative-play activities and growth-promoting teaching techniques.

Young children are motivated to learn to communicate and develop language skills from their earliest interactions with adults and the environment. At first, children use gestures and simple language to communicate their needs and feelings to adults as they go through a learning process that results in their becoming effective communicators who can receive information, express thoughts, and finally comprehend abstract and complex communication. To understand how young children develop language and how that development is supported through play, it is necessary to review the important developmental milestones in communication and consider ways in which the creative-play curriculum fosters the development of language and communication skills.

DEVELOPMENTAL MILESTONES IN COMMUNICATION _____

In no other domain of development do children reach adultlike behavior as quickly as they do in the development of communication. It is not until around the first birthday that children speak their first words, yet by age 6 most children have a compre-

hension vocabulary of 23,700 words and know and use correct rules of grammar (Smith, 1941). What knowledge and skills constitute effective communication? And what is the route to such sophisticated language skills? Language, the primary means by which we express our thoughts, is not the only essential component of communication. Language is simply the sounds arbitrarily assigned and agreed upon to refer to certain ideas that convey meaning.

Activities were written by Kathy Carlson, Amy R. Kerlin, and Anne Miller Stott; adaptations were written by Bobbie Beckmann.

Communication includes language, but it also encompasses gestures and nonverbal messages found in eye contact, pointing, and affectionate behaviors. For example, children's early gestures indicate that they understand that objects have names even before they can vocalize the names. In fact, early gesturing is related to children's later development of vocabulary (Acredolo & Goodwyn, 1988). Children who are effective communicators learn to understand others and express themselves using a variety of methods to communicate even before they use spoken language. The path to effective communication begins at birth in the stage called prespeech, which lasts until children utter their first words at about 1 year. Infants engage in early dialogue that may appear to be devoid of language. A reciprocal pattern of looking, smiling, or vocalizing (cooing, babbling) is an early indication to children that human interactions occur in dialogue or a pattern of taking turns: You smile, I smile back. You gurgle, I gurgle back. This pattern of dialogue also is seen in feeding. Babies will suck on a bottle and stop, then parents will jiggle the bottle. Babies will suck, then parents jiggle. This sucking-jiggling pattern also approximates a dialogue, and infants become accustomed to a pattern of social discourse (Kaye, 1982).

Infants engage in three behaviors in the prespeech stage—crying, gesturing, and babbling. Crying, cooing, and gurgling are sounds that communicate, usually either happiness or distress, but they are not considered speech sounds because they are not phonemes, which are vowel or consonant sounds. In the first six months, when infants babble they first produce vowel sounds, then later, consonant sounds. Children of all linguistic groups produce similar babbling sounds, as do deaf children, suggesting the importance of maturation in the early prespeech stage.

After six months, babbling becomes more systematic. Infants repeat certain sounds more frequently because they hear these sounds often and because caregivers reinforce certain sounds. A mother's gleeful reaction to the sound "mah," a father's proud response to the sound "dah," or a teacher's reinforcement of "bah" because it sounds as if the child is saying "ball" tell children that certain sounds, usually first produced without reference to mama, daddy, or ball, elicit positive reactions in others; and this reinforcement serves to increase their frequency. This method of language learning suggests the importance of environmental factors. During this prespeech stage, infants have begun to develop a comprehension vocabulary, or words that they understand. At about 1 year, when infants utter their first word with a clear referent, they are showing evidence of their production vocabulary, or words that children can use.

This first meaningful word signals progression into the second stage or speech stage, which comprises five substages (Wood, 1981):

- Sentencelike words, or *holophrases,* are single-word utterances that are not simply labels but suggest a complete idea. Children's one-word holophrases can communicate quite detailed information or forceful demands. For example, when a 14-month-old says "milk," it is not vocabulary practice but is usually meant to convey "I want milk," "I want more milk," or "The milk is dripping off the table onto the dog's head."

- Two-word sentences occur by about 18 months as children combine words to convey more meaning. These combinations are referred to as *telegraphic* because they convey meaning in an abbreviated manner. Examples of two-word sentences are "More milk," "Daddy gone," "All gone," and "That mine."

- Multiple-word sentences begin to occur around 2 years and indicate a transition to more linguistic sophistication. In this substage, children use complete sentences, articles, pronouns, and morphemes, which are words or parts of words that change the meaning of other words—for example—*-ed, -ing,* or *-es.* Children in this stage of language development also have progressed to the preoperational stage of cognitive development. They are learning how to use symbols and can begin to manipulate language playfully. LeFrancois (1995) describes the example of a young friend "who, having learned that 'pitch black' was very black, insisted that other things can be 'pitch clean,' 'pitch empty,' or 'pitch big' " (p. 324).

- A substage of more complex grammar and words begins around age 3 as children make transformations or changes in grammar, structure, and meaning by using conjunctions to combine sentences, embedding to insert words that alter meaning, and permutations—that is, changing the word order in a sentence to alter the meaning.

- The last substage of adultlike structures occurs after age 4. Children's speech becomes more meaningful and reflects correct grammar and language usage.

In addition to many experiences with socially oriented oral communication, children's development of language involves experiences with books and print. Children's rapid language development and natural interest in communication provide the important basis for fostering emergent literacy skills. The emergent literacy paradigm recognizes the integrative nature of language development, the importance of children's active construction of language knowledge, and the significance of viewing language development in a familial and cultural context (Spodek & Saracho, 1993).

The next step beyond oral language is the aspect of literacy that begins with print awareness. Young children's emergence into writing involves movement through three stages: emergent writing, beginning writing, and fluent writing. Children in the *emergent writing* stage explore through scribbling and drawing; children in the *beginning writing* stage use invented spelling and dictated stories; children in the *fluent writing* stage begin to use conventional spelling and develop early authoring skills. Young children's emergence into reading also involves movement into three stages: *emergent reading,* when children begin to recognize environmental print such as signs and labels; *beginning reading,* when children develop knowledge about word concepts and word recognition; and *fluent reading,* when children's reading activities are focused on comprehension.

Kontos (1986) has written an extensive review of the literature about preschool children's understanding of the reading process. Young children learn to distinguish print or written language from pictures and other graphic materials such as numbers at age 3. Some children at age 4 still may have difficulty distinguishing between print and pictures or what a reader looks at while reading. Print awareness, or knowing why and how printed words are used, is understood by most children at age 5. Another skill that children acquire is recognizing and reading words in the environment using context cues. For example, children as young as 3 can identify words in their usual context, such as the word *STOP* on an eight-sided sign, but are less able to identify words in isolation or out of this context. Although many 3-year-olds can recite letters of the alphabet, more important in later reading is children's ability to identify letters, or letter name knowledge. By age 3, children have begun to identify letters, and they have almost mastered letter names by age 5. This knowledge seems to be important both in differentiating letter shapes and forms and in developing phonetic or sound association with printed words.

Children's knowledge about reading develops through three levels: knowledge of the function of print, knowledge of the form of print, and knowledge of the conventions of print, such as book handling and terminology, oral language competence, and rules of classroom discourse—for example, taking turns (Mason, 1981, 1985). How do children progress through these three levels to reading? Kontos (1986) describes how literacy acquisition is fostered in an environment rich in literacy-related activities and experiences and by adults who assist and instruct children with more difficult aspects of reading. Activities and experiences that promote literacy interest and ability are story reading, discussion of stories, the number of adults who read to the child, and parents who model reading and writing and who are responsive to children's requests for information and help with reading. Classroom experiences that promote literacy include opportunities to use and practice communication skills with books, notes, lists, recipes, schedules, and labels. Reading and writing materials should be accessible and practical and have a real purpose and interest for children; experiences with them should be integrated in meaningful and imaginative ways into all aspects of the classroom (Kontos, 1986).

Children in the early stages of emergent and beginning reading and writing recognize that the purpose of print is communication. Their early writing grows out of their talk about everyday experiences and their early reading grows out of being read to and beginning to reread memorized portions of predictable or repetitive stories. Thus emergent reading and emergent writing are parallel or integrative components of emergent literacy that lead to a later stage of development in which children express meaning through reading and writing (Juel, 1991; Salinger, 1996; Thompkins, 1997; Williams & Davis, 1994).

RESEARCH ON CHILDREN'S COMMUNICATION SKILLS

Research on the influence of environment on children's language development has found that most of a child's early vocabulary consists of words that represent objects and behaviors in a child's immediate environment, such as familiar people or objects, actions ("give"), or reward and punishment ("good," "bad") (Nelson, 1973). Adults in the environment also influence children's language learning. When parents use simple communication, such as many nouns and simple grammar structure, rather than more complex language, such as many verbs and pronouns and more abstract language, children have better language skills (Furrow, Nelson, & Benedict, 1979).

Researchers have studied young children's egocentrism in their communication with others. Much of this research has focused on referential communication tasks, that is, requesting that the child communicate with another person about a specific object or occurrence about which the listener has a different perspective or amount of information than the child. In a well-known study, researchers asked 4-year-old children to show a new toy to a younger child and to an adult. With the 2-year-old, children used short, simple sentences and adapted their communication to the comprehension abilities of the younger child: "Look at this." "See this." "Look here." With the adult, children used more sophisticated language and requested information from the adult (Shatz & Gelman, 1973). Researchers also have found that children will adapt their communication to be more easily understood by children with mental retardation (Guralnick & Paul-Brown, 1977).

This research appears to refute Piaget's claim (Piaget & Inhelder, 1969) that preschool children are egocentric, or unable to consider the perspective of another person, in their communication. Actually, the issue is much more complex than it appears. In a study of 4- and 6-year-olds' ability to interpret the effect of an ambiguous and an informative message on a listener's ability to find a hidden object, 6-year-olds effectively distinguished the two types of messages and whether the listener would be able to locate the hidden object with the information given in each message. Four-year-olds more often responded based on their own knowledge of the hidden object rather than the listeners' knowledge (Sodian, 1988). This research shows that, given a very complex communication task, in this case having to evaluate both the message and its effect on the listener, is difficult for young children. Faced with such a challenge, they rely on a more egocentric mode of responding. But in simpler referential communication, children can and do adapt their communication to the informational needs and comprehension ability of their listeners.

Piaget described language learning as an outcome of the child's individual and internal cognitive development. Adult language influences children's language, but not beyond the limits of the child's own cognitive abilities. Children explore, discover, and manipulate language as they engage in word play, in the same way that they explore, discover, and manipulate their physical environment to learn about their world by their actions upon their world. Vygotsky (1962), however, described the learning of language as a social process. Children learn language as they interact with adults and peers. Piaget viewed language as developing from the individual to the social. Vygotsky viewed language as developing from the social to fostering internal cognitive and problem-solving skills.

Research in early childhood education has revealed curricular and program factors that relate to children's language development. Children who were encouraged to engage in structured sociodramatic play and given appropriate materials to use in such play had more effective communication skills during play (Griffing, 1980). For example, in a study of 4- and 5-year-olds, children produced more detailed language in dramatic-play centers, such as a doctor's office, than in construction centers, such as blocks. Children pretending to be in a doctor's office used more verbs and more details to describe their play. They were more likely to use future- and past-tense verbs to relate their behavior either to the past or to the future. As children's language moves their play beyond the immediate environment, they develop skills for more complex cognitive tasks (Pellegrini, 1986). In early childhood programs with low staff-child ratios, high levels of verbal interaction between teachers and children, and cognitive and social stimulation, children have more mature language comprehension and communication skills (Golden et al., 1978; McCartney, 1984; Phillips, Scarr, & McCartney, 1987). For example, teachers who encourage open, extended conversations; who avoid questions requiring only brief, factual answers; and who maintain longer, natural, child-centered conversations with children have more meaningful communication with and are more sensitive to young children's language learning (Rogers, Perrin, & Waller, 1987).

Research on young children's literacy suggests several effective ways to guide and respond to children's literacy development. Children who are read to and have easy access to books, who have paper and writing instruments, who play with magnetic letters and such materials, and whose parents use and discuss with children other examples of letters and words in the environment, such as books, magazines, newspapers, signs, and the like, have higher levels of literacy development (Schickedanz, 1986). Research on the role of teacher guidance in children's literacy development suggests that teachers can increase children's use of books and print-related materials by giving suggestions and modeling literacy behaviors. Morrow and Rand (1991) set up conditions in which teachers placed literacy materials such as pencils, markers, books, magazines, signs, cards, and calendars in a dramatic-play area equipped as a veterinarian office. They made suggestions such as, "You can read while you're waiting for your pet" or "Fill out a prescription card after you sign in on the form at the desk." Teachers also modeled literacy behaviors and the use of props, such as discussing a pamphlet in the office or looking at a calendar and writing an appointment card. Children were more involved with the print materials and related activities when teachers provided both the print-rich environment and the modeling and guidance than when they provided one but not the other.

Specific characteristics of books also increase children's literacy activities and use of print. Books that are predictable, with repetitive sentences, rhymes, familiar sequences, are selected by children twice as often than books without these features (Martinez & Teale, 1988). Young children ask more questions about a book's pictures than its meaning. But repeated reading of the same book tends to elicit additional questions about letters, sounds, words, or story meaning (Morrow, 1988; Yaden, 1988). When culturally diverse books are present in the classroom but are underused, teachers can increase children's use of books by "introducing" them to children. When teachers show children the books and talk about the title, the author and illustrator, the story, and pictures in the book that the teacher likes, children's use of the books increases (Reid & Twardosz, 1996).

With increasing cultural diversity in the preschool population, more children in our classrooms will likely speak more than one language—they will be bilingual. Teachers also will work with children who do not speak Standard English—they use a dialect. In both cases teachers must understand and make wise decisions about some important issues.

There is much value in being able to speak more than one language. Bilingual children should be encouraged in their learning of both languages. Fillmore (1991) found that when language-minority children were assimilated into English-speaking classrooms and not encouraged and supported to develop and use their primary language, they lost a significant means of socialization into their families' culture and values; they lost the ability to understand their own history and tradition. There were significant impacts on parent–child relationships. Children who are encouraged to develop and use primary-language skills, in fact, more easily learn a second language (Garcia, 1986). Soto (1991) has suggested some guidelines to help teachers working with bilingual children:

- Avoid pushing children to learn a second language quickly. Accept children's individual "language-learning time frames" (p. 34).

- Help children have many opportunities for conversations in both native and new languages in dramatic play, story time, social experiences with peers and adults, field trips, and other activities.

- Develop the attitude that both languages are important for the child's cognitive and social development. One language is not being learned to replace the other.

- Accept children's attempts to communicate, without correction or domination of conversations.

- Provide an accepting classroom climate and experiences that demonstrate to bilingual children and their classmates that all cultures are valued.

Another issue in children's language learning and use that teachers must consider is that of children who speak a dialect, a form of English that teachers once believed reflected a deficit in language and communication skills. Now, we know that dialect such as Ebonics—formerly called Black English—is a meaningful and powerful language for communication among many African-American children and their families. A dialect parallels Standard English in that it has definite rules, structure, grammar, and word play/word games. For example, inserting the word *be* into a sentence, such as "He be going home," is a *pronomial apposition;* deleting the word *is* from the sentence is a *copula deletion* (Genishi & Dyson, 1984). Children who use a dialect consistently can be as skilled communicators as those who use a language that sounds more familiar to us. Genishi and Dyson suggest that teachers allow many opportunities for "ordinary talk" (p. 11)—using language that lets children ask questions, make observations, share experiences, and create stories that are meaningful and that engage children in further opportunities to learn language and more about their world.

It is important for future schooling and work for children to be skilled speakers of English. There also is value in speaking one or more other languages. Acknowledge, respect, and even learn if you can a child's second language or dialect. Encourage children to use both. In fact, this skill of moving from one language or dialect to another when the listener or situation requires it is one of the most essential language skills children can learn.

FOSTERING COMMUNICATION THROUGH CREATIVE-PLAY CURRICULUM

Children learn language to be able to communicate with peers and adults and to be able to learn about and talk about the world. Language is the way we connect with

the world and build our bridges to each other. Children have many opportunities to learn and experiment with language in a creative-play curriculum that fosters interactions and conversations, opportunities for creative language expression, and a climate of respect for children's attempts at communication.

Conversational Time

One of the most important components of a classroom that supports the development of language in young children is the availability of conversational time. Children need time to talk and to be heard; they need encouragement to practice listening attentively to others; they need frequent opportunities to converse with both adults and peers. Teachers must ensure that their conversational time is distributed among all children and recognize the differing levels of ability and language competence in children in their classroom. Teachers who really listen to children's needs, concerns, and ideas will individualize their time with children and make talking and interacting with children a priority throughout every day. Teachers who are too busy to listen attentively to a child will miss a great deal of insight into what is special, unique, and meaningful in that child's world.

Teachers can enrich opportunities for language learning by providing a variety of activities that promote peer interactions, such as cooking activities, dramatic play, and other small-group projects. Children need to be able to converse with each other in individual, small-group, and large-group settings. Teachers also enrich language learning when they ask a variety of open-ended questions that require a thinking response, rather than closed-ended questions that require only a yes or no answer. For example, a teacher who approaches a child's block structure and says, "I see you've worked hard on this building. Is it a house?" will usually receive limited

Teachers stimulate children's interest in language by providing a climate of respect for children's attempts to express themselves.

response from the child. On the other hand, a teacher who approaches the same block structure and says, "What a large structure you've built! Tell me about the building. How did you get those big blocks on top? What do you want it to be? Who lives there?" will likely have several lively minutes of interesting conversation with the child, during which the teacher will learn more about the child's world.

Teachers facilitate children's use of language and attempts to communicate when they model appropriate language use but do not overemphasize errors that young children typically make in language usage. In addition, providing a rich, stimulating classroom environment with many choices of play material and activities will give young children something important to talk about and will facilitate their conversations with peers and adults.

Playing with Language

Young children learn about language in a variety of ways. They learn by imitating adults, by listening to others, and by expressing themselves. In a creative-play setting, children learn about the appropriate uses of language and how to communicate effectively with others, but they also learn about the magic of language.

There are many activities teachers of young children can use to stimulate an interest in language and help children learn to use language in creative and unique ways. Choosing lyrical and poetic children's books can help provide a useful model for children and can help them become sensitive to the aesthetic quality of language. Storytelling and dramatization activities put children in touch with the magic of verbal and nonverbal language usage. Effective storytellers and dramatists use words, voice inflection, and body movements to convey the message of their story. Young children can become involved as storytellers and use books, tape recorders, puppets, flannel-board stories, masks, and costumes to enact stories for themselves and their peers.

Children also learn about the magic of language when they begin to play with language, making up silly words and simple rhymes and dictating stories from their own experiences. Providing a variety of props for dramatic play, puppets, art, and drawing and writing experiences will facilitate children's ability to engage spontaneously in activities involving language. A classroom climate that encourages children to experiment with words and create stories helps children not only to learn language and develop emergent literacy skills but also to get in touch with their intuitive and creative selves. Winnie-the-Pooh aptly describes the creative process involving his Hums: "Poetry and Hums aren't things which you get, they're things which get you. And

Children learn the magic of language through a variety of storytelling activities.

all you can do is to go where they can find you" (Milne, 1957, p. 285). Helping children listen to the words they carry inside themselves and to share the magic of language with others is a vital part of developing competence in both creativity and communication.

Language in Sociodramatic Play

Children who are encouraged to engage in dramatic play with one or more peers, called sociodramatic play, must use language to choose and announce a play theme, assign characters and their responsibilities, and distribute play materials and props. In negotiating roles and clarifying behavior, children rehearse communication skills. For example, consider this sociodramatic-play episode:

Jasmyn: I have too many blocks in my house.
Carmen: Here, put them in my truck.
Denzil: I'm a driver; I'll take them to Cumberland. They're building a new school. They can use them.
Jasmyn: Who will use them?

Carmen: But it's my truck, and I'm the driver.
Denzil: The builders. They are building a new school. I saw it yesterday when I went there. I'll drive the blocks to the people building there.
Carmen: You drive to the school; I'll drive back.
Denzil: OK, where do I go?
Carmen: Go to Neyland Drive. Follow the orange signs to the school. Drive slow or we'll crash in the river.

In order for their play to continue, children must communicate their ideas, clarify their instructions, and suggest mutually satisfying options. As children's play themes become more complex, their language also becomes more complex and supports their efforts at interacting and playing in groups.

Whole Language

A whole-language approach to literacy development supports the integration of reading, writing, and listening. Language learning occurs in meaningful play situations and in a context that is relevant to children's everyday lives. Language learning is activity-based and is integrated into all aspects of the classroom and the curriculum through:

- the provision of a print-rich environment using signs and labels for classroom areas, objects, and dramatic-play props
- the availability of children's literature, including big books, taped books and stories, and interactive electronic books
- the use of writing or journaling about ideas and experiences using child-dictated stories, invented spelling, and simple word-processing programs

In a whole-language approach to literacy development, the purposeful use of language is emphasized, rather than a drill-and-practice approach to learning specific literacy skills (Saracho, 1993).

Play provides the optimal environment for enhancing literacy development throughout the curriculum: children choose from a variety of books in a welcoming and comfortable book area; children have access to many materials for drawing and writing in a writing center; and children practice verbal and written language skills in dramatic play and other creative activities. Play experiences provide an invitation to talk, listen, and share ideas through peer interactions; the opportunity to explore books, print, and words in order to make sense of the world; and the encouragement to create personal writing and stories by valuing imagination and individual backgrounds (Williams & Davis, 1994).

GOALS AND ACTIVITIES FOR COMMUNICATION _____

This section includes specific goals for children's communication in the areas of (1) receptive language, (2) expressive language, (3) nonverbal communication, and (4) auditory memory/discrimination; sample activities for infants, toddlers, and preschoolers and adaptations for children with disabilities are also included.

Receptive Language

The first subdomain in the area of communication is the development of receptive language. Children develop receptive language as they listen to adults and peers and engage in classroom activities that enhance their understanding of language usage. Specific developmental goals in this subdomain include the following:

1. Help children develop the ability to listen to stories, songs, and the like.

2. Help children identify concepts through understanding of the labeling words.

3. Increase children's ability to respond to directional instructions.

4. Help children learn to react to each other's communication (Bryen & Gallagher, 1983, pp. 84–85).

The development of receptive language can best be fostered by giving children a multitude of opportunities to interact with adults and peers and participate in a variety of storytelling and dramatic-play activities. In addition, specific activities can be developed for each age group to foster the development of receptive language skills. Here are some suggested sample activities for infants, toddlers, and preschoolers that can be adapted for a variety of developmental needs.

INFANT ACTIVITY
Conversations (Quiet Game)

This activity is most appropriate for younger infants who are beginning to experiment with vocalizations. Place the infant in a face-up position on your lap to facilitate eye contact. Establish eye contact and converse with the baby. Talk about the infant's facial expression, clothing, and bright eyes. Take turns by giving the baby opportunities to "converse" also. Comment on the sound of the infant's voice, pitch, and variations in tone. Continue to include pauses, to encourage taking turns.

Additional Skills:

Communication (receptive language); socialization (social interaction)

Adaptations for Children with Disabilities:

Physically Impaired: None needed.

Speech/Language Impaired: Praise any attempts at vocalizations.

Visually Impaired: None needed.

Hearing Impaired: Use signs and/or gestures while talking.

Behavior Disordered/Emotionally Disturbed: None needed.

TODDLER ACTIVITY
I Know My Name (Quiet Game)

Take pictures of the children and put all of them in a photo album. Also take pictures of the staff members. Pass the album around to the children and ask them to pick out their own picture. After they have pointed to themselves in the album, ask them to say their name. En-

courage them to say their first and last names. Then ask the children to identify the teachers by their faces as well as to say their names. Encourage the children to speak clearly and distinctly when they are identifying the pictures.

Additional Skills:

Cognition (imitation/memory); communication (receptive language)

Adaptations for Children with Disabilities:

Physically Impaired: If the child cannot point with a finger, accept a "look" as a point. Ask the child to look at the picture. Provide physical assistance as needed.

Speech/Language Impaired: Provide verbal prompts as needed. For example, if the child's name is Bob, prompt him by saying "B" to encourage him to say "Bob." If he cannot tell his name with the first sound prompted, try "Bo." If he still is unable to say his name, prompt with "Bob" and encourage him to imitate it.

Visually Impaired: Attach a tactile cue to the picture of the child who is visually impaired. Cues could include a ribbon bow, the Braille name of the child, a geometric shape from construction paper, a "smelly" sticker, and so forth. Choose a cue that would relate to the child. For example, if the child is a girl who wears ribbons in her hair, choose a ribbon bow.

Hearing Impaired: Use the child's signed name. Have the other children create signs for their names. Encourage them to use these during the activity.

Behavior Disordered/Emotionally Disturbed: None needed.

PRESCHOOL ACTIVITY
Mixed-Up Murphy (Storytelling)

Tell the children you have a friend (a puppet) named Murphy who is always getting mixed up! Ask them to help Murphy by listening to some things Murphy did and then suggesting what Murphy should have done instead. The "stories" can be written on pieces of colored paper. Children take turns choosing a story and offering a solution. Examples of stories are, "One day, Murphy":

1. "wanted a hamburger, so he went to the doctor's office."
2. "wanted to buy shoes, so he went to the library."
3. "needed to buy Band-Aids, so he went to McDonald's."
4. "ran out of gas in his car, so he went to the drugstore."
5. "wanted to go swimming, so he put on his mittens and snow boots."
6. "wanted to listen to records, so he got out the paintbrushes."

Encourage children to think of several alternative solutions to help Murphy.

Additional Skills:

Cognition (problem solving/reasoning); communication (receptive language)

Adaptations for Children with Disabilities:

Physically Impaired: None needed.

Speech/Language Impaired: Use pictures as prompts to help the child create solutions.

Visually Impaired: None needed.

Hearing Impaired: Use pictures and signs to tell the stories.

Behavior Disordered/Emotionally Disturbed: None needed.

Expressive Language

The second subdomain in the area of communication is the development of expressive language. As children develop expressive language skills, they increase their ability to communicate with others, express their needs and desires, and influence the world around them. Specific developmental goals in this subdomain include the following:

1. Help children express needs, wants, and feelings verbally.
2. Encourage children to speak clearly and distinctly so they are easily understood.

3. Encourage the development of verbal fluency (Hendrick, 1998).
4. Help children understand that their communications can actively affect their physical and social environments (Bryen & Gallagher, 1983).

The development of expressive language skills is best facilitated in an open, responsive classroom environment where children have many opportunities to converse with adults and peers in individual and group situations. Here are some suggested sample activities for infants, toddlers, and preschoolers that can be adapted for a variety of developmental levels (an asterisk [*] denotes an activity that is also appropriate for use in the outdoor play environment).

INFANT ACTIVITY
Oh Where, Oh Where? (Music)*

Use the song, "Oh Where, Oh Where Has My Little Dog Gone?" to encourage infants' receptive language skills. Choose objects that the infants are familiar with: a beach ball, a set of keys, a banana. Show them to the infants, then place them away from the infant, out of reach. Sing:

> Oh where, oh where, can our beach ball be,
> Oh where, oh where can it be?
> It's big and round and bounces so high.
> Oh where, oh where, can it be?

Older infants can go to get the beach ball and younger infants can point or look toward the ball. Looking in the direction of the object shows understanding or knowledge of that particular object. Other verses include:

> Set of keys: "They cling and clang and shine so bright."
> Banana: "It's long and yellow and tastes so good."

Additional Skills:

Cognition (association/classification); personal awareness (independence)

Adaptations for Children with Disabilities:

Physically Impaired: None needed.

Speech/Language Impaired: Provide physical or verbal prompts as needed to help the child find the object named.

Visually Impaired: Encourage the child to feel the various objects. While the child explores the object by touching it, point out the differentiating features that help the child identify it.

Hearing Impaired: Use signs and/or gestures to sing the song and describe the activity.

Behavior Disordered/Emotionally Disturbed: None needed.

TODDLER ACTIVITY
A Stuffed Animal's House (Quiet Game)

Make a house for a stuffed animal out of a shoebox. Place the animal in the house. Ask the child specific questions that encourage the child to follow the teacher's direction and to begin to understand the concepts of *in, out, above, below, beside,* and so forth. As you ask the questions, the child needs to show the teacher where the animal belongs. For example, "Can you put the stuffed animal on top of the house?" "Can you put the stuffed animal beside the house?" "Can you take the stuffed animal out of the house?" "Can you put the stuffed animal in the house?" "Can you put the stuffed animal underneath the house?"

Additional Skills:

Cognition (concept formation and imitation/memory)

Adaptations for Children with Disabilities:

Physically Impaired: Choose a box big enough for the child to use successfully in this activity. Provide assistance as needed.

Speech/Language Impaired: Provide verbal and physical prompts as needed.

Visually Impaired: Encourage the child to feel the house with one hand and place the stuffed animal with the other hand. Use raised edges or cutouts on the house for doors, windows, and so forth.

Hearing Impaired: Use signs and/or gestures to describe the activity and make requests.

Behavior Disordered/Emotionally Disturbed: None needed.

PRESCHOOL ACTIVITY
Sound-Effects Stories (Storytelling)

Provide a variety of instruments (tone bells, jingle bells, step bells, rhythm sticks, drum, sand blocks, and the like) and ask the children to choose an instrument that would sound like the following:

an alarm clock

someone running downstairs

walking upstairs

brushing teeth

jumping out of bed

raindrops on the window

thunder

wristwatch

grandfather clock

Accept any instrument children choose; there are no wrong answers. Tell the following story and point to a child to make the sound when needed. After children are familiar with the idea, encourage them to help you make up new stories.

Sound-Effects Story:

Erika was sound asleep in her bed when all of a sudden something woke her up. She listened and she heard thunder. Then big raindrops splashed against the window. Erika loved to listen to the raindrops, especially when she was in her warm bed. "Maybe I can sleep some more," she thought, and just as she drifted off to sleep again the alarm clock

rang. Erika jumped out of bed. She was very hungry so she ran downstairs to the kitchen. After a big breakfast, she walked upstairs to the bathroom and brushed her teeth. She got dressed for school and walked downstairs. In the hallway, the grandfather clock said it was 8:00. She checked her wristwatch; it said 8:00, too. Time to go to school!

Additional Skills:

Communication (expressive language)

Adaptations for Children with Disabilities:

Physically Impaired: If the child has difficulty manipulating objects, tie the jingle bells on the child's wrist or ankle. Provide assistance to activate the bells as needed.

Speech/Language Impaired: None needed.

Visually Impaired: None needed.

Hearing Impaired: Use musical instruments that provide tactile input such as a drum, tambourine, and the like, so that the child can feel the vibrations when the instrument is activated. Use signs and/or gestures to explain the activity, how the musical instrument is to be used, and to tell the story.

Behavior Disordered/Emotionally Disturbed: None needed.

Nonverbal Communication

The third subdomain in the area of communication encompasses the process of nonverbal communication. Nonverbal communication is a powerful tool for expressing emotions and understanding others' feelings. Children learn to be effective total communicators when they can match their nonverbal and verbal messages. Specific developmental goals in this subdomain include the following:

1. Help children express feelings and emotions through facial expressions.
2. Help children express wants and needs through body/hand gestures.

3. Encourage children to establish eye contact when initiating interactions with others.
4. Help children learn to send nonverbal communicative signals that are congruent with verbal messages.

The development of nonverbal communication skills proceeds when children have a variety of opportunities to practice interactions with peers in the classroom setting. Young children who develop nonverbal communication techniques and then receive helpful and supportive feedback from others become more effective communicators. Here are some suggested sample activities for infants, toddlers, and preschoolers that can be adapted for a variety of developmental levels.

INFANT ACTIVITY
Hello/Good-Bye (Music)

To encourage the nonverbal communication skill of waving with infants, use the song "Hello/Good-Bye" (to the tune of "Good Night, Ladies"). Sing:

> "Hello, babies (wave to all babies),
> Hello, babies,
> Hello, babies,
> We're gonna have fun today!"

or

> "Good-bye, babies (wave to all babies),
> Good-bye, babies,
> Good-bye, babies,
> We've had a lot of fun!"

Encourage the infants to wave in response. Praise all attempts: "That's right, that's the way to wave to me!"

Additional Skills:

Cognition (imitation/memory); socialization (social interaction)

Adaptations for Children with Disabilities:

Physically Impaired: Physically help the child wave.

Speech/Language Impaired: Provide physical and verbal prompts as needed.

Visually Impaired: Wave the child's hand while singing the song. Praise the child for waving.

Hearing Impaired: Use signs and/or gestures while singing. Use physical prompts to encourage waving as needed.

Behavior Disordered/Emotionally Disturbed: None needed.

TODDLER ACTIVITY
What Do You Do When . . . ? (Active Game)

This is a gesture activity. Ask the children to act out various feelings without speaking. For instance, "What do you do when you are happy?" If the children need an example, show a smile or a jump for joy. Here are some other examples of feelings that the children can act out: angry—a frown or stomping feet; excited—clapping, smiling or raising hands up into the air; sad—wiping eyes or frowning; sleepy—yawning or rubbing eyes; happy—smiling, jumping, or laughing. Encourage the children to make up their own actions.

Additional Skills:

Socialization (respect for others)

Adaptations for Children with Disabilities:

Physically Impaired: None needed.

Speech/Language Impaired: None needed.

Visually Impaired: None needed.

Hearing Impaired: Use signs and/or gestures to explain the activity and ask the questions.

Behavior Disordered/Emotionally Disturbed: Provide additional encouragement for the child who has difficulty recognizing or expressing emotions.

PRESCHOOL ACTIVITY
How Do They Feel? (Storytelling)

Find examples of faces in magazines that express a variety of emotions (happy, sad, scared, angry). Mount the faces on index cards or construction paper. Children take turns choosing a card and identifying the emotion. Ask children to think about what could have happened to make the person feel that way. Encourage them to make up a story that would explain what happened. Have children give the person a name and tell where the person was, who the person was with, what happened (what the person saw or heard), and what the person did next.

Additional Skills:

Emotional well-being (awareness, acceptance, and expression of emotions); communication (expressive language)

Adaptations for Children with Disabilities:

Physically Impaired: None needed.

Speech/Language Impaired: If the child has limited expressive language skills, enhance the receptive skill of identifying the emotions named. Using the same pictures of faces on the cards, have the child identify one emotion from a choice of two. Another activity is for the child to "show" the group a happy, sad, or scared face.

Visually Impaired: Use pictures on index cards with various expressions made with yarn or glue for child to feel. Have the child feel the face of a peer who is making an expression.

Hearing Impaired: Use signs and/or gestures to describe the activity and name the emotions.

Behavior Disordered/Emotionally Disturbed: Provide prompts and additional encouragement for the child who has difficulty expressing or coping with feelings.

Auditory Memory/Discrimination

The fourth subdomain in the area of communication is the development of auditory memory and discrimination. Helping children to discriminate sounds, recall events, and send understandable messages is a complex process and a critical component of developing communication skills. Specific developmental goals in this subdomain include the following:

1. Teach children to discriminate between types/pitches/intensity of noises.
2. Encourage children to repeat and imitate rhythmic patterns.
3. Help children learn to deliver a complex verbal message.

4. Increase children's abilities to recall and reconstruct the sequencing and sentence structure of stories and events.

Developing auditory memory and discrimination is best accomplished in a classroom environment where children have many opportunities to converse with others and become involved in activities such as storytelling, music, and dramatic play. Here are some suggested sample activities for infants, toddlers, and preschoolers that can be adapted for a variety of developmental levels (an asterisk [*] denotes an activity that is also appropriate for use in the outdoor play environment).

INFANT ACTIVITY
Band Concert (Music)*

Collect a variety of metal pots and pans, plastic bowls, metal spoons, and wooden spoons. Encourage infants to bang metal pots and pans with a metal spoon, bang metal pots and pans with a wooden spoon, and bang plastic bowls with metal and wooden spoons. The infants can be encouraged to swap utensils and they should be praised for sharing. Teacher can talk about the different sounds: "clink-clink," "clunk-clunk," "dump-dump," "dimp-dimp." Teachers can emphasize listening to the sounds.

Additional Skills:

Socialization (social interaction, cooperation); perceptual motor (eye-hand coordination, body management and control)

Adaptations for Children with Disabilities:

Physically Impaired: Provide physical assistance for banging with the spoon.

Speech/Language Impaired: None needed.

Visually Impaired: None needed.

Hearing Impaired: Use signs and/or gestures to explain the activity. Encourage the child to feel the pan with one hand and bang with the other in order to feel the vibrations.

Behavior Disordered/Emotionally Disturbed: None needed.

TODDLER ACTIVITY
Silly Words (Quiet Game)

This activity will help the children to listen carefully to a simple story and to stop the teacher when a silly word is used instead of the correct word. Read a simple story and throughout the story use a word that obviously does not fit into the context. For instance, "This is a story about a boy and his dog. One day, Billy was walking with his dog, Rover. They were walking through the grass and the dog said, 'Moo.'" At this point, say, "That's silly! What kind of sound does a dog really make?" Stories that are familiar to a child can be used for this activity so that the child easily can pick out the word that does not belong.

Additional Skills:

Communication (receptive language); cognition (imitation/memory)

Adaptations for Children with Disabilities:

Physically Impaired: None needed.

Speech/Language Impaired: None needed.

Visually Impaired: None needed.

Hearing Impaired: Use signs and/or gestures to explain the activity and tell the stories. Initially, use stories that are very familiar to the child and use the silly words for very concrete concepts/objects.

Behavior Disordered/Emotionally Disturbed: None needed.

PRESCHOOL ACTIVITY
Computer Storytelling (Storytelling)

Introduce an interactive CD-ROM storybook to the children (for example, *Just Grandma and Me* from the Living Books series). Encourage children to listen to and interact with the animated, interactive story. Extend the activity to include children's participation by providing props such as a beach ball, sand bucket, and beach towel for children to dramatize part of the story.

Additional Skills:

Communication (receptive and expressive language); socialization (cooperation); cognition (imitation/memory)

Adaptations for Children with Disabilities:

Physically Impaired: Provide assistive technology such as touch screens and pressure switches to facilitate use of the computer.

Speech/Language Impaired: If the child has limited expressive language skills, ask the child to point to the picture on the computer screen. If the child is developmentally ready to name the characters, use the pictures on the screen as prompts. Use assistive technology such as eye-gaze control devices if needed.

Visually Impaired: Use assistive technology such as screen magnifiers or speech synthesizers and digitizers to facilitate use of the computer.

Hearing Impaired: Use signs and/or gestures to tell the story and encourage participation.

Behavior Disordered/Emotionally Disturbed: None needed.

CHAPTER SUMMARY _____

Children who learn to use language appropriately and creatively are embarking on a lifetime of joy playing with and effectively using words. In a creative-play classroom environment, young children can learn to communicate effectively with peers and adults as well as learn to use language in order to share ideas, feelings, and scenarios through stories and dramatic play.

■ ■ ■ ■ ■ ■ ■ ■ ■

The development of language skills is critical for children to achieve success in interpersonal relationships, complete cognitive tasks, and develop a positive sense of self. Children like Trey, who are slow to develop language, are at a serious disadvantage with peers and adults in a classroom situation.

Comprehensive diagnostic testing of Trey determines that there is no physical reason for the language delay. You realize, however, that Trey probably has not started talking because his parents and older siblings have been meeting all his needs so quickly and thoroughly that he really has not had a need to talk. The teachers at school also have learned to "read" Trey and respond to him without his needing to talk. Understanding the problem helps you and Trey's parents to develop strategies for supporting Trey's language development:

• Gradually begin to require Trey to ask for what he wants. Say you do not understand and ask him to tell you, even using one word if necessary in the initial stages. Give Trey encouragement and praise for using two-word sentences.

• Give Trey many opportunities to practice his language skills by talking, sharing, dictating experience stories, and describing events. As Trey begins to use multiple-word sentences, praise him and involve him in higher-level language activities.

• Encourage Trey to interact more with his peers. Make sure there is ample conversational time between Trey and his peers as well as with his teachers.

• Provide a variety of books, storytelling props, dramatic-play props, and music activities to get Trey involved in feeling the magic of language and motivate him to more creative language usage.

• Help Trey to feel confident about his newly emerging language and communication skills. Enhance his self-image by helping him have increased success in social relationships and cognitive activities.

■ ■ ■ ■ ■ ■ ■ ■ ■

DISCUSSION QUESTIONS _____

1. Discuss the vignette at the beginning of the chapter. What other questions or concerns might you have? Discuss the vignette at the end of the chapter. Are there other responses you might have to this situation?

2. Describe children's language behaviors in the prespeech and speech stages.

3. Explain and give examples of telegraphic combinations.

4. How can adults promote better language skills in children?

5. Discuss the issue of egocentrism in children's communication.

6. Describe the development of children's emergent literacy skills.

7. What early childhood program features promote children's language development?

8. Describe ways in which conversational time in the classroom can enhance children's language development.

9. Describe examples of teacher questions and comments in response to a child saying, "Look at this bug!" that will more likely foster a dialogue than a simple yes or no response.

10. Describe ways that children's language development is fostered through sociodramatic play.

11. Describe the four subdomains of development in communication.

REFERENCES _____

Acredolo, L., & Goodwyn, S. (1988). Symbolic gesturing in normal infants. *Child Development, 59,* 450–466.

Bryen, D., & Gallagher, D. (1983). Assessment of language and communication. In J. Paget & B. Bracken (Eds.), *The psychoeducational assessment of preschool children* (pp. 81–144). New York: Harcourt Brace Jovanovich.

Fillmore, L. (1991). When learning a second language means losing the first. *Early Childhood Research Quarterly, 6,* 323–346.

Furrow, D., Nelson, K., & Benedict, H. (1979). Mothers' speech to children and syntactic development: Some simple relationships. *Journal of Child Language, 6,* 423–442.

Garcia, E. (1986). Bilingual development and the education of bilingual children during early childhood. *American Journal of Education, 11,* 96–121.

Genishi, C., & Dyson, A. (1984, Winter). Ways of talking: Respecting differences. *Beginnings,* pp. 7–11.

Golden, M., Rosenbluth, L., Grossi, M., Policare, H., Freeman, H., & Brownlee, M. (1978). *The New York City infant day care study.* New York: Medical and Health Research Association of New York City.

Griffing, P. (1980). The relationship between socioeconomic status and sociodramatic play among black kindergarten children. *Genetic Psychology Monographs, 101,* 3–34.

Guralnick, M., & Paul-Brown, D. (1977). The nature of verbal interactions among handicapped and nonhandicapped preschool children. *Child Development, 48,* 254–260.

Hendrick, J. (1998). *Total learning: Developmental curriculum for the young child* (5th ed.). Columbus, OH: Merrill/Prentice-Hall.

Juel, C. (1991). Beginning reading. In R. Barr, M. Kamil, P. Mosenthal, & P. Pearson (Eds.), *Handbook of reading research,* (Vol. 2, pp. 759–788). New York: Longman.

Kaye, K. (1982). *The mental and social life of babies.* Chicago: University of Chicago Press.

Kontos, S. (1986). What preschool children know about reading and how they learn it. *Young Children, 42*(1), 58–66.

LeFrancois, G. (1995). *Of children.* Belmont, CA: Wadsworth.

Martinez, M., & Teale, W. (1988). Reading in a kindergarten classroom library. *The Reading Teacher, 41,* 568–573.

Mason, J. (1981). *Prereading: A developmental perspective.* Urbana, IL: University of Illinois, Center for the Study of Reading.

Mason, J. (1985). Cognitive monitoring and early reading: A proposed model. In D. Forrest-Presley, G. MacKinnon, & T. Waller (Eds.), *Metacognition, cognition, and human performance* (pp. 77–101). Orlando, FL: Academic Press.

McCartney, K. (1984). The effect of quality of day care environment upon children's language development. *Developmental Psychology, 20,* 244–260.

Milne, A. A. (1957). *The world of Pooh: The complete Winnie-the-Pooh and the House at Pooh corner.* New York: Dutton.

Morrow, L. (1988). Young children's responses to one-to-one story readings in school settings. *Reading Research Quarterly, 23,* 89–107.

Morrow, L., & Rand, M. (1991). Promoting literacy during play by designing early childhood classroom environments. *The Reading Teacher, 44,* 396–402.

Nelson, K. (1973) Structure and strategy in learning to talk. *Monographs of the Society for Research in Child Development, 38* (Serial No. 162).

Pellegrini, A. (1986). Communicating in and about play: The effect of play centers on preschoolers' explicit language. In G. Fein & M. Rivkin (Eds.), *The young child at play* (pp. 79–91). Washington, DC: National Association for the Education of Young Children.

Phillips, D., Scarr, S., & McCartney, K. (1987). Child care quality and children's social development. *Developmental Psychology, 23,* 537–543.

Piaget, J., & Inhelder, B. (1969) *The psychology of the child.* New York: Basic Books.

Reid, K., & Twardosz, S. (1996). Use of culturally diverse books in daycare. *Early Education and Development, 7*(4), 319–348.

Rogers, D., Perrin, M., & Waller, C. (1987). Enhancing the development of language and thought through conversations with young children. *Journal of Research in Childhood Education, 2*(1), 17–29.

Salinger, T. S. (1996). *Literacy for young children* (2nd ed.). Englewood Cliffs, NJ: Prentice-Hall.

Saracho, O. (1993). Literacy development: The whole language approach. In B. Spodek & O. Saracho (Eds.), *Language and literacy in early childhood education* (pp. 42–59). New York: Teachers College Press.

Schickedanz, J. A. (1986). *More than the ABCs: The early stages of reading and writing.* Washington, DC: National Association for the Education of Young Children.

Shatz, M., & Gelman, R. (1973). The development of communication skills: Modifications in the speech of young children as a function of listener. *Monographs of the Society for Research in Child Development, 38* (Serial No. 152).

Smith, M. (1941). Measurement of the size of general English vocabulary through the elementary grades and high school. *Genetic Psychology Monographs, 24,* 311–345.

Sodian, B. (1988). Children's attribution of knowledge to the listener in a referential communication task. *Child Development, 59,* 378–385.

Soto, L. (1991). Understanding bilingual/bicultural young children. *Young Children, 46*(2), 30–36.

Spodek, B., & Saracho, O. (1993). Language and literacy programs in early childhood education: A look to the future. In B. Spodek & O. Saracho (Eds.), *Language and literacy in early childhood education* (pp. 196–200). New York: Teachers College Press.

Thompkins, G. (1997). *Literacy for the 21st century: A balanced approach.* Upper Saddle River, NJ: Prentice-Hall.

Vygotsky, L. (1962). *Thought and language* (E. Hanfmann & G. Vakar, Trans.). Cambridge, MA: MIT Press.

Williams, R., & Davis, J. (1994). Lead sprightly into literacy. *Young Children, 49*(4), 37–41.

Wood, B. (1981). *Children and communication: Verbal and nonverbal language development.* Englewood Cliffs, NJ: Prentice-Hall.

Yaden, D. (1988). Understanding stories through repeated read-alouds: How many does it take? *The Reading Teacher, 41,* 556–566.

ADDITIONAL RESOURCES _____

Buchoff, R. (1994). Joyful voices: Facilitating language growth through the rhythmic response to chants. *Young Children, 49*(4), 26–30.

Catron, C. E., & Parks, B. C. (1986). *Super storytelling.* Minneapolis, MN: Denison.

Cazden, C. (Ed.). (1981). *Language in early childhood education.* Washington, DC: National Association for the Education of Young Children.

Dyson, A., & Genishi, C. (1993). Visions of children as language users: Language and language education in early childhood. In B. Spodek (Ed.), *Handbook of research on the education of young children* (pp. 122–136). New York: Macmillan.

Galda, L., Cullinan, B., & Strickland, D. (1993). *Language, literacy and the child.* Fort Worth, TX: Harcourt Brace Jovanovich.

Garrard, K. R. (1987). Helping young children develop mature speech patterns. *Young Children, 42*(3), 16–21.

Garvey, C. (1979). Communication controls in social play. In B. Sutton-Smith (Ed.), *Play and learning* (pp. 109–125). New York: Gardner.

Genishi, C. (1988). Children's language: Learning words from experience. *Young Children, 44*(1), 16–23.

Genishi, C., Dyson, A., & Fassler, R. (1994). Language and diversity in early childhood: Whose voices are appropriate? In B. Mallory & R. New (Eds.), *Diversity and developmentally appropriate practices* (pp. 250–268). New York: Teachers College Press.

Goodman, Y. (Ed.). (1990). *How children construct literacy: Piagetian perspectives.* Newark, DE: International Reading Association.

Gullo, D. (1988). Guidelines for facilitating language development. *Day Care and Early Education, 16*(2), 10–14.

Han, E. (1991). "You be the baby bear": Story reenactments by young children. *Dimensions, 19*(2), 14–17.

Holmes, J. (1993). Teachers, parents, and children as writing role models. *Dimensions, 21*(3), 12–14.

Honig, A. (1989). Talk, read, joke, make friends: Language power for children. *Day Care and Early Education, 16*(4), 14–17.

Ishee, N., & Goldhaber, J. (1990). Story re-enactment: Let the play begin! *Young Children, 45*(3), 71–75.

Jalongo, M. (1996). Teaching young children to become better listeners. *Young Children, 51*(2), 21–26.

Lamme, L. & McKinley, L. (1992). Creating a caring classroom with children's literature. *Young Children, 48*(1), 65–71.

Manning, M., Manning, G., & Kamii, C. (1988). Early phonics instruction: Its effect on literacy development. *Young Children, 44*(1), 4–8.

Mason, J., & Sinha, S. (1993). Emerging literacy in the early childhood years: Applying a Vygotskian model of learning and development. In B. Spodek (Ed.), *Handbook of research on the education of young children* (pp. 137–150). New York: Macmillan.

McClune, L. (1985). Play-language relationships and symbolic development. In C. C. Brown & A. W. Gottfried (Eds.), *Play interactions: The role of toys and parental involvement in children's development* (pp. 38–45). Skillman, NJ: Johnson & Johnson.

Mills, H., & Clyde, J. (1991). Children's success as readers and writers: It's the teacher's beliefs that make the difference. *Young Children, 46*(2), 54–59.

Neugebauer, B. (1992). Reflecting diversity: Books to read with young children. In B. Neugebauer (Ed.), *Alike and different* (pp. 163–174). Washington, DC: National Association for the Education of Young Children.

Pellegrini, A. D. (1984). Children's play and language. In A. D. Pellegrini (Eds.), *Child's play and play therapy* (pp. 45–58). Lancaster, PA: Technomic.

Perlmutter, J., & Laminack, L. (1993). Sociodramatic play: A stage for practicing literacy. *Dimensions, 21*(4), 13–16, 31.

Sachs, J. (1980). The role of adult-child play in language development. In K. H. Rubin (Ed.), *New directions for child development: Children's play* (pp. 33–48). San Francisco: Jossey-Bass.

Schirrmacher, R. (1986). Talking with young children about their art. *Young Children, 41*(5), 3–7.

Stone, J. (1993). Caregiver and teacher language—Responsive or restrictive. *Young Children, 48*(4), 12–18.

Teale, W., & Martinez, M. (1988). Getting on the right road to reading: Bringing books and young children together in the classroom. *Young Children, 44*(1), 10–15.

Trawick-Smith, J. (1988). Some mysteries about child language learning. *Day Care and Early Education, 16*(2), 6–9.

Trawick-Smith, J. (1994). Authentic dialogue with children. *Dimensions, 22*(4), 9–16.

Trelease, J. (1993). The dos and don'ts of read-aloud. *Dimensions, 21*(3), 17–20, 39–40.

Walton, S. (1989). Katy learns to read and write. *Young Children, 44*(5), 52–57.

Waring-Chaffee, M. (1994). "RDRNT . . . HRIKM" ("Ready or not, Here I come!") Investigations in children's emergence as readers and writers. *Young Children, 49*(6), 52–55

Watkins, R., & Bunce, B. (1996). Natural literacy: Theory and practice for preschool intervention programs. *Topics in Early Childhood Special Education, 16*(2), 191–212.

Weed, J. (1991). Living daily in a whole language classroom. In Y. Goodman, W. Hood, & K. Goodman (Eds.), *Organizing for whole language* (pp. 84–94). Portsmouth, NH: Heinemann.

Wolter, D. (1992). Whole group story reading? *Young Children, 48*(1), 72–75.

Wood, D., Hough, R. A., & Nurss, J. R. (1987). Tell me a story: Making opportunities for elaborated language in early childhood classrooms. *Young Children, 43*(1), 6–12.

15.

Curriculum for Developing Cognition

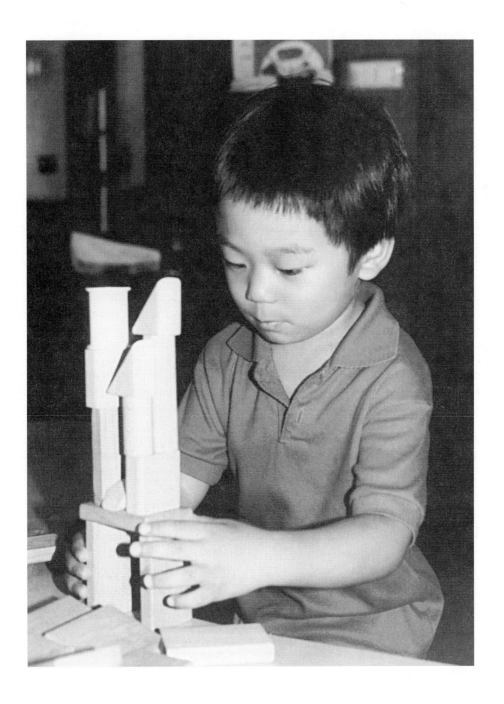

As a preschool teacher in a public school, you are very aware of how young children learn about and think about themselves, others, and their environment. You have organized your classroom so that children have many opportunities to actively explore the environment through a variety of manipulative and sensory activities, and you encourage children's involvement in problem solving and generating alternative ideas and solutions.

Upon entering the teachers' lounge after school one day, you encounter one of your colleagues, a kindergarten teacher, who is extremely frustrated because some of the children in her classroom seem incapable of successfully completing workbook and worksheet assignments. The teacher is complaining vehemently about how unprepared these children are for kindergarten work. You are very concerned about the teacher's remarks, and at home that evening you consider the following questions:

• How can you tactfully communicate to the kindergarten teacher that most of these children were very successful in

preschool and that the different teaching strategies from preschool to kindergarten might be partially responsible for the problem?

• Is there a way you can help the kindergarten teacher to recognize that 5-year-olds continue to need involvement with active manipulation of materials and exploration of the environment to learn effectively?

• Can you convince the kindergarten teacher that there is value in providing opportunities for children in her classroom to learn through play and exploration?

• Will you be able to help this teacher focus on teaching practices and classroom curriculum rather than on the difficulties with "problem children"?

• What might be done in your school to close the gap between the developmental hands-on preschool program and the academically oriented, paper-and-pencil kindergarten program?

Suggestions for responding to this classroom vignette will be shared at the end of the chapter.

When reading this chapter, focus on understanding the developmental milestones in the domain of cognition and the ways to foster young children's cognitive development. Also, become aware of the important role of play in the enhancement of children's learning about objects, other people, and the environment.

The development of cognition involves the process of growth in children's ways of thinking about and interacting with their environment. Young children initially learn about the world through active physical exploration and then gradually develop the ability to think symbolically and logically about their experiences. Children are curious explorers, and their cog-

nitive development involves learning new concepts and testing a variety of ideas. To facilitate young children's growth in the domain of cognition, it is important to review the milestones in children's cognitive development and consider teacher attitudes as well as curricular activities that foster the development of thinking, reasoning, and problem-solving skills.

DEVELOPMENTAL MILESTONES IN COGNITIVE DEVELOPMENT

Any discussion of cognitive development milestones is based on Piaget's description of children's development through sequential stages of cognitive activity

Activities were written by Kathy Carlson, Amy R. Kerlin, and Anne Miller Stott; adaptations were written by Bobbie Beckmann.

(Piaget & Inhelder, 1969). The first stage is the period of *sensorimotor* development, which lasts from birth to 18–24 months. In this stage, which Piaget divided into six substages, infants learn about their environment by their motor actions on the objects in the environment and the sensory experiences provided by the objects. In the first month, infants' involuntary or reflex actions are important physical movements that are repeated individually. More complex, coordinated movements involving two or more actions occur around 3 to 5 months. For example, infants first look at an object and may repeat this looking without additional actions or movements. This first substage Piaget labeled *exercising reflexes*.

Also in these first few months, in the *primary circular reactions* substage, infants discover that certain actions (for example, thumb-sucking) are pleasurable, and the infant repeats these. Beginning at 4 months, the *secondary circular reactions* substage, infants' actions extend beyond the self to objects, and actions that bring interesting sights or sounds from these objects are repeated by the infant (for example, when touching a mobile creates a musical sound, the infant will repeatedly touch the mobile).

Beginning at 8 months, in the *purposeful coordination* substage, infants combine actions, such as looking at and then reaching for an object. Parents, teachers, and others are recognized now as children distinguish the familiar from the unfamiliar; separation anxiety and stranger anxiety now may occur as children realize that a familiar person is leaving or that an unfamiliar person is nearby. Children also can now anticipate events—being dressed in a jacket signals a trip outside, jangling keys means someone is leaving in the car. This is an early understanding of causality and sequence, that one event or action leads to another.

Beginning at 12 months, in the *tertiary circular reactions* substage, children repeat earlier actions with intention and experimentation. They make deliberate changes in vocalizations or behavior in order to observe the outcome. For example, infants may repeat a "word," changing the vowel sound in it each time. By 18 months, in the *mental representation* substage, children begin to internalize, or think about, behavior so that its outcome can be considered without the actual behavior being performed. For example, a child may consider how to best make an escape from a playpen or crib before attempting it. This consideration can be noted as the child visually surveys either of several escape routes and leans over each side to assess potential falling distance. Children between 18 and 24 months are in transition to Piaget's second stage of cognitive development, the preoperational stage, lasting from ages 2 to 7. According to Piaget, logical thinking is an operation; therefore, the preschool child whose thinking lacks logic is using preoperational, or prelogical, thinking. There are two substages: the preconceptual and the intuitive.

In the first substage, from ages 2 to 4, children's thinking is characterized by transductive and syncretic reasoning. *Transductive* reasoning is based on developing a specific conclusion from a specific observation. This contrasts with the deductive reasoning and inductive reasoning used by other children and adults. Transductive reasoning often leads to inaccurate conclusions, such as "fish swim; Daddy swims; Daddy is a fish." *Syncretic* reasoning, also characteristic of the first substage, is the use of unclear and changing rules of classification. A 3-year-old might group the same collection of objects based on color, then switch to shape, then group by size.

By age 4, children begin to use intuitive thinking, or thought based on the child's perception and comprehension rather than logic. For example, Piaget developed a cognitive task in which children watch three different-colored beads on a string being inserted into a cardboard tube. The tube is held vertically and then turned one-half, one, or two rotations. At each turn, children are asked which color bead is on top. As long as children can mentally represent the rotations and the resulting position of the beads, they can correctly identify which color is on top. But children at this stage cannot arrive at a logical rule to explain why the yellow bead is on top with each even-numbered rotation, and the blue bead is on top with each odd-numbered rotation.

Although this description may appear to emphasize the limitations of preoperational thinking, children in the preoperational stage have reached the milestone of being capable of representational thought. Children's knowledge of the world comes not just from the result of their actions on objects, as in the sensorimotor stage, but from their thinking about objects and actions. Thus, children are able to develop concepts as they think about objects and classify related characteristics of those objects.

Piaget also described two additional stages that reflect children's cognitive development beyond the preschool years. The third stage, called the *concrete operations* stage, begins at about age 7 and lasts until age 11 or 12. In this stage, children understand logical classification schemes and number concepts; they are able to conserve—that is, to know that a change in appearance of a substance does not necessarily equate to a change in mass, size, volume, weight, or number. For example, in a classic Piagetian task, a preoperational child who acknowledges that two balls of clay are equivalent will change her opinion when one ball is rolled out into a snake or rope and appears to be larger. The older child in the concrete operations stage understands that the long coil of clay only appears to look larger and that the operation can be reversed by rolling the clay back into a ball, thus proving the equivalency of the two.

In the fourth stage, the *formal operations* stage, which begins around age 12, children can use deductive reasoning and propositional thought to ponder complex abstract and hypothetical situations.

As children progress through these stages, they learn about their physical and social world through a process Piaget labeled *adaptation*. All learning occurs as children discover new information that creates dissonance or confusion. Children then adapt to this new object or idea using either assimilation or accommodation. To assimilate, children consider and use what they already know and introduce the new information into an existing pattern, a way of thinking or acting, or a *scheme*, as Piaget labeled it. If the new object or idea is so different from existing knowledge that it cannot be assimilated into an existing scheme, then the child's pattern of thinking or acting must be changed to incorporate the new information.

Before most infants are 8 to 12 months old, they operate on the principle of "out of sight, out of mind." For example, if a ball rolls behind another object, an infant may fail to realize that the object exists once it is hidden. When a child can imagine or mentally represent an object, the child will then look for a hidden object. This object concept—the knowledge that an object has an identity and permanence—is an important milestone in cognitive development. It signifies that a child can internalize symbols (the spoken or written word *ball* or a picture of a ball)—that is, mentally consider them without requiring the physical presence of the object itself. When an infant realizes that a ball hidden under a blanket has not gone away, but that it is simply out of sight and can be retrieved, the infant must accommodate his or her thinking about hidden objects: "An object that moves from my line of vision does not cease to exist." Prior to this time, when a person or an object was no longer visible to the child, the information was assimilated into an existing pattern of thought or scheme of "All gone." This process of adaptation involves continually assimilating, or using existing knowledge and behavior, and accommodating, or changing existing knowledge and behavior, throughout life. According to Piaget, all learning occurs through these two complementary processes.

Other theorists have also offered descriptions of children's cognitive development. A contemporary of Piaget was Lev Vygotsky (1896–1934). He had a brief career as a psychologist in the Soviet Union, but his books and articles were not translated into English until the 1960s and 1970s. Vygotsky "was the chief architect of Soviet developmental psychology in the early years of the Communist regime" (Thomas, 1996, p. 320), and his theory offers insight into children's thought and language development. Just as Piaget described intellectual development in four major stages, Vygotsky identified a hierarchy of three major stages in children's thinking: (1) thinking in unorganized groups, (2) thinking in complexes, and (3) thinking in concepts, which is adultlike cognition that occurs in early adolescence. Vygotsky emphasized a socioinstructional process in which children learn by sharing problem-solving experiences with a teacher, parent, or peer (Belmont, 1989). He also emphasized the role of language in cognitive development. As children develop, the once separate functions of speech and thought begin to overlap. Rather than adult speech directing a child's behavior, the child's own internal language becomes the primary means for intellectual adaptation and development (Vygotsky, 1962).

Social learning theory also has been used to explain children's thinking. A major proponent of this view, known as social cognitive learning, is Albert Bandura. Social learning theorists disagree with the traditional behavioristic explanation for children's learning, which focuses only on the observable stimulus-response model. Instead, social learning theorists view children as more active in their learning. Children observe, model, and imitate what they see and hear. Important cognitive functions include paying attention, memory coding, memory permanence, motor actions, and motivation. According to social learning theorists, consequences (reward or punishment) do not automatically reinforce and result in certain behaviors; instead, consequences that children either observe or experience are sources of information for children to use in determining their actions (Bandura, 1969, 1977). Thus, social learning theory explains more effectively the complex behaviors that result from children's cognition or thinking.

More recently, children's cognition has been explained by the information-processing theory. This framework implies no developmental dimension to cognition—that is, people of all ages learn in the same way—and compares thought to a computer operation involving the senses, several types of memory, and behavioral output (Thomas, 1996). Sternberg's triarchic theory of intelligence is an example of an information-processing explanation of cognition (Sternberg, 1985). Another explanation is Gardner's (1983) proposition of the existence of at least six distinct human intelligences—linguistic, spatial, logical-mathematical, musical, bodily-kinesthetic, and personal. Sternberg's and Gardner's models address children's cognition less directly than Piaget's cognitive-development framework; however, they have gained wider acceptance for explaining children's cognitive development.

RESEARCH ON COGNITIVE DEVELOPMENT _____

A great deal of research in children's cognitive development has focused on children's egocentrism, a characteristic that limits children's ability to consider the perspective of another person, particularly when it differs from their own. Piaget found evidence of children's egocentrism in their thinking, language, and social interactions. A 3-year-old child who had witnessed a novel event would describe it to an adult unfamiliar with the event as if the adult had witnessed it also and had the pertinent information to understand an abridged or incomplete description. A 4-year-old sitting on one side of a block arrangement or pattern, when asked to describe a view of the blocks from the perspective of another child seated on the other side, would have difficulty taking the physical perspective of another person.

Researchers have found that children are not always as egocentric as Piaget described. For example, a group of 4-year-olds were asked to place a doll behind a partitioned screen so that it would be hidden from two police officers who were chasing it. To be successful, as most of the 4-year-olds were, the children had to consider the perspective of both police figures. The conclusion drawn to explain the children's success was that a game of chase is very familiar, and perhaps more motivating in the research task, to preschoolers (Donaldson, 1978). In another study, preschool children more accurately described a drawing to a person who was blindfolded than to a person also looking at the drawing. The blindfold functioned as a reminder to the child to consider the differences in perspective or knowledge between the child and the listener and to adjust the verbal explanation (Maratsos, 1973). The research suggests that preschoolers are sometimes limited by their egocentrism; however, efforts to reduce its influence on children's thinking often are effective, and children are more sensitive to differing perspectives than originally believed.

Researchers studying children's cognition have examined children's memory as a component of thinking and learning. Young children differ very little from adults in their short-term sensory memory, or the ability to use visual, auditory, or tactile perception to register a cognitive impression. Children also are similar to adults in their short-term memory, which is the ability to recall information such as words or numbers for a few seconds. Young children do differ, however, from older children and adults in their long-term memory, or the ability to recall information minutes, days, weeks, or years later (Flavell, 1970). Younger children do not rehearse and organize information well enough to facilitate its recall.

Asking children to think of a way to help them remember is somewhat effective; it signals to the child that remembering is important. Suggesting strategies to help the child to organize and recall, such as "think of all the blue things, then the red things, then the yellow things" is another way children's memory is enhanced.

Teachers of young children should be aware of the cultural influences on children's development that result in different cognitive and learning styles. In a review of relevant literature on the topic, Hale-Benson (1981) identified important teaching and learning issues for culturally sensitive programs. Most schools require children to use an analytical approach to learning, characterized by a long attention span, an objective attitude, and thinking that is stimulus-centered or object-centered and parts-specific, that is, examining and analyzing components of the whole. Many children, however, function with a relational style of learning, characterized by a short attention span, contextual and colorful language, nonverbal communication, personification, global thinking, and a more emotional, affective style of relating to peers and adults (Cohen, 1971; Hilliard, 1976). Teachers must better understand relational and other learning styles to structure experiences and interactions in the classroom for children with varying cognitive styles.

Children's cognition develops in and reflects the economic, family, and cultural context in which the children live (Rogoff, 1990). The assessment of children's cognition must also reflect an understanding of these cultural influences. In some cultures, adults do not ask children "known-answer" questions, or questions whose answers are already known by the adult. So in testing and assessment situations, children may give an answer that reflects the riddle or joke they think the question to be. Or, if answering the question would make it appear that the child knows more than the teacher, the child may not give the expected or correct answer (Rogoff & Mistry, 1985). Children's learning and cognitive development cannot be separated from the culture in which they occur. Teachers must support all children in their learning, and parents in their child-rearing practices, that reflect their family and cultural values.

Recent research focusing on young children's cognition and brain development has created a flurry of interest in children's experiences in the earliest years of life. On April 17, 1997, President and Mrs. Clinton hosted the White House Conference on Early Childhood Development and Learning: What New Research on the Brain Tells Us About Our Youngest Children.

Researchers, including those from neurobiology and child development, presented new findings on brain development that affirmed the importance of responsive, sensitive, and developmentally appropriate experiences and social interaction for young children. The new findings clarify ways in which children learn and the role that children's environments, relationships, and stressors play in enhancing or inhibiting brain development and learning. Information travels through the brain on neurons and synapses, or connections between the brain cells, that act as pathways in the brain. As teachers and the environment provide stimulation—through play, language, response, and reaction to the child, the neural pathways grow and strengthen. The synapses or pathways that are used become permanent; those that are unused are lost. The more pathways there are, then the more, and the more

easily, children can learn. Babies who are played with, held, and touched more often as infants develop more neural pathways than babies who receive less attention. Children's brains also react to physical and emotional trauma in the early years. Cortisol, a steroid hormone released by the body in response to stress, eliminates brain cells and the neural pathways in the brain through which information is processed. Children who receive warm, sensitive, and responsive attention from adults and who have strong emotional attachments have lower levels of cortisol in their brains. Other children, without this emotional bond and appropriate caregiving, suffer impaired cognitive capability as well as difficulty in developing effective coping strategies (Gunnar, Broderson, Krueger, & Rigatuso, 1996; Families and Work Institute, 1996; Leister-Willis, 1997; Newberger, 1997).

FOSTERING COGNITIVE DEVELOPMENT THROUGH CREATIVE PLAY CURRICULUM _____

What appears to be "just" play—that is, actively exploring and manipulating objects—is the means by which young children learn in the sensorimotor and preoperational stages of development. Play is the most important activity for children's cognitive growth. To learn, children must construct knowledge by exploring, experimenting, and discovering.

Young children's cognitive abilities are energized and expanded through a creative-play environment. Through play, children acquire answers to their questions about the world, test new ideas and concepts, practice problem-solving and reasoning skills, and develop a sense of delight in the process of learning.

Expanding Children's Curiosity

Young children are curious, and they ask hard questions. Infants and toddlers learn about the world by active exploration; preschoolers frequently ask "Why" and "How come?" Young children need teachers who listen to them and help them find answers to their difficult, thought-provoking, and essential questions about the meaning of life and death. A 3-year-old asked: "Did you know that when you have a flashlight in bed with you at night the robbers won't come? Why do robbers come?" Another preschooler asked: "Did you know that when people die God makes a whole lot of new ones? Where do they come from?"

These are important, serious questions to young children. An early childhood educator who expects to

follow a teaching manual or a lesson-planning guide to teach young children will have many surprises. Young children are just as likely to ask a question about the cosmos as they are to ask why blue and yellow paint mixed together make green. Teachers do not need to know all the answers to children's questions but must appreciate their inquiring minds and spirits and be prepared to help children become involved in a learning process to find the answers they seek. Teachers of young children must be intelligent, knowledgeable, sensitive, curious, and respectful of children's need to know. These teachers will create classroom environments where children can learn concepts and ideas through play as well as explore situations and solve problems together through play.

Learning New Concepts

The process of acquiring new information, testing the validity and usefulness of the information, and then applying the concepts learned in a variety of situations is critical in the development of cognitive skills. Young children are constantly learning about themselves in relationship to objects, activities, and other people—not just during planned activities but during all of their daily experiences.

Children do not make an idea or concept fully their own by just hearing about it; they must have the opportunity to touch, taste, smell, move, manipulate, and explore in order to completely grasp the mean-

Open-ended activities allow children to explore their individual abilities at their own pace.

ing of a new concept. For example, telling a child that rough things feel prickly, scratchy, or uneven and that smooth things feel soft, slick, or even is not enough for the concept to become real or the learning to be complete. The child must feel a variety of textures, such as burlap, silk, sandpaper, and plastic to fully understand the concepts of *rough* and *smooth*.

Effective teachers of young children support children's learning about new ideas and concepts by providing a variety of toys, materials, and activities that lend themselves to manipulation and exploration. Teachers also encourage the learning of new concepts by introducing information and ideas through stories, discussions, special visitors, and field trips and then extending children's learning through par-

ticipatory activities such as cooking, art, discovery activities, woodworking, sand and water play, and block building. For example, the teacher may use a book or flannel-board story that introduces the idea of measurement. The concept will begin to become real to young children only after they have actively participated in a follow-up cooking activity or water-play activity using a variety of measuring cups and spoons and different sizes of containers. Children also need repetitive experiences with these materials in order to explore and test these new concepts. Teachers will help children to solidify their learning by giving them opportunities to repeat their play with objects and to apply the concepts to a variety of other objects, activities, or situations. Learning new

Activities that encourage children's exploration and manipulation foster the learning of new concepts.

concepts through play experiences fosters cognitive development in young children.

Developing Problem-Solving Skills

Teachers who provide a flexible classroom environment where children are encouraged to experiment with ideas and search for alternative ways of approaching situations are setting the stage for the development of problem-solving skills. An atmosphere where there are many possibilities and numerous ways to be successful encourages young children to think, interact, and create. A climate that includes rigid, specific rules and a plethora of ways to be wrong does not provide such encouragement.

Teachers must find a balance between establishing guidelines necessary to ensure children's safety and enforcing an excessive number of rules that restrict children's freedom to experiment, take risks, and try alternatives. In addition, teachers who rush to rescue children from every possible mishap or frustration may prevent them from learning to solve their own problems. For example, a teacher who quickly comes to the aid of a young toddler who is having difficulty navigating a low climbing structure does eliminate any chance of a tumble but also does

not allow any opportunity for the toddler to determine a route over the climber. Sometimes waiting for a brief time and allowing children to attempt to find an alternative can make a significant difference in the development of problem-solving skills.

Teachers also enhance problem-solving capabilities when they encourage children to search for answers to their questions and explore a variety of possible alternatives rather than automatically giving children information, answers, and suggestions. Children also need to be encouraged to learn to resolve their own conflicts with peers instead of always expecting the teacher to be the referee. By preschool age, children can resolve many of their own conflicts if teachers have appropriately modeled and taught conflict resolution skills. A skilled and sensitive teacher will know when children really need help and support and also will know when they need encouragement to find their own solutions and resolutions.

Supporting Playfulness

Young children typically approach new activities and ideas with anticipation and eagerness. Teachers who also experience joy in learning and openly share their enthusiasm with children support the children's view of learning as a positive, enjoyable experience. On the other hand, teachers who view learning as a necessary but grim and serious task stifle children's spontaneity and soon squelch their interest in seeking new opportunities for learning and growing.

Children's enjoyment of learning is also supported when teachers choose activities that allow children to explore their unique capabilities, take their own time, and have fun. For example, a teacher who provides a variety of materials for an art project (for example, construction paper, yarn, fabric, pipe cleaners, tissue paper, and glue) encourages children to think, experiment, and create. This type of open-ended activity also allows all children to experience enjoyment and success regardless of their level of development. On the other hand, a teacher who provides precut colored circles and glue for children to produce a product that resembles the teacher's pattern limits children's ability to think for themselves and explore their individual talents. If, in addition, the teacher rewards children who carefully reproduce the pattern and berates children whose creations are different, children learn conformity rather than creativity and learn to mistrust their ideas rather than trust their perceptions.

Young children need teachers who have the capacity to be playful and spontaneous themselves and who recognize that children need to become intensely and actively involved with play experiences. Teachers should nurture children's sense of delight in play by providing open-ended and creative activities and props, allowing children to determine the length of time for their involvement in play, and modeling an attitude of enthusiasm and respect for the pursuit of learning through active exploration.

GOALS AND ACTIVITIES FOR COGNITION

This section includes specific goals for developing children's cognition in the areas of (1) problem-solving/reasoning, (2) concept formation, (3) imitation/memory, and (4) association/classification. Suggested activities for infants, toddlers, and preschoolers are included as well.

Problem-Solving/Reasoning

The first subdomain in the area of cognition encompasses the development of problem-solving and reasoning skills. Children acquire these cognitive skills when they learn to think, process information, solve problems, and sequence events as well as develop a positive attitude toward learning. Specific developmental goals in this subdomain include the following:

1. Help children learn to think for themselves (Hendrick, 1998).

2. Ask children to think of ways to solve problems and propose alternative possibilities (Hendrick, 1998).

3. Help children develop joy and interest in learning (Hendrick, 1998).

4. Enhance children's ability to extend a sentence, story, or sequence of events logically.

The development of problem-solving and reasoning skills can best be accomplished in an environment that allows for active exploration and by a teacher who supports children's individuality and their attempts to find multiple alternatives to solving problems. Here are some specific activities for infants, toddlers, and preschoolers that can be adapted for a variety of developmental levels (an asterisk [*] denotes an activity that is also appropriate for use in the outdoor play environment).

INFANT ACTIVITY
Hide-and-Seek (Quiet Game)*

Use a large brown paper bag and choose an interesting toy, such as a set of jingle bells. Show the child the set of jingle bells. (Be sure that the bells are securely attached to an object and are not small enough to be swallowed.) Put the object in the paper bag. Close the bag by folding or scrunching it shut. Say, "Where are the jingle bells? Find the jingle bells." Shake the bag so the infant can hear the bells. For very young infants, leave the bag open and encourage them to reach for the bells in the bag. For older infants, hide the entire bag and encourage the child to "find the jingle bells."

Additional Skills:

Perceptual motor (coordination); communication (auditory discrimination)

Adaptations for Children with Disabilities:

Physically Impaired: Cut the top from a large grocery bag so that the bag has a wide opening but short sides and easier access. If the child has difficulty grasping objects, attach the bells to a large ring, a rattle, or another object the child can grasp or manipulate.

Speech/Language Impaired: None needed.

Visually Impaired: Encourage the child to listen carefully, face the sound, and move toward it. Provide verbal and physical cues as needed.

Hearing Impaired: Encourage the child to watch you place the bells inside the bag. Using signs and/or gestures, ask the child, "Where are the jingle bells?"

Behavior Disordered/Emotionally Disturbed: None needed.

TODDLER ACTIVITY
Build a Tall Tower (Quiet Game)

Provide a variety of shapes and sizes of blocks for children to choose from. Have each child take a turn stacking a block on top of or beside the previously stacked block. When the structure gets tall and wobbly, encourage the other children to help decide where the block should go, how the child should place it, and so forth. When the tower falls, the children get their blocks back and start over again.

Additional Skills:

Socialization (cooperation); cognition (concept formation)

Adaptations for Children with Disabilities:

Physically Impaired: Use very large blocks and containers. Provide physical assistance as needed.

Speech/Language Impaired: None needed.

Visually Impaired: Physically assist the child to feel the structure and where to place the block. If you are using small blocks, structure the activity so the child's turn comes at the beginning of the activity to increase success at adding to the structure without knocking it down.

Hearing Impaired: Use signs and/or gestures to explain the activity.

Behavior Disordered/Emotionally Disturbed: None needed.

PRESCHOOL ACTIVITY
Boats and Bears (Science/Nature)

Provide plastic teddy bear counters, a variety of objects to make "boats" for the bears (jar lids, wood scraps, plastic eggs, Styrofoam trays, small aluminum pie containers, tongue depressors), and a "lake" (water table, dishpan, cat-litter box). Tell the following story: "Once upon a time some bears decided to go to the lake to have some fun. When they got there, they enjoyed playing in the water for a while (they were very good at floating!), and then they decided they needed a boat. They found several objects that might make a boat, so they experimented to see which object could hold the most bears and still float." Choose one of the lids and start adding bears. Keep adding bears until the boat sinks. Encourage children to try different objects to see which ones float and how many bears each can hold. Some children will enjoy counting the bears as they experiment.

Additional Skills:

Cognition (concept formation); perceptual motor (coordination)

Adaptations for Children with Disabilities:

Physically Impaired: Use large lids for the child who has a functional grasp so that it will be easier to place the

bears. If the child does not have a functional grasp, encourage the other children to place the bears for the child or assist the child yourself.

Speech/Language Impaired: This is an excellent activity to enhance the development of the concepts *on top of* and *under.* Encourage the child to tell you where the boats and bears are. If you use bears and lids of different colors, this also can be a color-matching game (put blue bears on the blue lid).

Visually Impaired: Verbally describe the activity while the child explores the water, lids, and bears. Encourage the child to feel the "boat" with one hand while adding bears with the other hand.

Hearing Impaired: Use signs and/or gestures to explain the activity. Encourage the child to tell you where the bears and boats are (on top of the water or under the water).

Behavior Disordered/Emotionally Disturbed: None needed.

Concept Formation

The second subdomain in the area of cognition is concept formation. Children learn new concepts through interactions with the environment and testing and applying new concepts. Specific developmental goals in this subdomain include the following:

1. Help children learn about the environment through perceptual processing.
2. Help children learn to identify colors and shapes.
3. Encourage children to learn to count and understand number concepts.

4. Strengthen children's ability to understand relationships of objects and their own bodies in space.

Concept formation is best facilitated in a classroom where children have opportunities to actively participate and to test out new ideas. Here are some sample activities for infants, toddlers, and preschoolers that can be adapted for a variety of developmental levels (an asterisk [*] denotes an activity that is also appropriate for use in the outdoor play environment).

INFANT ACTIVITY
Textured Balls (Science/Nature)*

Collect a variety of balls made from many different materials (yarn balls, sock balls, rubber balls, plastic balls). Use a large sheet or quilt to contain the activity. Encourage infants to feel, roll, and throw the balls. Talk about the differences in textures: soft, hard, smooth, and rough.

Additional Skills:

Socialization (cooperation/sharing); perceptual motor (eye-hand coordination)

Adaptations for Children with Disabilities:

Physically Impaired: None needed.

Speech/Language Impaired: None needed.

Visually Impaired: None needed.

Hearing Impaired: Use signs and/or gestures to make the comments.

Behavior Disordered/Emotionally Disturbed: None needed.

TODDLER ACTIVITY
Prepositions (Movement)

Find a big cardboard box for the children to play in and explore. As the children are playing, ask them several questions to help explain some simple prepositions. For instance, "Taja, can you play inside the box?" or "Kris, can you play beside (behind, in front of) the box?" The box also can be placed over a child so that the child is underneath the box.

Additional Skills:

Communication (receptive language); perceptual motor (locomotor skills)

Adaptations for Children with Disabilities:

Physically Impaired: Provide physical assistance as needed.

Speech/Language Impaired: Use verbal and physical prompts as needed.

Visually Impaired: Encourage the child to feel the box for tactile cues to determine his or her position in relation to the box. Provide detailed descriptions of where the child and the box are positioned.

Hearing Impaired: Use signs and/or gestures to explain the activity and ask the questions.

Behavior Disordered/Emotionally Disturbed: None needed.

PRESCHOOL ACTIVITY
Shapes Are Everywhere (Active Game)*

Provide paper cutouts of geometric shapes (triangle, circle, square, rectangle) and go on a shape hunt. Look for items in the room (or in magazines) that are shaped like the paper cutouts. For example, the record cover is square and inside there is a circle; the books are rectangles; the clock is a circle; the easel is a triangle when viewed from the side; hangers are triangles; and the tables are squares or rectangles.

Extend the activity by encouraging the children to look for shapes on the playground, at snack time, and at home.

Additional Skills:

Communication (receptive and expressive language)

Adaptations for Children with Disabilities:

Physically Impaired: None needed.

Speech/Language Impaired: None needed.

Visually Impaired: While the child is using various objects or playing with various toys, discuss the shapes. Encourage the child to feel the outside edges and talk about the differences in the shapes (squares have four sharp points or corners, circles are round and smooth, and so on).

Hearing Impaired: Use signs to explain the activity and describe the shapes.

Behavior Disordered/Emotionally Disturbed: None needed.

Imitation/Memory

The third subdomain in the area of cognition involves developing imitation and memory. Children's development of imitation and memory involves learning the skills of recall, imitation, representation, and sequencing. Specific developmental goals in this subdomain include the following:

1. Encourage children to recall familiar objects and events.
2. Increase children's ability to imitate and model behaviors, structures, and so forth.
3. Help children learn to visualize and represent an object, person, or event from their past.
4. Encourage children to recall sequencing of past experiences.

The development of imitation and memory occurs when children have a variety of opportunities to ask questions, describe events, and model behaviors. An open, exploratory classroom environment that facilitates communication and storytelling will foster the growth of imitation and memory. In addition, specific activities can be developed for each age group. Here are some sample activities for infants, toddlers, and preschoolers than can be adapted for a variety of developmental levels (an asterisk [*] denotes an activity that is also appropriate for use in the outdoor play environment).

INFANT ACTIVITY
Peek-a-Boo (Active Game)*

Save a large cardboard box. Hide in the box and surprise the infants with a big "peek-a-boo." Repeat several times. Let the infants take turns getting in the box and playing "peek-a-boo." Start slowly so as not to startle or frighten the infants and then build up to more unexpected "peek-a-boos."

Additional Skills:

Socialization (social interaction, conservation of resources)

Adaptations for Children with Disabilities:

Physically Impaired: None needed.

Speech/Language Impaired: None needed.

Visually Impaired: Encourage the child to feel and explore the box. Hide with child and pop up to play "peek-a-boo."

Hearing Impaired: None needed.

Behavior Disordered/Emotionally Disturbed: None needed.

TODDLER ACTIVITY
Guess What's Missing (Quiet Game)

Provide several objects that illustrate a concept or emphasize a thematic idea. If the theme is "People Who Help Us," for example, the objects could be tools that helpers use. Introduce the objects to the children one at a time and then cover all objects with a scarf or piece of fabric. Chant "Abracadabra, riddle dee ree, something's missing, look and see!" Pick up one object as you remove the scarf. Ask the children to recall what's missing. If they have difficulty, let them feel the object through the scarf. You may wish to follow the identification of the object with a brief discussion, such as "Tell us who uses this tool." Return the object and continue the game. Let the children take turns being the one who picks up the missing object.

Additional Skills:

Communication (receptive and expressive language); socialization (social interaction and cooperation)

Adaptations for Children with Disabilities:

Physically Impaired: None needed.

Speech/Language Impaired: None needed.

Visually Impaired: Provide time for the child to explore all of the objects to be used in the activity. Describe the

tactile differences of each object to help the child with identification. During the activity, encourage the child to feel the objects, going from the left side to the right side. (Placing the objects on a tray would provide more structure for the child.) Keep the objects in order as they are removed.

Hearing Impaired: Use signs and/or gestures to explain the activity.

Behavior Disordered/Emotionally Disturbed: None needed.

PRESCHOOL ACTIVITY
Zoo Parade (Quiet Game)

Provide several wooden or plastic zoo animals. Tell the following story using the animals as props: "Once upon a time there was a parade of animals from the zoo. The elephant was first in line, then the giraffe, then the tiger. The bear was last. Look closely at how they are lined up for the parade! Now I am going to mix them up and see if you can put them back in order." Select a child to put the animals back in order. If the child wants or needs help, encourage the others to provide it. Children may wish to take turns being the storyteller and placing the animals in different order for others to recall.

Variation: Use transportation toys.

Additional Skills:

Cognition (concept formation); communication (expressive language)

Adaptations for Children with Disabilities:

Physically Impaired: None needed

Speech/Language Impaired: None needed.

Visually Impaired: Provide time for the child to explore the objects to be used in this activity. Describe the tactile differences of each object to assist with identification. During this activity, encourage the child to feel the objects, going from the left side to the right side. Assist the child in finding the first object on the left side. Keep the objects in order when one is removed.

Hearing Impaired: Use signs and/or gestures to explain the activity.

Behavior Disordered/Emotionally Disturbed: None needed.

Association/Classification

The fourth subdomain in the area of cognition is the development of association and classification skills. Helping children develop specific cognitive capabilities in classifying groups of objects and events and learning to establish relationships between objects and events are major tasks in this subdomain. Specific developmental goals include the following:

1. Encourage children to develop specific mental abilities in matching, grouping, ordering, and classifying.
2. Encourage children to identify and classify uses and attributes of objects, events, weather, body parts, and so forth.

3. Help children learn to understand and complete analogy statements.
4. Enhance children's ability to establish relationships between objects.

Children can best establish the ability to practice association and classification skills in an environment where they have a variety of opportunities to engage in hands-on activities and games involving matching, grouping, and classifying. Here are some sample activities for infants, toddlers, and preschoolers that can be adapted for a variety of developmental levels (an asterisk [*] denotes an activity that is also appropriate for use in the outdoor play environment).

INFANT ACTIVITY
Smells (Science/Nature)

Save some old spice containers with the shaker tops and put a variety of "smelly" materials into them. Break up pieces of orange peel, save some whole cloves, soak a cotton ball in perfume, and break up an onion or garlic clove. Put each "smelly" item in a separate container. Label each and talk about the type of smell. Be sure to name each object several times and encourage the infants to try to vocalize the sounds. Model smelling the different containers and encourage the infants to try to smell each container. Let them explore the containers by mouthing, touching, and manipulating each.

Sample Comments:

"Oh, smell this one. This is an orange peel. It smells fruity!"

"This perfume has a strong smell. Do you smell it? It smells like a plant."

"This is an onion. It has a really strong smell, too. It may make your eyes water."

Additional Skills:

Communication (receptive language); perceptual motor (eye-hand coordination)

Adaptations for Children with Disabilities:

Physically Impaired: None needed.

Speech/Language Impaired: None needed.

Visually Impaired: None needed.

Hearing Impaired: Use signs and/or gestures along with comments to name smells.

Behavior Disordered/Emotionally Disturbed: None needed.

TODDLER ACTIVITY
Buried Treasure (Quiet Game)*

Fill a large laundry tub with sand. Add shells, plastic eggs, wooden cubes, large plastic keys, and wooden animal figures. Provide a muffin tin to hold items after they are found. Children take turns hunting through the sand to find the treasure and then place it in the container. Encourage children to put items that are the same in the same section of the muffin tin (same color, same shape, and so forth).

Additional Skills:

Cognition (concept formation)

Adaptations for Children with Disabilities:

Physically Impaired: If the container's sections are too close together, provide bowls or plastic plates for the child

to sort the objects. If the child has a tactile sensitivity, provide gloves to wear.

Speech/Language Impaired: Encourage the child to identify or name the various treasures.

Visually Impaired: Encourage the child to identify the objects by feeling. This is a great activity to teach the concepts of *same* and *different.*

Hearing Impaired: Use signs and/or gestures to explain the activity.

Behavior Disordered/Emotionally Disturbed: None needed.

PRESCHOOL ACTIVITY
Hide-and-Seek Matching Game (Active Game)

Use index cards and make duplicate sets by using stickers, shape designs, numerals, letters, and wallpaper designs. (Playing cards or paint chips also can be used.) Ask children to hide their eyes while you place (hide) one set of cards around the room. (Cards should remain visible but in unusual places.)

Distribute the other cards to the children. They look around the room to find the card that matches the one they have. Encourage children to help each other. When all cards are found, hide them again and repeat the game as long as children are interested. Children will enjoy taking turns hiding the cards.

Additional Skills:

Cognition (concept formation); socialization (social interaction and cooperation)

Adaptations for Children with Disabilities:

Physically Impaired: Place the cards around the room in places that are easily accessible to the child.

Speech/Language Impaired: None needed.

Visually Impaired: Use "smelly" stickers, shape designs, numerals, and letters cut from various textures. Encourage the child to feel the similarities. Ask another child to assist the child with finding the areas where the cards are hidden or provide a verbal "map" for the child to find the cards.

Hearing Impaired: Use signs to explain the activity.

Behavior Disordered/Emotionally Disturbed: None needed.

CHAPTER SUMMARY _____

Children's cognitive abilities are enhanced in a classroom environment that emphasizes play experiences. Play allows young children to manipulate objects, participate in activities, try out new ideas, practice solutions to problems, satisfy their curiosity, create new inventions, and develop their recall of events. A flexible and open atmosphere also supports children's sense of playfulness and delight in learning. "Have you ever seen a child who wanted to stop playing?" (Rogers & Sawyers, 1988, p. 59). Play is the way young children learn about the world.

■   ■   ■   ■   ■   ■   ■   ■   ■

Until at least age 7, young children need opportunities to actively explore the environment in order to develop their cognitive skills. As a preschool teacher who is concerned about the continuing success of children in your school, you must communicate, cooperate, and coordinate with the kindergarten and primary-grade teachers to develop an integrated educational program that recognizes the following:

• Young children from ages 2 to 7 are in the stage of preoperational thinking. Egocentrism characterizes their perspectives and relationships.

• Children develop knowledge as they assimilate and accommodate new information.

• A classroom environment that allows for active exploration of materials and activities encourages young children to develop and test new concepts.

• Play supports the development of young children's cognitive competence.

• The development of children as unique and creative individuals is fostered in a classroom setting that encourages playfulness, problem solving, and the exploration of alternatives.

• Young children's positive attitudes about learning are enhanced in an atmosphere that is open and responsive to children's needs, enthusiasm, and level of activity.

■   ■   ■   ■   ■   ■   ■   ■   ■

DISCUSSION QUESTIONS _____

1. Discuss the vignette at the beginning of the chapter. What other questions or concerns might you have? Discuss the vignette at the end of the chapter. Are there other responses you might have to this situation?

2. Describe Piaget's theory of four stages of cognitive development. What are the substages and developmental milestones in the first two stages?

3. Contrast Vygotsky's theory and stages of cognitive and language development with Piaget's theory and stages.

4. How do behaviorists and social learning theorists each explain children's thinking?

5. How do children's and adults' memory abilities differ?

6. Describe differences in children's learning styles that have been attributed to cultural differences.

7. Describe ways that teachers can foster children's curiosity and learning. What role do children's questions have in their learning?

8. How does children's concept knowledge develop?

9. How can teachers foster the development of children's problem solving skills?

10. Describe the four subdomains of development in cognition.

REFERENCES

Bandura, A. (1969). *Principles of behavior modification.* New York: Holt, Rinehart, & Winston.

Bandura, A. (1977). *Social learning theory.* Englewood Cliffs, NJ: Prentice-Hall.

Belmont, J. (1989). Cognitive strategies and strategic learning: The socio-instructional approach. *American Psychologist, 44,* 142–148.

Cohen, R. (1971). The influence of conceptual rule-sets on measures of learning ability. In M. Tumin, (Ed.), *Race and intelligence* (pp. 89–96). Washington, DC: American Anthropological Association.

Donaldson, M. (1978). *Children's minds.* New York: Norton.

Families and Work Institute. (1996, June). *Rethinking the brain: New insights into early development.* Executive summary of the Conference on Brain Development in Young Children: New Frontiers for Research, Policy, and Practice, University of Chicago.

Flavell, J. (1970). *Cognitive development.* Englewood Cliffs, NJ: Prentice-Hall.

Gardner, H. (1983). *Frames of mind: The theory of multiple intelligence.* New York: Basic Books.

Gunnar, M., Broderson, K., Krueger, K., & Rigatuso, R. (1996). Dampening of behavioral and adrenocortical reactivity during early infancy: Normative changes and individual differences. *Child Development, 67*(3), 877–889.

Hale-Benson, J. (1981). Black children: Their roots, culture, and learning styles. *Young Children, 36*(2), 37–50.

Hendrick, J. (1998). *Total learning: Developmental curriculum for the young child* (5th ed.). Columbus, OH: Merrill/Prentice-Hall.

Hilliard, A. (1976). *Alternatives to IQ testing: An approach to the identification of gifted minority children.* Final report to the California State Department of Education.

Leister-Willis, C. (1997). What new research on the brain tells us about our youngest children: Summary on the White House Conference on Early Childhood. *Dimensions, 25*(2), 20a–d.

Maratsos, M. (1973). Non-egocentric communication abilities in preschool children. *Child Development, 44,* 697–700.

Newberger, J. (1997). New brain development research—A wonderful opportunity to build public support for early childhood education! *Young Children, 52*(4), 4–9.

Piaget, J., & Inhelder, B. (1969). *The psychology of the child.* New York: Basic Books.

Rogers, C. S., & Sawyers, J. K. (1988). *Play in the lives of children.* Washington, DC: National Association for the Education of Young Children.

Rogoff, B. (1990). *Apprenticeship in thinking: Cognitive development in social context.* New York: Oxford University Press.

Rogoff, B., & Mistry, J. (1985). Memory development in cultural context. In M. Pressley & C. Brainerd (Eds.), *Progress in cognitive development.* New York: Springer-Verlag.

Sternberg, R. (1985). *Beyond IQ: A triarchic theory of human intelligence.* New York: Cambridge University Press.

Thomas, R. M. (1996). *Comparing theories of child development* (4th ed.). Belmont, CA: Brooks/Cole.

Vygotsky, L. (1962). *Thought and language.* Cambridge, MA: MIT Press.

ADDITIONAL RESOURCES

Bjorklund, D. (1995). *Children's thinking: Developmental function and individual differences.* Pacific Grove, CA: Brooks/Cole.

Brown, L., & Pollitt, E. (1996, February). Malnutrition, poverty, and intellectual development. *Scientific American,* pp. 38–43.

Bullock, J. (1988). Encouraging problem solving. *Day Care and Early Education, 16*(1), 24–27.

Campbell, K., & Arnold, F. (1988). Stimulating thinking and communicating skills. *Dimensions, 16*(2), 11–13.

Cartwright, S. (1988). Play can be the building blocks of learning. *Young Children, 43*(5), 44–47.

Caruso, D. A. (1988). Play and learning in infancy: Research and implications. *Young Children, 43*(6), 28–32.

Casey, M. B., & Lippman, M. (1991). Learning to plan through play. *Young Children, 46*(4), 52–58.

Egan, K. (1994). Young children's imagination and learning: Engaging children's emotional response. *Young Children, 49*(6), 27–32.

File, N. (1995). Applications of Vygotskian theory to early childhood education: Moving toward a new teaching-learning paradigm. In S. Reifel (Ed.), *Advances in early education and day care: Social contexts of early development and education,* (Vol. 7, pp. 295–319). Greenwich, CT: JAI Press.

Furman, E. (1990). Plant a potato—Learn about life (and death). *Young Children, 46*(1), 15–20.

Goffin, S., & Tull, C. (1985). Problem solving: Encouraging active learning. *Young Children, 40*(3), 28–32.

Harsh, A. (1987). Teach mathematics with children's literature. *Young Children, 42*(6), 24–29.

Jennings, C., & Terry, G. (1990). Children's stories: A natural path to teaching thinking. *Dimensions, 18*(2), 5–8.

Kantrowitz, B., & Wingert, P. (1989). How kids learn. *Young Children, 44*(6), 4–10.

Rogers, D., Martin, R., & Kousaleos, S. (1988). Encouraging science through playful discovery. *Day Care and Early Education, 16*(1), 20–23.

Shaw, J., & Cliatt, M. (1988). Questioning techniques to promote thinking. *Day Care and Early Education, 16*(1), 10–13.

Sprung, B., Froschl, M., & Campbell, P. (1986). What will happen if . . . : Young children and the scientific method. *Day Care and Early Education, 13*(4), 28–35.

Stone, J. (1987). Early childhood math: Make it manipulative! *Young Children, 42*(6), 16–23.

Trudge, J., & Caruso, D. (1988). Cooperative problem solving in the classroom: Enhancing young children's cognitive development. *Young Children, 44*(1), 46–52.

Zeece, P. D., & Graul, S. K. (1990). Learning to play. Playing to learn. *Day Care and Early Education, 18*(1), 11–15.

Ziemer, M. (1987). Science and the early childhood curriculum: One thing leads to another. *Young Children, 42*(6), 44–51.

16.

Curriculum for Developing Perceptual Motor Skills

Children in your preschool classroom enjoy many opportunities for the development of perceptual motor skills. The indoor classroom environment includes activities and equipment that let children develop and use both small- and large-motor skills. Children are encouraged to climb, jump, hop, skip, and balance. There also are activities that let children practice creative and expressive movement. In the outdoor environment there is plenty of space and more equipment that lets children practice motor skills. You see that children enjoy this component of your program, and you are pleased that the perceptual motor needs of the children are recognized and met.

During a discussion with one of the fathers of a 5-year-old in your class, it becomes clear that some of the parents have different goals and expectations for their children's physical development and education. The father asks you for advice about allowing his child to become involved in competitive physical activities. Specifically, he would like information about group or team sports such as baseball and soccer. Many children in the neighborhood are involved in group sports and practice regularly after school and on weekends, and neighborhood parents are very enthusiastic about supporting these teams. However, this father is concerned about encouraging his child to become involved in competitive sports at such an early age. You share the father's concerns and express your view that 5-year-olds are still developing and practicing skills in motor development, and their skill levels range widely. You also are concerned about the competitiveness inherent in team sports. It is clear that several issues must be considered as you and this parent discuss practices about children's motor development:

- What activities are most helpful to children as they develop and practice perceptual motor skills?
- How can teachers help children have positive feelings about their physical development and skills?
- What are ways to promote a sense of cooperation instead of competition in group games?
- How can teachers educate parents about the importance of open-ended, noncompetitive physical activities for young children?
- What are the possible negative consequences for children who become involved in competitive team sports at an early age?

Suggestions for responding to this classroom vignette will be shared at the end of the chapter.

When reading this chapter, focus on understanding major developmental milestones for young children in the perceptual motor domain. Also, consider ways that the development of perceptual motor skills can be fostered through creative-play activities and growth-promoting techniques.

Young children who develop perceptual motor skills can experience feelings of mastery and control over their bodies, develop a positive body image, practice a healthy lifestyle, and engage in active social experiences with others. Recent concern about children's sedentary lifestyles and stressful environments placing them at risk for health problems has created a renaissance in the concern for children's physical development. In order to plan the curriculum to foster the development of perceptual motor skills as well as facilitate young children's emotional and social development and overall physcial well-being, it is necessary to review important milestones in children's physical development.

Activities were written by Kathy Carlson, Amy R. Kerlin, and Anne Miller Stott; adaptations were written by Bobbie Beckmann.

DEVELOPMENTAL MILESTONES
IN PERCEPTUAL MOTOR SKILLS _____

Young children appear helpless at birth. They have no control over body movements, yet they engage in a variety of reflex behaviors that are precursors to later, intentional physical activity. At birth, infants display reflex behaviors that are involuntary muscle movement, usually stimulated by something in the near environment. A common one is the sucking reflex, triggered by placing a bottle or nipple in the infant's mouth. Related to sucking is the rooting reflex, which occurs when the baby's face is touched or stroked, causing the infant to turn toward the touch. Children also exhibit the Moro reflex, flinging the arms out and then pulling them in toward the body in response to loud noises; the Babinski reflex, spreading out the toes in response to being tickled on the bottom of the feet; and the stepping reflex, appearing to take steps when held above a flat surface such as a table. These reflex behaviors disappear in the first few months of life and are replaced by motor actions that are voluntary and under the child's control.

Within a few months after birth, most reflex behaviors disappear and development follows two principles of human growth. The first, *proximodistal development,* suggests that development proceeds from the center of the body outward. For example, children can control the movement of their trunk first, then their arms; finally, they gain small-motor control of their fingers. Evidence for this principle is found in the developmental sequence of infants' ability to roll over, then use their arms to reach for objects, and finally to actually grasp, hold, and manipulate objects. The second principle, *cephalocaudal development,* suggests that development occurs in an orderly sequence from the head to the feet. Evidence for this principle is found in the sequence of maturation to walking: infants lift the head, then the chest, then sit up, pull up, stand up, and finally walk unsupported, usually by 15 months.

Beyond infancy, into the preschool years, physical development slows. Children appear less babyish and more adultlike as fat tissue begins to disappear. Body proportions also change as the head appears smaller in relation to the body. Children's locomotor skills continue to develop as children expand their repertoire to include climbing stairs, hopping, and skipping. Other achievements for preschoolers are greater physical control and body management that permit refinement of nonlocomotor skills and coordination. The area of fine-motor-skill development is closely related to children's cognitive development and their use of classroom materials such as pencils and crayons. The development of these skills in handling objects begins in infancy and develops in four stages. In the first stage, children see, and are attracted by, an object, but they make no motor actions at all. In the second stage, children exhibit "motor excitement" when viewing the attractive object; they may move or wave their hands but use no coordinated motions to get the object. In the third stage, children touch and begin to manipulate the object. In the last stage children have much more control of their manipulation and actions on the object; for example, they may stack, throw, or line up several blocks. In the first three stages, the cognitive component of children's perceptual motor activity can be seen. Children must see and touch objects in order to learn about them. In the last stage, children begin to attach names or labels to objects and then vocalize these names. At this point, children no longer need to have and handle the object to be able to think and talk about it. The motor activity and sensory experiences in the first three stages have provided the opportunity to identify and learn about the object (Cratty, 1970).

Children also follow an identifiable sequence in developing the fine motor skills in drawing and writing. In the beginning, when children find or are given a writing instrument such as a pen, pencil, crayon, or marker, they may simply hold it. Then, either by being shown and helped to use the instrument or by accidentally marking with it and realizing this possible use, children begin to make random marks on paper (or walls or tables). These random markings are replaced with more intentional drawing of vertical, horizontal, and radiating lines as children respond to a model or stimulus. Children gain more control during the second year, and the lines become enclosed shapes and resemble circles, and later, squares. During the third year, children draw geometric shapes with more intention and control. The shapes are not always drawn in a continuous motion and may not be fully enclosed. Younger children draw their shapes larger. Older children draw figures smaller, and the more difficult the shape is to draw, the smaller it is drawn (Cratty & Martin, 1969). Gesell, in his studies of children's normative development, which yielded norms or average ages for skill acquisition, described older children's fine motor skills. He reported that by age 3, children can copy a circle and a horizontal line; 4-year-olds can copy a cross and a diamond; and by age 5, children can produce a triangle (Gesell, 1925). By age 4, most children have begun to write letters and numbers. They ignore a base line and write all over the page, sometimes slanting or turning the writing sideways. As children's fine motor skills mature, they gain control, first over size, then over spacing of their letters and numbers (Cratty, 1970). Other researchers have found similar results; where contradictions occur is in the direction of children producing these shapes later, not earlier, than Gesell reported. This suggests the importance of physical readiness and maturation before children can express in written form their understanding of cognitive concepts such as shape. Physical maturation is a necessary but not a sufficient component for the development of children's drawing and writing skills. Also necessary is an environment that encourages these skills: a variety of writing instruments such as crayons, pens, pencils, and markers; various surfaces such as paper, cardboard, or fabric on a table, floor, or wall; and adults who draw, write, and value the aesthetic and communicative functions of drawing and writing. As children's movements become increasingly skilled and coordinated, from early reflex responses to mastery of locomotor skills, they begin to develop body awareness. This involves the child's perception of her body and its fit and function in various spaces. This is not abstract learning; children begin to understand how their own size, weight, strength, and proportion relate to space and other people or objects in the environment. As children control and coordinate both small- and large-motor muscles with vision and hearing, they increase their ability to explore, and learn from, their environment in more complex, challenging, and creative ways.

Another important component of this domain is the development of perception and sensory capacities. The 1890 description by William James of the infant's world as a "blooming, buzzing mass of confusion" has been refuted by research that has shown the remarkable sensory and perceptual abilities present in newborns. Infants use all five of their senses at birth to begin to learn about their physical world. They detect light and dark contrasts, can discriminate among patterned figures, and prefer looking at the human face over other solid or patterned figures. Newborn infants hear well enough to differentiate among familiar and unfamiliar voices and to make distinctions among speech sounds.

Infants also have well-developed senses of smell and taste at birth; they distinguish among tastes and react differently to pleasant and unpleasant smells. Infants respond to touch, particularly those types of touch that soothe, comfort, and calm distressed or crying infants. Most of these sensory modes progress to mature functioning within a few months after birth, and children rely on their sensory ability to perceive important information about the people and objects, and the behavior of both, in their physical world.

RESEARCH ON PERCEPTUAL MOTOR DEVELOPMENT

Research on infants' sensory capabilities shows that children have fairly sophisticated mechanisms for perceiving their physical world with vision, hearing, taste, smell, and touch. Infants are born with less than "perfect" vision, between 20/400 and 20/800 (adult vision without defects is 20/20). By about 6 months, vision becomes normalized. In the first six months, infants prefer looking at the human face over several other patterns and colors, which indicates the ability to discriminate, or find differences, among several figures and to prefer more complex patterns over patternless figures; this is evident within a few hours of birth. Infants can follow a bright light with their eyes, even at birth in the delivery room. By 1 month, infants see best at a distance of eight to ten inches, the distance a teacher's face would be from the infant's face. Infants can track, or visually follow, moving objects fairly well by

8 weeks (McCall, 1980). By 2 to 4 months, infants have a well-developed sense of color perception and show color preferences by looking longer at reds and blues (Bornstein, 1978).

Infants have auditory acuity, or hearing ability, although they do not hear as well as adults do. At 1 month, infants can distinguish between very familiar sounds, such as "p (uh)" and "b (uh)." By 2 months, they recognize differences in vowel sounds. Infants also have the remarkable ability to recognize their mother's voice and distinguish it from another female voice two days after birth. By the second year of life, children's hearing ability is similar to that of adults (Fogel, 1991).

At birth, infants can distinguish between things with different tastes. They suck faster on a bottle when it contains sugar water than when it contains plain water. They detect differences between sour, bitter, and salty solutions two hours after birth (Rosenstein & Oster, 1988). They also distinguish between different smells. At one week, infants grimace and turn away from the smell of ammonia or vinegar. Breast-feeding infants only 5 days old turned toward a nursing pad previously worn by their mothers and away from an alternate pad. When the alternate pad was one from another breast-feeding mother, infants 6 days old still turned toward the pad of their own mother (MacFarlane, 1975).

Infants are sensitive to touch; this is demonstrated by their reflex responses to being stroked on the lips, cheek, feet, and hands. Touching, holding, and rocking also produce a response from the infant. Researchers do not agree on infants' sensitivity to painful touch, such as that which occurs when infants are pricked for a blood test or when male babies are circumcised without anesthesia. Some researchers believe that infants do not perceive pain at birth as adults do; research to answer this question would be unethical.

The timing of children's acquisition of motor skills varies widely, yet infants acquire their physical and motor skills in an invariant sequence. Early theories of physical development posited that infants' physical development occurred as a result of maturation, not learning. Subsequent research has shown that lack of experiences to simulate and allow practice of motor action can seriously delay motor development and result in children being unable to crawl or walk. Other research has shown an environmental influence. A study of 300 Ugandan infants found that these babies could sit up and hold their heads up two days after birth with an adult touching their elbows for support. This milestone is not reached until two months later by American infants and was apparently due to the Ugandan mothers giving birth without anesthesia (Gerber, 1985).

Specific links between motor activity and other domains of development have also been studied. Children who have better-developed locomotor or movement skills show greater interest in social stimuli and increased awareness of their mother's presence. In a study with 8-month-olds, some of whom could not crawl or walk, some of whom could crawl, and others who could walk with help, infants who had developed and had been using locomotor skills for the longest period of time had greater skills in searching for objects, a cognitive skill necessary for the development of object permanence (Kermoian & Campos, 1988).

Contemporary research has focused on the link between cognitive and perceptual motor development and how environmental factors influence motor development. "Skillful moving requires skillful thought on the child's part" (Stinson, 1992, p. 227). Developing control of movement patterns is strongly related to cognitive development. Children's potential for information processing is fostered through playful movement activities, open-ended motor practice, and movement exploration. Movement programs can be an effective vehicle for the development of problem solving skills and organizational thought as young children discover what their bodies can do and actively learn positional and directional concepts and relationships (Haywood, 1986). Early movement experiences provide a foundation for critical thinking. "As children solve movement problems, they are not only learning to move but moving to learn" (Stinson, 1992, p. 227).

Research on the role of the teacher and the environment in enhancing motor development is of interest to early childhood educators. The type of equipment used (for example, the size of a ball to be caught), the design of movement activities, and the teacher's role in facilitating play and movement all are factors that influence children's success and level of motor development. Contemporary practice in movement education focuses on the development of the child rather than the acquisition of a skill (Halverson, 1990; Herkowitz, 1978; Williams, 1983).

FOSTERING PERCEPTUAL MOTOR DEVELOPMENT THROUGH CREATIVE-PLAY CURRICULUM _____

It is not surprising that play has an essential role in promoting perceptual motor development. As a young child performs an action or behavior, the pleasure, novelty, or enjoyment found in that action will result in its repetition. Playing with an object affords practice of the behavior and skills involved in its performance. For example, an infant will reach for and grasp a rattle, then repeatedly shake it or knock it against the side of the crib. This repetition enhances the child's mastery and control of body and movements.

Teachers can use play to help children acquire and practice skills. Climbing steps to the slide or imitating animals helps children to practice climbing, running, and crawling. Just as children extend their play cognitively to include new themes, characters, and language, so do they expand their physical repertoire of movement and physical skills. Children with physical disabilities such as ambulatory problems, visual impairments, health impairments such as asthma, and obesity also need opportunities for developing endurance, movement tolerance, and relaxation techniques (Spodek & Saracho, 1994). Young children experiencing stress can learn to cope positively through play by exercising large muscles and releasing emotional energy (Honig, 1990; Johns & Johns, 1983). Teachers can facilitate movement activities for children with these special needs through consultation with health practitioners, physical therapists, and parents. Teachers must assess individual children's motor skill levels and patterns of movement and plan a curriculum that fosters development across levels.

Practice Play

The type and complexity of children's physical play changes as they grow and develop. Piaget classifies children's play during infancy to 18–24 months as

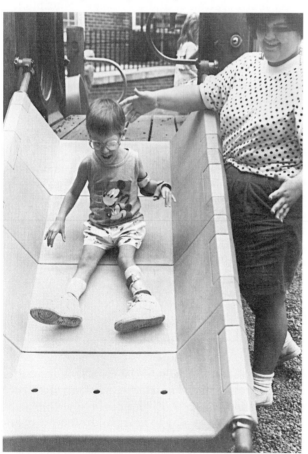

As children master locomotor skills, they develop increased levels of confidence and self-esteem.

being primarily practice play (Rogers & Sawyers, 1988). Infants and toddlers experiment with objects and materials as well as with newly emerging motor skills and control of the body. Teachers can enhance children's perceptual motor development through practice play by providing an environment rich with objects, materials, activities, and equipment that young children can explore freely. For example, infants who are confined to cribs, playpens, or swings for a large portion of the day are engaging in passive activities that do not allow for much exploration of the environment or discovery of motor skills. On the other hand, infants and toddlers who have access to many types of materials, objects, and equipment placed within their reach are able to grasp and explore the attributes of the materials as well as their own physical capabilities. As crawlers, children explore the variations in floor surfaces such as carpet and tile. They explore low soft spaces, such as large cushions and pillows, and harder spaces such as shelves and climbers. Moving to these areas and exploring them allows young children to test out and practice their motor skills.

Walkers can explore the environment in a different way. They are increasingly mobile, active, curious, and eager to practice their new motor skills. Walkers extend their learning through more sophisticated movement, such as dancing, running, and climbing. At the same time, fine motor skills are more highly developed and children are able to manipulate objects with more mastery and control and with greater success. Puzzles that would have been impossible to master earlier are now an enjoyable activity as well as a confidence builder. Play with blocks and other manipulative toys also becomes more complex, which helps children develop the physical skills that will prepare them for the transition to symbolic play.

Symbolic Play

As children's sensorimotor, cognitive, and language skills develop, their preference for type of play also changes. Young children ages 2 through 7 engage primarily in symbolic play. Symbolic play is characterized by an emphasis on pretend play from ages 2 to 4, and on dramatic play from ages 4 to 7. This stage of development corresponds with Piaget's classification of the preoperational stage for cognitive development (Rogers & Sawyers, 1988). Through pretend play, children extend development of their locomotor and body mastery skills. Children who pretend to be a variety of animals in the outdoor play setting are developing large-motor skills. Horses may gallop and chase each other; dogs and cats may creep, crawl, or scoot around on the ground. Putting on a pretend circus or parade allows children to take on the roles of animals such as elephants (walking slowly and swinging their trunks) and lions and tigers (running, jumping, and pouncing) as well as the roles of tightrope walker, ballerina, dancer, clown, juggler, baton twirler, and marching band member. The dramatic-play stage continues to offer opportunities for children to develop locomotor skills. Children may refine fine motor skills by engaging in dramatic-play schemes involving playing school or playing office, where they enact their roles with typewriters, computers, and a variety of writing and drawing utensils. Dramatic play gives young children the opportunity to explore roles and capabilities without fear of failure. As Winnie-the-Pooh said of his own fine motor skills, "[M]y spelling is Wobbly. It's good spelling but it Wobbles, and the letters get in the wrong places" (Milne, 1957, p. 78). In dramatic-play situations, it is all right for spelling to be a little wobbly. Children may also act out stories by using puppets, costumes, or masks and enhance their communication skills as well as the motor skills and body mastery involved in playing the part. Symbolic play, including pretend play and dramatic play, offers children many opportunities to extend and refine development of their motor skills while also developing confidence, creativity, and control over their bodies. Play is the arena that allows young children to become increasingly comfortable with their physical attributes as they explore their bodies, minds, and emotions through a variety of play scenarios.

Movement experiences that occur during play can focus on the aesthetic quality of movement and on bodily awareness. Through play, children experience the grace of movement, explore body motion, develop self-reliance and increased confidence in meeting physical challenges, and have opportunities for creativity and self-expression. Teachers' enthusiasm and enjoyment of physcial activity encourages children to be involved with large-motor movement during play (Laban, 1988; Spodek & Saracho, 1994).

Games with Rules

During the age span of 7 to 12, children develop an interest in games with rules. This stage of motor development corresponds with Piaget's classification of the period of concrete operations for cognitive development (Rogers & Sawyers, 1988). Although children in the preoperational stage of development may begin to show an interest in games, their play is generally less well organized and the rules more flexible than the

Creative movement activities enhance the development of children's motor skills.

games with rules in which children ages 7 to 12 become involved. When games with rules are used with 4- to 7-year-olds, several guidelines are important:

■ Introduce games with rules gradually and let children choose whether or not to participate.

■ Choose games that are fun, have flexible rules, and allow children to modify the rules in order to stay active and involved.

■ Choose several different games that encompass many levels of motor skill development, and emphasize the challenges inherent in the games rather than winning or losing (Rogers & Sawyers, 1988).

Many teachers are concerned about the appropriateness of group sports in early childhood programs. Objections focus on two issues. The first is the developmental appropriateness of organized team sports. Children's physical abilities and skills, such as running, throwing, kicking, and catching, vary widely in early childhood. Running, throwing, kicking, and catching are sophisticated actions requiring balance, coordination, and eye-hand and eye-foot coordination. Young children should engage in a variety of physical and motor actions and not overuse any one muscle group. The lengthy practice of motor actions required for accurate pitching in softball and baseball or for kicking in soccer should be avoided until bone growth is slowed or completed, around ages 11 to 13 in girls and ages 13 to 15 in boys (Stoner, 1978).

A second concern is the inevitable competition in team sports. The emphasis on winning rather than simple enjoyment and the development of skills, the negative emotions experienced by the "losers," and the many ways our society teaches competition rather than cooperation support this concern. Pressuring younger children to become involved in games with rules or competitive sports is not in the best interest of children and may heighten their levels of stress and frustration. Competition for young children "often results in isolating some [children] in favor of creating sports stars. Practices, uniforms, waiting a turn, specialized skills, strict rules, equipment, coaches, spectators, and choosing teams—where the worst player is chosen last—have no part in cooperative play" (Sobel, 1983, p. 30). Although parents may want their young children to develop an interest in sports or games at an early age, "generally it is parent need, not a child's authentic wish, that pushes children into team sports at an early age" (Elkind, 1988, p. 31). A number of researchers have found that less than 4 percent of preschoolers play games with formal rules (Rogers & Sawyers, 1988).

Cooperative games in which participants play together, rather than against one another, are appropriate for young children. The emphasis is on acceptance of all players; scores, standings, winning, and losing are de-emphasized. Some activities such as block building, dramatic play, and dance and movement are naturally cooperative. Other activities that have traditionally had competitive elements can be changed to reduce the competitive focus and to increase cooperation, inclusion, and fun. For example, change the traditional game Musical Chairs so that no one is excluded. When there aren't enough chairs for everyone after the music stops, then children can find a way to share chairs safely—two or three children sitting on a chair or in each other's laps, more children placing a hand or a foot on a chair, and so on. Teachers can devise new games or change familiar ones so that all children can participate and win (Sobel, 1983).

Although preschoolers may be frustrated and overwhelmed by group games, school-age children need the opportunity to organize their own games and establish their own rules. Teachers can foster healthy attitudes toward games by helping children emphasize the fun aspect of games and learn to handle both winning and losing (Kamii & DeVries, 1980). For older children, games and activities are an important component of cognitive and social development as well as a testing ground for their physical skills.

GOALS AND ACTIVITIES FOR PERCEPTUAL MOTOR DEVELOPMENT

Specific goals for children's development in the areas of (1) eye-hand/eye-foot coordination, (2) locomotor skills, (3) nonlocomotor skills, and (4) body management and control, as well as suggested activities for infants, toddlers, and preschoolers, are included in this section.

Eye-Hand/Eye-Foot Coordination

The first subdomain in the area of perceptual motor development encompasses the development of eye-hand and eye-foot coordination. Young children develop increasingly complex skills for manipulating and acting on objects in their environment. Specific developmental goals in this subdomain include the following:

1. Encourage the development of object-manipulation skills (Williams, 1983).

2. Help children learn the object-projection skills of throwing, catching, and striking (Williams, 1983).

3. Foster the development of fine motor skills such as scribbling, drawing, and writing.

4. Enhance the development of visual tracking skills.

The development of eye-hand and eye-foot coordination can best be fostered by providing an environment where children can manipulate and act on a variety of objects and materials. In addition, specific activities can be developed for each age group to facilitate the development of eye-hand and eye-foot coordination. Here are some suggested sample activities for infants, toddlers, and preschoolers that can be adapted for a variety of developmental levels (an asterisk [*] denotes an activity that is also appropriate for use in the outdoor play environment).

INFANT ACTIVITY

Stringing Bottle Rings (Quiet Game)*

Provide a variety of bottle rings (that secure a nipple on a bottle) and a long string. Encourage infants to put the string through the bottle rings. You may want to secure one end of the string to a large object so that the rings do not fall off. You also can tie the two ends of the string together to make a necklace. The larger holes in the bottle rings make it easier for infants to put a string through them. Experiment with different types and thicknesses of rope.

Additional Skills:

Cognition (problem solving/reasoning); communication (receptive language)

Adaptations for Children with Disabilities:

Physically Impaired: If the child has difficulty holding the string, attach a small ring, rattle, or another object that the child can grasp (and that will fit through the bottle rings). Provide physical assistance as needed.

Speech/Language Impaired: None needed.

Visually Impaired: None needed.

Hearing Impaired: None needed.

Behavior Disordered/Emotionally Disturbed: None needed.

TODDLER ACTIVITY

Balls in the Box (Active Game)*

Set up a big box with one open end. Allow the children to practice kicking balls into the box. Give the children a variety of sizes of balls to kick. Give children an opportunity to kick the ball in different ways—for example, both as it is rolling and as it is lying still.

Variation: Have the children throw the ball into the box using both hands or one hand.

Additional Skills:

Perceptual motor (locomotor skills)

Adaptations for Children with Disabilities:

Physically Impaired: If the child cannot kick, modify the activity to throw, push, or hit the ball into the box.

Speech/Language Impaired: Encourage the child to verbalize actions.

Visually Impaired: Explain the activity in detail. Tap the box to provide auditory cues. Have the child face the tapping sound, and then indicate to the child which foot is closer to the ball. Encourage independent kicking, but provide assistance as needed to prevent frustration.

Hearing Impaired: Use signs and/or gestures to explain the activity.

Behavior Disordered/Emotionally Disturbed: None needed.

PRESCHOOL ACTIVITY

Cutting Party (Art)

Encourage children to explore and practice using scissors by inviting them to a cutting party. Provide paper party hats for children to wear when they come to the table to cut. Use songs about cutting; for example, to the tune of "Open, Shut Them," sing: "Open, shut them, open, shut them; scissors open and shut. Open, shut them, open, shut them; this is the way to cut!" Or sing to the tune of "The More We Get Together": "The more we cut together, the happier we'll be." Children may cut pa-per scraps, newspaper, magazine pictures, old calendars, and the like. Children who are having difficulty should be given narrow paper strips so that one scissor cut will result in success.

Additional Skills:

Socialization (social interaction)

Adaptations for Children with Disabilities:

Physically Impaired: Provide squeeze or loop scissors for the child to use independently but provide assistance if needed. Stiffer paper might be easier for the child. Seat the child away from the table to cut in his or her lap if this is easier.

Speech/Language Impaired: None needed.

Visually Impaired: Use narrow paper strips to provide an opportunity for more success. Encourage the child to feel across the strip before cutting. Provide verbal directions as needed.

Hearing Impaired: Use signs and/or gestures to explain the activity.

Behavior Disordered/Emotionally Disturbed: None needed.

Locomotor Skills

The second subdomain in the area of perceptual motor development is locomotor skills. Young children need to develop increasingly complex and competent locomotor skills in order to successfully engage in a variety of play experiences. Specific developmental goals in this subdomain include the following:

1. Help children develop the ability to use the large muscles of the body in moving the total body horizontally through space (Williams, 1983).
2. Help children learn the body projection skills of running, jumping, hopping, skipping, galloping, leaping, and sliding (Williams, 1983).

3. Foster total body movement through creative dance (Hendrick, 1998).
4. Foster the ability to maintain the body in a state of equilibrium when moving (Williams, 1983).

The development of locomotor skills is best facilitated in a program that has a well-integrated indoor and outdoor play curriculum with many opportunities for moving and exploring the body in relationship to space, although specific activities in the indoor and outdoor classroom can emphasize the importance of developing locomotor skills. Here are some suggested sample activities for infants, toddlers, and preschoolers that can be adapted for a variety of developmental levels (an asterisk [*] denotes an activity that is also appropriate for use in the outdoor play environment).

INFANT ACTIVITY
Bouncing Babies (Movement)

The teacher should choose two or three large cushions or an old mattress and make a "bounding pit." Surround the cushions with carpeted blocks, platforms, small room dividers, snap walls, or even a cardboard box. Help babies to bounce on their cushions. Very young infants can bounce gently (do not shake) when lying down on their tummies, backs, or in a sitting position, holding a teacher's hands. Infants who are able to stand can bounce while standing and holding on to a teacher's hands. Walkers should be encouraged to bounce by themselves. The teacher can support an infant in a standing position to help the baby jump and get the feeling of bouncing and landing. Encourage infants to "bounce like a bunny." Infants also can explore on their own with the cushions.

Additional Skills:

Socialization (social interaction); cognition (imitation/memory)

Adaptations for Children with Disabilities:

Physically Impaired: None needed.

Speech/Language Impaired: None needed.

Visually Impaired: None needed.

Hearing Impaired: Use signs and/or gestures to explain the activity.

Behavior Disordered/Emotionally Disturbed: None needed.

TODDLER ACTIVITY
Animal Dancing (Movement)*

Encourage the children to pretend that they are specific animals and to make animal sounds as they are moving. Here are some examples of animal sounds and movements:

Cow: crawling—"Moooo"

Bunny: hopping—make ears by holding hands up to head

Dog: crawling—"Arf-Arf" (shake bottom to pretend to wag tail)

Monkey: hunched over walking with arms scratching side of body—"Eee-Eee"

Snake: wiggling on the floor—"Ssss-Ssss"

Bird: arms out to pretend to fly—"Tweet-Tweet"

Additional Skills:

Cognition (association/classification)

Adaptations for Children with Disabilities:

Physically Impaired: Provide physical assistance as needed, but encourage the child to move as independently and creatively as possible.

Speech/Language Impaired: None needed.

Visually Impaired: Verbally describe ways the animals move. Encourage the other children to suggest various body movements to use. Provide physical assistance if needed.

Hearing Impaired: Use signs and/or gestures to explain the activity.

Behavior Disordered/Emotionally Disturbed: None needed.

PRESCHOOL ACTIVITY
Let's Go Skating (Imaginary Play)

Set up the imaginary-play area to resemble a frozen lake. Use masking tape to outline the lake. At the lake's edge, provide a campfire (tape an oven rack to unit blocks and use rocks, sticks, and red tissue paper for the fire). Provide empty milk and cocoa containers, a pan to heat the cocoa, and spoons and cups. Also provide hats, scarves, and mittens. Children can enjoy painting large evergreen tree shapes on butcher paper on the wall. Cut $\frac{1}{4}$-inch masonite into pieces (approximately 6 by 12 inches) to use for "skates." Children skate by stepping on and scooting the boards.

Variation: Just provide the boards and use "magic dust" to transform the room into a frozen pond. Play music with a slow tempo and encourage children to skate to the music.

Additional Skills:

Socialization (social interaction and cooperation)

Adaptations for Children with Disabilities:

Physically Impaired: Attach the "skates" to the sides of the chair or walker so that the child will not slip while

skating but will be able to participate with the other children. Also, a cardboard box, cut out to fit around the wheelchair, can become a "sled" for the child to use.

Speech/Language Impaired: Encourage receptive identification and naming of the various props in this activity.

Visually Impaired: Provide a "tour" of the area to show the child what props are available, how the props are to be used, and where the props are located. Include a sighted child on this tour and ask that child to be the "tour guide" on the following days.

Hearing Impaired: Use signs and/or gestures to explain the activity and name the props.

Behavior Disordered/Emotionally Disturbed: None needed.

Nonlocomotor Skills

The third subdomain in the area of perceptual motor development is nonlocomotor skills. Children's ability to develop nonlocomotor skills is related to

their mastery over their bodies, including the ability to relax, control movements within a confined space, and maintain a state of equilibrium. Specific developmental goals in this subdomain include the following:

1. Help children develop the ability to move the body or body parts while stationary within a well-defined, small area of space (Williams, 1983).
2. Help children learn the body manipulation skills of pulling, pushing, lifting, turning, stretching, twisting, rolling, and bending (Williams, 1983).
3. Encourage children to learn how to relax and calm their bodies (Hendrick, 1998).
4. Foster the ability to maintain the body in a state of equilibrium when stationary (Williams, 1983).

The development of nonlocomotor skills occurs when children have a variety of opportunities to engage in play experiences that encourage movement as well as relaxation and control of the body. In addition, specific activities can be developed for each age group to foster the development of nonlocomotor skills. Here are some suggested sample activities for infants, toddlers, and preschoolers that can be adapted for a variety of developmental levels (an asterisk [*] denotes an activity that is also appropriate for use in the outdoor play environment).

INFANT ACTIVITY
Shakers (Science/Nature)

The teachers should make several shakers using plastic spice containers or plastic drink bottles. Fill the container with jingle bells or plastic beads and tape them together securely. Give each infant a shaker and demonstrate shaking them. Allow infants to explore with the shakers by touching, feeling, mouthing, and manipulating them. Talk about the sounds the shakers make. A record may be used to encourage infants to shake and feel a rhythm. For very young infants, hold their arms with the shaker and help them shake it. Encourage infants to shake the shakers when sitting, standing, stretching, and squatting.

Additional Skills:

Cognition (concept formation)

Adaptations for Children with Disabilities:

Physically Impaired: Make handles out of cardboard or plastic to help the child hold the shaker. If the child cannot grasp the strip handle, make the handle big enough for the wrist to slip into it.

Speech/Language Impaired: None needed.

Visually Impaired: None needed.

Hearing Impaired: Use signs and/or gestures to explain the activity.

Behavior Disordered/Emotionally Disturbed: None needed.

TODDLER ACTIVITY
Stretching (Movement)*

Give a colorful scarf to each child. Put on soft, slow music and ask the children to stretch to the music. Encourage them to hold the scarf in each hand and stretch high into the sky, then down toward their toes. Encourage the children to stretch to their right and to their left. Then have the children lie on their backs and stretch their scarves above their heads.

Additional Skills:

Communication (receptive language); emotional well-being (coping skills)

Adaptations for Children with Disabilities:

Physically Impaired: If the child cannot grasp the scarf, attach Velcro bracelets to each end and let the child "wear" the scarf on both hands. Provide physical assistance as needed.

Speech/Language Impaired: None needed.

Visually Impaired: None needed.

Hearing Impaired: Use signs and/or gestures to explain the activity and give the directions.

Behavior Disordered/Emotionally Disturbed: None needed.

PRESCHOOL ACTIVITY
Are You Twisting? (Movement)

Use the tune "Are You Sleeping?" and substitute nonlocomotor movements such as stretching, bending, swaying, twisting, and so on:

> Are you twisting? Are you twisting?
> Brother John, Brother John?
> Morning bells are ringing,
> Morning bells are ringing,
> Ding, ding, dong
> Ding, ding, dong.

Choose children to take turns being the leader and substitute the child's name in the song.

Additional Skills:

Communication (receptive language); emotional well-being (personality integration)

Adaptations for Children with Disabilities:

Physically Impaired: Include nonlocomotor movements the child can do independently.

Speech/Language Impaired: None needed.

Visually Impaired: Encourage the child to follow verbal directions, providing physical assistance as needed.

Hearing Impaired: Use signs and/or gestures to explain the activity and to sing the song.

Behavior Disordered/Emotionally Disturbed: None needed.

Body Management and Control

The fourth subdomain in the area of perceptual motor development is the process of acquiring body management and control. Helping children learn about their bodies in space and to manage motor skills in a variety of situations are major tasks of developing body management and control. Specific developmental goals in this subdomain include the following:

1. Encourage children's ability to manage daily motor skills (Hendrick, 1998).
2. Help children learn rhythm, static and dynamic balance, and temporal awareness (Hendrick, 1998).

3. Help children develop agility and coordination (ability to stop, start, change directions) (Williams, 1983).
4. Help children learn body and space perception (Hendrick, 1998).

Although developing body management and control is best accomplished in an environment where children can practice a variety of motor skills on a daily basis, specific activities can be developed for each age group to support the development of these abilities. here are some suggested sample activities for infants, toddlers, and preschoolers that can be adapted for a variety of developmental levels (an asterisk [*] denotes an activity that is also appropriate for use in the outdoor play environment).

INFANT ACTIVITY
Magic Carpet Ride (Movement)

The teacher should use a large blanket or quilt for the magic carpet. Older infants can be seated on the quilt and young infants can lie on their tummies. The teacher can pull the blanket around the classroom on a linoleum floor. The ride can be fast or slow. It can stop and pick up and drop off infants at certain destinations. Teachers can emphasize that the children are "riding together" or "taking turns" on the magic carpet. The carpet can travel on a

curvy ride or a straight ride, offering more of a challenge for infants to continue sitting.

Additional Skills:

Socialization (social interaction and cooperation)

Adaptations for Children with Disabilities:

Physically Impaired: Position the child in the safest position, in an infant seat or with another adult holding the child. Children with a history of seizures will need to move slowly.

Speech/Language Impaired: None needed.

Visually Impaired: None needed.

Hearing Impaired: Use signs and/or gestures to explain the activity.

Behavior Disordered/Emotionally Disturbed: None needed.

TODDLER ACTIVITY
Copycat Rhythms (Music)

Give the children a variety of musical instruments, such as cymbals, blocks, drums, sticks, and so on. Start with simple beats, such as two claps in a sequence, and ask the children to mimic or copy the sound they hear. Increase the difficulty of the beat to develop the children's rhythmic skills. As the children master the simple rhythmic patterns, encourage them to move around the room while using their musical instruments to the beat.

Additional Skills:

Perceptual motor (coordination); communication (receptive language, auditory memory/discrimination)

Adaptations for Children with Disabilities:

Physically Impaired: If the child cannot hold an instrument, tie a jingle-bell bracelet or shaker to the child's wrist. Encourage the child to imitate the pattern.

Speech/Language Impaired: None needed.

Visually Impaired: None needed.

Hearing Impaired: Use signs and/or gestures to explain the activity. Ask the child to imitate the rhythmic sequences. Use exaggerated movements to cue the child.

Behavior Disordered/Emotionally Disturbed: None needed.

PRESCHOOL ACTIVITY
Walk the Tightrope (Active Game)*

Attach 3 yards of 1 inch elastic to two 12-by-1-inch dowel rods. Two people hold the dowels so that the elastic is approximately 12 to 18 inches off the floor. Announce the tightrope walker: "Ladies and gentlemen, the amazing Steven Sutton will walk the tightrope above the center ring." As the child steps on the elastic, there is the illusion of walking on a tightrope even though each step lowers the elastic to the floor. The audience cheers the tightrope walker.

Additional Skills:

Emotional well-being (personality integration)

Adaptations for Children with Disabilities:

Physically Impaired: If needed, assist the child with walking on the elastic. Use wider elastic strips if the child uses a wheelchair or walker.

Speech/Language Impaired: None needed.

Visually Impaired: Ask another child to be the child's partner and lead the child across the tightrope.

Hearing Impaired: Use signs to explain the activity.

Behavior Disordered/Emotionally Disturbed: None needed.

CHAPTER SUMMARY _____

Teachers who want children to develop body mastery and control and become comfortable with their physi-cal selves will provide a variety of physical activities in the indoor and outdoor play environments. Young children, who receive support from teachers to master physical challenges regardless of their level of skill development, will be more likely to attempt new physical activities and to enjoy their involvement in these

activities. When competition and comparison are eliminated from physical endeavors, young children can develop good feelings about themselves and their physical capabilities, whatever their strengths may be.

■ ■ ■ ■ ■   ■ ■ ■ ■

In order to develop perceptual motor skills, young children need opportunities to actively explore the environment and engage in a variety of movement, large-motor, and small-motor activities. Teachers of young children must recognize children's level of physical, cognitive, emotional, and social development to plan developmentally appropriate and growth-promoting activities.

Specifically, it is important to do the following:

- Provide an environment where infants and toddlers can engage in practice play by exploring objects, activities, and equipment.

- Organize the indoor and outdoor classroom environment to facilitate opportunities for preschool children to develop motor skills through symbolic play.

- Allow children to develop an increase in group games as they are developmentally ready, rather than pushing participation in games or sports. When children become interested in and motivated by group games, place the emphasis on problem solving, creativity, and cooperation rather than teacher-imposed rules and competition.

- Encourage children to test their physical skills in an atmosphere that helps children achieve success regardless of their level of motor skill development.

- Enhance children's development of a positive physical self-image by planning activities that are appropriate for a wide range of skill levels and interests.

■ ■ ■ ■ ■   ■ ■ ■ ■

DISCUSSION QUESTIONS _____

1. Discuss the vignette at the beginning of the chapter. What other questions or concerns might you have? Discuss the vignette at the end of the chapter. Are there other responses you might have to this situation?

2. Describe reflex behaviors that are present at birth. What evolutionary value could be associated with each behavior?

3. Describe examples of *proximodistal* and *cephalocaudal* development.

4. Describe the development of children's skills in handling small objects.

5. What is the role of cognition and cognitive activity in the development of children's perceptual motor skills?

6. What is the sequence of the development of children's writing and drawing skills?

7. Describe a newborn's sensory capabilities.

8. How can teachers foster children's practice play?

9. What classroom equipment and props are likely to promote symbolic play?

10. Discuss the role and timing of games with rules and organized team sports for children related to their social, emotional, cognitive, and physical development.

11. Describe the subdomains of development in perceptual motor skills.

REFERENCES _____

Bornstein, M. (1978). Chromatic vision in infancy. In H. Reese & L. Lipsitt (Eds.), *Advances in child development and behavior* (Vol. 12, pp. 117–182). New York: Academic Press.

Cratty, B. (1970). *Perceptual and motor development in infants and children.* New York: Macmillan.

Cratty, B., & Martin, M. (1969). *Perceptual motor efficiency in children: The measurement and improvement of movement attributes.* Philadelphia: Lea & Febiger.

Elkind, D. (1988). *The hurried child: Growing up too fast too soon* (Rev. ed.). Reading, MA: Addison-Wesley.

Fogel, A. (1991). *Infancy.* St. Paul, MN: West.

Gerber, M. (1985). The psycho-motor development of African children in the first year of life and the influences of maternal behavior. *Journal of Social Psychology, 47,* 185–195.

Gesell, A. (1925). *The mental growth of the pre-school child.* New York: Macmillan.

Halverson, L. (1990). Motor development and phsycial education for young children. In B. Stinson (Ed.), *Moving and learning for the young child* (pp. 85–103). Reston, VA: American Alliance for Health, Physical Education, Recreation, and Dance.

Haywood, K. (1986). *Lifespan motor development.* Champaign, IL: Human Kinetics.

Hendrick, J. (1998). *Total learning: Developmental curriculum for the young child* (5th ed.). Columbus, OH: Merrill/Prentice-Hall.

Herkowitz, J. (1978). Developmental task analysis: The design of movement experiences and evaluation of motor development status. In M. Ridenour (Ed.), *Motor development: Issues and applications* (pp. 139–164). Princeton, NJ: Princeton Book Company.

Honig, A. (1990). Baby moves: Relation to learning. In B. Stinson (Ed.), *Moving and learning for the young child* (pp. 31–41). Reston, VA: American Alliance for Health, Physical Education, Recreation, and Dance.

James, W. (1890). *The principles of psychology.* New York: Henry Holt.

Johns, B., & Johns, M. (1983). Stress burns out kids, too. *Education Digest, 49*(2), 44–46.

Kamii, C., & DeVries, R. (1980). *Group games in early education: Implications of Piaget's theory.* Washington, DC: National Association for the Education of Young Children.

Kermoian, R., & Campos, J. (1988). Locomotor experience: A facilitator of spatial cognitive development. *Child Development, 59,* 908–917.

Laban, R. (1988). *The mastery of movement* (4th ed.). London: MacDonald & Evans.

MacFarlane, A. (1975). Olfaction in the development of social preferences in the human neonate. In Ciba Foundation Symposium (Ed.), *Parent-infant interaction* (pp. 103–117). New York: Elsevier.

McCall, R. (1980). *Infants.* New York: Random House.

Milne, A. A. (1957). *The world of Pooh: The complete Winnie-the-Pooh and the House at Pooh Corner.* New York: Dutton.

Rogers, C. S., & Sawyers, J. K. (1988). *Play in the lives of children.* Washington, DC: National Association for the Education of Young Children.

Rosenstein, D., & Oster, H. (1988). Differential facial responses to four basic tastes in newborns. *Child Development, 59,* 1555–1568.

Sobel, J. (1983). Everybody wins: Non-competitive games. *Day Care and Early Education, 13*(2), 30–34.

Spodek, B., & Saracho, O. (1994). *Dealing with individual differences in the early childhood classroom.* New York: Longman.

Stinson, B. (1992). Early childhood trends in movement development. In C. Seefeldt (Ed.), *The early childhood curriculum: A review of current research* (2nd ed., pp. 226–236). New York: Teachers College Press.

Stoner, L. (1978). Selecting physical activities for the young child, with an understanding of bone growth and development. In J. Shick & J. Klayman (Eds.), *Reviews of research for practitioners and parents* (pp. 32–42). Minneapolis, MN: Center for Early Education and Development.

Williams, H. G. (1983). Assessment of gross motor functioning. In J. Paget & B. Bracken (Eds.), *The psychoeducational assessment of preschool children* (pp. 225–260). New York: Harcourt Brace Jovanovich.

ADDITIONAL RESOURCES

Andress, B. (1991). From research to practice: Preschool children and their movement responses to music. *Young Children, 47*(1), 22–27.

Boucher, A. (1988). Good beginnings. *Journal of Physical Education, Recreation and Dance, 59*(7), 42.

Buschner, C. (1990). Can we help children move and think critically? In B. Stinson (Ed.), *Moving and learning for the young child* (pp. 51–66). Reston, VA: American Alliance for Health, Physical Education, Recreation and Dance.

Curtis, S. (1982). *The joy of movement in early childhood.* New York: Teachers College Press.

Eastman, W. (1997). Active living: Physical activities for infants, toddlers, and preschoolers. *Early Childhood Education Journal, 24*(3), 161–164.

Engstrom, G. (Ed.). (1971). *The significance of the young child's motor development.* Washington, DC: National Association for the Education of Young Children.

Frost, J., & Sunderlin, S. (Eds.). (1985). When children play: *Proceedings of the International Conference on Play and Play Environments.* Wheaton, MD: Association for Childhood Education International.

Gallahue, D. (1993). Motor development and movement skill acquisition in early childhood education. In B. Spodek (Ed.), *Handbook of research on the education of young children* (pp. 24–41). New York: Macmillan.

Grineski, S. (1993). Children, cooperative learning, and physical education. *Teaching Elementary Physical Education, 46,* 10–11, 14.

Hammett, C. (1992). *Movement activities for early childhood.* Champaign, IL: Human Kinetics.

Pica, R. (1997). Beyond physical development: Why young children need to move. *Young Children, 52*(6), 4–11.

Poest, C., Williams, R., Witt, D., & Atwood, M. (1990). Challenge me to move: Long muscle development in young children. *Young Children, 45*(5), 4–10.

Rivkin, M. (1995). *The great outdoors: Restoring children's right to play outside.* Washington, DC: National Association for the Education of Young Children.

Rodger, L. (1996). Adding movement throughout the day. *Young Children, 51*(3), 4–6.

Sanders, S. (1992). *Designing preschool movement programs.* Champaign, IL: Human Kinetics.

Sullivan, M. (1982). *Feeling strong, feeling free: Movement exploration for young children.* Washington, DC: National Association for the Education of Young Children.

Torta, S. (1994). Join my dance: The unique movement style of each infant and toddler can invite communication, expression and intervention. *Zero to Three, 15*(1), 1–11.

Werner, P., Timms, S., & Almond, L. (1996). Health stops: Practical ideas for health-related exercise in preschool and primary classrooms. *Young Children, 51*(6), 48–55.

FOUR . . . .

PROFESSIONAL ISSUES IN EARLY CHILDHOOD CURRICULA AND PROGRAMS

17.

Issues in Implementing
Early Childhood Curriculum

As a new preschool teacher in a public-school program, you are pleased to find that the majority of children in your classroom are excited about beginning their first school experience. However, you soon become extremely concerned about Joshua, a 4-year-old who has a very difficult time separating from his parents and seems to have tremendous anxiety about coming to school. Joshua's parents ask to talk with you, and with some difficulty they describe their family situation to you.

The parents recount the painful experience Joshua's older brother had during his first year of school when he entered a highly structured, rigid, and academically oriented preschool program, had an unsuccessful experience, and was retained in preschool for a second year. The parents realized how much of his brother's struggle Joshua had internalized when they started to prepare him for preschool. Joshua was very silent at first. Then he began to respond by saying, "I'm going to put a big book on my head so I will stay small and I won't have to go to school," or "I'm going to build a tunnel to go to Granddad's house, so when they come to take me to school they won't be able to find me," or "I'm not going to eat today so I won't grow bigger and I won't have to go to school." Indeed, some days Joshua did not eat much and his parents were beginning to worry about his physical health as well as his emotional well-being.

You and Joshua's parents make a commitment to work together to gradually transition Joshua into the classroom, offer him support, help him have successful experiences, and help him learn that school can be a good place to be. You are very troubled by this story, worried about Joshua and his family, and determined to help. You also realize that this family's experience raises broader questions and issues for you:

- How can you be sure that you are using your knowledge about children's development and curriculum planning to create a positive, stimulating, and appropriate classroom where children want to come each day?
- What will you do when you encounter a colleague who creates a rigid, academically oriented program? How will you relate to that teacher? How can you help convince that teacher that there is a better, more positive, and more productive way to teach young children?
- Is it possible to create an environment where the teachers agree about what to teach and how to teach—where they can have a shared vision about the education of young children?
- How will you react if your supervisor asks you to teach in a quiet, passive classroom environment with worksheets completed at desks, instead of the active classroom environment with learning centers you prefer? Will you have the knowledge to defend your practices and the courage to make the best choices for the children?
- What can you do to prevent other children from having unsuccessful school experiences? How can you become involved with other professionals to help ensure high-quality, developmentally appropriate programs for all young children?

Suggestions for responding to this classroom vignette will be shared at the end of the chapter.

When reading this chapter, focus on how to use the results of research and what you have learned about the components of curriculum to build a high-quality early childhood classroom. Also gain an understanding of how to develop a professional identity in the workplace and how to implement standards of excellence in the field of early childhood education.

The previous chapters have described how young children learn and develop and how the various components of the creative-play curriculum contribute to high-quality early childhood program environments. Teachers of young children are required to use their knowledge and skills to provide a comprehensive, integrated curriculum that facilitates the optimal creative development of young children. In order to make effective decisions about integrating and implementing creative-play curriculum, it is important to consider what research tells us about the effects of early childhood programs, to compare the types of programs for young children in the United States with program-delivery models in other countries, and to develop an awareness of professional issues affecting early childhood teachers and programs.

ANALYZING THE EFFECTS OF EARLY CHILDHOOD PROGRAMS _____

With the initiation of Head Start in 1965 and the growth of preschool programs in the 1970s and 1980s, there has also been a wealth of research studies to determine the effects of early childhood education on children and families. The early research of the 1960s and 1970s examined several outcomes, primarily developmental and behavioral factors such as IQ, language, and social behavior. In long-term research, children's later school achievement scores and grades were measured. When follow-up of these children was completed, these gains diminished, usually by the second and third grades. Researchers began to recognize the more complex set of influences on children's development and expanded the measurement outcomes in later research. These expanded measures included assessment of children's school and career aspirations and behavior beyond school, such as employment, college admission, or arrest record. Measures of parents' behavior and child-rearing practices were also included to assess the indirect influence of programs on children.

Although many unanswered questions remain, there is agreement in several areas about the effects of early childhood programs on children and families. Children's cognitive development has been the concern of many parents, teachers, and researchers. In general, high-quality programs have positive effects on children, particularly in language development. Children from disadvantaged backgrounds that place children at risk for developmental delays and school failure appear to benefit cognitively from most preschool programs. A second area of interest is children's social development. Children who have preschool experience, compared to children whose primary care was by a parent, are more social, have more positive and negative social interactions with other children, and engage in more cooperative and associative play. Some studies have found such children to be more aggressive; other studies have found them to be more assertive, but not necessarily aggressive.

A third area, that of children's emotional development, has received renewed emphasis in the last decade, particularly on the issue of parent–child attachment. Most of the early research suggested that children who are in nonparental care are able to form multiple attachments, with parents and other caregivers, and the attachments with other caregivers do not diminish the quality of infants' attachment to parents. More recent research has raised concerns about the effects of infant programs, particularly for children who enter in the first year of life for more than 30 hours a week. This research has been criticized for the small sample sizes or numbers of children in the studies and also for the measure used to assess children's attachment. The assessment instrument was developed in the 1960s to use with children who had little or no experience in nonparental care, and the appropriateness of its continued use with large numbers of children who have extensive experience in preschool programs is currently being debated.

Research has examined indirect effects of early childhood programs on children. For example, indirect effects occur when parents change the home environment, their verbal or physical interactions with children, or their child-rearing practices, such as discipline, as a result of the parents' involvement in early childhood programs. These changes at home have outcomes on children's development and behavior as a result of the program's effect on parents.

A review of program effects on children reveals that all programs do not have the same effects; all children are not affected in the same ways. These program-specific outcomes are a result of variations or differences in programs. One factor responsible for differences in programs and resulting differences in child outcomes is the variation in quality. Programs of higher quality foster children's cognitive, social, and emotional development and skills for thinking, learning, and interacting with others. Components of higher quality programs include a developmental curriculum, low child–staff ratio and small group size, developmentally appropriate assessment, and safe and adequate space and materials. Teachers also are an important part of quality programs; they should be trained in early childhood development and education, show a recognition of and sensitivity to the needs of children and parents, relate to parents as partners in children's education, and receive adequate compensation, in-service training, and supervisory support in order to be retained in their position and in the field of early childhood education (Schweinhart, 1988).

Another variable that results in different outcomes in children is the curriculum. The curriculum was examined as a variable in a study of the effects of preschool education on 54 children at age 15 and age 23. The children had been enrolled in preschool education as 3- and 4-year-olds from lower socioeconomic backgrounds. In the first year of preschool, the children's IQ had increased significantly; however, IQ gains and school achievement diminished over time. At age 15, there were important differences among the students based on the three curriculum models. Students who had been enrolled in programs using a behavioral, teacher-directed curriculum model had engaged in twice as many delinquent behaviors as had the children in the cognitive-development or free play models. Students in the behavioral model had poorer relationships with family members, participated in fewer school sports, and were less likely to seek help for personal problems (Schweinhart, Weikart, & Larner, 1986). By age 23, children who had been in the teacher-directed curriculum model had three times as many arrests for felonies, were almost eight times more likely to have been treated for emotional impairments, and were much less likely to have done volunteer work or to have voted in the 1996 presidential election. These results "suggest that specific curriulum models based on child-initiated learning activities are essential if preschool programs are to produce lasting benefits . . . and supports the preventive value of [appropriate] early childhood education" (Schweinhart & Weikar, 1997).

A valuable contribution to the literature is research that examines long-term, socially relevant outcomes of early childhood programs. Children from low socioeconomic backgrounds with preschool education, compared to children with similar backgrounds but with no preschool education, are less likely to be retained in a grade, require special-education placement, get pregnant as teenagers, have a juvenile arrest record, or drop out of high school; they are more likely to graduate, have higher career aspirations, and be employed after high school. Comparing the cost of preschool education to the costs associated with later services to children who lack preschool education reveals that the latter outweighs the former by seven times (Berrueta-Clement, Schweinhart, Barnett, Epstein, & Weikart, 1984; Consortium for Longitudinal Studies, 1983).

Future research on the effects of early childhood programs must be sensitive to the complex, interrelated ecological variables that influence children's development. For example, teachers in a program may influence parents' child-rearing practices, which later will affect children's behavior and development. Research also must focus on those elements that can be modified programmatically or administratively. Finally, research that is longitudinal and that examines the many outcomes for children, their families, and for society is essential for enlightened decision making about early childhood programs.

CROSS-CULTURAL PERSPECTIVES ON EARLY CHILDHOOD PROGRAMS _____

Much of the research that composes the knowledge base in early childhood education has focused on programs and curricula in the United States. A cross-cultural perspective on early childhood education, however, enriches and broadens our efforts and understanding, both in the policy arena and in the development of curriculum practices. Although the level of activity in research and rhetoric is high in the United States, our nation appears to lag behind many other countries in its examination of the nature of early care and education, particularly in quality, comprehensiveness, and governmental support and leadership. Most Western European nations provide services to young children up to the age of school entrance in a system of free programs available to all children if their parents choose to use them. In comparison, the United States has a child-care system that has been described as a "non-system," a chaotic system, one in which there is considerable confusion, varying quality, much overlap, and little or no government leadership or support (Kamerman & Kahn, 1978).

For example, Sweden has a comprehensive program of care and education for young children up to the age of 7, the age of school entrance. The system of "child centers" includes preschool, which may be either day nurseries (all-day child care) or part-time groups, and free-time centers (school-age child care both before and after the school day). Family day care is widespread, and there are also programs, referred to as "complementary preschool activities," to provide care for sick children of parents employed by the government, to provide supervision of children in public parks for parents who wish to leave children for a brief time, and to provide preschool education and services to children with special needs or a chronic illness who are unable to attend preschool. All these services are developed, monitored, and funded by local government, with leadership from national government authorities. Early childhood education and care is viewed as a "natural" component of a broad social responsibility that the government and its citizens have to ensure high-quality services that promote the health and development of all children. The Swedish program is "evidence that a high level of programming and imagination can be sustained over many local jurisdictions . . . through leadership, encouragement, and technical-financial aid from central authorities and commissions" (Kahn & Kamerman, 1975).

In Denmark, there are national guidelines for family day care. (The United States does not have national guidelines for center-based or home-based child care or early education.) Social-services supervisors have a case load of 50 or fewer children (not programs) whom they visit at least twice a month. Supervisors are available by phone at least two hours each day to talk to teachers, answer questions, and provide support. The government provides equipment, materials, liability insurance, workers' compensation, sick leave, paid vacation (five weeks), and paid release time for training to all family day-care providers. One-third of the providers' income is tax-free, to help with the costs of food, utilities, and "household wear and tear." The Danish model is one for comparison and emulation especially in the areas of regulation and supervision, training, and monetary support and compensation. "Comparing our largely unregulated system [in the United States] to the thoughtfully supported and supervised Danish one creates questions about our priorities" (Corsini, 1991, p. 15).

In addition, many European countries offer programs for young children that emphasize play and individualized learning. The emphasis on formal academic programs generally begins much later in a child's development, with some countries beginning formal schooling at age 7. For example, one curriculum area of great concern in public schools in the United States is the development of reading skills. Many parents and teachers begin focusing on reading readiness in the early years, but the United States still has a major problem with illiteracy. In Denmark, however, preschool classrooms include a focus on a variety of language experiences, and formal reading instruction is delayed until second grade. There is also a 100 percent literacy rate in Denmark (Elkind, 1987).

The British infant- and primary-school models also include an emphasis on individualized learning experiences. Classrooms have rich supplies of creative and concrete materials, manipulative toys, and a variety of learning centers. Early reading or number experiences are not forced and occur only if chil-

dren express an interest. This informal education model is based on teachers' planning for individual children and respecting children's unique styles of learning. This environment is also characterized by a high level of trust in children's ability to utilize a variety of learning experiences to enhance their development and allowing children "the fullest involvement that comes through pursuit of their own purposes and questions and choices" (Weber, 1971, pp. 134–135). Children clearly are active participants in their learning and in the life of the school.

In Hungary, an approach to infant care and education was developed by Dr. Emmi Pikler, and its use has extended into other countries; it has been called the Pikler model or the Resources for Infant Educarers model. The approach is based on the importance of respectful, responsive, and reciprocal interaction and communication between infants and adults. To grow into adults who respect themselves and others, infants must be treated with respect. Principles of this approach include meaningfully involving infants in routines and activities that concern them, letting infants solve problems through incidental learning opportunities, teaching trust by being dependable and consistent, and focusing on quality interactions and experiences at each stage of development rather than rushing children to reach developmental milestones (Gonzalez-Mena & Eyer, 1997).

In France the *école maternelle* (nursery school) is a system of 18,000 preschools that serve more than 2 million children ages 2 through 5. Including the 300,000 children enrolled in private and religious preschools, which also are subsidized by the government, 84 percent of all preschoolers in France are enrolled in state-supported early childhood education. The schools are available and free to all preschool children, regardless of income or citizenship. Preschool teachers must have the equivalent of a master's degree in early childhood education. Class size is typically larger than in the United States; most classes have 28 children. The sponsors argue, however, that the highly paid, well-qualified staffs, which experience little turnover, compensate for the less desirable teacher–child ratios. Research on 20,000 children who attended the *école maternelle* found that they had higher rates of promotion from 6th grade through high school compared to other children. Research on children's emotional development found that children entering school at age 2 did not have more difficulty with the transition than 3-year-olds did. Some researchers have noted concerns about the large class size and age of entrance, as well as unanswered questions about children's emotional development and parent–child relationships; yet

France's system of free, universal early childhood education represents an acceptance of governmental concern and responsibility for the care and education of all children, even the very young (McMahan, 1992).

A consideration of developmental and educational practices in other countries reinforces the view of developmental milestones as a guide to our understanding of children's development and as an aid in fostering their development. Supporting children's development does not mean pushing children to reach milestones "on time." Instead, teachers should use developmental milestones to know what children need from adults to support their development and learning, in order for children to reach their own level of development "in their own time," rather than "on time" (Gonzalez-Mena & Eyer, 1997).

INTEGRATING THE COMPONENTS OF CURRICULUM

The ability to offer high-quality, developmentally appropriate programs for young children depends on knowledge of research and program models, availability of program support and resources, and understanding of the components of curriculum. It can seem somewhat overwhelming to consider implementing the many components of the creative-play curriculum: the variety of teaching roles, parent participation strategies, classroom guidance techniques, and design and organization of the indoor and outdoor environments that compose the invisible curriculum, as well as the assessment processes, goal setting, and activity planning necessary to support the visible curriculum. In order to take the various components of the curriculum and integrate them into a total classroom environment that reflects an understanding of the whole child, it is necessary to demystify the concept of a curriculum and consider how to define the curriculum in a manner that leads to implementation.

The curriculum is what teachers and young children do together during the day. The curriculum is what happens—the interaction, the activities, the surprises, the ups and downs, the materials, the learning centers, the movement from one place to the next—with children and adults spending time and experiencing learning together. Implementing a curriculum necessitates knowing children—their characteristics, what they like to do, how they learn; and knowing teachers—the characteristics of the best teachers, how they interact with children, how they teach. Implementing the curriculum also requires integrating theory and practice, exhibiting flexibility and openness, and exercising professional judgment in order to do the following:

- Adapt the curriculum for a particular population of children and families, recognizing and valuing the diverse needs of individuals
- Search for new ideas and innovative activities to enrich curriculum offerings
- Evaluate and modify curriculum practices and teaching strategies as a result of new information and findings from current research

Integrating the curriculum involves preparing the classroom environment to meet overall program goals and planning daily and weekly activities to support children's individual developmental objectives. A truly integrated curriculum results in a day that flows smoothly, providing many opportunities for children to learn in all developmental areas, allowing for individual differences in learning styles and rates, and encouraging creativity through a variety of play experiences. In schools of the 21st century, there will be a growing need for children to develop creative skills and strengths that allow them to solve problems, generate new ideas, and adapt to a rapidly changing world (Tegano, Moran, & Sawyers, 1991). There also will be an increasing need for young children with disabilities to receive interventions in an inclusive program environment. An integrated, individualized curricular approach fosters the development of all children, regardless of developmental level (Odom & Warren, 1988).

CREATING A GOOD PLACE TO TEACH

As programs vary in the experiences they provide to children, so too do they vary in the work environment provided to teachers. Adults, like children, need positive, caring environments in order to be productive and creative and to continue to learn and develop. Even the most dedicated and knowledgeable teacher of young children cannot be effective without the support of colleagues and supervisors as well as the availability of program resources. In order to create optimal learning environments for children, the working conditions for teachers also must be optimal (Katz, 1977). Most teachers consider a good place to teach one that includes an open, flexible working environment, close and cooperative relationships with other adults, and adequate financial compensation.

Working Environment

Teachers of young children work in a helping profession that demands a constant expenditure of emotional, mental, and physical energy in order to meet the needs of children and families. A supportive and accepting working environment is necessary to help teachers be successful, refresh their perspectives, and facilitate continual growth.

Factors that increase teachers' well-being in the workplace include the following:

- Compatibility of personal views about teaching young children with the program philosophy
- Sufficient numbers of qualified staff members to provide individual educational experiences to small groups of children
- Availability of adequate program resources such as teaching materials, indoor and outdoor equipment, and classroom supplies
- Consistency in administrative support and encouraging, growth-promoting feedback on performance
- Continuing-learning and professional-development opportunities
- Participatory decision making that allows for teacher input and autonomy in the classroom
- Daily scheduling of work assignments that includes paid time for breaks, planning, and staff meetings
- Positive, cooperative, and empathic relationships with colleagues

Surveys of teachers' satisfaction and dissatisfaction with their salaries, benefits, and other conditions in their work environment have revealed several factors that produced high levels of satisfaction for teachers, such as job autonomy, relationship with one's supervisor and co-workers, and job clarity (Jorde-Bloom, 1988); daily work demands (Whitebook, Howes, & Phillips, 1990); working with children, intellectual challenge, and opportunities for creativity (Granger & Marx, 1988); contact with children (Kontos & Stremmel, 1988); and work schedule, relationship with other staff, job security, program resources, and agreement with program

goals and philosophy (Allen & Catron, 1987). In the last study, teachers also reported areas of greater dissatisfaction: salary, workload, and promotion opportunities. In studies that questioned teachers about what they did not like about their jobs, compensation—either salary or benefits or both—is mentioned most frequently.

Teachers' dissatisfaction also can be identified by the turnover rates in the profession (Phillips, Howes, & Whitebook, 1991). In a survey of 500 early childhood educators in Tennessee who were better educated and more satisfied than teachers in most other studies, over 30 percent of the teachers expected to leave the field within five to ten years (Allen & Catron, 1987). In a survey of 169 child-care workers in Pennsylvania, 41 percent reported that they planned to leave their job in the near future; one year later, 23 percent of them had. Teachers who perceived that other jobs were available to them or who had higher scores on a measurement of emotional exhaustion reported greater intent to leave; the former, perception of alternative jobs, was the best predictor of actual turnover (Manlove & Guzell, 1997).

Most studies of teacher turnover in early childhood education report annual rates of 26 to 41 percent (Whitebook, Phillips, & Howes, 1993). Clearly, annual turnover in child care is among the highest of all professions. And it also is clear that turnover is linked to low salaries. The National Child Care Staffing Study reported that salary was the most significant factor in predicting turnover. Programs with higher salaries and more benefits had teachers who reported more satisfaction and who were observed to engage in more positive, appropriate interactions with children (Whitebook, Howes, et al., 1990). In New York City, where state legislation mandated and funded a child-care salary enhancement and teachers received an average $1,200 increase in salary, the turnover rate was cut by half (Marx, Zinsser, & Porter, 1990).

The salaries and benefits provided to most early childhood teachers are inadequate compensation for positions that require a high level of training and experience and involve a high level of responsibility for the safety, well-being, and education of young children. In some studies, over a third of the child-care workers earned minimum wage or less. Most earn less for 12 months of work than public-school teachers do for nine months of employment. Numerous surveys have found that teachers of preschool children earn about half of the salary that teachers of older students do (Granger & Marx, 1988; Pettygrove, Whitebook, & Weir, 1984). In an NAEYC-sponsored survey of benefits provided to child-care workers, only 51 percent received social security, 26 percent received full medical coverage, 68 percent received sick days, and 53 percent received vacation days (NAEYC, 1984).

Acknowledging teachers' need for support, recognizing the importance of professional-development opportunities, and providing adequate salaries and benefits encourages the development of healthy program environments that result in higher levels of teacher satisfaction. Teachers whose basic needs for support and compensation are met are able to focus on planning and implementing developmentally appropriate, creative curricular activities with young children.

Relationships with Adults

Most early childhood teacher preparation programs devote the majority of time in course work and practicum experiences to helping students become effective at establishing relationships with children. However, an important component of teacher satisfaction in the workplace is the nature of relationships with other adults. Negative relationships with other teachers are often characterized by a lack of trust, an atmosphere of tension and conflict, and frequent misunderstandings that create a frustrating, unproductive working environment. Positive relationships, on the other hand, are characterized by trust, mutual respect, and emotional support that create a sense of well-being and productivity in the working environment.

In order to build effective teaching teams, increase the level of cooperation, and develop clear communication skills, it is necessary to be aware of differences in temperament, personality types, and styles of communication. The early childhood educator who wants to create positive relationships with other teachers needs to understand the uniqueness of personality traits.

One way to increase the understanding of self and others is to use a personality inventory, such as the Myers-Briggs Type Indicator (Myers, 1962), to learn about individual differences. The Myers-Briggs Type

Indicator is a personality survey based on the "psychological types" theory of Carl Jung (1923). Identifying psychological type involves determining individuals' preferences for knowing, relating, and acting. The four sets of preferences identified by Jung are classified as the *extroversion-introversion* preference, the *sensing-intuitive* preference, the *thinking-feeling* preference, and the *judgment-perception* preference. For example, the introvert is primarily oriented toward the inner world of concepts and ideas and the extrovert is oriented toward the outer world of people and things. The sensing individual becomes aware of things directly through the use of the senses and perceives the immediate, real, practical facts of experience, whereas the intuitive individual perceives possibilities, relationships, and the meaning of experiences and tends to rely on "hunches" or indirect perception by way of the unconscious. The thinker makes impersonal, objective judgments based on logic and principles and the feeler makes judgments subjectively and personally and is concerned with how decisions affect other people. The judging person prefers the order and control over events that come with decisiveness and closure, whereas the perceiving person prefers the flexibility and adaptability that comes with keeping options open (Myers, 1962; Myers & Myers, 1980; Kiersey & Bates, 1984; Lawrence, 1987).

People with opposite preferences often have great difficulty communicating effectively. Learning to understand each other involves realizing that thinkers may be impersonal, direct, and critical in their communication and may ignore people's feelings; feelers, on the other hand, value harmony and prefer agreeing with others but may ignore facts and statistics; intuitives often have flashes of inspiration and innovative ideas but may not communicate clearly and may jump from one idea to the next; and sensing types communicate logical thoughts and facts but may not give credence to inspirational ideas. A knowledge of personality preferences increases the possibilities of clear communication, "lessens friction and eases strain . . . [and] reveals the value of differences" (Myers & Myers, 1980, p. 210).

Utilizing the understanding of different personality types is one way of fostering effective communication; creating clear channels of communication for expressing concerns or problems is another. For example, when a teacher has a conflict with a colleague, the most appropriate course of action is to speak directly with the colleague. Discussing the problem openly and directly, without blaming or accusing, usually leads to participation in joint problem solving and resolution of the conflict. Alternative responses, such as talking about the problem with other teachers or doing nothing at all, usually lead to an escalation of the conflict and the creation of tension and mistrust in the relationship. It is also important that teachers have open channels of communication with supervisors, so that program problems can be discussed and solved in a timely and professional manner.

Teachers who understand and value the differences in people's preferences for being and behaving, appreciate individual strengths and gifts, and learn strategies for effective communication will increase their connectedness to other adults and deepen the sense of community in the workplace. Positive relationships with other teachers foster cooperation, joint problem solving, and productive work environments where teachers as well as children feel good about themselves. This type of enabling work environment allows teachers to focus on providing optimal early childhood programs that meet the needs of young children.

DEVELOPING A PROFESSIONAL IDENTITY

Early childhood educators who develop effective, growth-promoting collegial relationships; advocate for better working conditions, salaries and benefits; and create optimal program environments for children are helping to build a professional identity. Another important task facing teachers of young children today is helping to educate the public about the critical need for high-quality early childhood programs; this can best be accomplished by working together with others in the early childhood profession. Although tremendous progress has been made in the past two decades, the early childhood profession has been slow to gain an identity, and there is still much divisiveness and misunderstanding about the multitude of programs and services offered. Many different words are used to label early childhood programs, such as *preschool, kindergarten, day care, nursery school, child development center,* and *laboratory school.* Some programs have the label of "custodial care" or "babysitting services," and still others have the label of "school" or "educational program." It is important to recognize that the diversity of programs is a strength, because it offers parents alternatives, but it is also a weakness because of the lack of consistency in quality (Caldwell, 1990).

Before teachers can do the best job of educating parents and the public about quality programs, early childhood professionals must review knowledge about children and how they learn, and must stand together, united as a profession. The early years are critically important for development and education; young children learn from all their experiences and from their diverse, varied environments. These factors are instrumental in determining high program quality:

- Small groups and high ratios of teacher to children
- Well-trained teachers
- Safe and hygienic physical environments
- Cooperation and involvement of parents

- Frequent and consistent interactions between adults and children
- A curriculum that fosters learning within the context of self-regulation and play and that stresses social interactive skills and values (Bowman, 1990, p. 27)

It is time for teachers of young children to claim a professional identity with pride. Teachers of young children must become professionals in the very best sense of the word: not as distant, objective experts, but as knowledgeable and caring educators who are "involved with the human spirit" (Satir, 1988, p. 21). It is time to discard the often-misunderstood labels and call all programs early childhood education programs, to offer a resounding no to anyone who suggests that programs for young children are mere babysitting or to any program that offers only custodial care. Betty Caldwell has suggested the term *educare* to describe both the educational function and the caring role, which are equally important in high-quality programs for young children (Caldwell, 1990, p. 6). Opportunities for both learning and caring relationships are important for children to grow.

Young children are living and growing today; they can wait no longer for educators to debate and vacillate. Yes, a variety of programs is offered in order to meet the needs of diverse groups of children and families; that is a strength of the field. However, the profession must take a firm stand on the need to provide high-quality, developmentally appropriate programs that both care for and educate all young children. This task is the most critical task of the profession. Teachers must build linkages to each other, to parents, and to leaders. Early childhood professionals must stand together and demand higher standards in state licensing laws, a set of mandatory national standards, and resources and funding from government, business, and local school systems to make the vision for excellence in early childhood programming become a reality.

CREATING EXCELLENCE IN EARLY CHILDHOOD PROGRAMS _____

Most early childhood educators agree that all program environments, regardless of whether the program is classified as a child-care center, a preschool, or a kindergarten, should offer the highest-quality care and education for young children. The ingredients of excellence in early childhood programs can be described by outlining three major issues:

- Excellent early childhood programs never separate caring for young children from educating young children.

- To provide excellence for children, programs are flexible and curriculum and teaching methods are appropriate for the age and development of the children.

- Quality, compensation, and affordability are three interrelated components that are essential to achieving excellence in programs serving our young children. High-quality programs require qualified staff. Qualified staff require adequate compensation. Adequate compensation requires increased funding from a variety of sources and cannot be restricted to fees that parents can afford to pay (Smith, 1989, pp. 6–7).

In order to achieve excellence in programs for young children, professionals must support increased funding in combination with higher standards for early childhood programs. In addition, the field of early childhood education must train and license effective teachers, both professionals and paraprofessionals, who are skilled in the implementation of developmentally appropriate curricula (Bowman, 1990).

National Accreditation

The National Academy of Early Childhood Programs is a division of the National Association for the Education of Young Children created to develop and implement national standards for high-quality early childhood programs. The academy produced a set of criteria for high-quality early childhood programs that were adopted by the NAEYC governing board in 1984; the academy also designed and implemented a process for accrediting centers who meet the criteria (*Accreditation Criteria and Procedures,* 1991). The purposes of national accreditation are to facilitate

the involvement of early childhood professionals in a process that improves the quality of their programs and to evaluate program quality and accredit programs that "substantially comply with the criteria for high quality programs" (*Accreditation Criteria and Procedures,* 1991, p. 1).

National accreditation is a voluntary process that involves conducting a self-study to evaluate the classroom environment, program administration, staffing, and parent-involvement components of the early childhood program. The results of the self-study are used to set goals for program improvement; when the program goals are met, a final program description report is sent to the academy. The last steps in the accreditation process include an on-site visit by validators trained by the academy and an accreditation decision made by a team of the academy's commissioners. When national accreditation is awarded to an early childhood program, it is valid for three years (*Accreditation Criteria and Procedures,* 1991).

In the first decade of accreditation (1985–1995), 13,000 child-care programs participated in the accreditation process. More than 4,500 were accredited. However, there are 80,000 child-care programs nationwide that are eligible to be accredited, so accredited child-care programs and the higher standards they meet are available only to a small number of parents seeking quality child-care for their children (Bredekamp & Glowacki, 1996).

The success of the accreditation process thus far lies in the time and effort invested by early childhood professionals who serve in various roles as academy validators, who visit programs to determine compliance with national standards; mentors, who facilitate a center's involvement in the self-study process; and commissioners, who make judgments about programs' suitability for accreditation. The strength of the accreditation process lies in its ability to recognize the common components of high-quality environments for young children while supporting the diversity of early childhood programs.

Voluntary national accreditation of early childhood programs is an important step in creating and supporting high-quality environments, but it is not a system that is able to cope with the crisis in care and education of young children caused by inadequate licensing regulations and an overwhelming number of low-quality child-care programs. National accreditation has accomplished several major tasks: it has created consensus among early childhood professionals as they developed, field-tested, and implemented a set of program standards; and it has educated teachers, parents, and the public about the importance of high standards in programs for young children. However, it has not addressed the range in program quality created by the wide disparity among state licensing standards for child-care centers and state department guidelines for K–3 programs.

There is a critical need to apply developmentally appropriate curricula and program standards to all programs for young children—to close the gap between custodial and educational programs, to close the gap between programs serving children from birth to age 5 and programs serving children ages 5 to 8, and to close the gap between early childhood programs and special-education programs for young children. This can be accomplished by implementing a set of required national standards that will protect the right of all young children to learning environments that are healthy, growth-promoting, and developmentally appropriate and by recognizing the need to create stronger links between the fields of early childhood education and early childhood special education.

Training Teachers of Young Children

The most important factor in the implementation of high-quality program environments for young children is the expertise of the teachers. There are a number of ways in which teachers who work with young children receive their training. Colleges and universities offer teacher training programs in early childhood education through departments of education or child development. Some universities also offer specialized degrees in early childhood special education for teachers who plan to work primarily in programs serving young children with disabilities. Early childhood teacher training programs should provide a background in general education and professional studies as well as early and extended exposure to principles of child development and early childhood education. Training programs must include a variety of practical experiences culminating with student teaching, and must emphasize the integration of theory and practice (NAEYC, 1996). Specialized training or course work in special education is necessary to prepare all early childhood educators to effectively plan for and teach young children with disabilities who may be in their classroom. A more recent trend

in state teacher licensing requirements and in university teacher training programs is to combine programs in early childhood and early childhood special education in recognition of the emphasis on inclusion of children with disabilities in all programs for young children. These teacher training programs result in a bachelor's degree, which is necessary to obtain state certification to teach in early childhood education. Teachers with bachelor's degrees are the lead teachers who provide leadership in curriculum development in early childhood classrooms.

Many community colleges offer two-year early childhood training programs that result in an associate's degree. The programs typically do not include in-depth training in child development and teaching strategies, but they do include an emphasis on planning activities and provide a variety of practical experiences with children. Teachers with associate's degrees often have positions as assistant teachers in early childhood classrooms. In addition, teachers also may receive training and credentialing through the Child Development Associate (CDA) program. The CDA training is a competency-based program that allows teachers to be trained in a variety of settings, including field-based programs, college classes, and independent-study programs. CDA training is an alternative to traditional college- and university-based training and can enable teachers to move into positions that involve higher levels of responsibility in early childhood classrooms (Maxim, 1997). There is no consensus among early childhood educators about the importance of staffing programs with degreed teachers. Although few programs can afford to hire only college-educated teachers, hiring a lead teacher with extensive training in early childhood development and education for each classroom will increase the quality of the program for children and parents.

The Five C's of Effective Teaching

Early childhood educators will face a variety of challenges before all of the nation's young children have access to programs with developmentally appropriate, creative curriculum. Every teacher of young children has a role to play in improving the quality of young children's lives:

■ By providing the very best learning environment in every classroom for all young children

■ By educating parents, colleagues, and the public about early childhood education issues

■ By joining together with other professionals to advocate for higher program standards and increased funding for early childhood programs

To play this role effectively, early childhood educators need to have in abundance the qualities that can best be described as the five C's of effective teaching: caring, competence, creativity, commitment, and courage.

Caring. Teachers of young children must be warm, open, and caring individuals who have the capacity for nurturing children and supporting families. For most teachers, a primary motivation for entering the early childhood profession is their caring and concern for the well-being of young children.

The teaching profession has no place for adults who are impatient with the needs and demands of young children, who label or ridicule children because of their differences and level of ability, or who expect all children to conform to a specified standard of behavior and achievement. Young children need teachers who nurture their emerging selves, respect their individual differences, value their unique methods of learning, and reach out in welcome to their families. Young children need teachers with an enormous capacity for caring and compassion.

Teachers must also have the capacity to care for themselves in order to prevent excessive stress and professional burnout and to remain positive and enthusiastic contributors to the early childhood profession. Stress is common among teachers of young children and is created by the intense emotional demands, poor working conditions, and low level of support typical of many early childhood working environments. Burnout—which is characterized by symptoms that include reduced levels of energy, lack of interest in job-related tasks, lowered productivity levels, and increases in absenteeism as well as physical symptoms such as depression or sleeplessness—is often the result of extended periods of stress. Stress and burnout claim large numbers of teachers each year, but they can be effectively combated by taking time on a regular basis for personal and professional renewal. The ability to care for oneself as well as for others requires learning the art of balancing both personal and professional demands: meeting personal needs for relationships, creative pursuits, and spiritual fulfillment while also attending to the needs of children, families, and colleagues in the workplace.

Children need the very best teachers, and they need them not just for one or two years but for a lifetime. The early childhood profession suffers the loss of both knowledge and experience when teachers burn out and leave the field after a few years. To avoid becoming a casualty of burnout and to continue being effective and productive, teachers must exhibit caring attitudes and behaviors toward themselves in addition to the children and families they serve.

Competence. Early childhood educators must have the competence to put their knowledge of child development and early childhood teaching strategies into practice in the classroom. Competence, however, involves more than having the intelligence and knowledge necessary to learn the principles of early childhood education. In the words of Winnie-the-Pooh: " 'Rabbit's clever,' said Pooh thoughtfully. 'Yes,' said Piglet, 'Rabbit's clever.' 'And he has Brain.' 'Yes,' said Piglet, 'Rabbit has Brain.' There was a long silence. 'I suppose,' said Pooh, 'that that's why he never understands anything' " (Milne, 1957, pp. 270–271). Competence involves the capability to understand the principles of early childhood education as they influence the daily lives of children and teachers, the insight and ability to make effective decisions about program practices, and the teaching skills necessary to implement developmentally appropriate, creative curriculum in the classroom.

Competent teachers of young children do the following:

■ Formulate a thoughtful educational philosophy
■ Link developmental theory and educational practice
■ Develop child-centered, age-appropriate curricula
■ Evaluate the effectiveness of classroom practices and teaching strategies
■ Make well-informed decisions about the classroom environment based on children's needs and interests

Competent teachers of young children provide child-centered, age-appropriate curricular activities.

- Exhibit high personal and professional standards and adhere to the principles of ethical conduct
- Interact in a sensitive and empathic manner with children, parents, and colleagues
- Cope constructively with child and family crises and classroom problems
- Advocate effectively for program support and resources
- Contribute to the professionalization of the field of early childhood education

Perhaps most important, however, capable teachers use their knowledge of young children and their teaching competence to develop effective judgment and decision-making skills. Competent teachers have a clear focus on children, a grasp of what is fundamentally important to children, and the ability to make decisions based on what is best for children.

Creativity. Teachers of young children must be open, flexible, creative, and reflective people who value the unique gifts found in each child. Children flourish when they have creative teachers who provide an environment that cultivates their imagination, enables them to search for alternatives, and widens their circle of understanding about the world. These teachers are able to enter a child's world, share a child's perspective, and stretch a child's mind in new and delightful ways.

Early childhood educators help prepare children for a rapidly changing future when they model effective evaluation, problem-solving, and coping skills. Creative teachers are innovative and forward thinking; they consistently look for new challenges, invent new ideas, and try out new strategies. Teachers must help children learn to adapt to change by supporting divergent thinking, encouraging self-expression, and developing creative potential.

Young children need teachers who are alive with the joy of learning and eager to share their fresh ideas and insights. Children enjoy learning and growing in an experiential play environment with teachers who are connected to their own creative abilities and who remain enthusiastic about the pursuit of knowledge. The best, most creative teachers introduce children to learning as an exciting, lifelong journey of exploration, discovery, and growth.

Commitment. Teachers of young children must have a commitment to excellence, coupled with a clear vision of what young children need. In the world of a child, bigger is not better; larger group size, fewer teachers, and overflowing classrooms and

schools negate young children's needs for intimate, nurturing contact with adults. In the world of a child, faster is not better; accelerated learning groups and a schedule packed full of music lessons and group athletics do not allow young children to develop at their own pace and in their own time. In the world of a child, earlier is not better; structured academic programs and an emphasis on early standardized or readiness testing places demands on young children that are often beyond their capacity to cope (Bos, 1983; Elkind, 1987).

What young children need is small and flexible and warm and human and sane. They need to live this way every day. They need to live this way with wise, sensitive, and caring adults who are committed to creating a world where they are safe, nurtured, and enabled to learn through play.

Young children also need teachers who are committed to the lifelong pursuit of learning—to reading books and articles about the results of research and new teaching strategies; attending workshops and conferences for the purpose of gaining new insights and sharing ideas and information; visiting programs in order to explore alternative approaches to teaching and form growth-promoting partnerships with other early childhood educators; and listening closely to the wisdom of children and learning through experiences shared with children. The commitment to learning encourages teachers to continually evaluate their classroom environments and enables teachers to make the best decisions about program practices.

Courage. Early childhood educators must have the courage to respond to administrators who demand quiet, neat classrooms and higher test scores as evidence that children are learning, and to legislators who target children's programs for budget cuts when fiscal resources are lacking. Caring about children and families is not enough; knowing what is the best and most creative practice in early childhood classrooms is not enough; being dedicated to excellence in program standards is not enough. Young children need courageous, wise, and strong advocates if the early childhood profession is to meet its goals in the years ahead.

This means that teachers of young children will have to become comfortable with both "the tough and the tender" aspects of their personal and professional selves, to be able to integrate the warm, nurturing person and the strong, decisive person into a whole, effective, and courageous educator. Being courageous means having the capacity to be kind and generous as well as the ability to be clear and firm.

Young children cannot speak for themselves. They have no voice in the staff meeting when teachers plan how the children are to spend their days; they are not present in the administrator's office when decisions about allocating resources are made; and they cannot be seen in the halls of Congress when funding for early childhood programs is determined. Early childhood educators must have the courage to give young children a voice

CHAPTER SUMMARY _____

By far the biggest challenge ahead of us as early childhood educators is to make each day the best it can be for young children—to create the highest-quality programs staffed with the most exceptional teachers who provide the most appropriate, growth-promoting, and creative curriculum. We know how to meet this challenge. We know what young children need and how they learn. We know what characterizes effective teachers of young children. We know the components of a developmentally appropriate, creative curriculum. We must have the caring, competence, creativity, commitment, and courage to make all our children's days, and all our early childhood programs, the very best they can be.

■   ■   ■   ■   ■   ■   ■   ■   ■   ■

As a teacher of young children, you will be faced with a variety of decisions that will affect children's development as well as their attitudes toward learning and school environments. Your decisions about the use of curriculum practices and teaching strategies will also shape your personal and professional identity and contribute to the professionalization of the field of early childhood education. In order to be an effective early childhood teacher you will need to do the following:

• Understand the positive effects of high-quality early childhood programs on the development of young children.

• Integrate the components of the visible and invisible curriculum in order to implement a stimulating, developmentally appropriate classroom environment that will provide successful, supportive experiences for children rather than creating failure, mistrust, and lowered self-esteem.

• Advocate for higher teacher salaries and better working conditions to increase respect for early childhood educators and help retain the best teachers as members of the profession.

• Develop positive relationships with colleagues in order to give and receive emotional support and create optimal program environments.

• Support excellence in early childhood programming by advocating for national standards and implementing high standards in your classroom. Developing to your full potential as a teacher of young children; making wise, courageous decisions on behalf of children; and adhering to standards of excellence will benefit you, children and families, and the early childhood profession.

■   ■   ■   ■   ■   ■   ■   ■   ■   ■

DISCUSSION QUESTIONS _____

1. Discuss the vignette at the beginning of the chapter. What other questions or concerns might you have? Discuss the vignette at the end of the chapter. Are there other responses you might have to this situation?

2. What have been the different outcomes of early childhood programs that researchers have studied since the 1960s? Which do you think are most de-velopmentally relevant? Which are most socially relevant? Which are most politically relevant?

3. What can be concluded from research about the effects of early childhood programs on children's cognitive, social, and emotional development?

4. What is meant by "program-specific outcomes"?

5. Discuss the role of curriculum as a factor in child outcomes.

6. Describe the system of child-care in another country. Would this system be politically or economically feasible in the United States? Why or why not?

7. To what does "on time" versus "in their own time" refer? Describe a teacher's philosophy and attitude in a program based on the latter term.

8. Describe a good working environment for teachers in early childhood programs. What factors are obstacles in creating this optimal environment?

9. What is the value of using a personality inventory, such as the Myers-Briggs Type Indicator, with teachers in an early childhood program?

10. Describe the role of accreditation in program quality.

11. What are the "five C's of effective teaching"? Assess your skills in each of the five areas.

REFERENCES

Accreditation criteria and procedures of the National Academy of Early Childhood Programs. (1991). Washington, DC: National Association for the Education of Young Children.

Allen, J., & Catron, C. (1987, November). *For love or for money? Satisfactions and dissatisfactions among child-care workers.* Paper presented at the meeting of the National Association of Early Childhood Teacher Educators, Chicago, IL.

Berrueta-Clement, J. R., Schweinhart, L. J., Barnett, W. S., Epstein, A. S., & Weikart, D. P. (1984). *Changed lives: The effects of the Perry Preschool program on youths through age 19.* Monographs of the High/Scope Educational Research Foundation. Ypsilanti, MI: High/Scope Press.

Bos, B. (1983). *Before the basics.* Roseville, CA: Turn the Page.

Bowman, B. (1990). Child care: Challenges for the 90's. *Dimensions, 16*(4), 27–31.

Bredekamp, S., & Glowacki, S. (1996). The first decade of NAEYC accreditation: Growth and impact on the field. In S. Bredekamp & B. Willer (Eds.), *NAEYC Accreditation: A decade of learning and the years ahead* (pp. 1–10). Washington, DC: National Association for the Education of Young Children.

Caldwell, B. (1990). Educare: A new concept for our profession. *Dimensions, 16*(4), 3–6.

Consortium for Longitudinal Studies. (1983). *As the twig is bent: Lasting effects of preschool programs.* Hillsdale, NJ: Erlbaum.

Corsini, D. (1991). Family day care in Denmark: A model for the United States? *Young Children, 46*(5), 10–15.

Elkind, D. (1987). *Miseducation: Preschoolers at risk.* New York: Knopf.

Gonzalez-Mena, J., & Eyer, D. (1997). *Infancy and caregiving.* Palo Alto, CA: Mayfield.

Granger, B., & Marx, E. (1988). *Who is teaching? Early childhood teachers in New York City's publicly funded programs.* New York: Bank Street College of Education.

Jorde-Bloom, P. (1988). *A great place to work: Improving conditions for staff in young children's programs.* Washington, DC: National Association for the Education of Young Children.

Jung, C. G. (1923). *Psychological types.* New York: Harcourt & Brace.

Kahn, A., & Kamerman, S. (1975). *Not for the poor alone: European social services.* Philadelphia: Temple University Press.

Kamerman, S., & Kahn, A. (Eds.) (1978). *Family policy: Government and families in fourteen countries.* New York: Columbia University Press.

Katz, L. (1977). *Talks with teachers.* Washington, DC: National Association for the Education of Young Children.

Kiersey, D., & Bates, M. (1984). *Please understand me: Character and temperament types.* Del Mar, CA: Prometheus Nemesis.

Kontos, S., & Stremmel, A. (1988). Caregivers' perceptions of working conditions in a child-care environment. *Early Childhood Research Quarterly, 3*(1), 77–90.

Lawrence, G. (1987). *People types and tiger stripes: A practical guide to learning styles.* Gainesville, FL: Center for Applications of Psychological Type.

Manlove, E., & Guzell, J. (1997). Intention to leave, anticipated reasons for leaving, and 12-month turnover of child-care center staff. *Early Childhood Research Quarterly, 12,* 145–167.

Marx, E., & Zinsser, C., with Porter, T. (1990). *Raising child-care salaries and benefits: An evaluation of the New York state salary enhancement legislation.* New York: Bank Street College and the Center for Public Advocacy Research.

Maxim, G. W. (1997). *The very young: Guiding children from infancy through the early years* (5th ed.). Columbus, OH: Merrill/Prentice-Hall.

McMahan, I. (1992). Public preschool from the age of two: *The école maternelle* in France. *Young Children, 47*(5), 22–28.

Milne, A. A. (1957). *The World of Pooh: The complete Winnie-the-Pooh and the House at Pooh Corner.* New York: Dutton.

Myers, I. B. (1962). *The Myers-Briggs type indicator.* Palo Alto, CA: Consulting Psychologists Press.

Myers, I. B., & Myers, P. B. (1980). *Gifts differing.* Palo Alto, CA: Consulting Psychologists Press.

National Association for the Education of Young Children (NAEYC). (1996). *Guidelines for preparation of early childhood professionals.* Washington, DC: National Association for the Education of Young Children.

National Association for the Education of Young Children (NAEYC). (1984). Results of the National Association for the Education of Young Children survey of child-care salaries and working conditions. *Young Children, 40*(1), 9–14.

Odom, S. L., & Warren, S. F. (1988). Early childhood special education in the year 2000. *Journal of the Division for Early Childhood, 12*(3), 263–273.

Pettygrove, W., Whitebook, M., & Weir, M. (1984). Beyond babysitting: Changing the treatment and image of child-caregivers. *Young Children, 39*(5), 14–21.

Phillips, D., Howes, C., & Whitebook, M. (1991). Child care as an adult work environment. *Journal of Social Issues, 47,* 49–70.

Satir, V. (1988). Healing human spirits, creating joy in living. *Focus, 11*(5), 20–21, 28–32.

Schweinhart, L. (1988). Quality: The central issue in programs for young children. *Tennessee's Children, 30*(1), 18–23.

Schweinhart, L., & Weikart, D. (1997). The High/Scope Preschool Curriculum comparison study through age 23. *Early Childhood Research Quarterly, 12,* 117–143.

Schweinhart, L., Weikart, D., & Larner, M. (1986). Consequences of three preschool curriculum models through age 15. *Early Childhood Research Quarterly, 1,* 15–45.

Smith, M. (1989). Excellence and equity for America's children. *Tennessee's Children, 30*(2), 5–12.

Tegano, D. W., Moran, J. D., III, & Sawyers, J. K. (1991). *Creativity in early childhood classrooms.* Washington, DC: National Education Association.

Weber, L. (1971). *The English infant school and informal education.* Englewood Cliffs, NJ: Prentice-Hall.

Whitebook, M., Howes, C., & Phillips, D. (1990). *Who cares? Child care teachers and the quality of care in America.* Final report of the National Child Care Staffing Study. Oakland, CA: Child Care Employee Project.

Whitebook, M., Phillips, D., & Howes, C. (1993). *National child-care staffing study revisited: Four years in the life of center-based child-care.* Oakland, CA: Child Care Employee Project.

ADDITIONAL RESOURCES _____

Bredekamp, S. (1995). What do early childhood professionals need to know and be able to do? *Young Children, 50*(2), 67–69.

Bredekamp, S., & Copple, C. (Eds.). (1997). *Developmentally appropriate practice in early childhood programs.* Washington, DC: National Association for the Education of Young Children.

Bredekamp, S., & Willer, B. (Eds.). (1996). *NAEYC accreditation: A decade of learning and the years ahead.* Washington, DC: National Association for the Education of Young Children.

Brooke, G. (1994). My personal journey toward professionalism. *Young Children, 49*(6), 69–71.

Caulfield, R. (1997). Professionalism in early care and education. *Early Childhood Education Journal, 24*(4), 261–264.

Driscoll, A. (1995). *Cases in early childhood education: Stories of programs and practices.* Needham Heights, MA: Allyn & Bacon.

Dunn, L., & Kontos, S. (1997). What have we learned about developmentally appropriate practice? *Young Children, 52*(5), 5–13.

Eisenberg, J., & Jalongo, M. (Eds.). (1997). *Major trends and issues in early childhood education.* New York: Teachers College Press.

Elkind, D. (Ed.). (1991). *Perspectives on early childhood education.* Washington, DC: National Education Association.

Evans, J. (1993). Early childhood care and development: Issues from the developing country perspective. In B. Spodek (Ed.), *Handbook of research on the education of young children* (pp. 427–438). New York: Macmillan.

Galinsky, E., & Friedman, D. (1993). *Education before school: Investing in quality child-care.* New York: Families and Work Institute.

Green, M., & Widoff, E. (1990). Special needs child-care: Training is a key issue. *Young Children, 45*(3), 60–61.

Howard, V., Williams, B., Port, P., & Lepper, C. (1997). *Very young children with special needs: A formative approach for the 21st century.* Upper Saddle River, NJ: Prentice-Hall.

Jalongo, M., Hoot, J., Pattnaik, J., Cai, W., & Park, S. (1997). Early childhood programs: International perspectives. In J. Isenberg & M. Jalongo (Eds.), *Major trends and issues in early childhood education* (pp. 188–204). New York: Teachers College Press.

Jorde-Bloom, P. (1993). "But I'm worth more than that!": Addressing employee concerns about compensation. *Young Children, 48*(3), 65–68.

Kagan, S. L. (1991). Policy changes and their implications for early childhood care and education. *Dimensions, 19*(3), 3–7, 40.

Kagan, S. L., & Rivera, A. M. (1991). Collaboration in early care and education: What can and should we expect? *Young Children, 47*(1), 51–56.

Katz, L. (1984). The professional early childhood teacher. *Young Children, 39*(5), 3–11.

Lubeck, S. (1995). Policy issues in the development of child-care and early education systems: The need for cross-national comparison. In A. Hatch (Ed.), *Qualitative research in early childhood settings* (pp. 79–98). Westport, CT: Praeger.

National Association for the Education of Young Children (NAEYC). (1984). National Association for the Education of Young Children position statement on nomenclature, salaries, benefits, and the status of the early childhood profession. *Young Children, 40*(1), 52–59.

National Association for the Education of Young Children (NAEYC). (1987). National Association for the Education of Young Children position statement on guidelines for developing legislation creating or expanding programs for young children. *Young Children, 42*(3), 43–45.

National Association for the Education of Young Children (NAEYC). (1990). Predictors of quality: How accreditation criteria are interrelated. *Academy Update, 4*(3), 1, 7.

National Association for the Education of Young Children (NAEYC). (1991). Early childhood teacher certification: A position statement of the Association of Teacher Educators and the National Association for the Education of Young Children. *Young Children, 47*(1), 16–21.

National Association for the Education of Young Children (NAEYC). (1995). NAEYC position statement on quality, compensation, and affordability. *Young Children, 51*(1), 39–41.

Pattnaik, J. (1996). Early childhood education in India: History, trends, issues, and achievements. *Early Childhood Education Journal, 24*(1), 11–16.

Phillips, C. B. (1990). The CDA program: Entering a new era. *Young Children, 45*(3), 24–27.

Phillips, D., Lande, J., & Goldberg, M. (1990). The state of child-care regulation: A comparative analysis. *Early Childhood Research Quarterly, 5*(2), 151–179.

Schweinhart, L., Weikart, D., & Larner, M. (1986). Child-initiated activities in early childhood programs may help prevent delinquency. *Early Childhood Research Quarterly, 1,* 303–311.

Seefeldt, C. (1990). *Continuing issues in early childhood education.* Columbus, OH: Merrill.

Short, V. M., & Burger, M. (1987). The English infant/primary school revisited. *Childhood Education, 64*(2), 75–79.

Spodek, B., Saracho, O. N., & Peters, D. L. (Eds.). (1988). *Professionalism and the early childhood practitioner.* New York: Teachers College Press.

Swadener, E., & Bloch, M. (1997). Children, families, and change: International perspectives. *Early Education and Development, 8*(3), 207–218.

United States General Accounting Office. (1990). *Early childhood education: What are the costs of high-quality programs?* Washington, DC: Author.

Weikart, D. P. (1989). Hard choices in early childhood care and education: A view to the future. *Young Children, 44*(3), 25–30.

Willer, B. (Ed.). (1990). *Reaching the full cost of quality in early childhood programs.* Washington, DC: National Association for the Education of Young Children.

Willer, B., Hofferth, S. L., Kisker, E. E., Divine-Hawkins, P., Farquhar, E., & Glantz, F. B. (1991). *The demand and supply of child care in 1990.* Washington, DC: National Association for the Education of Young Children.

Zigler, E., Finn-Stevenson, M., & Stern, B. (1997). Supporting children and families in the schools: The school of the 21st century. *American Journal of Orthopsychiatry, 67*(3), 396–407.

Zigler, E., & Styfco, S. (Eds.). (1993). *Head Start and beyond.* New Haven, CT: Yale University Press.

A.

NAEYC Code of Ethical Conduct

NAEYC recognizes that many daily decisions required of those who work with young children are of a moral and ethical nature. The NAEYC Code of Ethical Conduct offers guidelines for responsible behavior and sets forth a common basis for resolving the principal ethical dilemmas encountered in early childhood education. The primary focus is on daily practice with children and their families in programs for children from birth to 8 years of age: preschools, child care centers, family day care homes, kindergartens, and primary classrooms. Many of the provisions also apply to specialists who do not work directly with children, including program administrators, parent educators, college professors, and child care licensing specialists.

Standards of ethical behavior in early childhood education are based on commitment to core values that are deeply rooted in the history of our field. We have committed ourselves to

- Appreciating childhood as a unique and valuable stage of the human life cycle

- Basing our work with children on knowledge of child development

- Appreciating and supporting the close ties between the child and family

- Recognizing that children are best understood in the context of family, culture, and society

- Respecting the dignity, worth, and uniqueness of each individual (child, family member, and colleague)

- Helping children and adults achieve their full potential in the context of relationships that are based on trust, respect, and positive regard

The code sets forth a conception of our professional responsibilities in four sections, each addressing an arena of professional relationships: (1) children, (2) families, (3) colleagues, and (4) community and society. Each section includes an introduction to the primary responsibilities of the early childhood practitioner in that arena, a set of ideals pointing in the direction of exemplary professional practice, and a set of principles defining practices that are required, prohibited, and permitted.

Feeney, S., & Kipnis, L. (1996). *Code of ethical conduct.* Washington, DC: National Association for the Education of Young Children. Reprinted by permission of NAEYC.

SECTION I:
ETHICAL RESPONSIBILITIES TO CHILDREN _____

Childhood is a unique and valuable stage in the life cycle. Our paramount responsibility is to provide safe, healthy, nurturing, and responsive settings for children. We are committed to supporting children's development by cherishing individual differences, by helping them learn to live and work cooperatively, and by promoting their self-esteem.

Ideals

I-1.1—To be familiar with the knowledge base of early childhood education and to keep current through continuing education and in-service training.

I-1.2—To base program practices upon current knowledge in the field of child development and related disciplines and upon particular knowledge of each child.

I-1.3—To recognize and respect the uniqueness and the potential of each child.

I-1.4—To appreciate the special vulnerability of children.

I-1.5—To create and maintain safe and healthy settings that foster children's social, emotional, intellectual, and physical development and that respect their dignity and their contributions.

I-1.6—To support the right of children with special needs to participate, consistent with their ability, in regular early childhood programs.

Principles

P-1.1—Above all, we shall not harm children. We shall not participate in practices that are disrespectful, degrading, dangerous, exploitative, intimidating, psychologically damaging, or physically harmful to children. *This principle has precedence over all others in this Code.*

P-1.2—We shall not participate in practices that discriminate against children by denying benefits, giving special advantages, or excluding them from programs or activities on the basis of their race, religion, sex, national origin, or the status, behavior, or beliefs of their parents. (This principle does not apply to programs that have a lawful mandate to provide services to a particular population of children.)

P-1.3—We shall involve all of those with relevant knowledge (including staff and parents) in decisions concerning a child.

P-1.4—When, after appropriate efforts have been made with a child and the family, the child still does not appear to be benefiting from a program, we shall communicate our concern to the family in a positive way and offer them assistance in finding a more suitable setting.

P-1.5—We shall be familiar with the symptoms of child abuse and neglect and know and follow community procedures and state laws that protect children against abuse and neglect.

P-1.6—When we have evidence of child abuse or neglect, we shall report the evidence to the appropriate community agency and follow up to ensure that appropriate action has been taken. When possible, parents will be informed that the referral has been made.

P-1.7—When another person tells us of their suspicion that a child is being abused or neglected but we lack evidence, we shall assist that person in taking appropriate action to protect the child.

P-1.8—When a child protective agency fails to provide adequate protection for abused or neglected children, we acknowledge a collective ethical responsibility to work toward improvement of these services.

P-1.9—When we become aware of a practice or situation that endangers the health or safety of children, but has not been previously known to do so, we have an ethical responsibility to inform those who can remedy the situation and who can keep other children from being similarly endangered.

SECTION II:
ETHICAL RESPONSIBILITIES TO FAMILIES _____

Families are of primary importance in children's development. (The term *family* may include others, besides parents, who are responsibly involved with the child.) Because the family and the early childhood educator have a common interest in the child's welfare, we acknowledge a primary responsibility to bring about collaboration between the home and school in ways that enhance the child's development.

Ideals

I-2.1—To develop relationships of mutual trust with the families we serve.

I-2.2—To acknowledge and build upon strengths and competencies as we support families in their task of nurturing children.

I-2.3—To respect the dignity of each family and its culture, customs, and beliefs.

I-2.4—To respect families' childrearing values and their right to make decisions for their children.

I-2.5—To interpret each child's progress to parents within the framework of a developmental perspective and to help families understand and appreciate the value of developmentally appropriate early childhood programs.

I-2.6—To help family members improve their understanding of their children and to enhance their skills as parents.

I-2.7—To participate in building support networks for families by providing them with opportunities to interact with program staff and families.

Principles

P-2.1—We shall not deny family members access to their child's classroom or program setting.

P-2.2—We shall inform families of program philosophy, policies, and personnel qualifications, and explain why we teach as we do.

P-2.3—We shall inform families of and, when appropriate, involve them in policy decisions.

P-2.4—We shall inform families of and, when appropriate , involve them in significant decisions affecting their child.

P-2.5—We shall inform the family of accidents involving their child, of risks such as exposures to contagious disease that may result in infection, and of events that might result in psychological damage.

P-2.6—We shall not permit or participate in research that could in any way hinder the education or development of the children in our programs. Families shall be fully informed of any proposed research projects involving their children and shall have the opportunity to give or withhold consent.

P-2.7—We shall not engage in or support exploitation of families. We shall not use our relationship with a family for private advantage or personal gain, or enter into relationships with family members that might impair our effectiveness in working with children.

P-2.8—We shall develop written policies for the protection of confidentiality and the disclosure of children's records. The policy documents shall be made available to all program personnel and families. Disclosure of children's records beyond family members, program personnel, and consultants having an obligation of confidentiality shall require familial consent (except in cases of abuse or neglect).

P-2.9—We shall maintain confidentiality and shall respect the family's right to privacy, refraining from disclosure of confidential information and intrusion into family life. However, when we are concerned about a child's welfare, it is permissible to reveal confidential information to agencies and individuals who may be able to act in the child's interest.

P-2.10—In cases where family members are in conflict we shall work openly, sharing our observations of the child, to help all parties involved make informed decisions. We shall refrain from becoming an advocate for one party.

P-2.11—We shall be familiar with and appropriately use community resources and professional services that support families. After a referral has been made, we shall follow up to ensure that services have been adequately provided.

SECTION III:
ETHICAL RESPONSIBILITIES TO COLLEAGUES _____

In a caring, cooperative work place human dignity is respected, professional satisfaction is promoted, and positive relationships are modeled. Our primary responsibility in this arena is to establish and maintain settings and relationships that support productive work and meet professional needs.

A—Responsibilities to Co-workers

Ideals

I-3A.1—To establish and maintain relationships of trust and cooperation with co-workers.

I-3A.2—To share resources and information with co-workers.

I-3A.3—To support co-workers in meeting their professional needs and in their professional development.

I-3A.4—To accord co-workers due recognition of professional achievement.

Principles

P-3A.1—When we have concern about the professional behavior of a co-worker, we shall first let that person know of our concern and attempt to resolve the matter collegially.

P-3A.2—We shall exercise care in expressing views regarding the personal attributes or professional conduct of co-workers. Statements should be based on firsthand knowledge and relevant to the interests of children and programs.

B—Responsibilities to Employers

Ideals

I-3B.1—To assist the program in providing the highest quality of service.

I-3B.2—To maintain loyalty to the program and uphold its reputation.

Principles

P-3B.1—When we do not agree with program policies, we shall first attempt to effect change through constructive action within the organization.

P-3B.2—We shall speak or act on behalf of an organization only when authorized. We shall take care to note when we are speaking for the organization and when we are expressing a personal judgment.

C—Responsibilities to Employees

Ideals

I-3C.1—To promote policies and working conditions that foster competence, well-being, and self-esteem in staff members.

I-3C.2—To create a climate of trust and candor that will enable staff to speak and act in the best interests of children, families, and the field of early childhood education.

I-3C.3—To strive to secure an adequate livelihood for those who work with or on behalf of young children.

Principles

P-3C.1—In decisions concerning children and programs, we shall appropriately utilize the training, experience, and expertise of staff members.

P-3C.2—We shall provide staff members with working conditions that permit them to carry out their responsibilities, timely and non-threatening evaluation procedures, written grievance procedures, constructive feedback, and opportunities for continuing professional development and advancement.

P-3C.3—We shall develop and maintain comprehensive written personnel policies that define program standards and, when applicable, that specify the extent to which employees are accountable for their conduct outside the work place. These policies shall be given to new staff members and shall be available for review by all staff members.

P-3C.4—Employees who do not meet program standards shall be informed of areas of concern and, when possible, assisted in improving their performance.

P-3C.5—Employees who are dismissed shall be informed of the reasons for their termination. When a dismissal is for cause, justification must be based on evidence of inadequate or inappropriate behavior that is accurately documented, current, and available for the employee to review.

P-3C.6—In making evaluations and recommendations, judgments shall be based on fact and relevant to the interests of children and programs.

P-3C.7—Hiring and promotion shall be based solely on a person's record of accomplishment and ability to carry out the responsibilities of the position.

P-3C.8—In hiring, promotion, and provision of training, we shall not participate in any form of discrimination based on race, religion, sex, national origin, handicap, age, or sexual preference. We shall be familiar with laws and regulations that pertain to employment discrimination.

SECTION IV:
ETHICAL RESPONSIBILITES TO COMMUNITY AND SOCIETY _____

Early childhood programs operate within a context of an immediate community made up of families and other institutions concerned with children's welfare. Our responsibilities to the community are to provide programs that meet its needs and to cooperate with agencies and professions that share responsibility for children. Because the larger society has a measure of responsibility for the welfare and protection of children, and because of our specialized expertise in child development, we acknowledge an obligation to serve as a voice for children everywhere.

Ideals

I-4.1—To provide the community with high-quality, culturally sensitive programs and services.

I-4.2—To promote cooperation among agencies and professions concerned with the welfare of young children, their families, and their teachers.

I-4.3—To work, through education, research, and advocacy, toward an environmentally safe world in which all children are adequately fed, sheltered, and nurtured.

I-4.4—To work, through education, research, and advocacy, toward a society in which all young children have access to quality programs.

I-4.5—To promote knowledge and understanding of young children and their needs. To work toward greater social acknowledgment of children's rights and greater social acceptance of responsibility for their well-being.

I-4.6—To support policies and laws that promote the well-being of children and families. To oppose those that impair their well-being. To cooperate with other individuals and groups in these efforts.

I-4.7—To further the professional development of the field of early childhood education and to strengthen its commitment to realizing its core values as reflected in this Code.

Principles

P-4.1—We shall communicate openly and truthfully about the nature and extent of services that we provide.

P-4.2—We shall not accept or continue to work in positions for which we are personally unsuited or professionally unqualified. We shall not offer services that we do not have the competence, qualifications, or resources to provide.

P-4.3—We shall be objective and accurate in reporting the knowledge upon which we base our program practices.

P-4.4—We shall cooperate with other professionals who work with children and their families.

P-4.5—We shall not hire or recommend for employment any person who is unsuited for a position with respect to competence, qualifications, or character.

P-4.6—We shall report the unethical or incompetent behavior of a colleague to a supervisor when informal resolution is not effective.

P-4.7—We shall be familiar with laws and regulations that serve to protect the children in our programs.

P-4.8—We shall not participate in practices that are in violation of laws and regulations that protect the children in our programs.

P-4.9—When we have evidence that an early childhood program is violating laws or regulations protecting children, we shall report it to persons responsible for the program. If compliance is not accomplished within a reasonable time, we will report the violation to appropriate authorities who can be expected to remedy the situation.

P-4.10—When we have evidence that an agency or a professional charged with providing services to children, families, or teachers is failing to meet its obligations, we acknowledge a collective ethical responsibility to report the problem to appropriate authorities or to the public.

P-4.11—When a program violates or requires its employees to violate this Code, it is permissible, after fair assessment of the evidence, to disclose the identity of that program.

STATEMENT OF COMMITMENT _____

As an individual who works with young children, I commit myself to furthering the values of early childhood education as they are reflected in the NAEYC Code of Ethical Conduct.

To the best of my ability I will

- Ensure that programs for young children are based on current knowledge of child development and early childhood education.

- Respect and support families in their task of nurturing children.

- Respect colleagues in early childhood education and support them in maintaining the NAEYC Code of Ethical Conduct.

- Serve as an advocate for children, their families, and their teachers in community and society.

- Maintain high standards of professional conduct.

- Recognize how personal values, opinions, and biases can affect professional judgment.

- Be open to new ideas and be willing to learn from the suggestions of others.

- Continue to learn, grow, and contribute as a professional.

- Honor the ideals and principles of the NAEYC Code of Ethical Conduct.

The Statement of Commitment expresses those basic personal commitments that individuals must make in order to align themselves with the profession's responsibilities as set forth in the NAEYC Code of Ethical Conduct.

B.

Developmental Checklist

The developmental checklist is to be used by teachers as a tool to provide a systematic approach to observing young children. It was designed to provide teachers with specific information regarding a child's development and to enhance program and curriculum development.

The results of this checklist should be used to set goals for individual children and to enhance the creative-play curriculum. When used as designed, this checklist can provide a teacher with relevant developmental information and assist in curriculum planning.

Results of this checklist do not yield a developmental age level. This is not designed to be a diagnostic tool; therefore, it is not an intelligence predictor. It is not the intent nor the purpose of this checklist to be used to label a child. This information is not intended for comparing a child's development with other children's development.

Administration of the checklist should begin at one developmental age level below the child's chronological age level, continue through the child's age level, and end at one age level above the chronological age. (For example, if a child is 22 months old, then the three developmental levels to be assessed would be 12 to 18 months, 18 to 24 months, and 24 to 30 months.) This method takes into account the variations in children's development. Evaluators may decide to extend the age range (further below or above the child's chronological age) if the child has very few (+) items or all (+) items.

The majority of the items on the checklist can be assessed by observing children in their natural classroom environment. A few items may need to be "staged" by taking special toys or materials into the classroom and asking a child specific questions while he or she is playing with the items. The checklist is scored with a (+) symbol to denote that the child can perform the task consistently and with confidence and ease or with a (−) symbol to denote that the child cannot perform the task at all or can perform it rarely or only with help. All (−) items should be reassessed during the next assessment period.

Items referenced in parentheses with an asterisk are direct quotes or are derived directly from the source. Items referenced in parentheses only are similar to items in the source. The items are used by permission of the following publishers: *Memphis Comprehensive Development Scale* by permission of Fearon/Janus Publishers; *Learning Accomplishment Profile* and *Learning Accomplishment Profile for Infants* by permission of Kaplan School Supply; *Portage Guide to Early Education* by permission of the Cooperative Education Service Agency; *First feelings,* copyright © 1985 by Stanley Greenspan and

This section was written by Bobbie Beckmann; Carol E. Catron also contributed to writing this section.

Nancy Thorndike Greenspan, used by permission of Viking Penguin, a division of Penguin Books USA Inc.; and *HELP (Hawaii Early Learning Profile) checklist* © 1984, 1988 by VORT Corporation (P.O. Box 60132, Palo Alto, CA 94306), used by permission of VORT Corporation (the HELP checklist covers 650+ skills for assessment and tracking of children from birth to age 3).

CREATIVE-PLAY CURRICULUM
DEVELOPMENTAL CHECKLIST _____

Name _____

Date of Birth _____

Personal Awareness

TEST DATE: _____ _____ _____ _____

1–2 months					

1–2 months

1. Pulls at clothing with hands. (SH) (*Memphis)
2. Anticipates feeding with increased activity. (I) (*LAP)
3. Opens mouth for breast and/or bottle. (SH) (HELP)
4. Has established routine for feeding and/or naps. (SH) (*First Feelings*)
5. Exhibits startle reflex to loud noises and/or sudden movements. (PS)
6. Anticipates being lifted via change in muscle tone, activity, etc. (I) (Memphis)

Observations:

_____

TEST DATE: _____ _____ _____ _____

2–4 months

1. Recognizes bottle visually. (SH)
2. Puts hand in mouth. (I) (Memphis)
3. Stays awake for longer periods without crying. (I) (*HELP)

Observations:

_____

Personal Awareness Subdomains:

SH Self-help skills
 I Independence
PH Personal health

PS   Personal safety

TEST DATE: _____ _____ _____ _____

4–6 months

1. Holds bottle with some help. (SH)
   (HELP)
2. Begins consistent naps two to three times per
   day. (SH)
   (HELP)
3. Brings toy to mouth. (I)
   (HELP)
4. Recognizes and reaches for bottle. (SH)
   (*HELP)

Observations:

TEST DATE: _____ _____ _____ _____

6–9 months

1. Drinks from a cup with help. (SH)
   (Memphis)
2. Begins to finger-feed foods. (SH)
   (HELP)
3. Holds own bottle. (SH)
   (Memphis)
4. Cooperates with changing clothes. (PH)
   (Early LAP)

Observations:

TEST DATE: _____ _____ _____ _____

9–12 months

1. Eats semisolid foods. (PH)
   (Early LAP)
2. May express awareness of and/or discomfort at being wet. (I)
   (Early LAP)
3. Begins to bring spoon to mouth. (SH)
   (HELP)
4. Finger-feeds self for a meal or snack. (SH)
   (*Early LAP)

Observations:

TEST DATE: _____ _____ _____ _____

12–18 months

1. Pulls off socks and/or shoes. (SH)
   (*Early LAP)
2. Chews most foods well. (PH)
   (Early LAP)
3. Holds own cup and drinks with some spilling. (SH)
   (Memphis)
4. Brings spoon to mouth and gets food off. (SH)
   (Memphis)
5. Cooperates with hand washing.
   (PH)
6. Points to one body part on a doll when asked. (PH)

Observations:

TEST DATE: _____ _____ _____ _____

18–24 months

1. Drinks from a cup—no longer uses bottle. (SH)
   (HELP)
2. Washes own hands. (H)
   (*HELP)
3. Begins to indicate toilet needs—may ask to go.
   (SH)
   (Early LAP)
4. Points to four body parts on a doll when
   asked. (PH)
   (Memphis)

Observations:

_____

TEST DATE: _____ _____ _____ _____

24–30 months

1. Puts on loose shoes. (SH)
   (Early LAP)
2. Takes off coat/shirt. (SH)
   (Early LAP)
3. Knows difference between edible and nonedible
   substances. (PH)
   (Early LAP)
4. Remains dry during day. (I)
   (Early LAP)

Observations:

_____

TEST DATE: _____ _____ _____ _____

30–36 months

1. Dries own hands. (PH)
   (HELP)
2. Puts on coat/shirt. (SH)
   (LAP)
3. Completely toilet trained during
   daytime. (SH)
4. Avoids simple hazards. (PS)
5. Shows curiosity about male/female
   body parts. (PH)

Observations:

TEST DATE: _____ _____ _____ _____

36–42 months

1. Wipes own nose with tissue. (PH)
   (LAP)
2. Removes clothes for toileting. (SH)
3. Pours from pitcher with little or no spilling.
   (SH)
4. Unbuttons front button—large size ($\frac{3}{4}$ inch
   or larger). (SH) (*LAP)
5. Willing to taste food provided at lunch or
   snack. (PH)

Observations:

TEST DATE: _____ _____ _____ _____

42–48 months
1. Washes hands and dries them. (PH)
   (*LAP)
2. Returns to classroom from outside play area, following teacher. (I)
   (*LAP)
3. Remembers to flush toilet without reminder. (SH)
   (*LAP)
4. Unbuckles seat belt. (PS)

Observations:

_____

TEST DATE: _____ _____ _____ _____

48–54 months
1. Tells street name. (PS)
2. Comprehends hypothetical safety events. (PS)
3. Distinguishes front from back of clothing. (SH)
4. Washes face thoroughly and without reminder. (PH)
5. Cleans up spills without assistance. (I)
6. Begins recognizing sexual differences between boys and girls. (PH)

Observations:

_____

TEST DATE: _____ _____ _____ _____

54–60 months
1. Dresses self except for tying shoes. (SH)
   (Portage)
2. Fastens shoes. (SH)
   (Portage)
3. Spreads with dull-tipped knife. (SH)
   (Portage)
4. Helps set the table for lunch and/or helps set out project materials. (I)
   (Portage)
5. Takes care of toys and materials. (I)

Observations:

TEST DATE: _____ _____ _____ _____

60–66 months
1. Zips a separated front zipper. (SH)
   (*LAP)
2. Uses a napkin. (SH)
   (*LAP)
3. Buckles a seat belt. (PS)
   (*Portage)
4. Remembers to look before crossing a street without reminder (adult present). (PS)
   (*Portage)
5. Shows responsibility for personal possessions. (I)

Observations:

TEST DATE: _____ _____ _____ _____

66–72 months

1. Tells complete address. (PS)
   (*HELP)
2. Can dress and undress completely
   without assistance. (SH)
   (*LAP)
3. Blows nose. (PH)
   (*LAP)
4. Demonstrates understanding that it is
   unsafe to accept rides, food, or money
   from strangers. (PS)
5. Points to at least eight body parts
   when asked. (PH)

Observations:

_____

TEST DATE: _____ _____ _____ _____

72–78 months

1. Brushes/combs hair. (PH)
   (*LAP)
2. Cuts food with a table knife and fork. (SH)
   (*LAP)
3. Bathes self with minimal assistance. (SH)
   (*LAP)
4. Knows telephone number. (PS)
5. Is comfortable with own gender. (PH)
6. Can dial 0 or 911 for emergency. (PS)

Observations:

_____

CREATIVE-PLAY CURRICULUM
DEVELOPMENTAL CHECKLIST _____

Name _____
Date of Birth _____

Emotional Well-Being

TEST DATE: _____ _____ _____ _____

1–2 months

1. Is increasingly able to calm down. (CS)
2. Exhibits distress, excitement, and/or delight. (AAEE)
3. Molds and relaxes body when held—cuddles. (PI)
   (*HELP)
4. Responds to a person other than a parent. (CS)
   (Early LAP)
5. Brightens to sights and/or sounds by alerting and focusing. (AAEE)
   (Early LAP)

Observations:

TEST DATE: _____ _____ _____ _____

2–4 months

1. Has a regular sleep pattern. (PI)
   (*First Feelings*)
2. Shows pleasure when touched or held. Looks in direction of a touch. (AAEE)
   (*First Feelings*)
3. Enjoys movements in space. (BV)
   (**First Feelings*)
4. Adjusts to routines. (CS)
5. Enjoys adult attention and demands it at times. (PI)
   (HELP)

Observations:

Emotional Well-Being Subdomains:

AAEE Awareness, acceptance, and expression of emotions
  CS Coping skills
  PI Personality integration
  BV Building values

TEST DATE: _____ _____ _____ _____

4–6 months

1. Begins to initiate interactions via vocalization, etc. (PI) (Early LAP)
2. Smiles in response to parent's or teacher's vocalizations and/or facial expressions. (AAEE) (Early LAP)
3. Begins having abrupt mood changes— primary moods are pleasure, complaint, and temper. (AAEE)
4. Smiles at a person's image in mirror. (PI) (HELP)

Observations:

TEST DATE: _____ _____ _____ _____

6–9 months

1. Begins to initiate exploration and assertiveness. (BV) (*First Feelings*)
2. Reaches out to be held. (AAEE) (Early LAP)
3. Repeats enjoyable activities. (CS) (*HELP)
4. Exhibits stable attachment to adult; is able to maintain a loving, cuddling exchange for five to ten minutes. (PI)

Observations:

TEST DATE: _____ _____ _____ _____

9–12 months

1. Exhibits a variety of emotions throughout the day, usually related to environmental stimuli. (AAEE)
2. Recovers from anger after a few minutes. (CS)
   (*First Feelings*)
3. Uses complex behavior to establish closeness. (PI)
   (*HELP)
4. Begins to understand cause and effect in relationships with others. (BV)
   (Brigance)

Observations:

TEST DATE: _____ _____ _____ _____

12–18 months

1. Uses own emotions to elicit specific adult emotional reactions. (AAEE)
   (*First Feelings*)
2. Demonstrates complex imitations of both behaviors and emotions. (AAEE)
   (*First Feelings*)
3. Begins to exhibit distal communication to maintain feelings of security. (CS)
   (*First Feelings*)
4. Shows increasing independence in exploring the environment. (PI)
5. Smiles at own image in mirror. (PI)

Observations:

TEST DATE: _____ _____ _____ _____

18–24 months

1. Uses words or complex gestures to communicate desire for closeness. (AAEE) (*First Feelings*)
2. Begins to engage in pretend play alone. (CS) (*First Feelings*)
3. Begins to show a fairly consistent emotional style. (PI)
4. Cares for, holds, and nurtures a doll or stuffed toy. (BV) (HELP)
5. Conveys emotions through facial expressions. (AAEE) (*First Feelings*)

Observations:

_____

TEST DATE: _____ _____ _____ _____

24–30 months

1. Smiles in recognition of own image in mirror. (PI) (HELP)
2. Voluntarily slows down for nap or rest. (CS) (*Memphis)
3. Begins to use words or complex gestures to express needs or feelings. (AAEE) (*First Feelings*)
4. Begins to exhibit ability to set limits for self. (CS) (HELP)
5. Begins to instigate activities based on own needs and desires rather than by imitation alone. (PI)

Observations:

_____

TEST DATE: _____ _____ _____ _____

30–36 months

1. Expresses emotions through pretend play. (AAEE)
2. Relates warmly and positively to adults but is not overly dependent. (BV) (*First Feelings*)
3. Begins to enjoy small-group activities and interactions. (PI)
4. Can describe a memory of an emotional situation or interaction. (CS) (*First Feelings*)

Observations:

TEST DATE: _____ _____ _____ _____

36–42 months

1. Verbalizes emotions he or she is feeling. (BV) (*Portage)
2. Is able to recover from anger or temper tantrum and be cooperative and organized. (CS) (*First Feelings*)
3. Expresses displeasure through verbalization rather than physical aggression. (BV) (*LAP)
4. Separates from parent without reluctance. (PI) (*LAP)

Observations:

TEST DATE: _____   _____   _____   _____

42–48 months

1. Recognizes emotions in others. (BV)
2. Verbalizes consequences of behaviors. (CS)
3. Maintains an appropriate, stable temperament most of the time. (PI)
   (*First Feelings*)
4. Begins to differentiate between fact and fantasy. (PI)

Observations:

TEST DATE: _____   _____   _____   _____

48–54 months

1. Responds to a specific need/desire when expressed by another child. (BV)
2. Is able to separate own emotions from those of other people. (AAEE)
3. Shows increasing levels of positive interactions and friendliness in small-group settings. (PI)
4. Sees humor in everyday situations. (CS)

Observations:

TEST DATE: _____   _____   _____   _____

54–60 months

1. Exhibits concern for fairness in what happens to others by sharing and/or taking turns. (BV)
2. Verbalizes and is comfortable expressing a wider variety of emotions. (AAEE)
3. Is able to return to equilibrium after experiencing stress. (CS)
4. Openly and warmly expresses affection to other children. (AAEE)

Observations:

TEST DATE: _____   _____   _____   _____

60–66 months

1. Demonstrates a greater ability to differentiate between fact and fantasy. (PI) (*First Feelings*)
2. Shows willingness to delay gratification and impulsive responses; shows evidence of internal locus of control. (CS)
3. Exhibits increasing flexibility and comfort in coping with change. (CS)
4. Comforts other children in distress. (AAEE)

Observations:

TEST DATE: _____ _____ _____ _____

66–72 months

1. Realizes and verbalizes the relationship between feelings and behavior. (AAEE) (*First Feelings*)
2. Is supportive and helpful to others in small-group settings. (BV)
3. Increasingly exerts individuality and uniqueness in relationships with others. (PI)
4. Distinguishes ranges of emotions. (AAEE)

Observations:

TEST DATE: _____ _____ _____ _____

72–78 months

1. Demonstrates increasing autonomy in decision making and problem solving. (PI)
2. Has a positive view of self; shows high comfort level with own feelings, behaviors, etc. (PI)
3. Increasingly demonstrates empathy for others experiencing pain, frustration, etc. (BV)
4. Shows exuberance and enjoyment and is more secure interacting freely in group settings. (PI)

Observations:

CREATIVE-PLAY CURRICULUM
DEVELOPMENTAL CHECKLIST _____

Name _____

Date of Birth _____

Socialization

TEST DATE: _____ _____ _____ _____

1–2 months
1. Begins to smile responsively. (SI)
   (Early LAP)
2. Regards adult's face and/or voice. (SI)
   (Early LAP)
3. Responds to a person other than a parent. (SI)
   (Early LAP)
4. Visually prefers a person to an object. (SI)
   (Early LAP)
5. Quiets to a person's voice or face, or in response to being held. (SI)
   (*Early LAP)

Observations:

_____

TEST DATE: _____ _____ _____ _____

2–4 months
1. Responds with total body to a face he or she recognizes. (SI)
   (HELP)
2. Begins to adjust responses to people. (SI)
   (HELP)
3. Begins to respond to interesting objects or animated facial expressions. (SI)
4. Smiles selectively—has "special" smile for parent/familiar adults. (SI)
   (*First Feelings*)

Observations:

_____

Socialization Subdomains:
- SI   Social interactions
- C   Cooperation
- CR   Conservation of resources
- RO   Respect for others

TEST DATE: _____ _____ _____ _____

4–6 months

1. Smiles responsively. (SI)
   (HELP)
2. Occupies self with a toy for a short period of time. (CR)
   (HELP)
3. Smiles and/or vocalizes to make social contact and/or gain attention. (SI)
4. Occasionally stops crying when talked to. (C)
   (HELP)
5. Begins to show recognition of mother, father, and/or familiar adult. (SI)
   (Memphis)

Observations:

TEST DATE: _____ _____ _____ _____

6–9 months

1. Desires personal attention beyond holding. (SI)
   (*Memphis)
2. Shows anticipation of play when familiar and/or interesting toy is seen (moving, laughing, etc.). (CR)
3. May offer toy to another child or adult but not necessarily release it. (C)
   (HELP)
4. Shows clear attachment to mother and/or father. (SI)
   (Early LAP)

Observations:

TEST DATE: _____ _____ _____ _____

9–12 months

1. May pull away from strangers. (SI) (HELP)
2. When encouraged to continue in play, child responds by repeating action. (SI) (HELP)
3. Gives toy to adult when asked. (C) (*Early LAP)
4. Indicates wants without crying. (C) (Battelle)
5. Imitates another child at play. (SI)
6. May be sensitive to other children. (SI)

Observations:

TEST DATE: _____ _____ _____ _____

12–18 months

1. Engages in parallel play. (SI) (Early LAP)
2. Takes part in games, such as pushing a car or rolling a ball with an adult. (CR) (HELP)
3. Plays in a focused, organized manner. (SI) (*First Feelings*)
4. Begins to accept adult limits. (C) (Memphis)

Observations:

TEST DATE: _____ _____ _____ _____

18–24 months

1. Generally follows adult requests, directions, etc. (C) (Memphis)
2. Plays effectively around other children. (SI) (*Memphis)
3. Requests adult attention—pulls adult to "show" something. (SI)
4. Waits for needs to be met at lunch table and/or changing table. (C)
5. Greets familiar adults and peers when reminded. (SI) (*Portage)

Observations:

TEST DATE: _____ _____ _____ _____

24–30 months

1. Plays with toys constructively; is not intentionally destructive. (CR)
2. Cooperates with adult requests most of the time. (C) (Memphis)
3. Begins to understand how behavior can be related to consequences. (SI) (*First Feelings)
4. Shares object with another child when requested. (SI) (Portage)

Observations:

TEST DATE: _____ _____ _____ _____

30–36 months

1. Plays cooperatively with one child. (SI)
   (*LAP)
2. Says "please" or "thank you" when reminded. (RO)
   (*Portage)
3. Makes a choice when asked. (C)
   (*Portage)
4. Participates in group time, most of the time. (C)

Observations:

_____

TEST DATE: _____ _____ _____ _____

36–42 months

1. Enjoys saying nursery rhymes, finger plays, singing simple songs with others. (SI)
2. Greets familiar adults or peers without reminders. (SI)
   (*Portage)
3. Attempts to help with clean-up activities. (C)
4. Plays simple group games. (SI)
   (*LAP)
5. Begins to take turns. (C)
   (*LAP)
6. Attends to short stories for five to ten minutes. (C)
   (*Portage)

Observations:

TEST DATE: _____ _____ _____ _____

42–48 months

1. Plays interactive games—exhibits associative play. (SI)
   (*LAP)
2. Plays with peers with a minimal amount of conflict. (SI)
3. Asks permission to use items belonging to others. (RO)
   (*Portage)
4. Interacts in a socially appropriate way with peers. (SI)
   (*First Feelings)
5. Interacts in a socially appropriate way with adults; cooperates with adult requests most of the time. (SI)

Observations:

TEST DATE: _____ _____ _____ _____

48–54 months

1. Asks for assistance when having difficulty. (SI)
   (*Portage)
2. Repeats songs, rhymes, etc., for others. (C)
3. Puts toys away without close supervision. (CR)
   (*LAP)
4. Says "please" and "thank you" without reminders. (RO)
   (*Portage)
5. Attends to a story for ten to fifteen minutes. (C)
6. Frequently participates in cooperative play with small groups of children. (SI)

Observations:

TEST DATE: _____ _____ _____ _____

54–60 months

1. Joins in conversation at mealtime. (SI)
   (Portage)
2. Uses play materials constructively—builds
   instead of tearing down. (CR)
3. Plays cooperatively with two or more
   children. (SI)
   (*LAP)
4. Initiates friendship relationships with peers.
   (SI)

Observations:

TEST DATE: _____ _____ _____ _____

60–66 months

1. Verbalizes emotions to resolve conflict with
   peers. (SI)
2. Takes turns and understands rules of simple
   games, such as hide-and-seek, red light/green
   light, etc. (C)
3. Shows a preference for some friends over
   others. (SI)
4. Initiates activities in small groups. (SI)

Observations:

TEST DATE: _____   _____   _____   _____

66–72 months

1. Helps adult with simple tasks. (C)
2. Addresses two familiar adults by name. (SI)
3. Responds verbally to social small talk initiated by adults. (SI)
4. Identifies people by characteristics other than name. (SI)
5. Exhibits positive interactions in group settings. (SI)
6. Assumes responsibility to stay within the rules of games/activities without reminders. (C)

Observations:

TEST DATE: _____   _____   _____   _____

72–78 months

1. Organizes a group to participate in games/activities. (SI)
2. Uses others in group to facilitate problem solving in conflict situations. (SI)
3. Takes responsibility for appropriate care of materials and the environment without reminders. (CR)
4. Demonstrates respect and understanding of differences in people (race, sex, cultural backgrounds). (RO)

Observations:

CREATIVE-PLAY CURRICULUM
DEVELOPMENTAL CHECKLIST _____

Name _____
Date of Birth _____

Communication

TEST DATE: _____ _____ _____ _____

1–2 months

1. Responds to voice. (RL)
   (*Early LAP)
2. Vocalizes other than crying. (EL)
   (Early LAP)
3. Reacts to loud sounds by startle, eye blink, crying, smiling, etc. (A)
   (Early LAP)
4. Exhibits differentiated cry. (EL)
   (HELP)
5. Begins to use vowel sounds (when not crying). (EL)
   (Early LAP)

Observations:

_____

TEST DATE: _____ _____ _____ _____

2–4 months

1. Searches for sound with eyes. (A)
   (HELP)
2. Shows positive response to being talked to. (RL)
   (Early LAP)
3. Laughs aloud. (EL)
   (*Early LAP)
4. Vocalizes in response to cooing sounds. (EL)
   (HELP)
5. Imitates cooing sounds. (EL)
   (HELP)

Observations:

_____

Communication Subdomains:

RL   Receptive language
EL   Expressive language
NV   Nonverbal communication
A   Auditory memory/discrimination

TEST DATE: _____   _____   _____   _____

4–6 months

1. Localizes sounds with eyes. (A)
   (HELP)
2. Vocalizes in response to babbling sounds. (EL)
   (HELP)
3. Changes activity level in recognition of a sign—
   at sight of bottle, bib, etc. (NV)
   (LAP)
4. Vocalizes displeasure in ways other than
   crying. (EL)
   (HELP)
5. Exhibits variation in pitch and rhythm of
   cry. (EL)
   (*HELP)

Observations:

TEST DATE: _____   _____   _____   _____

6–9 months

1. Begins to communicate with simple gestures.
   (NV)
   (HELP)
2. Changes pitch while vocalizing or talking. (EL)
   (HELP)
3. Localizes sounds or voices outside line of
   vision. (A)
   (Early LAP)
4. Produces various vowel sounds in vocal
   play. (EL)
   (Early LAP)
5. Exhibits babbling. (EL)
   (Early LAP)
6. Begins response with gestures. (NV)
   (HELP)

Observations:

TEST DATE: _____ _____ _____ _____

9–12 months

1. Vocalizes in response to familiar words (may use some similar sounds). (EL) (HELP)
2. Uses expressive jargon. (EL) (Early LAP)
3. Begins to shake head for "no" and/or "yes." (NV) (Early LAP)
4. Begins to imitate gestures. (NV) (HELP)
5. Says "mama" and/or "dada," specifically. (EL) (*HELP)
6. Imitates a simple rhythmic pattern. (A) (Early LAP)

Observations:

TEST DATE: _____ _____ _____ _____

12–18 months

1. Imitates babbling sounds and/or familiar words. (EL) (HELP)
2. Has functional vocabulary of at least ten words. (EL) (HELP)
3. Follows simple commands involving familiar objects. (RL) (*Early LAP)
4. Understands questions. (RL) (Early LAP)
5. Indicates wants or needs by vocalizing. (EL) (Early LAP)
6. Indicates wants or needs by pointing or gesturing. (NV) (*Early LAP)

Observations:

TEST DATE: _____ _____ _____ _____

18–24 months

1. Has functional vocabulary of 20 words. (EL)
   (Early LAP)
2. Names three objects from pictures. (EL)
   (Early LAP)
3. Follows simple directions. (RL)
   (Early LAP)
4. Uses pronouns. (EL)
   (*Early LAP)
5. Uses two-word combinations to form
   sentences/phrases. (EL)
   (Early LAP)

Observations:

TEST DATE: _____ _____ _____ _____

24–30 months

1. Uses regular plurals. (EL)
   (Early LAP)
2. Knows first name when asked. (EL)
   (*Early LAP)
3. Listens to a simple story, showing preference
   for one heard before. (A)
   (HELP)
4. Identifies object by use in pictures when
   asked. (RL)
   (Early LAP)
5. Responds to commands involving directions
   with modifier. (RL)
6. Uses three-word combinations to form
   sentences/phrases. (EL)
   (Memphis)

Observations:

TEST DATE: _____ _____ _____ _____

30–36 months
1. Answers simple "what" questions. (EL) (*LAP)
2. Discriminates noisemakers. (A)
3. Repeats a five-word sentence. (EL)
4. Identifies simple actions in pictures when asked. (RL)
5. Follows a one-step command. (A)
6. Uses four-word sentences consistently. (EL)

Observations:

TEST DATE: _____ _____ _____ _____

36–42 months
1. Gives first and last name. (EL) (*HELP)
2. Names three common actions. (EL) (*LAP)
3. Tells of a simple experience. (A) (*Portage)
4. When given a choice, names preferred object or activity. (EL)
5. Begins asking purposeful questions. (EL)
6. Uses complete sentences consistently. (EL)

Observations:

TEST DATE: _____ _____ _____ _____

42–48 months

1. Sings a simple song. (EL)
2. Asks a variety of questions using "who," "what," "where," etc. (EL)
3. Tells a story using a picture. (EL)
4. Answers "if this . . . then what" questions. (EL) (*Portage)
5. Delivers a one-part verbal message. (EL) (LAP)

Observations:

TEST DATE: _____ _____ _____ _____

48–54 months

1. Follows a two-step command. (RL)
2. Describes objects by function. (EL)
3. Discriminates "is" versus "is not" by pointing to objects when asked. (RL)
4. Uses possessive forms of nouns. (EL)
5. Uses conjunctions serially. (EL)
6. Averages five-word sentences in conversation. (EL)

Observations:

TEST DATE: _____ _____ _____ _____

54–60 months

1. Names at least six animals when asked to name all of the animals he or she can think of. (EL)
2. Repeats a series of four-digit numerals. (A)
3. Shows an interest in new or novel words. (EL)
4. Describes items and/or actions in books. (EL)

Observations:

TEST DATE: _____ _____ _____ _____

60–66 months

1. Follows commands involving three actions *in the sequence given.* (A)
2. Names sources of fifteen actions. (EL) (LAP)
3. Uses irregular plurals. (EL) (LAP)
4. Rhymes words after demonstration. (EL) (*LAP)

Observations:

TEST DATE: _____ _____ _____ _____

66–72 months
1. Sequences three pictures and tells a story. (A)
2. Delivers a two-part verbal message. (EL) (*LAP)
3. Distinguishes animals from pictures and descriptions. (RL)
4. Repeats a sentence of eleven or twelve syllables. (A) (Brigance)

Observations:

TEST DATE: _____ _____ _____ _____

72–78 months
1. Names at least eight animals. (EL) (LAP)
2. Builds sentences following demonstration. (A)
3. Comprehends left and right. (RL)
4. Tells a story without using pictures. (EL) (*Portage)

Observations:

CREATIVE-PLAY CURRICULUM
DEVELOPMENTAL CHECKLIST _____

Name _____

Date of Birth _____

Cognition

TEST DATE: _____ _____ _____ _____

1–2 months

1. Visually fixates on object held eight to ten inches in front of eyes. (CF) (Battelle)
2. Looks at lights. (CF)
3. Begins to visually inspect surroundings. (CF) (*HELP)

Observations:

TEST DATE: _____ _____ _____ _____

2–4 months

1. Tracks an object through a 180° arc. (CF) (Early LAP)
2. In a supine position, or seated in an infant seat, attempts to maintain visual contact after object has moved out of visual field. (PS/R) (HELP)
3. Increases/decreases activity upon seeing an object presented by an adult. (CF) (HELP)
4. Attends to gestures performed by an adult. (CF)
5. Imitates behaviors already in his or her repertoire. (I/M)

Observations:

Cognition Subdomains:

PS/R	Problem solving/reasoning
CF	Concept formation
I/M	Imitation/memory
A/C	Association/classification

TEST DATE: _____ _____ _____ _____

4–6 months

1. Visually searches for object at point of disappearance. (PS/R) (HELP)
2. Discriminates between strangers and parent/familiar adult. (A/C) (Early LAP)
3. Begins to show repetitive behaviors—will repeat a procedure to obtain the same result from an object or toy. (I/M) (Early LAP)
4. Plays with own hands, feet, fingers, toes, etc. (CF) (HELP)
5. Finds a partially hidden object. (PS/R) (*HELP)

Observations:

TEST DATE: _____ _____ _____ _____

6–9 months

1. Withdraws object held in his or her hand following covering of hand and object with cloth. (PS/R)
2. Finds object hidden under one screen. (PS/R) (Early LAP)
3. Activates a toy. (I/M) (Early LAP)
4. Shows evidence of early problem solving. (PS/R)
5. Follows path of object as it falls out of view. (PS/R) (Early LAP)
6. Inspects objects visually and tactilely. (CF)
7. Touches adult's hand or toy as a casual action in response to adult activating a toy. (PS/R)

Observations:

TEST DATE: _____ _____ _____ _____

9–12 months

1. Uses some form of locomotion to obtain an out-of-reach object. (PS/R) (*HELP)
2. Imitates complex gestures. (I/M) (HELP)
3. Drops or throws objects, with visual monitoring of results. (CF) (HELP)
4. Begins to show understanding of relationship between objects and events. (A/C)

Observations:

TEST DATE: _____ _____ _____ _____

12–18 months

1. Looks in correct place for toy or object that he or she has seen covered or rolled out of sight. (PS/R) (*Early LAP)
2. Uses a string to functionally pull a toy along the floor. (PS/R) (*Early LAP)
3. Imitates new and novel gestures. (I/M) (HELP)
4. Follows one direction. (I/M) (Early LAP)
5. Finds object hidden under one of two screens. (I/M)
6. Places objects in a cup and dumps out contents. (PS/R) (Memphis)
7. Recognizes and labels or points to a picture representing an object. (A/C) (Early LAP)
8. Places round shapes in a shape formboard. (CF) (*HELP)

Observations:

TEST DATE: _____ _____ _____ _____

42–48 months

1. Counts three objects. (CF) (*LAP)
2. Matches two colors. (CF) (*LAP)
3. Comprehends this question: "What do you do when you are ____?" (PS/R)
4. Knows own gender. (CF)
5. Knows concept of "one more" when asked to give "one more." (CF)
6. Knows concept of "empty." (CF)

Observations:

TEST DATE: _____ _____ _____ _____

48–54 months

1. Counts to ten by rote. (I/M) (*LAP)
2. Names picture that has been hidden. (I/M)
3. Draws a two-part person. (A/C)
4. Completes opposite analogy statements after explanation. (A/C)
5. Comprehends this question: "What do we do with our ____?" (A/C)
6. Works a twelve-piece puzzle. (PS/R) (*Memphis)

Observations:

TEST DATE: _____ _____ _____ _____

54–60 months

1. Counts four objects. (CF)
   (*LAP)
2. Knows difference between hard and soft surfaces. (CF)
3. Identifies four colors when named. (CF)
   (*LAP)
4. Identifies a circle. (CF)
5. Knows appropriate daytime versus nighttime activities. (A/C)
6. Draws a three-part person. (A/C)
   (*Memphis)
7. Extends sentence logically. (PS/R)

Observations:

TEST DATE: _____ _____ _____ _____

60–66 months

1. Names four colors. (CF)
   (*LAP)
2. Counts ten objects. (CF)
   (LAP)
3. Identifies eight colors when named. (CF)
   (*LAP)
4. Identifies a square. (CF)
   (*LAP)
5. Extends sequence of events logically. (PS/R)

Observations:

TEST DATE: _____ _____ _____ _____

66–72 months

1. Identifies the object in the "middle." (CF)
   (*LAP)
2. Describes the weather. (A/C)
   (LAP)
3. Counts thirteen objects. (CF)
   (*LAP)
4. Arranges objects in order from smallest to largest. (CF)
   (*LAP)
5. Tells which is "bigger." (CF)
   (*LAP)
6. Proposes alternative ways to solve peer problems. (PS/R)

Observations:

TEST DATE: _____ _____ _____ _____

72–78 months

1. Counts 20 objects. (CF)
   (LAP)
2. Names the seven days of the week. (I/M)
   (LAP)
3. Knows morning versus afternoon activities. (A/C)
   (*LAP)
4. Creates, structures, and solves problems in play situations. (PS/R)
5. Creates challenges for self by increasing the difficulty/complexity of tasks. (PS/R)

Observations:

CREATIVE-PLAY CURRICULUM
DEVELOPMENTAL CHECKLIST _____

Name _____

Date of Birth _____

Perceptual Motor

TEST DATE: _____ _____ _____ _____

1–2 months				

1–2 months

1. Performs equal movements of arms and/or legs. (BMC)
2. In prone position, lifts head 45°. (NLS) (*HELP)
3. Lifts head when held at shoulder. (NLS)
4. In supine position, turns head to both sides. (NLS)

Observations:

_____

TEST DATE: _____ _____ _____ _____

2–4 months

1. Has an awareness of hands. (EHC) (*Early LAP)
2. Brings hands together at midline. (EHC) (HELP)
3. Crudely grasps an object placed in hand. (EHC)
4. Rolls from side to back. (NLS) (*Early LAP)
5. While held in a sitting position, controls head. (BMC) (*Early LAP)

Observations:

_____

Perceptual Motor Subdomains:

EHC Eye-hand/eye-foot coordination
LS Locomotor skills
NLS Nonlocomotor skills
BMC Body management and control

TEST DATE: _____ _____ _____ _____

4–6 months

1. Reaches for nearby objects. (EHC) (HELP)
2. Brings two toys together in play at midline. (EHC)
3. Begins pushing up chest with arms when in prone position. (EHC) (*Early LAP)
4. Rolls from back to stomach. (NLS) (Early LAP)
5. Begins traveling by rolling or scooting. (LS)
6. Pulls to a sit with no head lag. (NLS) (*Early LAP)
7. Brings hand to mouth. (EHC) (Memphis)

Observations:

TEST DATE: _____ _____ _____ _____

6–9 months

1. Transfers a toy from hand to hand. (EHC) (*Early LAP)
2. When offered, grasps a one-inch cube with one hand. (EHC)
3. Uses raking grasp to obtain small objects. (EHC) (*Early LAP)
4. Sits unsupported for several minutes. (NLS) (*Memphis)
5. Pulls to a stand. (BMC) (*Early LAP)
6. Begins a commando crawl. (LS)

Observations:

TEST DATE: ____ ____ ____ ____

9–12 months

1. Utilizes pincer grasp. (EHC)
   (*Early LAP)
2. Removes pegs from a pegboard. (EHC)
   (*Portage)
3. Bangs two one-inch cubes together, holding one in each hand. (EHC)
   (HELP)
4. Creeps. (LS)
   (*Portage)
5. Stands alone, temporarily, without support. (BMC)
   (*HELP)
6. Walks holding on to furniture. (LS)
   (*HELP)

Observations:

TEST DATE: ____ ____ ____ ____

12–18 months

1. Holds a crayon, functionally. (EHC)
   (*Early LAP)
2. Builds a tower of two blocks. (EHC)
   (*Early LAP)
3. Turns pages of a cardboard book one at a time. (EHC)
   (Portage)
4. Walks without support. (LS)
   (*Portage)
5. Stoops and recovers balance without support. (BMC)
   (*HELP)
6. Sits in a small chair. (NLS)
   (*Portage)

Observations:

TEST DATE: _____ _____ _____ _____

18–24 months

1. Builds a four-block tower. (EHC)
   (*Early LAP)
2. Throws a small ball. (EHC)
   (*Early LAP)
3. Unwraps a small package. (EHC)
   (*Portage)
4. Runs well with only occasional falling. (LS)
   (*HELP)
5. Squats to play, balancing without hand
   support. (BMC)
   (*Memphis)
6. Pushes and pulls a large object while
   walking. (LS)
   (*Portage)

Observations:

TEST DATE: _____ _____ _____ _____

24–30 months

1. Builds a six-block tower. (EHC)
   (*HELP)
2. Pounds, squeezes, rolls, and/or pulls clay. (EHC)
   (Brigance)
3. Turns paper pages of a book, singly. (EHC)
   (*Early LAP)
4. Jumps with both feet off floor. (LS)
   (*Portage)
5. Walks up and down stairs using rail (both feet
   on same step). (LS)
   (*HELP)
6. Stands and kicks a ball. (EFC)
   (*Early LAP)

Observations:

TEST DATE: _____ _____ _____ _____

30–36 months

1. Builds an eight-block tower. (EHC) (*HELP)
2. Cuts with scissors functionally but not necessarily correctly. (EHC)
3. Begins to hold crayon or pencil with fingers in opposition to thumb. (EHC) (*HELP)
4. Pedals appropriate-size tricycle. (LS) (*HELP)
5. Stands on one foot momentarily. (BMC) (*LAP)
6. Climbs over objects and obstacles. (BMC)

Observations:

TEST DATE: _____ _____ _____ _____

36–42 months

1. Builds a nine-block tower. (EHC) (*HELP)
2. Strings one-inch beads. (EHC) (*LAP)
3. Stirs liquid with spoon. (EHC) (*LAP)
4. Jumps down from low object (six to eight inches). (LS) (*Portage)
5. Throws a ball a distance of at least two yards. (EHC)
6. Catches a six- to eight-inch ball using arms (not necessarily extended). (EHC)
7. Makes wide turns around obstacles while running and/or riding a tricycle. (LS)

Observations:

TEST DATE: _____ _____ _____ _____

42–48 months
1. Easily uses scissors to cut paper into two pieces. (EHC)
2. Builds with Lincoln Logs, Snap-Lock Blocks, etc. (EHC)
3. Walks up and down stairs, one foot per step, without rail or adult assistance. (LS)
4. Balances on one foot for four to five seconds. (BMC) (*LAP)
5. Throws a ball overhanded *and* underhanded for a distance of at least two yards. (EHC)
6. Folds and creases an $8\frac{1}{2}$-by-11-inch piece of paper in half. (EHC) (Brigance)

Observations

TEST DATE: _____ _____ _____ _____

48–54 months
1. Holds paper in place with one hand while writing with the other. (EHC)
2. Cuts with scissors along a thick line. (EHC) (LAP)
3. Jumps over a stationary rope held six inches above the ground. (EHC)
4. Balances on one foot for five to ten seconds. (BMC)
5. Pedals a tricycle around sharp corners and obstacles. (LS) (*LAP)
6. Catches a ball in hands, arms flexed. (EHC) (*LAP)
7. Holds a crayon with grasp of fingers in opposition to thumb. (EHC)

Observations:

TEST DATE: _____ _____ _____ _____

54–60 months
1. Laces shoes and/or lacing board. (EHC)
2. Cuts along a thick curved line. (EHC)
3. Throws a ball with close accuracy. (EHC)
4. Jumps a moving rope. (LS)
   (Portage)
5. Walks backward, heel-to-toe walk. (BMC)
   (LAP)

Observations:

TEST DATE: _____ _____ _____ _____

60–66 months
1. Ties a single knot. (EHC)
   (LAP)
2. Cuts out a three-inch square using scissors. (EHC)
   (LAP)
3. Crumples paper into ball with one hand. (EHC)
   (*LAP)
4. Walks up and kicks ball. (EFC)
   (*LAP)
5. Stands on tiptoes. (BMC)
   (*LAP)
6. Jumps backward. (LS)
   (LAP)
7. Draws/writes recognizable objects or letters. (EHC)

Observations:

TEST DATE: _____ _____ _____ _____

66–72 months

1. Writes own first name. (EHC)
2. Skips, alternating feet. (LS) (*LAP)
3. Runs on tiptoes. (LS) (*HELP)
4. Hops forward on one foot. (LS) (*LAP)
5. Jumps a turning rope. (EFC)

Observations:

TEST DATE: _____ _____ _____ _____

72–78 months

1. Cuts out magazine picture following the shape of the object. (EHC) (LAP)
2. Jumps and turns in midair. (LS)
3. Bounces ball with one hand and catches with two hands. (EHC)
4. Holds on to and hangs from climber bar. (BMC)

Observations:

REFERENCES _____

Bluma, S., Shearer, M., Frohman, A., & Hilliard, J. (1976). *Portage guide to early education.* Portage, WI: Portage Project.

Brigance, A. (1978). *Brigance diagnostic inventory of early development.* Woburn, MA: Curriculum Associates.

Furuno, S., Inatsuka, T., O'Reilly, K., Hosaka, C., Zeisloft, B., & Allman, T. (1984). *HELP (Hawaii early learning profile) checklist.* Palo Alto, CA: VORT Corporation.

Greenspan, S., & Greenspan, N. T. (1985). *First feelings.* New York: Viking Press.

Griffin, P. M., & Sanford, A. R. (1975). *Learning accomplishment profile for infants.* Winston-Salem, NC: Kaplan Press.

Newburg, J., Stock, J. R., & Winek, L. (1984). *Battelle developmental inventory.* Allen, TX: DLM Teaching Resources.

Quick, A. D., & Campbell, A. A. (1974). *Memphis comprehensive development scale.* Belmont, CA: Fearon.

Sanford, A. R., & Zelman, J. G. (1981). *Learning accomplishment profile.* Winston-Salem, NC: Kaplan Press.

For further information about the assessments that are referenced, contact the following organizations.

LAP—Learning Accomplishment Profile

Kaplan School Supply
P.O. Box 609
Lewisville, NC 27023

The LAP is a criterion-referenced assessment tool for both young children with special needs and normally developing children in the developmental range of 36 to 72 months. The developmental areas assessed are gross motor, fine motor, prewriting, cognitive, language, self-help, and personal/social skills. The LAP for Infants assesses children younger than 36 months.

Portage Guide to Early Education

Portage Project
Cooperative Education Service Agency
P.O. Box 564
Portage, WI 53901

The Portage checklist is a developmental inventory that assesses young children's behaviors in six areas of development: infant stimulation, socialization, language, self-help, cognitive, and motor skills. The Portage checklist assesses development in children from infancy through age 6.

Memphis Comprehensive Developmental Scale

Fearon/Janus Publishers
500 Harbor Blvd.
Belmont, CA 94002

The Memphis scale assesses young children's perceptual-cognitive, language, fine motor, gross motor, and personal/social skills. The Memphis scale assesses the development of young children from 3 months to 5 years.

HELP—Hawaii Early Learning Profile

VORT Corporation
P.O. Box 60132
Palo Alto, CA 94306

The HELP is a developmental checklist to assess skills in young children from birth to 36 months in the areas of cognitive, language, gross motor, fine motor, social-emotional, and self-help skills. The HELP is designed to promote individualized child assessment and to aid in program planning.

Brigance Diagnostic Inventory of Early Development

Curriculum Associates, Inc.
5 Esquire Rd.
North Billerica, MA 01862

The Brigance inventory is a criterion-referenced and norm-referenced assessment for young children of developmental levels up to 7 years. The Brigance inventory is designed to assess children's development and facilitate instructional planning. The inventory assesses development in the areas of preambulatory motor skills and behaviors, gross motor skills and behaviors, fine motor skills and behaviors, self-help skills, prespeech, speech and language, general knowledge and comprehension, readiness, reading, manuscript, and basic math.

Battelle Developmental Inventory

DLM Teaching Resources
One DLM Park
Allen, TX 75002

The Battelle Developmental Inventory (BDI) is a standardized, individually administered assessment designed to be used by infant, toddler, preschool, and primary teachers, as well as by special educators. The BDI assesses key developmental skills in children from birth to age 8 and consists of 341 test items in the personal-social, adaptive, motor, communication, and cognitive domains.

C.

Guidelines for Child Observations

GUIDELINES FOR WRITING INFANT (6 WEEKS TO 15 MONTHS) OBSERVATIONS

Personal Awareness

Self-Help Skills
(increases skill to feed and dress self and regulate toileting and sleeping)

Dressing

How does the infant help with dressing: touch or pull at clothes, push arm through sleeves, lift leg for pants, put sock or shoe toward foot, or cooperate when dressed by someone else?

Nap / Rest Time

How does the infant relax or put self to sleep: alone, with bottle, while rocking, with patting, crib rocking? How does the infant indicate a need for sleep: rubbing eyes or face, whining, crying, tossing head in crib, yawning, playing with blankets, singing/vocalizing? How does the infant indicate nap is finished: standing in crib, crying, vocalizing, pushing up and looking around, rolling over and playing in crib, reaching for teacher? How does the child put self back to sleep: find pacifier or fingers to suck on, cry? Does the child wake frequently and go back to sleep?

Mealtime

How does the child help with bottle or breast feeding? Does the child push the bottle in and out of his/her mouth to regulate flow of formula? Does the child use a spoon to pick up finger foods, open mouth eagerly for food, move or turn head away when full or when food is offered too quickly? Does the older infant help with serving and pouring at mealtime? Does the infant use a cup? Does the child spill or choke frequently or rarely? Does the child use two hands or one hand? Does the child put cup back down on table/tray, rarely spilling? Is cup use functional or is infant just mouthing or reaching for the cup?

This section was written by Anne Miller Stott, Kathy Carlson, and Amy R. Kerlin; Jan Allen also contributed to writing this section.

Toileting

Is the child always wet when diaper is checked or is the child staying dry for short periods of time? Does the child signal need for a diaper change and indicate discomfort when diaper is wet or soiled? Is the infant completely dependent on adult for help with diaper changes? Does the child reach for or pull wet/soiled diaper or help to get diapering supplies?

Independence
(exhibits control of self and mastery of environment)

Acceptance of Responsibility

Does the infant hold on to a toy if another child tries to take it away? Is the child beginning to follow simple tasks, such as helping teacher with a task or putting a toy in a container?

Separation from Family

How does the child separate from parents at arrival time? Does the child cry? For how long? Does the child eagerly reach for teachers or for toys? Does the child wave good-bye or ignore the parent? Does the child cling or try to "fake a cry"? Does the child cooperate by not reacting to being handed from the parent to the teacher? Does the child react differently if separating from a different person or when being taken by a different teacher?

Interactions with Environment

Does the child choose own activities or does the child need help choosing an activity? What kind of help is needed—verbal or physical? How often is adult help needed to begin play or exploration? Is help needed when the infant is tired or hungry, or at other times?

Control over Environment

How does the infant meet own needs? Are nonverbal communication, gesturing, or crying used? How much assistance does the child require getting wants met? How does the infant enlist adult assistance? With which activities or routines is adult assistance needed?

Personal Health
(develops knowledge of body parts, nutrition, hygiene, drug abuse prevention, wellness)

Body Image

How does the infant react when an adult names, touches, and talks about different parts of the child's body? Does the child smile, listen with interest, or act shy and pull away? How does the infant react to talk of own clothes or body? Does the infant show pride?

Sexual Identity

Does the infant reach for, touch, or explore own genitals? How does the infant react to an adult talking about gender, such as "You are a girl. _____ is a boy."? How does the infant react when an adult names and discusses genitals during diaper changes?

Hygiene

How does the infant show an awareness of clean versus dirty, such as a need for hand washing or nose wipes? How does the infant take part in or cooperate with diaper changes, face washing, and hand washing? Does the infant show an awareness of wet/dirty clothes? Describe how you know this awareness exists.

Nutritional Habits

Does the infant show beginning nutritional habits, such as eating on a regular schedule, being willing to try new foods, and eating a variety of both baby and table foods? Does the infant show an active interest in the discussion of foods? Does the infant limit intake of foods or refuse to eat more when full? Does the infant continue to eat until an adult limits intake? Does the infant eat more at certain times of the day? What foods does the infant seem to prefer?

Personal Safety
(learns child abuse prevention and passenger and pedestrian safety practices; develops an awareness of environmental hazards)

Passenger Safety Rules

Does the infant cooperate or protest riding in a car seat? How does the infant respond to being strapped into a cart or stroller for walks?

Pedestrian Safety Rules

Does the child listen as pedestrian safety rules are explained? Does the child show a recognition of pedestrian safety rules by watching as teachers "look both ways"? How does the child react when adults practice pedestrian safety rules or discuss them? Is there an awareness of traffic?

Safe / Unsafe Interactions with Adults

Is the child aware of differences in people? How does the child react to different situations with people? How does the child react to strangers? When does the child react most strongly?

Right to Privacy / Ownership of Body

How does the infant react to having personal space "invaded"? How does the child react to extended interactions with adults? How does the infant react to being left alone (with adult nearby) for periods of time? How does the child react to "crowding" by another child or adult?

Emotional Well-Being

Awareness, Acceptance, and Expression of Emotions
(identifies a variety of feelings and expresses feelings to others)

Recognition and Verbalization of Emotions

Does the infant vocalize anger, excitement, pleasure, delight, or discomfort? How does the child vocalize these emotions? Are there differences in cries for different emotions?

Separation of Emotions

How does the infant respond to other children's and adults' expressions of emotion? Is the child aware or beginning to be aware of others' expressions? How do you know? Is the child focused primarily on his or her own emotions and their expression? Does the child watch another person expressing one type of emotion and then express a very different emotion for self?

Contact and Control of Feelings

Is the infant beginning to be able to calm self in certain situations? Describe these situations. Is the child still primarily dependent on adults to help calm down? Is the infant ever able to express anger or displeasure in ways other than intense crying? Describe.

Expression of Emotion

What variety of emotions do you see the infant express—anger, fear, delight, affection, pleasure, or distrust? Describe what the infant does when expressing these emotions. How does the child express these emotions—verbally, nonverbally, with cries, with gestures, or combinations?

Coping Skills
(shows adaptive and healthy response to stressors, conflict, or change; uses relaxation techniques; resolves emotional conflict and issues)

Use of Play and Creative Materials

How does the infant use play materials to calm self? Can the child be calmed by distraction with an interesting or special activity? Describe how this is done.

When is it most likely to occur? What types of toys or activities can be used effectively to help the infant calm self? Which type of activity—slow, calm, or energetic—is best for helping the child to release tension, anger, or frustration?

Internal Locus of Control

In what types of situations is the infant able to calm self? How is the child beginning to do this? In what ways does the infant exhibit internal control? In what types of situations is this most likely to occur?

Facing Reality and Adjusting to Change

How does the infant cope with change in the daily routines, in transitions, in different adult interactions, or in new environments? How does the infant react to verbal "warnings" or explanations of change? Do these help the infant to cope? How easily can the infant be redirected? In what types of situations is this most effectively carried out?

Response to Stress and Crisis Situations

How does the infant cope with stressful situations, such as fire drills, several crying babies, or a worker hammering in the classroom? When is the child better able to cope with these situations—when rested and fed, when in the company of a teacher or with parents? What responses does the infant exhibit in these situations—moving to an adult, crying, startling, ignoring, and looking around?

Personality Integration
(exhibits general adjustment, autonomy, positive self-concept)

Self-Esteem

Does the infant have positive or negative feelings about self? How is this exhibited behaviorally? Does the infant take pride in own accomplishments—by smiling when praised or by repeating a new behavior or skill just accomplished? How much adult encouragement does the infant need to take part in a new activity? Is the child eager to do something new or does the infant pause, watch, or need an adult close by to take part in new activities?

Feelings about Gender and Ethnic or Cultural Heritage

How does the infant react to an adult talking about the child being a boy or girl or being from a particular ethnic, cultural, or racial background? Does the infant show an early precursor skill of simply being interested in all people, including self?

Relationships with Others

How is the infant a unique individual in relationships with others? What unique aspects of relationships with others does the infant exhibit—unusual interactions, establishing closeness with adults, demanding attention other than holding, relaxing body when held, cuddling, or showing dependence or independence? Is the infant attached to a parent? How is that attachment different with caregivers?

Autonomy

How much autonomy does the infant use in daily interactions and explorations (for example, in problem solving and decision making)? Is the infant insistent on doing a task his or her own way?

Building Values
(develops empathy, trust, reverence, respect)

Attitudes

What attitudes does the infant exhibit—trust, autonomy, initiative, independence, flexibility, curiosity? Does the young infant prefer people or toys? When and how do these attitudes appear as behaviors by the infant?

Empathy

Is the infant showing early precursor skills that will help later to develop the skill of empathy, such as showing an active interest in other adults and children, an awareness of other children's emotional stages (anger, joy), or an interest in helping others? How does the infant react to another crying baby? Does the infant exhibit any behaviors that show a concern or an awareness of adults' feelings? Does the older infant pat a crying child or offer a toy?

Understanding and Valuing Life

Does the infant exhibit early precursors to understanding and valuing life, such as an active interest in people, special creatures, and things outside? How does the infant react to discussions of the importance of respecting and caring for living creatures? Does the infant need physical or verbal prompts to touch gently when exploring another baby, an animal, or bugs and flowers outside?

Awareness of Others' Emotions

Does the infant exhibit an awareness of others' emotions, such as stopping to watch a crying child; patting, hugging, or laughing when another child or adult laughs; or getting excited when someone else is excited or enthusiastic? How often and when is it likely to happen?

Socialization

Social Interactions
(interacting with peers and adults; resolving conflict)

Adults

How does the infant interact with adults? Does the infant reach or move toward, smile, vocalize, calm, or use eye contact? How does the infant initiate interactions with adults? How does the child respond to adults' interactions? Are there differences in the infant's interactions with familiar and unfamiliar adults or with parents? How frequent and how long are the infant's interactions with adults?

Peers

How does the infant interact with other infants? Does the child watch, smile, touch, vocalize, imitate, reach toward, follow, play "chase," or show or give a toy? Are peer interactions initiated or are they a response to another infant? Describe examples of these. How long and how frequent are the infant's interactions with peers? Is there a difference in the infant's interactions with familiar and unfamiliar peers?

Conflict Resolution

In what types of conflict with adults and with peers is the infant typically involved? How much adult assistance does the infant need to resolve these conflicts? What types of adult assistance is needed—verbal prompts, physical prompts, redirections, or restraints? In what way is the infant beginning to resolve conflict—moving away or expressing displeasure to other child? Describe.

Cooperation
(helping, sharing, taking turns)

Satisfaction in Helping

How does the infant help teachers and adults clean up, take bottles, or give a toy? How much adult prompting is needed in these situations? How does the infant react to praise for this behavior? Does the child repeat it for additional praise? When do these helping behaviors occur?

Communicating Needs/Wants

How does the infant communicate wants or needs—crying, going to an adult, pointing, vocalizing, or reaching toward the need? What methods does the infant use to obtain what is wanted? How socially appropriate are these methods?

Understanding the Individual's Place in the World

How does the infant view self as a single individual and as a member of the group? Is the infant's viewpoint still clearly egocentric or is there a beginning awareness of another's needs and wants? Can the child be redirected and have gratification for short periods of time? Is the infant beginning to share?

Functioning as a Part of the Group

Does the older infant take part in small-group activities? How much adult prompting is needed? Does the very young infant watch group activities with interest? How does the infant react to sitting with the "group" at snacks and lunch? What group skills does the infant exhibit—sharing, taking turns (with prompts), walking around several people on the floor, moving to a cluster of people in the classroom, or listening to a story with other children?

Conservation of Resources
(using and caring for materials and the environment appropriately)

Use of Play Materials

What types of toys and materials does the infant typically choose? What toys does the child never choose on his or her own but needs an adult's prompt to engage in play? How does the infant play with toys? Does the child change toys frequently, use one toy for prolonged periods, or always try to put a toy in mouth?

Care of Materials and Environment

How is the infant exhibiting early skills that will later lead to care of materials and the environment? Is the infant gentle and careful with manipulation of materials? Is the child gentle with materials when an adult prompts and praises? Does the infant show an active interest in materials and the environment? Will the infant "help to pick up" or "clean up" when prompted?

Respect and Care for the Natural World

Does the child show an active interest in the outdoor world or carefully manipulate natural materials with or without an adult prompt? How does the young infant react to discussions of the importance of care of the outdoor environment?

Awareness of Ecological Problems and Conservation Practices

What precursor skills does the child exhibit—an interest and an awareness of the outdoors; a special enjoyment of walks and outdoor play; listening, watching, helping when an adult waters the grass or feeds the fish; helping to clean up outside; gentle exploration of outdoor materials?

Respect for Others
(understanding and accepting individual differences, multicultural issues)

Responding to Others' Needs

Does the infant exhibit precursor skills that will later lead to responding to others' needs—an awareness that other people exist, pleasure and delight in seeing and interacting with others, or looking or touching when another child cries or an adult is upset? Does the infant bring a toy or tissue to another child?

Understanding Similarities and Differences in People

Does the infant demonstrate a knowledge of familiar and unfamiliar people? How is this knowledge demonstrated—fear, pulling away, crying, moving to a familiar person—when an unfamiliar person comes near the infant? Does the infant exhibit different behavior when parents are near? Describe. Does the infant exhibit an interest in or awareness of children with special needs?

Respecting and Understanding Differences in People

Does the infant respond differently to people of a different gender or people with different voice tones or accents? How does the infant respond differently? Is the infant aware of and interested in differences, such as hair, clothes, and jewelry? Does the older infant exhibit an awareness of differences in tiny infants and older infants or other children and older siblings?

Nurturing Behaviors toward Others

What nurturing behaviors—hugs, pats, kisses, reaching toward—does the infant exhibit toward other people? When are these most likely to occur? Are these behaviors spontaneous or in response to other nurturing behaviors? Does the very young infant show delight, hug or cuddle, or increase activity when nurtured? Does the young infant hug back when given a hug?

Communication

Receptive Language
(follows directions; understands basic concepts)

Understanding Stories and Songs

Does the infant respond when an adult reads, tells a story, or sings a song? How does the child respond to the stories or songs? Does the infant try to imitate simple gestures in finger plays? Does the infant watch or listen to songs or finger plays or come over to sit by the adult who is singing or reading? Is there a difference in the infant's reaction to familiar or unfamiliar songs?

Understanding Concepts

Does the infant show an understanding of concepts, such as in and out, up and down, under and over, and hot and cold? How does the child demonstrate this understanding? Does the infant respond to concepts such as "going outside," "eating snack," "diaper change," "special toy"? Describe the infant's response. Does the child respond to single words, such as a name called or "look at this"?

Following Instructions

Does the infant follow simple one-part instructions, such as *go, bring, take, pick up?* Does the older infant follow two-part instructions? Does the young infant listen, increase activity, or watch while the adult gives the instructions?

Reacting to Communication

How does the infant react to others communicating with the child? Is there increased activity, smiles, laughter? Does the infant ignore communication? When? Does the infant work to maintain or continue communication? Does the infant react differently to adults', parents', or children's communication or to verbal or nonverbal communication?

Expressive Language
(expresses needs, wants, feelings; uses words, phrases, sentences; speaks clearly and distinctly)

Verbalizations

What types of verbalizations does the infant make? Are they mainly vocalizations (vowel, consonant, or combinations) or are there words also? When do most verbalizations occur—in response to an adult or initiated spontaneously? What voice inflections are used? Are they loud or soft? Does the child cry to express needs? Does the child laugh? When?

Intelligibility

How clearly and distinctly does the child verbalize? Do these verbalizations help the child to communicate needs? What vowel and consonant sounds and words can be clearly distinguished? What sounds are the least easily distinguished? Does crying change when the child's needs change? How does the tone and variation of pitch and rhythm change in the child's verbalizations and cries?

Verbal Fluency

How many (and which) sounds and words does the infant use functionally or with ease? Are these spontaneous or are they encouraged? How frequently does the infant use these words and sounds? Does the infant babble? When and with which sounds?

Effect of Communication

Does the infant use crying to communicate a need? How? In what ways? Does the infant "take turns" vocalizing with an adult in a conversational manner? Does the infant vocalize other than crying to have a need met?

Nonverbal Communication
(uses congruent communication, facial expressions/affect, body gestures, hand gestures)

Facial Expressions

What types of facial expressions does the infant use—smiles, frowns, wrinkling nose or forehead, wide eyes, or use of eyebrows? When are these expressions used? What types of situations elicit these expressions? Are these facial expressions made spontaneously or do they need encouragement?

Body/Hand Gestures

What types of body or hand gestures does the infant use—pointing, shaking head yes or no, reaching toward something wanted, or waving? Does the infant increase body activity (kicking, waving arms) at the sight of a bottle, a parent or a special toy? Does the infant use hand or body gestures alone or in combination with verbalizations? Are these gestures spontaneous or in imitation of another person? How does the infant use these gestures to communicate a need?

Eye Contact

When does the infant make eye contact with adults—in response to adult interactions or to initiate interactions with others? How long does the infant maintain eye contact? What situations make the infant break eye contact with an adult?

Congruent Verbal and Nonverbal Messages

Do the hand or body and facial expressions the infant makes match the verbalizations and emotions the infant is expressing—for example, rigid, tense, jerky when infant is angry, or smooth, calm when infant is relaxed and content? Are there situations when the infant's verbal and nonverbal messages are not congruent? Describe these situations.

Auditory Memory/Discrimination
(understands spoken language; discriminates different sounds)

Auditory Discrimination

Does the child react differently to very loud, sudden noises as opposed to soft, quiet noises? Describe these different reactions. Does the infant differentiate noises of various pitches—shrill cries or dull thuds? What about the infant's response to a voice as opposed to object noises, or familiar sounds as opposed to unfamiliar sounds? How does the infant react differently?

Rhythm

Can the infant imitate or repeat a rhythm heard by clapping or beating? How complex a rhythm can be repeated (*da, da, da,* and so on)? What types of rhythmic patterns does the infant beat or bang when involved in free play? Does the infant clap and "rock" body in response to music?

Complex Verbal Message Delivery

Is the infant beginning to develop skills that will later lead to delivering complex verbal messages, such as making verbalizations or vocalizations, listening to spoken speech, or following simple instructions?

Story or Event Sequencing

Is the infant beginning to develop early precursor skills that will later lead to properly sequencing stories and events, such as listening to spoken speech, making own vocalizations, listening to stories or showing an active interest in books, and imitating a sequence of vocalizations made by an adult?

Auditory Memory

Can the child repeat a simple sound, such as an animal sound? Can the child repeat multiple (different) sounds in a sequence?

Cognition

Problem Solving/Reasoning

(uses divergent thinking; suggests solutions to peer problems, "what if" situations; answers questions; extends sentence or story logically)

Thinks Independently

How does the infant exhibit independent thought processes, such as doing something without an adult suggestion or prompt, choosing toys or activities independently, ignoring redirection, or exploring independently? When do these behaviors usually occur? Does the infant try to solve a cognitive problem in more than one way? Does the infant observe something being done and try it without a prompt or encouragement?

Solves Problems / Proposes Alternative Possibilities

How does the child solve cognitive problems, such as retrieving a dropped object, uncovering a partially hidden object, trying to maintain eye contact with a person or visual contact with an object that moves out of the line of vision, or finding a hidden object? How much adult prompting does the infant need? Does the child try several ways to solve these problems? Describe.

Attacks Cognitive Problems Confidently

Does the infant confidently and happily attack cognitive problems and seem interested and eager to take part in these activities? Does the infant hesitate to take part, become easily frustrated, or need lots of adult prompting to continue with this type of play? Does the infant smile, clap, or vocalize when successful or praised for participating in cognitive tasks?

Extends Sentence, Story, or Sequence of Events

What precursor skills does the infant exhibit that will later lead to extending a sentence, story, or sequence of events—continuing a vocalization when an adult stops, listening with interest to an adult read or tell a story, following a sequence of events in a task (for example, hand washing, getting coat when parent arrives, or retrieving a ball after it bounces)?

Concept Formation
(understands spatial relations; identifies color, number, shape)

Perceptual Processing

Describe examples of the infant's behavior that are Piagetian tasks in the sensorimotor stage, such as shifting from passive responsiveness to active search in very young infants, repeating events for the pleasurable response, intentional goal-directed activity, object permanence, and endless search for variations in how things happen.

Color/Shape Identification

What precursor skills does the infant exhibit that will later result in identifying colors and shapes? Does the infant attempt to work a shape sorter or attempt to put shaped objects inside other same-shaped objects? Does the infant actively explore different-colored objects? How much adult assistance does the infant need in working a simple shape sorter? Does the very young infant mouth all objects to feel their shape or actively explore objects of different shapes?

Number Concepts

What precursor skills does the infant exhibit that will lead to an understanding of number concepts? Does the infant ask for "more" by pointing, reaching, or vocalizing? Does the infant get "another" ball (or other toy) when asked for "another" or "one more"?

Spatial Relationships

How aware is the infant of his or her own body in space or in relation to other objects and people in space? Does the infant judge spaces and go around things or go right through the middle of things? Does the infant climb carefully on top of blocks or equipment? Does the infant get too close to the edge and tumble often? Does the infant use hands to stop a fall? Does the infant crawl or walk into objects or easily maneuver around them? Does the young infant blink when objects come too close to the face?

Imitation/Memory
(imitates, recalls past events, sequences events)

Recalling Familiar Objects / Events

Does the infant look toward or point toward the object when asked "Where is the _____?" Which objects does the infant identify in this way? Does the infant identify people in this way? Which people? Does the infant name some objects? Does the young infant increase activity or reach for certain familiar objects (for example, a bottle, pacifier, parent, or special toy)?

Imitating and Modeling Behavior Structures

What behaviors does the infant imitate—vocalizing, smiling, waving, clapping, or patting the head? How much adult prompting does the infant need? Does the infant imitate precisely or with approximation? Can the infant imitate a sequence of two or more behaviors? Describe. How often does the infant imitate?

Visualizing / Representing Object, Event, or Person from Past

What precursor skills does the infant exhibit that will later lead to performing this skill? Does the infant exhibit recognition (increased activity or smiles) when he or she sees a picture of someone or something from the past? Does the infant exhibit recognition (moving to the person or reaching for them) when he or she sees a person recently known? How long ago was the person known and how long was the relationship the infant had with the person?

Sequencing Past Events

Describe precursor skills to sequencing past events—knowing what comes next after a task (for example, parts of hand washing, going outside, repeating an activity in the same sequence it was done before, or manipulating parts of a toy in the same order).

Association/Classification
(matches, sorts, groups, classifies, establishes relationships between objects)

Mental Abilities

Do precursor skills to matching, grouping, ordering, and classifying of objects exist? Does the infant actively explore different properties of objects and listen to adult explanations of what objects are alike, why they are alike, and how they are different? Does the infant ever put two of the same things together (for example, two cube blocks)? Is it done with or without a prompt?

Uses / Attributes Identification

Does the infant use typical objects in the way they are intended to be used—for example, eating from a spoon, rolling a ball, drinking from a cup, pushing a car, putting a hat on his or her head, trying to put baby bear's pacifier in its mouth? Is the infant beginning to know body parts? Does the infant go to get coat when parent arrives or when an adult says "outside"?

Analogous Relationships

What types of precursor skills exist that will enable the infant to later understand analogous relationships? Does the infant listen to analogous situation examples given and explained by an adult? Does the infant actively explore the environment to gain knowledge of many situations and properties of objects for later comparison?

Relationships between Objects

Does the infant show an understanding of size (bigger/smaller)? Does the infant discard a large object for a smaller one that will fit into the mouth better? Does the infant try putting different-sized objects inside each other? Does the infant use a spoon to try to get food from the bowl to his or her mouth?

Perceptual Motor

Eye-Hand/Eye-Foot Coordination
(drawing, writing, manipulation of objects, visual tracking, throwing, catching, kicking)

Object Manipulation

How specifically does the child handle objects? Does the child use a palmar grasp? Do all fingers curve around the object? Does the child use a pincer or raking grasp when picking up small objects? Which hand(s) is (are) used to reach or grasp? Does the child transfer objects from hand to hand? Does the child do this easily, routinely, or with difficulty? What size objects are manipulated more easily, large or small? Are the objects soft or hard? Do they rattle or squeak? Does the child bring toys or hands to the mouth to explore? When the child grasps a toy, is it merely held or is it shaken, waved, thrown, dropped, or patted? Does the child bring hands or toys into midline and bang them together?

Object Projection

Does the child roll, throw, or kick objects? Which hand(s) or foot (feet) is (are) used? Does the child watch as an object is rolled, thrown, or kicked? Does the child push large or small objects? Does the child receive a toy that has been rolled toward him or her? How does the child play with objects such as cars, trucks, and wagons?

Fine Motor Skills

How does the child hold a crayon—with full fist or fingers? Can the child make marks, such as points or scribbles? Which hand does the child use? Does the child have a pincer or raking grasp? Can the child turn pages of a book? Can the child build a block tower? How many blocks? Does the child do this confidently, routinely, or with difficulty? Can the child pick up small things, such as pieces of paper, rocks, leaves, or foods? Does the child clap?

Visual Tracking Skills

Does the child track 45°, 90°, or 180° and horizontally, vertically, or circularly? Can the child follow complex patterns such as zigzags and diagonals? Does the child turn the head to keep an object in view? Does the child follow adult gestures or movements? Does the child watch a caregiver clap or walk across the room? Does the child focus on certain or preferred objects, stare intently at an object or person, alternate glance between two objects, or monitor a toy as it falls out of view or rolls away?

Locomotor Skills

(moving body through space: walking, jumping, marching, skipping, running, hopping, galloping, rolling, crawling, creeping)

Moving Body through Space

How does the child use rolling, crawling, creeping, or walking to move through space? Does the child roll over several times? Does the child roll to obtain an object out of reach? How often? Does the child crawl or creep functionally? Does the child crawl or creep up and down off large blocks? Does the child fall forward on face often or have difficulty coordinating arms and legs? Does the child crawl or creep backward or forward? Is the child walking functionally? Can the child walk with support of caregiver's hands? Does the child walk or cruise holding on to something? How many steps can the child take without support? Does the child do this only when prompted or also spontaneously? Does the child walk better on flat, bumpy, or cushiony surfaces (indoors and outdoors)? Does the child walk confidently and with ease, or stop and start often?

Body Projection

Does the child jump when supported by a caregiver? Does the child slide or attempt to jump on the trampoline?

Creative Dance

How does the child respond to music? Does the child bounce up and down on legs or sitting on bottom? Does the child sway side to side, wiggle hips, or shake shoulders? Does the child turn around, wave arms, clap, or flail arms and legs? Does the child jump, dance, or twist with support? Does the child raise arms? Does the child make motions to the songs when appropriate? Does the child follow directions for movement within a song?

Equilibrium

How does the child maintain balance when walking? Does the child hold arms out, squat, or stop? Does the child balance confidently? Can the child balance on the edge of a large block, on a climber, or standing on a chair? Is it easier for the child to balance on flat or bumpy surfaces? How does the very young infant control head and neck muscles?

Nonlocomotor Skills
(static: bending, reaching, turning, twisting, stretching, swaying, squatting, sitting, standing)

Movement in Defined Space

How does the infant react when on the edge of a climber or when the teachers say that the child is close to the edge?

Body Manipulation

How does the child stretch—using one or both arm(s) and leg(s), arching the back, or using a facial expression? When and how often does the child stretch? How does the child twist—at the waist, from side to side, or to only one side? Does the child move or raise arms and head when twisting? Does the child do this spontaneously or only when prompted? How specifically does the child roll—side to side, front to back, or back to side? How does the child use the arms, legs, and head when rolling—hold arms out or push and straighten legs? When does the child roll? Does the child bend over and return to a standing position or does the child fall?

Relax and Calm Body

How does the child react when tired or frustrated? Is the infant able to calm self and go to sleep independently? How much adult assistance is needed?

Equilibrium When Stationary

How does the child balance when standing still or sitting? Does the child hold out his or her arms or bend legs? How much support is needed? How does the child balance on uneven surfaces or while sitting in the beanbag? Does the young infant use the arms to steady self when about to fall? Does the infant move from a sitting to a standing position? How often?

Body Management and Control
(exhibits body awareness, space awareness, rhythm, balance, and ability to start, stop, and change directions)

Body Parts

How does the infant control movement of specific parts of the body? Is movement random, haphazard, and accidental, or is it precise and with purpose? Can the infant move more than one part of the body at a time? What combinations of movements are exhibited? How does the older infant control body parts when given specific instructions, such as: "Reach for the _____," "Kick the ball," "Throw the ball," "Clap your hands"?

Daily Motor Skills Management

How does the infant control the body throughout the day in general movements? How secure or insecure is the child? Does the child fall often or rarely? How much assistance from adults does the infant need?

Rhythm, Balance, and Temporal Awareness

How does the infant use rhythm? What are the infant's reactions to music and different types of music (fast and slow)? How does the infant react to songs, finger plays, and musical instruments? Does the infant clap hands or make dancing movements in response to music? Describe.

Body and Space Perception

How does the infant show an awareness of own body in space and in relation to other objects? Does the child crawl over the top of other children and toys or go around them? Does the child allow enough room when sitting down or does the child sit on another child? Does the infant frequently or rarely bump into other objects when walking, crawling, or cruising? How does the infant react to being crowded or having others "invade personal space"?

GUIDELINES FOR WRITING TODDLER (15 MONTHS TO 3 YEARS) AND PRESCHOOL (3 TO 5 YEARS) OBSERVATIONS _____

Personal Awareness

Self-Help Skills
(increases skill to feed and dress self and regulate toileting and sleeping)

Dressing

Can the child zip, buckle, button, and fasten shoes, shirt, and pants? Does the child help or cooperate with an adult when assistance is required?

Nap/Rest Time

Can the child regulate own needs for calming, resting, sleeping, and duration of nap? What does the child do when awakened from nap?

Mealtime

Does the child serve own food, use a variety of utensils, and clean self and materials? What other behaviors does the child exhibit during eating?

Toileting

How does the child regulate patterns of and indicate need for toileting? How much help does the child need?

Independence
(exhibits control of self and mastery of environment)

Acceptance of Responsibility

How does the child exhibit responsibility for personal possessions, toys, clothing, and so on?

Separation from Family

What types of behaviors does the child exhibit when separating from parent(s) at arrival time? How much time is needed to regain calm and control?

Interactions with Environment

How does the child make choices and decisions? For what reasons and in what situations does the child make choices? What are typical choices made by the child—peer play preference, selecting play materials, or choosing one activity over another?

Control over Environment

How does the child meet own needs? What level of assistance is needed? What does the child try to control and when is the child likely to show control?

Personal Health
(develops knowledge of body parts, nutrition, hygiene, drug abuse prevention, wellness)

Body Image

How does the child perceive self or body? How does the child question and talk about body parts? How does the child react to talk about the body? How does the child talk about clothes, hair, body size, weight, height?

Sexual Identity

How does the child show an awareness of gender differences? Does the child talk comfortably about gender difference or sexual identity?

Hygiene

How does the child show awareness of need for cleanliness? Does the child wash hands and face, brush teeth, clean self after toileting, and care for hair and clothes?

Nutritional Habits

What types of foods does the child eat? Is the child willing to try new foods or a variety of foods? Does the child regulate or limit amount of food? How?

Personal Safety
(learns child abuse prevention and passenger and pedestrian safety practices; develops an awareness of environmental hazards)

Passenger Safety Rules

Does the child ride in child-restraint seat or use a seat belt? How does the child respond to passenger restraint? Does the child show an awareness of safety rules? How does the child respond to discussion of safety rules?

Pedestrian Safety Rules

Does the child role-play, answer questions, or respond to picture situations when discussing safety roles? When outside, does the child show an awareness of traffic? Does the child "look both ways," with or without adult prompting, when approaching a street?

Safe / Unsafe Interactions with Adults

Does the child show an awareness of various situations, respond to questions, and respond to picture representations of interactions about safe and unsafe situations? Does the child comment spontaneously about situations or concerns?

Right to Privacy / Ownership of Body

How does the child exhibit the value of privacy? How does the child protect self? How does the child show ownership of body? Does the child take unnecessary risks on the playground or inside? Does the child walk in front of swings or trikes, climb beyond ability, or run inside or run without being aware of obstacles?

Emotional Well-Being

Awareness, Acceptance, and Expression of Emotions
(identifies a variety of feelings and expresses feelings to others)

Recognition and Verbalization of Emotions

Which emotions does the child recognize, express, and discuss—sadness, happiness, fear, anger, joy, pride, and so on? Does the child know varying emotions or just happy and sad?

Separation of Emotions

How does the child differentiate own feelings from others' feelings? How does the child respond to emotions in others? How does the child respond when another's emotions are different from his or her emotions?

Contact and Control of Feelings

How does the child remain in contact with feelings while learning to control what is done about them? Can the child express emotions, rather than repressing them, in safe, appropriate ways?

Expression of Emotion

In what ways does the child express emotions? Does the child use a variety of ways of expression, such as verbal and nonverbal? Which emotions does the child express more frequently or more easily?

Coping Skills

(shows adaptive and healthy response to stressors, conflict, or change; uses relaxation techniques; resolves emotional conflict and issues)

Use of Play and Creative Materials

In what ways does the child clarify feelings and resolve emotional problems? How is this done? When does it occur? What prompts the child to do this?

Internal Locus of Control

In what way is control exhibited? When and how does the child use locus of control? What is the frequency of and what situations cause tantrums?

Facing Reality and Adjusting to Change

How does the child accept what cannot be changed? Is the child satisfied with alternative solutions? Is the child able to cope with transitions? When and why does adjusting occur?

Response to Stress and Crisis Situations

In what ways does the child respond to stress? What coping mechanisms are used—relaxation, humor, talking, exercise, play, and so on? When does the child use them?

Personality Integration

(exhibits general adjustment, autonomy, positive self-concept)

Self-Esteem

How does the child talk and view self—in a positive or negative way? Is the child willing to try new activities and take part? How does the child feel about self? What judgment is made of self? How does the child react when pleased with self?

Feelings about Gender and Ethnic or Cultural Heritage

In what ways does the child express feelings about gender and ethnic or cultural heritage? How does the child view others and discuss their gender, ethnicity, and cultural heritage? How does the child respond to others discussing gender, ethnicity, or cultural heritage?

Relationships with Others

How does the child view and expect individuality and uniqueness of roles in relationships? How does the child relate differently to different people?

Autonomy

How much autonomy does the child use in making decisions and solving problems? When does the child use more or less autonomy? In which centers and in what activities does the child spend time?

Building Values
(develops empathy, trust, reverence, respect)

Attitudes

What types of attitudes does the child exhibit—trust, autonomy, initiative? When are attitudes typically exhibited and how are they exhibited?

Empathy

In what ways does the child show empathy for others? When and why does showing empathy occur? Does the child know the difference between gentle and rough touch? How does the child care for dolls, other children, and adults?

Understanding and Valuing Life

In what way does the child show understanding of, respect for, and value of living things? How does the child show a special interest in people, pets, and plants?

Awareness of Others' Emotions

How does the child recognize, understand, and exhibit concern for the emotions of others? When does the child do this and how often does it occur? How many different emotions are recognized in others? Does the child verbalize another's emotions or respond in appropriate ways to these emotions?

Socialization

Social Interactions
(interacting with peers and adults; resolving conflict)

Adults

In what ways does the child interact with adults? What is the frequency, length, and quality of interactions? How does the child initiate interactions and respond to an adult's initiation of interactions?

Peers

In what ways does the child interact with peers? What is the frequency, length, and quality of interactions? Does the child initiate interaction? What is the incidence of parallel and cooperative play?

Conflict Resolution

In what ways does the child resolve conflicts? What type of assistance is needed? Is the child satisfied with resolution that is a compromise?

Cooperation
(helping, sharing, taking turns)

Satisfaction in Helping

In what ways does the child help others, individually or as a group? What behaviors indicate satisfaction with helping? Where, when, and how does the child help others?

Communicating Needs/Wants

How does the child get his or her own needs and wants met? Does the child use socially appropriate means to obtain these?

Understanding the Individual's Place in the World

How does the child view self in relationships with others, both one-on-one and in group settings? Does the child show a sense of self as part of a group? How does the child respond or act in group situations—withdrawn, outgoing, as a leader?

Functioning as a Part of the Group

How does the child use such skills as communicating, negotiating, and compromising to be a part of group? What skills are used? When are these skills most likely to be used? How much adult prompting is needed?

Conservation of Resources
(using and caring for materials and the environment appropriately)

Use of Play Materials

Does the child use materials constructively and appropriately? Describe examples of material use. Does the child initiate appropriate use of materials or only with adult prompts?

Care of Materials and Environment

How much responsibility does the child take for caring for materials and the environment? When is this done? Does it occur independently or with prompts?

Respect and Care for the Natural World

How does the child demonstrate respect and care for the natural world? Does it occur independently or with prompts? With which materials or in what activity does the child show this?

Awareness of Ecological Problems and Conservation Practices

How does the child show awareness and caring for the outdoor world and conservation, such as in caring for plants in a garden? How is the concern shown? Does the child understand the need to care for and keep the environment clean?

Respect for Others
(understanding and accepting individual differences, multicultural issues)

Responding to Others' Needs

How does the child recognize and respond to others' needs? What types of responses are used—affirmative, supportive? In what situation does the child typically recognize and respond to others?

Understanding Similarities and Differences in People

How does the child demonstrate understanding of similarities and differences in people? What does the child say and do? What similarities or differences are understood?

Respecting and Understanding Differences in People

How does the child exhibit respect and understanding for differences in sex, culture, ability, age, personality, and race?

Nurturing Behaviors toward Others

How does the child respond to others? Does the child show kindness, generosity, or compassion?

Communication

Receptive Language
(follows directions, understands basic concepts)

Understanding Stories and Songs

How does the child perform songs, relate stories, and understand and identify concepts of stories or songs?

Understanding Concepts

How does the child demonstrate an understanding of concepts? Which concepts does the child understand?

Following Instructions

How does the child follow directions? What types of complex directions can the child follow—one-part, two-part, three-part, in order or out of sequence?

Reacting to Communication

How does the child react to adults' and peers' communicative messages? What does the child do? How does the child respond to various communicative messages?

Expressive Language
(expresses needs, wants, feelings; uses words, phrases, sentences; speaks clearly and distinctly)

Verbalizations

How does the child use language to express ideas, needs, wants, and feelings?

Intelligibility

How clearly and distinctly does the child speak? How well is the child understood? How well are ideas communicated?

Verbal Fluency

How many functional vocabulary words does the child have? How does the child use words to communicate? Are there difficulties with fluent verbalizations? Remember that normal disfluency occurs between ages 3 and 4.

Effect of Communication

How does the child use language to control physical and social environments? How is this done? What are the social effects of the child using effective communication? How does the child use words to solve problems?

Nonverbal Communication
(uses congruent communication, facial expressions/affect, body gestures, hand gestures)

Facial Expressions

How does the child use facial expression to show emotions? What types of facial expressions are used? How often are they used?

Body/Hand Gestures

How does the child use gestures to express needs and wants—alone, with verbalization, and so on? What types of gestures are used?

Eye Contact

When does the child give eye contact to initiate interactions? Are there other times the child does this? How long is eye contact maintained?

Congruent Verbal and Nonverbal Messages

How does the child use nonverbal cues in conjunction with verbalizations? What type of body language is used? Does body language match verbal cues?

Auditory Memory/Discrimination
(understands spoken language; discriminates different sounds)

Auditory Discrimination

How does the child exhibit awareness of differences in noises or noisemakers? Can the child identify the source of noise?

Rhythm

How does the child imitate or repeat a rhythm? What types of rhythmic patterns are imitated? Which are easier and harder?

Complex Verbal Message Delivery

How much does the child remember? How accurately does the child convey the message?

Story or Event Sequencing

How does the child reconstruct a story that has been heard? How accurately does the child sequence story events? What types of prompts does the child need and use?

Auditory Memory

What is the child's ability to recall word strings, numbers, instruments sounds, and so on that have been presented by someone else (for example, "Say 4-3-8-6.")?

Cognition

Problem Solving/Reasoning
(uses divergent thinking; suggests solutions to peer problems, "what if" situations; answers questions; extends sentence or story logically)

Thinks Independently

How often does the child exhibit independent thought processes? In what ways is this ability shown? Does the child express independent thinking by choosing activities, solving problems, or exploring materials in new ways?

Solves Problems / Proposes Alternative Possibilities

How does the child approach solving problems? Does the child ask for help? Does the child propose alternatives? Is prompting needed? In what situations (physical problems, social problems) can the child solve problems?

Attacks Cognitive Problems Confidently

How does the child exhibit confidence and ease or happiness with cognitive abilities? In what situations is this evident? Are prompts needed? Does the child show an understanding of cause and effect?

Extends Sentence, Story, or Sequence of Events

How does the child extend stories, sentences, and so on? Does the child use logic? How much prompting or modeling is needed?

Concept Formation
(understands spatial relations; identifies color, number, shape)

Perceptual Processing

How does the child interact with and perceive the environment? Is there evidence of concrete learning that takes place?

Color / Shape Identification

Which colors and shapes does the child know? Does the child name these or indicate knowledge of color and shape by use of them?

Number Concepts

How high can the child count? Is the child's knowledge rote, or does the child use one-to-one correspondence? What other number concepts are known? How does the child approach counting?

Spatial Relationships

How does the child show awareness of body in space, relationship of body to objects, and objects to each other? Does the child respond correctly to requests such as "Put the car on, behind, beside, under the chair"?

Imitation/Memory
(imitates, recalls past events, sequences events)

Recalling Familiar Objects / Events

What can the child recall? How much prompting or modeling is needed to recall accurately?

Imitating and Modeling Behavior Structures

How does the child imitate? What does the child imitate? When is imitation likely to occur? Are prompts needed? Does the child extend behavior or do something differently? Can the child imitate an exact model if asked?

Visualizing / Representing Object, Event, or Person from Past

How does the child describe objects, events, or people from the past? In what ways is this done? Does the child use visual terminology?

Sequencing Past Events

How does the child relate sequences of past events? Are prompts needed? Does the child tell order accurately?

Association/Classification
(matches, sorts, groups, classifies, establishes relationships between objects)

Mental Abilities

How does the child match order or classify groups? Are prompts needed? In what ways is this done?

Uses / Attributes Identification

How does the child describe uses and attributes of objects, events, weather, or body parts? Can the child identify an object by its description?

Analogous Relationships

How well does the child complete analogy statements? What types of analogy statements are completed? Are prompts needed? What is the child's ability to compare objects, events, and attributes?

Relationships between Objects

How does the child show an understanding of interrelationships and grouping of objects? Does the child know what objects go with an activity or with other similar objects?

Perceptual Motor

Eye-Hand/Eye-Foot Coordination
(drawing, writing, manipulation of objects, visual tracking, throwing, catching, kicking)

Object Manipulation

How does the child use hands to manipulate objects? What size of objects are most easily handled? Which hand is primarily used or does the child use either hand or both?

Object Projection

How does the child throw, catch, strike, or kick objects to move them through space? What hand or foot is used?

Fine Motor Skills

How does the child scribble, draw, or write? What hand does the child typically use? What type of writing instrument does the child choose? How is the instrument held? What types of figures does the child draw or scribble?

Visual Tracking Skills

How well does the child use eyes to follow objects? What path does the child track—horizontal, vertical, circular, and so on?

Locomotor Skills
(moving body through space: walking, jumping, marching, skipping, running, hopping, galloping, rolling, crawling, creeping)

Moving Body through Space

How does the child use rolling, crawling, creeping, walking, and so on, to move through space?

Body Projection

How does the child run, jump, hop, skip, gallop, leap, slide, and so on?

Creative dance

How does the child use total body in dancing, creative movement of body, and so on?

Equilibrium

How does the child exhibit balance and control of the body in various locomotor skills? When does it appear easier for the child?

Nonlocomotor Skills
(static: bending, reaching, turning, twisting, stretching, swaying, squatting, sitting, standing)

Movement in Defined Space

How does the child respond to directions to move specified body parts inside his or her confined space? When and where does the child do this? Are prompts needed?

Body Manipulation

When and how does the child stretch, twist, roll, bend?

Relax and Calm Body

Does the child use nonlocomotor skills (stretching, rocking, and so on) to relax? Can the child pace self? How does the child identify and respond to tension or tiredness? Are adult prompts or assistance needed?

Equilibrium When Stationary

How does the child balance on one foot, balance beam, and so on?

Body Management and Control
(exhibits body awareness, space awareness, rhythm, balance, and ability to start, stop, and change directions)

Body Parts

How is the child able to control movement of specific parts of the body, particularly when given specific directions?

Daily Motor Skills Management

How does the child control body movement throughout the day? What amount or type of adult assistance is needed?

Rhythm, Balance, and Temporal Awareness

How does the child use rhythm and use instruments? Does the child keep time to music?

Body and Space Perception

How does the child exhibit awareness of the body in space? How does the child show an awareness of the relationship of space the child is occupying to others' space? How does the child show an ability to judge the size of space to the size of body?

D.

Creativity Indicators

Some indicators of creativity in preschool-age children are[*]:

- Child is willing to take risks, do things differently, try new things. Willing to try the difficult.

- Child has an extraordinary sense of humor in everyday situations.

- Child is opinionated, outspoken, willing to talk openly and freely.

- Child is flexible, able to accommodate to unexpected changes in situations.

- Child is self-directed, self-motivated.

- Child is interested in many things, is curious, questioning.

- Child engages in deliberate, systematic exploration, develops a plan of action.

- Child is able to make activities uniquely his or her own, personalizes what he or she does.

- Child is imaginative, enjoys fantasy.

- Child is a nonconformist, does things his or her own way.

- Child comes up with many solutions to a problem.

- Child is uninhibited, has a freewheeling style.

[*]From Tegano, D. W., Moran, J. D., & Sawyers, J. K. (1991). *Creativity in early childhood classrooms*. Washington, DC: National Education Association. Reprinted by permission of NEA.

Activity Index

ACTIVE GAMES

ACTIVITY NAME	PAGE	PA	E	S	CM	CG	PM
What Do You Do When . . . ?	263			x	X		
Shapes Are Everywhere	279				x	X	
Peek-a-Boo	280			x		X	
Hide-and-Seek Matching Game	282			x		X	
Balls in the Box	295						X
Walk the Tightrope	300		x				X

ART

Painting with Cars	211	X				x	x
What's My Name and How Do I Feel?	223		X		x		
Roll-on Deodorant Bottles	241			X			x
Let's Do It Together	243			X		x	
Cutting Party	295			x			X

X—Primary Domain
x—Additional Domains

PA Personal Awareness Domain
 E Emotional Well-being Domain
 S Socialization Domain
CM Communication Domain
CG Cognitive Domain
PM Perceptual Motor Domain

DISCUSSION

ACTIVITY NAME	PAGE	PA	E	S	CM	CG	PM
Let's Use the Tape Recorder	208	**X**		x	x		
Three Little Children Climbing on the Climber	211	**X**			x	x	
How Would You Feel? What Would You Do?	224	x	**X**		x		
Pictures of My Friends	227		**X**	x	x		
Empathy	228		**X**	x			
Helping Others	229		**X**	x	x		
Baby Faces	246		x	**X**		x	
Hard Things/Easy Things	247		x	**X**	x		

STORYTELLING

Baby Emmy	223		**X**		x	x	
Guess-Who Stories	227		**X**	x	x		
Familiar Tales a New Way	229		**X**	x	x		
Gingerbread Hunt	242			**X**	x		
The Clean-Up Club	245			**X**	x		
Mixed-Up Murphy	260				**X**	x	
Sound-Effects Stories	262				**X**		
How Do They Feel?	263		x		**X**		
Computer Storytelling	265			x	**X**	x	

X—Primary Domain
x—Additional Domains

SCIENCE/NATURE

ACTIVITY NAME	PAGE	PA	E	S	CM	CG	PM
Pouring Party	206	**X**				x	x
Washing	209	**X**		x		x	
Friendship Soup/Salad	210	**X**		x		x	x
Tiny Bubbles	225		**X**			x	
Grass Watering	244			**X**		x	x
Washing Toys and Equipment	245			**X**			x
Boats and Bears	278					**X**	x
Textured Balls	279			x		**X**	x
Smells	282				x	**X**	x
Shakers	298					x	**X**

QUIET GAMES

Sock Party	205	**X**		x			x
Good-Bye Book	208	**X**			x		
Conversations	259			x	**X**		
I Know My Name	259				**X**	x	
A Stuffed Animal's House	261				**X**	x	
Silly Words	265				**X**	x	
Hide-and-Seek	277				x	**X**	x
Guess What's Missing	278				x	**X**	
Zoo Parade	280			x	x	**X**	
Buried Treasure	281					**X**	
Stringing Bottle Rings	282				x	x	**X**
Build a Tall Tower	295			x		**X**	

X—Primary Domain
x—Additional Domains

MUSIC

ACTIVITY NAME	PAGE	PA	E	S	CM	CG	PM
Zip-a-Dee-Doo-Dah	206	**X**					x
All by Yourself	207	**X**			x	x	
The Washing Hands Song	209	**X**			x	x	
If You're Angry and You Know It	226		**X**		x	x	
Where Is _____?	227		**X**		x		
A-Visiting We Will Go	241		x	**X**			
Oh Where, Oh Where?	261	x			**X**	x	
Hello/Good-Bye	263			x	**X**	x	
Band Concert	264			x	**X**		x
Copycat Rhythms	300				x		**X**

MOVEMENT

Wagon Rides	243		x	**X**			x
Prepositions	279				x	**X**	x
Bouncing Babies	296			x		x	**X**
Animal Dancing	297					x	**X**
Stretching	298		x		x		**X**
Are You Twisting?	299		x		x		**X**
Magic Carpet Ride	299			x			**X**

X—Primary Domain
x—Additional Domains

IMAGINARY/DRAMATIC PLAY

ACTIVITY NAME	PAGE	PA	E	S	CM	CG	PM
Buckle UP	211	**X**		x			x
Hammering	225		**X**				x
Different Clothes	246			**X**	x		
Puppet Show	243			**X**	x		
Let's Go Skating	297			x			**X**

X—Primary Domain
x—Additional Domains

Index